CIMA

STRATEGIC

PAPER P3

PERFORMANCE STRATEGY

This kit is for exams in 2013.

In this Kit we:

- Discuss the **best strategies** for revising and taking your P3 exam

- Show you how to be well prepared for the **2013 exams**

- Give you **lots of great guidance** on tackling questions

- Demonstrate how you can **build your own exams**

- Provide you with **three** mock exams

FOR EXAMS IN 2013

First edition 2010
Fourth edition January 2013

ISBN 9781 4453 6622 7
(Previous ISBN 9781 4453 8095 7)
e-ISBN 9781 4453 9285 1

British Library Cataloguing-in-Publication Data
A catalogue record for this book
is available from the British Library

Published by

BPP Learning Media Ltd
BPP House, Aldine Place, 142/144 Uxbridge Road
London W12 8AA

www.bpp.com/learningmedia

Printed in the United Kingdom by Polester Wheatons

Hennock Road
Marsh Barton
Exeter
EX2 8RP

Your learning materials, published by BPP Learning
Media Ltd, are printed on paper obtained from
traceable, sustainable sources.

The contents of this book are intended as a guide and
not professional advice. Although every effort has been
made to ensure that the contents of this book are correct
at the time of going to press, BPP Learning Media
makes no warranty that the information in this book is
accurate or complete and accepts no liability for any loss
or damage suffered by any person acting or refraining
from acting as a result of the material in this book.

We are grateful to the Chartered Institute of
Management Accountants for permission to reproduce
past examination questions. The answers to past
examination questions have been prepared by BPP
Learning Media Ltd.

BPP
LEARNING MEDIA

Contents

Question index

The headings in this checklist/index indicate the main topics of questions, but questions often cover several different topics.

Questions set under the old syllabus's *Risk and Control Strategy (RCS) exam* are included because their style and content are similar to those that appear in the Paper P3 exam.

Mock exam 1
Questions 81 – 84

Mock exam 2 (September 2012 Resit examination)
Questions 85 – 88

Mock exam 3 (November 2012 examination)
Questions 89 – 92

Planning your question practice

Our guidance from page xx shows you how to organise your question practice, either by attempting questions from each syllabus area or by **building your own exams** – tackling questions as a series of practice exams.

Topic index

Listed below are the key Paper P3 syllabus topics and the numbers of the questions in this Kit covering those topics.

If you need to concentrate your practice and revision on certain topics or if you want to attempt all available questions that refer to a particular subject you will find this index useful.

Syllabus topic	Question numbers
Information technology risks	6, 16, 52, 54, 56, 63, 67, Mock exam 2 Q3, Mock exam 3 Q1(b)
Inherent risk	68(a)
Internal audit	1(b), 3(c), 5(c), 22(b), 23(b), 28(b), 53(b), 59, 62(a), 64, 65, 67-72, 75(c), 80(c), Mock exam 1 Q4, Mock exam 2 Q1(b), Mock exam 3 Q4
Internal control review	14, 22, 66
Internal control systems	4, 11, 12, 14-27, 58, 69, 70, 74(b)
Interest rate futures	34(b), Mock exam 1 Q2(a)
Interest rate options	34(b), Mock exam 1 Q2(a)
Interest rate parity (Expectations theory)	38(b), 42, 46, 50
Interest rate risk	30-34, 47(c), 71(b), Mock exam 1 Q2
Interest rate swaps	30-34, 71(b), Mock exam 1 Q2(b)
Management audit	23
Management control systems	17, 23, 26, 60, Mock exam 1 Q4, Mock 2 Q2
Money market hedges	36, 40(a), 45, 46, 50, 72(c)
Multilateral netting	39(a)
Non-executive directors	9(a), Mock exam 1 Q1(c), Mock exam 3 Q2(c)
Outsourcing	57(b), 61, 69(b), Mock exam 1 Q1(a)
Political risk	4, 43(b), 73(c), Mock exam 3 Q1(a)
Post-completion audit	78(b)
Post-implementation review	53(a)
Project risk	61, 62
Purchasing power parity	42, Mock exam 2 Q4
Quality control	24, 65, Mock exam 2 Q2
Quality of control	69
Return on capital employed	Mock exam 2 Q2
Risk appetite	5(b)
Risk assessment	3-6, 8(a), 15(a), 17(a), 18(b), 21(a), 22(a), 24(a), 31(a), 34(a), 35, 41(a), 51(a), 56(a), 64, 67, 68, 71-80, Mock exam 1 Q1, Mock exam 2 Q1, Mock exam 3 Q1
Risk categorisation	3, 6, 12
Risk management	1-6, 10-12, 19(b), 27, 35, 43, 48, 54(a), 56(b), 66, 72-78, Mock exam 1 Q1(b), Mock exam 1 Q4, Mock exam 3 Q1
Risk mapping	18(b), 68(a), 75(a), Mock 2 Q1(a)
Risk profile	4
Sampling	68(b)
System-based audits	5(c)
Systems development	51(b), 53, 57, 59, 62, 63(c), 74(c)
Total quality management	24
Transfer prices	25(b)
Translation risk	34(a), 41(b)
Treasury function	4(b), 28, 37, Mock exam 3 Q3(c)
Value at risk	29(c), 41(c), 45(d)
Value for money	65

Using your BPP Learning Media Practice and Revision Kit

Tackling revision and the exam

You can significantly improve your chances of passing by tackling revision and the exam in the right ways. Our advice is based on feedback from CIMA. We focus on Paper P3; we discuss revising the syllabus, what to do (and what not to do) in the exam, how to approach different types of question and ways of obtaining easy marks.

Selecting questions

We provide signposts to help you plan your revision.

* A full **question index**

* A **topic index**, listing all the questions that cover key topics, so that you can locate the questions that provide practice on these topics, and see the different ways in which they might be examined

* **BPP's question plan**, highlighting the most important questions

* **Build your own exams**, showing you how you can practise questions in a series of exams

Making the most of question practice

We realise that you need more than questions and model answers to get the most from your question practice.

* Our **Top tips** provide essential advice on tackling questions and presenting answers

* We show you how you can pick up **Easy marks** on questions, as picking up all readily available marks can make the difference between passing and failing

* We include **marking guides** to show you what the examiner rewards

* We summarise **Examiner's comments** to show you how students coped with the questions

* We refer to the **BPP 2012 Study Text** (for 2013 exams) for detailed coverage of the topics covered in each question

Attempting mock exams

There are three mock exams that provide practice at coping with the pressures of the exam day. We strongly recommend that you attempt them under exam conditions, as they reflect the question styles and syllabus coverage of the exam. To help you get the most out of doing these exams, we provide guidance on how you should have approached the whole exam.

Our other products

BPP Learning Media also offers these products for practising and revising for the P3 exam:

Passcards	Summarising what you should know in visual, easy to remember, form
Success CDs	Covering the vital elements of the P3 syllabus in less than 90 minutes and also containing exam hints to help you fine tune your strategy
i-Pass	Providing computer-based testing in a variety of formats, ideal for self-assessment
Interactive passcards	Allowing you to learn actively with a clear visual format summarising what you must know
Case Study Kit	The compulsory question in each strategic level exam is based on a common pre-seen case study issued in April and October each year. The BPP Case Study Kit provides analysis of this pre-seen case study and special practice questions based on the themes in the case study.

You can purchase these products by visiting www.bpp.com/learningmedia

Revising P3

Risk and control

Risk and control are central to this paper and hence should be central to your revision.

On risk you need to know:

- The main risks businesses face, not just accounting risks, but also wider strategic, business, operational, financial, economic and IT risks, also reputation risk (often forgotten by students)
- Components of an organisation's risk management strategy
- All the stages of the risk analysis process
- Types of response to risk

Controls – potentially you may have to discuss and evaluate a wide range of controls in any question:

- Control environment (lack of knowledge of what the control environment is may be a serious weakness)
- Corporate governance
- Strategic controls, management supervision and review
- Accounting area controls
- Organisational controls including appropriate structure and communication, controls over outsourcing
- Human resource and behavioural controls including recruitment and training
- Security controls
- Quality controls and customer feedback
- Business continuity controls
- The main financial risk hedging instruments
- Information systems strategies and controls – does the system produce appropriate information? Is it appropriately used (eg budget and actual figures compared), and is action taken if variances are found? Are there appropriate controls over systems development? You need to focus on issues that affect computerised information systems and not manual systems
- The main internal audit objectives and techniques
- Interaction between internal and external audit
- Ethical codes, particularly CIMA's code

Regard this as a checklist to give you ideas but don't expect to use them all in the exam.

Exam questions may group controls under the headers financial, non-financial quantitative and non-financial qualitative; you should be able to think of examples of each.

Question practice

You should use the Passcards and any brief notes you have to revise these topics, but you mustn't spend all your revision time passively reading. Question practice is vital; doing as many questions as you can in full will help develop your ability to analyse scenarios and produce relevant discussion and recommendations. The question plan on page xix tells you what questions cover so that you can choose questions covering a variety of organisations and risk situations.

Researching the preseen

Part of the Section A question (the preseen) will be issued some weeks before the exam, and will be common to all three strategic papers. This will give you the opportunity to research the industry in which the organisation covered in Section A operates. However **DO NOT** spend all your revision time on the preseen. CIMA has stated that students should not spend excessive time on research. Your priority should be lots of question practice. As well as practising Section A questions, you should do plenty of Section B questions, as Section B is also worth 50% of the marks for the paper.

Passing the P3 exam

Displaying the right qualities

The examiner will expect you to display the following qualities.

Qualities required	
Show risk-based perspective	You must be able to **identify**, **classify** and **evaluate** major risks in a variety of scenarios; your answers must be **clearly related to the scenarios.**
Make reasonable recommendations	The controls and other measures you recommend must be **appropriate** for the organisation and deal with the risks it faces; you will need to discuss their strengths and weaknesses, as there may be costs of adopting them. The recommendations should clearly state what has to be done.
Synthesise knowledge	You may see questions that relate quite strongly to other Strategic level papers or lower level exams. The examiners expect you to use knowledge from these papers to answer questions in P3.
Carry out appropriate calculations	You will need to perform calculations that directly indicate risk levels or that give insights into the scenario described in the question. The examiner has emphasised that you must learn the main financial risk calculations. They may appear in either section of the exam.
Show strategic awareness	Remember this is a Strategic level paper, and the organisation's strategies will determine not only the risks it faces, but also how it responds to those risks.

Avoiding weaknesses

You will enhance your chances significantly if you ensure you avoid these mistakes, in particular:

- Failing to provide what the question verbs require (discussion, evaluation, recommendations) or to write about the topics specified in the question requirements

- Making general points rather than relating answers to the scenario; regurgitation of definitions and lists with no application to the question. Questions will contain specific information about the organisation which is meant to be used in the answer

- Spending too much time discussing accounting controls and not enough time on other sorts of control

Other weaknesses you should avoid include:

- Unrealistic or impractical recommendations

- Vague recommendations (instead of just saying improve risk management procedures, you should discuss precisely **how** you would improve them)

- If the question asks for a discussion, providing a series of single line bullet points without enough depth

- Repeating the same material in different parts of answers

- Brain dumping all that is known about a topic (no credit is given for this)

- Listing all possible risks or risks not apparent from the scenario rather than concentrating on the significant ones in the scenario

- Failing to answer sufficient questions because of poor time management

- Not answering all parts of optional questions

Using the reading time

Whilst you're reading the paper, remember to keep thinking risks and controls for every scenario that you read.

We recommend that you spend the first part of the reading time choosing the Section B questions you will do, on the basis of:

- Your **knowledge** of the syllabus area tested
- Your **understanding** of the business and the terms used in the question
- The availability of **easy marks** (see below)
- Whether you can **fulfil all the question requirements** (including any calculations)

We suggest that you should note on the paper any ideas that come to you about these questions.

However don't spend the reading time going through and analysing the Section B question requirements in detail; leave that until the three hours writing time. Normally Section B requirements are more step-by-step than Section A requirements and so require less planning and thinking time. Instead you should be looking to spend as much of the reading time as possible looking at the Section A scenario, highlighting and annotating the key points on the question paper.

Choosing which questions to answer first

Spending most of your reading time on the Section A scenario will mean that you can get underway with planning and writing your answer to the Section A question as soon as the three hours start. It will give you more actual writing time during the one and a half hours you should allocate to it and it's writing time that you'll need.

During the second half of the exam, you can put Section A aside and concentrate on the two Section B questions you've chosen.

However our recommendations are not inflexible. If you really think the Section A question looks a lot harder than the Section B questions you've chosen, then do those first, but **DON'T run over time on them.** You must leave yourself an hour and a half to tackle the Section A question. When you come back to it, having had initial thoughts during the reading time, you should be able to generate more ideas and find the question is not as bad as it looks.

Tackling questions

Scenario questions

You'll improve your chances by following a step-by-step approach to Section A scenarios along the following lines.

 STEP 1 — Read the opening paragraph to set the scene

Look out in particular for changes from the preseen that the opening paragraph highlights, or factors influencing the business decisions you may be discussing in your answer (business strategies, financial resources and controls).

 STEP 2 — Read the requirements

You need to identify the knowledge areas being tested and what information will therefore be significant. In particular you need to identify which aspects of risk management you will have to cover in your answer.

 STEP 3 — Identify the action verbs

These convey the level of skill you need to exhibit. See the list on page xvi. Make sure you have highlighted **all** the verbs in the question; often question parts have more than one verb, and students take no notice of the second verb.

 STEP 4 — Identify what each part of the question requires

When planning, you will need to make sure that you aren't reproducing the same material in more than one part of the question.

Check the mark allocation to each part

This shows you the depth and number of points anticipated and helps allocate time.

 Read the scenario carefully

You need to highlight significant new information that the unseen provides.

- New data may give you a fresh perspective compared with the preseen
- The unseen may build on hints given in the preseen
- The unseen may give information about changes in situations described in the preseen

Also look out for risks and weaknesses, also procedures, systems and controls that are currently in place. Any risks that have been highlighted are likely to be very relevant to your answer. Terms such as exposure, variable, volatility, uncertainty and probability are likely to highlight key risks.

Put points under headings related to requirements (eg by margin notes). Consider the techniques you'll need to use.

 Consider the consequences of the points you've identified

Remember that in the answer you will often have to provide recommendations based on the information you've been given. Consider the limitations of any analysis you undertake or other factors that may impact upon your recommendations.

Also think how significant the points you identify are. Not everything you highlight will be vital to answering the question, and you may need to prioritise the points if you are under time pressure.

 Write a plan

You may be able to do this on the question paper as often there will be at least one blank page in the question booklet. However any plan you make should be reproduced in the answer booklet when writing time begins.

You must ensure when planning your answer to the Section A question that you use the unseen information appropriately. You can bring in the preseen information as well if it's relevant. The results of your research can also be used, but **only if relevant.** You must be prepared not to use any of your research if it doesn't help you answer the question. **DO NOT** brain dump all your research into your answer no matter what the question requirements are. Sadly you will receive **no marks** for irrelevant material, however much time you've spent researching it.

Assess quickly before you start writing that your plan covers **all necessary points** and **excludes irrelevant material**, and that you are happy with the **structure** of the answer and how much **detail** you will include, bearing in mind the **time constraints.** Make sure also that there is **no duplication** between answers to different question parts.

 Write the answer

Make every effort to present your answer clearly. Paragraphs should have **headers** that relate to the question requirements or key information in the scenario.

Numerical questions

Expect to see some numbers. The most likely place you will see them is in questions on financial risk. Questions will also be set on expected values and calculation of exposure to other sorts of risk. Questions may include interpretation of data. Don't be put off doing a question by the fact that there are numbers in it, as the techniques may not be too complex, and the numbers may not be worth very many marks.

Remember that **depth of discussion** is also important. Discussions will often consist of paragraphs containing 2-3 sentences. Each paragraph should:

- **Make a point**
- **Explain the point** (you must demonstrate **why** the point is important)
- **Apply the point** (with material or analysis from the scenario, perhaps an example from real-life)

Gaining the easy marks

There are likely to be easier marks available for stating the risks you've spotted in the scenario, also for defining key topics. On some papers you may see an essay question that doesn't link into a scenario and this type of question may well be easier than other scenario-linked questions on that paper.

The easier marks may be in the first part(s) of the question. If they are in subsequent parts, we would not recommend that you do these parts first, as question requirements and hence answers will generally have a logical flow to them. However you must give yourself enough time on these parts, and not get bogged down in the more difficult question parts.

The exam paper

Format of the paper

		Number of marks
Section A:	1 compulsory question, totalling 50 marks, with all subsections relating to a pre-seen case study and further new unseen case material	50
Section B:	2 out of 3 questions, 25 marks each. These do not relate to the pre-seen case study	50
		100

Time allowed: 3 hours, plus 20 minutes reading time

CIMA guidance

CIMA has stated that credit will be given for focusing on the right principles and making practical evaluations and recommendations in a variety of different business scenarios, including manufacturing, retailing and financial services.

A likely weakness of answers is excessive focus on details. Plausible alternative answers could be given to many questions, so model answers should not be regarded as all-inclusive.

Numerical content

The paper is likely to have about a 25% numerical content, mainly in questions relating to Section D *Management of financial risk*. Financial risk hedging will be covered in the majority of papers. The May 2010 post exam guide stated that financial risk will 'inevitably' be a part of Question 1.

Calculations may also be set involving expected values and exposure to other sorts of risk. Questions may also include the interpretation of data.

Breadth of question coverage

Questions in *both* sections of the paper may cover more than one syllabus area.

Knowledge from other syllabuses

Candidates should also use their knowledge from other Strategic level papers. One aim of this paper is to prepare candidates for the TOPCIMA T4 – Part B Case Study.

November 2012
Section A
1   Political and legal risks; online booking; currency risks

Section B
2   Role of board and non-executive directors

3   Arbitrage; treasury function

4   Independence of internal audit; internal audit work

This exam is Mock exam 3 in this Kit.

September 2012 (Resit exam)
Section A

1   Health and safety risks; audit planning; currency hedging; countertrade

Section B
2   ROCE; quality control

3   IT security and data protection

4   PPP; purchasing policy; government action

This exam is Mock exam 2 in this Kit.

May 2012

Section A

1 Shareholder relationships; cultural risk; interest rate risk and swaps; anti-fraud technology

Section B

2 Expert system development

3 Forward contract; corporate treasurership

4 Total quality management; quality control

March 2012 (Resit exam)

Section A

1 Reputation and legal risks; control environment and expenses; currency hedging

Section B

2 Balanced scorecard; transfer pricing

3 Disaster planning

4 Foreign borrowing; interest rate parity; currency swaps

November 2011

Section A

1 Bribery; plagiarism; political risk

Section B

2 Directors'remuneration

3 Tendering fraud

4 Multilateral netting; international cash management

September 2011 (Resit exam)

Section A

1 Reputation risk management; control procedures; inventory system development; loan risks

Section B

2 Management of value streams; lean management accounting

3 Value for money audit

4 Money market hedge; internal hedging

May 2011

Section A

1 Reputation risk; protection of intellectual property; role of internal audit; currency risk management

Section B

2 Culture and quality of service; partnership governance

3 Economic risk; translation risk; value at risk

4 Prevention and detection of fraud; control systems; human resource and systems controls

March 2011 (Resit exam)

Section A

1 Board structure; shareholders' interests; mission statement; currency risks

Section B

2 Risk avoidance; ethical dilemma

3 Post implementation review; internal audit; parallel running

4 Interest rate swaps

November 2010

Section A

1 New customer; operational risks; currency risk

Section B

2 Operational risks; EDI

3 Non-executive directors; Directors' remuneration

4 Exchange rate forecasts; Currency risk management

September 2010 (Resit exam)

Section A

1 Sales risk; post-completion audits; futures

Section B

2 Information systems; weaknesses in systems

3 Management control systems; human resources ethics

4 Currency risks; political risks

May 2010

Section A

1 Overseas investment risks; management information systems; foreign exchange risk management; ethical systems

Section B

2 Directors' remuneration; lending risk management

3 Forward contracts; economic risks

4 IT systems risks; IT fraud

> **Examiner's comments.** Poorer students failed to fulfil the requirements of questions, either because they did not understand what was being asked or because they were trying to obtain marks for repetition of memorised facts and information. Another weakness was failure to apply knowledge to a scenario. Students are expected to use information given in the scenario to illustrate the main points in their answers. Students will waste time if they fail to be specific in their answers.
>
> It is important to use the reading time well, to plan answers and ensure questions are read carefully.
>
> Another significant problem was students missing out parts of questions, suggesting a lack of knowledge of syllabus areas. There is limited choice, so students must be comfortable with all syllabus areas, particularly financial risk as it accounts for 35% of the syllabus.
>
> **BPP note.** The examiner has made very much the same general points after every exam up until September 2012 (the most recent post-exam guide available when this kit was published).

Specimen paper

Section A

1   Information strategy; overseas investment risks; environmental audits and reporting

Section B

2   Production control systems; risk mapping

3   Product launch risks; interest rate swaps

4   Internal control systems, control environment and risk management; analytical procedures

What the examiner means

The table below has been prepared by CIMA to help you interpret exam questions.

Learning objective	Verbs used	Definition	Examples in the Kit
1 Knowledge			
What you are expected to know	• List	• Make a list of	
	• State	• Express, fully or clearly, the details of/facts of	
	• Define	• Give the exact meaning of	
2 Comprehension			
What you are expected to understand	• Describe	• Communicate the key features of	63
	• Distinguish	• Highlight the differences between	
	• Explain	• Make clear or intelligible/state the meaning or purpose of	18
	• Identify	• Recognise, establish or select after consideration	58
	• Illustrate	• Use an example to describe or explain something	34
3 Application			
How you are expected to apply your knowledge	• Apply	• Put to practical use	
	• Calculate/compute	• Ascertain or reckon mathematically	44
	• Demonstrate	• Prove the certainty or exhibit by practical means	Mock exam 1 Q1
	• Prepare	• Make or get ready for use	2
	• Reconcile	• Make or prove consistent/ compatible	
	• Solve	• Find an answer to	
	• Tabulate	• Arrange in a table	
4 Analysis			
How you are expected to analyse the detail of what you have learned	• Analyse	• Examine in detail the structure of	67
	• Categorise	• Place into a defined class or division	
	• Compare and contrast	• Show the similarities and/or differences between	4
	• Construct	• Build up or complete	40
	• Discuss	• Examine in detail by argument	15
	• Interpret	• Translate into intelligible or familiar terms	
	• Prioritise	• Place in order of priority or sequence for action	
	• Produce	• Create or bring into existence	42
5 Evaluation			
How you are expected to use your learning to evaluate, make decisions or recommendations	• Advise	• Counsel, inform or notify	80
	• Evaluate	• Appraise or assess the value of	14
	• Recommend	• Propose a course of action	13

Planning your question practice

We have already stressed that question practice should be right at the centre of your revision. Whilst you will spend some time looking at your notes and the Paper P3 Passcards, you should spend the majority of your revision time practising questions.

We recommend two ways in which you can practise questions.

- Use **BPP Learning Media's question plan** to work systematically through the syllabus and attempt key and other questions on a section-by-section basis

- **Build your own exams** – attempt the questions as a series of practice exams

These ways are suggestions and simply following them is no guarantee of success. You or your college may prefer an alternative but equally valid approach.

BPP's question plan

The plan below requires you to devote a **minimum of 50 hours** to revision of Paper P3. Any time you can spend over and above this should only increase your chances of success.

 Review your notes and the chapter summaries in the Paper P3 **Passcards** for each section of the syllabus.

 Answer the key questions for that section. These questions have boxes round the question number in the table below and you should answer them in full. Even if you are short of time you must attempt these questions if you want to pass the exam. You should complete your answers without referring to our solutions.

 Attempt the other questions in that section. For some questions we have suggested that you prepare **answer plans or do the calculations** rather than full solutions. Planning an answer means that you should spend about 40% of the time allowance for the questions brainstorming the question and drawing up a list of points to be included in the answer.

 Attempt Mock exams 1, 2 and 3 under strict exam conditions.

Syllabus section	2012 Passcards chapters	Questions in this Kit	Comments	Done ☑
Risks and risk management	1-2	1	Answer in full. This March 2011 question is a good test of your understanding of different approaches to risk management and also includes a difficult ethical dilemma.	☐
		3	Answer in full. This question illustrates the wide variety of risks businesses can face, and how a systematic approach to categorising risks can help control them.	☐
		6	Prepare a plan for this question.	☐
Corporate governance	3	7	Answer in full. This is a topical question from November 2011, covering executive share schemes that many companies use.	☐
		8	Answer in full. This May 2011 question tests your understanding of the importance of an organisation's culture.	☐
		9	Answer in full. This question from November 2010 is a good illustration of the way the examiner includes plenty of relevant detail in the scenario, which students must use well in their answers.	☐
		10	Answer in full. This May 2010 question is a good indication of how topical subjects may be tested and provides useful practice in analysing scenarios for risks.	☐
		13	Answer in full. This is quite a challenging question, requiring you to apply governance requirements to a charity and ethical principles to acting as a director.	☐
		14	Prepare a plan for this question.	☐
Ethics	4	15	Answer in full. This scenario provides a good ethical problem to be solved, as well as requiring you to think carefully about the relevant risks in the situation.	☐
Control systems	5-6	11	List the controls the business would use.	☐
		12	Prepare a plan for part (a).	☐

Syllabus section	2012 Passcards chapters	Questions in this Kit	Comments	Done ☑
		16	Answer in full. This question from May 2011 is an excellent example of a question on fraud, with weaknesses in systems clearly highlighted.	☐
		17	Answer in full. Part (a) of this question is a good illustration of the risks that can arise from a new system. Part (b) provides useful practice on ethics.	☐
		18	Answer in full. This specimen paper question demonstrates the importance of reading question requirements carefully, and also provides useful practice in analysing control systems.	☐
		19	Answer in full. This specimen paper question pulls together a number of the topics you have covered so far in your revision.	☐
		20	Answer in full. This question provides is good practice in identifying weaknesses and suggesting improvements in control systems.	☐
		21	Answer in full. A good test of fraud and human resource issues.	☐
		22	Prepare a plan for this question.	☐
Management accounting control systems	7	24	Answer in full. This question is a very good test of your knowledge of total quality management and also covers some change management issues.	☐
		25	Answer in full. This question covers important areas in management accounting control systems, the balanced scorecard and transfer pricing.	☐
		26	Answer in full. This is a good test of your understanding of the principles of management accounting systems, as it involves changing to a more appropriate system for the business featured.	☐
		27	Answer in full. This question shows how risk management links in practice with product investment and development.	☐
Financial risk management	8	29	Answer in full. A challenging question, including a general discussion on derivatives, and also requiring specific knowledge of IAS 39 and value at risk.	☐

Syllabus section	2012 Passcards chapters	Questions in this Kit	Comments	Done ☑
Interest rate risk management	9	30	Answer in full.	☐
		31	Answer in full.	☐
		32	Answer in full. These questions provide handy practice of interest rate swap calculations, and also require consideration of wider financial risk management issues.	☐
		34	Answer in full. This is a good wide-ranging question on different types of financial risk.	☐
International risk management	10	35	Answer in full. The question covers quite a tricky situation for you to apply your knowledge of risk, and includes calculations.	☐
Transaction risk management	11-12	36	Answer in full. Attempt this preparation question to remind you of the most important currency risk calculations.	☐
		37	Answer in full. This recent question covers forward contracts and the establishment of a treasury function.	☐
		38	Answer in full. This question is a comprehensive test of your knowledge of currency swaps.	☐
		39	Answer in full. This question tests your understanding of how treasury arrangements work in a multinational organisation.	☐
		40	Answer in full. This September 2011 question is a good test of your knowledge of hedging currency risk without using derivatives.	☐
		41	Answer in full. This question provides very useful practice of financial risk areas (economic risk and value at risk) that students often find difficult.	☐
		42	Answer in full. This November 2010 question demonstrates that financial risk questions can reward simple calculations generously.	☐
		43	Answer in full. A good illustration of various issues that a company investing and trading abroad faces.	☐
		44	Answer in full. This May 2010 question covers economic risk. The examiner commented that it was not done very well and emphasised that there would be further questions on economic risk in future.	☐

Syllabus section	2012 Passcards chapters	Questions in this Kit	Comments	Done ☑
		45	Answer in full. This question tests your knowledge of various financial risk management concepts, and also involves calculations that require some thought.	☐
		46	Answer in full. There is good coverage here of the theories underlying foreign exchange risk, as well as a look at some of the simpler hedging methods.	☐
		47	Answer in full. This question is an example of how more complex techniques could be examined. As well as calculations being tested, the question provides practice in analysing the most appropriate strategy for different types of company.	☐
Risk and control in information systems	13-14	51	Answer in full. This May 2012 question tests not only systems development, but also your understanding of how expert systems work.	☐
		52	Answer in full. This March 2012 question covers practical problems that firms organising a disaster simulation may encounter.	☐
		53	Answer in full. A good mainstream question on systems development from March 2011.	☐
		54	Answer in full. The examiner emphasised that this November 2010 question was designed to test important real-world issues.	☐
		55	Answer in full. Another practical question from a 2010 exam, concerning the controls for a branch that is heavily dependent on its information systems.	☐
		56	Answer in full. This is a wide-ranging question from May 2010.	☐
		58	Prepare a plan for this question.	☐
		59	Answer in full. A good test, as this question covers this part of the syllabus quite widely.	☐
		60	Prepare a plan for this question.	☐
		61	Answer in full. This scenario provides good coverage of the important topic of outsourcing.	☐
		63	Prepare a plan for this question.	☐

Syllabus section	2012 Passcards chapters	Questions in this Kit	Comments	Done ☑
Audit and review	15-16	64	Answer in full. This question covers internal audit work in an area where there can be a significant risk of fraud, the bidding process.	☐
		65	Answer in full. This is rather an unusual audit and quality control question, but is a good test of your knowledge of value for money issues.	☐
		66	Answer in full. This is a rather tough question, as it requires application of corporate governance principles to a charity.	☐
		67	Answer in full. This is a wide-ranging question that covers a number of issues relevant to the internal audit section of the syllabus and also brings in IT considerations.	☐
		68	Prepare a plan for this question.	☐
		69	Answer in full. Another test of your ability to describe relevant audit work. This question gives you a lot of information which you have to sort out in order to come up with an appropriate plan.	☐
Case studies		71	Answer in full.	☐
		72	Answer in full.	☐
		74	Answer in full.	☐
		76	Answer in full.	☐
		78	Answer in full. These questions mirror the format of the actual exam so they are essential practice for this paper.	☐

Build your own exams

Having revised your notes and the BPP Passcards, you can attempt the questions in the Kit as a series of practice exams. You can organise the questions in the following ways.

- Either you can attempt complete past exam papers; recent papers are listed below:

	Past papers								
	Spec	5 /10	9 /10	11 /10	3 /11	5 /11	9 /11	11 /11	3 /12	5 /12
Section A										
1	80	79	78	77	76	75	74	73	72	71
Section B										
2	18	10	55	54	1	8	26	7	25	51
3	31	44	17	9	53	41	65	64	52	37
4	19	56	43	42	30	16	40	39	38	24

- Or you can make up practice exams, either yourself or using the suggestions we have listed below.

	Practice exams								
	1	2	3	4	5	6	7	8	9	10
Section A										
1	79	80	75	76	77	78	71	72	73	74
Section B										
2	18	44	42	54	30	56	64	65	51	52
3	1	16	55	31	53	19	40	7	38	24
4	41	9	10	17	8	43	25	39	26	37

Whichever practice exams you use, you must attempt **Mock exams 1, 2 and 3** at the end of your revision.

QUESTIONS

RISKS

Questions 1 to 6 cover risks, the subject of Part A of the BPP Study Text for Paper P3.

1   Grove (3/11)   45 mins

Grove Council is the local government authority responsible for the running of public services in a district of approximately 200 square miles and with a population of over 300,000. The Grove district comprises a mixture of towns, villages and rural areas.

The Council employs approximately 13,000 staff in a wide variety of occupations. The Council is responsible for the maintenance of the entire public infrastructure in its area of responsibility, including the roads and sewerage systems. The Council also manages education and care for vulnerable residents such as the elderly and infirm. The Council has a divisional structure, with divisions taking responsibility for specific matters such as education, roads and so on throughout the Grove district.

Injury statistics

Employment law requires that every employer, including Grove Council, must maintain a register of all workplace injuries sustained by employees. There is no precise definition of a reportable injury, but Council guidelines indicate that anything that requires a dressing, such as a bandage or sticking plaster, must be reported as minor injuries. Injuries are classified as "serious" if they require the victim to be absent from work for more than three days and "severe" if they require admission to hospital or involve a fatality.

The latest injury statistics show that there were 150 injuries during the year ended 31 December 2010, of which 20 were serious injuries and 3 were severe. The Council's Director of Operations is satisfied with these figures because the number of injuries is no worse than in previous years. He holds the view that such figures are to be expected given the diverse range of jobs, many of which are risky, throughout the Council. The Chief Executive of the Council does not share these views: he thinks that the Council should try to prevent all injuries by eliminating accidents in the workplace.

Internal audit of injury reporting procedures

The Chief Executive asked Grove Council's internal audit department to review the systems for reporting injuries. As part of the response to that request a CIMA qualified member of internal audit was sent to investigate the repair depot that maintains the Council's fleet of vehicles. The depot employs a team of over 40 mechanics and is equipped with a full range of welding and lifting equipment.

The depot's injury register had only two entries for the year prior to the internal audit visit. Both injuries were severe and each involved an injury that required an ambulance to be called and an employee to be admitted to hospital.

On enquiry, several of the mechanics explained that the small number of reports is due to the depot manager refusing to record injuries unless they are either serious or severe. Several of the depot mechanics are trained in first aid and no records are kept of any injuries that they treat. All of the mechanics refused to put these allegations in writing for the internal auditor.

The internal auditor asked the Head of Internal Audit to send an urgent report to the Chief Executive, but the Head of Internal Audit refused to do so on the grounds that there was insufficient evidence of manipulation. The Head of Internal Audit threatened to suspend the internal auditor if she repeated these allegations to anyone else either inside or outside of the Council. The internal auditor is dissatisfied with the Head of Internal Audit's response and is considering whether to take the matter further.

Required

(a) (i) Discuss the Director of Operations' view that it is impossible to prevent all workplace injuries.

(5 marks)

(ii) Discuss the Chief Executive's view that it is unacceptable for Grove Council to tolerate any workplace injuries.

(5 marks)

(b) (i) Analyse the ethical dilemma faced by the internal auditor.

(8 marks)

(ii) Recommend the course of action that the internal auditor should take if she is unable to persuade the Head of Internal Audit to draw these allegations of underreporting of injuries to the attention of the senior management of Grove Council.

(7 marks)

(Total = 25 marks)

2 JDM (RCS, 5/09)   45 mins

JDM Construction is a UK-based construction company. The company completed the building of 30 apartments in December 20X3 and immediately sold 15 of them for £125,000 each. However, no apartments have been sold since that date.

The total cost of building the apartments was £75,000 each. It is thought that the only additional cash flows that will arise will be for marketing and selling the remaining 15 apartments.

The Marketing Director of JDM has forecast the following changes in property prices during the next five years:

Market Forecast

20X4   10% decrease

20X5   2% decrease

20X6   5% increase

20X7   8% increase

20X8   5% increase

In response to the declining market, the Marketing Director has proposed and financially evaluated the two possible alternative marketing strategies shown below.

Marketing Strategy 1

Sell the properties at a discounted price of £115,000 each. This would require a marketing campaign that involves spending £210,000. Market research suggests that there is a 70% chance that all of the apartments would be sold within six months but a 30% chance that none will be sold. Under this strategy all money will be paid and received by 31 December 20X4.

Marketing Strategy 2

This strategy requires spending £75,000 on advertising. The Marketing Director expects that all the remaining 15 apartments will be sold under this strategy. Marketing Strategy 2 involves offering potential buyers the choice of three different deals, as detailed below:

Deal 1

Customers can buy an apartment at a reduced price of £95,000, if they agree to a rapid transfer of ownership. A 10% deposit is payable immediately, and the remaining balance is payable in eight weeks' time.

The Marketing Director expects that eight apartments will be sold under this arrangement.

Deal 2

Purchasers will be given the opportunity to purchase an apartment for £110,000, with a guarantee that if they wish to sell at any time during the next five years, JDM will purchase the property back at this initial price. Under this deal all sales receipts will be received within the next three months.

The marketing director expects to sell five apartments under this arrangement and that they will all be repurchased by 20X7.

Deal 3

Customers will be given the opportunity to purchase an apartment for £105,000, payable in three months' time, plus a further payment of £25,000 payable after 10 years, or when the customer sells the apartment, whichever occurs first.

The Marketing Director expects that two apartments will be sold under this arrangement.

Financial evaluation of Strategies 1 and 2

	NPV
	£000
Strategy 1	950
Strategy 2	
Immediate advertising	(75)
Deal 1	750
Deal 2	103
Deal 3	240
Total for Strategy 2	1,018

Required

(a) Discuss the relative merits of the two marketing strategies proposed by the Marketing Director of JDM.

(10 marks)

(b) Recommend, with reasons, which strategy JDM should adopt.

(5 marks)

(c) JDM is a relatively new company, which until now has operated in a buoyant market. In view of the recent economic downturn, the Board has realised that JDM needs a more formal system for considering risk.

Prepare a memo for the Board of Directors of JDM that explains an appropriate risk management process for the company.

(10 marks)

(Total = 25 marks)

3 LXY (RCS, 5/08)   45 mins

LXY is a company, which has a five-year contract to operate buses in and out of the city bus station in Danon, France. The station has 60 bus piers and an average of 90 buses per hour leave Danon for local and national destinations.

Services operate between 06.00 and 22.00 daily. All buses are operated solely by the driver, who loads and unloads luggage and checks that all passengers have a valid ticket. LXY only permits travel with a pre-paid ticket.

Local buses provide a suburban service to areas within a 20 kilometre radius of Danon. The national services cover distances of up to 500 kilometres and so drivers are frequently required to stay overnight at certain destinations before covering the return service the following day.

Required

(a)   You have recently been appointed Head of Risk and Internal Audit at LXY.

    (i)   Identify, with a brief justification, three categories which may be used to classify and manage the risks faced by LXY.   **(3 marks)**

    (ii)   For ONE of the categories that you have selected in (i) above, identify three possible risks and recommend appropriate tools for their control.   **(9 marks)**

(b)   A café owner in Danon has approached LXY with a proposal to provide food and drink facilities on board long-distance bus services.

    Identify the additional risks that need to be considered by LXY in the evaluation of the proposal, and how they might be managed.   **(4 marks)**

(c)   Many companies are too small to justify the existence of separate risk management and internal audit functions.

    Briefly explain the distinctive roles performed by each of these functions and recommend ways of maintaining their separate effectiveness within a combined department.   **(9 marks)**

(Total = 25 marks)

4   A and B (RCS, 11/06)   45 mins

The following information relates to two companies based in the United States of America, both of which are listed on the New York stock exchange. Each company had an annual turnover of approximately $800 million in 20X5.

Company A

This company sells into a mix of business-to-business and end-user markets across a total of 15 countries in North America and Europe. Business-to-business sales predominate and 40% of turnover comes from two key European customers.

Manufacturing, assembly and delivery is managed geographically rather than by product type, via three separate subsidiaries with their own CEO based in Canada, France and the UK respectively. Research and all Treasury operations for the arrangement of loan finance and hedging of foreign exchange risk are both fully centralised.

The company has a diverse shareholder base that includes two major pension funds, one of which has a representative entitled to be present as an observer at the board meetings of Company A.

Company B

This company operates in the same product market as Company A, but earns most of its income from end user sales, many of which are initiated by on-line direct orders. 80% of the internet sales originate in the United States of America. Company B's largest single customer, a Canadian company, represents 15% of its annual sales revenue, but no other customer exceeds 1% of total sales. Research and sales facilities are based at the US headquarters, but manufacturing and assembly is all undertaken by separate subsidiaries in China, where the company also has a joint venture business that manages all the global distribution. Treasury operations are fully decentralised, but run as cost rather than profit centres.

The company was started ten years ago, and the Board of Directors remains dominated by members of the founding family. The CEO and the Finance Director are husband and wife, and together own 35% of the company's shares.

Required

Using the information contained in the above scenario to develop your arguments, answer each of the following questions:

(a)   Discuss how decisions about company structure, market types and location can impact upon the risk profile of a company.

(12 marks)

(b)   Compare and contrast the risks associated with the differing approaches to the Treasury function adopted by the two companies in the above scenario.

(4 marks)

(c)   For either Company A or Company B as described in the scenario, taking into account its current structure and size, recommend one example of each of financial, non-financial quantitative, and non-financial qualitative controls that may be useful tools in monitoring exposure to either strategic or operational risks. You should briefly justify your choices.

(9 marks)

(Total = 25 marks)

5   Doctors' practice (RCS, 11/05)   45 mins

A large doctors' practice, with six partners and two practice nurses, has decided to increase its income by providing day surgery facilities. The existing building would be extended to provide room for the surgical unit and storage facilities for equipment and drugs. The aim is to offer patients the opportunity to have minor surgical procedures conducted by a doctor at their local practice, thus avoiding any unfamiliarity and possible delays to treatment that might result from referral to a hospital. Blood and samples taken during the surgery will be sent away to the local hospital for testing but the patient will get the results from their doctor at the practice. It is anticipated that the introduction of the day surgery facility will increase practice income by approximately 20 per cent.

Required

(a)   Identify the additional risks that the doctors' practice may expect to face as a consequence of the introduction of the new facility and explain how a model such as CIMA's risk management cycle might be used to understand and control such risks.

(12 marks)

(b)   Explain the meaning of the term 'risk appetite' and discuss who should take responsibility for defining that appetite in the context of the scenario outlined above.

(5 marks)

(c)   Critically discuss the role of systems-based internal auditing in relation to the assessment of risk management procedures in any organisation.

(8 marks)

(Total = 25 marks)

6   HOOD   45 mins

HOOD sells a wide range of coats, anoraks, waterproof trousers and similar outdoor clothing from its 56 stores located in one country. The company is profitable, although the gross profit in some stores has declined recently for no apparent reason.

Each store uses EPOS to maintain control of stock and provides the facility to use EFTPOS for payments. However, about 55% of all transactions are still made by cash. Details of sales made and stock below re-order levels are transferred to head office on a daily basis where management reports are also prepared.

Inventory is ordered centrally from Head Office, details of requirements being obtained from the daily management information provided by each store. Orders are sent to suppliers in the post, with inventory arriving at each store approximately 10 days after the re-order level is reached.

Recent newspaper reports indicate one of the chemicals used to waterproof garments releases toxic fumes after prolonged exposure to sunlight. The board of HOOD are investigating the claim, but are currently treating it with some degree of scepticism. The product range has generally sold well, although there has been little innovation in terms of garment design in the last 4 years.

Required

(a)   Identify the different risks facing the HOOD Company, placing the risks into suitable categories.

(10 marks)

(b)   Evaluate the potential effect of each risk on the company, recommending how the impact of that risk can be minimised.

(15 marks)

(Total = 25 marks)

MANAGEMENT AND INTERNAL CONTROL SYSTEMS

Questions 7 to 27 cover management and internal control systems, the subject of Part B of the BPP Study Text for Paper P3.

7   VV (11/11)   45 mins

VV is a quoted company. Its board comprises an equal number of both executive and non-executive directors. The company has a remuneration committee, comprised entirely of non-executives.

A major institutional investor in VV has written to the chair of the remuneration committee to raise some concerns about the manner in which the performance of VV's executive directors is controlled and rewarded.

At present, each of the executive directors receives a fairly substantial fixed annual salary combined with options granted under an executive share option scheme ("ESOS"). The ESOS is designed in order to align the directors' interests with those of the shareholders:

- The remuneration committee reviews each director's performance during the financial year and grants a number of share options in accordance with performance.

- The options are issued "at the money" (that is, the exercise price is the same as the market price) so that the directors have an incentive to increase the share price.

- The options can only be exercised on a specified date that falls three years after their issue.

- If a director leaves the company then any outstanding options will lapse without compensation.

The institutional investor has expressed concern about the ESOS arrangement because of the underlying financial implications of the scheme. VV first introduced ESOSs in order to motivate the executive directors to act in the shareholders' interests. If the directors work towards maximising VV's share price then the options will provide higher returns if they are in the money when they come due for exercise. In addition, VV's directors are much less likely to reject positive net present value investment opportunities if they hold options. Normally the directors are more risk averse than the shareholders when it comes to project appraisal, but holding options makes risk-taking more appealing.

The institutional investor is concerned that the options may have encouraged dysfunctional behaviour by the directors, although it is difficult to be certain that that has arisen because of the limited information that is available to the shareholders.

The institutional investor has suggested that the executive directors should be rewarded with a simpler scheme, such as an annual profit-related bonus. At present, it is unclear whether the reward system in place provides the executive directors with meaningful feedback on their performance. As a shareholder, the investor wishes to see a clearer link between the directors' performance and their remuneration.

Required

(a)   (i)   Explain why the introduction of ESOSs could motivate VV's executive directors to accept positive net present value (NPV) projects.   **(7 marks)**

(ii)   Explain how an ESOS scheme could affect the actions taken by the directors (other than the project appraisal decision).   **(8 marks)**

(b)   Evaluate the advantages AND disadvantages of rewarding executive directors by paying a bonus based on a simple and transparent measure such as profit.   **(10 marks)**

(Total = 25 marks)

8 C (5/11)   45 mins

C is a partnership that offers a range of consultancy services involving structural engineering. The firm specialises in examining plans prepared by architects to ensure that the buildings being planned are structurally sound. This requires careful consideration of the design and the materials being used to ensure that the resulting building will be stable and can withstand the effects of the wind and other forces of nature. C specialises in major contracts and the firm often advises on complex designs that use innovative building techniques.

C has a reputation for having a competitive culture. The firm offers salaries that are much higher than the industry average. There is an "up or out" culture which means that qualified staff must demonstrate the potential to be promoted to the next level of seniority within a relatively short period or they will be encouraged to leave.

C has 45 partners, all of whom are qualified structural engineers, and approximately 400 professional staff. C's professional staff comprises engineers at different stages in their careers, ranging from team leaders to junior trainees. The team leaders are all experienced engineers who are eligible for promotion to partnership in the event that a vacancy arises. Selection for partnership depends on the ability to consistently complete assignments to a high standard and within budget.

Trainee engineers are appointed on a three year contract, during which time they are expected to pass their professional exams. C takes on approximately 50 trainees every year. Those trainees who demonstrate the necessary qualities to succeed in C are offered the opportunity to stay with the firm at the conclusion of their training contracts. Those who do not receive such an offer must leave.

Each partner is responsible for a portfolio of assignments, and each portfolio is accounted for as a profit centre. Partners are expected to be aware of the opportunities to bid for assignments and to win new business despite competition from other engineering firms. C has a reputation for bidding aggressively and accepting tight deadlines. Each partner is responsible for a portfolio of assignments, each of which will involve a team leader and several assistants. Professional staff time is charged to assignments on an absorption costing basis and the firm's time recording system calculates a notional profit for each assignment based on the cost of time charged against the fee generated.

At the end of every financial year each partner receives an equal share of the firm's annual profit, but it is a matter of pride for each partner to generate more profit for the firm than he or she receives from the annual profit share.

All partners enjoy equal seniority and major strategic decisions are decided by a simple majority vote of the partnership. The firm is managed on a day to day basis by a management committee which comprises three partners. Every partner is expected to take a turn as a member of the management committee at some stage in his or her career. One person joins the committee every year to take over from the committee member whose term of office has expired. The third year of service on the management committee is spent as the firm's managing partner. There is no additional reward for serving on the management committee, but during that year the committee members are not expected to be responsible for a full complement of assignments and the managing partner is not expected to be responsible for any assignments.

Required

(a)   Evaluate the risks to the quality of service offered to C's clients arising from the competitive nature of the firm's culture.   **(12 marks)**

(b)   Evaluate the strengths and weaknesses of C's governance arrangements with respect to the partnership and its management committee.   **(13 marks)**

(Total = 25 marks)

9   P (11/10)   45 mins

P is a major quoted company that manufactures industrial chemicals. The company's Board comprises a Chief
Executive and five other executive directors, a non-executive chairman and four non-executive directors.   6+5

Two of the non-executive directors have served on P's board for five years. The company has a policy of asking
non-executive directors to stand down after six years and so the Chairman has established a Nominations
Committee to start the process of selecting replacements.

Three replacements have been suggested to the Nominations Committee. The nominees are:

- S, who is on the main board of C Pensions, an investment institution which owns 5% of P's equity. S has
  worked for C Pensions for 20 years and has always worked in the management of the company's
  investments, initially as an analyst and more recently as director in charge of investments. Before working
  for C Pensions, S was an investment analyst with an insurance company for 15 years.

- T, who is a CIMA member, is about to retire from full-time work. T has had a varied career, completing
  the CIMA qualification while working as a trainee accountant with a food manufacturer, then as a
  management accountant with an engineering company and finally as a senior accountant with a
  commercial bank. T was promoted to the bank's board and has been Finance Director for eight years.

- U, who is a former politician. After a brief career as a journalist, U became a member of parliament at the
  age of 35. After spending 20 years as a politician, including several years as a government minister, U
  has recently retired from politics at the age of 55. U already holds two other non-executive directorships
  in companies that do not compete with and are not in any way connected to P.

The Chairman of P is keen to recruit more non-executive directors as a matter of priority because the
Remuneration Committee faces a difficult task. The executive directors are presently remunerated with a
combination of a salary and executive stock options. P's shareholders have expressed concern about the
pressures created by these stock options and have asked that they be replaced by individual bonuses that reflect
the personal contribution made by each of the executive directors.

The Chairman and the non-executive directors are discussing the level of bonus that should be awarded for the
current year. This has been complicated because P made a loss for the first time. The Chief Executive has stated
that it would not be appropriate to accept a bonus from a loss-making company, but the other executive directors
claim that the loss was attributable to economic and industrial conditions and that their leadership minimised
the loss. All of the executive directors other than the Chief Executive have asked for substantial bonuses to reflect
their leadership in difficult times.

Required

(a)   Evaluate the suitability of each of the three nominees.

    Your answer should include arguments for and against each of the nominees.   **(15 marks)**

(b)   Discuss the problems associated with determining a suitable level of bonus for each of P's executive
    directors.   **(10 marks)**

                                                                          (Total = 25 marks)

10   B Bank (5/10)   45 mins

Introduction

The B Bank is a large international bank. It employs 6,000 staff in 250 branches and has approximately
500,000 borrowers and over 1,500,000 savers. The bank, which was founded in 1856, has an excellent
reputation for good customer service. The bank's share price has increased, on average, by 12% in each of the
last 10 years.

Directors' remuneration

There has been much adverse media coverage in many countries, including B Bank's home country, about the
alleged excessive bonuses received by the directors of banks. A meeting of central bank governors from many
nations failed to reach agreement on how to limit the size of directors' bonuses. The governor of the central bank
in B Bank's home country is particularly concerned about this issue, and consequently put forward the following
proposal:

Directors of banks will be asked to pay a fee to the bank for the privilege of being a director. This fee will be set by the remuneration committee of each bank. Directors will be paid a bonus based solely on appropriate profit and growth indicators. The more the bank succeeds, the higher will be the bonus. This proposal directly links performance of the bank to directors' pay. I see this as a more realistic option than simply limiting salaries or bonuses by statute as proposed at the recent central bank governors' conference."

<u>B Bank board and strategy</u>

The constitution of the board of B Bank is in accordance with the internationally agreed code of corporate governance.

Overall board strategy has been to set targets based on previous (profitable) experience, with increased emphasis on those areas where higher potential profits can be made such as mortgage lending (this is discussed below). The bank's executive information systems are able to compute relative product profitability, which supports this strategy. This strategy generated substantial profits in recent years. The last major strategy review took place four years ago. Non-executive directors do not normally query the decisions of the executive directors.

In recent years, the profile of the major shareholders of the bank has moved. Traditionally the major shareholders were pension funds and other longer term investors but now these are overshadowed by hedge funds seeking to improve their short-term financial returns.

One of the major sources of revenue for the bank is interest obtained on lending money against securities such as houses (termed a "mortgage" in many countries) with repayments being due over periods varying between 15 and 25 years. Partly as a result of intense competition in the mortgage market, the values of the mortgages advanced by B Bank regularly exceed the value of the properties, for example B Bank has made advances of up to 125% of a property's value. Internal reports to the board estimate that property prices will reverse recent trends and will rise by 7% per annum for at least the next 10 years, with general and wage inflation at 2%. B Bank intends to continue to obtain finance to support new mortgages with loans from the short-term money-markets.

Required

(a) Evaluate the proposal made by the governor of the central bank. **(10 marks)**

(b) Evaluate the risk management strategy in B Bank (except for consideration of directors' remuneration). Your evaluation should include recommendations for changes that will lower the bank's exposure to risk. **(15 marks)**

(Total = 25 marks)

11 AFC (RCS, 5/09)   45 mins

AFC is a global engineering business with a $1 billion turnover, employing 5,000 people in 15 countries. It is listed on stock exchanges in New York and London. AFC carries out major construction projects that typically take several years to complete. Examples of the kinds of projects carried out by AFC are power stations, dams and bridges.

Most of AFC's customers are governments. Negotiations leading to the winning of tenders are extensive and the terms and conditions of the resulting contracts are very comprehensive. The negotiated price is most often a fixed price contract. Subsequent variations requested by the customer are invoiced to the customer at cost plus a 20% profit margin for AFC.

The major risks faced by AFC could arise from:

- Professional indemnity claims arising from technical errors that have caused faulty work and/or rectification. AFC's insurance premiums for professional indemnity are several million dollars each year.

- Downturns in business due mainly to the reductions in government funding of large construction projects.

- Cost over-runs, which erode profit (however, cost increases that result from specification changes requested by customers are invoiced to them as contract variations).

- Penalties that apply under the contract for late completion of the project.

Required

Recommend the controls that AFC should implement in order to minimise the risks identified in the scenario.

You should consider separately each of the four major risks faced by AFC, and for each risk recommend controls in each of the following categories:

- financial
- non-financial quantitative
- qualitative

There are approximately 2 marks available for each risk/control combination. **(Total = 25 marks)**

12 CM (RCS, 5/09) 45 mins

CM is an owner-managed restaurant in a student area of a university city. The menu lists a wide range of dishes, which are individually priced. The restaurant also offers, at certain times, a fixed price "eat as much as you like" buffet. The opening times for the restaurant and the times for the "all you can eat" buffet are shown below:

CM Opening Hours		"Eat as Much as You Like" opening hours
Monday – Friday	Noon – 11pm	5pm – 8pm
Saturday	Noon – Midnight	1pm – 3pm
		6pm – 8pm
Sunday	Noon – 7pm	1pm – 6pm

When the "eat as much as you like" buffet is closed, customers can choose individually priced dishes from an extensive menu. The owner thinks that about 85% of CM's customers come for the buffet.

CM offers free jugs of water but also sells a wide range of alcoholic and non-alcoholic drinks, which carry a high mark up on delivered cost.

In an effort to keep operating costs as low as possible, the restaurant employs only part-time staff aged under 21, who are paid the national minimum wage. Their terms of employment require them to be willing to work on any of a range of tasks including preparation and cooking in the kitchen, serving on tables, replenishing the buffet, and working on the reception and payment desk. Staff turnover rates are very high, with the average employee only working two months for CM. The provision of a daily free meal for each member of staff plus a friend has recently been introduced in an attempt to reduce high staff turnover. No records are kept of the number of free meals provided.

The restaurant manager has nationally recognised qualifications in catering and food hygiene. Externally accredited courses in food hygiene for employees are available at local colleges. However, the manager considers them to be too expensive in view of the high staff turnover. Consequently, he takes sole responsibility for training new staff.

The restaurant accepts only cash from its customers. Customers pay on departure, giving cash to whoever is working the payment desk at the time. The cash is not processed through a till and receipts are not issued.

Required

(a)   Identify the potential risks in the current operation of CM and recommend appropriate control measures to reduce those risks in each of the following areas of CM's operations:

- Record keeping;
- Working capital management;
- Human resource policy. **(19 marks)**

(b)   Explain three possible reasons why the manager of CM may choose not to implement any controls.

(6 marks)

(Total = 25 marks)

13 HFD (RCS, 11/08)   45 mins

HFD is a registered charity with 100 employees and 250 volunteers providing in-home care for elderly persons who are unable to fully take care of themselves. The company structure has no shareholders in a practical sense although a small number of issued shares are held by the sponsors who established the charity many years previously. HFD is governed by a seven-member Board of Directors. The Chief Executive Officer (CEO) chairs the Board which comprises the Chief Financial Officer (CFO) and five independent, unpaid non-executive directors who were appointed by the CEO based on past business relationships. You are one of the independent members of HFD's Board.

The CEO/Chair sets the Board agendas, distributes Board papers in advance of meetings and briefs Board members in relation to each agenda item. At each of its quarterly meetings the Board reviews the financial reports of the charity in some detail and the CFO answers questions. Other issues that regularly appear as agenda items include new government funding initiatives for the client group, and the results of proposals that have been submitted to funding agencies, of which about 25% are successful. There is rarely any discussion of operational matters relating to the charity as the CEO believes these are outside the directors' experience and the executive management team is more than capable of managing the delivery of the in-home care services.

The Board has no separate audit committee but relies on the annual management letter from the external auditors to provide assurance that financial controls are operating effectively. The external auditors were appointed by the CEO many years previously.

HFD's Board believes that the company's corporate governance could be improved by following the principles applicable to listed companies.

Required

(a)   Recommend how HFD's board should be restructured to comply with the principles of good corporate governance.   **(16 marks)**

(b)   Explain the aspects of CIMA's ethical principles and the conceptual framework underlying those principles which you would consider relevant to continuing in your role as an independent member of HFD's board.   **(9 marks)**

(Total = 25 marks)

14 PKG High School (RCS, 5/07)   45 mins

The PKG High School has 900 pupils, 40 teachers, 10 support staff and a budget of $3 million per annum, 85% of which represents salary and salary-related costs. The local authority for PKG's area is responsible for 34 schools, of which six are high schools. The local authority allocates government funding for education to schools based on the number of pupils. It ensures that the government-approved curriculum is taught in all schools in its area with the aim of achieving government targets. All schools, including PKG, are subject to an independent financial audit as well as a scrutiny of their education provision by the local authority, and reports of both are presented to the school governing body.

The number of pupils determines the approximate number of teachers, based on class sizes of approximately 30 pupils. The salary costs for teachers are determined nationally and pay scales mean that more experienced teachers receive higher salaries. In addition, some teachers receive school-specific responsibility allowances.

PKG is managed on a day-to-day basis by the head teacher. The governance of each school is carried out by a governing body comprising the head teacher, elected representatives of parents of pupils, and members appointed by the local authority. The principles of good corporate governance apply to school governing bodies which are accountable to parents and the local authority for the performance of the school.

The governing body holds the head teacher accountable for day-to-day school management, but on certain matters such as building maintenance the head teacher will seek expert advice from the local authority.

The governing body meets quarterly and has as its main responsibilities budgetary management, appointment of staff, and education standards. The main control mechanisms exercised by the governing body include scrutiny of a year-to-date financial report, a quarterly non-financial performance report, teacher recruitment and approval of all purchases over $1,000. The head teacher has expenditure authority below this level.

The financial report (which is updated monthly) is presented to each meeting of the governing body. It shows the local authority's budget allocation to the school for the year, the expenditure incurred for each month and the year to data, and any unspent balances. Although there is no external financial reporting requirement for the school, the local authority will not allow any school to overspend its budget allocation in any financial year.

PKG's budget allocation is only just sufficient to provide adequate educational facilities. Additional funds are always required for teaching resources, building maintenance, and to upgrade computer equipment. The only flexibility the school has in budget management is to limit responsibility allowances and delay teacher recruitment. This increases pupil-contact time for individual teachers however, and forces teachers to undertake preparation, marking and administration after school hours.

Note: A local authority (or council) carries out service for the local community and levies local taxes (or council tax) to fund most of its operations. Many of the local authority functions are regulated by central government and considerable funding also comes from that source. The range of local authority services include education, community health, refuse collection, and maintenance of footpaths and public parks.

Required

(a)   Explain why the review and audit of control systems is important for the governing body of a school such as PKG. **(5 marks)**

(b)   Evaluate the effectiveness of the governing body's control over PKG High School and recommend ways in which it might be improved. **(20 marks)**

(Total = 25 marks)

15 Pensions (RCS, 5/07)   45 mins

Under international accounting conventions, the rules on accounting for employee benefits are based upon the principle that the cost of providing such benefits, should be recognised in the period in which the benefit is earned by the employee, rather than when it is paid or payable. The rules laid down in International Accounting Standard 19 (IAS 19) *Employee benefits* apply to a wide range of employee benefits, of which the most common form is pensions.

A significant number of pension plans are classed as defined benefit plans, under which the pension payable by the organisation on the retirement of an employee is linked to his/her salary. The salary used for the calculation of the benefit may be either an average or a final salary, although final salary is still the most common.

Under IAS 19, a company's statement of financial position must record the present value of the future benefits payable, net of the value of the pension fund assets. The discount rate used to arrive at a present value for the liabilities is equal to the interest rate payable on AA rated corporate bonds. The valuation are carried out by actuaries, who are required to make a number of assumptions about current economic conditions, life expectancy, the rate of salary increase over time, and the expected rate of return on the pension fund assets.

In the UK, the requirement to put the value of the pension fund's net assets or liabilities on the face of the statement of financial position has resulted in a number of companies reporting pension fund deficits in excess of £1 billion and has led to concerns over a 'pensions crisis'.

Required

(a)   A company has a pension fund deficit equal to ten per cent of its market capitalisation. Explain and discuss the nature of the risks posed to **both** the company and its current employees by the existence of such a substantial pension fund deficit. **(10 marks)**

The Finance Director of a UK listed company is concerned about the sensitivity of the company's pension fund deficit to changes in life expectancy. If the company's advising actuaries use the most up-to-date life expectancy table, the company's pension deficit will increase by 30%, to approximately 60% of its market capitalisation. The Head of Financial Reporting is therefore considering requesting the actuaries to continue using tables which are now deemed out of date.

Required

(b) (i) Discuss the proposal to request the actuaries to use out-of-date tables. **(8 marks)**

(ii) Identify the internal and external financial reporting controls that could be used to prevent the manipulation of the liability valuation in the manner suggested by the Head of Financial Reporting. **(7 marks)**

(Total = 25 marks)

16 College fraud (5/11)
45 mins

A large college has several sites and employs hundreds of teaching staff. The college has recently discovered a serious fraud involving false billings for part-time teaching.

The fraud involved two members of staff. M is a clerk in the payroll office who is responsible for processing payments to part-time teaching staff. P is the head of the Business Studies department at the N campus. Part-time lecturers are required to complete a monthly claim form which lists the classes taught and the total hours claimed. These forms must be signed by their head of department, who sends all signed forms to M. M checks that the class codes on the claim forms are valid, that hours have been budgeted for those classes and inputs the information into the college's payroll package.

The college has a separate personnel department that is responsible for maintaining all personnel files. Additions to the payroll must be made by a supervisor in the personnel office. The payroll package is programmed to reject any claims for payment to employees whose personnel files are not present in the system.

M had gained access to the personnel department supervisor's office by asking the college security officer for the loan of a pass key because he had forgotten the key to his own office. M knew that the office would be unoccupied that day because the supervisor was attending a wedding. M logged onto the supervisor's computer terminal by guessing her password, which turned out to be the registration number of the supervisor's car. M then added a fictitious part-time employee, who was allocated to the N campus Business Studies department.

P then began making claims on behalf of the fictitious staff member and submitting them to M. M signed off the forms and input them as normal. The claims resulted in a steady series of payments to a bank account that had been opened by P. The proceeds of the fraud were shared equally between M and P.

The fraud was only discovered when the college wrote to every member of staff with a formal invitation to the college's centenary celebration. The letter addressed to the fictitious lecturer was returned as undeliverable and the personnel department became suspicious when they tried to contact this person in order to update his contact details. By then M and P had been claiming for non-existent teaching for three years.

The government department responsible for funding the college conducted an investigation and concluded that the college's management had relied excessively on the application controls programmed into administrative software and had paid too little attention to the human resources aspects of the system.

Required

(a) Evaluate the difficulties associated with preventing and/or detecting this fraud. **(10 marks)**

(b) Advise the college on the weaknesses in its systems and procedures. **(8 marks)**

(c) Discuss the suggestion that the human elements of control systems are frequently more important than the software elements in ensuring that records are correct. **(7 marks)**

(Total = 25 marks)

17 M (9/10)   45 mins

M is the leading retailer of mobile telephones in its home country. The company has almost 100 branches, with at least one branch in every major town and city. Some branches are located within walking distance of one another.

M has a highly aggressive management team. It views sales growth as the key to the company's continuing success. It believes that increasing their share of the retail market will enable M to negotiate large discounts from manufacturers and network providers. It also creates economies of scale in the advertising and promotion of the company and its services.

Two years ago the directors abandoned traditional budgeting and target setting. They decided that budgets did not necessarily give branch staff a sufficient incentive to maximise sales because they tended to work towards achieving but not surpassing sales targets. They introduced a new management control system with the following features:

- Shop sales are recorded using electronic point of sales (EPOS) cash registers that are linked to head office. Every sale indicates the branch and the member of staff responsible for the sale. These transactions are recorded in real time during the course of the day.

- A terminal in every shop lists a running total of that shop's sales for the day, analysed between each member of sales staff. The terminal also indicates the shop's ranking for the day relative to all of M's other shops.

- Every shop manager must be at work at least an hour before the shop opens. During that hour the manager receives a telephone call from the regional sales manager to discuss the previous day's sales and likely sales during the day ahead.

- Each shop manager is permitted considerable freedom to introduce special offers and promotions, subject to achieving an acceptable margin on each sale made.

- At the end of every week the manager and staff of the ten shops with the highest sales are given a substantial bonus. The manager and staff at the ten shops with the poorest sales are given one week's notice to improve or they face being moved to other shops or even dismissal.

- Sales have grown rapidly since this system was introduced, although the rate of growth has been declining recently.

The Director of Human Resources has investigated staff absenteeism and turnover and has discovered that many of M's branch managers and sales staff have been with the company for several years. They seem to thrive in the competitive environment and the company pays staff with good sales records a substantial salary compared with other retailers. M also suffers a high staff turnover every year and some members of staff are frequently absent for health reasons, with their doctors certifying them as ill due to stress-related conditions.

M's Chief Accountant is concerned that the company's management accounting systems are unethical and she has provided the board with a copy of CIMA's *Code of Professional Ethics*. Performance Strategy 17 September 2010

Required

(a) Discuss the operational risks that could arise as a result of the new management control system. Your discussion should include the potential risks associated with this new system.   **(15 marks)**

(b) Advise M's directors on the ethical implications of their approach to personnel management.   **(10 marks)**

(Total = 25 marks)

18 Y (Specimen paper)   45 mins

The Y company produces a range of dairy products such as yoghurts, cream and butter from one factory. The main ingredient for these products is milk, which is obtained from 27 different dairy farms (fields where cows are allowed to graze and produce milk) within a 60 km radius of the factory. Y requires that milk must be delivered within 6 hours of being obtained from the cows and that the farms themselves use "organic" principles (farming without using manmade pesticides, growth hormones etc.). Transportation systems in Y's country are good and milk is rarely delivered late.

Each farm provides a quality certificate on each batch of milk produced confirming adherence to these standards (this is important to Y although customer satisfaction surveys show Y products are sold on taste, not sourcing of ingredients).

In Y's factory, yoghurt is produced in batches. The inputs to each batch such as milk, fruit, *appropriate* bacteria and other ingredients, are recorded in the batch database showing the source of that ingredient, that is the specific farm. During production, Y's quality control department tests each batch for purity (lack of contamination from *harmful* bacteria etc) and acceptable taste, with the results being recorded in the quality control database. Any batches not meeting quality standards are rejected and destroyed. Y's costing systems have maintained a 5% failure rate in production for the last 6 years which is now well in excess of the industry average.

On completion of each batch, the quality control department again undertakes purity control and taste testing. Batches are rejected where standards are not met; a further 2% failure rate is expected at this stage.

Batches of yoghurt etc are packed on Y's premises and then despatched for sale via retail outlets such as supermarkets; Y does not sell direct to the consumer. However, Y has an excellent brand name resulting from innovative advertising and high product quality. Product reviews in magazines and news websites have always been favourable meaning that Y does not need to pay much, if any, attention to customer feedback.

Required

(a) Evaluate the control systems in Y for the manufacture of yoghurt, recommending improvements to those systems where necessary.   **(12 marks)**

(b) Explain the process of risk mapping and construct a risk map for Y. Discuss how risk mapping can be used within the Y organisation.   **(13 marks)**

(Total = 25 marks)

19 X (Specimen paper)   45 mins

X is an organisation involved in making business-to-business sales of industrial products. X employs a sales team of 40 representatives and assigns each a geographic territory that is quite large. Sales representatives search for new business and follow up sales leads to win new business, and maintain contact with the existing customer base.

The sales representatives spend almost all their time travelling to visit clients. The only time when they are not doing this is on one day each month when they are required to attend their regional offices for a sales meeting. Sales representatives incur expenses. They have a mobile telephone, a fully maintained company car and a corporate credit card which can be used to pay for vehicle expenses, accommodation and meals and the cost of entertaining potential and existing clients.

The performance appraisal system for each sales representative is based on the number and value of new clients and existing clients in their territory. All sales representatives are required to submit a weekly report to their regional managers which gives details of the new and existing clients that they have visited during that week. The regional managers do not get involved in the daily routines of sales representatives if they are generating sufficient sales. Consequently, sales representatives have a large amount of freedom.

The Head Office Finance department, to whom regional managers have a reporting relationship, analyses the volume and value of business won by sales representatives and collects details of their expenses which are then reported back monthly to regional managers. At the last meeting of regional managers, the Head Office Finance department highlighted the increase in sales representatives' expenses as a proportion of sales revenue over the last two years and instructed regional managers to improve their control over the work representatives carry out and the expenses they incur.

BPP
LEARNING MEDIA

Required

(a) Explain what an internal control system is, how it relates to the control environment and its likely costs, benefits and limitations. **(8 marks)**

(b) Discuss the purposes and importance of internal control and risk management to the X company and recommend action that should be taken to overcome any perceived weaknesses identified in internal control and/or risk management systems. **(12 marks)**

(c) Recommend how substantive analytical procedures could be used in the internal audit of X's sales representatives' expenses. **(5 marks)**

(Total = 25 marks)

20 KSP (RCS, 11/09) 45 mins

KSP has sales of about €100 million per annum. Sales are 'business-to-business' and payments are required on 30 day net terms. The sales representatives of KSP are set demanding targets that require them to win new customers and also to increase the size of individual orders.

The sales representatives have considerable autonomy over the amount of discount they allow as a deduction from the published list price to their customers. The list price is the only price that is held in KSP's computer system. Sales, and discounts, are frequently negotiated over the telephone. The sales representatives note the discounts they have agreed with each customer on an order form completed by the sales representatives. The credit limit for each customer is approved by the Sales Manager.

Each one of the sales representatives is paid a commission. This is based on the sales they have made, but the commission is calculated on a sliding scale according to the discount that they have granted. A high discount results in a low commission (and a low discount gives a higher commission).

There are 20 staff in KSP's Accounts Receivable Department, which is headed by the Accounts Receivable Manager. The department relies heavily on information technology for processing and management of invoicing and accounts receivable. All accounts receivable staff are multi-skilled, working in small teams with customer-specific rather than single-function responsibilities. For each team, which looks after a defined group of customers, responsibilities include invoicing, and data entry to customer accounts of customer payments paid direct into KSP's bank account or received by cheque through the post. In addition, Accounts Receivable staff carry out debt collection activity by telephone and letter.

The performance of the Accounts Receivable Department is measured against three targets:

- Ensuring that credit notes are no greater than 1% of sales value. At present aggregate credit notes across the company amount to three times this level.

- Achieving an average days sales outstanding (DSO) of 45. Actual DSOs over the past year have ranged between 56 and 62 days at the month ends.

- Keeping bad debt write-offs below 2% of sales turnover. Actual bad debt write-offs over the last two years have averaged 3·5%.

An internal audit report has recently identified the below-target performance of the Accounts Receivable Department. The Accounts Receivable Manager has responded by explaining that a significant number of customers dispute their accounts due to the prices charged on the invoice. This results in slower collections whilst the query is being investigated, and subsequently a large number of credit notes have to be issued. The Accounts Receivable Manager also stated that bad debts should not be her responsibility as the department has no control over the credit limit granted to customers.

Required

Internal control weaknesses throughout KSP may have led to KSP's Accounts Receivable Department not achieving its performance targets.

(a) Recommend, with reasons, controls that KSP should implement to improve the Accounts Receivable Department's performance in relation to its targets. **(18 marks)**

(b) Discuss the importance of the internal control environment for KSP. **(7 marks)**

(Total = 25 marks)

21 SRN (RCS, 11/08)   45 mins

SRN is a small listed clothing retailer operating a chain of 18 stores in suburban shopping centres together with a city-based Head Office. Orders for stock are placed centrally by Head Office and are delivered to Head Office by suppliers. Details of goods received are entered by Head Office employees to the company's computer system. The goods are then despatched to the retail locations.

There are typically between two and three full-time employees in each store (one of whom is the store manager) plus part-time employees during the busiest periods. They are responsible for display and sales. All sales are processed using the electronic point of sale (EPOS) terminals which have the facility for cash, and debit and credit card sales. Cash sales are banked daily by store employees and each day Head Office reconciles bank deposits with the EPOS reports for each store.

Sales through the EPOS terminals automatically reduce stock levels and support Head Office purchasing and stock replenishment decisions. A physical stocktake is carried out by store employees six monthly. Usually the stocktakes reveal stock shortfalls for almost half the stores. Store employees attribute this to theft.

Prices are set initially by Head Office as a standard mark-up on the purchase cost. This price is automatically displayed on the EPOS terminals. However, employees have the authority to discount prices based on the length of time stock has been in their store and the need to ensure constant stock rotation. Sales revenue and price discounts are monitored weekly by Head Office to ensure that sales levels and margins are on target and that excessive discounting does not take place.

Sales, gross profits and net profits are reported quarterly for each store. A Head Office manager visits each store once per week, typically on the same day and at the same time, so that store employees can discuss any problems with the Head Office manager.

Required

(a)   Identify the risks of fraud and theft faced by SRN in relation to its employees.   **(6 marks)**

(b)   Recommend (with reasons) the policies and internal controls that SRN could implement to prevent employee fraud and theft. In making your recommendations, you should consider both

  (i)   Working conditions and the role of the Human Resource function; and
  (ii) Operational internal controls.   **(19 marks)**

                                                                        (Total = 25 marks)

22 CSX (RCS, 5/08)   45 mins

CSX is a distribution company, which buys and sells small electronic components. The company has sales of $200 million per annum on which it achieves a profit of $12 million.

Central Warehouse Department

The company has a large Central Warehouse Department employing 100 staff over 2 shifts. The warehouse contains 30,000 different components, which are of high value and are readily saleable. Technological change is commonplace and components can become obsolete with little warning. Twice a year, the Purchasing Manager authorises the disposal of obsolete inventory. Inventory control is carried out through a computer system that has been used by the company for the last ten years.

Purchasing and receiving

Inventory is ordered using manual purchase orders based on tender prices. Goods received into the Central Warehouse are recorded on a manual Goods Received Note which is the source document for computer data entry. Data entry is done by clerical staff employed within the Central Warehouse.

Customer orders

Orders from customers are entered into the computer by clerical staff in the Sales Department. The computer checks inventory availability and produces a Picking List which is used by Central Warehouse staff to assemble the order. Frequently, there are differences between the computer inventory record and what is physically in the store. The Picking List (showing the actual quantities ready to be delivered) is used by clerical staff to update the computer records in the Central Warehouse. A combined Delivery Note/Invoice is then printed to accompany the goods.

<u>Accounting</u>

At the end of each financial year, a physical check of inventory is carried out which results in a significant write-off. To allow for these losses, the monthly operating statements to the Board of Directors include a 2% contingency, added to each month's cost of sales.

<u>Internal Audit Department</u>

The company's Internal Audit Department has been asked by the Board to look at the problem of inventory losses. Managers in the Central Warehouse believe that inventory losses are the result of inaccurate data entry, the old and unreliable nature of the computer system and the large number of small inventory items which are easily lost, or which warehouse staff throw away if they are obsolete or damaged.

Required

(a)   Explain the risks faced by CSX in relation to its inventory control system and recommend specific improvements to the system's internal controls.   **(15 marks)**

(b)   Recommend (without being specific to the CSX scenario) the tests or techniques, both manual and computerised, that internal auditors can use in assessing the adequacy of inventory controls. **(10 marks)**

(Total = 25 marks)

23   HIJ (RCS, 5/06)   45 mins

HIJ is a new company that provides professional services to small businesses. Apart from the Principal, a qualified accountant who owns 100% of the business, there are four professionally qualified and two support staff. The business model adopted by HIJ is to charge an annually negotiated fixed monthly retainer to its clients in return for advice and assistance in relation to budgeting, costing, cash management, receivables and inventory control, and monthly and annual management reporting. The work involves weekly visits to each client by a member of staff and a monthly review between HIJ's Principal and the chief executive of the client company. In delivering its client services, HIJ makes extensive use of specialist accounting software.

The Principal continually carries out marketing activity to identify and win new clients. This involves advertising, production of brochures and attending conferences, exhibitions, and various business events where potential clients may be located.

The management of HIJ by its Principal is based on strict cost control, maximising the chargeable hours of staff and ensuring that the retainers charged are sufficient to cover the hours worked for each client over the financial year.

Required

(a)   Recommend management controls that would be appropriate for the Principal to have in place for HIJ.
                                                                                              (12 marks)

(b)   Discuss the need for various types of audit that are appropriate for HIJ.   **(8 marks)**

(c)   Discuss the costs and benefits for HIJ that are likely to arise from a system of internal controls. **(5 marks)**

(Total = 25 marks)

24   GG (5/12)   45 mins

GG manufactures a range of valves that are used in the manufacture of car braking systems. GG sells its components to several major car manufacturers. It is difficult to manufacture a perfectly serviceable valve every time because the manufacturing process is complicated and involves several steps. After each step has been completed the company runs a series of quality checks and valves that fail are discarded before they go on to the next stage or are accepted into inventory. The rejection rates vary from step to step, but can be as high as 5% in some stages of the production process. Overall, GG budgets for a 20% rejection rate when estimating the size of production runs.

There are substantial costs associated with quality checks and rejections. Approximately 20% of staff time is devoted to quality control. The rejected components have no scrap value and so GG has to pay to dispose of them in an environmentally acceptable manner.

Staff morale appears to have a role in the determination of quality. Failure rates are higher on Friday afternoons and Monday mornings when employees are distracted by looking forward to the weekend or demotivated by the start of the working week. Also major televised sporting events broadcast late at night can lead to deterioration in the quality of the following day's output because staff have stayed up to watch the event.

The failure rate depends largely upon the care with which the manufacturing machinery has been set up and calibrated before a batch of parts is processed, although that is not the only factor. For example, a defective part may have passed through earlier quality checks unnoticed and could cause a failure at a later stage.

GG's board is keen to enjoy the benefits associated with total quality management (TQM), but has not committed itself to a full implementation of TQM. As an initial step the board asked production supervisors to come into work an hour early once a week for a quality circle meeting. The board had intended to devote more time and effort to TQM if this initial step had proved successful, but the directors have been disappointed by the initial feedback, which can be summarised as follows:

- The supervisors have proposed that the working week be reorganised so that staff can leave early on a Friday afternoon and have longer breaks on a Monday. This proposal is supported by a revised schedule that would make up for this time by having staff work longer hours in the middle of the week. GG's board has rejected this proposal because there would be some additional administrative costs associated with the proposed new working arrangements.

- The supervisors wish to reallocate some of the present quality control staff to production so that more staff time would be available to permit production processes to be properly set up. The supervisors believe that production staff have to work at close to 100% of their capacity and that such effort is not consistent with producing high quality work. Reducing the pressure would lead to a dramatic reduction in failed parts and so the company would need fewer quality inspectors. GG's board has rejected this proposal because it believes that staff should be encouraged to work harder and not to slow down. Also, the board would expect any reduction in the quality control staff to offer the opportunity to reduce staffing and save costs.

Required

(a)   (i)   Advise GG's board on the shortcomings of the approach that it has taken to TQM.   **(8 marks)**

      (ii)   Recommend, stating reasons, the actions that GG's board should have taken in order to successfully introduce TQM within GG.   **(7 marks)**

(b)   Advise GG's board on the risks associated with reducing the number of quality control staff in the factory.

     (10 marks)

     (Total = 25 marks)

25   D (3/12)   45 mins

D is currently a large business which sells cars. D was established almost 30 years ago when the founder started buying and selling used cars. The company has expanded steadily since then. It now owns 32 vehicle dealerships that are spread across the country.

All of the dealerships now sell new cars. Each dealership has a franchise from a specific motor manufacturer. The dealerships do not compete with one another. Those which sell luxury models are well distanced from one another, as are those which sell more basic models. D has at least one dealership for each of the major manufacturers.

All of the dealerships accept customers' old cars as trade-ins against the cost of their new car. Trade-in cars are resold at the dealerships if they are less than four years old and are in good condition. If they do not meet these criteria then they are sold through a third party's car auction. It is company policy that each trade-in is serviced and repaired by the dealership that accepted the car from the customer.

D's inventory of second hand cars is organised in order to maximise selling prices. Cars are often moved across the country in order to ensure that each dealership has a balanced inventory on offer. High quality luxury cars are sold through the dealerships that specialise in luxury models. Other cars are sorted according to manufacturer. Second hand cars tend to attract higher selling prices if they are sold through a dealership that sells new cars of the same make.

The founder of the business remains in place as D's Chief Executive. He has always been closely involved in the day to day supervision of the business but he has now decided to change things. He is thinking about setting up a divisional structure, with four regional divisions for dealerships in the North, South, East and West of the country. Each division will be managed by its own divisional manager and there will be a small executive team based at D's head office to take charge of the business as a whole. The founder's intention is that the divisional managers will be left free to manage without interference from the centre, but performance will be observed and monitored closely.

Required

(a)   The founder has decided that each of the divisional managers will be evaluated using a balanced scorecard system.

Recommend, with reasons, TWO measures that should appear under each perspective:

- Financial

- Customer

- Learning and growth

- Internal business processes   **(16 marks)**

(b)   (i)   Evaluate the potential for dysfunctional behaviour arising from the transfer of trade-ins between dealerships and divisions.   **(6 marks)**

(ii)   Explain how the problems identified in (i) might be overcome.   **(3 marks)**

(Total = 25 marks)

26   HH (9/11)   45 mins

HH is a large marketing consultancy that provides a range of services including developing marketing campaigns, designing web pages, managing media relations and so on. There are approximately 300 professional staff working in departments such as advertising and media relations and 600 support staff in areas such as administration and information technology (IT). HH operates from a large office block in the centre of a major city.

In common with similar agencies, HH is successful because it can offer clients an integrated service for all of their marketing and public relations needs. Sometimes those needs are related. For example, advertising staff may work alongside public relations staff to ensure that a new product is advertised effectively and that any positive press publicity, such as the consumers' favourable reaction at the product's launch, can be maximised.

HH has a traditional management accounting system. Each department has its own detailed management accounts, which show financial transactions and chargeable hours. Financial transactions include all revenue from billings invoiced to clients and all costs.   Included in the costs are substantial amounts for overheads associated with the running costs of the office building and the business as a whole. Chargeable hours are monitored for each member of staff. The hourly charge-out rate varies according to the seniority of the staff member and is set so that all costs are recovered and a healthy profit is charged on top. Any work undertaken for another department is charged internally at the staff member's full charge-out rate.

The media buying department of HH buys and sells advertising space in newspapers and airtime on radio and television. The department sells this space and time to its clients at cost plus a mark-up and also makes it available at the same price to other departments in HH. This means that HH can offer to plan and implement a marketing campaign from the initial design all the way through to the publication or broadcast of the finished advertisement.

HH's board is concerned that the company's traditional management accounting system is encouraging dysfunctional behaviour and causing disputes between managers. The following examples have been debated at recent board meetings:

- The public relations department is paying external web designers to design "blogs" on behalf of clients rather than using the web designers from HH's web design department. The web design business has seasonal peaks and troughs and there are times when there is spare capacity, but the hourly rates charged by the web design department are more expensive than those available from third parties.

- The staff coffee shop was closed to create additional work space. Since the closure the space has been empty because none of HH's department heads wish to be charged with the cost of additional overheads.

- Account executives within HH are keen to earn as much profit for themselves from each sale. Consequently they are dealing directly with major broadcasters and newspapers and are not using the media buying department. These individual deals are taking away the bargaining power of the media buying department.

HH's board is keen to consider whether the implementation of lean manufacturing and lean management accounting techniques might improve matters. In particular, the following principles have been identified as being relevant to HH:

- HH should be managed through processes or value streams rather than traditional departmental structures. The board believes that the two value streams are the sale of professional services and the sale of media space.

- The consultancy should maximise the flow of services through the value streams while eliminating waste.

- Lean management accounting should provide the value stream leader with performance measurement information to both control and improve the value stream.

Required

(a) (i)   Advise HH's board on the differences between managing value streams and managing departmental profits.   **(5 marks)**

     (ii) Recommend, stating reasons, the changes that HH should make to its management accounting systems and policies in order to improve the management of the value streams.   **(10 marks)**

(b) Advise HH's directors on the difficulties that are likely to be associated with implementing the changes that a move towards lean management accounting will create. Your advice should include recommendations as to how those difficulties might best be dealt with.   **(10 marks)**

(Total = 25 marks)

27   Product choice (RCS, 5/07)   45 mins

You work in the new product development division of a USA based global consumer electronics company. You are employed as the accountant responsible for costing and project appraisal of all new product proposals. All costs and revenues are based on information provided by the electronic engineers and marketing staff responsible for each individual project. It is assumed that all development is fully completed prior to initial marketing, and so no redesign costs are allowed once a product is launched. The rapid rate of technology change within the industry has led the company to assume a maximum product life of seven years.

The tables below give details of the company-wide incremental cash flows for two new consumer products. All cash flows are assumed to occur at the year end. Regulatory constraints mean that the company cannot invest in both developments. The company-wide hurdle rate for capital investments is 7.5% per year but the Finance Director is considering introducing risk-adjusted rates, which would give a discount rate of 8.5% per year for Product 1 and 10% per year for Product 2. The net present values generated by each of the products, using both the standard hurdle rate and the risk-adjusted hurdle rates, are also given in the tables.

Product 1 would be manufactured and assembled in China and transferred to company-owned retail outlets in the USA. Product 2 would be assembled in the Czech Republic from components shipped in from Taiwan and then sold to third party distributors across Western Europe.

Product 1	Year(s)	Annual sales revenue $ Million (based on ex factory prices)	Design and development costs $ Million	Annual manufacturing and distribution costs $ Million
	1	Nil	200	Nil
	2	Nil	400	Nil
	3	280		120
	4-7	420		180
NPV at 7.5% pa	$244 million			
NPV at 8.5% pa	$217 million			

Product 2	Year(s)	Annual sales revenue $ Million (based on ex factory prices)	Design and development costs $ Million	Annual manufacturing and distribution costs $ Million
	1	Nil	6,400	Nil
	2	1,250	Nil	600
	3	2,000	Nil	750
	4-6	3,500	nil	1,200
NPV at 7.5% pa	$430 million			
NPV at 10% pa	($45 million)			

Required

(a)   Recommend three ways of improving your company's internal control systems to ensure better management of risks throughout the product life cycle.   **(10 marks)**

(b)   Prepare a memo for your Head of Division recommending which product your company should support. You should clearly explain and justify your recommendations in the context of risk management.

(15 marks)

(Total = 25 marks)

MANAGEMENT OF FINANCIAL RISK

Questions 28 to 50 cover management of financial risk, the subject of Part C of the BPP Study Text for Paper P3.

28 VTB (RCS, 11/09)   45 mins

VTB sells canned vegetables to large stores and supermarkets. The company operates by monitoring crop harvests throughout the world. It identifies countries where there are surpluses of particular crops and then takes advantage of the situation by buying at low prices. VTB then arranges for local companies to process and can the vegetables before shipping them back to VTB's home country. This strategy has been successful because VTB can supply good quality products at prices lower than those of other food processing companies. VTB has grown rapidly since it was founded five years ago. The company has several major supermarkets in its home country as its customers and is continuing to expand.

VTB has to manage its cash flows very carefully. Its buying strategy does not permit it to develop long-term relationships with any of the growers or factories that it uses and so it does not have trade credit. VTB must pay for goods at the time of purchase. Conversely, the supermarkets which buy from VTB often take significant periods to pay for the goods that they have purchased. There is a further complication because VTB buys from a host of different countries and so it needs to enter into transactions in a variety of currencies.

The Finance Director and Chief Accountant have shared the responsibility for managing VTB's cash position since VTB's creation. This is a major responsibility because the company must keep a substantial cash surplus, with balances in several currencies. This can be very time consuming because VTB must constantly convert cash between currencies to meet operating requirements, without building up excessive balances in any of them. There is also a complicated bookkeeping process in order to reconcile the effects of exchange differences. It has been decided that the cash position should be managed by a dedicated team.

The board has agreed to establish a corporate treasury department, with a full-time Treasurer who will be appointed to deal with the cash flows, supported by a small staff who will undertake the associated administration. None of VTB's existing employees are suitably qualified for any of these posts and so all will have to be appointed externally. The Chief Accountant is concerned that this team of new employees will have a great deal of discretion over making payments which will increase the risk of fraud. The Finance Director feels that the Internal Audit department can monitor the Treasury department on a day to day basis. The Finance Director also feels that the new Treasury department will give VTB the opportunity to profit from currency movements by actively taking positions in currencies that are going to appreciate in value.

Required

(a) Explain the steps that the HR department of VTB should take when appointing the Treasurer and support staff for this new department.   **(12 marks)**

(b) Discuss the merits of the suggestion that VTB should control its planned Treasury department by having the Internal Audit department monitor its routine activities.   **(8 marks)**

(c) Discuss the merits of VTB attempting to earn profit from speculating on currency movements.   **(5 marks)**

(Total = 25 marks)

29 Derivatives (RCS, 5/06)   45 mins

Warren Buffett, the stock market investor, views derivatives as a 'time bomb', but many corporate treasurers clearly perceive them as very useful tools for reducing risk.

Required

(a) Explain and discuss the reasons for such divergent viewpoints. **(13 marks)**

The International Accounting Standard on Financial Instrument Recognition and Measurement (IAS 39) includes a fair value option that permits a company to designate certain types of financial instruments as ones to be measured at fair value on initial recognition, with changes in fair value recognised in profit or loss. The designation is irrevocable. Additionally, all financial assets and liabilities held for trading are measured at fair value with the associated changes in value passing through profit and loss.

This method of accounting is defended on the grounds that it ensures that the disclosures better reflect the risks that are being taken, thereby improving the information available to the stock market.

Required

(b) Explain the additional risks arising from these rules that may be faced by companies which choose to exercise the fair value option and/or regularly trade derivatives for profit. **(5 marks)**

An investor owns a portfolio of shares that has varied in value over the last twelve months between £1·5 million and £1·8 million. All stock is highly liquid and can be sold within one day. The daily profit and loss distribution is assumed to be normally distributed with a mean of zero and a standard deviation of £60,000.

Required

(c) (i) Explain the meaning of the term 'value at risk' from the perspective of a fund manager. **(4 marks)**

     (ii) Calculate and comment upon the value at risk of the portfolio, assuming a 95% confidence level and a one day holding period. **(3 marks)**

(Total = 25 marks)

30 W Bank (3/11)   45 mins

W Bank is a small bank which offers a range of banking and credit facilities to both individual and business customers. W Bank generates most of its funds for lending by taking deposits from customers who are paid a variable rate of interest in line with market conditions.

W Bank generates revenue from acting as an intermediary for interest rate swaps. In order to give itself maximum flexibility, W does not necessarily identify two clients who have matching requirements. Instead, the bank will act as a counterparty to any entity who meets its credit criteria. Ideally, the bank's portfolio of swaps will tend to balance one another in terms of the mix of fixed and floating positions and the maturity of the arrangements.

W Bank has been approached by P, a major quoted company with a sound credit rating. P has a £50m loan outstanding on which it is paying a variable rate of interest of LIBOR + 0.8% per annum. This loan has four years remaining and P's directors are concerned that interest rates may rise. P's directors have asked W Bank to arrange a swap that would give P a fixed rate of interest.

W Bank has offered P a swap arrangement whereby W bank will borrow £50m from P at LIBOR + 0.8% per annum and will lend £50m to P at a fixed rate of 5.0% per annum. The two parties will pay the net sum due to one another at the end of each of the next four years. W Bank will charge P an annual commission of 0.2% on the £50m loan at the end of each year. The present LIBOR is 4.1% per annum.

The swaps department of W Bank is conducting some scenario planning in order to determine W Bank's exposure arising from this arrangement. The swaps department envisages three likely scenarios:

- LIBOR will remain at 4.1% per annum for the duration of the swap

- LIBOR will remain at 4.1% per annum for one year and will then fall to 3.9% for the remaining duration of the swap

- LIBOR will remain at 4.1% per annum for one year and will then rise to 5.6% for the remaining duration of the swap

Required

(a) Calculate the net present value (NPV) of the cash flows that W Bank will generate from this swap under each of the three scenarios identified by the swaps department. W Bank discounts cash flows from such projects at 7%. **(8 marks)**

(b) (i) Advise W Bank on the risks that will arise from this swap arrangement. **(6 marks)**

(ii) Explain how W Bank might mitigate the risks arising from this swap and identify the difficulties in doing so. **(6 marks)**

(c) Evaluate the benefits to P of entering into this swap arrangement. **(5 marks)**

(Total = 25 marks)

31   A (Specimen paper)   45 mins

A is a small company based in England. The company had the choice of launching a new product in either England or France but lack of funding meant that it could not do both. The company bases its decisions on Expected Net Present Value (ENPV) and current exchange rates. As a result of this methodology, and the details shown below, it was decided to launch in England (with an ENPV of £28,392) and not France (with an ENPV of £25,560).

England	Probability	France	Probability
Launch Costs		*Launch Costs*	
£145,000	0·1	£190,000	1·0
£120,000	0·9		
Annual Cash Flows		*Annual Cash Flows*	
£65,000	0·4	£90,000	0·5
£42,000	0·4	£70,000	0·2
£24,000	0·2	£30,000	0·3

Required

(a) Discuss the risks associated with each launch option. Advise how these risks may be managed by the company. **(12 marks)**

Company A wishes to raise 3 year £500,000 floating rate finance to fund the product launch and additional capital investments. Company A has a choice between:

Alternative A: floating rate finance at LIBOR + 1·2% or

Alternative B: fixed rate finance at 9·4%, together with an interest rate swap at a fixed annual rate of 8·5% against LIBOR with a swap arrangement fee of 0·5% flat payable up front

Required

(b) (i) Discuss the potential benefits and hazards of interest rate swaps as a tool for managing interest rate risk. **(8 marks)**

(ii) Ignoring the time value of money, calculate the total difference in cost between the two alternative sources of finance available to Company A. **(5 marks)**

(Total = 25 marks)

32 RGT (RCS, 11/09)   45 mins

RGT is a large industrial construction company with several branches throughout the world. It has a large centralised Treasury department which ensures the company is making the most advantageous financial arrangements possible, while keeping financial risk at an acceptable level.

It has some cash flow difficulties at the moment as it has been building in the Middle East and some customers are having problems keeping to their payment schedules. Two customers have gone into liquidation and the buildings they had ordered are half completed. RGT has a full order book and the directors have decided that it can continue in business.

This does mean that RGT will have to be extremely efficient and make the best use of all its resources in order to meet payment commitments and make profits in these difficult times.

RGT took out a $10m loan at LIBOR plus 3%, repayable after ten years. This loan still has eight years to run. The Directors of RGT are now concerned that there is likely to be a substantial rise in interest rates. They would prefer to pay a fixed interest rate.

RGT could take out an eight year loan at a fixed rate of 10%. However a swap broker identified a counterparty which needs to borrow $10m, and is able to get a loan for eight years either at LIBOR plus 1·5% or at a fixed rate of 8%.

The swap broker will require a commission of 20 basis points for arranging this swap. The commission, along with any remaining benefit, will be shared equally by RGT and the counterparty.

Required

(a)   (i)   Explain how a swap arrangement would work using the figures in the scenario and calculate the effective rate that RGT will pay if it enters into the swap arrangement with the counterparty.

(6 marks)

(ii)   Discuss the advantages to RGT of entering into this arrangement.   **(3 marks)**

(b)   Explain why a company might choose to borrow at a floating interest rate when there is always greater certainty concerning the amounts payable with fixed rate loans.   **(8 marks)**

Coincidentally, RGT has just repaid a 12 year floating rate loan that matured earlier in this financial year. The directors of RGT had entered into a swap arrangement at the end of the fifth year of that loan to fix the rate payable. With the benefit of hindsight it is now apparent that RGT would have paid less over the remainder of that loan if they had continued with the floating rate. Some of the shareholders are annoyed that the directors have wasted money on this arrangement and have suggested that the Treasury department is not doing its job properly.

(c)   Discuss the shareholders' concerns that the directors of RGT wasted money when they entered into the swap arrangement on the 12 year loan.   **(8 marks)**

(Total = 25 marks)

33 LXN (RCS, 11/05)   45 mins

LXN is a large book retailer in France and as a result of recent rapid sales growth has decided to expand by opening six new branches in the south of France. The estimated set up cost per branch is €250,000 and LXN wishes to raise the required funding (plus an additional 20% for increased working capital requirements) via borrowing. The Treasurer of LXN is concerned about interest rate risk however, and is unsure about whether to opt for a fixed or floating rate loan. LXN's Board of Directors has indicated that it wishes to maximise the company's use of opportunities to hedge interest rate risk.

LXN currently has €2,000 million of assets and the following long-term debt in its statement of financial position.

€15 million [(6% fixed rate) redeemable 20X9]
€18 million [(Sterling LIBOR plus 3%) redeemable 20X7]

All rates are quoted as an annual rate. The current exchange rate is €1 = £0.684.

Required

(a)   Discuss the factors that should be taken into account by the Treasurer of LXN when deciding whether to raise fixed rate or floating rate debt for the expansion project and whether to hedge the resulting interest rate exposure.   **(10 marks)**

LXN's Treasurer has negotiated a fixed rate of 6% or a variable rate of Euro LIBOR plus 1.5% for the required borrowing. In addition, a counterparty (MGV) has offered to convert any new fixed rate debt that LXN takes on into synthetic floating rate debt via a swap arrangement in which the two companies will share the quality spread differential equally.

MGV, the counterparty, can borrow at a fixed rate of 7.2% or at a variable rate of Euro LIBOR plus 2.5%.

Euro LIBOR is currently 5%. All rates are quoted as an annual rate.

Required

(b)   (i)   Briefly discuss the advantages and disadvantages of interest rate swaps as a tool for managing interest rate risk.   **(5 marks)**

(ii)   Draw a diagram to illustrate how the transactions between LXN and MGV and the two lenders will operate if the swap is agreed.   **(4 marks)**

(iii)   Calculate the interest rate terms payable by LXN. Evaluate the potential annual saving resulting from borrowing at a fixed rate and engaging in an interest rate swap, as against a straightforward floating rate loan.   **(6 marks)**

(Total = 25 marks)

34   Listed services group   45 mins

A listed services group with a UK head office and subsidiaries throughout the world reports in Sterling and shows the following liabilities in its notes to the accounts.

Liabilities All figures are in £ million	Total liabilities	Floating rate	Fixed rate liabilities	Weighted average interest rate	Weighted average years for which rate is fixed
£ Sterling	98	98			
$ US	41	8	33	7.25%	5
Euro	4	4			
Total	143	110	33		

Maturity All figures are in £ million	Total	Maturing within 1 year	Within 1-2 years	Within 2-5 years	Over 5 years
£ Sterling	98	73	3	18	4
$ US	41				41
Euro	4	1	1	1	1
Total	143	74	4	19	46

Interest rates are currently about 5%.

Required

(a)   (i)   Evaluate the main sources of financial risk for this group (assuming there are no offsetting assets that might provide a hedge against the liabilities).

(ii)   Quantify the transaction risk faced by the group if sterling was to depreciate against the $US and Euro by 10%.

(iii)   Evaluate how transaction risk relates to translation risk and economic risk in this example.

(13 marks)

(b)   Discuss the use of exchange traded and Over The Counter (OTC) derivatives for hedging and how they may be used to reduce the exchange rate and interest rate risks the group faces. Illustrate your answer by comparing and contrasting the main features of appropriate derivatives.   **(12 marks)**

(Total = 25 marks)

35 ZX
45 mins

ZX is a UK-based retailer and manufacturer that also owns a limited number of outlets in the USA, but is anxious to expand internationally via the use of franchising agreements. The enterprise plans to open five franchised shops in each of France, Italy, Germany, Belgium and Holland over the course of the next twelve months. ZX will provide loan finance to assist individuals wishing to purchase a franchise, the average cost of which will be €100,000. Loans will also be available (up to a maximum of 50% of the purchase price) to cover the cost of the franchisee acquiring suitable freehold or leasehold premises. The total sum required for the property loan facility is estimated by the treasurer of ZX to equal €4.8 million. The opportunity cost of capital in the UK is 10% per annum but, in recognition of the lower rates of interest available in the Eurozone, ZX will only charge the franchisees a fixed rate of 7.0% each year on all loans. Repayments will be made in equal Euro-denominated instalments.

ZX charges commission to the franchisees at a rate of 1% of sales revenue, and also earns a net margin of 12% (of retail value) on the products supplied to the outlets from its UK manufacturing plant.

Planned sales from the new European outlets equal €26 million over the next twelve months, but the enterprise recognises that its profits are dependent upon both sales revenue and the extent of loan defaults amongst franchisees (if any). Estimates of the likelihood of a range of scenarios are detailed below.

Probability	Sales	Number of loan defaults	Comment
0.1	10% below plan	2	Economic difficulties reduce sales and cause problems for some franchisees
0.3	20% below plan	4	Severe economic problems lead to low sales and higher loan defaults
0.4	As per plan	0	'Base case'
0.2	As per plan	1	The weak German economy causes problems for one franchisee

Loan default is assumed to mean total write-off and ZX expects 80% of the new franchisees to take full advantage of the loan facilities offered to them.

The current Sterling: Euro exchange rate is £1 = €1.3939 and the Euro is expected to strengthen against Sterling by 5% over the next twelve months.

In addition to the cash required to fund the foreign loan facility, a further £3.65 million of working capital will be required for the expansion project and the treasury department of ZX requires a minimum annualised return of 15% on all overseas projects.

Required

(a) Use the table of possible scenarios given above to calculate the expected sterling value of the additional profit that ZX will earn if the store openings are completed as planned and the foreign exchange rate forecast is fulfilled. (You should use the average exchange rate over the year for the calculation.)

You should evaluate whether this profit yields the return required for international operations. **(7 marks)**

(b) Discuss the risks that ZX might face in choosing to expand into Europe via the use of franchising.
(8 marks)

(c) Evaluate methods of managing/minimising the risks involved in granting Euro denominated loans to the franchisees. **(10 marks)**

(Total = 25 marks)

36   Preparation question: Bruce SA

14 June data

Bruce SA, a French company, makes a sale of $2,350,000 to a US company on 3 months' credit.

Currency Market Rates

Spot Rate €1 = $	1.2354 – 1.2362
Forward premium	0.0035 – 0.0028

Money Market Rates p.a.

Euro	2.2%	US		1.2%

Futures Prices (contract size = €125,000)

June	1.2347	September		1.2321

Currency options (contract size = €62,500; premia stated in cents per Euro)

	CALLS		PUTS	
Strike	June	September	June	September
12300	2.51	3.59	2.24	3.55
12350	2.27	3.36	2.50	3.82
12400	2.04	3.15	2.77	4.10
12450	1.83	2.75	3.06	4.70

Bruce receives the payment in mid-September when the spot rate is €1 = $1.2450. The September futures price in mid-September is 1.2439.

Required

Recommend appropriate methods for Bruce SA to use to hedge its foreign exchange risk for the next three months. Your answer should include appropriate calculations to support your recommendations.

Tutor's hints. This question gives you enough data to consider all the main methods of hedging currency risks other than swaps. The key things you have to consider include:

- Which spot and forward rate to use if you are receiving dollars when you want Euros?

- If you're using the money markets, is the first stage to invest or borrow in the home or foreign markets?

- For futures, which contract to choose?

- For options do you choose a June or September, and a put or a call option?

- For options, would you exercise the option you've chosen given what you know about the closing spot rate?

---

37   JJ (5/12)   45 mins

JJ manufactures specialised electronic equipment in the UK. The company has just won its first export order and will receive payment of USD 15 million in three months. JJ's Chief Executive is concerned that the USD may decline against the GBP during the three months and has asked the company's bank to offer a guaranteed price for the currency when it is received.

The bank has offered to enter into a forward contract with JJ at a rate of GBP1 = USD 1.65.

JJ's Chief Executive is unhappy with this offer because the present exchange rate is GBP1 = USD 1.60. Given the size of the transaction, this constitutes a major additional cost that JJ had not budgeted for when setting its selling price. JJ's Chief Executive would rather wait until the payment is received in the hope that the spot rate at that time is better than the GBP1 = USD 1.65 offered by the bank.

JJ's Chief Executive is concerned that the differential rate being charged by the bank is unfair. He believes that global economics are so complicated that it is impossible to forecast exchange rate movements and the

movements in the exchange rate are just as likely to be favourable as unfavourable to JJ over the next three months.

JJ's bank manager has pointed out that the rate offered is in line with market expectations and that it is unrealistic for the Chief Executive to ask the bank to commit itself to guaranteeing that today's exchange rate can be obtained on a transaction that will occur in three months.

The bank manager has recommended that JJ appoints a full-time corporate treasurer to take on the responsibility of the treasury function and relieve the Chief Executive of that burden.

All of JJ's directors come from an electronic engineering background and the small administrative staff provides basic clerical and book-keeping support.

Required

(a) Evaluate the respective arguments of JJ's Chief Executive and the bank manager about the rate offered by the bank on the forward contract. **(9 marks)**

(b) Evaluate the bank manager's recommendation to appoint a corporate treasurer. **(8 marks)**

(c) Recommend, stating reasons, the steps that the directors of JJ should take in the selection of a suitable person for the role of corporate treasurer. **(8 marks)**

(Total = 25 marks)

38 Q (3/12)   45 mins

Q is a Sri Lankan company that manufactures machine parts. Q plans to establish a wholly-owned French subsidiary that will manufacture its range of products in France for distribution across the European Union (EU). Q has been established for many years, but it is not widely known outside of Sri Lanka despite the fact that its product range has a very good reputation.

Q's Finance Director visited Paris recently in order to discuss the financing arrangements for the subsidiary with a number of French banks. Q could easily borrow the funds at an attractive rate in Sri Lankan Rupees (LKR), but Q's board would prefer to borrow in Euros (EUR). Unfortunately, the French banks felt that they would be taking a risk if they were to back a foreign borrower who was unknown to them and so they either refused Q's loan application or they offered to lend at a high rate of interest.

On the flight home the Finance Director entered into a conversation with P, the passenger in the next seat. P is the founder of a French design company that wishes to build a factory in Sri Lanka. All of Sri Lanka's banks have refused to lend to P. One French bank has agreed to make the loan, but at a high rate of interest. P would prefer to raise the finance in LKR and has decided to travel to Sri Lanka in the hope that a face to face meeting with the bank lending officers will be more successful than a negotiation by telephone and email.

When Q's Finance Director and P realised that they had complementary requirements they started to discuss the possibility of a currency swap that might be mutually beneficial.

- They each require to borrow the equivalent of €20 million for six years to establish their respective businesses.

- The current spot rate is LKR 155.0 to the EUR.

- Q can borrow in LKR at an annual rate of 9% for six years or in EUR at an annual rate of 12%.

- A French accountant has told Q that a similar French business would be able to borrow €20 million for six years at 6%.

- P can borrow in EUR at a rate of 10% for six years.

- All of the proposed loans would be repayable in one lump sum at the end of the borrowing period.

P proposes borrowing EUR 20 million from a French bank at 10%. Q would borrow LKR 3,100 million at 9% from the Sri Lankan bank. The two companies would swap these principal sums and would each pay the interest on the other's borrowings. P is confident that both parties will generate sufficient surpluses from their new foreign operations to raise the necessary currency to meet the interest payments and to accumulate sufficient funds to swap the principal sums back at the end of six years.

Required

(a)   Explain THREE reasons why Q would wish to borrow in EUR in order to finance the proposed French subsidiary.   **(6 marks)**

(b)   Calculate an estimated LKR to EUR exchange rate at the date of repayment in six years. Note: your answer should include an explanation of your method.   **(4 marks)**

(c)   Calculate the net present value of Q's cash flows associated with financing if it accepts P's swap arrangements, assuming a required discount rate of 9% and that the anticipated change in exchange rates will occur evenly over the six year period.   **(7 marks)**

(d)   Evaluate the risks to Q from P's swap arrangement.   **(8 marks)**

(Total = 25 marks)

39   WW (11/11)   45 mins

WW is a multinational professional services company. Many of WW's clients are also multinational companies. Each client is assigned to a specific engagement partner who is generally based in the client's home country. Client work overseas is frequently referred to the local WW office to avoid the travel and accommodation costs that would be associated with sending consultants from the home country. It would also ensure that the work is undertaken by a local consultant who understands the business culture.

All billings are made to the client's home office. If work is undertaken by an overseas office of WW then the overseas office invoices the engagement partner, who includes the cost of that work in the total invoice. The engagement partner then agrees to pay the local office out of the proceeds of the client's settlement of that invoice.

WW has so many clients that there can be substantial inter-office payments. WW's treasurer has decided to experiment with multilateral netting to reduce the overall number of inter-office payments. The treasurer plans to undertake this experiment for herself rather than involve a netting centre.

The net inter-office balances as at 31 October 2011 were agreed at:

Paying office	UK (GBP)	France (EUR)	US (USD)	Japan (JPY)
Receiving office				
UK (GBP)	-	GBP 0.9 million	-	-
France (EUR)		-		EUR 1.1 million
US (USD)	USD 3.1 million	USD 2.7 million	-	-
Japan (JPY)	JPY 180.0 million	-	JPY 190.0 million	-

At the same date WW's treasury department set the following indicative exchange rates:

	France (EUR)	US (USD)	Japan (JPY)
GBP 1 =	1.13	1.61	135.5

Quite apart from the transactions between offices, WW's London office frequently has to engage independent consultants in eurozone countries that do not have a local WW office. The London office also frequently receives commissions from clients based in the eurozone who wish to deal directly with a UK consultant. The amounts of € receipts and payments vary significantly, but receipts average €1m per month and payments €0.8m. WW's treasurer is considering opening a € bank account for the London office.

Required

(a)   (i)   Calculate the net payments that will be required in order to settle all inter-office balances, assuming that the process is managed by WW's London-based treasury department.   **(11 marks)**

       (ii)   Advise WW of the advantages and disadvantages of offsetting balances using multilateral netting.
                                                                                                (8 marks)

(b)   Evaluate the suggestion that WW's London office should open a EUR bank account to deal with EUR receipts and payments. **(6 marks)**

(Total = 25 marks)

40   KK (9/11)   45 mins

KK farms heat in the UK. KK has discovered a new piece of farm equipment that is manufactured overseas in a developing country where the national currency is the P$. KK has agreed to buy the equipment. The equipment will take eight months to manufacture and ship to the UK. The terms of the agreement are that KK must pay for the equipment when it clears UK customs.

The equipment is priced at P$2m. The current exchange rate is 1 GBP = 2 P$. The exchange rate for the P$ is extremely volatile and KK's managers are concerned that the effective price could move dramatically.

KK's bank has advised that it will not sell P$2m forward for eight months, nor is there a specific financial instrument that KK could use to cover this payment. The bank manager has offered the following three possible suggestions:

*   KK could create a money market hedge by borrowing an appropriate amount in GBP and opening a P$ bank account with a bank in the vendor's country. KK's bank would charge a rate of 10% per annum on this loan and it has been established that the banks in the vendor's country would pay a rate of 13% per annum. KK could engage a local lawyer or accountant to open the deposit account overseas.

*   KK could offer to pay the manufacturer the P$2m immediately, perhaps asking for a discount for prompt payment.

*   KK could retain the risk of a currency movement.

Required

(a)   (i)   Construct the transactions that KK would have to undertake in order to create a money market hedge. Your answer should include calculations of all relevant figures, ignoring transaction costs.
                                                                        (5 marks)

        (ii)   Advise KK on the costs that are likely to be associated with this hedge and also the risks that will be involved.   **(8 marks)**

(b)   (i)   Evaluate the suggestion that KK should pay the P$2m immediately. Your evaluation should consider the risks and also the costs of doing so.   **(7 marks)**

        (ii)   Explain whether the manufacturer would be likely to accept payment of GBP1m in GBP, payable when the contract is signed instead of the current agreement. **(5 marks)**

(Total = 25 marks)

41   G (5/11)   45 mins

G is a large retail organisation that imports goods from the US for sale in its home market, where the currency is the R$.

The directors of G are aware that the company is subject to significant economic exposure to movements on the US$ because any appreciation of the US$ will increase the cost of goods for resale. G has attempted to create a partial hedge against this by placing all of its cash reserves in a US$ bank account. That way the losses associated with any increase in cost prices will be partially offset by a gain on the bank account.

The directors are concerned that the translation gains and losses on the US$ bank balance are visible to shareholders, whereas the offsetting of economic exposure is not and so their hedging policy may be misunderstood.

The US bank account has a balance of US$30m. The exchange rate is presently R$3 to US$1. The daily standard deviation of the balance when it is translated to R$ is R$450,000.

Required

(a) Advise the directors on the matters that they would have to consider in order to determine the extent of G's economic exposure. **(5 marks)**

(b) Evaluate the validity of the directors' concern that "the translation gains and losses on the US$ bank balance are visible to shareholders, whereas the offsetting of economic exposure is not and so their hedging policy may be misunderstood". **(10 marks)**

(c) (i) Calculate the 95% daily value at risk (VaR) of G's US$ bank balance. **(3 marks)**

(ii) Use your answer to (c)(i) to calculate the 95% 30 day VaR of G's US$ bank balance.

(2 marks)

(iii) Advise the directors on the relevance of the VaR statistic to their consideration of the risks associated with retaining this US$ bank balance. **(5 marks)**

(Total = 25 marks)

42 V (11/10)   45 mins

V is a marketing consultancy based in an Asian country, where the local currency is the Y$. V is negotiating a contract with a large Canadian company that wishes to launch a major advertising campaign in V's home country. V will be responsible for designing the campaign and also for buying the associated advertising space in magazines and on television and radio.

V's client will pay 10% of the total value of the contract immediately and the remainder in one year's time, when the product will be launched. The client insists on paying in Canadian Dollars (C$).

The total value of the contract is C$10m.

V's Finance Director is considering whether to hedge the value of the C$9m that it will receive in twelve months' time or whether it would be better simply to accept the spot rate when the payment is received. To that end, the Finance Director has gathered the following information in order to forecast the spot rate:

- The present spot rate Y$ / C$ = 2.020 (Y$1 = C$2.020).

- The one year forward rate Y$ /C$ = 2.121.

- The interest rates for one year deposits in Y$ and C$ are 5.7% and 11.0% respectively.

- Various economic forecasts suggest that the rate of inflation in V's home country will be 2% over the next year and 8% in Canada.

- The Canadian customer plans to sell its product for C$420 in Canada and for Y$200 in V's home country after the launch.

The Finance Director is concerned that each of the forecast exchange rates implied in the various models differs from the others. She is unsure whether that suggests a hedge is appropriate.

V has been offered an option to exchange C$9m at a rate of Y$/C$ = 2.150. The premium on this option would be Y$270,000, payable immediately.

Required

(a) (i) Use the information gathered by the Finance Director to produce three alternative forecasts of the expected spot rate when the payment is received. **(9 marks)**

(ii) Recommend with reasons the forecasting model that you regard as the most reliable for V's purposes. **(5 marks)**

(b) Discuss the advantages and disadvantages of buying the currency option.

Your answer should include calculations to show the benefit of exercising the option. **(6 marks)**

(c) The management of V are thinking of changing their policy so that all customers will be required to pay in Y$.

Discuss the advantages and disadvantages of this policy change for V. **(5 marks)**

(Total = 25 marks)

43 E and N (9/10)   45 mins

N manufactures fire engines. It has a reputation for excellent build quality and has been successful in its home market for many years. N is based in Asia.

Five years ago N introduced a new fire engine that is superior to any competing product. The factors that make N's design superior are protected by patent and are unlikely to be matched by competitors in the foreseeable future. N has had growing interest from overseas customers and it has recently been asked to consider two major contracts, both of which will provide N with a significant increase in revenue and profit. These will be N's first significant export contracts.

South American contract

E, a South American country, requires several hundred fire engines in order to re-equip its emergency services. E's government cannot afford to purchase these fire engines directly from N and has proposed a mutually beneficial agreement.

The government of E proposes that N will establish a subsidiary in the South American country that will assemble fire engines using parts imported from N's Asian factory and local labour. N will buy as many parts and materials as possible locally in E. For example, E has a factory that manufactures diesel engines that are almost identical to those used by N and these would be suitable alternatives to the standard engines.

N's Production Managers have estimated that 50% (by value) of the parts and 60% of the labour could be sourced in E. Complex parts will continue to be sourced from N's main factory and skilled assembly work will still be undertaken there. N has found a suitable factory in E that can be rented for the duration of the contract. It will take four years to build the entire order.

This arrangement will help the economy because parts and labour will be purchased locally.

The government of E insists that N must invoice it in the E Peso. This currency is freely exchanged on international currency markets, although it is regarded as rather weak.

It is anticipated that N will complete ten fire engines per month and will invoice for deliveries on a monthly basis. All payments will be made to N's subsidiary in E. The subsidiary will pay for all local wages and purchases and will remit any cash surplus back to N on a monthly basis.

The selling price has been fixed in terms of E Pesos for the duration of the contract.

European contract

S, a European country, also requires several hundred fire engines. The country's senior fire-fighters have argued that they should be equipped with N's fire engine despite the fact that they have always purchased from K, a company located in S that manufactures a range of vehicles including fire engines.

The government of S is concerned about the political implications of placing such a large order with a foreign supplier because doing so will risk the loss of jobs at K. The government of S proposes that N should sell K a licence to manufacture its fire engine. Under this arrangement K will provide 100% of the labour and will purchase 90% by value of the parts and materials. Only 10% of the parts will be purchased from N. The part sales form a very minor part of the contract and will not have a material effect on N's business.

Under the licence K will make an annual payment, in Euros, to N. The annual payment will vary in line with the number of fire engines completed during the year and has been negotiated at a sum that is slightly more than the profit that N normally makes on the manufacture and sale of that number of fire engines.

It will take K approximately four years to manufacture the order. Performance Strategy 19 September 2010

Required

(a) (i) Evaluate the currency transaction risks that will arise under each of these contracts. Your answer should indicate why the nature of the currency risk associated with each of the contracts differs.

(6 marks)

(ii) Recommend, with reasons, an appropriate strategy for the management of each of the currency transaction risks you have identified. **(9 marks)**

(b) Recent newspaper reports have documented the high levels of corruption and economic instability in E. N's directors are concerned that they will be exposed to significant risks if they establish a subsidiary in E and have identified two possible strategies for managing the risks:

(i) Entering into a joint venture with a company located in E
(ii) Borrowing in E Pesos

Discuss the advantages and disadvantages of each of the two strategies for N. **(10 marks)**

(Total = 25 marks)

44 N (5/10) — 45 mins

N is based in the UK. The company manufactures advanced braking systems for trains. N has just sold a test system with a value of US$1,755,250 to L, a company based in the USA. L insisted on being invoiced in US$; N agreed to this request in an attempt to generate goodwill with its new customer. The directors of N hope to obtain significant sales with L in the future if the test system is found to meet that company's requirements. Payment is due in 90 days.

This is N's first significant overseas order. The Management Accountant has taken advice on hedging the transaction risk and concluded that a forward contract is the best method available.

Information relevant to this decision: *sell   buy*

- Current spot rates £1 = US$1·6000 – 1·6050.
- There is a three month discount forward of 2·30 cents – 2·50 cents.
- The actual spot rate 90 days later was £1 = US$1·6585 – 1·6635.

Required

(a) (i) Discuss the advantages and disadvantages of the use of a forward contract by N. **(8 marks)**

(ii) Calculate for N whether, in retrospect, purchasing a forward contract was actually beneficial for the company. **(4 marks)**

(b) (i) Explain why N's competitive position could be exposed to movements on the US$. **(4 marks)**

(ii) Discuss why exposure to economic risk as a result of exchange rate fluctuations is hard to quantify. **(9 marks)**

(Total = 25 marks)

45 Arbitrage (RCS, 5/08) — 45 mins

A foreign exchange dealer working in a London-based investment bank wishes to take advantage of arbitrage opportunities in the international money markets.

The following data is available relating to interest rates and exchange rates for Australia and the USA:

Spot	£1 = US$2.0254	£1 = Aus$2.3180
6 Month Forward	£1 = US$1.9971	£1 = Aus$2.3602

The effective six-month Australian dollar interest rate is 3.32% and the equivalent US $ rate is 3.68%. These rates apply to both borrowing and lending.

Assume that in six months' time the actual exchange rate between sterling and Australian dollars is £1 = Aus$2.32.

The dealer is authorised to buy or sell up to US$5 million per transaction. The costs for this type of currency trading are charged in sterling at a rate of £3,000 per transaction.

Note. Each currency conversion counts as one transaction.

Required

(a) Calculate the spot and six-month forward cross rates between the Australian and US dollar. **(4 marks)**

(b) Explain the meaning of the term "arbitrage profit" and explain why such profits may be available in the scenario outlined above. (No illustrative calculations are required). **(6 marks)**

(c) Calculate the profit available to the dealer from exploiting the opportunity shown above, clearly showing all of your calculations. **(10 marks)**

(d) Explain the importance of "trading limits" and "value at risk" as tools for managing the risks within a financial trading operation. **(5 marks)**

(Total = 25 marks)

46 VQR (RCS, 5/07)   45 mins

You are the newly-appointed treasurer of VQR Ltd, a medium-sized importing and exporting company, based in Singapore. The company imports goods from Australia and New Zealand and exports these goods to the United States. A subsidiary company, based in Sydney, Australia is partly financed by an Australian dollar denominated floating rate bank loan. VQR uses the forward or money markets to hedge its foreign currency risk. Most customers are allowed, and take, 3 months' credit.

You need to respond to the points raised in the following memo from your Chief Executive Officer:

MEMORANDUM

From: CEO
To: Treasurer
Date: 24 May 20X7

I have been reading the financial section of the local business press and note the following in respect of interest rates and other economic data:

Exchange rates
Spot rate   US$1 = Sing$1.565   US$1 = Aus$1.311
1 month forward   US$1 = Sing$1.562   US$1 = Aus$1.312

	Singapore	USA	Australia
Annual inter-bank offer rate	3.44%	5.38%	6.2%

(a) As interest rates are higher in the USA than here in Singapore, surely the US$ should be trading forward at a premium to the Sing$, not at a discount?

(b) The newspaper did not quote a 3-month forward rate. We have recently sold goods to a customer in the US to the value of US$ 3 million. What 3 month forward rate of exchange is implied by the information we do have, and therefore what will be the receipt in Singapore dollars in 3 months' time?

(c) Can we save money by buying Aus$ on the spot market as and when we need them to pay for imports, rather than taking out forward contracts, and are there any disadvantages to this strategy?

(d) Would it be in our interests to borrow Sing$ and use the proceeds to pay off our Aus$ loan given that rates of interest in Australia are higher than those in Singapore?

Please respond to these questions by the close of today.

Required

Produce a response to the CEO.

Note. Your response should include a brief explanation of theories and appropriate calculations to support your discussion. 5 marks will be allocated for explanation of appropriate theories. The balance of 20 marks is for application of those theories and relevant calculations. **(25 marks)**

47 MNO (RCS, 11/06) — 45 mins

uk
spot

MNO is a UK based company that has delivered goods, invoiced at $1,800,000 US dollars to a customer in Singapore. Payment is due in three months' time, that is, in February 20X7. The finance director of MNO is concerned about the potential exchange risk resulting from the transaction and wishes to hedge the risk in either the futures or the options market.

The current spot rate is £1 = $1.695. A three month futures contract is quoted at $1.690 per £1, and the contract size for $/£ futures contracts is £62,500.

A three month put option is available at a price of $1.675 per £1.

Required

(a) Assuming that the spot rate and the futures rate turn out to be the same in February 20X7, indicating that there is no basis risk, identify the lowest cost way of hedging the exchange rate risk (using either futures or options) where the exchange rate at the time of payment is:

(i)   £1 = $1.665
(ii) £1 = $1.720

Note. Your answer should show all the calculations used to reach your answer, including the extent (if any) of the uncovered risk. **(10 marks)**

(b) Briefly discuss the problems of using futures contracts to hedge exchange rate risks. **(6 marks)**

(c) Identify and explain the key reasons why small versus large companies may differ in terms of both the extent of foreign exchange and interest rate hedging that is undertaken, and the tools used by management for such purposes. **(9 marks)**

(Total = 25 marks)

48 SDT (RCS, 5/05) — 45 mins

SDT plc is a UK based manufacturer of a wide range of printed circuit boards (PCBs) that are used in a variety of electrical products. SDT exports over 90% of its production to assembly plants owned by large multinational electronics companies all around the world. Two companies (A and B) require SDT to invoice them in a single currency, regardless of the export destination of the PCBs. The chosen currencies are the Japanese Yen (Company A) and the US$ (Company B) respectively. The remaining export sales all go to European customers and are invoiced in Euros.

The variable cost and export price per unit PCB are shown below.

Market	Unit variable cost (£)	Unit export sales price
Company A	2.75	Yen 632.50
Company B	4.80	US$ 10.2678
Europe	6.25	Euro 12.033

Goods are supplied on 60 day credit terms.

The following receipts for export sales are due in 60 days:

Company A	Yen 9,487,500
Company B	US$ 82,142
Europe	Euro 66,181

The foreign exchange rates to be used by SDT in evaluating its revenue from the export sales are as follows. All rates are quoted per £1.

	Yen	US$	Euro
Spot market	198.987 – 200.787	1.7620 – 1.7826	1.4603 – 1.4813
2 months forward	197.667 – 200.032	1.7550 – 1.7775	1.4504 – 1.4784
3 months forward	196.028 – 198.432	1.7440 – 1.7677	1.4410 – 1.4721
1 year forward	188.158 – 190.992	1.6950 – 1.7311	1.4076 – 1.4426

The Managing Director of SDT believes that the foreign exchange markets are efficient and so the likelihood that SDT will make foreign exchange gains is the same as the likelihood that it will make foreign exchange losses. Furthermore, any exchange risk is already diversified across three currencies, each from countries in very different economic regions of the world. The Managing Director has therefore recommended that the Treasury Department should not hedge any foreign exchange risks arising from export sales.

Required

(a)   Critically comment on the validity of the views and recommendations expressed by the Managing Director and explain how currency hedging might nevertheless be beneficial to SDT.   **(6 marks)**

(b)   (i)   Calculate the sterling value of the contribution earned from exports to each of the customers (A, B and Europe) assuming that SDT:

             (1)   Hedges the risk in the forward market;   **(3 marks)**

             (2)   Does not hedge the risk and the relevant spot exchange rates in two months' time are as follows:

Two month spot
£1 = Yen 200.18 – 202.63
£1 = US$ 1.7650 – 1.7750
£1 = Euro 1.4600 – 1.4680

                                                            (3 marks)

     (ii)   Calculate the average contribution to sales ratio in each of the above scenarios and advise SDT accordingly on whether to hedge its foreign exchange exposure.   **(3 marks)**

(c)   Comment on why (based on relative risk analysis) a company might seek to generate higher rates of return from export sales compared to domestic sales.   **(6 marks)**

(d)   If the payment from Company B is received late, briefly explain what risk SDT is taking in hedging B's payment in the forward market, and how this risk could be avoided.   **(4 marks)**

(Total = 25 marks)

49   OJ   45 mins

OJ is a supplier of leather goods to retailers in the UK and other western European countries. The company is considering entering into a joint venture with a manufacturer in South America. The two companies will each own 50% of the limited liability company JV (SA) and will share profits equally. £450,000 of the initial capital is being provided by OJ, and the equivalent in South American dollars (SA$) is being provided by the foreign partner. The managers of the joint venture expect the following net operating cash flows which are in nominal terms.

	SA$'000	Forward rates of exchange to the £ Sterling
Year 1	4,250	10
Year 2	6,500	15
Year 3	8,350	21

For tax reasons JV (SA), the company to be formed specifically for the joint venture, will be registered in South America.

Ignore taxation in your calculations.

Assume you are a financial adviser retained by OJ to advise on the proposed joint venture.

Required

(a)   (i)   Calculate the NPV of the project under the two assumptions explained below. Use a discount rate of 16% for both assumptions.

     Assumption 1

     The South American country has exchange controls which prohibit the payment of dividends above 50% of the annual cash flows for the first three years of the project. The accumulated balance can be repatriated at the end of the third year.

Assumption 2

The government of the South American country is considering removing exchange controls and restrictions on repatriation of profits. If this happens all cash flows will be distributed as dividends to the partner companies at the end of each year.

(ii) Recommend whether or not the joint venture should proceed based solely on these calculations.

(7 marks)

During a meeting to discuss the joint venture, the following questions are raised by the managers of OJ.

(i) 'In reality we will exchange our SA$ cash flows into Sterling at the spot rate prevailing at the end of each year. How reliable are forward rates of exchange as predictors of spot rates?'

(ii) 'If exchange controls exist we will not get much of our cash for three years. Surely we should be using a higher discount rate for Assumption 1?'

(iii) 'Under either assumption we have to accept substantial exchange rate risk. Could we use a currency swap to help us minimise this risk?'

Required

(b) Discuss the three questions raised by the managers of OJ and advise them of any other practical issues which should be considered before they decide to proceed. **(18 marks)**

(Total = 25 marks)

50 YZ   45 mins

YZ is a specialist food manufacturing company based in the south of England. It trades with companies within the European common currency area. The following receipts and payments are due within the next three months:

	Euros (€)
Due in 1 month:	
Payments to suppliers	600,000
Receipts from customers	400,000
Due in 3 months	
Payments to suppliers	800,000
Receipts from customers	1,200,000
Exchange rates as at today:	
Spot	£1 = €1.6186 – 1.6202
1 month forward	0.0006 – 0.0002 premium
3 months forward	0.0013 – 0.0008 premium

Interest rates (annual):		
(assumed to apply throughout the common currency area)	*Borrowing*	*Lending*
£ sterling	4.25	3.75
€ (Euro)	3.50	3.00

Required

(a) Calculate the *net* Sterling currency receipts or payments that YZ might expect for *both* its one-month and three-month transactions if it:

(i) Hedges the risk using the forward market

(ii) Hedges the risk using the money market

(iii) Does not hedge the risk and the spot exchange rates in one and three months' time are £1 = € 1.6192 – 1.6208 and 1.6200 – 1.6220 respectively **(14 marks)**

(b) Discuss the advantages and disadvantages of the three courses of action being considered in (a) and recommend which you consider to be the most appropriate for YZ.

[Note: alternative (iii) is not to hedge. You would not of course know what the actual exchange rates will be when you offer this advice.] **(11 marks)**

Note. A report format is NOT required in answering this question. **(Total = 25 marks)**

RISK AND CONTROL IN INFORMATION SYSTEMS

Questions 51 to 63 cover risk and control in information systems, the subject of Part D of the BPP Study Text for Paper P3.

51 H (5/12)   45 mins

H is a legal firm that specialises in pursuing small claims for compensation for personal injuries that its clients have suffered. The company advertises its services on television and guarantees that its clients do not have to pay any legal fees even if they lose the case. The losing side is normally liable for the other party's legal fees and so H's fee is paid by the negligent party who caused the injury, provided H wins the case for its client.

H has to take great care when evaluating applications from potential clients. If H loses the case it will not be paid for any of the work it has done on the case and H will also be liable for the other side's legal fees. To reduce the risk of taking on cases that it might subsequently lose, H uses highly trained legal staff to conduct telephone interviews with applicants. These staff work in a telephone call centre and ask each potential client a series of questions to establish the likelihood of winning that case. This procedure has proven to be very reliable: H has won more than 80% of the cases that it has accepted. Unfortunately, this system is expensive because H has to pay high salaries in order to recruit suitably qualified legal staff.

H's Head of Information Technology (IT) has suggested that the legal staff in the call centre could be replaced by an 'expert system'. Such a system could be manned by operators who would not require a great deal of training or expertise. The expert system will be an interactive software package that will provide call centre staff with a series of questions to ask potential clients. The call centre operators will be trained to explain the meaning of the questions if necessary and to input the responses into the system in a consistent way. The expert system will choose the questions that are asked to reflect information that has already been input. For example, if a case involves a road traffic accident then there will be different questions depending on whether the police were involved in the incident and whether either party has been charged with a motoring offence. Once all of the questions have been answered the software will provide the operator with a recommendation as to whether the case should be accepted, rejected or referred to a lawyer in H's legal department for further consideration.

H's Head of IT believes that a well-designed expert system will be as reliable as the legal staff who are presently employed. It will be expensive to develop, but it will save a great deal of money in the long term because the call centre operators will be cheaper to employ.

The expert system would be developed by an external consultant who would act as a "knowledge engineer". The knowledge engineer would work with the senior lawyers in H's legal department to identify the logic that runs through the evaluation of a potential client's case and codify that logic using a standard expert system package. H's senior lawyers would then have to assist in testing the expert system. Finally, call centre staff will have to be trained in the operation of the expert system.

Required

(a)   Advise H's directors on the risks of using an expert system instead of legal staff at the call centre.

(13 marks)

(b)   Recommend, giving reasons, the procedures that should be in place to ensure the successful design and testing of the expert system.   **(12 marks)**

(Total = 25 marks)

52 AHB (3/12)   45 mins

AHB is a major travel agent that specialises in holiday travel. AHB's sales are all made either online or through a call centre.

AHB's primary data processing centre is located in a large office building close to a major city centre. This data processing centre houses the computers and the staff who operate and maintain the website that enables customers to make online bookings. The data processing centre also houses the call centre that handles bookings made by telephone.

The website operates continuously. The call centre operates six days per week from 8.00 in the morning until 10.00 at night. There are 120 call centre operators who work on a two shift basis. The call centre staff work at terminals that are linked through a local network to the same data servers that provide the online service. AHB's system runs on the standard software package that is used across the travel industry to enable travel agents, airlines and hotels to communicate with one another. All holiday sales are recorded in real-time to prevent overbooking.

Data processing is a key part of AHB's operations. Consequently AHB has two data processing sites one central and one remote. The primary site is in the city centre and employs 60 systems staff, who operate a three shift system to ensure that the website is always available and up to date.

The remote site is located in an industrial estate 40 miles away; it has the same hardware as the primary site. The two sites are linked electronically and data is backed up frequently. There is a full back up every Sunday and incremental backups occur several times every day.

The remote site has a small team of systems operators and their shift patterns ensure that there is always at least one of them onsite at all times to ensure that hardware and software are maintained and backups are secure.

AHB's directors decided to test the operation of the backup site by conducting the company's first ever full-scale disaster simulation. The first Tuesday in September is usually the quietest day of the year with a low volume of activity and so that was designated as the test day. All systems and call centre staff were asked to arrive at the primary data processing centre two hours before their normal start time on the test day so that they could be taken to the remote site by chartered buses. The chartered buses would then operate a shuttle service to the city centre site to allow for shift changes and to enable staff to get home at the end of their shift.

Systems and call centre staff were warned several weeks in advance that the primary data processing centre would be taken offline at 6.00 on the morning of the test day, immediately after the scheduled incremental backup. The website would go offline at that time. That would simulate a disaster such as a major fire that had disrupted power and communications. It was planned that the systems operators at the remote site would be asked to recreate the data files at 6.30 on the morning of the test day by combining the most recent backup copy with the subsequent incremental backups. The website would be brought back online from the remote site within an hour and the call centre operated from the remote site for a full working day.

There was an unexpected 40% absenteeism rate on the day of the simulation, which made it impossible to operate a full service during the simulation. Many of the staff had been concerned that they would find it difficult to travel to and from work at the proposed times because there would be little or no public transport. Furthermore, many would find it disruptive to their childcare arrangements. Almost all of those who were absent emailed their supervisors on the day of the simulation to say that they had minor illnesses and that they would return to work next day.

Required

(a)   (i)   Discuss the advantages and disadvantages to AHB of running a disaster simulation.   **(8 marks)**

       (ii)   Discuss the weaknesses of the planned approach taken by AHB to its simulation.   **(7 marks)**

(b)   Recommend, stating reasons, ways in which AHB could ensure that the remote centre would be fully staffed in the event that a genuine disaster occurs.   **(10 marks)**

(Total = 25 marks)

53 T (3/11) 45 mins

T is a retail organisation that owns six large shops that are located in different areas of a major city. Each shop has approximately 50 sales staff. T also has a central head office, located in that city, which houses all of the accounting and administrative departments. These departments include a Purchasing Department and an Accounts Payable Department. There is also an Internal Audit Department which has five staff. T has recently upgraded its accounting and inventory management systems.

Old system

In the old system the electronic tills in the shops transmitted details of sales transactions to a central computer at head office. That computer recorded details of all payments received, both in terms of cash and those made by debit or credit card. It also held details of inventory movements and was used to identify when orders were needed to replenish inventory. The accounting staff at head office used a different computer to maintain the nominal ledger. Sales information had to be entered manually into this computer.

The Purchasing Department placed orders using pre-numbered order forms which were mailed to suppliers and copies were sent to the shops and to the Accounts Payable Department. Goods are delivered directly to shops. The shops sent "goods received notes" to head office when the inventory arrived. Those documents were used to validate suppliers' invoices before they were recorded in the payables files in the bookkeeping system. The information from the goods received notes was also used to update the inventory records.

The old accounting system generated sales reports at the end of every month. These showed details of the sales made by each shop and the types and volumes of products sold. If additional reports were required by T's senior management, special programmes had to be written at considerable expense.

New system

T's new system integrates all record keeping into a single software package that is run on a central system. Data from the tills is recorded directly into the system. The Purchasing Department places orders electronically with suppliers. Shop staff input details of the goods received into the system directly from the new networked PCs that have been installed in all of the shops. Suppliers' invoices are input directly into the system by the Accounts Payable staff and the software checks that the related inventory was ordered and received before it allows invoices to be paid.

The new system generates the same routine reports as were produced by the old system, but it can be interrogated quickly and easily to produce other reports that T's management might need.

The software that forms the basis of the new system was purchased from a recognised vendor. It is a standard package that required very little adaptation to meet T's requirements. The software vendor has agreed to provide a telephone helpdesk function for the first three months of the system's operation.

Implementation issues

The new system has only been live for just over a week. It was not run in parallel with the old system because T's finance director deemed that a parallel run would have been too expensive and disruptive to T's operations.

The head of T's internal audit department offered to conduct a post-implementation review of the system to confirm that user needs are being satisfied, but T's finance director declined this offer. She argued that any problems with the new system will quickly become apparent after it goes live.

Required

(a) Evaluate the argument put forward by T's finance director for refusing to have a post-implementation review. **(10 marks)**

(b) Evaluate the suitability of the internal audit department to conduct T's post-implementation review in the event that such a review is conducted. **(5 marks)**

(c) Discuss the problems that might arise if an entity does not conduct a parallel run when implementing a new system. **(10 marks)**

(Total = 25 marks)

54 W (11/10)   45 mins

W is a leading manufacturer of consumer electronics devices. The company has a significant share of the markets for mobile phone and personal music players ("mp3 players").

W's main areas of expertise are in design and marketing. The company has a reputation for developing innovative products that set the trend for the market as a whole. New product launches attract a great deal of press interest and consequently W spends very little on advertising. Most of its promotional budget is spent on maintaining contact with leading technology journalists and editors.

W does not have a significant manufacturing capacity. New products are designed at the company's research laboratory, which has a small factory unit that can manufacture prototypes in sufficient quantity to produce demonstration models for test and publicity purposes. When a product's design has been finalised W pays a number of independent factories to manufacture parts and to assemble products, although W retains control of the manufacturing process.

W purchases parts from a large number of suppliers but some parts are highly specialised and can only be produced by a small number of companies. Other parts are standard components that can be ordered from a large number of sources. W chooses suppliers on the basis of price and reliability.

All assembly work is undertaken by independent companies. Assembly work is not particularly skilled, but it is time consuming and so labour can cost almost as much as parts.

W has a large procurement department that organises the manufacturing process. A typical cycle for the manufacture of a batch of products is as follows:

- W's procurement department orders the necessary parts from parts suppliers and schedules assembly work in the electronics factories.

- The parts are ordered by W but are delivered to the factories where the assembly will take place.

- The finished goods are delivered directly to the customer.

This is a complicated process because each of W's products has at least 100 components and these can be purchased from several different countries.

W insists on communicating with its suppliers via electronic data interchange (EDI) for placing orders and also for accounting processes such as invoicing and making payment. This is necessary because of the degree of coordination required for some transactions. For example, W may have to order parts from one supplier that have to be delivered to another so that the other supplier can carry out some assembly work. Both suppliers have to be given clear and realistic deadlines so that the resulting assemblies are delivered on time to enable W to meet its own deadlines.

W recently launched a new range of mp3 players. The launch of the first batches of players attracted a great deal of adverse publicity:

- The supplier which produces the unique memory chips used in the mp3 player was unable to meet the delivery deadlines and that delayed the launch. The supplier owns the patent for the design of these memory chips.

- Supplies of the memory chip are now available. The assembly factories have been asked to increase their rates of production to shorten the timescale now that the memory chips have become available.

Required

(a) Evaluate THREE operational risks associated with the manufacture of W's products. (Your answer should include an explanation of how each of these risks could be managed.)   **(15 marks)**

(b) Evaluate the risks associated with the use of EDI for managing W's ordering and accounting processes.
                                                                                              (10 marks)

                                                                                     (Total = 25 marks)

55 J (9/10)

45 mins

J rents cars and small vans to individual and business customers. The company has twelve branches located in large towns spread across J's home country.

Each of J's branches has its own computer network which stores details of all vehicles located at the branch, advanced bookings and current rentals. The only paper records held at branches are the signed rental agreements. Everything else is held electronically. Each branch has several PCs that are linked to a branch server where all of the files are stored. The files on each branch server are backed up to the head office computer system after the close of business every evening.

Customers can book rentals in advance by telephoning their local branch or by logging onto the branch web page. Customers details are initially collected on the branch network but all details including verification of identity and driver's licence are checked when the customer collects the car. Details of the vehicle, including any dents or scrapes on the bodywork or minor mechanical defects, are printed on the rental agreement form and the member of staff and the customer check the vehicle together before the customer signs the agreement.

The branch network keeps track of all vehicles that are supposed to be returned each day. If a vehicle is overdue without good reason then the police are informed that the vehicle has been stolen.

All returned vehicles are checked for damage that was not listed on the rental agreement. Customers have to pay for any damage that occurred while the vehicle was in their possession.

The manager in charge of J's information systems (IS) at the company's head office has been asked to investigate two potential problems that occurred at the Southtown branch. A member of the IS team visited the branch in order to carry out some routine maintenance and discovered the following:

- The Branch Manager had a notebook computer plugged into the branch network. The manager explained that the notebook computer was his own personal property. He found it useful to copy branch files so that he could work on writing his monthly management reports at home.

- One of the PCs in the branch was not the standard model used throughout J. The branch manager explained that there were never sufficient PCs in the branch and so he had used part of the branch equipment budget to purchase an inexpensive PC from a local computer store. The inexpensive PC came equipped with the latest version of a standard operating system. The PCs communicate with the branch network using a specially written program. The branch staff loaded a copy of that program from a CD that had been left behind by a member of the head office IS team during an earlier visit.

J's system uses an older version of the standard operating system and the branch network software installed on the PC was not the latest version, although the Branch Manager insisted that the PC worked perfectly. It has also been useful because the other PCs in the branch were not fitted with optical drives (i.e. they cannot read CDs or DVDs) and he has found it useful to be able to use this machine to install software to other machines over the branch network in order to enhance efficiency. *Performance Strategy 15 September 2010*

Required

(a)   Advise the branch manager on the importance of adequate information systems (IS) for J.

Your answer to part (a) should NOT discuss the specific matters identified by the member of the IS team during the branch visit.

(10 marks)

(b)   Evaluate the control implications of each of the matters discovered by the member of the IS team.

(15 marks)

(Total = 25 marks)

56 K (5/10)
45 mins

K is a provider of music downloads on the Internet (also called MP3 downloads). K is based in a European country.

The company's financial statements are ready for statutory audit and the external auditors have just commenced work.

The company has an electronic library of 19 million different songs in 23 different languages which are available for downloading or listening to online.

Customers register online with K for a fee of $10 a month. This fee allows customers to listen to songs online at any time during that month and also gives the right to download 10 songs each month to their own MP3 players. Additional songs can be downloaded for $1 each.

When K's customers register they must enter into an agreement that permits K to collect the monthly fee from their credit card accounts. Customers who wish to cancel their agreement can do so at any time using a link on K's website. A member of K's administration staff then has to cancel the monthly payment from the customers' credit cards. Customers cannot cancel their monthly payments by contacting their credit card providers directly. This arrangement is standard practice in the provision of online services. It simplifies the relationships between customers, online vendors and credit card companies.

K purchases the rights to distribute and sell some songs outright (normally songs more than 10 years old). This is a flat fee paid by K. Other songs are paid for by K on a royalty basis: the artists are paid a fee of 25 cents every time one of their songs is downloaded by one of K's customers (irrespective of whether it is one of the 10 songs per month allowed in the monthly fee or an additional purchase).

K's music library, website, customer information and all financial accounting systems are maintained on K's own computer systems, which are located at K's head office.

Required

(a)   Discuss FIVE factors that the external auditors should consider when performing a risk assessment of K's IT systems.
(15 marks)

K has been told by a major credit card company that several hundred of its customers had complained that fraudulent charges had been made to their credit card accounts for downloads from K's site. Initial investigations in K have been unable to determine either the validity of these claims or why additional charges may have been made.

Required

(b)   Evaluate the risks to K of such complaints, explaining how those risks could be alleviated.   **(10 marks)**

(Total = 25 marks)

57 FDS (RCS, 11/08)
45 mins

FDS is a large diversified company whose information technology and information management activities are carried out by a shared service centre. FDS 25 is one of many business units operating as an investment centre within FDS. FDS 25 has developed a new business strategy which requires a major new investment in information technology to support its business strategy. FDS 25 needs to implement the new system as quickly as possible and within budget in order to meet its objectives.

Required

(a)   Recommend the controls that could be implemented by a business unit like FDS 25 to mitigate against risk at each stage of information system design and implementation.
(15 marks)

(b)   From the perspective of FDS 25, identify the risk management advantages and disadvantages of each of

(i)   Utilising the shared service centre; and
(ii)   Outsourcing for the design and implementation of a new information system.
(10 marks)

(Total = 25 marks)

58 VWS (RCS, 11/07)

45 mins

VWS is a company manufacturing and selling a wide range of industrial products to a large number of businesses throughout the country. VWS is a significant local employer, with 2,500 people working out of several locations around the region, all linked by a networked computer system.

VWS purchases numerous components from 750 local and regional suppliers, receiving these components into a central warehouse. The company carries about 10,000 different inventory items, placing 25,000 orders with its suppliers each year.

The accounts payable department of VWS has six staff who process all supplier invoices through the company's computer system and make payment to suppliers by cheque or electronic remittance.

Required

(a)   Discuss the purpose and value of an internal control system for accounts payable to a company like VWS.
(10 marks)

(b)   Identify the information systems controls that should be in place for accounts payable in a company like VWS.
(10 marks)

(c)   Explain the risks of fraud in a computerised accounts payable system for a company like VWS and how that risk can be mitigated.
(5 marks)

(Total = 25 marks)

59 STU (RCS, 11/06)

45 mins

STU is a large distribution business which provides logistical support to large retail chains. A significant problem currently faced by STU is the number of legacy systems[1] in use throughout the organisation. The various legacy systems, each of which tends to be used by a single business function, hold data that is inconsistent with other systems, leading to an inconsistent approach to decision making across the business. The problem is made worse by many managers having developed their own PC-based databases and spreadsheets because of the lack of suitable information produced by the legacy systems.

STU's Board of Directors has recently approved the feasibility study presented by the Finance Director for the in-house development of a new Strategic Enterprise Management (SEM) system. The SEM system will use real-time data entry to collect transaction data from remote sites to maintain a data warehouse storing all business information which can then be accessed by various analytical tools to support strategic decision making. The SEM system will be developed and implemented over a three year period within a budget approved by the Board. Three phases have been identified: design of the new system; development of the software; and delivery of the finished system into business units. The Board considers that designing, developing and delivering the SEM system will be crucial to business growth plans in a competitive environment.

[1]*Note:* A legacy system is a computer system which continues to be used because the information it provides is critical to a business. However, the high cost of replacing or redesigning the system has led to it being retained by the business. It is typically an older design, is not compatible with more up-to-date software, and because of its age, provides information that is not as complete or reliable as it should be.

Required

(a)   Assuming that you are STU's Head of Internal Audit, recommend the actions that should be taken in connection with the design, development and delivery of the SEM system.
(13 marks)

(b)   Advise the audit committee of STU about:

(i)   Possible approaches to auditing computer systems; and
(ii)   The controls that should exist in an IT environment.
(12 marks)

(Total = 25 marks)

60 CDE (RCS, 5/06)   45 mins

CDE is a manufacturer of almost one hundred different automotive components that are sold in both large and small quantities on a just-in-time (JIT) basis to the major vehicle assemblers. Business is highly competitive and price sensitive. The company is listed on the stock exchange but CDE's share performance has not matched that of its main competitors.

CDE's management accounting system uses a manufacturing resource planning (MRPII) system to control production scheduling, inventory movements and stock control, and labour and machine utilisation. The accounting department carries out a detailed annual budgeting exercise, determines standard costs for labour and materials, and allocates production overhead on the basis of machine utilisation. Strict accounting controls over labour and material costs are managed by the detailed recording of operator and machine timesheets and raw material movements, and by calculating and investigating all significant variances.

While the information from the MRPII system is useful to management, there is an absence of integrated data about customer requirements and suppliers. Some information is contained within spreadsheets and databases held by the Sales and Purchasing departments respectively. One result of this lack of integration is that inventories are higher than they should be in a JIT environment.

The managers of CDE (representing functional areas of sales, production, purchasing, finance and administration) believe that, while costs are strictly controlled, the cost of the accounting department is excessive and significant savings need to be made, even at the expense of data accuracy. Managers believe that there may not be optimum use of the production capacity to generate profits and cash flow and improve shareholder value. CDE's management wants to carry out sensitivity and other analyses of strategic alternatives, but this is difficult when the existing management accounting system is focused on control rather than on decision support.

Required

(a) (i) Outline the different types of information system available to manufacturing firms like CDE; and

   (ii) Recommend with reasons the information system that would be appropriate to CDE's needs.

(10 marks)

(b) Given the business environment that CDE faces, and the desire of management to reduce the cost of accounting,

   (i) Critically evaluate the relevance of the current management accounting system; and

   (ii) Recommend how the system should be improved. **(15 marks)**

(Total = 25 marks)

61 AMF (RCS, 5/05)   45 mins

AMF is a market leading, high technology manufacturing organisation producing components for the computer industry. AMF has adopted a 'lean' approach to all its functions and has already made a decision to implement a new enterprise resource planning system (ERPS) to support the management of its customers, suppliers, inventory, capacity planning, production scheduling, distribution and accounting functions. The Board of AMF is considering the outsourcing of the design, delivery, implementation and operation of the ERPS to a specialist contractor that has an excellent reputation within the computer industry. A team would be set up within AMF to manage the transition.

Required

Write a formal report to the Board of AMF that:

(a) Discusses the advantages and disadvantages of outsourcing the ERPS system as suggested above.

(5 marks)

(b) Identifies the main risks involving in outsourcing the ERPS and suggests how these risks might be mitigated through internal controls and internal audit. **(10 marks)**

(c) Recommends the processes and controls that AMF should adopt to manage a project for successful transition to a chosen outsource supplier should that be the decision of the Board. **(5 marks)**

(Total = 25 marks)

(Total marks include 5 marks for style, coherence and presentation of the report.)

62 KL   45 mins

KL Group has developed rapidly from a wholesaler supplying specialist stores in one region of the country into a much larger organisation with a significant share of the national market. This has been achieved by:

(a)   Acquiring other regional wholesalers

(b)   Acquiring local groups of retail shops

(c)   Making long-term agreements with stores to act as exclusive suppliers

The group is in the process of consolidating its position, and plans to introduce as quickly as possible an integrated computer system for the whole business, to replace all the current mixture of systems. The main justification for this is to enable central purchasing to use the combined volumes to obtain the best prices and minimise stockholdings. It is envisaged that the integrated system will enable the number of warehouses to be rationalised and reduced.

The finance director has expressed his concern to you, as chief internal auditor, regarding the progress of the project. He fully agrees the need for speed, and the general direction of the project, but does not consider he is adequately informed of the progress made, or of the steps taken to ensure that accounting (and audit) problems will not arise on implementation of the integrated system.

Required

(a)   Explain what steps should be taken in the management of a major project, such as the project described above, to ensure that all senior managers are fully aware of the progress made, and any problems arising.

(7 marks)

(b)   Explain briefly the potential accounting and audit problems arising from the implementation of the new integrated system, and recommend the actions required to deal with these problems.   **(18 marks)**

Note. You are not required to discuss the design of the new integrated systems.

(Total = 25 marks)

63 ROS   45 mins

You are in charge of information security in ROS Inc., a company which writes bespoke computer applications for a number of clients. The most recent application is production of a software control program for nanotechnology used in medical research. The software is highly confidential and has only been used on the internal private network in ROS; this network has no connections outside of the company.

As part of your monitoring, you have noticed private emails being sent by one employee Mr X, to a series of apparently related addressees in the BSTR company, a firm in competition with ROS. On further investigation, you found that the emails contained sections of the code of the new software control program. When challenged Mr X confirmed that the emails did contain sections of the code and asked you for a reference of good conduct prior to leaving the company. Mr X indicated that if this reference was not forthcoming, a timebomb virus hidden in the software control program would erase the entire program sometime in the next two weeks. You are informed that the virus can also be activated immediately by a series of keystrokes on the keyboard.

Required

(a)   Recommend the actions that must be taken as a result of the breach of security up to and including removal of the virus.   **(10 marks)**

(b)   Discuss the main features of a personnel security policy that would be appropriate for ROS Inc, indicating the likely effectiveness of each section of the policy in preventing the introduction of a virus into the software control program.   **(6 marks)**

(c)   Describe the main elements of a software testing strategy designed to prevent a virus being included in software, and explain the problems in implementing this strategy successfully.   **(9 marks)**

(Total = 25 marks)

AUDIT AND REVIEW

Questions 64 to 70 cover audit and review, the subject of Part E of the BPP Study Text for Paper P3.

64 Z (11/11)   45 mins

Z is a government agency that is responsible for promoting road safety. Z needs to buy a fleet of 24 buses that have been converted into mobile exhibition spaces so that they can be driven around to educate community groups about the importance of safe road use.

The management board of Z has decided to use a sealed bid system to tender for this fleet of buses. The sealed bid system is as follows:

- Suppliers who wish to bid for the contract to supply and modify 24 buses should submit a sealed bid to Z's chief buyer.

- The bid should be submitted in a plain envelope with a typed label stating "Bus Bid". There should be no other writing on the envelope.

- The bid should identify:

    o   The supplier
    o   The type of bus to be modified
    o   Details of all the modifications to be undertaken
    o   The price of supplying 24 modified buses

- On receipt of the sealed envelope the chief buyer of Z will sign across the flap of the envelope and place the bid in the safe.

Z's chief executive contacted the head of internal audit immediately before the end of the bidding process and requested that the internal audit department attend the meeting at which the envelopes would be opened. A senior member of the internal audit department was assigned to the task. In addition, the meeting would be attended by the chief buyer, the head of operations and the departmental manager who would be responsible for managing the exhibitions.

At the meeting the chief buyer announced that four bids had been received. The envelopes were opened in random order by the internal auditor. The contents were:

Envelope 1   Bid of GBP 2.8 million from supplier L
Envelope 2   Bid of GBP 3.0 million from supplier K and a letter to withdraw a previously submitted bid of GBP 2.0 million
Envelope 3   Bid of GBP 3.2 million from supplier M
Envelope 4   Bid of GBP 2.0 million from supplier K

The details of the bids in envelopes 2 and 4 from supplier K were identical except for the price.

Supplier L's bid of GBP 2.8million was rejected immediately because the bidder was planning to use a slightly smaller model of bus than the others and planned to use poor quality materials for the modifications. It was, therefore, agreed that the winning bid would be the revised offer to supply the buses for GBP 3.0 million from supplier K.

The head of internal audit was concerned that there could be some irregularities in this bidding process and asked the chief executive to postpone placing an order for the buses until the internal audit department had undertaken an investigation.

Required

(a)   Explain THREE factors that could have caused the head of internal audit to be concerned about the bidding process for the buses.   **(6 marks)**

(b)   Recommend, with reasons, the work that the internal auditor should undertake if the bidding process for the buses is investigated.   **(11 marks)**

(c)   Advise the chief executive about TWO advantages and TWO disadvantages of the internal auditor being actively involved in the investigation of suspected fraud.   **(8 marks)**

(Total = 25 marks)

65 Seatown (9/11)   45 mins

Seatown is located on the coast. The town's main industry is tourism with an emphasis on family holidays and consequently the cleanliness of the town's beaches is a major factor in the town's success.

The town council, which is the local government authority, has a cleaning department that is responsible for keeping the beaches clean and tidy. Early every morning, as soon as the tide has gone out, the beaches are swept using equipment that is towed behind tractors. This equipment skims the top layer of sand and runs it through a filter to remove any litter before returning the cleaned sand to the beach. Most litter takes the form of paper and plastic packaging, but it can include glass bottles and aluminium cans.

To try to prevent litter being left on the beach the town council also places bins on the beaches above the high water mark. Litter bins need to be emptied regularly otherwise holidaymakers pile their rubbish beside the bins and that leads to litter being spread by the wind or by seabirds scavenging for food scraps.

The cost of cleaning the beaches is a major expense for the town council. The management team of the town council has asked the internal audit department to investigate whether the town is getting good "value for money" from this expenditure. The head of internal audit has sought clarification from the town managers on whether the audit should focus on the economy and efficiency of the cleaning operations or their effectiveness. Economy and efficiency audits generally focus on whether cost can be reduced for the same level of service and effectiveness audits ask whether better service can be achieved for the same cost.

Required

(a) Recommend, giving reasons, the matters that the town council's internal audit department should study in order to evaluate the economy and efficiency of the beach cleaning activities.

Your answer should include advice on how to obtain the necessary data and information.   **(10 marks)**

(b) Recommend, giving reasons, the matters that the town council's internal audit department should study in order to evaluate the effectiveness of the beach cleaning activities.

Your answer should include advice on how to obtain the necessary data and information.   **(10 marks)**

(c) Explain why it is easier to investigate the economy and efficiency rather than the effectiveness of the cleaning activities.   **(5 marks)**

(Total = 25 marks)

66 LMN (RCS, 5/06)   45 mins

LMN is a charity that provides low-cost housing for people on low incomes. The government has privatised much of the home building, maintenance and management in this sector. The sector is heavily regulated and receives some government money but there are significant funds borrowed from banks to invest in new housing developments, on the security of future rent receipts. Government agencies subsidise much of the rental cost for low-income residents.

The board and senior management have identified the major risks to LMN as: having insufficient housing stock of a suitable type to meet the needs of local people on low incomes; making poor property investment decisions; having dissatisfied tenants due to inadequate property maintenance; failing to comply with the requirements of the regulator; having a poor credit rating with lenders; poor cost control; incurring bad debts for rental; and having vacant properties that are not earning income. LMN has produced a risk register as part of its risk management process. For each of more than 200 individual risks, the risk register identifies a description of the risk and the (high, medium or low) likelihood of the risk eventuating and the (high, medium or low) consequences for the organisation if the risk does eventuate.

The management of LMN is carried out by professionally qualified housing executives with wide experience in property development, housing management and maintenance, and financial management. The board of LMN is composed of volunteers with wide experience and an interest in social welfare. The board is representative of the community, tenants and the local authority, any of whom may be shareholders (shareholdings are nominal and the company pays no dividends). The local authority has overall responsibility for housing and social welfare in the area. The audit committee of the board of LMN, which has responsibility for risk management as well as internal control, wants to move towards a system of internal controls that are more closely related to risks identified in the risk register.

Required

For an organisation like LMN:

(a) Discuss the purposes and importance of risk management and its relationship with the internal control system. **(8 marks)**

(b) Explain the importance of a management review of controls for the audit committee. **(5 marks)**

(c) Discuss the principles of good corporate governance as they apply to the Board's role

    (i) in conducting a review of internal controls; and

    (ii) reporting on compliance. **(12 marks)**

Illustrate your answer with examples from the scenario.

(Total = 25 marks)

67 SPQ (RCS,11/05)   45 mins

As a CIMA member, you have recently been appointed as the Head of Internal Audit for SPQ, a multinational listed company that carries out a large volume of internet sales to customers who place their orders using their home or work computers. You report to the Chief Executive, although you work closely with the Finance Director. You have direct access to the Chair of the Audit committee whenever you consider it necessary.

One of your internal audit teams has been conducting a review of IT security for a system which has been in operation for 18 months and which is integral to internet sales. The audit was included in the internal audit plan following a request by the chief accountant. Sample testing by the internal audit team has revealed several transactions over the last three months which have raised concerns about possible hacking or fraudulent access to the customer/order database. Each of these transactions has disappeared from the database after deliveries have been made but without sales being recorded or funds collected from the customer. Each of the identified transactions was for a different customer and there seems to be no relationship between any of the transactions.

You have received a draft report from the internal audit manager responsible for this audit which suggests serious weaknesses in the design of the system. You have discussed this informally with senior managers who have told you that such a report will be politically very unpopular with the chief executive as he was significantly involved in the design and approval of the new system and insisted it be implemented earlier than the IT department considered was advisable. No post-implementation review of the system has taken place.

You have been informally advised by several senior managers to lessen the criticism and work with the IT department to correct any deficiencies within the system and to produce a report to the audit committee that is less critical and merely identifies the need for some improvement. They suggest that these actions would avoid criticism of the chief executive by the Board of SPQ.

Required

(a) Explain the role of internal audit in internal control and risk management. **(5 marks)**

(b) Analyse the potential risks faced by SPQ that have been exposed by the review of IT security and recommend controls that should be implemented to reduce them. **(8 marks)**

(c) Discuss the issues that need to be considered when planning an audit of activities and systems such as the one undertaken at SPQ. **(5 marks)**

(d) Explain the ethical principles you should apply as the head of internal audit for SPQ when reporting the results of this internal review and how any ethical conflicts should be resolved. **(7 marks)**

(Total = 25 marks)

68 CFB   45 mins

You work in the Internal Audit department of CFB, a company producing a variety of fruit drinks from cheap orange squash to 100% pure fruit juices. It operates from one location on the edge of a major city.

The main accounting and operational systems of CFB are maintained on an online computer with terminals in all of CFB's departments. The software was written in-house two years ago and is currently supported by a team of 5 programmers, who make amendments to the software as necessary.

Most of the company's sales are made on account to wholesalers and distributors of drinks. However, a small retail shop is maintained on the premises where customers can purchase CFB products. Sales are made on a cash basis with total sales representing about 4% of the total income of the company.

The work of internal audit encompasses not only the financial systems of the company, but also monitoring of the quality of drinks produced in conjunction with the quality control department. Internal audit receives reports on raw materials purchased from the buying department, prices paid from the purchasing department, production quantities from the manufacturing department and quality reports from the quality control department. This information is collated and checked to ensure that poor quality inputs do not result in poor quality outputs. A low price followed by high wastage and poor quality reports could indicate poor quality of product.

The Internal Audit department is required to monitor the cleaning of the vats used for mixing drinks. These vats are cleared every three weeks and discharged into the sewer system. Relatively large amounts of fruit juice are sometimes lost as a result of mixing but no environmental damage has ever occurred.

The Finance Director has recently complained about the efficiency of the Internal Audit department. In his view, the department does not make sufficient use of sampling, and he believes that some members of the internal audit department need to be briefed on how sampling should be used.

Required

(a)   Analyse how audit risk can be ranked using the severity/frequency (likelihood/consequences) matrix, using examples from CFB to support your analysis. You should also provide recommendations on how CFB should manage risk.   **(17 marks)**

(b)   Prepare a briefing for other members of the Internal Audit team explaining the sampling process, covering:

(i)   The basis to use to select items for testing
(ii)   The number of items that should be tested
(iii)   The actions to be taken if errors are found in the test   **(8 marks)**

(Total = 25 marks)

69 JJJ   45 mins

You are the senior audit officer in the newly formed internal audit department of JJJ, a generally well run company which operates a chain of 30 juice bars in the capital city and the South East. Details of the contribution to total revenue that these outlets make are as follows:

Kings Cross Station	24%	Thame Station	8%
Marylebone Station	13%	Bicester Shopping Centre	2%
Hammersmith Station	12%	Banbury Station	2%
Ealing Common Station	10%	Other	19%
Gerrards Cross Café	10%		

The outlets sell fruit and vegetable juices and have more recently introduced a range of smoothies onto the menu. Customers may also choose from a limited range of luxury snacks including muffins and bagels. In a number of locations purchases can be consumed on the premises but the majority operate as kiosks based in shopping centres and railway stations.

Station kiosks are in operation from 6am-12 midnight Monday to Saturday and from 9am-6pm on Sunday. Those in shopping centres are open from 9am-6pm Monday to Saturday. Two members of staff work each shift, one of whom is the manager with responsibility for cash and inventory. Management at Head Office are becoming concerned about the high level of staff turnover at the Ealing kiosk which has had four new managers in the last six months.

All transactions must be paid for in cash. Takings are banked after each nine hour shift. All sales and takings are recorded by computerised tills with the information transferred to Head Office on a daily basis where all the accounting records are maintained.

Reconciliations performed at Head Office have highlighted a number of discrepancies relating to the kiosk at Princes Risborough station, a relatively new outlet which has failed to perform. There have been several instances where there has been a shortfall in cash banked as compared to takings recorded by the till. In addition, information from the till shows that even though the kiosk opens at 6 am often the first transaction is not recorded until 8 am or later.

Standard menus and price lists are used throughout the organisation with the exception of the café style bars whose prices are 10% higher to cover the additional premises cost. On the whole the launch of the smoothie range has been successful. Analysis showing a breakdown of revenue of the five major kiosks has shown the following:

	Juice	Smoothies	Other
Kings Cross	70%	19%	11%
Hammersmith	69%	21%	10%
Ealing	73%	17%	10%
Gerrards Cross	86%	2%	12%
Marylebone	68%	20%	12%

All ordering and purchases are dealt with from Head Office. The manager of each outlet places an order on a daily basis. The order is processed and delivered from regional warehouses the following day. Detailed inventory records are not maintained.

On a weekly basis a physical inventory count is performed and the results returned to Head Office. Each café and kiosk has a separate storeroom with the exception of the Kings Cross Station site where two kiosks operate and share a store. At Head Office stock reconciliations are performed and stock losses calculated. These reconciliations have shown significant losses at the Kings Cross and Ealing sites.

Required

(a)   Explain the matters you would consider in planning the internal audit work for JJJ.   **(13 marks)**

The directors are considering outsourcing the IT requirement, including the accounting function, of JJJ.

Required

(b)   Explain how this would affect the internal audit approach.   **(12 marks)**

(Total = 25 marks)

70   APS   45 mins

APS has grown in recent years from a small business to a medium sized manufacturing business.

APS employs over 200 hourly paid staff in the factory. In that period the payroll system, as described below, has remained basically unchanged, except that certain routines are now computerised. Controls over the system include daily backup, and also backup after each payroll is produced.

Payroll system

(i)   On Monday mornings each employee takes a blank time card from a pile and writes his or her name and number at the top. Each day of the week they record their starting and finishing times. The following Monday each department supervisor collects the cards and forwards them to the wages clerk.

(ii)   Personnel and wages records are maintained by the wages clerk on a personal computer. From the time cards he calculates the hours worked by each employee and enters them into a payroll program on the computer. This program, using data from personnel records as to wage rates and deduction, produces the weekly payroll and a payslip for each employee.

(iii)   The wages clerk prepares a cheque requisition for the total net pay for the week, which is sent to the company accountant together with a copy of the payroll. The accountant draws up the cheque, made payable to cash, and has it countersigned by a director. The wages clerk takes the cheque to the bank and uses the cash to prepare the wage packets. Wage packets are given to the department supervisors for distribution to the employees in their department as they see fit.

(iv)   There is no personnel department. Each department supervisor has the authority to engage new employees and to determine changes in wage rates with the verbal consent of a director.

(v)   Gross weekly wages never exceed $500 for any employee, the total hours never exceed 50 hours a week and increases in hourly rates of pay never exceed 10%.

When APS was a small business it was felt that the directors maintained a reasonable level of supervision over all aspects of the business. Now that the business has expanded, the directors felt that a small internal audit function needed to be set up, and you have recently been recruited to join the newly established internal audit function.

During the planning phase of the first internal audit it became apparent that reliance on management supervision may no longer be sufficient in the area of wages and payroll. There are now too many employees for them to be personally known to the directors who, in any event, now rarely find the time to visit the factory. Recognising this, the directors have appointed a factory manager to oversee the day to day running of the factory. The factory manager's job description includes responsibility for hiring factory staff and determining their rates of pay. Since the directors feel that the company is not sufficiently large to require a separate personnel department, appropriate functions are to be assigned to the factory manager.

The internal audit manager asks you to draft a note to form the basis of a report concerning the wages system. She suggests that the note should identify each of the principal weaknesses of the existing system, possible consequences if the weakness is not remedied and recommend changes that should be made including functions to be assigned to the factory manager.

Required

(a)   Prepare the note suggested by the audit manager. (You are not required to draft the report)   **(18 marks)**

In their last audit the external auditors recommended the introduction of access controls and programmed application controls into the computer system. If such controls are introduced the external auditors might be able to place more audit reliance on computer controls.

Required

(b)   Prepare paragraphs for a report to the directors:

(i)   Describing access and programmed application controls that could be included in the computer system   **(3 marks)**

(ii)   Explaining the use of test data in verifying the computer processing of payroll, including a description of the test data you would use.   **(4 marks)**

Note. You do not have to answer part (b) in a report format.   **(Total = 25 marks)**

CASE STUDIES

Case study questions 71 – 80 combine preseen and unseen material, in the same format as you will see in your P3 exam. The preseen material is also included in BPP's E3 and F3 kits.

71   B Supermarkets (5/12)   90 mins

Preseen case study

Introduction

B Supermarkets (B) was founded as a grocery retailer in a European country in 1963. Its sales consist mainly of food and household items including clothing. B now owns or franchises over 15,000 stores world-wide in 36 countries. The company has stores in Europe (in both eurozone and non-eurozone countries), Asia and North America. B's head office is located in a eurozone country. B has become one of the world's largest chains of stores.

B's Board thinks that there are opportunities to take advantage of the rapid economic growth of some Asian countries and the associated increases in demand for food and consumer goods.

Structure

The B Group is structured into a holding company, B, and three subsidiary companies which are located in each of the regions of the world in which it operates (Europe, Asia and North America). The subsidiary companies, referred to as "Regions" within B, are respectively B-Europe, B-Asia and B-North America.

Store operations, sales mix and staffing

B operates four types of store: supermarkets, hypermarkets, discount stores and convenience stores. For the purpose of this case study, the definition of each of these types of store is as follows:

A *supermarket* is a self-service store which sells a wide variety of food and household goods such as washing and cleaning materials, cooking utensils and other items which are easily carried by customers out of the store.

A *hypermarket* is a superstore or very large store which sells the same type of products as a supermarket but in addition it sells a wide range of other items such as consumer durable white goods, for example refrigerators, freezers, washing machines and furniture. Hypermarkets are often located on out-of-town sites.

A *discount store* is a retail store that sells a variety of goods such as electrical appliances and electronic equipment. Discount stores in general usually sell branded products and pursue a high-volume, low priced strategy and aim their marketing at customers who seek goods at prices which are usually less than can be found in a hypermarket.

A *convenience store* is a small shop or store in an urban area that sells goods which are purchased regularly by customers. These would typically include groceries, toiletries, alcoholic beverages, soft drinks and confectionery. They are convenient for shoppers as they are located in or near residential areas and are often open for long hours. Customers are willing to pay premium prices for the convenience of having the store close by.

B sells food products and clothing in its supermarkets and hypermarkets at a higher price than many of its competitors because the Board thinks that its customers are prepared to pay higher prices for better quality food products. B also sells good quality consumer durable products in its supermarkets and hypermarkets but it is forced to sell these at competitive prices as there is strong competition for the sale of such goods. B's discount stores sell good quality electrical products usually at lower prices than those charged in its supermarkets and hypermarkets, B only sells electronic equipment in its discount stores. Customers have a greater range from which to choose in the discount stores as compared with supermarkets and hypermarkets because the discount stores specialise in the goods which they sell. B's convenience stores do not have the availability of space to carry a wide range of products and they charge a higher price for the same brand and type of goods which it sells in its supermarkets.

Although B owns most of its stores, it has granted franchises for the operation of some stores which carry its name.

Nearly 0.5 million full-time equivalent staff are employed world-wide in the Group. B tries when possible to recruit local staff to fill job vacancies within its stores.

Value statement and mission

In recognition of the strong competitive and dynamic markets in which it operates, B's Board has established an overall value statement as follows: "We aim to satisfy our customers wherever we trade. We intend to employ different generic competitive strategies depending on the market segment in which our stores trade."

The Board has also produced the following mission statement:

"B practises sustainable investment within a healthy ethical and thoughtful culture and strives to achieve customer satisfaction by giving a courteous and efficient service, selling high quality goods at a reasonable price, sourcing goods from local suppliers where possible and causing the least damage possible to the natural environment. By this, we aim to satisfy the expectations of our shareholders by achieving consistent growth in our share price and also to enhance our reputation for being an environmentally responsible company."

Strategic objectives

The following objectives have been derived from the mission statement:

1   Build shareholder value through consistent growth in the company's share price.

2   Increase customer satisfaction ratings to 95% as measured by customer feedback surveys.

3   Increase commitment to local suppliers by working towards achieving 40% of our supplies from sources which are local to where B stores trade.

4   Reduce carbon emissions calculated by internationally agreed measures by at least 1% per year until B becomes totally carbon neutral.

5   Maximise returns to shareholders by employing different generic competitive strategies depending on the market segment in which B stores trade.

Financial objectives

The Board has set the following financial objectives:

1   Achieve consistent growth in earnings per share of 7% each year.

2   Maintain a dividend pay-out ratio of 50% each year.

3   Gearing levels as measured by long-term debt divided by long-term debt plus equity should not exceed 40% based on book value.

Governance

The main board comprises the Non-executive Chairman, the Chief Executive and nine Executive directors. These cover the functions of finance, human resources, corporate affairs (including legal and public relations), marketing, planning and procurement. There is also one executive director for each of the three regions, being the Regional Managing Directors of B-Europe, B-Asia and B-North America. There are also nine non-executive main board members in addition to the Chairman.

The main Board of Directors has separate committees responsible for audit, remuneration, appointments, corporate governance and risk assessment and control. The Risk Assessment and Control Committee's tasks were formerly included within the Audit Committee's role. It was agreed by the Board in 2009 that these tasks should be separated out in order not to overload the Audit Committee which has responsibilities to review the probity of the company. B's expansion has been very rapid in some countries. The expansion has been so rapid that B has not been able to carry out any internal audit activities in some of these countries to date. The regional boards do not have a committee structure.

Each of the Regional Managing Directors chairs his or her own Regional Board. All of the Regional Boards have their own directors for finance, human resources, corporate affairs, marketing, planning and procurement but their structure is different for the directors who have responsibility for the stores. In B-Asia, one regional director is responsible for the hypermarkets and supermarkets and another is responsible for discount stores and convenience stores. In B-North America, one regional director is responsible for the hypermarkets and supermarkets and another is responsible for discount stores (B does not have any convenience stores in North America). In B-Europe there is one regional director responsible for supermarkets and hypermarkets, one for discount stores and one for convenience stores. In all regions the regional directors have line accountability to their respective regional managing director and professional accountability to the relevant main board director. There are no non-executive directors on the regional boards. Appendix 1 shows the main board and regional board structures.

Treasury

Each of B's three regions has a regional treasury department managed by a regional treasurer who has direct accountability to the respective Regional Director of Finance and professional accountability to the Group Treasurer. The Group Treasurer manages the central corporate treasury department which is located in B's head office. The Group Treasurer, who is not a main board member, reports to the Director of Finance on the main board.

Shareholding, year-end share prices and dividends paid for the last five years

B is listed on a major European stock exchange within the eurozone and it wholly owns its subsidiaries. There are five major shareholders of B, including employees taken as a group, which between them hold 25% of the 1,350 million total shares in issue. The major shareholders comprise two long term investment trusts which each owns 4%, a hedge fund owns 5%, employees own 5% and the founding family trust owns 7% of the shares. The remaining 75% of shares are owned by the general public.

The year-end share prices and the dividends paid for the last five years were as follows:

	200 €	2008 €	2009 €	2010 €	2011 €
Share price at 31 December	47.38	25.45	28.68	29.44	31.37
Net Dividend per share	1.54	1.54	1.54	1.62	1.65

Planning and management control

B has a very structured planning process. Each regional board produces a five year strategic plan for its region relating to specific objectives set for it by the main board and submits this to the main board for approval. The main board then produces a consolidated strategic plan for the whole company. This is reviewed on a three yearly cycle and results in a revised and updated group five year plan being produced every three years.

B's management control system, which operates throughout its regions and at head office, is well known in the industry to be bureaucratic and authoritarian. Strict financial authority levels for development purposes are imposed from the main Board. There is tension between the main Board and the regional boards. The regional board members feel that they are not able to manage effectively despite being located much closer to their own regional markets than the members of the main Board. The main Board members, on the other hand, think that they need to exercise tight control because they are remote from the markets. This often stifles planning initiatives within each region. This tension is also felt lower down the organisation as the regional board members exercise strict financial and management control over operational managers in their regions in order to ensure that the main Board directives are carried out.

Competitive overview

B operates in highly competitive markets for all the products it sells. The characteristics of each of the markets in which it operates are different. For example, there are different planning restrictions applying within each region. In some countries, B is required to operate each of its stores in a partnership arrangement with local enterprises, whereas no such restriction exists within other countries in which it trades. B needs to be aware of different customer tastes and preferences which differ from country to country. The following table provides a break-down of B's stores in each region.

	B Europe	B Asia	B North America
Supermarkets and hypermarkets	3,456	619	512
Discount stores	5,168	380	780
Convenience stores	4,586	35	

B is one of the largest retailing companies in the world and faces different levels of competition in each region. B's overall market share in terms of retail sales for all supermarkets, hypermarkets, discount stores and convenience stores in each of its regions is as follows:

	Market share
Europe	20%
Asia	1%
North America	1.5%

The following table shows the sales revenue and net operating profit earned by B in each of its regions for the year ended 31 December 2011:

	B Europe € million	B Asia € million	B North America € million
Revenue	89,899	10,105	9,708
Net Operating Profit	4,795	743	673

B is constantly seeking other areas of the world into which it can expand, especially within Asia where it perceives many countries have an increasing population and strengthening economies.

<u>Corporate Social Responsibility (CSR)</u>

B is meeting its CSR obligations by establishing environmental targets for carbon emissions (greenhouse gas emissions), careful monitoring of its supply chain, undertaking sustainable investments and investing in its human capital.

Environmental targets for carbon emissions

B's main board is keen to demonstrate the company's concern for the environment by pursuing continuous improvement in the reduction of its carbon emissions and by developing ways of increasing sustainability in its trading practices. A number of environmental indicators have been established to provide transparency in B's overall performance in respect of sustainability. These published measures were verified by B's statutory auditor and are calculated on a like-for-like basis for the stores in operation over the period measured.

In the year ended 31 December 2011, B reduced its consumption of kilowatt hours (kWh) per square metre of sales area as compared with the year ended 31 December 2008 by 9%. The target reduction for that period was 5%. In the same period it reduced the number of free disposable plastic bags provided to customers per square metre of sales area, by 51% against a target of 60%. Its overall greenhouse gas emissions (measured by kilogrammes of carbon dioxide per square metre of sales area) reduced by 1% in 2011 which was exactly on target.

B provides funding for the development of local amenity projects in all of the countries where B stores operate. (An amenity project is one which provides benefit to the local population, such as providing a park, community gardens or a swimming pool.)

Distribution and sourcing

Distribution from suppliers across such a wide geographical area is an issue for B. While supplies are sourced from the country in which a store is located as much as possible, there is nevertheless still a requirement for transportation across long distances either by road or air. Approximately 20% of the physical quantity of goods sold across the group as a whole is sourced locally, that is within the country in which the goods are sold. These tend to be perishable items such as fruit and vegetables. The remaining 80% of goods are sourced from large international manufacturers and distributors. These tend to be large items such as electrical or electronic equipment which are bought under contracts which are set up by the regional procurement departments. B, due to its size and scope of operations, is able to place orders for goods made to its own specification and packaged as under its own brand label. Some contracts are agreed between manufacturers and the Group Procurement Director for the supply of goods to the whole of the B group world-wide.

B's inventory is rarely transported by rail except within Europe. This has resulted in lower average reductions in carbon emissions per square metre of sales area by stores operated by B-Asia and B-North America than for those stores operated by B-Europe. This is because the carbon emission statistics take into account the transportation of goods into B's stores.

Sustainable investments

B aspires to become carbon neutral over the long term. The Board aims to reduce its carbon emissions by investing in state of the art technology in its new store developments and by carrying out modifications to existing stores.

Human Resources

B prides itself on the training it provides to its staff. The training of store staff is carried out in store by specialist teams which operate in each country where B trades. In this way, B believes that training is consistent across all of its stores. In some countries, the training is considered to be at a sufficiently high level to be recognised by national training bodies. The average number of training hours per employee in the year ended 31 December 2011 was 17 compared with 13 hours in the year ended 31 December 2010. In 2011, B employed 45% more staff with declared disabilities compared with 2010.

Information systems and inventory management

In order to operate efficiently, B's Board has recognised that it must have up-to-date information systems including electronic point of sale (EPOS) systems. An EPOS system uses computers or specialised terminals that can be combined with other hardware such as bar-code readers to accurately capture the sale and adjust the inventory levels within the store. EPOS systems installation is on-going. B has installed EPOS systems in its stores in some countries but not in all its stores world-wide.

B's information systems are not perfect as stock-outs do occur from time-to-time, especially in the European stores. This can be damaging to sales revenue when stock-outs occur during peak sales periods such as the days leading up to a public holiday. In Asia and North America in particular, B's information technology systems sometimes provide misleading information. This has led to doubts in the minds of some head office staff about just how robust are B's inventory control systems.

As is normal in chain store groups, there is a certain degree of loss through theft by staff and customers. Another way that loss is suffered is through goods which have gone past their "sell-by" date and mainly relates to perishable food items which are wasted as they cannot be sold to the public. In most countries, such food items which cannot be sold to the public may be sold to local farmers for animal feed.

Regulatory issues

B's subsidiaries in Asia and North America have sometimes experienced governmental regulatory difficulties in some countries which have hindered the installation of improved information systems. To overcome some of these regulatory restrictions, B-Asia and B-North America have, on occasions, resorted to paying inducements to government officials in order for the regulations to be relaxed.

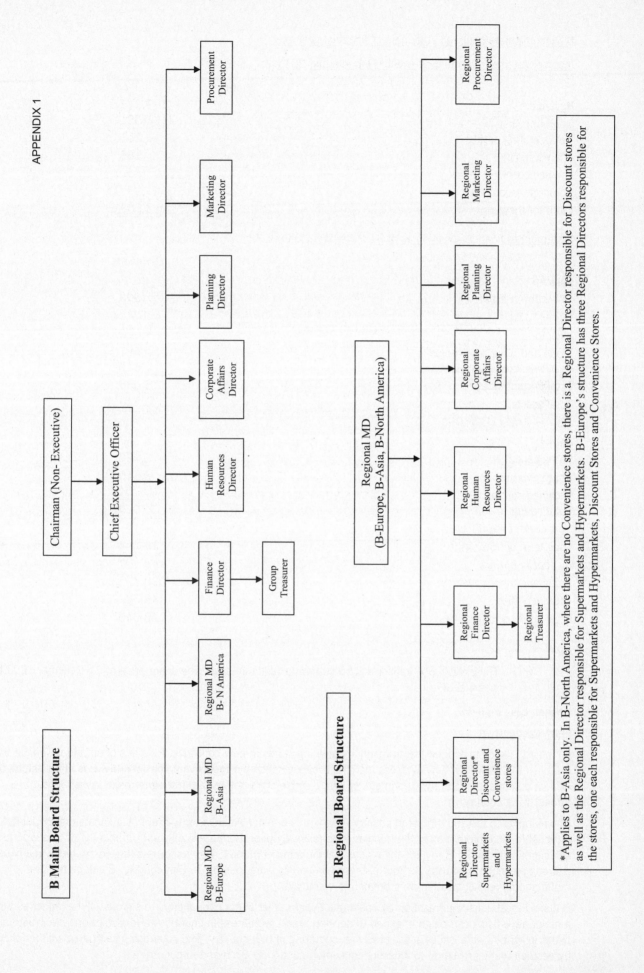

APPENDIX 1

B Main Board Structure

B Regional Board Structure

*Applies to B-Asia only. In B-North America, where there are no Convenience stores, there is a Regional Director responsible for Discount stores as well as the Regional Director responsible for Supermarkets and Hypermarkets. B-Europe's structure has three Regional Directors responsible for the stores, one each responsible for Supermarkets and Hypermarkets, Discount Stores and Convenience Stores.

B's income statement and statement of financial position.

Income statement for the year ended 31 December 2011

	Notes	€ million
Revenue		109,712
Operating costs		(103,501)
Net operating profit		6,211
Interest income		165
Finance costs		(852)
Corporate income tax		(1,933)
Profit for the year		3,591

Statement of financial position as at 31 December 2011

		€ million
ASSETS		
Non-current assets		57,502
Current assets		
Inventories		7,670
Trade and other receivables		1,521
Cash and cash equivalents		3,847
Total current assets		13,038
Total assets		70,540
EQUITY AND LIABILITIES		
Equity		
Share capital	1	2,025
Share premium		3,040
Retained earnings		18,954
Total equity		24,019
Non-current liabilities		
Long term borrowings		15,744
Current liabilities		
Trade and other payables		30,777
Total liabilities		46,521
Total equity and liabilities		70,540

Notes:

1. There are 1,350 million €1.50 shares currently in issue. The share price at 31 December 2011 was €31.37.

Unseen case material

Entry to country A

B's board is keen to expand the company by opening stores in new countries. Retailers often find it difficult to establish themselves in new overseas markets because consumer tastes vary considerably. It is often helpful to explore potential markets by experimenting with a single store before committing to major investments throughout a country.

B is planning to test the market in country A, which is a major Asian country that has a substantial population. Although a large proportion of the population is relatively poor there are significant numbers of people who are sufficiently affluent for B to view them as a profitable target market. Two major retailing companies already have a strong presence in country A. Both of these companies were founded in that country. B will be the first multinational retailer to attempt to break into country A.

B plans to test consumer reaction by opening a hypermarket in A's capital city. This store will be launched with a major advertising campaign intended to develop brand awareness in country A and also to provide B with a better insight into the issues associated with operating in that country. The advertising campaign will be followed by detailed market research to measure consumer reaction to B's brand in country A.

B's plans to enter country A have been heavily publicised in the business news in B's home country. B's press release indicated that the board is confident that the new store will be the first of many in country A and that further overseas markets are under consideration.

B's hypermarkets have a standard layout and they tend to stock the same ranges of goods regardless of the country in which they operate. Both the layout and the range of goods can be modified if there is a possibility that local tastes and culture make it inappropriate or unprofitable to sell the standard range or to promote products that are unlikely to appeal to local markets. For example, B sells its own "Beebrand" range of goods with white packaging in most countries, but a different colour is used in Asian countries because white is often associated with mourning in Asia.

B's marketing department has suggested that before the hypermarket is opened B should seek advice from a retail consultancy that is based in country A's capital city in order to gain an awareness of any major issues. For example, many of the products that B sells in Europe and America could be considered offensive by a large proportion of the population of country A. B's chief executive is concerned that taking the advice of such consultants would defeat the purpose of the investment in country A. The objective of the investment is to establish B's style of retailing in country A and promote B's values with the intention of changing consumer attitudes in country A.

Long-term borrowings

B's long-term borrowings include a variable rate loan of EUR 7,000 million on which interest of EURIBOR plus 3.8% is being charged. This loan was taken out four years ago and is not due for repayment for another six years.

B's Finance Director did not work for B when the loan was taken out. She believes that the company should have taken out a fixed rate loan even though the fixed rate that was available then was higher than the variable rate. She is concerned that B is vulnerable to an increase in interest rates for two reasons: firstly, borrowing heavily using variable rate debt means that an increase in interest rates will prove expensive and, secondly, consumer demand can be affected by rising interest rates. The Finance Director believes that the company should have taken out a fixed interest loan and she has investigated some of the ways in which B might reduce the risks associated with the variable rate borrowing.

A major commercial bank has given B an indication that it would be possible to arrange a swap whereby the bank would enter into a swap arrangement under which B would pay a fixed rate of interest of 7.2% for the remaining six years of its existing variable-rate loan. At present EURIBOR is 1.1%.

B's Finance Director believes that the EURIBOR will soon rise to 2.0%, despite most economic commentators stating that interest rates are unlikely to increase by much within the next twelve months.

The Finance Director's assistant has suggested that the company should investigate the use of alternatives to a swap, such as forward rate agreements or interest rate options. The Finance Director has stated that there is very little point in such an investigation because the alternatives to swaps tend to be designed to deal with short term interest rate movements and so they would offer very little protection against the movements that could occur over the next six years. The Finance Director does not believe that there is any point in purchasing a sequence of short term instruments over the next six years.

IT system

B's accounting system is based around a smart-retailing package that incorporates both hardware and software in all stores. At present all of the inventory that arrives at each store is tracked using barcodes. Whenever a consignment of inventory is received, a staff member uses a handheld barcode reader to scan the codes printed on the packaging. That information is transmitted from the reader to the store's inventory management system. Similarly, all goods are scanned at the point of sale (or point of despatch for large items, such as televisions, that are purchased in store but dispatched from the store's warehouse). Consequently the inventory system is updated with relatively little human effort.

One area of inventory management that remains very labour-intensive is the physical counting of inventory that is necessary to identify any losses that may have occurred due to theft or damage. Every store is required to conduct frequent checks on high-value items by having staff conduct physical counts of specific items. The results of these counts are then compared to the inventory records. The counting can be time-consuming because items such as small electrical goods may have some inventory displayed and available for sale in the store while bulk supplies are held in one or more locations in the store's warehouse. Such items can have high unit costs and so the count must be accurate and must also involve teams of two members of staff so that each can corroborate the accuracy of the count.

B's Finance Director is keen to introduce a new system for managing inventory. Many manufacturers attach Radio Frequency Identification (RFID) tags to their products. These are self-adhesive tags that have circuitry embedded in them that allows the data they contain to be read by a device that emits a radio wave that is capable of powering any RFID tags within short range. When powered in this way the tags transmit a code back to the reader. All of the suppliers who produce B's electrical and electronic goods for resale already fit RFID tags to all of their products. Large items, such as cookers and freezers, have the tags stuck to the back of the items themselves. Smaller items, such as shavers and hairdryers, have the tags stuck to the inside of each individual item's packaging.

There is a standard format for the data that is embedded in an RFID tag. That makes it easy for a retailer such as B to be certain of being able to capture all the information that is required for inventory management purposes. Each tag also carries an individual tag number that makes it possible for the reader to count the precise number of items of the same type without any risk of double counting. For example, a reader fitted to the door of the goods received area can scan a pallet of goods being delivered and immediately record the arriving inventory without B's staff having to take any action. Another reader attached to the door leading from the warehouse to the retail area will track the movement of the goods when they are taken for display or sale. Finally, readers at the point of sale can identify when tagged items are sold.

Inventory counts would be undertaken by using portable readers that count tagged inventory and log the unique code numbers of each item held. That means that one member of staff can check holdings of a particular product by taking the reader to the areas where that product is stored and activating the reader. The tags themselves cannot be reprogrammed after they have been manufactured and the software in the reader cannot be tampered with and so the system is claimed to be secure.

The Finance Director believes that the RFID technology will simplify the management of inventory and will reduce the time that has to be spent on inventory control. She has commissioned a pilot programme to test this system in the management of electrical goods at one of B's hypermarkets.

Required

(a)	(i)	Discuss TWO ways in which B's investment in country A could adversely affect the relationship between B's board and the shareholders of B.	**(8 marks)**
	(ii)	Evaluate the risk that B's venture in country A will fail because of cultural differences.	**(8 marks)**
(b)	(i)	Evaluate the risks for B arising from interest rate fluctuations.	**(6 marks)**
	(ii)	Discuss the potential risks and benefits that could arise from the swap arrangement with the major commercial bank. Your answer should be supported by calculations that show the effects of the swap a) assuming that EURIBOR remains constant and b) assuming that the rate increases to 2%.	**(6 marks)**
	(iii)	Evaluate the Finance Director's statement that there is no point in purchasing a sequence of short term instruments to lower exposure to interest rate risks over the remaining six years of the loan.	**(6 marks)**
(c)	(i)	Evaluate the potential effectiveness of RFID technology for the identification and prevention of fraud by staff.	**(8 marks)**
	(ii)	Recommend tests that B's internal audit department could conduct to evaluate the effectiveness of the RFID technology while the pilot programme is operating.	**(8 marks)**

(Total = 50 marks)

72 M Newspapers 1 (3/12) 90 mins

Note: This Preseen applies to Questions 72 and 73

Preseen case study

Introduction

M plc is a long established publisher of newspapers and provider of web media. It is based in London and has had a full listing on the London Stock Exchange since 1983. The company has three operating divisions which are managed from the United Kingdom (UK). These are the Newspapers Division, the Web Division and the Advertising Division.

Newspapers Division

The Newspapers Division publishes three daily newspapers and one Sunday newspaper in the UK. The Division has three offices and two printing sites. Between them the three offices edit the three daily newspapers and the Sunday newspaper. The Newspaper Division has two subsidiary publishing companies, FR and N. FR is based in France within the Eurozone and N in an Eastern European country which is outside the Eurozone. Printing for all the Division's publications, except those produced by FR and N, is undertaken at the two printing sites. FR and N have their own printing sites.

Web Division

The Web Division maintains and develops 200 websites which it owns. Some of these websites are much more popular in terms of the number of "hits" they receive than others. Web material is an increasing part of M plc's business. In the last ten years, the Web Division has developed an online version of all the newspapers produced by the Newspapers Division.

Advertising Division

The sale of advertising space is undertaken for the whole of M plc by the Advertising Division. Therefore, advertisements which appear in the print media and on the web pages produced by the Newspapers Division (including that produced by FR and N) and the Web Division respectively are all handled by the Advertising Division.

Group Headquarters

In addition to the three operating divisions, M plc also has a head office, based in the UK, which is the group's corporate headquarters where the Board of Directors is located. The main role of M plc's headquarters is to develop and administer its policies and procedures as well as to deal with its group corporate affairs.

Mission statement

M plc established a simple mission statement in 2005. This drove the initiative to acquire FR in 2008 and remains a driving force for the company. M plc's mission is "to be the best news media organisation in Europe, providing quality reporting and information on European and world-wide events".

Strategic objectives

Four main strategic objectives were established in 2005 by M plc's Board of Directors. These are to:

1   Meet the needs of readers for reliable and well informed news.

2   Expand the geographical spread of M plc's output to reach as many potential newspaper and website readers as possible.

3   Publish some newspapers which help meet the needs of native English speakers who live in countries which do not have English as their first language.

4   Increase advertising income so that the group moves towards offering as many news titles as possible free of charge to the public.

Financial objectives

In meeting these strategic objectives, M plc has developed the following financial objectives:

(i) To ensure that revenue and operating profit grow by an average of 4% per year.

(ii) To achieve steady growth in dividend per share.

(iii) To maintain gearing below 40%, where gearing is calculated as debt/(debt plus equity) based on the market value of equity and the book value of debt.

Forecast revenue and operating profit

M plc's forecast revenue and net operating profit for the year ending 31 March 2012 are £280 million and £73 million respectively.

Extracts from M plc's forecast income statement for the year ending 31 March 2012 and forecast statement of financial position as at 31 March 2012 are shown in the appendix.

Comparative divisional performance and headquarters financial information

The following information is provided showing the revenue generated, the operating profit achieved and the capital employed for each division and the operating costs incurred and capital employed in M plc's headquarters. This information covers the last two years and also gives a forecast for the year ending 31 March 2012. All M plc's revenue is earned by the three divisions.

Newspapers Division	Year ended 31.3.2010 £million	Year ended 31.3.2011 £million	Forecast for year ending 31.3.2012 £million
Revenue external	91	94	94
Revenue internal transfers	90	91	96
Net operating profit	45	46	48
Non-current assets	420	490	548
Net current assets	4	8	(10)

Web Division	Year ended 31.3.2010 £million	Year ended 31.3.2011 £million	Forecast for year ending 31.3.2012 £million
Revenue internal transfers	55	60	66
Net operating profit	10	13	16
Non-current assets	37	40	43
Net current assets	1	1	(2)

Advertising Division	Year ended 31.3.2010 £million	Year ended 31.3.2011 £million	Forecast for year ending 31.3.2012 £million
Revenue external	162	180	186
Internal transfers	(145)	(151)	(162)
Net operating profit	10	18	19
Non-current assets	3	6	7
Net current assets	1	1	(2)

Headquarters	Year ended 31.3.2010 £million	Year ended 31.3.2011 £million	Forecast for year ending 31.3.2012 £million
Operating costs	8	9	10
Non-current assets	37	39	43
Net current assets	1	1	(1)

Notes

1   The Advertising Division remits advertising revenue to both the Newspapers and Web Divisions after deducting its own commission.

2   The Web Division's entire revenue is generated from advertising.

3   The revenues and operating profits shown for the Newspapers Division include those earned by FR and N. The converted revenue and operating profit from N are forecast to be £20 million and £4 million respectively for the year ending 31 March 2012. FR is forecast to make a small operating profit in the year ending 31 March 2012. The Board of M plc is disappointed with the profit FR has achieved.

Additional information on each of M plc's divisions

Newspapers Division

FR is wholly owned and was acquired in 2008. Its financial statements are translated into British pounds and consolidated into M plc's group accounts and included within the Newspaper Division's results for internal reporting purposes.

Shortly after it was acquired by M plc, FR launched a pan-European weekly newspaper. This newspaper, which is written in English, is produced in France and then distributed throughout Europe. M plc's board thought that this newspaper would become very popular because it provides a snapshot of the week's news, focused particularly on European issues but viewed from a British perspective. Sales have, however, been disappointing.

N, which publishes local newspapers in its home Eastern European country, is also treated as part of the Newspapers Division. M plc acquired 80% of its equity in 2010. At that time, M plc's board thought that Eastern Europe was a growing market for newspapers. The subsidiary has proved to be profitable mainly because local production costs are lower than those in the UK relative to the selling prices.

The Newspapers Division's journalists incur a high level of expenses in order to carry out their duties. The overall level of expenses claimed by the journalists has been ignored by M plc in previous years because it has been viewed as a necessary cost of running the business. However, these expenses have risen significantly in recent years and have attracted the attention of M plc's internal audit department.

There has been significant capital investment in the Newspapers Division since 2009/10. The printing press facilities at each of the two printing sites have been modernised. These modernisations have improved the quality of output and have enabled improved levels of efficiency to be achieved in order to meet the increasing workloads demanded in the last two years. Surveys carried out before and after the modernisation have indicated higher levels of customer satisfaction with the improved quality of printing.

The increased mechanisation and efficiency has reduced costs and led to a reduction in the number of employees required to operate the printing presses. This has led to some dis-satisfaction among the divisional staff. Staff in the other divisions have been unaffected by the discontent in the Newspapers Division. Staff turnover has been relatively static across the three divisions, with the exception of the department which operates the printing presses in the Newspapers Division where some redundancies have occurred due to fewer staff being required since the modernisation.

Web Division

The web versions of the newspapers are shorter versions of the printed ones. There is currently no charge for access to the web versions of the newspapers. Revenues are generated from sales by the Advertising Division of advertising space on the web pages. Some of the websites permit unsolicited comments from the public to be posted on them and they have proved to be very popular. The Web Division is undertaking a review of all its costs, particularly those relating to energy, employees and website development.

The Web Division's management accounting is not sophisticated: for example, although it reports monthly on the Division's revenue and profitability, it cannot disaggregate costs so as to produce monthly results for each of the 200 websites. The Division is at a similar disadvantage as regards strategic management accounting as it lacks information about the websites' market share and growth rates. This has not mattered in the past as M plc was content that the Web Division has always been profitable. However, one of M plc's directors, the Business Development Director (see below under The Board of Directors and group shareholding) thinks that the Web Division could increase its profitability considerably and wants to undertake a review of its 200 websites.

Advertising Division

The Advertising Division remits advertising revenue to both the Newspapers and Web Divisions after deducting its own commission. In addition, the Advertising Division offers an advertising service to corporate clients. Such services include television and radio advertising and poster campaigns on bill boards. Advertisements are also placed in newspapers and magazines which are not produced by M plc, if the client so wishes. An increasing element of the work undertaken by the Advertising Division is in providing pop-up advertisements on websites.

Planning process

Each division carries out its own planning process. The Newspapers Division operates a rational model and prepares annual plans which it presents to M plc's board for approval. The Web Division takes advantage of opportunities as they arise and is operating in a growth market, unlike the other two divisions. Its planning approach might best be described as one of logical incrementalism. Increased capital expenditure in 2010/11 helped the Advertising Division to achieve an 11% increase in revenue in that year. The Divisional Managers of both the Web Division and the Advertising Division are keen to develop their businesses and are considering growth options including converting their businesses into outsource service providers to M plc.

The Board of Directors and group shareholding

M plc's Board of Directors comprises six executive directors and six non-executive directors, one of whom is the Non-executive Chairman. The executive directors are the Chief Executive, and the Directors of Strategy, Corporate Affairs, Finance, Human Resources and Business Development. The Business Development Director did not work for M plc in 2005 and so had no part in drafting the strategic objectives. She thinks that objective number four has become out- dated as it does not reflect current day practice. The Business Development Director has a great deal of experience working with subscription-based websites and this was one of the main reasons M plc recruited her in March 2011. Her previous experience also incorporated the management of product portfolios including product development and portfolio rationalisation.

There are divisional managing directors for each of the three divisions who are not board members but report directly to the Chief Executive.

One of M plc's non-executive directors was appointed at the insistence of the bank which holds 10% of M plc's shares. Another was appointed by a private charity which owns a further 10% of the shares in M plc. The charity represents the interests of print workers and provides long-term care to retired print workers and their dependents. Two other non-executive directors were appointed by a financial institution which owns 20% of the shares in M plc. The remaining 60% of shares are held by private investors. The board members between them hold 5% of the shares in issue. None of the other private investors holds more than 70,000 of the total 140 million shares in issue.

It has become clear that there is some tension between the board members. Four of the non- executive directors, those appointed by the bank, the charity and the financial institution, have had disagreements with the other board members. They are dissatisfied with the rate of growth and profitability of the company and wish to see more positive action to secure M plc's financial objectives.

Some board members feel that the newspapers market is declining because fewer people can make time to read printed publications. Some of the non-executive directors think that many people are more likely to watch a television news channel than read a newspaper.

Editorial policy

M plc's board applies a policy of editorial freedom provided that the published material is within the law and is accurate. The editors of each of the publications printed in the UK and France and of the websites have complete autonomy over what is published. They are also responsible for adhering to regulatory constraints and voluntary industry codes of practice relating to articles and photographs which might be considered offensive by some readers.

There is less scrutiny of the accuracy of the reporting in N's home country than in other countries. The Eastern European country in which N is situated has become politically unstable in the last two years. Much of this unrest is fuelled by the public distaste for the perceived blatant corruption and bribery which is endemic within the country's Government and business community. It is well known that journalists have accepted bribes to present only the Government's version of events, rather than a balanced view. There is

also widespread plagiarism of published material by the country's newspapers and copyright laws are simply ignored.

Corporate Social Responsibility

A policy is in place throughout M plc in order to eliminate bribery and corruption among staff especially those who have front line responsibility for obtaining business. This policy was established 15 years ago. All new employees are made aware of the policy and other staff policies and procedures during their induction. The Director of Human Resources has confidence in the procedures applied by his staff at induction and is proud that no action has ever been brought against an employee of M plc for breach of the bribery and corruption policy.

M plc is trying to reduce its carbon footprint and is in the process of developing policies to limit its energy consumption, reduce the mileage travelled by its staff and source environmentally friendly supplies of paper for its printing presses. The Newspapers Division purchases the paper it uses for printing newspapers from a supplier in a Scandinavian country. This paper is purchased because it provides a satisfactory level of quality at a relatively cheap price. The Scandinavian country from which the paper is sourced is not the same country in which N is situated.

Strategic Development

The Board of Directors is now reviewing M plc's competitive position. The Board of Directors is under pressure from the non-executive directors appointed by the bank, the charity and the financial institution (which between them own 40% of the shares in M plc), to devise a strategic plan before June 2012 which is aimed at achieving M plc's stated financial objectives.

APPENDIX 1

Extracts from M plc's forecast group income statement and forecast statement of financial position

Forecast income statement for the group for the year ending 31 March 2012

	Notes	£ million (GBP million)
Revenue		280
Operating costs		(207)
Net operating profit		73
Interest income		1
Finance costs		(11)
Corporate income tax	1	(19)
Forecast profit for the year		44

Forecast statement of the group financial position as at 31 March 2012

	Notes	£ million (GBP million)
ASSETS		
Non-current assets		641
Current assets		
Inventories		2
Trade and other receivables		27
Cash and cash equivalents		2
Total current assets		31
Total assets		672
EQUITY AND LIABILITIES		
Equity		
Share capital	2	140
Share premium		35
Retained earnings		185
Non-controlling interest		16
Total equity		376
Non-current liabilities		
Long term borrowings	3	250
Current liabilities		
Trade and other payables		46
Total liabilities		296
Total equity and liabilities		672

Notes:

1   The corporate income tax rate can be assumed to be 30%.

2   There are 140 million £1 shares currently in issue.

3   The long-term borrowings include £83 million of loan capital which is due for repayment on 1 April 2013 and the remainder is due for repayment on 1 April 2019.

Unseen case material

The following information relates to M plc.

Web site

M plc publishes a Sunday newspaper that is popular throughout the UK. The newspaper has recently launched an online version which can be downloaded by subscribers who pay a monthly fee that is slightly less expensive than buying the printed version of the newspaper. There are approximately 80,000 subscribers to this service.

The online version of the newspaper allows subscribers to post comments concerning any of the articles published in the most recent version of the newspaper. This has been a popular facility that readers appear to value. There has been an average of 15,000 posts per week since the posting facility was introduced.

Subscribers must log in using their user names and passwords before they can make a post. M plc does not edit such posts because it would be prohibitively expensive to do so. Instead, M plc relies on software that scans

each draft post for offensive language and any post that does not trigger that software appears in a text box underneath the article and can be read by all subscribers.

Subscribers to the online version of this newspaper must register using a credit card in order to obtain a subscription. They have to tick a box onscreen to acknowledge that they have read and agreed to M plc's terms and conditions, which include the following:

- Subscribers accept M plc is not responsible for any offensive or incorrect comments posted on the site.

- Subscribers agree that any posts they place on the site will be honest, accurate and not intended to cause any harm or offence. Authors agree that all responsibility for comments they post remains with the author not M plc.

- The copyright to all posts to the site belongs to M plc and nobody is permitted to copy, print or publish them for any purpose without first seeking M plc's permission.

Last month a post was made underneath an article about J, a famous pop singer, who endorses a range of vegetarian meals. The post's author claimed to have seen J eating a meat dish in a restaurant. The post was read and copied by a journalist from a rival newspaper. The journalist sought reactions from J and the manufacturer of the vegetarian meals and published the story on the front page of the Monday edition of the rival newspaper under the headline "Famous vegetarian eats principles". The article was careful to state that the only foundation for the story is the post to M plc's site.

J's lawyers have contacted M plc to inform the company that the vegetarian meals manufacturer has cancelled J's advertising contract. J is seeking compensation from M plc for the loss of these earnings and also for the damage to her reputation. M plc has rejected the claim on the grounds that it had taken all reasonable steps to prevent any harm to J's reputation when it drafted its terms and conditions. The offending post was removed from the site as soon as it was drawn to M plc's attention.

Expenses audit

M plc's directors receive monthly management accounts which show major categories of income and expenditure. The level of journalists' expenses has been growing dramatically. The Board of Directors has insisted that the internal audit department carry out regular reviews of the journalists' expenses starting as soon as possible.

The directors also asked the Head of Internal Audit to investigate immediately the increase in journalists' expenses. The investigation revealed no evidence of fraud but did uncover a culture in which job-related expenses were being incurred with no regard to the cost. For example, if a journalist wished to conduct an interview outside of a contact's office for the sake of privacy, it had become accepted that the interview would be conducted in an expensive restaurant. Journalists make their own travel arrangements: this was considered to be necessary in order to avoid slowing down work on a breaking story. It had become common practice for all rail journeys to be booked first class and all flights to be taken in business class even though that cost a great deal more than standard or economy class travel. Overnight stays tended to be booked in five star hotels.

Journalists had also claimed for items of equipment ranging from mobile phones and laptops to expensive televisions and office furniture for home offices. They usually bought the latest and most expensive technology and justified it on the basis that it would make news gathering more efficient.

Expense claims must be submitted on official claim forms with receipts attached. Each claim must be signed by the journalist's editor before the accounts department will process it. Editors told the Head of Internal Audit that journalists' attitudes had changed over the past four or five years and that they were making ever more substantial claims. Editors did not wish to risk demotivating journalists by restricting expenses and so spending had tended to escalate.

M plc has a formal policy on expenses, with guidance on the maximum costs that can be incurred for entertaining or travel without seeking specific approval. The investigation found that no one in the company has paid any attention to that policy.

Wood pulp

M plc purchases its paper from a Scandinavian company. Paper is manufactured from wood pulp. Most of the pulp sold in Europe comes from specially grown forests in Scandinavia. Wood pulp is a commodity that is traded around the world at prices set in USD. That means that M plc is quite heavily exposed to fluctuations in the USD exchange rate against GBP because paper is one of the company's biggest expenses.

M plc's board reviews its policies on currency risk on a regular basis. It has called for a discussion of three possible methods of managing the company's exposure:

- <u>Switch to a UK supplier</u>

  There are three or four UK-based paper manufacturers with which M plc could do business. M plc buys paper in such large quantities that the Production Director believes that it will be possible to negotiate a contract under which the manufacturer will offer a price set in GBP that will be fixed for, say, three years.

- <u>Invest in USD</u>

  M plc has a small cash reserve that it can increase by borrowing a substantial amount in GBP. If the resulting balance is deposited in a USD bank account then the interest received will go some way to compensating for the increased cost of borrowing. If the USD strengthens then the deposit will appreciate in value and that will compensate for the additional cost of paper.

- <u>Take the risk</u>

  M plc can accept that the price of paper will fluctuate as the GBP fluctuates against the USD. If the movement in the exchange rate is either small or short-lived then M plc's profits will be depressed or enhanced slightly. If the USD appreciates significantly then the additional cost may require the cover price of newspapers to increase.

Required

(a) (i) Evaluate the risks to M plc associated with allowing subscribers to post comments and views on the newspaper website. **(10 marks)**

    (ii) Recommend, stating reasons, appropriate controls that might be put in place in future to minimise the risks to M plc associated with malicious and inaccurate posts. **(10 marks)**

(b) (i) Explain the importance of a robust control environment for M plc. **(3 marks)**

    (ii) Explain THREE ways in which weaknesses in the control environment appear to have contributed to the problems with journalists' expense claims. **(7 marks)**

    (iii) Explain the difficulties that could arise from the board's directive that the internal audit department should carry out regular reviews of journalists' expenses. **(7 marks)**

(c) Discuss the THREE stated possible methods of managing M plc's exposure to movements of the USD against the GBP. Your answer should include an evaluation of the costs and risks associated with each of the three methods. **(13 marks)**

(Total = 50 marks)

73 M Newspapers 2 (11/11)   90 mins

Unseen case material

M plc owns 80% of the equity in N, the company's Eastern European subsidiary. The remaining 20% is owned by J, a local entrepreneur who has many business interests in the Eastern European country in which the company operates. J has a seat on the subsidiary's board and he takes an active interest in the running of the company. He has no other involvement with M plc.

Bribery

M plc receives monthly management accounts from N. One of the expense headings is "fees and professional charges". One of M plc's directors remarked that there is always a payment of approximately 3% of the subsidiary's monthly revenue under this heading. On investigation, M plc's directors discovered that this is a monthly payment to a government official in the Eastern European country.

The directors emailed N's Chief Executive for clarification and he revealed that newspapers can only be published in the country if their publishers hold a publishing permit issued by the government. The government official responsible for issuing permits was helpful and cooperative when N first started publishing newspapers in the country five years ago. However once printing was underway he threatened to withdraw the publishing permit unless he received a personal monthly payment. N's Chief Executive called a board meeting and N's directors agreed that the official's demands would be met. The members of N's board did not consider this bribe to be a particularly unusual issue because it is common practice for such officials to abuse their power in this manner.

N's Chief Executive claims that he did not report the bribe to M plc when it acquired N because he believed that the government official's behaviour is known by his superiors within the Government. It is tolerated because he shares the bribe with those superiors and this is accepted practice. The situation has created a serious dilemma for M plc's directors. N's Chief Executive has advised M plc's board that the Government will almost certainly close the subsidiary down in the event that the monthly payments are discontinued.

Plagiarism

N's most popular newspaper is printed in English. The newspaper staff have created a website that publishes a selection of articles that have appeared in print. These articles can be read by anybody without the need to subscribe or enter a password. Articles are never placed on the site until the day after they have appeared in the printed edition of the newspaper so that the free internet access does not discourage readers from buying a printed copy.

N provides the website as an additional source of advertising revenue. Most of the site's visitors are expatriates from the Eastern European country and advertisers are willing to pay to advertise to that audience. The site is also a useful promotional tool because much of the advertising space in the newspaper is sold to foreign multinationals which wish to stimulate sales for their products in N's home country. The website makes it easy for potential advertisers to develop an understanding of the newspaper's editorial position.

The editor of N's newspaper has recently received a formal complaint from the legal section of a South American embassy. The complaint concerns a series of articles that had been published in N's newspaper concerning a successful charity that had been established in a town 100 kilometres from N's head office, which is in the country's capital city. The problem is that the articles are almost exact copies of articles published on the website of a South American newspaper. The only differences are the name of the town and the names of the charity workers have been changed for N's version of the story.

The duplication of the story was discovered when the South American journalist who had been responsible for the original version typed a technical term that had been used in the article into an internet search engine. The search results had included N's story.

N's journalist admitted that the article had been stolen. He claimed that he had been under intense pressure to complete several assignments and that it had been a simple matter to search the internet for some suitable stories.

The South American newspaper wishes N to make a substantial donation to the charity that was the inspiration for the original article. It also wishes N to publish an admission of guilt in both the print edition of N's newspaper and the home page of N's newspaper's website.

Political risk

The board of M plc is concerned that a potential change in the government of the Eastern European country may lead to significant risks for N.

When the plans to establish the subsidiary were first developed, M plc's board was relaxed about doing business in that country because the Government had been in place for many years and it appeared to be stable. Since then the fact that the company has established a newspaper means that it now has a much deeper insight into the social and political environment. It appears that the forthcoming elections could lead to a change of government and that could be disastrous for foreign investors because the party that has the greatest chance of winning control of the country has pledged to nationalise (take into government ownership) all foreign businesses. The election is still several months away.

M plc does not own 100% of N because press laws in the Eastern European country forbid newspapers based in the country to be owned outright by foreign nationals. J was selected to be M plc's partner because J has an established track record as a successful business person and also because J has close links to the country's government.

The board of M plc invited J to London for a meeting and, at that meeting, J confirmed that there are serious grounds for concern. J has said that he will do his best to protect N's interests no matter what happens. During these discussions he also offered to purchase M plc's 80% holding in N for a sum that is approximately 30% of the amount that M plc paid for its original investment.

Required

(a)   (i)   Evaluate the ethical AND commercial implications of N's bribery of the government official.

(9 marks)

       (ii)   Advise M plc's board on an appropriate course of action with respect to the continuing bribery.

(9 marks)

In considering the ethical implications you may wish to reflect on the extent to which CIMA's Fundamental Principles of Integrity, Objectivity, Professional Competence and Due Care, Confidentiality and Professional Behaviour could be relevant.

(b)   (i)   Evaluate the implications for N of the duplication of the story about the charity and of the demand for an admission of guilt and a donation.   **(8 marks)**

       (ii)   Recommend ways in which M plc could utilise information technology across all of its newspapers to reduce the risk of journalists stealing or fabricating news stories in the future.   **(9 marks)**

(c)   (i)   Recommend a course of action for the board of M plc with respect to reducing the risk of N being nationalised in the event of a change of government. You should assume that M plc will not sell its investment to J.   **(9 marks)**

       (ii)   Discuss J's offer to buy M plc's equity in N.   **(6 marks)**

(Total = 50 marks)

74 F1 (9/11)

90 mins

Note: This Preseen applies to Questions 74 and 75

Preseen case study

Introduction

F plc is a food manufacturer based in the United Kingdom. It generates its revenue from three divisions named the Meals, Snacks and Desserts divisions. Each division specialises in the production of different types of food and operates from its own factory located on three different sites in England. F plc's head office is located in a remote part of England and is about equidistant from each of the company's three divisions.

Currently, F plc has a total employment establishment of about 10,000 full-time equivalent employees, about 97% of whom are employed in its three divisions. It is constantly running with about 700 full-time vacancies, mostly in the Desserts Division. This vacancy factor in the Desserts Division impedes its productivity.

The company was founded over 150 years ago by an entrepreneurial farmer who saw the opportunity to expand his farming business by vertically integrating into food production. Instead of selling his crops on the open market, he established a mill and produced flour. From this, it was a natural progression to diversify into producing other crops which were then processed into different ingredients for food products.

The company grew steadily and it became clear at the beginning of the 20th Century that increased production facilities were needed. It was at this point that the company built its first factory which at the time was a state of the art manufacturing facility. As demand continued to grow during the 20th Century, the company required additional manufacturing facilities and made a public offering of shares in 1960 to finance this expansion. The public offer was successful and F Limited was established. The original family's holding in the company fell to 25% at this point. Although a second factory was opened with the capital that had been raised, F Limited continued to manage the company on a centralised basis.

The next phase of development came in the late 1980's when F Limited became F plc. After this, F plc had a successful rights issue which raised sufficient capital to enable a third factory to be built. It was at this point that the divisionalised and de-centralised structure was established. Prior to this, the company managed its factories directly from its head office. The family shareholding fell to 20% at this point, with one family member holding 10% of the shares and family trusts holding the other 10%.

The environment in which F plc trades is dynamic, particularly with regard to the growth of legislation relating to food hygiene and production methods. F plc now exports many of its products as well as obtaining ingredients from foreign producers, which means that F plc must observe legislative requirements and food standard protocols in different countries.

Mission statement

F plc's mission statement, which was set in the year 2000, is as follows:

"F plc is committed to continually seek ways to increase its return to investors by expanding its share of both its domestic and overseas markets. It will achieve this by sourcing high quality ingredients, using efficient processes and maintaining the highest standards of hygiene in its production methods and paying fair prices for the goods and services it uses."

Strategic aims

The strategic aims are set in order to enable F plc to meet the obligations contained in its mission statement.

F plc aims to:

(a)   increase profitability of each of its divisions through increased market share in both domestic and overseas markets

(b)   Source high quality ingredients to enhance product attractiveness

(c)   Ensure that its factories adhere to the highest standards of food hygiene which guarantee the quality of its products

(d)   Strive to be at the forefront in food manufacturing techniques by being innovative and increasing efficiency of production with least waste.

Corporate Social Responsibility

F plc takes Corporate Social Responsibility (CSR) seriously. The post of Environmental Effects Manager was created two years ago and a qualified environmental scientist was appointed to it. The Environmental Effects

Manager reports directly to the Director of Operations. The role of the Environmental Effects Manager is to develop initiatives to reduce environmental impacts, capture data on the environmental effects of divisional and head office operations and report to the Board of Directors on the progress towards the achievement of F plc's CSR targets. An extract from F plc's internal CSR report for 2010 is shown in Appendix 1. F plc does not publish its CSR report externally.

Last year, F plc received criticism in the national press in England and in other countries for exploiting some of its suppliers in Africa by paying low prices for ingredients. This resulted in an extensive public relations campaign by F plc to counter these accusations. It established a programme to channel funds to support farmers in Africa via payments made through African government agencies. The programme, which is managed through F plc's head office, received initial financing from F plc itself and is now widening its remit to draw funding from other sources including public funding from the European Union.

The Board of Directors

The Board of Directors comprises five executive and five non-executive members all of whom are British. No member of the Board is from an ethnic minority.

The Chairman is a senior non-executive director and a retired Chief Executive of a major quoted retail clothing company based in England. He received a knighthood two years ago for services to industry.

The Chief Executive is 52 years old and was Director of Operations at F plc before taking up his current post three years ago.

The Finance Director is 49 years old and a qualified CIMA accountant. He has experience in a variety of manufacturing and retail organisations.

The Director of Operations is 65 years old and is a member of the original family which founded the business. He has been employed by F plc for all of his working life. He took up his current post three years ago following the promotion of the previous post holder to the role of Chief Executive.

The Marketing Director is 43 years old and has held various positions in sales and marketing for different organisations before being appointed to the Board. He came to the attention of the Chief Executive when he was instrumental in a successful initiative to market a new shopping complex in the city in which F plc's head office is based. At the time, the Marketing Director was the Chief Marketing Officer for the local government authority in the area.

The Director of Human Resources, the only female member of the Board, is 38 years old and holds a recognised HR professional qualification. Last year she was presented with a national award which recognised her achievements in the development of human resource management practices.

In addition there are four other non-executive directors on the Board. Two of them previously worked in senior positions alongside the Chairman when he was Chief Executive of the retail clothing company. One of them was the clothing company's finance director, but is now retired and the other was its marketing director but is now the sales and marketing director for a pharmaceutical company. One of the other non-executive directors is a practising lawyer and the other is a sports personality of national renown and a personal friend of the Chairman.

The Divisional General Managers, responsible for each of the three divisions, are not members of F plc's board. The Divisions are organised along traditional functional lines. Each division is managed by a Divisional Board which is headed by a Divisional General Manager. Each Divisional Board comprises the posts of Divisional Operations Manager, Divisional Accountant, Divisional Marketing Manager and Divisional Human Resources Manager. Each division undertakes its own marketing and human resource management. The divisional accountants are responsible for the management accounting functions within their divisions. Each member of the divisional boards is directly accountable to the Divisional General Manager but have professional accountability to the relevant functional F plc executive board members.

Financial position and borrowing facilities

Extracts from F plc's financial statements for the year ended 31 December 2010 are shown in Appendix 2.

F plc's long term borrowings are made up of a £160 million bank loan for capital expenditure and a £74 million revolving credit facility (RCF).

The bank loan is secured on F plc's assets and is repayable on 1 January 2018.

The RCF allows F plc to borrow, make repayments and then re-borrow over the term of the agreement. This provides F plc with flexibility because it can continue to obtain loans as long as it remains at or below £80 million, being the total amount agreed for this facility. The RCF expires on 31 December 2013.

Planning process

The planning process employed by F plc is one which can be described as adhering to classical rational principles. This has been the method of planning used for many years and culminates in the production of a five year forecast. The annual budget cycle feeds in to the strategic plan which is then updated on an annual basis. All F plc's revenue is derived through the operations of the three divisions. The only income generated by F plc's head office is from investments. The five year forecast for sales revenue and net operating profit for each division and F plc in total, after deduction of head office operating costs, is shown in Appendix 3. This shows that F plc is seeking to increase its sales revenue and net operating profit over the five year plan period.

Competition within the industry

F plc is one of the largest food production companies in England. It had an overall share of about 6% of its home market in 2010. Its nearest competitors held 5% and 7% market share respectively in 2010. The products in the industry have varying product life cycles. Competition is intense and there is a high failure rate for new products. Usually, new products require significant marketing support particularly if a new brand is being established.

Organisational culture within each division

Different cultures have emerged within each division.

Meals Division

In the Meals Division, each function operates with little direct interference from the Divisional Board members. The approach is to allow each function to operate with as little control as possible being exercised by the Divisional Board.

Snacks Division

In the Snacks Division, the emphasis of the Divisional Board is on product research and development and marketing. The Snacks Divisional Board expects its divisional marketing staff to undertake market research into customer tastes and preferences and then for products which satisfy these to be developed by its divisional research staff.

Desserts Division

In the Desserts Division, the finance function is the dominant force. The finance functions in the other two divisions exert less influence over operations than is the case in the Desserts Division. It is not unusual for the Divisional Accountant in the Desserts Division to have confrontational meetings with managers of other functions. Such confrontation is particularly evident in the monthly meetings between the Divisional Accountant and the Divisional Marketing staff. It is clear that within the Desserts Division, the Divisional General Manager, a food technologist by profession, and the Divisional Accountant, formerly an auditor with a local government authority, maintain strict control over the operation of the division.

Further details relating to the three divisions are as follows:

Meals Division

The Meals division is located in the South of England. It specialises in manufacturing frozen meals, which are designed to be easy for consumers to quickly heat up and serve. The meals are sold to supermarkets and other retail outlets. Some are manufactured under F plc's own brand and others are manufactured under supermarkets' own labels. The division is also increasing its sales to welfare organisations which support elderly and infirm people. These organisations purchase simple frozen meals in bulk which they then heat up to provide a hot meal each day to those people in their care. In 2010, the Meals Division earned 14% of its revenue from outside the United Kingdom.

One of the Meals Division's most profitable products is a steak pie that is flavoured with special gravy that was developed by one of F plc's founding family members in the early part of the 20th Century. F plc's competitors cannot copy this gravy because the ingredients have to be combined in a very precise manner and then cooked in a particular way. The recipe for this gravy is known only to F plc's Director of Operations and the manager of the pie factory.

Two of the Meals Division's products are currently subject to investigation by the Food Standards Authority of a European country. Please see Appendix 1 under the heading "Food labelling" for more information on this.

Snacks Division

The Snacks Division, located in the East of England, mainly manufactures confectionery such as packet savouries and chocolate bars. Its main customers are supermarkets and retail shops. It has a growing market in continental

Europe and in 2010 the division earned 19% of its revenue from non-United Kingdom sales. Many of its products are F plc's own brands, although, similarly with the Meals Division, it supplies products to supermarkets under their own label.

The Snacks Division successfully launched a new premium brand of chocolate bars in the UK in 2010.

Desserts Division

The Desserts Division is located in the North of England where road, rail and air links are not well developed. This has resulted in high transportation costs for goods into and out of the factory. Originally, this location was chosen because the lease terms for the factory were very competitive but in recent times the local taxes placed on the factory have become expensive. There is some limited room for expansion on the site the factory occupies but the local government authority has repeatedly rejected the expansion plans when the Division has sought the necessary planning permission to put its plans into action. This has caused the Divisional Board to consider whether it should move its entire operation to another part of England where its expansion plans may be more easily accomplished.

The Division has experienced technical and managerial staff shortages. The workforce of the Division has an establishment of 4,700 full-time equivalent employees. Despite there being a ready supply of manual labour for production work, the Desserts division runs with an average of 385 full-time vacancies at any one time.

The Division's products range from cold desserts, particularly ice cream, which can be eaten directly from the packaging, to those which require some preparation by the final purchaser before the product can be consumed. The Divisional Marketing Department has been investigating the possibility of negotiating 'Freezer deals' by which the Desserts Division would supply ice cream freezers to independent retailers which sell the Division's ice cream products. An independent retailer is a shop or outlet that is not part of a larger chain. This is in order to investigate the possibility of increasing the Division's share of the ice cream market sold by independent retailers.

The Division's sales increase in the periods which lead up to national and international festive periods such as Christmas and Chinese New Year. The Division is constantly researching new markets in an effort to increase its foreign earnings. Revenue from outside the United Kingdom in 2010 represented 23% of the Division's total revenue.

Inventory control and IT systems

There have been a number of problems across all three divisions in respect of inventory control. Poor inventory control has led to high levels of wastage and obsolete inventory being carried. This has been particularly problematic in respect of perishable ingredients. In the case of the Desserts Division, the Divisional Accountant has estimated that 5% of the Division's potential revenue has been lost as a result of not being able to satisfy customer orders on time, due to poor inventory control.

F plc operates a standard information management system across all the Divisions and at Head Office. The Information Technology in use has been unreliable due to technical malfunctions since the information management system was installed in 2001. Monthly management accounts, provided by each division to head office are often late, sometimes not being made available for up to three weeks into the subsequent month.

Internal audit

Until now, F plc's Internal Audit function, which is based at Head Office, has tended to concentrate its efforts on reviewing activities in the Meals and Snacks divisions as they each produce lower revenues and net operating profits in absolute terms compared with the Desserts division. The Internal Audit function's approach of applying a "light touch" to the Desserts Division is also in recognition of the influence exerted by the Divisional Finance function over the Division's operational activities.

Strategic development

The Board of Directors is now midway through its strategic planning cycle and is considering how the company should move forward. There is a proposal to build and operate a factory in West Africa to reduce air kilometres being flown in supplying the Meals Division with fresh vegetables. It is intended that the African factory will freeze the vegetables and then transport them to the Meals Division's factory in England by refrigerated ship.

APPENDIX 1

Extracts from F plc's internal Corporate Social Responsibility report for the year ended 31 December 2010.

This report was produced by the Environmental Effects Manager and presented to the Board of F plc in January 2011.

Fair trading

In accordance with its mission statement, F plc is committed to paying a fair price for the ingredients it uses in its products, particularly to farmers in the less developed economies of the world.

Waste reduction and recycling

F plc set a target for the financial year 2010 that waste of ingredients should be cut by 2%, measured by weight, from the 2009 levels. The actual ingredient waste was 2.5% lower in 2010 than in 2009 as measured by weight.

A target was also set for F plc to recycle 90% of its used packaging in the year 2010. It was recorded that 85% of total used packaging in 2010 was actually recycled.

Food labelling

Legal requirements demand accuracy in food labelling, in respect of ingredients, product description and cooking instructions in many countries. F plc employs a Compliance Manager

to ensure that relevant labelling laws in each country, with which the company trades, are adhered to. A target is set for F plc to justify 100% of its claims in food labelling. Two products manufactured in the Meals Division are currently undergoing investigations by the Food Standards Authority of a European country following allegations that the labelling is inaccurate.

Transportation

Following adverse press coverage relating to the high number of kilometres travelled when importing and exporting goods from and to overseas countries, F plc introduced a target that its use of air travel should be reduced by 10% in 2010 compared with the amount used in 2009. F plc fell short of its target by only reducing air kilometres travelled by 3% in 2010 compared with 2009. Road kilometres travelled increased by 5% in 2010 compared with 2009.

Efficiency of energy usage in production

In an effort to reduce carbon emissions from the three divisions and head office, a target was set that by 2015, F plc will become carbon neutral in terms of its usage of energy. Energy usage in 2010 was at the same level as in 2009. It has been proposed that energy efficient lighting should replace the current energy inefficient lighting at all three factories and at head office in 2011 and smart meters should be installed in all of F plc's premises to keep the waste of electricity to a minimum.

APPENDIX 2

Extracts from F plc's income statement and statement of financial position

Income statement for the year ended 31 December 2010

	£ million
Revenue	986
Operating costs	(938)
Net operating profit	48
Interest income	1
Finance costs	(16)
Corporate income tax Notes	(10)
Profit for the year	23

Statement of financial position as at 31 December 2010

	Notes	£ million
ASSETS		
Non-current assets		465
Current assets		
Inventories		90
Trade and other receivables		112
Cash and cash equivalents		20
Total current assets		222
Total assets		687
EQUITY AND LIABILITIES		
Equity		
Share capital	1	140
Share premium		40
Retained earnings		61
Total equity		241
Non-current liabilities		
Long term borrowings	2	234
Current liabilities		
Trade and other payables		212
Total liabilities		446
Total equity and liabilities		687

Notes

1 There are 560 million ordinary shares of £0.25 each in issue.

2 The long term borrowings comprise £160 million loan for capital expenditure which is repayable on 1 January 2018 and a £74 million revolving credit facility which expires on 31 December 2013.

APPENDIX 3

Five year forecast of sales revenue and net operating profit for each division and F plc in total and operating costs for head office

	2010 (Actual)	2011	2012	2013	2014	2015
Meals Division						
Sales revenue	266	287	310	335	362	391
Net operating profit	31	34	40	47	54	63
Snacks Division						
Sales revenue	176	194	213	234	258	283
Net operating profit	44	48	53	58	64	71
Desserts Division						
Sales revenue	544	571	600	630	661	694
Net operating profit	72	80	90	101	112	125
Head Office						
Operating costs	(99)	(107)	(112)	(118)	(124)	(130)
F plc total						
Sales revenue	986	1,052	1,123	1,199	1,281	1,368
Net operating profit	48	55	71	88	106	129

Unseen case material

African factory

F plc's Meals Division also produces frozen vegetables. Fresh vegetables are purchased from farmers in West Africa because the climate there enables vegetables to be grown throughout the year.

Fresh vegetables are flown to the United Kingdom within 24 hours of being harvested. The vegetables are perishable and therefore must be processed and frozen within hours of arriving in the UK. After they have been frozen the vegetables are packaged and stored ready for sale.

F plc's board has decided to build a factory in West Africa to process the vegetables. Fresh vegetables will be delivered to the factory, where they will be processed and packaged in the same way as they are in the UK factory. The packaged vegetables will then be transported in refrigerated shipping containers to the UK and will be ready for immediate sale.

The board of F plc believes that building a factory in West Africa will demonstrate a commitment to sound corporate social responsibility. The factory will create jobs in the West African country and so more of the wealth created by its farmers will circulate in the local economy. Furthermore, environmentalists will have fewer objections to shipping than air freighting.

There will be no significant difference in the total cost of manufacturing and transporting the finished product compared to the present arrangements.

Staffing

The factory will be highly mechanised and therefore most of the labour will be unskilled. Manual workers are needed to move vegetables and finished products. The staffing plan prepared by the Director of Operations shows that the unskilled labour will be recruited locally in West Africa.

However, there are some posts that require staff with considerable education and training. For example, the UK factory currently employs several qualified food technicians who have university degrees. They are responsible for testing batches of vegetables when they arrive to ensure that they are suitable for freezing. This work is very important because factors such as the water content and acidity of a batch of vegetables can affect the quality of the final product. There is also a significant number of skilled supervisors who are responsible for quality control, health and safety and other tasks.

The staffing plan shows that the skilled posts will initially be filled by sending staff from the UK factory to West Africa. It is proposed that the staff will work for four weeks in West Africa and then be flown home for two weeks of leave before being flown back to West Africa for another four weeks. The Director of Operations has planned for this pattern to continue for the first two years. During this period F plc will work with local West African colleges to develop intensive courses on food technology, management and other skills to provide a local pool of skilled labour with the required qualifications.

F plc has already determined that there are local colleges that teach relevant subjects and so there is the basis of an educational programme. It would not be particularly expensive for F plc to sponsor courses at these colleges so that they could develop their course content to ensure that F's requirements are met in terms of both syllabus coverage and rigorous assessment.

At the end of the two year transitional period, the UK staff will either be transferred to other posts in the UK or they will be made redundant.

When the proposal to transfer production was announced the UK skilled staff were unhappy with the planned arrangements. Many of them have said that they will not work in West Africa because the proposed work patterns are too disruptive to family life and that F plc will either have to find them suitable alternative employment in the UK or make them redundant.

Information systems

Inventory management is very important for the success and profitability of producing frozen vegetables. Frozen vegetables can be stored for a very long time but it is expensive to do so and therefore inventory levels are closely monitored and managed through the Meals Division's information system. Sometimes major customers are offered substantial discounts in order to clear inventory and thereby reduce holding costs.

The inventory management system will need to be adapted significantly when production is transferred to West Africa because additional data will have to be collected at the West African factory and also when finished goods are loaded onto ships in refrigerated shipping containers.

Finance

F plc has the choice of two ways to fund the investment needed for the factory in West Africa:

- The company has banked with a UK commercial bank for many years and the bank has offered to grant a loan denominated in GBP. The loan would be secured against F plc's UK assets.

- The government of the West African country has also offered to make a loan for the same amount, but denominated in the local currency. The loan would be secured against the West African factory.

Risk evaluation

F plc has a policy of conducting all formal risk evaluations in accordance with CIMA's Risk Management Cycle. The first four stages of the cycle are:

- Set goals
- Identify risk areas
- Understand and assess scale of risk
- Develop risk response strategy

Required

(a) F plc's directors are concerned about the risks to F plc's reputation arising from moving production to West Africa.

    (i)   Use CIMA's Risk Management Cycle to evaluate FOUR possible risks to F plc's reputation.

(8 marks)

    (ii)   Recommend appropriate actions to manage those risks.   **(8 marks)**

(b) Advise the board of F plc on the control procedures that should be established over the development and running of the food technology courses that will be provided by the West African colleges for F plc.

Your answer should consider the following areas:

- Governance
- Staffing
- Support facilities
- Course content

(10 marks)

(c) Advise the board on the controls necessary during the development and implementation of the changes to the inventory management system. **(12 marks)**

(d) Evaluate both the currency and the non-currency risks associated with each of the two loan packages for the financing of the West African factory. **(12 marks)**

(Total = 50 marks)

75 F2 (5/11)   90 mins

Unseen case material

Meals Division

The sale of pre-packaged oven-ready meals to charities and government-funded organisations generates 15% of the revenue of the Meals Division. The Division produces a range of frozen meals that are designed to meet the nutritional requirements of elderly and infirm people. The meals are packaged so that they can be cooked in bulk in catering ovens before being delivered as ready to eat meals to the homes of the elderly and infirm.

The Meals Division sells a large quantity of these meals and enjoys significant economies of scale. Consequently, even though the selling price of these meals is much lower than any other products, this is a very profitable business segment.

Unfortunately, the Meals Division suffered a significant setback in February 2011. A charity that works with elderly people received complaints that several cases of severe food poisoning had occurred. Eight of the victims were so ill that they had to be admitted to hospital for emergency treatment. Samples of the frozen meals remaining in the charity's freezer, all of which had been supplied by the Meals Division, were sent to an independent laboratory for analysis. It was discovered that they were contaminated by bacteria that can cause severe abdominal illness.

The Meals Division conducted its own analysis of the meals purchased by the charity. The presence of the bacteria was confirmed, but it was found to be a common organism that is present in almost all meat. If the charity had cooked the frozen meals in accordance with the instructions printed on the packaging then the bacteria would have been killed and the consumers would not have been harmed in any way. Furthermore, the contamination was only very slight. A healthy person who ate a meal containing small quantities of these bacteria would not become ill because of the body's immune system.

This case has been reported widely in newspapers and on television. F plc's directors have asked for an analysis of the risks to the company's reputation. The Meals Division's management team has recommended that F plc's defence should be based on the following two arguments:

- All meat products contain these bacteria. Those manufactured by F plc contain a lower concentration than the industry average and comply with all relevant hygiene regulations.

- The frozen meals supplied by the Meals Division should not have caused any harm unless they had been prepared negligently by the charity. The charity should be blamed for the food poisoning and not F plc.

Secret recipe

One of F plc's most popular and profitable products is a steak pie that is flavoured with a special gravy that was developed by one of F plc's founding family members in the early part of the 20th Century. The gravy is manufactured using a very specific mixture of herbs and spices. F plc's competitors cannot copy this mixture because the ingredients have to be combined in a very precise manner and then cooked in a particular way.

The recipe for this herb and spice mix is known only to F plc's Director of Operations and the manager of the pie factory. There is no written record anywhere. The factory manager has worked for F plc for more than 30 years and he is a trusted member of staff. Twice a year, the director and the manager of the pie factory close part of the factory to all other staff and the two of them make sufficient quantity of the mix to last for the next six months.

The factory manager was recently offered a job by one of F plc's largest rivals. The job would double the factory manager's salary and he would be guaranteed the opportunity to retire on full pay within two years of taking up the post. He declined this offer and informed the Director of Operations that he received this approach.

The chief executive of F plc is concerned that a competitor could have acquired the factory manager's knowledge of the recipe in such an easy and inexpensive manner. He is also concerned that F plc does not have a record, other than the memories of two senior members of staff. He has asked for recommendations on the most appropriate way to secure this knowledge.

Internal audit

The external auditor has noted concerns expressed by the management accountant in the Desserts Division concerning weaknesses in the IT system associated with inventory and the relative lack of attention paid to the division by the internal audit department. The partner in charge of the external audit has held a meeting with the finance director and has requested that the internal audit department investigates the concerns voiced by the management accountant.

The head of internal audit has responded that it is inappropriate for the divisional management accountant to comment on the allocation of internal audit resources and that the external auditor should offer to cooperate more fully with internal audit before making such requests.

F plc currency risks

Most of F plc's sales are to customers in the United Kingdom. F plc imports many of the ingredients that it uses from a variety of countries. The vast majority of F plc's foreign suppliers insist on invoicing F plc in their own currency and it has proved impossible to insist on paying for imported ingredients in British Pounds.

The board of F plc has always refused to devote any attention to the currency risks associated with importing. It has always absorbed minor fluctuations by taking a slightly larger or smaller profit on sales. Larger fluctuations have been passed on to customers in the form of increased or decreased selling prices. Certain members of the board have always argued that F plc's competitors are subject to the same currency risks and so the market will always be forced to accept the impact of currency movements, in which case there is very little point in taking active steps to manage currency risks.

Required

(a) (i) Evaluate the risks arising from the outbreak of food poisoning to F plc's reputation in terms of their likelihood and impact of occurrence. **(8 marks)**

(ii) Advise the directors of F plc on the suitability of the two arguments proposed by the managers of the Meals Division for defending the company's reputation. **(8 marks)**

(b) (i) Advise the board on the implications of the secret recipe being obtained by a competitor. **(4 marks)**

(ii) Recommend, stating reasons, suitable precautions for preventing the recipe from being obtained by a competitor. **(6 marks)**

(c) (i) Evaluate the head of internal audit's statement that the divisional management accountant should not comment on the allocation of internal audit resources. **(6 marks)**

(ii) Discuss the validity of the head of internal audit's assertion that the external auditor should be prepared to cooperate with the internal audit department. **(6 marks)**

(d) Evaluate the views of certain board members concerning there being no need to manage F plc's currency risks. **(12 marks)**

(Total = 50 marks)

76 DEF 1 (3/11)　　　　　　　　　　　　　　　　　　　　90 mins

Note: This Preseen applies to Questions 76 and 77

Preseen case study

Overview

DEF Airport is situated in country D within Europe but which is outside the Eurozone. The local currency is D$. It is located near to the town of DEF. It began life in the 1930s as a flying club and was extended in 1947, providing scheduled services within central Europe. A group of four local state governments, which are all in easy reach of the airport (hereafter referred to as the LSGs), took over the running of the airport in 1961. The four LSGs are named North (NLSG), South (SLSG), East (ELSG) and West (WLSG). These names place their geographical location in relation to the airport. In the early 1970s flights from the airport to European holiday destinations commenced with charter flights operated by holiday companies. In 1986, the first transatlantic flight was established and the airport terminal building was extended in 1987.

By 1989 the airport was handling 500,000 passengers per year which is forecast to increase to 3.5 million for both incoming and outgoing passengers in the current financial year to 30 June 2011. The airport mainly serves holidaymakers flying to destinations within Europe and only 5% of the passengers who use the airport are business travellers.

DEF Airport was converted into a company in 1990 and the four LSGs became the shareholders, each with an equal share. The company is not listed on a stock exchange. The airport has undertaken extensive development since 2000, with improvements to its single terminal building. The improvements have mainly been to improve the airport's catering facilities and to increase the number of check-in desks. There has also been investment in the aircraft maintenance facilities offered to the airlines operating out of the airport.

Governance

The Board of Directors has four Executive directors: the Chief Executive, the Director of Facilities Management, the Finance Director and the Commercial Director. In addition there is a Company Secretary and a Non-Executive Chairman. In accordance with DEF Airport's Articles of Association, the Non-Executive Chairman is drawn from one of the four LSGs. The Non-Executive Chairman is the sole representative of all four LSGs. The Chairmanship changes every two years with each of the four LSGs taking turns to nominate the Chair.

The four LSGs have indicated that they may wish to sell their shareholdings in the airport in the near future. If any LSG wishes to sell its shares in the airport it must first offer them to the other three LSGs. Any shares that are not purchased by the other LSGs may then be sold on the open market. A local investment bank (IVB) has written to the Chairman expressing an interest in investing in the airport in return for a shareholding together with a seat on the Board.

Mission statement

The Board of Directors drew up a mission statement in 2008. It states "At DEF Airport we aim to outperform all other regional airports in Europe by ensuring that we offer our customers a range of services that are of the highest quality, provided by the best people and conform to the highest ethical standards. We aim to be a good corporate citizen in everything we do."

DEF Airport development plan

The Board of Directors produced a development plan in 2009. The Board of Directors consulted with businesses in the area and followed central government airport planning guidelines. It was assumed that the views of other local stakeholders would be represented by the four LSGs which would feed comments to the Board through the Chairman.

The plan relates to the development of DEF Airport and its forecast passenger growth for the next two decades. The Board proposed that future development of the airport will be phased and gradual in order to avoid unexpected consequences for the local communities and industry.

Strategic objectives

The following strategic objectives have been established in the development plan:

1   Create a planning framework which enables DEF Airport to meet the demands of the forecast passenger numbers

2   Reduce to a minimum the visual and audible impacts of the operation of the airport on the local environment

3   Ensure that the airport is financially secure

4   Improve land based access to the airport

5   Minimise the pollution effects of the operation of the airport

6   Maintain / increase employment opportunities for people living close to the airport

By the year ending 30 June 2015, DEF Airport is expected to support about 3,000 local jobs and have a throughput of 5 million passengers per year, an increase of 1.5 million from the 3.5 million passengers forecast for the current financial year ending 30 June 2011. In order to accommodate the forecast increased number of passengers and attain the development objectives, it will be necessary for the airport to extend its operational area to the east of the land it currently occupies.

Financial objectives

Extracts from DEF Airport's forecast income statement for the year ending 30 June 2011 and forecast statement of financial position as at that date are presented in the Appendix. The four LSGs have made it clear to the Board of Directors that the airport must at least achieve financial self-sufficiency. The financial objectives of the airport are to ensure that:

1   The airport does not run at a loss

2   All creditors are paid on time

3   Gearing levels must not exceed 20% (where gearing is defined as debt to debt plus equity) and any long-term borrowings are financed from sources approved by the four LSGs.

Corporate Social Responsibility

A key feature of DEF Airport's development plan is to develop "Sustainable Aviation" initiatives in order to reduce the effects of flying on the environment. One effect on the environment is that the airport is subject to specific planning restrictions affecting flights between the hours of 11 p.m. (2300 hours) and 7 a.m. (0700 hours) to reduce aircraft noise. Flights are permitted between these times, but must be specially authorised. Typically, flights between these times would be as a result of an emergency landing request.

A leading international consultancy, QEG, which specialises in auditing the corporate social responsibility (CSR) issues of commercial enterprises, has offered to provide a CSR audit to DEF Airport free of charge. QEG is based in the USA and hopes to expand by offering its services to European enterprises.

DEF Airport's competitors

TUV Airport is located about 100 kilometres away from DEF Airport and serves a highly populated industrial city. The Board of Directors of DEF Airport considers TUV Airport to be its main competitor. There are another three competing airports within 80 kilometres of DEF Airport. TUV Airport purchased one of these three competitor airports and subsequently reduced services from it in order to reduce the competitive threat to itself.

Airlines

Airlines are keen to negotiate the most cost effective deal they can with airports. DEF Airport applies a set of standard charges to airlines but is aware that some of its competitor airports have offered inducements to airlines in order to attract DEF's business.

Airlines across the world are facing rising fuel and staff costs as well as strong competition from within the industry. There has been an overall increase in customer demand for air travel in recent years and low-priced airlines have emerged and are threatening the well-established, traditional airlines. Consequently, the traditional airlines have begun to cut the number of destinations to which they fly.

There are several low-priced airlines that serve DEF Airport's competitors, but only one, S, also operates out of DEF Airport. S is exploring ways in which it might increase its flights to and from DEF Airport.

DEF's Board of Directors has been approached by a North American airline that wishes to operate services from DEF Airport. This airline specialises in flights for business and first class passengers. However, this airline insists that it would pay DEF Airport in US$. This is contrary to the airport's policy of accepting payment only in D$, which is the local currency.

Analysis of revenue by business segment

The forecast split of total revenue of D$23.4 million by business segment for the current financial year ending 30 June 2011 is:

	%
Aviation income	48
Retail concessions at the airport	20
Car Parking	15
Other income	17

(Other income includes income from property rentals, and other fees and charges.)

DEF Airport offers discounts for prompt payment.

Aviation income

In addition to the standard charges, which are set out below, there is a range of surcharges which are levied on airlines for such items as "noisy aircraft" (charged when aircraft exceed the Government limits for acceptable noise levels), recovery of costs and expenses arising from cleaning or making safe any spillages from aircraft and extraordinary policing of flights (for example, arrests made as a result of anti-social behaviour on aircraft).

Standard charges made by DEF Airport to the airlines:

Charges per aircraft

Landing charges – large aircraft:	D$300
Landing charges – medium aircraft:	D$170

Parking charges for the first two hours are included in the landing charge. Thereafter, a charge of D$200 per hour is imposed for each large aircraft and D$250 per hour for each medium aircraft. The parking charge is lower for large aircraft because they take at least two hours to clean and refuel, so they almost always have to pay for an hour's parking, and also because there is less demand for the parking areas used for large aircraft. Medium aircraft tend to take off again within one hour of landing. Approximately 10% of medium sized aircraft landings result in the airline incurring parking charges for one hour. This is normally either because their scheduled departure time requires them to park or because of delays imposed by air traffic restrictions, technical malfunctions or problems with passengers.

Charges per passenger
Passenger Load:

Flights to European destinations:	D$1.60 per departing passenger
Flights outside Europe:	D$4.00 per departing passenger
Passenger security	D$1.20 per passenger arriving or departing

Retail concessions

DEF Airport provides the facilities for a range of shops, bureau de change (dealing in foreign exchange currency transactions for passengers), bars and cafes for the budget conscious passenger.

DEF Airport has a monopoly in the provision of retail concessions and therefore faces no competition.

Car parking

Car parking is an important source of DEF Airport's revenue. The airport has extended its own car parking facilities for customers over recent years. Car parks occupy a large area of what was green belt land (that is land which was not previously built on) around its perimeter. The land was acquired by the airport specifically for the purpose of car parking. A free passenger bus service is provided to take passengers to and from the car parks into the airport terminal building.

Competitors have established alternative car parking facilities off-site and provide bus services to and from the airport's terminal. The parking charges made by the competitors are lower than those levied by the airport. Competitor car park operators offer additional services to passengers, such as car maintenance and valeting, which are undertaken while the car is left in their care.

DEF Airport does not have a hotel on its premises. There is a hotel within walking distance of the airport which offers special rates for passengers to stay the night before their flight and then to park their cars at the hotel for the duration of their trip.

Other income

This heading contains a mixture of revenue streams. The Commercial Director reported that some have good growth prospects. Property rental income is likely to decline though as there has been much building development around the airport perimeter.

DEF Airport security

Passengers and their baggage are required to go through rigorous security checks. There is a fast track service provided which can be accessed by all passengers at an extra charge. This is intended to speed up the security process. However, on some occasions this leads to passengers on the normal route becoming frustrated because they are required to wait in lengthy queues to pass through the security checks. Airport security staff are required by law to search all departing passengers and their baggage for suspicious or dangerous items. On the very rare occasions that they discover anything they report their concerns to the police. There are always several police officers on patrol at the airport at any given time and so the police can respond to any report very quickly.

In addition to passenger and baggage screening, DEF Airport security staff are responsible for the security of parked aircraft and airport property. They do this primarily by monitoring all arriving and departing vehicles and their drivers and by monitoring the many closed circuit television cameras that cover the airport.

The airport has had a good record with regard to the prevention of theft from passenger baggage. This is frequently a serious matter at other airports, but DEF Airport has received very few complaints that baggage has been tampered with. DEF Airport's Head of Security regards the security of baggage as very low risk because of this low level of complaints.

The Head of Security at DEF Airport was appointed to his current role in 1990, when the airport was very much smaller than it is today. He was a police sergeant before he joined the airport staff. Immediately before his appointment he was responsible for the front desk of DEF town's main police station, a job that involved managing the day-to-day activities of the other police officers on duty. He was happy to accept the post of Head of Security because the police service was starting to make far greater use of computers. He had always relied on a comprehensive paper-based system for documenting and filing reports.

The Head of Security is directly responsible for all security matters at DEF Airport. In practice, he has to delegate most of the actual supervision of staff to shift managers and team leaders because he cannot be expected to be on duty for 24 hours per day or to manage the security arrangements in great detail while administering the security department. The overall responsibilities of the Head of Security have not been reviewed since his appointment.

Strategic options

The Board of Directors is now actively considering its strategic options which could be implemented in the future in order to meet the strategic objectives which were set out in the airport's development plan.

APPENDIX 1

Extracts of DEF Airport's forecast income statement for the year ending 30 June
2011 and statement of financial position as at 30 June 2011

Forecast income statement for the year ending 30 June 2011

	Note	D$000
Revenue		23,400
Operating costs	1	(25,450)
Net operating loss		(2,050)
Interest income		70
Finance costs		(1,590)
Corporate income tax expense		(130)
Loss for the year		(3,700)

Forecast statement of financial position as at 30 June 2011

	D$000
ASSETS	
Non-current assets	150,000
Current assets	
Inventories	400
Trade and other receivables	9,250
Cash and cash equivalents	3,030
Total current assets	12,680
Total assets	162,680

	Note	D$000
EQUITY AND LIABILITIES		
Equity		
Share capital	2	17,700
Share premium		530
Revaluation reserve		89,100
Retained earnings		23,200
Total equity		130,530
Non-current liabilities		
Long term borrowings	3	22,700
Current liabilities		
Trade and other payables		9,450
Total liabilities		32,150
Total equity and liabilities		162,680

Notes

1   Operating costs include depreciation of D$5.0 million.

2   There are 17.7 million ordinary shares of D$1 each in issue.

3   The long-term borrowings comprise a D$6.3 million loan for capital expenditure which is repayable on 1
     July 2015 and D$16.4 million owed to the 4 LSGs. This has no fixed repayment schedule and is not
     expected to be repaid in the next year.

Unseen case material

Potential buyer

DEF Airport's chairman met with Max, a senior partner in a major firm of consultants. Max represents a client whose identity must remain confidential at this stage. Max's instructions are to investigate the airport's business affairs in some detail and then to assist the client in the purchase of a controlling interest. Max's client is indifferent to the proportion of shares obtained from each of the four local state governments (LSGs). It may be that two of the LSGs will sell their entire holdings so that only a small number of shares will be required from a third or perhaps all four LSGs will sell a proportion of their stake. The client will expect to appoint an executive director immediately and will also wish to appoint a new non-executive chairman who will not have any direct relationship with any of the LSGs.

DEF's chairman was concerned about the nature of Max's questions during the meeting. Max was not particularly interested in the commercial activities of the airport itself. He was, however, keen to know exactly what land the airport owned, how many employees the company had and their length of service, their entitlement to pensions and so on. Max was also keen to know which of the LSGs had jurisdiction over the airport for the purposes of authorising development on the site.

DEF's chairman feels that Max's client has no particular interest in the airport business itself. He suspects that the plan is to buy control and then to close down the airport and use the site for some other purpose. Max's questions tended to indicate that he was trying to estimate the costs associated with making the airport's staff redundant and to determine how difficult it would be to obtain permission to use the site to build a retail development or houses for sale.

The chairman called a meeting of DEF's Board. At the meeting he suggested that the Board should actively resist any attempt by Max to facilitate the purchase of shares until the identity of the third party client is known and the Board is satisfied that there are no plans to fundamentally alter the airport's mission, as expressed in its mission statement and financial objectives. He also suggested that the Board should not communicate Max's interest in buying shares to the LSGs themselves.

Bureau de change

DEF operates a bureau de change in the airport, which exchanges currencies. Most passengers fly within Europe, but approximately 1,000 passengers fly to the USA every day and many exchange D$ for US Dollars (US$) at the airport. DEF exchanges D$ for US$ on a daily basis at its local bank. DEF sets its exchange rate so that it makes a small profit on every US$ exchanged. For example, today's US$ were purchased from the bank at D$/US$1.227 (that is, D$1 = 1.227 US$) and DEF sold them to customers at D$/$US1.150.

The Chief Executive has suggested that the bureau de change may provide a means of resolving the dilemma created by the North American airline who wishes to start a new service to DEF. The airline has made it clear that it will only use DEF if the airport agrees to invoice in US$, but airport policy is to accept payment in D$ only.

The Chief Executive proposes that DEF agrees to invoice the North American airline in US$ and also to offer the other airlines the same opportunity. It is anticipated that total US$ receipts from aviation income, rental of property to US airlines and cargo handling will total approximately 60% of DEF's US$ requirements for the bureau de change. This sum will be paid into a US$ bank account, and that will be used to fund the daily US$ requirements whenever there is sufficient US$ in the account. If the balance in the US$ bank account is insufficient then DEF will exchange currency with its local bank as at present.

Retail activities

DEF rents out spaces in the shopping area to a number of independent cafes and shops. These make most of their profit from large volumes of small sales, such as snacks, cups of coffee, newspapers and magazines. Many passengers are in transit and are on journeys that commenced outside of Europe. They often have only foreign currency. The shops and cafes will accept any major currencies, but the exchange rates offered are always very poor from the passengers' perspective. The passengers are prepared to accept these rates in return for the convenience of being able to shop without having any D$.

Every point of sale has a list of currencies that will be accepted along with the rates on offer. Any change is given in D$ notes and coins. The foreign currencies have to be counted and banked separately, but these are often quite profitable sales because of the high margins on the goods being sold and the poor exchange rates offered to the customers. All shops and cafes bank all of their receipts on a daily basis.

Required

(a) (i)   Evaluate the present structure of DEF's board, as described in the Governance section (page 2) of the pre-seen. Your evaluation should reflect all relevant facts provided about DEF. **(9 marks)**

     (ii) Evaluate the Chairman's arguments that the board should not cooperate with Max unless it can be determined that the client whom he represents will not change the airport in any fundamental way. **(8 marks)**

     (iii) Discuss the risks associated with pursuing the airport's mission statement (as provided in page 2 of the preseen) as a basis for the board's strategic management of DEF. **(8 marks)**

(b) (i)   Discuss the risks and benefits to DEF of the Chief Executive's proposal to accept payments in US$ which would then meet part of the airport's US$ outgoings. **(8 marks)**

     (ii) Explain the benefits of internal hedging methods for managing foreign currency risk over external methods involving financial instruments. **(8 marks)**

(c) Evaluate the risks to the retailers of accepting foreign currency payments at their shops and cafes.

  (9 marks)

  (Total = 50 marks)

77 DEF 2 (11/10)   90 mins

Unseen case material

S proposal

DEF Airport has been approached by S, the only low-priced airline that currently operates from the airport.

At the moment S operates two flights per day to each of two destinations (i.e. four landings and four take-offs per day or eight flights). These flights have been popular and S is considering an expansion to its operations.

S wishes to create a network of routes to European destinations from DEF Airport. Over the next few years the number of flights arriving and departing would increase from 8 per day to 26. DEF Airport presently operates just over 80 flights per day and is operating at approximately 80% of its capacity. The additional activity by S would take the airport close to its capacity. DEF Airport operates on 360 days per year.

In return for choosing to expand operations from DEF Airport, S has asked for the following:

*   DEF Airport will build a special departure lounge for passengers flying with S. This will be a small, basic facility that could accommodate up to 300 passengers. S has a policy of offering the lowest fares and passengers do not expect to enjoy the same degree of comfort as those flying on premium airlines. S commissioned an architect to design a suitable extension to the main terminal building on land that already belongs to DEF Airport. It is estimated that the building costs would be D$800,000.

*   DEF Airport will modify its charges for S:

    –   Landing charges will be D$140 per aircraft. S uses one type of aircraft which is medium-sized and carries up to 130 passengers, with each flight being 90% full on average.

    –   The passenger loading charge will reduce to D$0.80 per passenger because S does not require any facilities at the airport. Passengers will check-in online from home and print out their own boarding passes, so there is no need to provide check-in desks. S does not permit passengers to check luggage into the aircraft, so its passengers will have hand luggage only and will not require baggage handling facilities.

    –   Security charges will remain at D$1.20 per passenger.

    –   S will not pay aircraft parking charges. Typically, each aircraft will land with a load of passengers and will take only 30 minutes to refuel and pick up the next load before departing. It will simplify administration for S if it does not have to monitor time spent parking for each flight. (According to DEF Airport's records, S has a poor record for delays, with 14% of its flights in 2009 having had to pay an hour's parking charges.)

S has stated that the reduced rates are fair because the additional flights will give DEF Airport an increased throughput of passengers and therefore increase its revenues from car parking and the retail outlets at the airport.

S will not negotiate these terms in any way and has given DEF Airport 30 days to make a decision, after which time S will make this offer to a competing airport.

DEF Airport's Business Development Manager is currently trying to find ways of utilising the airport's current spare capacity and is in discussion with a number of other airlines. For example, an Asian airline is considering operating two flights per day to its home country (i.e. two landings and two take-offs per day). Each flight will arrive and depart with an average of 300 passengers. This operator uses large aircraft. It is unlikely that any of these discussions will reach a conclusion within the 30 day deadline for reaching an agreement with S.

Head of Security

The Head of Security is due to retire in March 2011. The Operations Manager of DEF Airport has overall responsibility for all aspects of the smooth running of the airport, including the airport security service. She is responsible for appointing a suitable replacement Head of Security.

Currency risks

DEF Airport's Directors have previously stated that they do not need to take steps to manage currency risks because all costs and revenues are priced in D$.

A consultant, who was engaged to review the operation of the airport's financial systems, recommended that a comprehensive review of currency risks should be undertaken as a matter of some priority. The consultant stated:

- 20% of all passengers live in country D and travel on internal flights within country D.

- 30% of all passengers travel to or from countries within the Eurozone.

- 90% of all passengers are holidaymakers.

- Aviation fuel is priced in US$ by suppliers who sell it directly to the airlines.

- There are only two manufacturers of aircraft which supply the airline companies who fly from DEF Airport. One is European, based within the Eurozone, and the other is based in the US.

Required

(a) DEF's board is seriously considering the proposal offered by S, but the Directors are unsure whether the risks that it will create are justified by the associated revenues.

    (i) Calculate the impact on DEF Airport's annual revenues of:

        • Accepting S's proposal

        • Winning the contract with the Asian airline that is currently in discussion with the Business Development Manager. **(6 marks)**

    (ii) Evaluate S's proposal using your calculations in (a)(i) above and also the other information provided in the scenario. **(10 marks)**

    (iii) Discuss the operational risks that DEF Airport could face if it accepts the proposal made by S.

        (12 marks)

(b) Discuss the advantages and disadvantages of the airport Operations Manager being directly responsible for the supervision of airport security. **(10 marks)**

(c) (i) Advise the directors of DEF Airport on the reasons why the airport is exposed to currency risk.

        (7 marks)

    (ii) Recommend an approach to managing the risks that you have identified in (c)(i) above.

        (5 marks)

        (Total = 50 marks)

78 Aybe 1 (9/10)   90 mins

Note: This Preseen applies to Questions 74 and 75

Preseen case study

Background

Aybe, located in Country C, was formed by the merger of two companies in 2001. It is a listed company which manufactures, markets and distributes a large range of components throughout Europe and the United States of America. Aybe employs approximately 700 people at its three factories in Eastern Europe and supplies products to over 0·5 million customers in 20 countries. Aybe holds stocks of about 100,000 different electronic components.

Aybe is regarded within its industry as being a well-established business. Company Ay had operated successfully for nearly 17 years before its merger with Company Be. Company Ay can therefore trace its history back for 25 years which is a long time in the fast moving electronic component business.

The company is organised into three divisions, the Domestic Electronic Components division (DEC), the Industrial Electronic Components division (IEC) and the Specialist Components division (SC). The Domestic and Industrial Electronic Components divisions supply standard electronic components for domestic and industrial use whereas the Specialist Components division supplies components which are often unique and made to specific customer requirements. Each of the three divisions has its own factory in Country C.

Composition of the Board of Directors

The Board of Directors has three executive directors, the Company Secretary and five non-executive directors. The Chairman is one of the five independent non-executive directors. The executive directors are the Chief Executive, Finance Director and Director of Operations. There is also an Audit Committee, a Remuneration Committee and a Nominations Committee. All three committees are made up entirely of the non-executive directors.

Organisational structure

Aybe is organised along traditional functional/unitary lines. The Board considers continuity to be a very important value. The present structure was established by Company Ay in 1990 and continued after the merger with Company Be. Many of Aybe's competitors have carried out structural reorganisations since then. In 2008, Aybe commissioned a review of its organisational structure from a human resource consultancy. The consultants suggested alternative structures which they thought Aybe could employ to its advantage. However, Aybe's Board felt that continuity was more important and no change to the organisational structure took place.

Product and service delivery

Customers are increasingly seeking assistance from their component suppliers with the design of their products and the associated manufacturing and assembly processes. Aybe's Board views this as a growth area. The Board has recognised that Aybe needs to develop web-based services and tools which can be accessed by customers. The traditional method of listing the company's range of components in a catalogue is becoming less effective because customers are increasingly seeking specially designed custom made components as the electronics industry becomes more sophisticated.

Financial data

Aybe's historical financial record, denominated in C's currency of C$, over the last five years is shown below.

	Year ended 31 December:				
	2009	2008	2007	2006	2005
	C$m	C$m	C$m	C$m	C$m
Revenue	620	600	475	433	360
Operating profit	41	39	35	20	13
Profit for the year	23	21	16	9	5
Earnings per share (C$)	0·128	0·117	0·089	0·050	0·028
Dividend per share (C$)	0·064	0·058	0	0	0

Extracts from the 2009 financial statements are given at Appendix A. There are currently 180 million ordinary shares in issue with a nominal value of C$0·10 each. The share price at 31 December 2009 was C$0·64. No dividend was paid in the three years 2005 to 2007 due to losses sustained in the first few years after the merger in 2001.

BPP
LEARNING MEDIA

Aybe's bank has imposed an overdraft limit of C$10 million and two covenants: (i) that its interest cover must not fall below 5 and (ii) its ratio of non-current liabilities to equity must not increase beyond 0·75:1. Aybe's Finance Director is comfortable with this overdraft limit and the two covenants.

The ordinary shareholding of Aybe is broken down as follows:

	Percentage of ordinary shares held at 31 December 2009
Institutional investors	55
Executive Directors and Company Secretary	10
Employees	5
Individual investors	30

The Executive Directors, Company Secretary and other senior managers are entitled to take part in an Executive Share Option Scheme offered by Aybe.

Performance review

Aybe's three divisions have been profitable throughout the last five years. The revenue and operating profit of the three divisions of Aybe for 2009 were as follows:

	DEC Division C$m	IEC Division C$m	SC Division C$m
Revenue	212	284	124
Operating profit	14	16	11

Financial objectives of Aybe

The Board has generally taken a cautious approach to providing strategic direction for the company. Most board members feel that this has been appropriate because the company was unprofitable for the three year period after the merger and needed to be turned around. Also, most board members think a cautious approach has been justified given the constrained economic circumstances which have affected Aybe's markets since 2008. While shareholders have been disappointed with Aybe's performance over the last five years, they have remained loyal and supported the Board in its attempts to move the company into profit. The institutional shareholders however are now looking for increased growth and profitability.

The Board has set the following financial objectives which it considers reflect the caution for which Aybe is well known:

(i)   Dividend payout to remain at 50% of profit for the year;
(ii)   No further equity shares to be issued over the next five years in order to avoid diluting earnings per share.

Capital budget overspends

Aybe has an internal audit department. The Chief Internal Auditor, who leads this department, reports directly to the Finance Director. Investigation by the Internal Audit department has revealed that managers with responsibility for capital expenditure have often paid little attention to expenditure authorisation levels approved by the Board. They have justified overspending on the grounds that the original budgets were inadequate and in order not to jeopardise the capital projects, the overspends were necessary.

An example of this was the building of an extension to the main factory at the DEC division that was completed in 2009 at a final cost of nearly C$3 million which was almost 50% over budget. The capital budget for the extension was set at the outset and the capital investment appraisal showed a positive net present value. It subsequently became apparent that the site clearance costs and on-going construction expenditure were under-estimated. These estimates were provided by a qualified quantity surveyor who was a contractor to Aybe. The estimates supplied by the quantity surveyor were accurately included in Aybe's capital investment appraisal system which was performed on a spreadsheet. However, no regular checks were carried out to compare the phased budgeted expenditure with actual costs incurred. It came as a surprise to the Board when the Finance Director finally produced the capital expenditure project report which showed the cost of the extension was nearly 50% overspent.

Strategic development

Aybe applies a traditional rational model in carrying out its strategic planning process. This encompasses an annual exercise to review the previous plan, creation of a revenue and capital budget for the next five years and instruction to managers within Aybe to maintain their expenditure within the budget limits approved by the Board.

Debates have taken place within the Board regarding the strategic direction in which Aybe should move. Most board members are generally satisfied that Aybe has been turned around over the last five years and were pleased that the company increased its profit in 2009 even though the global economy slowed down. Aybe benefited from a number of long-term contractual arrangements with customers throughout 2009 which were agreed in previous years. However, many of these are not being renewed due to the current economic climate.

The Board stated in its annual report, published in March 2010, that the overall strategic aim of the company is to:

"Achieve growth and increase shareholder returns by continuing to produce and distribute high quality electronic components and develop our international presence through expansion into new overseas markets."

Aybe's Chief Executive said in the annual report that the strategic aim is clear and straightforward. He said "Aybe will strive to maintain its share of the electronic development, operational, maintenance and repair markets in which it is engaged. This is despite the global economic difficulties which Aybe, along with its competitors, has faced since 2008. Aybe will continue to apply the highest ethical standards in its business activities."

In order to facilitate the achievement of the strategic aim, Aybe's Board has established the following strategic goals:

1.   Enhance the provision of products and services which are demanded by customers
2.   Invest in engineering and web-based support for customers
3.   Maintain the search for environmentally friendly products
4.   Pursue options for expansion into new overseas markets

The Board has also stated that Aybe is a responsible corporate organisation and recognises the social and environmental effects of its operational activities.

Concern over the rate of growth

Aybe's recently appointed Director of Operations and one of its Non-Executive Directors have privately expressed their concern to the Chief Executive at what they perceive to be the very slow growth of the company. While they accept that shareholder expectations should not be raised too high, they feel that the Board is not providing sufficient impetus to move the company forward. They fear that the results for 2010 will be worse than for 2009. They think that Aybe should be much more ambitious and fear that the institutional shareholders in particular, will not remain patient if Aybe does not create stronger earnings growth than has previously been achieved.

Development approaches

The Board has discussed different ways of expanding overseas in order to meet the overall strategic aim. It has, in the past, been reluctant to move from the current approach of exporting components. However the Director of Operations has now begun preparing a plan for the IEC division to open up a trading company in Asia. The DEC division is also establishing a subsidiary in Africa.

Appendix A

Extracts of Aybe's Income Statement and Statement of Financial Position

Income statement for the year ended 31 December 2009

	2009 C$million
Revenue	620
Operating costs	(579)
Finance costs	(4)
Profit before tax	37
Income tax expense	(14)
Profit for the year	23

Statement of financial position as at 31 December 2009

	2009 C$million
ASSETS	
Non-current assets	111
Current assets	
Inventories	40
Trade and other receivables	81
Cash and cash equivalents	3
Total current assets	124
Total assets	235
EQUITY AND LIABILITIES	
Equity	
Share capital	18
Share premium	9
Other reserves	8
Retained earnings	75
Total equity	110
Non-current liabilities	
Bank loan (8% interest, repayable 2015)	40
Current liabilities	
Trade and other payables	73
Current tax payable	8
Bank overdraft	4
Total current liabilities	85
Total liabilities	125
Total equity and liabilities	235

Unseen case material

New market opportunity

Two years ago IEC, a division of Aybe, established a special parts department ("SPD") to undertake the manufacture of customised components, such as a microprocessor that has been programmed with a specific set of instructions supplied by the customer. SPD can also make complex parts and assemblies. For example, a customer might require a circuit board for a computer or a control panel. Making such an assembly involves overlaying a plastic sheet with copper tracks to carry electrical current and signals and attaching components and connectors.

SPD does not generate a large proportion of Aybe's revenue, but it has been very profitable since it began 2 years ago because SPD can charge high profit margins. SPD employs 18 highly skilled technicians who work in a sophisticated electronics workshop.

Almost all of the work undertaken by SPD is 'jobbing work' i.e. for very small quantities, sometimes only a single unit. This is because SPD's customers often build prototypes of products that they plan to test before committing themselves to full-scale production. If the prototype is successful and the customer then requires larger quantities of the component SPD directs them to Aybe's IEC division. IEC has a highly automated electronics factory and consequently uses mainly semi-skilled employees. IEC's equipment can mass-produce almost anything that SPD's workshop can design. However because of the very high set-up costs associated with each new order, IEC needs the order to be for a significant volume.

SPD has been approached by Q, a specialist manufacturer of extremely expensive high performance cars. Q is in the process of developing a new car that will be one of the fastest in the world. The car will be designed to be driven on public roads, but the owners of such cars often take them to private race tracks where they can be driven at very high speeds.

Q has designed an electronics system to enable an average driver to drive the car safely at high speed. The system will monitor the engine, brakes and steering and will compensate for errors that could cause a crash. The system will, for example, sense that the car is about to skid and will compensate for that. The electronics system will be based on a circuit board that Q wishes to have built by SPD.

Building Q's circuit board will pose a number of challenges for SPD. The circuit board will be subject to a great deal of vibration when the car is driven at speed. The cars are expected to last for a very long time and so there could be problems if the circuit boards deteriorate with age. The circuit board will be installed in an inaccessible part of the car where it will be difficult to inspect or maintain.

Many of the components on the board will be manufactured by SPD, but some crucial components will be supplied by a third party that has already been selected by Q.

Q is prepared to order a large number of circuit boards but only if they are hand built by SPD. That is partly because the cars will not be built in sufficient volume to make it possible for IEC to mass-produce the boards and partly because Q wishes to be able to update and modify the design of the circuit boards in response to feedback from owners. SPD's Production Manager believes that the Q contract will create sufficient work to keep four technicians almost fully occupied. SPD will have to recruit and train additional staff in order to service this contract. Performance Strategy 9 September 2010

Post-completion audit

The members of Aybe's Audit Committee are very concerned about the Chief Internal Auditor's report on the capital budget overspends (see preseen case study page 4). The Audit Committee is keen to introduce a system of post-completion audits as a matter of priority.

For the sake of clarity, the Audit Committee wishes to adopt the CIMA definition of post-completion audits:

> *Post-completion audit: This is an objective and independent appraisal of the measure of success of a capital expenditure project in progressing the business as planned. It should cover the implementation of the project from authorisation to commissioning and its technical and commercial performance after commissioning. The information provided is also used by management as feedback which aids the implementation and control of future risk projects.*

The Head of the Audit Committee has asked the Chief Internal Auditor to consider the matter and to brief the Audit Committee on the following matters:

• The approach that the internal audit department would take to the planning and execution of post-completion audits. For example, how will projects be selected for investigation and what aspects will be examined?

• What difficulties does the Chief Internal Auditor envisage in conducting these post-completion audits?

The Audit Committee has informed the main board of its intention to commission post-completion audits. The Chief Executive is worried that some managers might be reluctant to propose projects if they know that such actions could be subjected to an audit

Copper futures

Aybe's manufacturing processes use a huge amount of copper. The board of Aybe anticipated that the price of copper would rise towards the end of 2010 and it hedged against a significant rise by purchasing 150 copper futures, each of which makes Aybe the purchaser of 25 tonnes of copper at a price of US$7,800 per tonne.

An earthquake at a major copper mine has caused a degree of panic in the copper market. The prevailing prices for a future with the same expiry date as those held by Aybe are US$8,300 per tonne (buyer) and US$8,310 (seller). Aybe's Director of Operations believes that the markets have overreacted to the news of the earthquake and that the company should sell its copper futures before the price falls. Aybe could then protect itself by waiting until the markets have settled down and prices have gone back to their equilibrium levels before purchasing an option to buy the same quantity of copper at the end of 2010.

Required

(a)   (i)   Evaluate FOUR significant risks associated with accepting the order from Q.   **(12 marks)**

      (ii)   Recommend, with reasons, an appropriate response to each of the risks identified in (a)(i) above.
                                                                            (12 marks)

(b)   (i)   Recommend an appropriate approach to the selection and investigation of projects for post-completion audits by the internal audit department.   **(8 marks)**

      (ii)   Discuss the possibility that the introduction of post-completion audits will deter capital investment.
                                                                            (5 marks)

(c)   (i)   Calculate the gain that Aybe would realise if it sells its copper futures.   **(3 marks)**

      (ii)   Discuss the validity of the Director of Operation's suggestion. Your answer should focus on the risks associated with the proposal.   **(6 marks)**

      (iii)   Explain whether your answer to (c)(ii) above would be any different if you knew whether or not Aybe's competitors had hedged against movements in the cost of copper.   **(4 marks)**

                                                                      (Total = 50 marks)

79   Aybe 2 (5/10)   90 mins

Unseen case material

DEC: New subsidiary

Following Aybe's desire to expand overseas, DEC has established a subsidiary in a central African country. The subsidiary manufactures products to be sold within that country and for export to neighbouring countries. The products manufactured in the African factory use components and raw materials that are purchased directly from DEC (in Aybe's home country). Payments for the components and raw materials will be made to DEC in the currency of the African subsidiary but DEC's accountant is concerned about the high level of inflation in the African country and the consequent impact on future receipts. He is particularly worried because it has been stated that the subsidiary will only make three payments each year for components and materials and therefore each payment will be for a high value. Profits from the subsidiary will be remitted to DEC on request and in accordance with any exchange control regulations of the African country.

The African factory was developed with a government-owned joint venture partner. All new foreign companies entering the African country are required to establish joint ventures in this way. This stipulation means that the African government effectively dictates the terms of the investment to the foreign investor.

DEC has just received payment for all of the shipments to the African subsidiary to date (as stated earlier, the subsidiary will in future only make three payments each year). The accountant has noticed that the amount remitted was in excess of the invoice value of the goods sent to the subsidiary. Initial investigations show that the prices were inflated on the invoices by a manager in DEC at the headquarters in Aybe who was attempting to increase his profit-related bonus.

The factory has just started selling its output within its home country but sales volumes are low. Export sales to other African countries have not yet commenced and forecasts for future export sales have yet to be produced. The product range offered by the African subsidiary is similar to DEC's European range.

The information systems within the African subsidiary are not fully developed. The priority was to set up control systems for inventory and production. These systems became operational within the last month. Consequently the sales staff in the subsidiary are already benefiting from knowledge of inventory levels and are able to provide accurate information to customers about product availability. However due to over-optimistic initial sales forecasts, significant levels of inventory have accumulated. The African sales staff are concerned that the shortfall in sales is having an adverse impact on their bonuses because they are not meeting their targets.

African sales staff are reluctant to offer discounts to promote sales and reduce the excessive inventory. Their bonuses, which make up the majority of their remuneration packages, are based on average profit per unit sold and sales volumes.

This information system problem referred to above is not the only issue affecting DEC's information systems in recent years. A factory extension previously referred to under "Capital budget overspends" (see page 4) was 50% overspent party due to lack of regular checks of budget to actual costs.

DEC: New service

The DEC Division in Europe and its African subsidiary have started to offer a new service in response to pressure from environmental campaigners. Up to five years ago, many of the components sold by DEC contained toxic materials. Recent legislation in Europe and the African country requires components to be recycled in specific ways to minimise any environmental damage. DEC has told customers that when they purchase new components they can give the old components to DEC and then the company will recycle them in accordance with the new legislation.

This service has provided some good publicity for DEC and has featured in its recent social and environmental report. However, a review of DEC's recycling procedures by Internal Audit Department identified that many components, including some that contain toxic materials, are simply thrown away by DEC staff rather than being recycled.

Required

(a)   Identify and evaluate FIVE risks affecting DEC's new African subsidiary.   **(15 marks)**

(b)   Discuss, in respect of the extension to the factory and the new African subsidiary, the strengths and weaknesses of DEC's management information system.   **(9 marks)**

(c)   (i)   Discuss the methods DEC and the African subsidiary could use to mitigate the foreign exchange risk when trading with other foreign countries.   **(10 marks)**

       (ii) Discuss the accounting implications for both DEC and the African subsidiary of each method identified in (i).   **(6 marks)**

(d) . Discuss the safeguards that should exist within any company to prevent the unethical manipulation of transactions. (You should refer to examples from DEC in your answer.)   **(10 marks)**

(Total = 50 marks)

80   PU (Specimen paper)   90 mins

Preseen case study

Background

Power Utilities (PU) is located in a democratic Asian country. Just over 12 months ago, the former nationalised Electricity Generating Corporation (EGC) was privatised and became PU. EGC was established as a nationalised industry many years ago. Its home government at that time had determined that the provision of the utility services of electricity generation production should be managed by boards that were accountable directly to Government. In theory, nationalised industries should be run efficiently, on behalf of the public, without the need to provide any form of risk related return to the funding providers. In other words, EGC, along with other nationalised industries, was a non-profit making organisation. This, the Government claimed at the time, would enable prices charged to the final consumer to be kept low.

Privatisation of EGC

The Prime Minister first announced three years ago that the Government intended to pursue the privatisation of the nationalised industries within the country. The first priority was to be the privatisation of the power generating utilities and EGC was selected as the first nationalised industry to be privatised. The main purpose of this strategy was to encourage public subscription for share capital. In addition, the Government's intention was that PU should take a full and active part in commercial activities such as raising capital and earning higher revenue by increasing its share of the power generation and supply market by achieving growth either organically or through making acquisitions. This, of course, also meant that PU was exposed to commercial pressures itself, including satisfying the requirements of shareholders and becoming a potential target for take-over.
The major shareholder, with a 51% share, would be the Government. However, the Minister of Energy has recently stated that the Government intends to reduce its shareholding in PU over time after the privatisation takes place.

Industry structure

PU operates 12 coal-fired power stations across the country and transmits electricity through an integrated national grid system which it manages and controls. It is organised into three regions, Northern, Eastern and Western. Each region generates electricity which is sold to 10 private sector electricity distribution companies which are PU's customers.

The three PU regions transmit the electricity they generate into the national grid system. A shortage of electricity generation in one region can be made up by taking from the national grid. This is particularly important when there is a national emergency, such as exceptional weather conditions.

The nationalised utility industries, including the former EGC, were set up in a monopolistic position. As such, no other providers of these particular services were permitted to enter the market within the country. Therefore, when EGC was privatised and became PU it remained the sole generator of electricity in the country. The electricity generating facilities, in the form of the 12 coal-fired power stations, were all built over 15 years ago and some date back to before EGC came into being.

The 10 private sector distribution companies are the suppliers of electricity to final users including households and industry within the country, and are not under the management or control of PU. They are completely independent companies owned by shareholders.

The 10 private sector distribution companies serve a variety of users of electricity. Some, such as AB, mainly serve domestic users whereas others, such as DP, only supply electricity to a few industrial clients. In fact, DP has a limited portfolio of industrial customers and 3 major clients, an industrial conglomerate, a local administrative authority and a supermarket chain. DP finds these clients costly to service.

Structure of PU

The structure of PU is that it has a Board of Directors headed by an independent Chairman and a separate Managing Director. The Chairman of PU was nominated by the Government at the time the announcement that EGC was to be privatised was made. His background is that he is a former Chairman of an industrial . conglomerate within the country. There was no previous Chairman of EGC which was managed by a Management Board, headed by the Managing Director. The former EGC Managing Director retired on privatisation and a new Managing Director was appointed.

The structure of PU comprises a hierarchy of many levels of management authority. In addition to the Chairman and Managing Director, the Board consists of the Directors of each of the Northern, Eastern and Western regions, a Technical Director, the Company Secretary and the Finance Director. All of these except the Chairman are the Executive Directors of PU. The Government also appointed seven Non Executive Directors to PU's Board. With the exception of the Company Secretary and Finance Director, all the Executive Directors are qualified electrical engineers. The Chairman and Managing Director of PU have worked hard to overcome some of the inertia which was an attitude that some staff had developed within the former EGC. PU is now operating efficiently as a private sector company. There have been many staff changes at a middle management level within the organisation.

Within the structure of PU's headquarters, there are five support functions; engineering, finance (which includes PU's Internal Audit department), corporate treasury, human resource management (HRM) and administration, each with its own chief officers, apart from HRM. Two Senior HRM Officers and Chief Administrative Officer report to the Company Secretary. The Chief Accountant and Corporate Treasurer each report to the Finance Director. These functions, except Internal Audit, are replicated in each region, each with its own regional officers and support staff. Internal Audit is an organisation wide function and is based at PU headquarters.

Regional Directors of PU

The Regional Directors all studied in the field of electrical engineering at the country's leading university and have worked together for a long time. Although they did not all attend the university at the same time, they have a strong belief in the quality of their education. After graduation from university, each of the Regional Directors started work at EGC in a junior capacity and then subsequently gained professional electrical engineering qualifications. They believe that the experience of working up through the ranks of EGC has enabled them to have a clear understanding of EGC's culture and the technical aspects of the industry as a whole. Each of the Regional Managers has recognised the changed environment that PU now operates within, compared with the former EGC, and they are now working hard to help PU achieve success as a private sector electricity generator. The Regional Directors are well regarded by both the Chairman and Managing Director, both in terms of their technical skill and managerial competence.

Governance of PU

Previously, the Managing Director of the Management Board of EGC reported to senior civil servants in the Ministry of Energy. There were no shareholders and ownership of the Corporation rested entirely with the Government. That has now changed. The Government holds 51% of the shares in PU and the Board of Directors is responsible to the shareholders but, inevitably, the Chairman has close links directly with the Minister of Energy, who represents the major shareholder.

The Board meetings are held regularly, normally weekly, and are properly conducted with full minutes being taken. In addition, there is a Remuneration Committee, an Audit Committee and an Appointments Committee, all in accordance with best practice. The model which has been used is the UK Corporate Governance Code which applies to companies which have full listing status on the London Stock Exchange. Although PU is not listed on the London Stock Exchange, the principles of the Code were considered by the Government to be appropriate to be applied with regard to the corporate governance of the company.

Currently, PU does not have an effective Executive Information System and this has recently been raised at a Board meeting by one of the non-executive directors because he believes this inhibits the function of the Board and consequently is disadvantageous to the governance of PU.

Remuneration of Executive Directors

In order to provide a financial incentive, the Remuneration Committee of PU has agreed that the Executive Directors be entitled to performance related pay, based on a bonus scheme, in addition to their fixed salary and health benefits.

Capital market

PU exists in a country which has a well developed capital market relating both to equity and loan stock funding. There are well established international institutions which are able to provide funds and corporate entities are free to issue their own loan stock in accordance with internationally recognised principles. PU is listed on the country's main stock exchange.

Strategic opportunity

The Board of PU is considering the possibility of vertical integration into electricity supply and has begun preliminary discussion with DP's Chairman with a view to making an offer for DP. PU's Board is attracted by DP's strong reputation for customer service but is aware, through press comment, that DP has received an increase in complaints regarding its service to customers over the last year. When the former EGC was a nationalised business, breakdowns were categorised by the Government as "urgent", when there was a danger to life, and "non-urgent" which was all others. Both the former EGC and DP had a very high success rate in meeting the government's requirements that a service engineer should attend the urgent break-down within 60 minutes. DP's record over this last year in attending urgent breakdowns has deteriorated seriously and if PU takes DP over, this situation would need to improve.

Energy consumption within the country and Government drive for increased efficiency and concern for the environment

Energy consumption has doubled in the country over the last 10 years. As PU continues to use coal-fired power stations, it now consumes most of the coal mined within the country.

The Minister of Energy has indicated to the Chairman of PU that the Government wishes to encourage more efficient methods of energy production. This includes the need to reduce production costs. The Government has limited resources for capital investment in energy production and wishes to be sure that future energy production facilities are more efficient and effective than at present.

The Minister of Energy has also expressed the Government's wish to see a reduction in harmful emissions from the country's power stations. (The term harmful emissions in this context, refers to pollution coming out of electricity generating power stations which damage the environment.)

One of PU's non-executive directors is aware that another Asian country is a market leader in coal gasification which is a fuel technology that could be used to replace coal for power generation. In the coal gasification process, coal is mixed with oxygen and water vapour under pressure, normally underground, and then pumped to the surface where the gas can be used in power stations. The process significantly reduces carbon dioxide emissions although it is not widely used at present and not on any significant commercial scale.

Another alternative to coal fired power stations being actively considered by PU's Board is the construction of a dam to generate hydro-electric power. The Board is mindful of the likely adverse response of the public living and working in the area where the dam would be built.

In response to the Government's wishes, PU has established environmental objectives relating to improved efficiency in energy production and reducing harmful emissions such as greenhouse gases. PU has also established an ethical code. Included within the code are sections relating to recycling and reduction in harmful emissions as well as to terms and conditions of employment.

Introduction of commercial accounting practices at EGC

The first financial statements have been produced for PU for 2008. Extracts from the Statement of Financial Position from this are shown in **Appendix A**. Within these financial statements, some of EGC's loans were "notionally" converted by the Government into ordinary shares. Interest is payable on the Government loans as shown in the statement of financial position. Reserves is a sum which was vested in EGC when it was first nationalised. This represents the initial capital stock valued on a historical cost basis from the former electricity generating organisations which became consolidated into EGC when it was first nationalised.

Being previously a nationalised industry and effectively this being the first "commercially based" financial statements, there are no retained earnings brought forward into 2008.

Appendix A

EXTRACTS FROM THE PRO FORMA FINANCIAL STATEMENTS OF THE ELECTRICITY GENERATING CORPORATION

Statement of financial position as at 31 December 2008

	P$ million
ASSETS	
Non-current assets	15,837
Current assets	
Inventories	1,529
Receivables	2,679
Cash and Cash equivalents	133
	4,341
Total assets	20,178
EQUITY AND LIABILITIES	
Equity	
Share capital	5,525
Reserves	1,231
Total equity	6,756
Non-current liabilities	
Government loans	9,560
Current liabilities	
Payables	3,862
Total liabilities	13,422
Total equity and liabilities	20,178

Unseen case material

New investment

Following the privatisation of PU, the board are now considering the investment needed to retain and improve the productive capacity available to the company. Currently, PU operates 12 power stations which were all built over 15 years ago. Life expectancy for coal fired power stations is around 25 to 30 years. This means that all 12 power stations will need replacing within 10 to 15 years. This will be a significant capital cost for PU which will almost certainly have to be financed by borrowing or other forms of external investment.

Although the Asian country PU operates in does have coal reserves to fuel new coal fired power stations, the board are keen to investigate other methods of power generation such as gas, nuclear and more environmentally friendly alternatives such as wind and wave power. If coal fired power stations are built they will have to meet new environmental legislation in the Asian country, as well as global agreements to decrease the amount of Carbon Dioxide emissions from this type of power station. This will mean that the cost per power station will be higher in real terms than when the power stations were first built.

The non-executive directors in PU have recently identified that there is a lack of an effective Executive Information System for the Board. This means that board members cannot either monitor the current management and financial information produced within PU, or appraise new investment projects. One option to replace coal fired power stations is coal gasification. In this process, coal is mixed with oxygen and water vapour under pressure, normally underground, and then pumped to the surface where the gas can be used in power stations or converted into petrol and other similar fuels. The process has the benefit of significantly reducing carbon dioxide emissions although the technology is not widely used at present and not on any significant commercial scale.

One of the non-executive directors is aware that country Zee is a market leader in coal gasification processes. Country Zee is located in Africa; while Zee appears to be financially stable, there is some political unrest caused partly from ethnic divergence and issues of inequitable income distribution. Country Zee appears keen to retain its lead in this technology; at present the technology has only been made available to one other company in another country. The government of country Zee required this company to establish a subsidiary in Zee and manufacture the gasification equipment in Zee prior to export to the other country. This is the only method currently available to obtain the technology. To repeat the process, an initial investment will be required in Zee$, although the government guarantees to purchase the subsidiary at prevailing market prices in Zee after five years. A further requirement was that 80% of the workforce had to be drawn from the population of country Zee.

Environmental information

Legislation in the Asian country requires PU to provide environmental information each year on its activities, with specific reference to emissions of carbon dioxide from its power stations. This environmental information is collated at each power station and then forwarded to PU's head office for inclusion within PU's overall environmental report. Information from each power station is audited on a rotational basis by PU's internal audit department.

This year, power station N3 was part of the rotational audit. The internal audit department discovered significant discrepancies between the published emissions information and actual information obtained from the records maintained in the power station itself. The manager of the power station indicated that emissions were actually higher than expected due to faulty extraction filters fitted to the power station. Although PU's head office was aware of the problem, funds were not made available to rectify this. The matter was reported by the head of internal audit to the Managing Director with the recommendation that the emissions information was amended to show actual emissions.

Required

Working as a consultant to the board of PU:

(a) The board of PU needs to assess methods of power generation in preparation for replacing the existing coal fired power stations. Advise the board how to develop an Information strategy to support this objective. **(12 marks)**

(b) Evaluate the financial and other risks affecting PU if a subsidiary is established in Zee to manufacture coal gasification equipment. **(16 marks)**

(c) (i) PU's internal audit department may be asked to participate in the environmental audit of PU.

Explain the term "environmental audit" and evaluate the attributes that PU's internal audit department should have prior to carrying out this work. **(8 marks)**

(ii) There is a discrepancy in environmental returns from power station N3. Recommend the actions (apart from reporting to the Managing Director) that the internal audit department of PU should undertake regarding this situation. **(8 marks)**

(d) Discuss the extent to which false reporting of environmental information is a source of risk to PU and explain control mechanisms that may be used to avoid false reporting. **(6 marks)**

(Total = 50 marks)

ANSWERS

108

1 Grove

(a)

(i)   Points in favour of view

Human error

Even if Grove has strong risk management systems in place, they may still be **undermined by human error**. An isolated lapse in concentration could result in an accident.

Credible policies

In order to minimise or eliminate risks, more onerous health and safety procedures may be introduced, including investigation of the factors that have led to injuries. However staff **may not take these procedures seriously** if they feel they are impractical. Staff failing to operate onerous procedures properly may result in greater risk than staff operating less strict procedures effectively.

Points against view

Complacency

The director's view appears to be **complacent.** The current injury statistics seem to be high. There is scope for reducing injuries towards zero, even if Grove can never prevent all injuries.

Reduction measures

Practical measures can be taken to reduce injuries. **Health and safety training** can be improved. Grove can introduce **requirements for staff** performing certain tasks, for example lifting heavy objects.

Negligence claims

The Director's toleration of an 'acceptable' level of injuries may leave the council **vulnerable to legal claims**. Staff who have been injured could use the Director's statements as evidence of a negligent attitude by senior management towards employee safety.

(ii)   <u>Points in favour of view</u>

<u>Consequences of breaches</u>

A strong argument in favour of zero tolerance is the **consequences of accidents,** possibly serious injury or death. Although a lapse may only have resulted in a minor injury on one occasion, the same lapse another time could have much more severe consequences.

<u>Duty of council</u>

However health and safety law is drafted, the Council has a **clear moral duty** to ensure its employees' safety.

<u>Safety culture</u>

Aiming towards eliminating injuries can **help promote a strong culture of safety**. If staff understand that there is no such thing as an acceptable level of injuries, they are unlikely to become complacent and will take steps to reduce the level of accidents further.

<u>Points against view</u>

Employee involvement in hazardous activities

The extent of the Council's responsibilities make it inevitable that some staff will have to be **involved in hazardous activities.** This will mean that there will always be a risk of injuries occurring, even if it can be reduced to very small levels.

<u>Costs</u>

Some risk prevention procedures, for example requiring staff to wear cumbersome clothing, may be **impractical**. The costs and time taken to investigate minor problems may be excessive.

(b)

Top tips. Analyse, the verb in (b) (i), means use a structured approach to explore the ethical dilemma by highlighting key issues, explaining the ethical problems and demonstrating how the ethical principles in CIMA's ethical code apply. That does **not** mean list CIMA's ethical principles without referring to the scenario. It is likely that the depot was chosen for audit because of health and safety risks that were inevitably higher than for some other departments. The depot is certainly breaching the Council's guidelines. Senior management at the Council should also be concerned about the suppression of evidence at the depot and the climate of intimidation. There don't appear to be any whistleblowing channels to protect the auditor if she reports the problems internally. Note also that CIMA's ethical guide doesn't provide an entirely simple solution to the issues. The auditor is under a duty of confidentiality and she would be disobeying a clear instruction if she went above her boss's head.

The recommendations in (b) (ii) need to be clear, logical and ethical. The allocation of 7 marks suggests that you will need to recommend more than one action, depending on whether the situation can be resolved. This is reinforced by the examiner's criticism that many students merely suggested that the auditor should resign without exploring other possible actions. Our answer takes a staged approach, starting with the auditor at least considering whether her boss is right.

(i)   <u>Key issues</u>

<u>Breaches of laws and guidelines</u>

The depot's team may be breaking the law, though this is not completely clear. Staff are certainly **breaching Council guidelines** for reporting injuries.

<u>Unwillingness to deal with problem</u>

There is no sign that the depot manager will **change his views** or depot staff will **keep records themselves.** As well as the safety risks, the unwillingness of staff to speak out suggests that there is a **culture of intimidation** at the depot.

Ethical problems

False health and safety record

By refusing to report injuries, staff are **giving a false picture** of the depot's health and safety record to Grove's senior management. The Council's directors are relying on the reports to decide the extent of safety problems throughout the Council's operations and therefore the actions required to reduce risks.

Auditor silence

The auditor has been ordered by her boss not to report the problems further. However she believes that not reporting the problems will mean that **practices at the depot will not improve** and staff will continue to be at risk of serious injury.

CIMA's code

Professional competence and due care

If the auditor does not report the problems and there is a serious injury at the depot, she could be accused of **failing to demonstrate competence and care.** She was been sent to the depot presumably because of concerns about injuries there, but will not have highlighted the problems she has found.

Confidentiality

The auditor has been ordered not to report the problem to anyone inside or outside the Council. If she **discloses the information to external parties**, she could be accused of failing to keep information confidential without good reason, since her boss has forbidden her to disclose it.

Professional behaviour

If the auditor ignores her boss's instructions and reports directly to senior management, she could be seen to be **acting unprofessionally.** She is unlikely to be able to support her claims without evidence from depot staff. An unsubstantiated report could reflect badly on the whole internal audit department.

Objectivity

The internal auditor's decision may be influenced by the threat of her boss to suspend her. She may be deterred from taking the course of action she would otherwise believe to be right by the **threat to her employment prospects.**

(ii) Review of evidence

The auditor should firstly have **another look** at the evidence of minor injuries that she has found and consider why they occurred. If the problems are unlikely to result in serious injuries on another occasion, then the Head of Internal Audit's decision may be correct and the auditor should not take the issue any further.

Resolution of problem

The auditor may be able to resolve the problem by **talking to the depot manager**, which she does not appear to have done yet. If she can persuade the depot manager to make a commitment to follow the Council's guidelines in future, she may feel that the problem has been resolved.

Reporting to senior management

If nothing is done at the depot and the auditor believes there is a high risk of serious injury, she should **report the matter to senior management at the Council**, even though she may risk being suspended. Because of the auditor's obligation to maintain the confidentiality of her employer's affairs, external reporting, for example to the Health and Safety Executive, can only be justified if she feels further serious injuries are very likely and is sure that no effective action will be taken internally to deal with the risks.

Resignation

The auditor should regard resignation as a **last resort.** However if the auditor believes that no effective action will be taken internally, she may be forced to resign. Resignation would signify that she disassociated herself from a culture that puts employees at serious risk.

2 JDM

Text references. Chapters 1, 2 and 8.

Top tips. In (b) the examiner criticised students for repeating the points they made in (a); however it is difficult to see how you can totally avoid overlap. One way of scoring well in (b) is to use the suitable, acceptable, feasible framework to support your recommendation. CIMA also allows a couple of marks for non-financial factors influencing the decision.

(c) should have represented largely basic knowledge, though you would have limited the marks you scored by not using a memo format or making any reference to JDM in your answer. CIMA's guide indicated that you would have scored marks for discussing the establishment of the process and the responsibilities for it, as well as the steps in the process.

It's worth noting that the economic recession is a significant factor in this question and was also a material issue in other questions in the exam in which this question appeared (the May 2009 exam). It's probable that the poor economic climate will also feature in other exams over the next couple of years, in the other strategic exams as well as in P3.

Easy marks. You must revise Chapter 2 of the text urgently if you couldn't generate ideas for (c).

Examiner's comments. Most students scored poorly on (a) and (b) and very well on (c). Answers to (a) were too general and often did not compare the two strategies. In (b), most students just reported the same points as in (a) and recommended one strategy without justifying it.

(a)   Amounts of cash flows

Strategy 1 offers a 70% chance of **maximising revenues** if all the apartments are sold. JDM should make a surplus of roughly £1.5 million (115,000 × 15 – 210,000). Strategy 2 has a higher **expected NPV**, although the NPV for Strategy 1 is an average figure that is very different from either of the two possibilities.

Uncertainties

The market may be **sufficiently sensitive to price** that the all or nothing possibilities under Strategy 1 are the only likely ones. The figure of 70% may be debatable. The forecasts do not consider what will happen under Strategy 1 if **none of the properties are sold.**

The forecasts for Strategy 2 appear to have been based **only on the outcome forecast** by the Marketing Director. However there are various uncertainties relating to his figures that forecasts should have taken into account. How can the Marketing Director be sure that the **demand for each deal** will be as predicted? What are the chances of a **buyback at greater than current market value** under Deal 2? What are the **chances of customer default** under Deal 3, something that is not possible under Strategy 1?

Cash flow patterns

Strategy 1 involves **higher initial marketing expenditure,** which may be significant if JDM is facing tight liquidity over the next few months. The **first receipts** should be received quicker under Strategy 2 than Strategy 1. However all the receipts will have been received under Strategy 1 by the end of this year, whereas £25,000 per apartment is due under Strategy 2 Deal 3, and Deal 2 may involve a buyback sometime over the next five years. The **greater length of time to settle payments due this year** under Strategy 1 may also make it more feasible for purchasers than the requirements to settle within weeks.

Complexity of strategies

Strategy 1 offers a **simple package** to buyers that should be easy to market and understand. The different possibilities under Strategy 2 may **confuse buyers** although it may increase JDM's chances of selling all the properties if one of the deals proves particularly appealing.

Impact of economic conditions

If the building industry is expected to come out of recession soon, this may make Strategy 1 more viable, as if JDM **cannot sell the apartments initially**, eventually it will be able to in the future at increased prices. However financing the increased working capital until the apartments are sold may be problematic under current conditions. If customers expect the **deflation in house prices to continue** for some time, they may wait until they believe that the market price has reached its lowest level before buying.

Economic conditions over the next five years may make it difficult for JDM to **fund the buybacks** should buyers choose Strategy 2 Deal 2 and exercise their options. However the **protection offered to buyers** under each of the deals may make Strategy 2 much more appealing in the current climate.

(b) Factors influencing strategy

Risk appetite

JDM's directors should take into account what they have decided **acceptable risks and risk levels** are, and their attitudes towards **risk levels versus return levels.** If the directors are risk-seeking, then arguably they will choose Strategy 1 as it offers the possibility of maximising returns. If they are risk-averse, then Strategy 2 may be chosen on the grounds that its expected net present value is higher, and its risks may not be significantly, if at all, higher.

Information risk

The directors will also consider the information supporting the predictions for each strategy. In particular they need to review the **market research** supporting Strategy 1 and the **evidence supporting the Marketing Director's** expectations in relation to Strategy 2, also the **strengths of the market forecasts** (if forecasts are wrong and prices fall more than expected or for longer than expected, there will be a loss under Strategy 2, Deal 2). If more customers than expected take up Strategy 2, Deal 3 the board will need some evidence of **customers' long-term creditworthiness**.

Recommendation

I recommend that the board adopts Strategy 1.

Reasons for recommendation

Suitable

The greater **simplicity** of Strategy 1 makes it a more suitable strategy. Purchasers may struggle to decide which the best option for them is, and the numbers choosing each deal may differ from the Marketing Director's estimate. Strategy 2 also requires JDM to commit to outcomes with significant future uncertainties.

Acceptable

Maximising revenue in a time of recession is clearly acceptable, and Strategy 1 offers a 70% chance of doing so. It is not the worst case scenario that JLS will receive £0. If property prices eventually rise as expected, then consumers may wish to buy the apartments in future. There is also an option to delay in the decision. The board **can reconsider their strategy** if the properties don't sell.

Feasible

The **significant marketing expenditure** relating to Strategy 1 does not appear to threaten JDM's liquidity.

(c) Memorandum

To: Board
From: Accountant
Subject: Risk management process
Date: 29 September 20X4

The purpose of this memorandum is to set out a **more formal risk management process** for JDM to establish.

Risk appetite

The board should first establish risk appetite, the **attitude to risks** and the relationship between **risk and return**. This may be determined by the risks directors feel comfortable taking or shareholder views. It will be affected by significant environmental issues such as the current recession. The board should ensure that risk appetite is directly **related to their business strategy**. It should feed into JDM's policies and procedures.

Establishment of risk management process

Formal systems for **monitoring and managing risk** need to be established. These systems require clear **board support**, and also **information and training** being provided to managers and staff to ensure that they operate effectively.

Responsibilities for risk management process

Specifying responsibilities is also a key part of establishing the risk management process. These include **responsibilities for monitoring the overall process** that the board, risk committee and the risk management function assume. It also includes establishing who is responsible for **controlling risks on a day-to-day basis**. The **risk register** should set out who is responsible for managing specific risks.

Risk identification

Risk management processes need to **identify what specific risks JDM faces.** JDM's board of the company also needs to be aware that the risks will change over time, so it must be on the lookout for new risks, for example those arising from more stringent building requirements or new health and safety legislation.

Risk assessment

Risk involves the use of various procedures to assess **the nature of the risk** and the **consequences** of the risk materialising. For a downside risk, the extent of any loss depends on:

(i)   The **probability of the outcome of the loss making event**, and
(ii)   The **size of the loss in the event that the risk crystallises** – that is occurs

The assessment may also cover the **expected loss**, the **probability that losses will occur** and the **largest predictable loss**.

Risk profiling

Risk profiling involves **mapping different risks** in terms of the **frequency** that they will crystallise, and the **severity** of the outcome if they do. Where the probability of the outcome is remote and the actual loss small, then no action may be taken regarding that risk. However, a high probability of the event occurring and potentially large losses will mean that serious risk management measures are required.

Risk management measures

Measures taken will vary depending on the risk:

*   **Abandonment/avoidance** of risks with high likelihood of occurring and serious consequences if they do occur – for example failing to sell any properties in a development in an unpopular area.
*   **Transfer**, for example by insurance, risks that have little chance of occurring, but will have serious consequences if they do materialise, for example major damage to properties whilst they are being built.
*   **Control** measures to reduce risks that are likely to materialise, but with limited consequences if they do, for example delays in construction.
*   **Acceptance** of risks with insignificant consequences, and little possibility of materialising.

Risk reporting

JDM's board needs to **establish a system of risk reporting.** Internally the frequency of reporting will depend on the significance of the risks, with key risks being monitored daily or weekly, less significant risks being monitored monthly or quarterly. There also needs to be a system for reporting to higher levels of management risks that are not being managed well. A key element of this is **residual risk reporting**, reviewing the risk exposure remaining after risk management activities have been implemented.

I hope these suggestions are helpful; please contact me if you need further information.

3 LXY

Text references. Chapters 1, 2 and 15.

Top tips. A good example of a question spanning strategic and operational risks.

Easy marks. The responsibilities of risk management and internal staff are likely to be examined quite frequently, so (c) should have been straightforward, particularly also as no application to the scenario was required.

Examiner's comments. Students generally scored well in (a) and (b), suggesting a wide variety of relevant risks.

In (c) students could describe the roles of the two functions, but struggled to come up with suggestions on how to maintain their separate effectiveness.

Marking scheme

			Marks
(a)	Choice of suitable risk categories – 1 mark per distinct reasonable category	3	
	Identification of risks that are reasonable for the category chosen and the company described in the scenario – 1 mark per risk	3	
	1 mark per control that relates to risk identified and is appropriate for the company. Up to two controls per risk	6	
			12
(b)	1 mark per reasonable risk related to the new service max	2	
	1 mark per control that relates to risk	2	
			4
(c)	1 mark for each relevant point about roles of functions max	4	
	Up to 2 marks for methods of maintaining separate effectiveness max	6	
	max		9
			25

(a)

Top tips. Two obvious categories in (a) are strategic and operational risks; the answer identifies the COSO ERM model as the source of the third category, compliance. You could also have chosen reporting from the COSO model. Alternatively other classifications of risk include regulatory, health and safety and financial. Given that there are only 3 marks in (a) your justification needs to be short, but you do need at least a sentence on each category.

The best way to plan (a) (ii) would be to choose the category that generates the most risks, bearing in mind that you not only have to discuss the risks, but recommend how they might be controlled. We've chosen operational risks as that seems to us to generate a lot of ideas, but we have listed alternative suggestions for other categories of risk.

(i) The three categories chosen are three categories in the COSO enterprise risk management model.

Strategic – business

Strategic risks are the **risks of volatility in profits** caused by the decisions the directors take about the business activities in which LXY is involved. Taking the wrong strategic decisions, such as deciding to **operate unprofitable routes**, can threaten LXY's existence in the long-term.

Operational

Operational risks are the risks arising from the **day-to-day activities** of LXY. If they are not managed effectively, they can result in significant costs over time, or lost revenue if buses are delayed or cancelled.

Compliance – strategic non-business

Compliance risks are the risks arising from **non-compliance with legislation or other obligations**, such as the contract to provide bus services. LXY should take these risks very seriously, as non-compliance could mean the company being fined heavily or stopped from running buses.

(ii) Operational risks

Bus breakdown or accidents

If buses break down or have accidents, LXY faces loss of revenue, customer dissatisfaction and sanctions for breaching its contract. Measures to limit this risk include:

- **A programme of regular inspection and maintenance** so that the engines, tyres are kept in good condition, and **ceasing to operate buses** once they reach a **certain age**
- Having **spare buses and staff available** so that buses that break down can be substituted as quickly as possible. Alternatively **hire contracts** for staff and vehicles may be cheaper and just as effective.

Weather disruption to long-distance routes

Poor weather may cause delays or cancellations, particularly to the national routes that LXY operates, resulting in **lost revenue** from not operating the routes or **customer refunds** on late journeys. Measures to limit this risk include:

- **Monitoring weather and road conditions**, also vehicle locations by radio or mobile phone
- **Building slack into bus timetables** to allow for delays at certain times, and having **contingency plans** to operate buses on **alternative routes** if some routes are particularly prone to delay

Poor driver performance

There may be **delays to return journeys on national routes**, and hence customer dissatisfaction, caused by drivers who have stayed away overnight not taking the return journey out on time. Measures to limit this risk include:

- **Making alarm calls** to drivers to ensure that they are awake and **having the driver check in** to central control before he takes the return journey out
- **Surprise inspections** to check buses are departing on time and **disciplinary action** against drivers who consistently take buses out late

Alternative solutions

We summarise below possible risks and controls for other categories of risk:

Risks	Control
Strategic	
Choosing unprofitable routes	<ul><li>Detailed management accounting information about profitability</li><li>Forecasting of likely future trends in passenger traffic</li></ul>
Competition from other transport providers	<ul><li>Obtaining intelligence about plans of other providers</li><li>Sensitivity analysis of alternative strategies to combat competition</li></ul>
Losing the contract	<ul><li>Reporting of breaches of contract terms to senior management.</li><li>Liaison with key stakeholders (Danon local government, passengers)</li><li>Customer complaint scheme and compensation for customers whose journeys are cancelled or delayed</li></ul>

Risks	Control
Operational	
Driver fraud by carrying extra passengers/freight/luggage	• References for all new drivers • Spot checks on buses
Compliance	
Breaching regulations about the maintenance of buses	• Regular maintenance programme • Service records and testing
Breaching regulations about driver training, licensing or hours	• Training programmes • Checks on police database • Time records, drivers clocking in tacographs
Breaching health and safety regulations – access, facilities, fire protection	• Staff training and manuals • Employment of health and safety specialists • Spot checks of buses by inspectors • Inspection of facilities • Disciplinary action
Breaching environmental regulations on emissions	• Regular vehicle maintenance • Emission monitoring
Failing to fulfil the requirements of the contract	• Monitoring of potential problems, eg bad weather • Spare drivers and buses/hire contracts
Reporting	
Incorrect decisions because of poor quality information	• Detailed breakdown of information from different routes • Information covering qualitative details such as customer satisfaction as well as financial data
Failure to report all income received	• Segregation of ticket issuing from maintenance of records • Reconciliation of passenger numbers with ticket records
Incorrect external reporting of results	• Qualified accounts staff • Internal audit function/audit committee review

(b)

> **Top tips.** (b) offers opportunities to go over time. It's only worth four marks, which means that you would get one mark for the risk and one mark for describing how it could be managed, so just two risks plus good suggestions about how they should be managed should generate maximum marks. It's rather a pity that more marks were not allocated to this part.

Breaches of food hygiene regulations

LXY may suffer fines if it is found to have breached hygiene regulations, even if the café owner is **ultimately responsible**.

LXY should ensure that the food and drink the café owner supplies is **regularly checked for quality** by its internal audit function and it has **sufficient storage facilities** for food and drink on buses with overnight stops. Staff responsible for supplying the food and drink during the journey should be given **appropriate training in food hygiene**.

Failure to deliver promised quality

Customers will be **dissatisfied**, and may **demand refunds**, if the food and drink promised by LXY for the journey is not delivered by the café owner.

The **contract** with the café owner should specify strictly what he will provide for each journey. If he fails to reach the standards demanded, LXY should **reduce the amount** he is paid, or make him **liable for any refunds to dissatisfied customers**.

Alternative solutions

You would also have scored marks if you had discussed the following risks and controls.

Damage to vehicles

Spillages of food and drink may cause **damage to buses** and **inconvenience passengers**.

Food and drink should be kept in **secure accommodation** which minimises the risks of leakages. Staff should be trained appropriately in **handling food and drink**. Coaches may need to be modified so that passengers have **enough space** to put their food and drink down safely.

Cafe owner ceasing to trade

If the cafe owner suddenly ceases to trade, LXY will not be able to supply the food and drink it has promised to customers.

LXY may be able to take out insurance against this possibility. The board should also have a **contingency plan** in place, **identifying possible alternative suppliers** so that they can be asked to **substitute quickly** if necessary.

(c)

Top tips. The main point to get across in the first part of (c) is that risk management is primarily responsible for design and implementation, internal audit for confirmation and review. Not auditing one's own work is an ethical, as well as an effectiveness, point.

Risk management

Objectives

The risk management function has responsibility for **implementing the objectives** of risk management that the board and audit and risk committees have decided.

Role

Risk management will be responsible for **building a risk aware culture** throughout the organisation by **information provision and training**. Risk management will provide **guidelines on overall risk policy** and **coordinate the various functional activities that deal with risks.**

Risk management will also be responsible for **designing and reviewing risk analysis procedures and risk response processes**. They should ensure not only their **recommendations** for improvements, but the recommendations of the board, board committees and internal audit functions are **implemented.**

Internal audit

Objectives

Internal audit will be responsible for **confirming** that appropriate risk management systems are being implemented, and that **risks associated with major business objectives** are being **managed effectively.**

Role

Internal auditors will be looking for evidence that risk management and internal control systems will be **able to take effective steps to counter major risks**. They will also review whether the systems are **working as they are supposed to work**. This includes **reviewing the activities of the risk management function itself**. Internal audit will be responsible for making **recommendations for improvements,** but will not be responsible for implementing these improvements. They should be acting in accordance with **internal auditing standards** as well as the requirements of the organisation.

Maintaining separate effectiveness of both functions

Different staff for risk management and internal audit

Although staff work for a combined department, managers can try to organise the department so that as far as possible **different staff** work on risk management and internal audit activities.

Different training and staff development programmes

Staff could follow **different training programmes** and **train for different qualifications**.

Supervision and management

Different line managers should manage risk management staff and internal audit staff. Risk management staff and managers should report to the **risk committee**, internal audit to the **audit committee**.

Restrictions on what staff can audit

Where staff have both internal audit and risk management responsibilities, they should **not be allowed to review systems in specific functional areas** that they themselves have **designed or implemented**.

4 A and B

Text references. Chapter 1 on risks for (a) and Chapter 7 on control measures for (c), though other chapters are relevant (Chapter 5 contains material on the impact of organisational structure, Chapter 6 on research and development).

Top tips. This is a good example of a question where material from all three Strategic level papers is relevant, also material from lower level papers. Remember that Performance Strategy is in the management accounting pillar of the exam structure so you will need to remember what you learnt in P1 and P2, but this questions also illustrates the need to retain financial accounting knowledge from F1 and F2.

Interestingly the question does not tell us what the two companies actually manufacture.

Easy marks. If you remembered what you have learnt in F3, (b) should be an easy 4 marks.

Examiner's comments. Most students answered this question reasonably well, although some failed to make the link to strategy. Some students' discussion of pros and cons in (b) was limited.

(a)

Top tips. (a) may appear to belong on E3 rather than this paper. However before you start bringing in all the E2 and E3 theories, you must remember that this paper focuses on risks and controls. This should lead you to read the question as saying what do the strategic decisions the boards take on structure, markets and location imply for the risk profile, the nature and level of risks that the two companies bear. It is a good example of what we stressed in the front pages about demonstrating strategic awareness.

(i)   Company structure

The decisions the boards make on company structure will have a particular influence on the following issues.

Effectiveness of risk management

The extent to which decision-making is diversified can determine the ways in which risks are managed. The more autonomy local managers have, the more they are likely to develop **differing risk appetites** and also **differing ways of managing risks**. A also has to ensure that effective control is maintained over the **central functions** of treasury and research and development. In B's case this is complicated by distribution being run as a joint venture. The joint venture partner may have attitudes to risk management and the relationship between risk and return with which B's central management differs, and the partner's attitude may influence the joint venture's activities.

Cooperation between subsidiaries

The board of A's decision to structure its operations geographically rather than by product indicates that it believes that there is a low risk of **production inefficiencies** caused by lack of co-ordination and co-operation between the different subsidiaries. A's board appears to believe that running the company using autonomous subsidiaries for different parts of its operations will not result in dysfunctional behaviour.

Performance measurement systems

The significance of the structure will depend on the performance measurement systems used as means of management control, and whether these are appropriate. **Profit centres, cost or investment centres, return on capital employed** and **residual income** all have advantages and disadvantages, but choosing the most appropriate method should reduce organisational risks such as non-congruent behaviour by subsidiaries.

(ii)   ### Market types

The type of markets the companies operate in will particularly influence the following risks:

Competition risks

A's greater involvement in the business to business market appears to have had the consequence that it is more dependent than B on demand from one or two **large customers**. This decision may mean that it is **less exposed to the risk of competition** since some potential competitors may not be big enough to service customers of such a size. However the **consequences** of losing either or both of its large customers are likely to be **more damaging to A** than B losing one of its customers other than perhaps the Canadian customer. Similarly the opportunities the two companies have to gain customers from competitors may differ significantly.

Customer risks

The risks of losing customers due to **inadequate service** in the different types of market may differ because of the differing expectations of customers in each market. Evidence suggests that B2B customers have increasingly demanding expectations of what suppliers should offer in terms of use of electronic links and local customer support.

Liquidity risks

Clearly loss of a customer will have a much more **violent effect on A's liquidity** than B. However B may face problems associated with a **higher cost base** necessary to maintain sales, for example the need for advertising spend with uncertain returns to attract more customers.

Information technology controls

B faces costs associated with maintaining an effective on-line presence. These include **security and data integrity risks**. They also include the risks arising from the **need to meet changing expectations of customers**, such as the need to enhance the website to reduce response and transaction times.

(iii)   ### Location

Choice of location may particularly impact on the following risks.

Political risk

Choosing to produce in China indicates that B's board is prepared to tolerate a possibly significant level of **political risk**. Political links between China and the USA are sensitive, and B's links with its subsidiaries may be **forcibly disrupted by the US government** if relations deteriorate. There is also the risk of a change in China to a regime that is **less welcoming to links with western companies**.

Legal risk

Company A may be more likely to suffer **legal compliance costs** in areas such as health and safety to fulfil statutory and regulatory requirements that risks be minimised. The manufacturing and assembly activities of Company B may be subject to a less rigorous regime in China. However the fact that Company A is obliged to adhere to more rigorous regulations may mean that it is **less likely to suffer a major health and safety breakdown** which a strict regime is designed to prevent.

Transportation risk

Both companies appear to be tolerating the risks of transport links being disrupted, as production and sales **take place in different countries**. Company A is possibly more likely to **suffer disruption at an earlier stage**, since the major stages of the production process take place in different continents. However B is more likely to **suffer distribution disruption**, since it is distributing from China to the USA whereas much of A's sales are distributed from the UK to elsewhere in Europe.

Alternative solutions

You would also have scored marks if you had discussed the following risks:

Infrastructure risk

Company B seems to be tolerating the risk that operations may be disrupted by problems with the **Chinese infrastructure**. In Autumn 2006 it was reported that Western companies that were manufacturing in China toys for the Christmas market were facing the risk of being unable to fulfil demand, as problems with the electricity supply had led to electricity rationing and factories only being able to work a certain number of hours per week.

Foreign exchange risks

Both companies make the bulk of their sales in one area, and both will suffer **foreign exchange risks** that are not mitigated by diversification. A will suffer them on sales for which it receives European currencies, B will suffer them on **production costs in China.** Both may be vulnerable to **longer-term economic risks** in the geographical markets in which they sell, and B may also be subject to rising production costs in China as the Chinese economy develops.

Reputation risk

Company B appears to have accepted a risk that its reputation may be damaged because it uses Chinese labour for manufacturing. It may receive **adverse publicity** for using underpaid labour and taking jobs away from the American economy, resulting in consumer boycotts.

(b)

Top tips. (b) is a very standard question on the key decisions about the treasury function. 4 marks is not a very generous mark allocation and it would be easy to run over time on this part. The question requirement **Compare and contrast** means that the best answer structure is a point-by-point comparison under the same headings.

Areas other than those covered in our answer that would have gained you credit include centralisation increasing opportunities for fraud and demotivating local staff, decentralisation meaning greater responsiveness to local needs.

Staff risk

Company B may be exposed to a greater risk of staff errors; the local divisions may not be able to employ staff with the **expertise necessary** to handle complex treasury issues. As the treasury function is centralised in Company A, resources can be focused on employing treasury specialists and the duplication that decentralising activities will involve should be avoided.

Speculation risk

The recognition of treasury operations as profit making activities implies that treasury activities may be undertaken for the sake of creating profits. **Trading in instruments** such as **derivatives speculatively** implies a **higher risk tolerance** of treasury activities on Company A's part. By contrast in B, treasury is a **service function**; local treasury functions support the activities of local operations and are more likely to use derivatives as a means of **minimising the financial risks** associated with trading.

Organisational risk

Centralisation in A provides a means of exercising **better control through use of standardised procedures** and **pooling and netting; monitoring of operational risks** is likely to be easier if operations are concentrated in one place. Distance may make controls in B weaker. However If the department in Company A's is to be a true profit centre, then **market prices** should be charged for its services to other departments. It may be difficult to decide realistic prices, and this may cause disputes.

Currency risk

Foreign currency risk management is likely to be improved by treasury centralisation. A's central treasury department can **match** foreign currency income earned by one subsidiary with expenditure in the same currency by another subsidiary. In this way, the risk of losses on adverse exchange rate changes can be avoided without the expense of forward exchange contracts or other 'hedging' (risk-reducing) methods. However if wrong decisions are made, the amounts at risk will be greater in A than B.

(c)

> **Top tips**. In (c) you were asked to give three controls for Company A or three controls for Company B; we have given three for both companies to cover both possibilities. The question is looking for performance measures that indicate risk levels. What is important is that you don't just state the measure, you also explain what it is and you **justify using the data in the scenario**, why the measure is important.
>
> Note the stress in the question requirements on taking into account current structure and size. Markers will be alert for recommendations that are unrealistic for the company you choose, and will not reward them. You should mark your answers against those criteria, as obviously there are other controls that you could have included that we haven't mentioned.
>
> Other possibilities for A include:
>
> - Financial – transfer pricing, responsibility accounting in subsidiaries
> - Non-financial quantitative – sales targets in different market segments
> - Non-financial qualitative – repeat business
>
> Other possibilities for B include:
>
> - Financial – profit margin per customer, on-line sales revenue
> - Non-financial quantitative – % of sales on-line
> - Non-financial qualitative – mystery shopper

Company A

Financial

A major task of A's treasury department is to manage foreign exchange risk, so therefore A needs to measure what its exposure to financial price risks might be. **Value at risk** calculations indicate the maximum loss that A may incur due to normal market movements in a set period of time with a set probability. The risk of losses greater than the value at risk should under normal market conditions be very small and hence be tolerated by A.

Non-financial quantitative

Monitoring and targeting production lead and waiting times will be key indicators of whether A risks failing to fulfil customer demands. Because of the complications of having manufacturing and assembly on different continents, data is needed on whether **target times for manufacturing and assembly** are being fulfilled, and where any delays are occurring that impact on other stages of the production process.

Non-financial qualitative

A is clearly **dependent on sales from two major customers** and therefore requires controls that will establish as quickly as possible whether these customers are dissatisfied. **Feedback** should therefore be obtained on a regular basis, both by meetings between A's and customers' senior management, and those on both sides who have the main responsibility for maintaining the relationship. These customers should also be able to communicate concerns between meetings, possibly with named managers who are not normally involved in maintaining the relationship. The board should **review** on a regular basis the **feedback** obtained along with **quantitative data** of those customers' demand and how long it has taken to fulfil their requirements.

Company B

Financial

Benchmarking B's cost data against cost data about major competitors will give an indication of how great the threat from competitors is. If competitors have a **high fixed cost structure** then they are likely to respond aggressively to threats to sales volumes; high operational gearing will mean that falls in sales revenues will significantly decrease profits. If competitors appear to have **high unit costs**, there may be a low risk that they can respond effectively to price cuts; this may be a particularly significant issue for B if it has located in China because it wishes to minimise its own unit costs.

Non-financial quantitative

Monitoring and targeting delivery time of completed products is a key measure of risk for B. The transport of goods to different continents may mean that there is a significant risk of delivery delays, and the fact that distribution is handled by a joint venture may mean B is able to exercise less control over it. The directors of B will wish to **measure actual delivery times** against those **budgeted** and also try to **benchmark delivery times against those of competitors**. Possibly cost advantages B gains through manufacturing in China need to be weighed against the risks that competitors will be able to provide a speedier, more reliable delivery service.

Non-financial qualitative

Research and development appears to be a significant area for B; its customer base is more diverse so it is possibly more dependent on new ideas. B's board needs to monitor carefully whether research and development efforts are being wasted, and the possibility that projects are late, over budget or have not delivered the planned benefits. A **post-implementation review** of projects that have been completed is a significant control to assess:

- How **projects performed** against plans
- Whether the R and D department complied with **internal guidelines**
- Whether R and D fulfilled the **strategic objectives** laid down by the board
- Whether **board monitoring** of projects whilst they were going on was regular and rigorous enough

Actions taken as a result of the recommendations of the review should enhance the value given by R and D and also may suggest stronger board monitoring to identify earlier on and terminate R and D activities that will not deliver significant benefits.

5 Doctors' practice

Text references. Chapter 1 discusses controls and general risk issues. Chapter 15 describes different types of audit.

Top tips. Our answers to (b) and (c) are rather shorter than some of the other parts for equivalent marks in this paper. In the exam you may well come across some disparities in the length of answer required to obtain a good mark.

Easy marks. (c) should be easiest, as it's a general part not related to the circumstances described in the question.

Examiner's comments. This question was unpopular and poorly done. In (a) students showed a lack of understanding of what a doctor's practice does, and demonstrated a lack of knowledge of CIMA's risk management cycle or other risk management models. (b) was well done but many answers to (c) were very bad indeed, with students demonstrating a lack of knowledge of systems or other types of auditing.

(a)

(i) Additional risks

A number of additional risks arise from the introduction of the new facility, including the following.

Operational risks

Surgical equipment failure

The practice may face threats to its income through **failures of its surgical equipment**, meaning that it cannot provide surgical procedures whilst the equipment is unavailable.

Storage facilities failure

Environmental failures in the storage facilities for equipment and drugs may also lead to a **loss of income** if surgical procedures cannot be provided. The practice may also face the **costs of replacing the equipment** and drugs that have been contaminated.

Alternative solutions

You would also have gained marks if you discussed the following operational risks:

Security

The additional equipment and drugs stored may make the practice more vulnerable to theft.

Transportation risks

The blood and samples taken may be contaminated by storage facilities problems at the surgery, and also by deterioration during transportation. This may result in misdiagnosis of illness and hence the costs of giving patients the wrong treatment.

High demand

High demand at certain times of the year may mean that the practice loses income through being unable to meet the demand, or incurs increased costs through having to pay for extra medical and nursing care.

Hospital delays

The practice may lose income through not being able to provide care because of delays in testing blood and samples at the local hospital.

Staff

Existing staff may not have the collective skills necessary to operate the new unit. If new staff are employed, there may be a risk of staff dissatisfaction and hence retention problems with existing staff if new staff are employed on better terms.

Effect on existing care

The resources required by the new facilities may mean less resources are available for existing work; hence the areas of care currently provided may suffer and income from these be threatened.

Non-business risks

Legal risks

Providing more procedures may increase the risk of problems arising during treatment, and hence losses through the **costs of fighting or settling negligence claims**.

Financial risks

The new **facilities** will have to be **financed**. As the practice buildings will need to be extended, the partners will have to borrow, probably from a bank. The partners, not the practice, will have **ultimate liability** for this debt. The partners may face problems in **meeting any finance costs** that it has to incur, particularly if the return on investment is not as good as forecast. Financing the investment may mean funds are lacking when required for other purposes, such as buying out a retiring partner.

Business risks

Practice development risks

The practice may not achieve the income growth expected if the **standard of treatment is believed to be lower** than would be available in the hospital, or if because of operational difficulties **patients were forced to wait longer** for treatment than they would in a hospital.

Regulatory risks

If shortcomings arise in the treatment provided, the practice's **regulatory body** may **intervene** and prevent the practice providing the surgical procedures it currently wishes to offer.

(ii)   Uses of risk management model

Iterative model

The most important feature of models such as CIMA's is that it demonstrates how risk management is a **continual process** and experience gained from carrying out all stages can impact upon all other stages of the cycle. Review by the **risk manager** or all of the doctors of the **effectiveness of risk management** needs to be built into the process.

Organisation– wide application

Models are used to assess **organisation-wide risks** and also **specific process or unit risks**. They also are used to assess the **interaction** between risks.

Logical process

Models show that risk management is a logical process, taking the organisation through **initial risk identification,** then **identification of events** that may cause **risks to crystallise, assessment** of **how great losses** might be and in the light of these how best to **respond to risks**. This will help identify who should be responsible for which aspects of the risk management cycle.

Role of monitoring and feedback

Models emphasise the importance of **monitoring risk management procedures** and controls once they are in place. The feedback from this monitoring will **impact upon future risk assessments** and also lead to **continuous improvements in processes**, following the **principles of feedforward control**.

Decision-making

Models emphasise that the results of all stages of the risk management process should impact upon **the organisation's decision-making process** and consequently **affect strategy** and also **the appetite the organisation has for risk**. The decisions taken as a result of this will in turn feed through to the risk assessment and management processes, modifying the views taken on **key risks** and the best ways to **respond to them**.

(b)

Risk appetite

Risk appetite is the amount of risk that the team of doctors **as a whole** is prepared to **accept in exchange for returns** (the clientele effect). The new arrangements here are expected to **increase income**, and the risk appetite defines what risk levels will be acceptable in exchange for the increased income. Risk appetite also infers that the practice is willing to accept that risk has a downside as well as an upside, and the consequences of both are culturally acceptable.

Risk appetite decisions

In this situation, one of the senior partners in the practice would act as the risk manager and be responsible for analysing risk and recommending what **acceptable risk levels** might be in the **changed circumstances** for each of the major risks. However as the decision results from a major change in what the practice is doing, the recommendations should certainly be approved by a majority of the doctors, and preferably be unanimous. If risks materialise, it could have **significant adverse financial and reputational consequences** for all the partners. The practice may also have to act within **constraints** imposed by government or regulator, which effectively limit the maximum amount of risk the practice can bear.

(c)

Purposes of systems-based auditing

Systems-based auditing focuses on the **overall functioning of the organisation's systems**. The level of risk of each of the systems that the organisation operates is assessed, the resources required to audit each system are determined and a decision is taken on how often each system should be audited.

Usefulness of systems-based auditing

Systems-based auditing concentrates on:

(i)   **Procedures** in place to **achieve an organisation's objectives**
(ii)   **Controls** that are in place to **manage the risks** that threaten the achievement of objectives

The systems-based audit will assess whether the **controls and procedures** in place are **appropriate** in the light of the **objectives management has decided** and the **risk management procedures** that managers have adopted. It then tests whether procedures and controls are operating effectively.

Limitations of systems-based audits

A major limitation of systems-based auditing can be a **lack of focus** on the **underlying risk-taking decisions** and **risk management framework**. A risk-based approach would assess whether the risk management processes are sufficient to **assess and manage risk.** A risk-based audit would question the **appropriateness of each system** as a means of managing risk and would question whether the **assessment of each system's risk** on which systems-based audits are based was itself appropriate. Audit of operational systems therefore needs to be combined with an **audit of the risk management system** itself.

6 HOOD

Text references. Chapter 1, with Chapter 14 also being particularly relevant on IT risks.

Top tips. A definition of a key subject relating to the answer can add value; however don't just repeat the requirement. Splitting the risks between operational and strategic risks is a good way of identifying the most important risks. Other frameworks may be used, although it will be important to ensure that the risks identified are clearly related to the situation outlined in the scenario. Enterprise Strategy knowledge about the influences on demand is helpful here.

In (a) where you're asked to identify the risks, you should focus on what causes them to arise. In (b) evaluate requires assessment of financial consequences.

For (b) if you are faced with a question of the format:

Part (a) Identify risks

Part (b) Evaluate effects of identified risks and recommend what the organisation can do to mitigate them, ensure your answer plan shows consistency in format. Your answer to (b) needs to be a mirror image of your answer to (a).

Don't worry also if you haven't thought of all the possible risks we have. Remember a score of 15 out of 25 is a comfortable pass. It's safer from the viewpoint of passing to cover each risk in reasonable depth, making reference to the scenario rather than just briefly listing all possible risks. A long list of risks without any explanation carries the possibility of obtaining no marks as you haven't shown why what you said is relevant.

Easy marks. Evidence suggests most students find it easier to identify risks than to come up with ways of reducing and controlling them. However to improve your chances of passing, you must be able to come up with ways of tackling risks that are realistic for the company described in the scenario.

Risk can defined as the possibility that events or results will turn out differently from is expected.

(a) The risks facing the HOOD Company are outlined below.

Operational risks

These are risks relating to the business's day-to-day operations.

(i) Accounting irregularities

The unexplained fall in gross profit in some stores may be indicative of **fraud** or **other accounting irregularities**. Low gross profit in itself may be caused by **incorrect inventory values** or loss of **sale income**. Incorrect stock levels in turn can be caused by **incorrect inventory counting** or **actual stealing of inventory** by employees. Similarly, **loss of sales income** could result from **accounting errors** or employees **fraudulently removing cash** from the business rather than recording it as a sale.

(ii) Delays in inventory ordering

Although inventory information is collected using the EPOS system, **re-ordering of inventory takes a significant amount of time**. Transferring data to head office for central purchasing may result in some discounts on purchase. However, the average 10 days before inventory is received at the store could result in **the company running out of inventory**.

(iii) Event

HOOD may be vulnerable to losses in a **warehouse fire**.

Strategic risks

These risks relate to factors affecting Hood's ability to trade in the longer term.

(i) Production

The possibility of sunlight making some of HOOD Company's products potentially dangerous may give rise to **loss of sales** also inventory recall.

(ii)   Corporate reputation

Risks in this category relate to the overall **perception of HOOD in the marketplace** as a supplier of (hopefully) good quality clothing. However, this reputation could be damaged by **problems with the manufacturing process** and a consequent high level of returns.

(iii)   Macro-economic risk

The company is dependent on one market sector and vulnerable to competition in that sector.

(iv)   Product demand

The most important social change is probably a **change in fashion**. HOOD has not changed its product designs for 4 years indicating some lack of investment in this area. Given that fashions tend to change more frequently than every four years, HOOD may experience falling sales as customers seek new designs for their outdoor clothing. HOOD may also be vulnerable to **seasonal variations** in demand.

(b)   The potential effects of the risks on HOOD and methods of overcoming those risks are explained below.

Operational risks

(i)   Accounting irregularities

The potential effect on HOOD is **loss of income** either from stock not being available for sale or cash not being recorded. The overall amount is unlikely to be significant as employees would be concerned about being caught stealing.

The risk can be minimised by introducing additional controls including the necessity of producing a **receipt for each sale** and the **agreement of cash received** to the **till roll** by the shop manager. Loss of stock may be identified by more frequent stock checks in the stores or closed-circuit television.

(ii)   Delays in inventory ordering

The potential effect on HOOD is **immediate loss of sales** as customers cannot purchase the garments that they require. In the longer term, if stock outs become more frequent, **customers may not visit** the store because they believe stock will not be available.

The risk can be minimised by letting the stores **order goods directly** from the manufacturers, using an extension of the EPOS system. Costs incurred relate to the provision of Internet access for the shops and possible increase in cost of goods supplied. However, this may be acceptable compared to overall loss of reputation.

(iii)   Event

The main effects of a warehouse fire will be a **loss of inventory** and the incurring of costs to replace it. There will also be a **loss of sales** as the inventory is not there to fulfil customer demand, and perhaps also a loss of subsequent sales as customers continue to shop elsewhere.

Potential losses of sales could be avoided by **holding contingency inventory** elsewhere, and losses from the fire could be reduced by **insurance**.

Strategic risks

(i)   Production

The effect on HOOD is the possibility of having to **reimburse customers** and the loss of income from the product until the problems are resolved.

The risk can be minimised by HOOD taking the claim seriously and **investigating its validity**, rather than ignoring it. For the future, **guarantees** should be obtained from suppliers to confirm that products are safe and **insurance** taken out against possible claims from customers for damage or distress.

(ii)   Corporate reputation

As well as **immediate losses of contribution from products** that have been returned, HOOD faces the consequence of loss of future sales from customers who believe their products no longer offer quality. Other clothing retailers have found this to be very serious; a **reputation for quality**, once lost, undoubtedly **cannot easily be regained**. The potential effect of a drop in overall corporate reputation will be falling sales for HOOD, resulting eventually in a **going concern problem**.

HOOD can guard against this loss of reputation by **enhanced quality control procedures**, and introducing processes such as **total quality management**.

(iii)   Macro-economic risk

The potential effect on HOOD largely depends on HOOD's **ability to provide an appropriate selection of clothes**. It is unlikely that demand for coats etc. will fall to zero, so some sales will be expected. However, an **increase in competition** may result in **falling sales,** and without some diversification, this will automatically affect the overall sales of HOOD.

HOOD can minimise the risk in two ways: by **diversifying into other areas**. Given that the company sells outdoor clothes, then commencing sales of other outdoor goods such as camping equipment may be one way of diversifying risk. It can also look to **reduce operational gearing**, fixed cost as a proportion of turnover.

(iv)   Product demand

Again the **risk of loss of demand and business to competitors** may undermine HOOD's ability to continue in business.

This risk can be minimised by having a **broad strategy** to **maintain** and **develop** the **brand** of HOOD. Not updating the product range would appear to be a mistake in this context as the brand may be devalued as products may not meet changing tastes of customers. The board must therefore allocate appropriate investment funds to updating the products and **introduce new products** to maintain the company's image.

7   VV

Text references. Chapter 3.

Top tips. Unusually the examiner uses the verb explain in both parts of (a) rather than CIMA's higher level verbs. The verb explain indicates that the answer should make clear why or how, and this is not something you can do just with single line bullet points. Underlying (a) (i) is one of the most important problems of governance, the agency problem. An important point to take away from this question is that directors and shareholders' interests may differ in terms of the risks the company should take as well as the ways in which directors should be remunerated.

One point in (a) (ii) that applies to all remuneration schemes is that if an individual element of a remuneration package is much more valuable than any other element, this could well have a dysfunctional impact on directors' behaviour. Thus ESOSs may end up being too successful in their aim of encouraging directors not to be excessively risk-averse. They could encourage directors to choose the highest risk options available. Another important issue is whether the directors believe that their ESOS will give them the rewards they feel they've earned and what they can do if it does not.

There is quite a lot of help in the scenario for (a) (ii) and most of the discussion should be based around the key features of this scheme.

(b) picks up some of the detail mentioned in the scenario, for example the simplicity of the profit-based bonus. Although the advantages appear to outnumber the disadvantages, probably the most important point discussed is how directors can manipulate a bonus based on a single measure for their own short-term ends.

Easy marks. (a) (i) is probably the most difficult part as it's the most specific.

Examiner's comments. Generally answers were good, although some gave the impression of reproducing rote learning rather than application to the scenario. Some answers to (a) ignored NPV.

(a)   (i)   How ESOSs (Executive Share Option Schemes) work

ESOSs are designed to provide incentives for directors to manage a company in a way that ensures its **share price increases.** If the share price exceeds the option exercise price at the date the options can be exercised, then directors can buy shares at less than market price. They can either then realise an immediate capital gain or retain the shares in the hope that share prices will increase further. Directors will only face an **upside risk**, because if the share price is less than the exercise price when the option expires, they will not suffer any losses.

Agency

An ESOS is a way of **aligning shareholder and manager goals.** Shareholder goals are often **focused around share price**, whereas management will often focus on **maximising their remuneration and benefits**. It should overcome the agency problem of having different owners and managers (directors), as the managers would enjoy the **benefits of ownership.**

Impact on risk-taking

Efficient investors should have a diversified portfolio. They should therefore be most concerned about the link between the **risk and return** of the investments the company makes. However directors may be more **risk-averse** than investors, as they are in VV. They may be excessively concerned with the **downside risk** of projects, fearing that they will be blamed if a project fails and they will lose their jobs. They may evaluate projects at **higher implicit rates of return** than shareholders, leading them to reject projects that shareholders would regard as acceptable. They may not therefore invest in projects that offer an acceptable combination of risk and return for shareholders. An ESOS is designed to overcome this problem, by making directors' remuneration dependent on the returns of projects and hence encouraging them to take into account the risk-return relationship.

(ii) Share price rises

The options will only become valuable if **share prices rise**. In an **efficient stock market**, the market value of a company's shares should be determined by the **long-term value of the investments** it makes. Therefore investing in projects with positive net present values should mean that the company's market value should increase. This should in turn mean that the value of share options should rise.

Long-term nature

The options cannot be exercised **until 3 years** after the date that they are offered. This will mean that directors have to be concerned with longer-term growth, rather than just focusing on the results for the next year.

Exercise on specific date

Requiring options to be **exercised on a specific date** will mean that directors have to ensure share price increases are sustained, to guarantee increases in share prices. However directors may have an **opportunity to manipulate results** and hence share prices around the date of exercise. There is also the issue that different directors will have options that mature at **different times.** This may cause disagreement amongst the directors, for example directors who have a lot of options coming up in the near future may fight plans that could cause a short-term fall in the share price.

Options lapsing on departures

Options lapsing on directors leaving the company will deter directors from departing suddenly and hence losing **potentially significant rewards.** This will help with long-term board succession planning, as the nomination committee will not need to allow for a significant possibility of directors leaving without warning.

(b) Advantages of profit-related bonuses

Link with performance

Paying a bonus based on performance means that part of directors' remuneration packages are based on what they have **achieved during the year**. Profitability figures provide a simple measure of **feedback** on performance. Directors can be **held to account** if they have failed to reach target profitability. Bonuses can vary year-by-year if performance varies. They can be used flexibly to encourage and reward performance that is not taken into account in long-term incentive schemes, but is still important. Bonuses contrast with rewarding directors solely by salaries, as salary levels are not determined by actual performance.

Clarity of disclosure

Readers of the accounts may find it **easier to understand** profit-based bonuses than the rewards conferred by share-based schemes. **Directors' motives** may be **clearer.** The amount of information disclosed about complex schemes may make their nature and scale difficult to understand.

Limitation of profit-related bonuses

The size of bonuses can be restricted to whatever **limit is considered desirable** by shareholders. Under an ESOS, where the directors' rewards depends on the difference between share price and exercise price, the maximum reward directors can earn is not limited by the company.

Disadvantages of profit-related bonuses

Manipulation of measures

Directors can **use questionable accounting policies** to distort profit. This issue would become less significant if a range of different measures was used to determine performance, so that manipulation of individual measures would have less impact. However it would then be more difficult to decide how important each measure used should be and whether the relative importance of each should vary by individual director. A scheme based on multiple measures might also be more difficult for shareholders to understand.

Encouragement of short-term outlook

Cash bonuses encourage directors to focus on **annual, short-term, performance**. This may mean their decision-making is distorted from the viewpoint of shareholders. Directors may choose shorter-term projects with quick gains, rather than projects that offer shareholders the best combination of risk and return over the longer-term.

Publicity

Large bonuses may be more likely to attract **adverse publicity** because they are more visible. They may be particularly unpopular in a poor economic climate when they are based on profits that have increased because of cutbacks in staff.

8 C

Text references. Chapters 1, 3, 5 and 6.

Top tips. The fundamental performance issue is the balancing of cost limitations and quality. Any reference to competitive culture in requirements is likely to indicate that quality or control will be undermined by partners and staff trying to maximise profitability.

(b) requires you to think how the broad principles underlying the UK Corporate Governance Code and other governance guidance can be applied outside listed companies. In fact many of the principles relating to boards – forum for long-term decision-making, aptitude of directors, breadth, role of managing director – can be applied very widely. Non-executive directors may seem excessive for a partnership like this, but remember that the wider perspective they provide and here the continuity as well.

Easy marks. Hopefully you found plenty to say about the board in (b).

Examiner's comments. Answers were generally good, though some students missed key points in the scenario.

(a) Quality of service risks

Innovation

C operates in an area of **new developments and cutting-edge techniques**. The **uncertainties** surrounded with these new areas increase the risks of errors being made.

Rejection of plans

Errors by C's staff could have a number of consequences. Firstly they could **recommend rejection of designs** that are sound. This will mean that architects' time and efforts are wasted and the clients **do not get the design that would be best for their circumstances.**

Over-specification of materials

The second error that C's staff could make is to **recommend acceptance of a design but over-specify the materials** that will be needed to implement it. This will mean that the architects' clients do not obtain value for money, although they may not be aware of this.

Under-specification of materials

C's staff might alternatively **recommend acceptance of a design that should be rejected** or under-specifying materials for that design. This could result in an **unsafe building** being constructed, ultimately with the risk of a very visible catastrophe if it cannot withstand extreme weather. Such a disaster could ruin C's reputation and leave it open to very large damages.

Impact of culture on errors

Quality metrics

In a number of ways it seems likely that the culture of C will encourage **errors or negligence** by its staff. Although selection for partnership depends partly on the ability to complete work to a high standard, quality metrics generally appear to be less important than financial success and minimising time spent.

Pressure on trainees

Trainees are expected to **show the necessary qualities** in order to be retained by C. At their level this would have to mean completing assignments as quickly as possible, although this may increase the risk of errors.

Pressure on staff

Once qualified, staff face pressure to show they are **high performers** or else they will be dismissed and **lose their high salaries.** In particular admission to partnership appears to be determined competitively. This may influence the behaviour of potential partners, ensuring that they **focus on achieving maximum profits** by reducing the time their teams spend on assignments, even though this increases the risks of cutting corners and errors being made. Their team members may be concerned with making sure that they have taken the minimum time in order to promote their own prospects, rather than being concerned with the success of the project as a whole. This may mean that they rush necessary tests or even produce fictitious results in order to avoid problems and more time being taken.

Pressures on partners

There also appears to be **peer pressure** on partners to do what is required to **deliver maximum profits.** There is no incentive for partners to promote quality if it results in time budgets not being met.

Bid standards

There appears to be a lack of guidance over the partnership on the **contents and realism of bids**. Partners seem to be **encouraged to bid aggressively** and promise deadlines that may only be met by excessively limiting the time spent.

Relationships with architects

Focusing on maintaining good relations with architects and hence continuing to obtain work from them may also influence decision-making. Partners and team leaders may be **reluctant to reject architect designs**, since it may mean that the architects use other firms, diminishing the profit opportunities for C.

(b)   Strengths

No domination

The requirement for regular rotation of committee membership and the requirement for major decisions to be subject to a whole-partnership vote, means that **a single partner or small clique of partners cannot dominate** the partnership over any length of time. This means that the members of the management committee should not be able to run the partnership for their own ends. The members are also accountable for major decisions.

Lack of remuneration

The condition that committee members are **not remunerated for their committee work** and receive the same income share as other partners means that their financial interests are **congruent with other partners**. This will avoid committee decisions being influenced by a desire to maximise their remuneration.

Experience on management committee

The requirement that every partner serves on the committee means that the partnership will include former committee members. Their **professional skills and perspective** should have been **enhanced** by being given the responsibility of managing the partnership.

Qualifications of management committee

All of committee members are engineers with significant experience within the partnership. They all should have the **necessary knowledge of the business and operational matters** that is needed for them to make an effective contribution.

Continuity on management committee

The system of three year service means that the management committee is **refreshed systematically** each year. It should avoid the situation where two or even all three members leave the committee together.

Weaknesses

Lack of aptitude

It is possible that some of the partners, although being very good engineers, **lack the strategic awareness** necessary to lead the practice well. Members of the management board need to be aware of how strategies could be developed in the longer-term, and have a wider perspective on developments in the profession and major risks.

Lack of nomination procedures

Although all partners are meant to serve on the committee, nominating members does **not appear to be done systematically**. This could cause disputes within the partnership. Partners who could contribute well to the committee may seek to avoid service for as long as possible to protect their portfolios. Partners who are able to serve because they have more time may not be as suitable for membership.

Lack of breadth

Because the board only consists of engineers, a **number of key functions**, particularly finance and marketing, are **not represented** on the board. This may mean that the board does not spend enough time considering important issues connected with these areas and lacks the expertise to come to the right decisions about them.

Lack of non-executive directors (NEDs)

Appointing one or two NEDs from outside the partnership would also **enhance the breadth of experience** of the board. The NEDs could challenge any group-think existing within the partnership. They would have the authority to advise on controversial issues, such as paying different remuneration to different partners.

Lack of motivation

Partners who find themselves obliged to serve on the management committee may **not spend sufficient time on partnership issues,** as they are not rewarded for the time that they spend on the management committee. Although they are meant to reduce their responsibility for their portfolios, there appears to be no formal mechanisms for forcing them to make an effective reduction. Some committee members may therefore retain too much work and not spend enough time on their committee duties.

Timeframe of membership

Members of the committee may focus on issues **within the timeframe of their remaining membership of the committee**, which is a maximum of three years. The committee may spend insufficient time on issues that are vital to the partnership's success in the longer-term.

Role of Managing Partner

The Managing Partner is only in office for one year. This is likely to be an **insufficient time to make an effective contribution** in various areas that a Chief Executive would normally lead, such as development of strategy and managing the risk profile of the partnership.

Determining strategy

The committee's role in developing strategy will always be limited by the requirement for all strategic decisions to be approved by a majority of the partners. This may result in a **lack of long-term decision-making**, and **lack of a consistent approach to risk appetite**, as partners vote according to their own self-interest.

9 P

Text references. Chapter 3.

Top tips. (a) is a very full question on non-executive directors covering the qualities they can bring, their role on the board and independence issues. The requirements of the question to discuss the factors for and against indicate that these may well be in conflict. Most significantly here, S clearly has the expert knowledge that T and U lack, but does not fulfil the independence criteria of governance best practice. As many codes stress the importance of the contribution of independent non-executive directors, this is a very serious drawback to appointing S.

In (b), directors' remuneration was examined in May 2010 as well as in November, and will continue to be tested frequently if controversies over arrangements appear regularly in the news. Again different factors have to be weighed up. As well as discussing incentives and shareholder concerns, you need to discuss the difficult areas of determining what the contribution of individuals actually is, and also how important different aspects of that contribution should be when determining remuneration levels.

Easy marks. If you have a good knowledge of the role and qualities of non-executive directors, you should be able to identify a lot to discuss in the scenario.

Examiner's comments. (a) was generally done well. Some students limited their marks in (b) by discussing the directors collectively rather than each director separately.

(a)   <u>S</u>

<u>Arguments for appointment</u>

<u>Knowledge of P</u>

S has **exceptionally good long-term knowledge** of P through S's involvement with the investment over 20 years. S's knowledge should mean that S can provide **expert scrutiny** of the performance of executive management.

<u>Knowledge of industry</u>

Because of S's long experience as investment analyst, S should have **wide knowledge of the industry and economy** as well as of P, although he has not worked in the manufacturing sector. This should mean that S is able to make an informed contribution to board discussions about strategy, and have the weight of knowledge to be able to challenge effectively the plans of executive directors from the perspective of an institutional investor.

<u>Arguments against appointment</u>

<u>Independence</u>

As the representative of a significant institutional investor in P, S cannot be regarded as an independent non-executive director under governance best practice such as the UK Corporate Governance Code. S has maybe been suggested because current board members believe, based on their previous dealings with S, that S will be reluctant to challenge their strategies. Also S does not appear to be stepping down from C's board. If S does not do so, S's duties to **promote the best interests of C and P may conflict.** Other significant investors may consider that S's appointment would give C a privileged position and demand board representation themselves.

<u>Lack of fresh perspective</u>

S may **not be able to bring a fresh perspective** to the affairs of P. As C's representative, S already has had chances to raise concerns about P's strategies or how P is being governed. Possibly S is unlikely to raise new issues if appointed as a director.

Recommendation

S's connections mean that S cannot be regarded as an **independent non-executive director**. This would limit S's contribution to the board, as S could not serve on **audit or remuneration committees** under governance best practice. The board would be some way short of fulfilling the requirement of governance best practice that at least half the board should be independent non-executive directors. For this reason S should not be appointed.

T

Arguments for appointment

CIMA membership

T's membership of CIMA means that T is subject to **CIMA's ethical code**. This should guarantee that T brings to the Board essential qualities such as **integrity and objectivity,** Adherence to CIMA's **continuing professional education requirements** will obligate T to make sure that T has the relevant, up-to-date, knowledge needed to contribute effectively as a director.

Wide experience

T can bring a **fresh perspective** to the board, based on experience of a number of different sectors. T's experience as Finance Director on the bank's board, together with CIMA membership, means that T has the **recent financial knowledge** highlighted by governance reports as a requirement for the audit committee. T will also bring contacts in the banking sector, which may be useful when P is dealing with major lenders.

Arguments against appointment

Independence

T is about to retire. We are **not given details of any other sources of income** that T has, although T probably has a pension from the bank.

T's fees as non-executive director may be a **significant proportion of his income** going forward. There is the risk that T may be less willing to challenge and upset other directors and jeopardise this source of income.

Lack of previous involvement in sector

T does not appear to have had **previous involvement** in this specific sector. T will need to have a **more extensive induction programme** than S would.

Recommendation

T should qualify as an independent non-executive director. The benefits that T's CIMA membership and wider experience will bring should mean that T is offered a directorship. T's role should include chairing the audit committee.

U

Arguments for appointment

Political knowledge

U should be able to bring expert knowledge of the **political and legal environment** to the Board, helping the board assess risks in this area. P may be able to use the political contacts that U has, and use U's expertise to lobby against damaging changes to legislation.

Other directorships

U is currently on **two other boards**. The perspective U gains from serving on these boards may inform U's contribution to P's board. U may be able to **benchmark** what P is doing against practice elsewhere. U should also have gone through an **induction process** at these companies and be aware of responsibilities in law and under governance best practice.

Arguments against appointment

Time

U is already a director of two other companies and this may limit the time that can be spent as a director of P to an **unacceptably low level.**

Lack of previous involvement in sector

U does not appear to have had any previous experience in the chemical sector unlike S. U also appears to lack T's financial knowledge.

Recommendation

U should be considered for one of the vacant directorships. However before U is appointed the board should obtain **guarantees that U will spend sufficient time** on P's affairs.

(b)   Reputation risk

The chief executive's decision indicates a fear that P may suffer **adverse criticism** if bonuses are awarded despite a loss being made. It may be very difficult to **justify to shareholders** who are already concerned about directors' remuneration the justification for appearing to award failure, particularly if the losses made have impacted adversely on the **dividends** directors recommend. P's remuneration committee will need to demonstrate that it has **considered the case for awarding a bonus for each director separately.**

Uncontrollable factors

Directors' rewards should be measured against factors that they can control. The other executive directors may be broadly right and P has performed better than could have been expected in the **tough economic climate.** However it is very difficult to assess the **impact of broad economic forces** and apply them separately to each director.

Incentives

If any of the directors feel that they are **unlikely to receive a bonus** because of poor results and that their salary will be their only reward, they may be **less motivated** to make significant efforts to improve performance.

Retention of directors

How directors view their bonuses may also be determined by the bonuses and remuneration paid to directors elsewhere in this sector. Some of the board may need to be paid some bonus in order to **guarantee they remain with P.** The remuneration committee would have to weigh up the consequences of these directors leaving, versus the risks of upsetting shareholders and other directors who have not been so generously rewarded.

Contribution of board as a whole

Another complication of rewarding directors is separating the contribution of the board as a whole from those of individuals. Corporate governance reports suggest that **key strategic decisions** should be made by the board as a whole. Therefore if poor decisions have been made, all members should bear some responsibility and this should be reflected in how they are rewarded.

Individual contribution

It may be very difficult to assess how directors should be rewarded relative to each other, because of the **different criteria** used to assess what each has done. Some directors may be assessed by quantitative means, for example the sales director being assessed by the level of **sales and market share.** However other directors, such as the human resources director, may be assessed by **qualitative criteria.** Even when directors perform together, for example in the contribution each makes to the board, it may be difficult to make judgements using objective criteria and to decide how significant an element this should be in directors' packages. There is also the risk that directors may **act dysfunctionally**, for example by withholding information, to improve the appearance of their own performance at the expense of other directors.

Balance of package

Shareholders appear to want stock options replaced by **performance bonuses** and the remuneration committee must take into account their wishes. Performance bonuses may be a better way of differentiating rewards between directors. However stock options are a way of rewarding an **increase in company value in the longer-term**. Balancing packages towards bonuses may mean that directors **concentrate excessively on short-term factors**, with the risk that they will try to manipulate these to guarantee good bonuses.

10 B Bank

Text references. Chapter 3 covers directors' remuneration, and also Chapter 5 on management rewards is relevant for (a).

Top tips. The question is on a topical area, with the scenario including some risk management weaknesses that have been identified recently in financial institutions. Some of the recommendations in the answer tie in with the 2009 UK Walker review of corporate governance in banks and other financial institutions.

(a) highlights recent concerns about corporate governance weaknesses, but also involves other important syllabus issues – controllability, short-term vs long-term performance and the risk/return relationship.

(b) combines corporate governance issues on strategy determination and the role of non-executives with control considerations relating to loans. An important point is that lenders should only lend to borrowers whom they expect to meet their commitments. Security is a method of limiting the impact of borrower default, but it won't be required if all borrowers repay on time.

Easy marks. A few fairly obvious hints in the scenario of (b).

Examiner's comments. Students generally scored enough marks to pass the question, although their answers lacked sufficient detail to score very high marks. A reason for many students scoring satisfactorily was that they had read about the worldwide banking crisis in the financial press. The main omission in (a) was discussion about the undesirability of banks having as directors high risk-seeking individuals who were only interested in their own rewards. In (b) some students failed to discuss the mortgage policy as a risk, which made it difficult to them to pass the question.

Marking scheme

		Marks
(a)	Advantages from shareholders ' viewpoint – demonstration of commitment, link between remuneration and performance max	3
	Disadvantages	
	Deter desirable recruits particularly NEDs	2
	Attract individuals who will seek excessive risks	2
	Excessive focus on short-term rewards	2
	Directors may manipulate profits	2
	Bank profits depend partly on key economic forces which directors can't control and which should not determine their remuneration	2
	max	10
(b)	Generally award 1 mark for explanation of each problem and a further 1 mark for recommendations for improvement	
	Poor strategic planning	3
	Failure to take into account current trends	2
	Inadequate performance by non-executive directors	2
	Establishment of relations with new shareholder base	2
	Lending to poor credit risks	2
	Inadequate security	2
	Lack of risk and scenario analysis	2
	max	15
		25

(a)   <u>Arguments in favour of proposal</u>

<u>Response to stakeholder demands</u>

The proposal may be popular with **shareholders** and other significant **stakeholders, such as government and the media**. If the banks do not make profits, directors will be exposed to the risk of the loss of their fee.

Clear link

The **link** between bank performance and directors' remuneration appears **clear**. Directors will not be given substantial rewards if their bank fails to perform well.

Arguments against proposal

Deterrence of fee

Having to pay an initial fee may put off some potential directors who would otherwise be good candidates. This particularly applies to **non-executive directors**. They should be recruited on the basis of the **independence, financial industry capability and critical perspective** that they can bring to the board, and also the time commitment they can make. Because they should be assisting shareholders and other stakeholders by scrutinising executive directors' actions, it would be inappropriate for them to be charged a fee. If non-executives' remuneration is linked to performance, they will face a **conflict of interest** when advising on potentially profitable but risky strategies, and may be less willing to disagree with executive directors' proposals.

Risk and return

The scheme appears to encourage behaviour that has been criticised over the past few years, banks putting excessive resources into **speculative or uncertain activities**, and as a result making large losses. The reward system proposed would seem to appeal most to directors who are willing to take excessive risks for the chance of achieving high returns. Such individuals may regard the fee they have to pay as an acceptable charge for the chance to obtain high remuneration. A better way to ensure director commitment to long-term success may be to require them to maintain a holding of a **minimum number of shares**.

Short and long-term

Rewarding directors by bonuses based on annual profits rewards short-term performance, and does not take account of the **long-term effects** of directors' decisions. Incentives should be balanced so that a **significant proportion of remuneration** takes the form of a **long-term incentive scheme** such as **share options** with rewards only being due after a number of years has elapsed. Even shorter-term bonuses should be **paid over more than a year**, with a **limit to the proportion paid** in the first year.

Manipulation of profits

Directors may try to **manipulate profits** to maximise their bonuses in a particular year. This risk could be lessened by **clawback** provisions, where directors have to **repay bonuses based on misleading accounts**.

Controllability of profits

The reward scheme should link to the factors directors can control. However economic factors such as **interest rates and inflation** will have a significant impact on the volume of lending and borrowing and hence on a bank's results. The decisions directors make may therefore have **less impact on profits** than external influences.

(b)   Review of strategy

Reviews of strategy should be conducted **more regularly than once every four years.** They are fundamental to a business's success over the long-term. Decisions on mortgages can affect the bank's results for up to 25 years. Strategic decisions impact greatly on risk management, since they are influenced by the **risk appetite** of the directors and impact upon the **risks borne** and the **ways risks are managed**. Therefore board consideration of strategy and risk needs to cover regularly current and future risk appetite.

Impact of current trends

In particular the board appears to be relying too much on policies that have been successful in the past in managing predictable financial risks. It does not seem to be taking enough notice of the implication of current economic trends, where **house price inflation is greater than wage inflation.** If this trend continues, it will mean that mortgages become less affordable. A decrease in demand for mortgages will threaten bank profits. The board should consider **diversification** into other products, particularly short-term loans, as it may presently be over-committed to longer-term lending.

Role of non-executive directors

Guidance such as the Higgs and Walker reports has identified scrutiny as a key duty of non-executive directors. Ideally executive directors should formulate strategy and it should then be **rigorously discussed and challenged** if necessary by non-executive directors. The failure of non-executive directors to do this at B may lead to strategies being implemented that are not in the bank's best interests. Non-executive directors should play a much more active role in deliberations about strategy.

Relations with shareholders

B's shareholder base is changing and the board does not seem to be considering the full implications of this. The changes could lead to the **risks faced by B increasing** as the new shareholder base demands higher returns. This could result in dangerous decisions being taken as B's board tries to fulfil unrealistic expectations. **Increased communication** with shareholders should help keep expectations under control. This will be a particularly important role for senior non-executive directors. Lending excessive amounts

B's **lending policy** seems to be primarily determined by competition. This increases its riskiness, as it seems that not enough attention is being given to the ability of **borrowers to repay**. Even if the value of loans is backed by adequate security, the best way to limit the riskiness of loans is only to lend to those who can provide **sufficient evidence of ability to repay.**

Inadequate security

B's policy of lending in excess of the properties' value increases the risk that the **security** provided by the properties will be **inadequate.** The security will only be enough if property prices continue to rise. If prices fall and borrowers default, B will be left with property assets that do **not cover the value of the loan**, are **declining in value and may be difficult to sell**. Lending up to a percentage that is some way short of 100% of property value should mean that the loan can be realised even if there is some fall in prices. The commitment mortgage payers have made of providing a certain amount of the property's value from their own resources should increase their **commitment to meet repayments** and avoid the loss of the property.

Scenario analysis

B's lending policy appears to be based on a scenario where property prices are **continuing to rise**. B does not appear to have adequately considered the possibility of **alternative scenarios** and developed plans for the possibility that prices fall.

11 AFC

Text references. Chapters 6 and 7.

Top tips. You do not need to spend any time worrying about the structure of the answer as the question makes it absolutely clear what's required. The main issues are to decide in how much detail to describe each control and to come up with controls under the three categories specified in the question. The examiner's comments highlighted an important failure of exam technique with many students just listing controls without allocating them under each header.

CIMA's guidance suggests that you will get two marks for each risk/control combination. To gain both marks however, you will need to explain how the control you recommend addresses the risk. Referring to the core risk management strategies (avoid, transfer, reduce) is useful. Considering whether the controls you recommend relate to input, processes or output is also helpful.

Remembering what you have learnt about project management will help you answer this question.

Easy marks. If you found it much easier to come up with financial controls than other types of control, you need to revise non-financial quantitative and qualitative controls, as these are very important in this exam.

Examiner's comments. Answers were generally poor. Students had a lot of problems splitting the controls up under each heading. 'If candidates did not show what heading the control was being discussed under, they did not get a mark.' Students were also penalised for putting controls under the wrong heading. Even when controls were put under the right heading, the answers often contained insufficient detail.

(a) <u>Premium charges</u>

<u>Financial</u>

The premiums clearly have a severe financial impact upon AFC. AFC must therefore look for ways to **reduce the premiums**. One way is to negotiate an **increased excess** on its policies, although then the financial consequences of a large claim would be more severe. Therefore **other risk reduction measures** are required to make the chances of a large claim remote, and also to provide evidence to the insurance company that claims are less likely, with the result hopefully of lower premiums.

<u>Quantitative</u>

AFC needs to implement effective controls over project output, so that problems can be **detected and rectified** before the projects are signed off. Methods of measurement could include Six Sigma, which seeks to eliminate the defects that could result in claims.

<u>Qualitative</u>

AFC should introduce controls over **inputs** to **prevent** the problems that cause overruns happening in the first place. These include **supervision and training** of AFC's staff, with training focused on areas where problems are most likely to occur. AFC will use subcontractors, and should, when recruiting subcontractors, obtain evidence that the **subcontractors' control procedures** and **quality of work** are likely to be satisfactory.

(b) <u>Economic downturn</u>

<u>Financial</u>

AFC needs to keep **tight control** over the costs of each project. It should introduce **target costing**, with the **target revenue being adjusted downwards** in order to respond to expected reductions in government funding and the need to quote lower tender prices. After subtracting a profit margin, AFC should aim to **reduce target costs continuously** by reviewing the material and labour inputs employed, and seeing if the amount or costs of these resources can be reduced.

<u>Quantitative</u>

AFC should **review the economic indicators** in countries in which it operates. It may be wary of doing business in countries where the economic outlook is particularly poor and there may be an increased risk of default.

<u>Qualitative</u>

AFC's main method of reducing risk should be to try to **diversify** in terms of the **types of project** it carries out, the **length of projects** and the **countries in which it operates.** It needs to avoid being committed to too many long-term projects on poor terms or projects in a single country, which may be particularly badly hit by a downturn.

(c) <u>Cost over-runs</u>

<u>Financial</u>

The **project budget** needs to be **sufficiently detailed** so that **variance analysis** will identify each material cost variance. Variances need to be investigated regularly during the contract to **obtain evidence** of the reasons for variations. This should mean that AFC is able to present clients with a detailed breakdown of the reasons for additional charges, reducing the chances that customers will refuse to accept those charges.

<u>Quantitative</u>

Managers should make **regular comparisons of time** actually taken with budgeted time. Overruns on time will indicate probable cost overruns.

<u>Qualitative</u>

A further check to ensure that customers are charged for **changes in the specification** of contracts should be **comparison between the final structure** and the **specification agreed** by customers when the contract was signed. This comparison and investigation of the cost implications should be part of a **post-completion audit** that should be undertaken for every major project. The audit should also recommend improvements, so that cost overruns that should have been controllable are avoided on future projects.

(d)   <u>Financial penalties</u>

AFC should try to negotiate **contract terms** that limit penalties to delays that relating to factors that AFC can control. For example AFC should not be held responsible for delays caused by extreme weather. If AFC subcontracts work, **contracts with the subcontractors** should also include penalties if the subcontractors fail to honour their obligations.

<u>Quantitative</u>

Methods of project analysis such as **Network charts and Gantt charts** should be used to track progress, so that possible delays can be identified as early as possible and action taken to prevent or rectify them. **Forecasts of future activity levels**   should identify activity peaks, and action can be planned to obtain extra resources if necessary at these times.

<u>Qualitative</u>

Serious delays are likely to be caused by problems with quality that are not dealt with until late on in the project. **Regular inspection of work** should **identify any problems** at an early enough stage for them to be rectified quickly.

12   CM

Text references. Chapters 5 and 6.

Top tips. The main issue in structuring in (a) is whether to list all the risks and all the controls under each header, or list each risk and then a control(s) to counter that risk. Trying to match controls to risk should help you generate effective controls but the danger is that you repeat the same control. You need therefore to plan your answer to ensure that you say something new under each risk-control heading.

In (b) it is legitimate to question whether the owner-manager is being honest. Saying that controls aren't being maintained because the owner-manager can't be bothered to operate them wouldn't gain any marks, however tempting making that suggestion is.

Easy marks. Perhaps the human resources risks and controls offer easy marks, as they are well signposted in the scenario. The examiner's comments indicated that many students scored heavily on all parts of this question.

Examiner's comments. Students generally scored well in this question, most making several relevant and practical suggestions for controls. Some answers to (b) needed to be more detailed.

(a)   (i)   <u>Record keeping</u>

<u>Profitability analysis</u>

Although the owner is aiming for high margins on drinks, the lack of sales records means that he cannot tell if the restaurant is **failing to achieve the desired margins**.

To manage this (and other risks listed) an **EPOS system** should be introduced. The system should include **codes for different items of food and drink**. Waiters should input data and bills be produced automatically. This should help ensure the mark-up on drinks is achieved. Although waiters may feed in incorrect data, the fact that most customers will **check their bills and query mistakes** should reduce the risk of mistakes not being corrected.

<u>Customer analysis</u>

The restaurant is making no attempt to find out how customers rate their meal or the service they received. It could be losing income through **dissatisfied customers failing to return**.

The restaurant should carry out regular **customer satisfaction surveys** and could also introduce **loyalty cards** as a means of tracking how much repeat business it is getting.

<u>Records for taxation purposes</u>

The restaurant may be at risk of suffering various penalties imposed by the tax authorities. Its poor recordkeeping may mean that it fails to register for sales tax when it should do, and it may be **fined** for not doing so. It may also be **fined** for failing to **charge sales tax when required** or **failing**

to keep proper records of **sales tax charged**. If the tax authorities are not satisfied with the information they are receiving from the restaurant, they may levy an estimated assessment, and as a result the restaurant may **suffer an excessive tax liability**.

The EPOS system should be able to **calculate and record sales tax** automatically. The EPOS records should be **retained and period totals calculated** as necessary. The restaurant should also keep records of **sales tax paid to suppliers to ensure it minimises its liability**.

(ii) <u>Working capital management</u>

<u>Theft of inventory and cash</u>

The **lack of sales records** mean that it is impossible to keep track of inventory and staff may take the opportunity to **steal inventory and cash**.

The risk of theft can be reduced by obtaining evidence that staff are honest, and so **references** should be obtained and checked for all staff employed. Till records should be **reconciled with inventory records** and **significant differences investigated. Allowing use of debit and credit cards** through an EFTPOS system will also reduce the amounts of cash that could be lost. If **significant losses** are **discovered**, **random** searches of staff as they leave may have to be introduced.

<u>Over/under ordering of inventory</u>

The **lack of records of amounts consumed in the buffet and the free meals** eaten by staff may mean that inventory is over-ordered and hence **goes to waste**, or under-ordered, meaning that **part of the menu is not available to customers**.

The EPOS system should **record the number of buffet meals eaten.** The restaurant should also **keep records of food quantities consumed each day in the buffet**. A comparison of the two should indicate the amount of inventory that should be ordered. The EPOS system should also record details of free meals obtained.

<u>Abuse of free meals</u>

Staff may take advantage of the free meals opportunity by **eating and drinking as much as they can** and also **allowing more than one friend** to obtain a free meal.

Free meals should all be **recorded**. Supervisors should **authorise free meals. Limits** could be placed on what can be obtained for free, particularly alcoholic drinks.

(iii) <u>Human resources policy</u>

<u>Staff numbers</u>

The frequent turnover of staff may mean that the business is **understaffed at busy times**, such as the start and end of university terms. The lack of records of customer numbers also makes it more difficult to gauge what the right staffing level is to **provide a satisfactory level of service**.

Staff should be put on **longer-term contracts**, maybe covering a university term. **Staff morale** should be measured by regular chats to staff. Staff leaving should have an **exit interview** to ascertain why they are going, for example whether they are taking another job with better wages. The EPOS system should **record the number of customers covered by each bill**. This should facilitate comparison of customer numbers with staff levels.

<u>Poor performance</u>

The owner-manager may have **insufficient time to train staff** with the result that they fail to carry out key tasks satisfactorily, for example allocating customers to the right tables. Poor performance may also not be identified due to **inadequate supervision**. The low wages paid mean staff have **little incentive to improve performance**.

The owner-manager should appoint some staff as **supervisors,** putting them on **longer-term contracts and higher wages**. They should be given responsibility for **training new staff and monitoring staff performance**. A **reward system**, performance-related bonuses or awards to employee of the month, should be introduced to **encourage good performance**.

<u>Inefficient working practices</u>

Staff are expected to cover **different roles if necessary**, and may be **unsure at times** what they should be doing. As a result **important tasks** such as taking orders may be neglected. It will also be difficult to make **staff accountable** if problems arise.

Staff could be given specific **job descriptions** or supervisors could **allocate work** at the start of each shift.

<u>Food hygiene breaches</u>

Staff working in the kitchen may have **insufficient knowledge of food hygiene regulations** and breach legal requirements. As a result the restaurant may be liable to **fines and threats of closure** from the government authorities and also a **loss of reputation** if customers fall ill due to poor hygiene.

All staff handling food should **attend the courses in food hygiene** at local colleges, and no-one should be **allowed to handle food without the necessary training**.

(b)   <u>Cost</u>

The owner-manager may not wish to bear the costs of **investing in a computerised record-keeping system** or **employing higher-paid** supervisory staff. He may prefer to maintain control solely by supervising the business himself.

<u>Risk acceptance</u>

The owner-manager may be prepared to accept risks such as **cash loss or abuse of the free meals system** rather than implement controls, if he believes these risks are low impact low likelihood risks.

<u>Understatement of profit</u>

The owner-manager may believe that failing to keep adequate records means that he can **declare a low profit figure** on his tax return and have less risk of the tax authorities successfully querying it.

13 HFD

Text references. Chapters 3 and 4.

Top tips. A good example of how governance and ethical guidance applies outside the corporate sector (in fact here most of the issues would also have been relevant to companies).

Easy marks. Hopefully you picked up the more obvious hints in (a): CEO/Chairman being the same person, questionable independence of NEDs, lack of scrutiny by NEDs of operational matters.

Examiner's comments. (a) was generally done well with many students identifying problem areas, although fewer then discussed why restructuring was needed. Answers to (b) were not very good, even though students could have discussed any issue they could reasonably justify as relevant. Students who discussed the ethical principles without mentioning the scenario scored poorly. The examiner noted that previous ethics question had not been done well and commented that this area of the syllabus appeared to require more revision.

Marking scheme

		Marks
(a)	2 marks for each recommendation. To score 2 marks recommendation must be justified by reference to the scenario. Reward discussion of composition of board, roles of executive and non-executive directors	16
(b)	Up to 3 marks for each issue from CIMA's code discussed. To score 3 marks issue must be related to scenario	$\frac{9}{25}$

(a)

> **Top tips.** (a) requires some care. The board wants to be more like a listed company board. However you need to remember that HFD is a fairly small charity, so you should be careful what you recommend. For example it would be fine to recommend the charity appoints 1 or 2 more executive directors but not 7 or 8. Your answer should also go beyond just quoting the UK Corporate Governance Code and emphasise the benefits to the charity of adopting the recommendations.

Split of role of chairman and chief executive

Governance reports recommend that the roles of chief executive and chairman should be split between different individuals, to avoid there being an excessive concentration of power in the hands of one individual. At present the chief executive is able to **manipulate the information** the board receives, to protect his position. It seems best for one of the existing NEDs to be appointed as chairman. Splitting the roles emphasises the two jobs are distinct, with the **chief executive running the charity** and the **chairman running the board**. The chairman can ensure the chief executive is **accountable** for his actions, by for example ensuring the board **has enough information** to exercise oversight of the chief executive.

Appointment of secretary

The board's functioning would be better if someone acted as company secretary. The secretary could undertake a number of tasks currently undertaken by the CEO including **distributing board minutes** in advance of meetings and **briefing board members in relation to each agenda item**. This would free up the time of the CEO or chairman. The secretary should be accountable to the board collectively, and should if necessary have the **independence** to come into conflict with the CEO if the secretary believes it is in the interest of HFD.

More executive directors

The UK Higgs report commented that there is a greater risk of distortion or withholding of information, or lack of balance in the management contribution, when there is only one or a very small number of executives on the board. HFD should consider appointing one or two more executive directors, for example an Operations Director; this would also help with **succession planning**, and lead to a greater emphasis on **risk management** and **operational control** at board level.

Audit committee

Appointing a **separate audit committee** will enable the main board to concentrate more on strategic and operational matters, leaving the audit committee to undertake the **detailed financial review** that is a major part of current board meetings. The audit committee should also be **responsible for appointment of auditors** and **liaison with them about further work including review of controls**. At present the auditors' ability to exercise independent scrutiny could be questioned, since they have been appointed by the CEO. Governance reports recommend that all members of the committee should have sufficient financial expertise to contribute effectively, and that one member should have **relevant and recent financial experience**. New directors may therefore need to be recruited to fulfil this requirement or existing members **receive training**.

Nomination committee

A nomination committee of NEDs would **oversee the appointment of the new directors** that HFD's board appears to need. The committee would also review other important issues of board functioning that have not been considered recently, such as:

- The **balance between executives and NEDs**
- Whether there are **gaps between the skills, knowledge and experience** possessed by the current board and what the board ideally should have
- The need to **attract board members from a variety of backgrounds**
- Whether HFD will need to pay **some NEDs** to attract the right candidates

Independent NEDs

Governance reports recommend that at least half the board are **independent NEDs**, without business or financial connections who face re-election regularly. Independent NEDs will be particularly important for HFD as it is a charity, and stakeholders will rely on NEDs to provide unbiased scrutiny of how the

executive directors are conducting its affairs. It is possible that none of the current NEDs can be classed as independent, since they have all been appointed on the basis of previous business connections.

Expert NEDs

NEDs with **experience of the charity sector** need to be appointed. The reason given for not discussing operational matters, that these are outside the directors' experience, indicates that as a body the NEDs have **insufficient expertise** at present. The CEO's belief that the executive management team is more than capable of managing the delivery of the in-home care services misses the point. NEDs should **scrutinise**, and if necessary **challenge**, the way the CEO is running operations, drawing on their own experience.

Stakeholder representation

There appears to be a **lack of stakeholder representation** on the board; with fund providers, volunteer helpers and users of HFD's services not being represented. Having a user representative on the board would mean that the board received **direct feedback on the effectiveness of the charity's activities**. Stakeholder representatives could also **provide feedback** to the stakeholders they represent on the reasoning behind board decisions and HFD's current strategy.

Changes in board membership

It seems that new NEDs need to be appointed to provide the **expertise and independence** the board is currently lacking. Corporate governance reports recommend that the board should not be so large as to be unwieldy; therefore some of the new board members may have to replace existing board members.

(b)

Top tips. If you struggled with (b), the fundamental principles and conceptual framework (based on ethical conflicts) are covered in Chapter 4 of the Study Text. Using the OPPTIC mnemonic would have helped you remember the relevant ones. The great majority of the points in these two sections are relevant; the main omission from our answer is confidentiality. To score good marks you need to use material in the scenario to show why they are relevant. Given that the question is concerned with whether you should continue, you also need to bring in the safeguards that are designed to counter the threats identified in the conceptual framework. Knowledge of the UK Corporate Governance Code can be used to reinforce your answer in (b), as well as being very important in (a).

Fundamental principles

Objectivity

My **objectivity** may be seen to be threatened if I have a relative or close friend who is dependent on the care HFD provides. This need not stop me acting as a director; however I should register an **interest** with the rest of the board and **not participate in discussions** on matters that affect my relative or friend.

Professional competence and due care

I need to ensure that I have **sufficient knowledge** about charities generally and the sector in which HFD operates. At present the chief executive does not believe I or the other NEDs have the knowledge to **scrutinise the charity's operations effectively**. **Appropriate training** should help remedy the deficiencies in my experience.

Conceptual framework

CIMA's conceptual framework states that accountants may face threats to compliance with the fundamental principles and need to **identify, evaluate and respond appropriately to these threats**.

Self-interest

I need to consider whether my **business relationship** is significant enough to mean that my **personal interests would be seriously threatened** if a disagreement with the CEO severed the relationship. The existence of the business relationship could mean that I could not be seen as an independent non-executive director.

Intimidation

Intimidation may become an issue if I feel that the CEO is being unduly **aggressive** in his attempts to prevent the NEDs from discussing important operational matters. A possible solution to deal with this problem is to **resign** and **publicise the reasons for resignation**, maybe reporting to the appropriate regulatory body. However stakeholder interests may be better served by my continuing on the board and **standing up to the chief executive**.

14 PKG High School

Text references. Chapters 3 and 6.

Top tips. This question is a good test of your understanding of the controls all organisations should have. Remember we stressed in the front pages that you need to know about a large variety of controls. This question is also a good illustration of the importance of choosing questions carefully. The examiner's comments indicated that the question was popular but not done well, indicating many students made the wrong choice. It seems students had insufficient understanding of the non-corporate sector, and how a governing body would differ from a company board.

Easy marks. Quite difficult to identify on this question.

Examiner's comments. This question was answered poorly. Answers needed to consider a broad range of issues, not just financial ones. However students seemed unable to discuss corporate governance in the context of a school, instead discussing governance procedures that would have been appropriate for a limited company. In (b) students failed to pick up many of the points in the scenario, including the need to control the head teacher and problems with the information received by the governing body.

(a)

Top tips. In (a) the stakeholders are different to those of a company, but they still need the assurance provided by an objective review. Benchmarking is likely to be a particularly important aspect of the audit, given that the governing body is responsible for educational standards.

Independent and objective assurance

Having an external review carried out should provide an **unbiased view** of how the school is performing. In particular this provides **reassurance to stakeholders such as parents and the local authority** that the school is providing education of sufficient quality and expenditure is being properly controlled.

Aid to monitoring

Like the board of directors in a listed company, the governors are responsible for establishing and maintaining a sound system of internal control and risk management. The review should provide **feedback** to the head teacher and governing body to enable them to set priorities for systems improvements, based on the areas of **greatest risk**. It should also highlight where the head teacher and governors should **focus their own monitoring activity.**

Expert opinion

The external reviewers can make recommendations based on their **knowledge of best practice in other schools.** This can provide the school with **benchmarks** that it can incorporate into financial and non-financial performance indicators.

(b)

Top tips. It is very easy in (b) to stray from the subject and talk too generally about controls – the question asks you to evaluate (often as here concentrate on the weaknesses), and recommend what the governing body should be doing. Our answer is based around the structure of:

* How the governing body is constituted and how it operates
* The data it gets (financial/non-financial, internal-external)
* The decisions it takes and the monitoring it carries out

which is a useful way of analysing how any governing body works.

You may have felt that the question could have given more detail about what the governing body is doing and the information it receives. It is valid to assume that if you're not told anything about key aspects of governance such as a committee system, then they aren't being operated when they should be.

It's also easy in (b) to fail to consider whether financial and other resources are being used to maximum efficiency. Spending limits often mean that expenditure is often made to the limits set down, with little consideration of whether value for money has been obtained.

(i) Structure and workings of governing body

Membership

The governing body includes representatives of the key stakeholder group of parents and the local authority.

However it may be a **more effective monitor** if it includes representation from key internal stakeholders. Certainly it should include staff representatives and perhaps also might include pupil representatives as well.

Committee system

Having the full governing body consider all relevant items at every meeting may not be the most efficient way of operation, and it may mean that some **key risk areas receive insufficient attention.**

Although committees may be difficult to staff, a **committee system** with each committee concentrating on certain key aspects of running the school may be the best way to conduct decision-making, with committees reporting into the main governing body. Certainly it may provide a good mechanism for parent representatives to use their particular expertise.

(1) Audit committee

An **audit committee**, including members with financial expertise, could be responsible for detailed scrutiny of expenditure and liaising with auditors. Its remit could also cover **compliance with legislation** and the **operation of internal controls.** This would leave the main governing body to concentrate on the split of expenditure and the overall review of control systems.

(2) Staff recruitment committee

Because of the significance of staffing the board should establish a separate recruitment committee. The committee should be involved in specific recruitment decisions, and should also proactively consider **staffing needs.** For example are there **sufficient experienced members** of staff and does the staff body as a whole have an **appropriate range of skills** in key areas such as IT. The committee must consider how **staffing headcount needs** can be **reconciled with planned staff expenditure.**

The committee should also consider the **balance between teachers and other support staff,** whether support staff, with specific skills, need to be recruited or whether their numbers could be reduced and more teachers recruited. It should also be involved in **internal promotion decisions** and consider the effectiveness of the **system of responsibility allowances.**

Induction of governing body members

There appear to be **no induction procedures** for new governing body members that would enhance their knowledge of what the school does and the requirements the governing body has to meet.

Certainly parent governors will need this understanding if they are be **effective governors** (hopefully the local authority will have selected suitably qualified and knowledgeable members).

(ii) Information received by governing body

Financial information

It is unclear whether the financial information is sufficiently detailed. The governing body needs to ensure that it receives **sufficient information about expenditure,** particularly because of the wide discretion the Headmaster has and the lack of **segregation of duties.**

Expenditure should be **classified** into **different categories** depending on its materiality and the ways it is controlled. The information should include what **has been spent,** and **expenditure commitments,** also **phasing of expenditure during the year;** not all expenditure will be made in even amounts over the year. The governing body also needs to ensure that the **reliability** of the

monthly financial report is reviewed because of its importance for decision-making. As the external auditors may not spend time on this, this review should perhaps be carried out by members of the audit committee.

Financial variances

Although the governors receive information about variances from budgeted expenditure, there is nothing mentioned about how they are, as they should be, informed of action planned if an over-spend appears likely.

They should have input into what should be done.

Non-financial information

There appears to be a lack of non-financial information that the governors need to **ensure educational standards** are being **maintained.** An **annual inspection by the local education authority** would not be frequent enough.

Governors should be supplied with the results of internal methods of assessing the effectiveness of teaching such as **termly exams** and **internal quality reviews** of teaching programmes. Since staffing is both a major element of expenditure and vital in ensuring standards, governors should be receiving details about staff such as **results of appraisals** and **staff development programmes**. Having parent, staff and pupil representatives on the governing body will help measure the **satisfaction levels** of these key stakeholder groups; the governors ought to consider other methods such as regular staff and parent surveys.

External information

No mention is whether the governing body is receiving the external information which it will need for longer-term decision-making.

The governing body should be receiving details of population trends in the area and the impact of changes in schools provisions. It should also be considering specific information about other schools in the area that it can use for **benchmarking purposes** such as pupil numbers, disposition of staff, facilities and exam results.

(iii) Actions taken by governing body

Strategic decision-making

The governing body's time horizon appears to be limited to a year, and it does not appear to be considering longer-term issues; there seems to be **no strategic plan.**

Better information should help it **modify** its strategy in response to local issues such as changes in pupil numbers, the opening of new schools, particularly specialist schools or government-promoted schools (such as UK academies) and changes in educational practice (such as increased use of information technology).

Flexibility of decision-making

The governing body needs to consider whether its decision-making is too constricted; the governors may have the flexibility to take decisions that ensure **better use of resources** and **better risk management.**

For example it may consider whether class sizes can be increased in the lower age ranges to allow smaller class sizes and greater preparation time for more advanced teaching. Also it should consider whether to include a **contingency fund** for urgent items of additional expenditure on staff, buildings and IT.

Review of small items of expenditure

The governing body does not appear to take any interest in expenditure under $1,000. There may be scope for the head teacher to abuse this by **spreading significant expenditure** out so that individual items are below $1,000, but the total sum is quite substantial.

The governors should **review all expenditure** below $1,000 even if they don't approve it in advance. There may be scope for raising the limit on certain types of expenditure, so that the governing body does not spend time considering what is essentially non-discretionary expenditure.

Communication

The governing body needs to consider how its **work should be communicated**; there is **no evidence** of how this is happening at present.

Clearly the head teacher will have prime responsibility for communicating and what the governing body publishes should be consistent with what the head teacher is saying. However **communication of what the governing body is doing** and the **issues it is considering** should prove to staff, pupils and current and prospective parents that the school is **well-run.** It should also aid **future recruitment** onto the governing body.

15 Pensions

Text references. Chapter 1, 4, 6 and 15.

Top tips. The examiner noted that this question was unpopular. It seems many students were put off it by mention of IAS 19 and the fear that they needed detailed knowledge of the standard to pass the question. In fact the question is about risks, ethics and controls, not the fine print of IAS 19.

Easy marks. (b) (ii) is based round the key figures in a large company's system of financial reporting.

Examiner's comments. Despite being the least popular question on the paper, this question was very well-answered.

(a)

Top tips. The key question in (a) is the financial consequences of the actions that need to be taken to combat the risks. Note that employees may suffer even if they are not making any contributions to the scheme themselves. (a) is also a good illustration of reputation risk, where risk levels depend upon the impact stakeholder actions can have on the company.

Risks to employer

(i) Financial risks

The employer will have to take action to **remedy a long-term deficit**. The nature of the risk will depend on the action taken. A **lump sum payment** will provide a quick fix, but may mean that the employer has **insufficient resources** to take advantage of major profitable investment opportunities. **Gradual repayment** may be easier on cash flow, but represents a **continuing drain** and means that the employer has to live with the other consequences of a deficit. Ultimately if the employer cannot meet the deficit, it could lead to the **employer's insolvency**.

(ii) Stock market risk

The company's **market value** may fall as a result of investors perceiving the company to be of **higher risk** because of the deficit. This fall may occur even if the underlying causes of the deficit are not long-term. For example if the pension fund is invested to a significant extent in equities, the effect of a few weeks of falling share prices may give an exaggeratedly pessimistic picture of the scheme funding at the year-end.

(iii) Financial provider risk

The reaction of other finance providers is likely to be similar to stock market investors. They may well perceive the employer to be of higher risk because of the liabilities on the statement of financial position, and hence be **less willing to provide funds** if they feel that the funds will be diverted to clearing the deficit. Alternatively funds provided may be on less favourable terms, causing **finance costs** to **rise.**

(iv) Employee risks

Threats to benefits or the possibility of increased contributions may cause **staff to leave** and make **recruiting new staff more difficult.** Staff who remain may be more unhappy and less co-operative because of the retrenchment necessary to resolve the deficit. Leavers and staff who remain may

decide to **transfer their entitlements** out of the pension fund to **another pension arrangement,** putting further pressure on it.

(v)   Information risks

The employer may take some significant decisions on the basis of actuarial forecasts that include significant uncertainties. In particular if **investment values** are in **flux,** or the **average age and past service of employees alter** as a result of **significant transfers out of the scheme,** the assumptions on which forecasts are made and decisions based may become misleading quite rapidly.

Risks to employees

(i)   Increased contributions

The employees too may face adverse financial consequences from a deficit **having to be remedied.** They may face **increased contributions themselves** to remedy the deficit.

(ii)   Salary costs

Even if they don't have to contribute, their **salaries** may be **capped,** not only to reduce operating costs, but also to limit the benefits that the scheme will ultimately have to pay. They may face an increased threat of redundancy.

(iii)   Employment risks

Other employment risks may be more indirect. If the employer is concentrating on resolving the deficit, then there may be **less development opportunities** because of the cutting back of expansion plans or reduction in training.

(iv)   Transfer risks

If staff member leave the pension scheme, and transfer to another pension arrangement, then there is a risk that the new arrangements will **provide less favourable benefits** than the old scheme at a higher risk. In particular, **transferring to a defined contribution scheme,** where the employee's contributions go into an individual 'pot' of investments out of which benefits are paid, means that the employee **bears the whole risk** of the investments fluctuating in value.

(v)   Non-payment of pensions

Ultimately if the scheme problems lead to the employer's bankruptcy, there is a risk that the staff will not receive the pensions they expect.

(b)

Top tips. (b) (i) follows the method suggested in Chapter 4 of the text; identifying the key facts, discussing the ethical issues, looking at possible actions and making justified recommendations. It's easy in ethics questions to fall into the weakness we highlighted in the Passing the P3 exam section of making vague and impractical recommendations. One problem is that it is not clear who the discussion should be aimed at – another member of the Financial Reporting team perhaps?

In (b) (ii) we are talking about how the system deals with a high level accounting issue, and is therefore a good test of top-level internal controls. Most governance reports specifically include consideration of significant accounting treatments within the audit committee's remit. The mention of external controls should indicate the need to discuss what external audit can do. Although knowledge of auditing standards on using the work of an expert would have helped you a bit, application of your general understanding about what external auditors are trying to achieve should hopefully have meant that you came up with the points we made.

(i)   Action proposed

The action proposed is problematic in two respects.

(1)   The actuary is being asked to prepare a valuation that is clearly not reasonable, since it is **based on out-of-date information.**

(2)   The valuation will be used in the accounts in a way that means that the accounts **do not show a true and fair view.**

Although the Finance Director might argue that the high valuation of the deficit is unfair, using the wrong information is clearly unacceptable, as it cannot be seen as reliable. If the accounts contain a lower valuation than appropriate, this will persuade investors that the company's value is higher

than it is, also perhaps that it is a lower risk investment. Both of these will **unfairly inflate the share price**.

Ethical principles

A number of ethical issues are at stake in this question. The Head of Financial Reporting is proposing action that will mean that he, and the Finance Director if he agrees, are not acting with **integrity** – acting in a **straightforward and honest manner**. This clearly constitutes **unprofessional behaviour by all parties**. In addition the fact that the Head of Financial Reporting believes that he will be able to influence the actuary may indicate the actuary lacks **objectivity,** something the Head of Financial Reporting is exploiting.

Lastly there is the issue of **confidentiality** that faces other members of the Financial Reporting team that know what has happened. If out-of-date information is used and misleading accounts are prepared, how should they weigh up their duty of confidentiality to their employer against the desirability of reporting unethical, and probably fraudulent, behaviour.

Actions taken

The actuary should obviously decline the request; his **professional ethical code** and **employer's code of conduct** will require him to decline. If he feels that undue pressure is being put upon him he should consider resigning.

Staff members who know about the fraud should consider the internal reporting options available. If the Finance Director has agreed to the arrangement, then the matter cannot be reported to him. The **head of the audit committee** should however have the independence and knowledge to challenge the treatment used. If satisfactory action is not taken internally, the **public interest issue** of the market being misled would appear to override confidentiality, and indicate reporting to the local equivalent of the UK's Financial Reporting Review Panel.

Recommendations

The threat to the actuary's integrity and professional position is such that resignation may be the most sensible course.

For Financial Reporting staff members, they should first consider reporting the situation to the **audit committee**, as an independent audit committee should be able to take action. Not only will this be making use of procedures within the organisation, if done in time publication of the **misleading information** may be **prevented** and the **damage limited**. However **whistleblowing to external regulators** is likely to be necessary if the accounts are published using the wrong information. Either way, staff should consider **resigning** because of possible future problems of working for senior management who lack integrity.

(ii)   Internal financial reporting

Recruitment of expert

There should be internal procedures in place governing the **recruitment of the expert**, the **qualifications** required, who makes the decision to recruit and retain the expert and to whom the expert reports.

Internal audit

The effectiveness of any internal audit work on the actuary's valuation will depend partly on internal auditors' level of expertise, also whether they themselves can employ external expert help. There are some things that internal audit should be able to assess well, including the **professional competence of the expert** and the **scope of the expert's work**. They may be able to carry out some work on the **data and assumptions** that the expert has used; this may be sufficient to identify the problem over the wrong table being used if internal auditors themselves are able to obtain sufficient information.

Internal audit committee

Corporate governance reports require the audit committee to review the **published accounts**. This should involve assessment of the **key accounting policies** and **major areas of judgement**. Hopefully some committee members should be able to review the actuary's work effectively. In

addition, the audit committee should act as a **forum for staff**, internal audit or actuary to raise concerns about being pressurised by senior management.

Financial statement controls

There should be a review of the **financial statements** for **compliance with accounting standards, disclosure requirements** and **consistency with internal information**, undertaken by staff who have not been responsible for its preparation. This review may highlight problems with the underlying evidence that require further investigation.

External financial reporting controls

External audit evidence

The work of the external auditor is a **fall-back** if internal controls have not worked satisfactorily. External auditors will be obliged by auditing standards to obtain sufficient evidence about all material items in the accounts. Clearly the valuation will be very material. External auditors should consider carefully not only the **work** the expert has done, but also the expert's **objectivity**.

External audit valuation

External auditors may need to call upon **expert assistance of their own** if they believe that the actuary's work does not represent sufficient audit evidence, because of doubts about the assumptions used or objectivity.

External reporting

Ultimately external auditors can qualify their audit report if they have not obtained satisfactory evidence. This may act as a **deterrent** preventing manipulation.

16 College fraud

Text references. Chapters 6 and 14.

Top tips. (a) and (b) follow the evaluate weaknesses/recommend solutions model. (c) is probably the most difficult part of the question, as it requires consideration of wider control issues. The answer gives some useful insights into the limitations of computer controls.

Easy marks. The controls in (b) should not have been difficult to identify, as the problems which the controls should be combating are clearly flagged in the scenario.

Examiner's comments. (a) was done poorly. Clearly students need to revise fraud better. (b) and (c) were done better, though some students failed to focus on the question requirements in (c).

(a)

Top tips. If you're asked as in (a) to evaluate the difficulties, the likelihood is that there will be some significant difficulties included in the scenario. In fact the scenario includes a number of widely-quoted examples of factors that can undermine internal controls including collusion, falsification of records, limited segregation of duties and involvement of management.

Small amounts

The college employs hundreds of teaching staff on full and part-time contracts. Payments for one fictitious employee **would not be large enough** to attract the attention of auditors automatically. Even if auditors had checked a random sample of payments each year, given the large population the probability was that the fictitious employee would not be discovered for some time, as indeed happened.

Falsification of records

The records of the employee appeared to be **genuine and also a routine payment to a lecturer,** entered on the payroll supervisor's log-in and signed off by P. There was **nothing unusual** about these payments that auditors could have identified.

Use of payroll supervisor's log-on

The payroll supervisor would normally have been the third person involved with this transaction because of his or her involvement at the initial stage. However P was able to **by-pass the need for the supervisor's involvement** by taking advantage of her absence and correctly guessing how to enter the computer on the supervisor's password.

Collusion

Once the fictitious lecturer's details had been entered, the college's systems meant that **two people** had to be involved for each payment to a lecturer to be made, the head of department and the payroll clerk. The involvement of both in the fraud meant that the **segregation of duties** between the two staff, that P authorised the payment and M entered it, was **lost**.

Involvement of senior staff

The system also depended on the **authorisation** of payments by P. The system would have produced for P a record of the lecturers who had been paid for working in P's department. However review of this by P would have been worthless as he would not have reported the fictitious lecturer. The system effectively **relied on P's honesty**. Many systems are designed on the basis that senior staff act honestly. As P had been appointed to a senior position, there presumably was no indication in his previous record that suggested he could not be trusted.

(b)

> **Top tips**. It's important to appreciate in (b) the distinction between design and operation of systems and not therefore spend the whole time criticising the controls in place. The system has some strong features, but is undermined by failure to operate the controls properly as well as the activities of the two people involved. One further suggestion for strengthening the controls would be for passwords to be allocated centrally rather than selected by individual staff.

Controls over keys

Security should **not be allowed** to make **pass keys** that can access a number of offices available to staff. The college could operate a system of duplicate keys for each office and staff only be allowed to use duplicates for their own offices. Alternatively if staff forget their keys, a security guard should unlock their office for them. Pass keys should only be used by security and cleaning staff.

Passwords

Staff must be told **not to use passwords that can easily be guessed**. This includes passwords that are **commonly in use** (such as user123) or passwords that **relate to information that is publicly available**, such as car registration details or information available on Facebook. Staff should also have to change their passwords periodically. Staff should also be **held responsible** for input made on their electronic identities, even if they did not make the input themselves. This should encourage staff to take steps, such as logging out, to ensure that no-one accesses the system on their identity.

Authorisation

Recruitment of new staff should **not just be authorised by a Head of Department** but by central management as well. This should help limit staffing costs and ensure that departments are **not over-staffed**. It should also **strengthen the recruitment process** by ensuring that staff who have been recruited have appropriate qualifications and experience.

Budgets

The system needs to be amended so that teaching time, rather than class time, is budgeted. This should provide a closer control over the **value** that staff give, as well as **reducing the risk of fraud**. Senior college management above the Head of Department should **approve the budgets** and review the actual teaching hours against budgets.

(c)

> **Top tips**. In (c) it's useful to think about what the computer can and cannot do. For example it can recognise a valid password, but cannot see that the wrong person has entered that password. The computer also cannot make judgements about the honesty and competence of staff.

Authorisation

One of the most important controls in most systems is authorisation. The computer cannot exercise judgement over whether lecturers have earned their fees if they have been **authorised as valid recipients** by the college staff.

Competence for role

Human judgement is also required to determine whether staff are able to **perform the tasks connected with the computer system** that are allocated to them.

Existence

Generally computer systems cannot confirm that someone physically exists. It is programmed to judge someone as a **valid person** if they fulfil the criteria that have been programmed, for example that they have entered a **valid password.** Here the fraud was identified because the Post Office could not locate the person who had been sent the invitation.

Access

Computers **cannot prevent themselves from being turned on** by someone who has no right to operate them. To be protected from this, they require measures to prevent the wrong people accessing them, for example ensuring the **rooms** where they are kept are **locked** at all times that staff permitted to use the computers are absent. This fraud arose partly because of lax security over keys.

Standing data

Amendments to standing data require **judgement and care** by the person making them. For example, if pay rates of individuals are changed, the computer may recognise as valid a 10% increase, but that may not be in line with what the operator has been told. An individual's address may be changed to somewhere that is a valid address, but the individual does not live there.

Transactions occurred

The computer system processed the false payments because they **fulfilled the requirements for payments for lecturers**. The system could not recognise the payments as fraudulent because the classes did not occur.

Honesty

The system also depends on the **honesty** of the people operating it, particularly senior management. Human judgement is required to examine people's previous history and current circumstances to see whether they should be placed in a position of trust. This will reduce (though not eliminate) the risk of dishonesty.

---

17 M

Text references. Chapters 4 and 7.

Top tips. (a) seems to require you to use a fairly loose definition of operational risk, since some of the issues relating to the performance measures are connected with M's longer-term strategy. You will have to discuss dealing with key stakeholders (staff and customers) in (a) and (b) so you need to be careful not to repeat yourself. (a) should focus on the operational consequences of poor treatment, (b) why it is wrong ethically.

You may feel in (b) that CIMA's code is not much help, and indeed much of it isn't relevant. You won't get credit for trying to stretch your answer to discuss all the categories. However it is important to mention professional behaviour and link professional competence with the poor decision-making in (a). Some of the ethical threats and safeguards (intimidation, disciplinary procedures) are also very relevant. Note the answer also brings in various stages of the ERM model. The poor internal environment underpins the answer, and under professional competence and due care the answer discusses objective setting and monitoring. Directors must have significant involvement in these stages for the ERM to function effectively.

Easy marks. Nothing that easy, success in the question depends on thinking through the implications of all you are told in the scenario.

Examiner's comments. (a) was done well with students picking up the issues in the scenario. (b) was not done so well, with many students just discussing the headings in CIMA's ethical guide, without relating them to the scenario. Some headers such as objectivity were not relevant.

Marking scheme

			Marks
(a)	Up to 2 marks per risks discussed. Risks can relate to:		
	Limitations of performance standards		
	Failure to use strategic measures		
	Internal competition		
	Lack of clear message		
	Treatment of customer		
	Treatment of staff		
	Reputation risk		
	Technological issues		
		max	15
(b)	Up to 2 marks per ethical issue discussed. Areas can include		
	Duty to customers		
	Duty to staff		
	Fairness		
	Legal issues		
	Poor performance by board (professional competence)		
	Integrity		
		max	10
			25

(a) <u>Lack of objective performance standards</u>

The measures do not provide an indication of how M is **performing against its competitors.** Although particular shops may do well through high discounting, as a result M's profit margins may be lower than its competitors achieve. The allowed margin on discounting does **not appear to be regularly reviewed**, which means it may become less appropriate over time.

<u>Suboptimal performance standards</u>

The maximisation of sales approach may have been more appropriate when M was seeking to gain market share, but is less appropriate as a long-term measure now that M is the dominant company in the market. There is no attempt to review factors that may significantly contribute to M being successful in the longer-term, for example the **amount of repeat business** and the **sales of higher margin or new products.** No account also appears to be taken of customers cancelling contracts and returning products because they are dissatisfied with them.

<u>Competing stores</u>

The close proximity of several stores will inevitably mean that some stores are **competing against each other** rather than combining against competitors, using the advantages of advertising and visibility that M enjoys. Customers who live near to several M stores may shop around and buy from the store that offers the cheapest deal on a particular package, **minimising M's revenues.**

<u>Customer messages</u>

Customers may be confused by the different messages coming from stores, with **different stores having promotions on different products.** The emphasis on special offers generally may result in a **loss of customer confidence** in the quality of the product that M is selling.

<u>Customer care</u>

Customers may react poorly to the approach employed in M's shops. They may find the **selling tactics too aggressive** and not enough time being spent on finding out their requirements. Customers may be particularly dissatisfied if they are **sold a package that does not fulfil their needs** and may not return to M's shops. The lack of repeat business could be a reason why M's growth is slowing.

Staffing

M may suffer **sudden staff shortages** if staff report sick due to stress. This may have an adverse impact on the service that stores offer, and put additional pressure on staff at short-staffed shops, increasing the risk that they too will suffer from stress.

Reputation risk

A poor reputation may damage M in various ways. A **bad reputation for customer care** may deter potential customers from shopping at M's stores in the first place. A **poor reputation for staff treatment** may deter individuals who are potentially good salespersons from applying to work at M.

Technology

M is dependent on the **functioning of its EPOS system.** There do not appear to be backup facilities available if the system breaks down.

(b) #### Duty to customers

It seems likely that in order to maximise sales, staff may be making **exaggerated claims** for the products they are offering and possibly disparaging references to others, which CIMA identifies as unethical. Staff may also be showing customers a **lack of due care** if they fail to identify customer requirements, and do not resolve after-sales queries.

Duty to staff

Managers also appear to be guilty of unprofessional behaviour in dealing with staff. No account appears to be taken of the impact of stores and staff competing with each other and the **excessively pressurised working environment** that has resulted. Although stress problems have been identified as a cause of high turnover and staff absence, managers have not addressed the causes of stress.

Staff performance measurement

The measurement of staff performance seems to be particularly unfair. Staff are mainly judged it seems by the performance of their shop rather than themselves as individuals. No account seems to be taken of **factors** that staff **cannot control** that could influence sales, such as location of shops and staffing levels. **Threatening disciplinary action** when staff have not done anything wrong seems particularly unjustified, and may well be illegal under employment law.

Objective setting and business monitoring

Directors may also be guilty of showing a **lack of competence and due care** by perpetuating performance measures that seem less and less in line with the needs of **M's business.** By not externally benchmarking and **failing to consider the long-term strategic position** of M, the directors are **not fulfilling their responsibilities to set proper strategic objectives and targets**, and **monitor the business effectively.**

Lack of central guidance

The board has also shown a lack of due care by failing to give enough guidance in areas where central guidance is required, for example **use of promotions.** This may have meant that revenues are less than they could have been, also that the advantages in promotion and advertising that M should enjoy are not being realised because of a lack of clarity of messages.

18 Y

> **Text references**. Chapters 2 and 6.
>
> **Top tips**. The focus in the scenario is on a process, suggesting very clearly that you ought to think about controls over input, processing and output. The answer looks at areas where controls are non-existent (independent verification of farm certification and obtaining customer feedback), inadequate (clear hints that 5% rejection rate is unacceptably high) and inefficient (testing by Y occurs too late in the process). It's worth noting that lack of use of feedback is an important issue at various points here.

In (b) it's likely that the marks would be split fairly evenly between the description of the process, the risk map for Y and the advantages for Y. Description of one risk in each quarter of the quadrant should have earned you the marks for risk mapping for Y, provided your assessment of risk levels was reasonable. Remember that the more serious risks are likely to be due to strategic factors, factors having a major impact upon demand and major operational failures such as delays in production.

Easy marks. The description of risk mapping is core knowledge.

(a)   Input

Farm self-certification

Y relies on farms to certify their adherence to its quality standards. Y does not **attempt** to **verify the accuracy** of the information that farms supply.

In order to ensure that it maintains its name for sourcing organically, Y should **obtain independent evidence** of the accuracy of the certification by farms, either through carrying out testing itself or outsourcing the testing to independent examiners.

Testing before production begins

At the moment 5% of batches are **rejected** after some processing has already taken place. The problems found could have been **picked up before the production process starts**.

Y should begin the **quality testing of milk before processing starts**. This should reduce the failure rate and costs of production, and also make it easier to **trace poor quality milk back to specific suppliers.**

Processing

Lack of use of information

Although information about rejections is **recorded on the quality database,** no further use appears to be made of that information.

The information about failure should be analysed to see if there are any **patterns or common features** in the batches that have been rejected. This information should be compared with information about inputs, to see if any problems can be traced back to specific suppliers.

High rejection rate

The rate of 5% is **high by industry standards** and has **not changed over the last six years**. The cost of this processing is money wasted, and appears to have been tolerated for too long.

Earlier testing and better use of information should bring down the rejection rate. Y should also have a target each year for **continuous improvement, reducing the rate incrementally,** certainly to at **least as low as the industry average.**

Output

Testing of output

Tests on **batch completion** lead to further batches being rejected, this time after they have incurred all the costs of processing.

Again the **reasons for rejection** at this stage should be **carefully analysed.** In particular the results of output testing should be compared with the results of testing during processing, to see why batches that passed during processing were rejected at the completion of the process.

Consumer reaction

At present no attempt is made to **gauge consumer views** on a large-scale basis. Relying on old reviews may mean that Y is **slow to identify customer dissatisfaction** and **longer-term shifts in consumer tastes**.

Y should try to **obtain consumer feedback on a continuous basis,** by surveys or by forums on websites.

(b)   <u>Risk mapping</u>

Risk mapping involves **organising the results of a risk assessment** by **grouping risks into families** on the basis of the **likelihood or frequency** of the risks materialising and the **severity** of the consequences if they materialise. The risk map can then be used to determine what actions should be taken:

- No action may be taken against risks identified as **low likelihood, low severity**
- Risks that are identified as **high likelihood, low severity** may be **reduced** by control procedures designed to **prevent the risks materialising** or designed to **minimise their consequences** if they do occur
- The organisation may seek to **transfer risks** that are **unlikely to materialise** but will have **severe consequences** if they do, by, for example, insuring them
- The organisation will try to **avoid high likelihood, high severity risks** by, for example, not undertaking the activities that generate these risks

		Severity	
		Low	**High**
Likelihood	**Low**	Lack of availability of milk supplies (diverse supplier base should ensure supplies maintained).	Late delivery of milk, leading to production delays and threats to quality. Customers' taste change, they no longer regard Y's products as tasty and Y fails to identify changes quickly.
	High	Farms do not supply quality certificate with milk – quality relates to adherence to organic principles about which customers care little.	Quality control procedures fail to identify problems and pass output that should fail. Customers may fall ill and Y be liable for fines and a collapse in its reputation. Unscrupulous supplier being discovered using non-organic methods, threatening Y's reputation.

<u>Uses of risk mapping</u>

<u>Identifying all risks that need to be met</u>

Analysing risks in this way emphasises the need to **take some action** in relation to all risks other than low: low risks. The process may identify risks where **insufficient action** has been taken.

<u>Determining priorities</u>

The risk map should help determine the **priorities for tackling risks**, with higher risks being tackled first and more resources being utilised to manage them.

<u>Aiding board review</u>

A risk map is important evidence for the board when it conducts **regular and annual reviews of risk**, as required by corporate governance best practice.

<u>Strategic decision-making</u>

Higher risks will often derive from **key strategic decisions** that the board takes. Risk mapping provides evidence for strategic decision-making, and the balancing of acceptable risk levels versus acceptable returns.

19 X

(a)

Internal control system

The internal control system includes the **policies and procedures** adopted by the directors and management of an entity to assist in achieving their objective of ensuring the **orderly and efficient conduct of its business**.

The internal control system extends beyond those matters that relate directly to the accounting system and should **evolve over time** in response to changing risks. The internal control system consists of two main elements, the **control environment** and **control procedures**. Control procedures include operational controls, communication, reports to management and review.

Control environment

The control environment is the **overall attitude, awareness and actions of directors and management regarding internal controls** and their importance in the entity. The control environment encompasses the **management style**, and **corporate culture and values** shared by all employees. It provides the background against which the various other controls are operated.

Costs

The main costs of the internal control function are the salary costs of staff employed to operate controls, such as **internal audit or compliance staff**. Other costs include **training** and **IT investment**. The costs are also the **lost revenues** as a result of operational staff operating internal controls, such as the managers carrying out expense reviews rather than being employed on profit-making activities. There may also be **intangible costs**, such as authorisation procedures **limiting the organisation's flexibility** to respond to new business.

Benefits

The benefits of internal control are **avoidance of losses** caused by disruption of operations, assets being stolen or losing their value through neglect, also as here **reducing or eliminating unnecessary expenditure** and **improving the utilisation of resources and employee performance**.

Limitations

The main limitations of internal controls are **poor design** leading to controls being set up which are **inadequate or inappropriate**. Controls that depend on the judgement of those operating them are **vulnerable to human error**. Controls may be overridden as a result of **collusion between employees or bypassed by directors or senior managers**. Even a **well-designed control system** will be designed with 'normal' transactions or 'normal' risks in mind and may not be able to cope with unusual transactions or unexpected occurrences.

(b)

> **Top tips.** (b) is a good example of a question part with more than one verb (discuss and recommend). You can't afford not to register the second verb and fail to recommend controls. Your answer, however, should have covered not just control of expenses but control of sales representatives' time, as the finance department raised the issue of control over work as well as expenses. Some of the controls we recommend are general, some are standard accounting system controls. Some seek to prevent problems by taking away from sales representatives the decisions over expenses, and some seek to identify problems (principally the review by regional managers).

Internal control and risk management systems

The internal control systems in X should ensure that salesman's activities are carried out in accordance with the **policies and procedures operated** by X, and that the key risks that relate to sales representatives' activities, particularly **not following policies or procedures**, are **avoided or reduced.**

Key risks

Sales representatives are an important feature of X's business. Unless X adopts an alternative B2B model, the sales force will have to be maintained. However greater control is needed for the following reasons.

Excessive costs

The risks of excessive costs include claims for **expenses not incurred**, **claims for private expenses** and **claims for excessive expenses**.

Inefficiencies

In pursuit of new customers and hence higher remuneration, sales representatives may try to **spend amounts to woo them** that are **higher than is desirable** given the chances of picking up their business or the volume of business they are likely to generate. There is also a **risk of inefficiencies** in sales representatives' practices, particularly in the distances they travel. They may be able to concentrate on smaller geographic areas each day.

Controls

Recruitment and training

Proper **references** should be obtained, and sales representatives trained in **selling techniques**.

Employment contracts

Sales representatives should have **employment contracts** detailing the behaviour expected and how their performance will be measured. There should be **disciplinary procedures** for employees who transgress.

Expense policies

Formal policies should clarify the **distinctions between business and personal expenditure**, and also what else constitutes **acceptable and unacceptable expenditure**. Policies should include recovery of expenditure charged but used for private purposes such as private motoring.

Targets

Employees should be set **budgetary targets** for expenditure and **variances** between **budgeted and actual expenditure** should be **investigated**.

More regular review of expenses

Regional managers could collect the data themselves, and be required to review expenses more regularly than they have been doing, maybe **weekly or fortnightly**. The difficulty may be that regional manager success is primarily judged by **how much** business their sales representatives have picked up, so **head office review** will continue to be required and regional managers' performance assessment should be considered (see below).

More detailed review of expenses

However regular they are, manager reviews will only be effective if managers undertake a detailed review of expenses and are prepared to take queries up with the sales representatives. Managers should review **records of all expenditure above a certain limit**, and **compare sales representatives' expenses over time and with other sales representatives under** their authority. Expenses should be **clearly related** to **customers**.

<u>Prior authorisation</u>

Proposed expenditure of certain types, particularly **entertainment**, above a certain limit should require prior authorisation by managers, and would have to be justified by sales representatives on the grounds of the business it was expected to generate.

<u>Central control</u>

Certain costs could be limited by taking decisions from sales representatives and having them **dealt with centrally**. **Hotels** for example could be booked by a single employee, who might be able to obtain discounts from hotel chains as well as limiting the hotels sales representatives can use. More generally, there could be a system of web-based expense authorisation, where sales representatives scan in receipts and invoices. They could then be authorised centrally and payment made.

<u>Alternative solutions</u>

You would also have scored marks if you had discussed the following controls.

<u>Payment means</u>

The risk of **non-existent expenses** would be **reduced by payment on invoice or by credit card settlement** rather than employee reimbursement.

<u>Time spent with customers</u>

Regional managers should review sales representatives' call records to see that an **acceptable volume** of calls has been made, and excessive time has not been spent on certain customers. They should monitor how successful the salesman has been in **turning potential customers into actual customers**.

<u>Customer satisfaction</u>

They should also check with customers to confirm their **satisfaction** with the salesman's efforts.

<u>Performance assessment</u>

A key control may be to change the way sales representatives, and possibly regional management, are assessed. Performance measures should be written into sales representatives' employment contracts, and should cover:

(i) **Targets for sales calls and business generated**, with assessment being made of whether the salesman has been instrumental in winning the business.

(ii) **Comparing the expenses incurred** to generate new clients and keep existing clients with the **volume of business generated**. Depending on how generous the remuneration is, this should reduce the risk that illegitimate expenses will be charged, and will encourage sales representatives not to spend excessive amounts on low volume business.

(c)

Top tips. In (c) the limited number of marks suggests that your discussion needed to concentrate on reasonableness comparisons; from the scenario there is plenty of evidence available for these. A definition of analytical procedures may earn 2 marks but no more, so don't spend too much time on this.

<u>Substantive analytical procedures</u>

Substantive analytical procedures are comparisons of ratios, trends and patterns **over time** and **between different businesses,** for example **departments or people**. They can be used by internal audit at the planning stage, as a means of **highlighting key risk areas**. They can also be used as part of detailed audit testing to spot unusual trends, inconsistencies or areas where fraud may have taken place.

Tests at X

Auditors should examine the level of sales representatives' expenditure and consider whether expenditure levels appear reasonable and are in accordance with the **expectations of the auditors**.

(i)   **Over time**, that there are not wide variations in expenditure and they appear reasonable in relation to sales revenue

(ii)   **In comparison with other sales representatives** reporting to different regional managers. Auditors would expect the levels of certain types of expenditure to be reasonably consistent between different sales representatives

(iii) **In the light of the sales representatives' circumstances**, for example fuel claims fairly reflecting the area the salesman chooses to travel, also the **car make** and **frequency of visits to clients**

20   KSP

Text reference. Chapter 6.

Top tips. The scenario highlights weaknesses at the key stages of the sales cycle including:

- Acceptance of customers
- Recording of transactions and receipts
- Collection of bad debts

The question asks for recommendations with reasons, so you need to explain what the problem is with the current situation or why current controls aren't adequate, as well as recommending improvements. Although the recommendations are designed to improve the Accounts Receivable department's performance, they don't all relate to that department, as not all the problems are its responsibility. However a reduction in the level of queries should help the department operate better in other ways.

Maybe about half the marks would be available in (b) for the definition of the control environment, and you can use the definition to expand on the points you need to discuss in relation to KSP. Remember that you are looking for points that relate to KSP as a whole and influence its culture and tone, including structuring and performance measurement, as well as the role of central functions such as internal audit and also business ethics.

Easy marks. A straightforward definition of the internal control environment would certainly earn you marks in (b). However the examiner's comments indicated that many students did not know what the internal control environment was.

Examiner's comments. In (a) students were very good at suggesting weaknesses, less good at recommending controls that would combat those weaknesses. (b) was not answered well, as many students appeared not to know what the internal control environment was and discussed internal controls in detail instead.

(a)   Acceptance of customers and credit limits

Sales managers may be tempted to offer credit to customers who are poor credit risks in order to maximise sales, increasing the risk of bad debt write-offs. If the Accounts Receivable (AR) manager is to be responsible for the level of bad debts, she should be responsible for deciding whether to **grant credit and setting credit limits**.

Recording of orders

The **recording of orders by sales representatives** may be a **significant reason for the disputes** that have prevented the AR department from achieving its targets. **Independent evidence** should be obtained to support orders, either insisting customers **place orders in writing** or **recording all phone calls**. The sales order forms used should show the **full sales price** and the **discounts given**.

Setting discounts

Sales representatives should **not be responsible for setting discounts**, as it will lead to a **lack of a consistent policy** and result in **disputed invoices, slower collections and more credit notes**. **Sales managers** should be responsible for **authorising customer discounts**.

Recording of discounts

Only holding the **list price** in the computer system means that senior managers **cannot monitor the level of discounts**, and the discounts given cannot be easily checked. The **discounts** should be **recorded separately** on the computer system as well as the gross sales amounts.

Checking invoices

Incorrect invoicing appears to be a significant cause of **disputes and credit notes. Invoices** therefore need to be **compared with sales order forms** before they are issued.

Segregation of duties

The **multi-tasking** by members of the AR department could lead to **fraud or individual staff colluding with customers. Segregation of duties**, having the key tasks of invoicing, recording receipts and debt collection done by different staff, acts as a **check on the work of individual staff** and makes **fraud and collusion less likely**.

Monitoring of debts

It seems that the AR department may not spend enough time on monitoring of the sales ledger. Customer accounts should be **reconciled regularly,** as this may highlight discrepancies that can cause disputes. **Statements** should be issued to customers at least monthly. An **aged receivables analysis** should highlight which customers have balances that are overdue, and should form part of a regular report to senior management along with details of **actions taken** to pursue these debts.

Dealing with discrepancies

A **reduction in the number of discrepancies** should mean that those that arise can be **investigated more quickly.** The AR department should **establish targets** for the time it should take to resolve queries, and **communications with customers** should be **recorded**. If credit notes have to be issued, they should be **authorised by managers.**

Pursuing overdue debts

The high level of receivables days appears to be partly due to the AR department **not spending enough time pursuing slow-paying customers.** The figures can be improved by the AR department focusing on **chasing high value debts.** It may be more effective to **hand debt collection over to an outside agency,** though cost may be an issue. **Bad debt write-offs** should be authorised by management only if there is **strong evidence** that the debt will not be received, such as the customer's liquidation or other evidence of financial difficulties. The **level of bad debts** should be **reported regularly** to senior management.

(b) ### Internal control environment

The internal control environment is the **overall attitude, awareness and actions** of directors and management towards internal controls, reflecting their importance in the organisation. The control environment includes the **management style and corporate culture and ethical values** shared by employees. It provides the background against which **other controls** are **operated.** It includes the **philosophy and operating style** of management, **organisational structure,** the **directors' methods of imposing controls**, and the **integrity and competence** of directors and staff.

Features of KSP's control environment

Pressures to increase sales

The targets set reflect pressures to increase sales, which may result in **excessive risk-taking,** with credit given to customers who could be poor credit risks.

Organisational structure

The structure of the **AR department** is geared towards **servicing customers efficiently.** However it seems to prevent control being exercised by **different staff being involved at different stages of the transaction** and being therefore able to check each other's work.

Target-setting

The manager of the AR department has justifiably criticised the targets the department has been set, on the grounds that the achievement of those targets is too heavily **influenced by actions and decisions taken outside the department**. This may indicate a general weakness in control systems, that the link between targets set for departments and departments' ability to control the factors affecting the targets may be too tenuous.

Internal audit

Internal audit's work may be limited to investigating whether **targets have been achieved** rather than probing more deeply into the reasons **why** targets have not been achieved, given that the AR manager had to supply explanations for the department's failure to achieve its targets. Internal audit work has also **failed to identify significant control weaknesses** such as lack of segregation of duties, or its **recommendations have not resulted in actions** to correct these weaknesses.

21 SRN

Text references. Chapters 5 and 6.

Top tips. Hopefully there are fairly obvious hints in the scenario that you should have been able to identify to use in your answer, for example:

- The apparent readiness of head office to accept (external) theft as an explanation for inventory losses
- Inventory being counted by the stores staff in charge of holding the inventory
- Store discretion to set discounts
- The predictability of current checks (store staff always know when the head office manager will visit and inventory will be counted)

You can assume in scenarios like this that if a control is not noted in the question, that it does not operate.

Easy marks. (a) did not require in-depth explanation and so should have been straightforward.

Examiner's comments. Most candidates scored very well on this question.

Marking scheme

			Marks
(a)		Up to 2 marks for each kind of theft or fraud discussed. Discussion should highlight scenario information that identifies opportunity for dishonesty	6
(b)	(i)	Up to 2 marks for each issue discussed (1 for description, 1 for explanation) Working conditions – credit discussion of culture, motivation, human resource controls, whistleblowing	10
	(ii)	Up to 2 marks for each issue discussed (1 for description, 1 for explanation) Operational controls – credit discussion of authorisation, segregation of duties, security arrangements, checks on inventory	10
		max	19 / 25

(a)

Top tips. One way to generate ideas in (a) is to think where in the process fraud and theft can occur; there are opportunities at Head Office, between Head Office and the stores, and at the stores.

Surprisingly it seems that theft (presumably by external parties) is accepted at present as a valid explanation for inventory losses. This allows staff a number of opportunities for theft.

Theft by head office staff

It appears possible for head office staff to receive and enter the goods, and then despatch them. Head office staff could **enter the amount received, steal some of that inventory and send a lower amount to the stores**. There is no evidence that anyone reconciles the inventory received by stores with the inventory received by head office.

Theft by delivery drivers

The failure to reconcile the inventory received by head office with the inventory received by stores also provides opportunities for **those responsible for delivering the inventory to stores** to steal some of it. It appears that stores staff can **simply blame third parties** for the theft of inventory that they themselves have stolen.

Theft covered up by stores staff

The responsibility stores staff have for counting inventory means that they have the **opportunity to steal inventory but report it as still present** at the stores.

False discounts

Store staff could offer **discounts on inventory** to friends who could then sell this inventory at a higher price and share the proceeds. If store staff knew what was considered as 'excessive' discounting by head office, they could set these discounts so that they were within the limits tolerated by head office.

(b)

> **Top tips.** In (b) the best way to ensure you score marks for the operational controls you give is to link those controls as directly as possible with the risks identified in (a).

(i)   Working conditions and the role of the human resources function

Zero toleration of theft

Head office management should try to deter theft by making it clear that **theft of inventory or cash is unacceptable** and staff who are discovered stealing anything will be **dismissed and prosecuted**.

Conditions and pay

Staff may be less inclined to steal inventory if **working conditions and pay** are **comparable with, or better than, competitors**. Instances have been publicised of staff theft of inventory being regarded as a fair perk in stores where pay and conditions were very poor. These thefts were **condoned by management**, demonstrating a **very bad control environment**. Introducing discounts for employees may increase **staff motivation**.

Recruitment

All staff recruited should provide **references** and be asked when they apply if they have been **convicted of any indictable offences**. Human resources staff should confirm **references** are genuine by **contacting referees themselves** and should investigate any details about referees that appear to be unusual (for example a school head teacher's address not being the address of his or her school).

Whistleblowing

The human resources function should **operate and publicise a channel of communication** so that staff who know that other staff have been **stealing inventory** can report thefts in confidence. Staff should be assured that they will not be victimised for reporting instances of theft.

Staffing levels

If stores are understaffed, staff may be **too busy to keep track of inventory** when it is delivered. Human resources need to assess whether staffing levels are adequate, in order for the **operational controls** described below to be effective.

Performance measures

The **performance measures used to judge the performance of store managers should include the % of inventory recorded** as stolen in their stores. The human resources function could benchmark practices at other store chains to see if manager and staff remuneration might be linked to the % of inventory stolen at their stores.

(ii) Operational internal controls

Segregation of duties at head office

To limit the opportunity for theft of inventory at head office, different staff should be responsible for **receiving inventory from suppliers** and **despatching it to stores**. Other staff should reconcile the **amounts shown as received by head office** with the **amounts shown as supplied on supplier documentation**.

Reconciliations

Inventory is not held at head office but **immediately despatched to stores once deliveries to Head Office are recorded**. It should therefore be possible to compare easily the inventory delivered and then despatched. This should prevent inventory being stolen at head office. A simpler solution may be to cut out the seemingly superfluous delivery to head office and have the **suppliers deliver directly to stores**. To **deter delivery staff** from **stealing inventory on route**, the **inventory despatched** to each store and the **inventory received** by each store should be **recorded**, and the **amounts compared** by separate head office staff.

Inventory counts

To remove the opportunity for **stores staff** to **record higher amounts in count records** to those held in inventory, each store's **regular counts** should be **conducted by staff from another store** or **head office**. To deter staff from stealing inventory between counts and seeking to cover up theft at the counts, **surprise inventory counts** could be **carried out** by other staff more frequently than every six months. These counts should not follow a predictable pattern, both in terms of **how frequently they happen** and the **items counted**.

Improved security arrangements

To limit the opportunity for inventory theft by staff, **access to shop inventory store rooms** could be **limited to store managers. Closed circuit television recordings**, reviewed by head office, could be used to **spot theft by staff of inventory on display in stores. Security tagging** of inventory with tags being removed at the point of sale would make it harder for staff to steal goods. Although it may offend some staff, management should consider introducing **random checks on staff bags and lockers**.

Head office authorisation of discounts

To ensure that illegitimate discounts are not given by stores, head office could remove from stores the discretion to give discounts on slow-moving inventory. Head office could **prescribe a set scale of discounts**, or **approve in advance any discounts store managers recommended**. This would also help store to store benchmarking as all % would be the same, so **making it easier for Head Office to spot theft.**

---

22 CSX

Text references. Chapters 6, 15 and 16.

Top tips. Our answer to (a) links risks with controls designed to counter them, which is the neatest way to tackle this question. The amount of detail given about data entry and the fairly casual attitude to inventory write-offs indicates that these are significant problems. CIMA's model answer also suggested that you would have received credit for discussing various general and application controls over computer activities.

(b) needs to be read quite carefully; the examiner wants a general answer about use of different audit tests in inventory work. You therefore need to think beyond CSX and consider work done at the inventory count. The question requirements include a very strong hint about discussing computer-assisted audit techniques, so you need to spend time describing how they are used to test inventory.

Easy marks. Provided you understood what the examiner wanted, and had a good knowledge of the basics of auditing, (b) should have been quite reasonable.

Examiner's comments. Students scored very well on (a), but disappointedly poorly on (b).

In (b) many answers just discussed internal controls, rather than internal audit tests and techniques, which was what the question required. A number of answers to (b) duplicated the answers to (a) and merely added that the auditors should check whether the control was operating. Students would have gained credit for general suggestions and detailed work on inventory. Future students would be well-advised to study internal audit well.

Marking scheme

		Marks
(a)	1 mark for each risk identified and 1 mark for each well-explained internal control linked with the risk. Issues discussed could include segregation of duties, recording, theft and disposal of inventory	15
(b)	Up to 3 marks for each audit test discussed. To score marks, tests must give assurance on inventory. Award marks for control testing, inventory count attendance, analytical review, CAATs	10
		$\overline{25}$

(a) <u>Risks and improvements</u>

<u>Incorrect quantities received</u>

There is no indication that the quantities received are matched with the quantities ordered. Suppliers may **over or under deliver amounts.** If too much inventory is delivered, then **inventory may be held for excessive time and the risk of obsolescence** may **increase.** If inventory is under-ordered, there may be **insufficient quantities in inventory to fulfil customer demand**.

Records of goods received should be **matched with purchase orders and supplier invoices.** The purchasing function should resolve matters with suppliers if incorrect quantities are delivered or deliveries that **do not match orders** could be **refused and returned**.

<u>Incorrect amounts paid</u>

The **actual price paid to suppliers** may be **greater than the tender price** on which the purchase order is based. This could also mean that **inventory is incorrectly valued** if it is valued at tender price.

The purchasing function should **compare the values of purchases invoiced by suppliers** with the **tender prices** to ensure that they are identical.

<u>Misposting of inventory</u>

Clerical staff could post **incorrect quantities of inventory received**. If amounts are over-posted, there is a risk that inventory actually available may be **insufficient to meet customer demand**. If amounts are under-posted, unnecessary extra orders may be made, resulting in **increased purchase and holding costs**, and **greater risk of obsolescence**. If data on picking lists have to be posted manually by warehouse staff, there is also a risk that **quantities delivered to customers** may be entered **wrongly**.

Purchase ordering should be **computerised** and **quantities entered on delivery matched** with **specific purchase orders.** The computer should identify any differences between **amounts ordered** and **deliveries entered.** The GRNs and picking lists should **automatically update warehouse records** without the need for further data entry by warehouse staff.

<u>Loss of inventory</u>

The company is suffering **increased costs** through inventory **being lost. More orders** may have to be made, and CSX may be **unable to satisfy customer demand** because there is insufficient inventory available. Also staff may be stealing inventory said to be lost, since components are **high value, small, portable** and **easily saleable.**

Inventory counts should be carried out **monthly due to technological changes** that rapidly render parts obsolete; if costs are an issue, different types of inventory should be counted each month, with all inventory perhaps being counted over a **three month cycle**. Excessive losses should be investigated. Steps taken to **prevent losses** should include **surveillance** by security staff, ensuring that there is **no access to inventory** by unauthorised staff and **searching staff** who are allowed access to inventory.

Collusion between staff

Collusion to hide loss or theft of inventory between staff handling goods and staff entering data may be easy to arrange as they work together in the warehouse.

There should be stricter **segregation of duties,** with staff entering data being based away from the warehouse and reporting to different managers.

Disposal of obsolete inventory

There appears to be no control over staff throwing away inventory that is obsolete or damaged. **Good inventory** could be **incorrectly classified** as obsolete, and again staff could use throwing away inventory as a cover for stealing good items.

Managers **should authorise the disposal of inventory**; staff should **not throw obsolete items away** on their own initiative. **All write-offs** should be **recorded**.

Loss of data

The age of the computer system may make **computer crashes and loss of data** more likely. There is no evidence of controls to counter these threats.

Data should be **backed up daily** and back up copies kept off site. CSX should also have **contingency arrangements** in place for processing data if the computer system breaks down. Other **appropriate general** and **application controls** should be in place to limit risks to data.

Accounting

There are various risks of **incorrect external reporting of accounting data** including **incorrect valuation of inventory** and use of a **potentially inaccurate general provision** of 2%. This provision may be contrary to the **requirements of IAS 37** and in the context of a **profit margin of $12 million** may be **material**. The lack of care taken over it may indicate a **poor control environment in relation to accounting**.

Inventory should be valued at **actual price paid to suppliers or net realisable value** if this is lower due to obsolescence. The provision against inventory should be **limited to specific losses**; this should also emphasise to management the extent of the problem of inventory loss and encourage them to take steps to reduce it.

(b)   Walkthrough tests

Auditors should confirm that the systems and documentation for **recording inventory** are operating as it should be. They should **trace** a limited number of items **through inventory records** to see whether their understanding of the system and controls is correct.

Tests of controls

Auditors should carry out **compliance tests** on controls in areas where risks are significant and the organisation needs controls to reduce these risks. Auditors should examine evidence such as **manual signatures or computer cross-references** to see that **comparisons are being made** between different inventory records, for example purchase orders and delivery notes. Auditors should also assess whether **inventory is being kept in secure accommodation**, and **observe security measures** such as **searches of staff** that are in place.

Substantive tests – attendance at inventory counts

Auditors should **observe inventory counts**, seeing whether count procedures are being followed by staff. They should carry out **test counts.** Auditors should also check that **differences between records** and **actual amounts** in inventory are **investigated** and **adequate explanations obtained,** both at the counts they attend and other counts held during the year. They should also check that **cut-off** is **correct,** that inventory movements are recorded in the right period.

Analytical review

Auditors should **review inventory levels at the count** and **records of inventory levels** during the year. They should obtain evidence that inventory is only ordered when amounts held are below **minimum levels. Analytic review** of different inventory figures can also highlight problems with certain types of inventory. Auditors can compare the **holding periods** and **write-offs** of specific types of inventory, inventory held in different locations or inventory ordered from certain suppliers. They can thus highlight areas of concern, poor control of inventory held in certain places for example.

Computer assisted audit techniques

As many inventory systems are computerised, auditors will need to use computer-assisted audit techniques to audit inventory effectively. Examples include:

(i)   Test data

Test data can be used to test controls over inventory data entry, such as reasonableness checks ensuring that entry of **excessive inventory quantities** is **queried**, or only items with permitted inventory line or supplier codes can be processed.

(ii)   Audit software

Audit software can be used to **make comparisons**, for example inventory levels at different locations, or **carry out analytic review calculations**, for example ranking inventory lines by % write-offs. Audit software can also be used to **compare versions of programs** that are used at different locations where inventory is held.

(iii)   Integrated test facility

An integrated test facility involves the creation of a **fictitious entity.** Transactions are put through using existing programs and actual results are compared with predicted results, for example whether inventory has been **costed correctly**.

(iv)   Systems control and review file

This posts **transactions with certain characteristics**, for example orders above a certain amount or unusual orders from specific suppliers to a file for **later auditor review**.

23   HIJ

Text references. Chapter 6 gives general guidance on internal controls and Chapter 7 will help with the management accounting aspects. Chapter 15 discusses the approach to different types of audit.

Top tips. Success in this question depends on using your imagination to make the most of the limited data available.

Easy marks. The discussion of cost-benefits in (c) covers the considerations that you would normally cover on cost-benefit questions. Note in (c) that benefits can be classified as positive benefits or means of reducing risks/avoiding losses. For costs your answer needs to mention direct financial costs and opportunity costs.

Examiner's comments. Again many students failed to apply their knowledge to the scenario, with some suggesting an internal audit department (which was unrealistic given the size of the company), others suggested that all expenses over £2 be approved. 'Reading the scenario and planning a sensible answer bearing in mind the organisation in the question would be a huge benefit to candidates.'

In (a) some answers failed to discuss management controls, in (b) some answers just listed the various types of audit rather than using the scenario to discuss the need for audits in terms of the risks identified.

(a)

Top tips. (a) asks for management controls; because of the small size of the company the Principal will have to implement most of the controls himself rather than rely on others. There are various ways in which you could group the controls; our broad headings relate to environmental and organisational controls, performance measurement controls and asset protection controls.

To achieve good marks, you need some explanation of each control as you are making recommendations, but it is important also to cover a range of controls. You need to cover financial, non-financial quantitative and qualitative controls. If you define and recommend each control well, you could probably score a couple of marks for each, so would need six controls to score the maximum twelve marks.

Exercise of controls

The small size of the organisation means it is likely that the Principal will operate most of the controls himself, although he will use the support staff to assist him.

Environment and organisational controls

How effective the control environment is and the organisational controls are will be very dependent on the Principal. He will be responsible for **setting standards** (and example) of **client care** and **cost consciousness**, and the **organisational structure** depends on his active involvement, as staff will report into him. If he is busy with marketing activity, it may be appropriate to **delegate certain responsibilities** to another senior member of staff such as guiding newer members of staff.

Budgets and comparison with actual data

Budgets should be prepared annually, and also amended to take account of changes in staff and client based. The following elements will be particularly important:

(i)   **Chargeable hours targets** for staff
(ii)   **Income and hours targets** for clients
(iii)   **Major expenses** including staff salaries, marketing, travel and office upkeep

The Principal should **compare budgeted and actual figures** monthly for hours and income targets, less frequently for less regular expenditure. The Principal should take appropriate action if there are **variances** (counselling staff who are not reaching their chargeable hour targets, using budgeted vs actual data when establishing fees).

Balanced scorecard

Using a balanced scorecard approach should mean using a **variety of indicators** and thinking in terms of **perspectives** across the whole organisation.

(i)   **Customer** – measures include **number of new clients won through marketing activity**, whether **any clients have been lost** and **feedback received** at the Principal's meetings with Managing Directors, also the results of **quality reviews** carried out by the Principal.

(ii)   **Internal** – measures include **chargeable hours as a percentage of total hours**, **average charge-out rate** per hour and **comparisons of time spent on each client**, also **deadlines** for producing information are met.

(iii)   **Innovation and training** – this can be judged by the **labour turnover rate**, also the **new or improved services** offered to clients.

(iv)   **Financial** – apart from total revenues, earnings, cash flow and return on capital employed indicators; other measures include percentage of clients that have not **been profitable**.

Debtor management

Billing must be kept up on a monthly basis, and **credit periods** established as part of the **annual negotiations.** Slow payers should be chased in a series of stages, and these should include **stopping Principal and staff visits** until the debts are paid.

Human resource management

Clearly the employees of HIJ are a key asset and controls are needed over the lifetime of their employment. Recruitment controls should include **references** and also an **interview process** that provides evidence of the **knowledge and communication skills** required. **Training** should include **induction processes** for all new staff and a **personal development programme**. **Remuneration levels** should be influenced by the staff member's success in meeting client profitability and chargeable hours targets. **Employment contracts** should include clauses that prevent staff poaching HIJ's clients if they move elsewhere.

Knowledge management

Human resource management is a key part of knowledge management but there are other issues including **transfer and retention of knowledge.** There should be **specific guidance on the level of detail** that needs to be recorded about each client, and also about the need for **regular updating** of information. Whenever staff are introduced to clients, there should be an **induction process** to ensure they have sufficient knowledge to deal satisfactorily with the clients.

(b)

Need for audit

Audit work should focus on areas where there is a high risk of loss or serious consequences if risk crystallises, or areas (particularly in dealings with clients) where value could be added.

As the Principal is a qualified accountant, he could carry out internal audit work himself, but given his already extensive role in control, it is difficult to see how additional work by himself will add value, and so the audit should be carried out by external auditors or consultants (the company is too small to warrant an internal audit function).

Financial audit

As cost control is a key priority, audit work needs to cover financial controls. However whether a separate audit is required is doubtful, as assurance can be gained from the work done by the external auditors.

The external auditors will be concerned with the **recoverability of receivables**, and hence will examine the **credit control procedures.** They will also be concerned with the **validity of expenditure,** so will check by reviewing documentation that the expenditure by the Principal and staff is for **business purposes.** Their analytical review should highlight **discrepancies in numerical information**, for example variations in figures between accounting periods, differences between sources of internal data.

Management audit

A management audit is an appraisal of the **effectiveness of managers** and the corporate structure in the achievement of entity and corporate objectives. As there is no effective internal review of the Principal's own role, an **external review by management consultants** will be necessary to highlight any areas of potential weakness. Areas might include:

- **Supervision**. Is the Principal exercising **sufficient supervision** over other staff; are the reviews of their work regular enough and have problems been identified early?
- **Information**. Is the Principal being given sufficient **timely information**?
- **Delegation**. Would management be more **effective** if the Principal **delegated** some of his work to a senior staff member?
- **Decisions**. Do the **judgments** that the Principal has made appear reasonable?
- **Principal's work**. What is the **quality of the Principal's own work** in advising clients in terms of the contents of reports?

Marketing audit

As marketing activity is central to HIJ's expansion, and much of the Principal's time is spent on it, an independent review will provide assurance of its **effectiveness.** A marketing specialist will be able to bring in knowledge of the sector to judge the **activity** at conferences and the **effectiveness of the brochures and advertising** as methods of communication.

Computer security audit

Loss of confidential information could be very serious for HIJ in terms of the **financial compensation** it may have to pay and **loss of reputation.** An independent check on the **robustness of security controls** will be valuable. Other key areas where an IT audit may add value is the **quality of output and adequacy of back-up procedures.**

(c)   <u>Benefits</u>

Benefits of internal controls will include fulfilment of the objectives established by the Principal including:

- **Cost control**
- All **clients being profitable**
- **Improved chargeable hours of staff**

Other benefits include:

- **Reduced losses through computer or security problems**
- **Bad debt reduction**
- **No loss of clients or key staff**
- Having **motivated staff** working to their full potential
- Producing **reliable financial information**

<u>Costs</u>

There will be costs involved in establishing most of the controls in (a), for example setting up **information sources for the balanced scorecard**. Ongoing costs include **monies paid** to anyone supplying a **control function**, for example a dedicated credit controller or internal auditor, or **fees** paid to an external auditor for services supplied. There may also be costs in **maintaining back-up computer facilities.**

Opportunity costs will include the loss of the **Principal's time**; his **chargeable hours** and hence **fee-earning capacity** will be **reduced** by the time he has to spend on internal controls. There are also the losses involved in diverting other staff to operate controls and away from more profitable activities.

24   GG

Text references. Chapters 5-7.

Top tips. The first issue in (a) (i) is the lack of commitment by the board. Remember this is an important part of the control environment and is particularly important here as GG clearly needs to make changes. Secondly the supervisors' suggestions demonstrate a clear understanding of the types of changes that need to be made if TQM is to be introduced successfully.

(a) (ii) is about an effective change management process for implementing TQM. It draws upon issues that you will have covered in E1 and E3. It also brings in a number of issues across control systems, for example feedback on processes, promotion of a favourable internal environment and culture by clear management commitment and HR issues (training and performance recognition). It is legitimate to discuss the quality circles that GG did run as they are a step that GG should have taken, but you need to demonstrate how they should be better implemented (principally by listening to the supervisors!)

In (b) it is not completely clear whether the reduction in quality control staff arises from the supervisors' suggestions being adopted. If they are, this should mean that a lower proportion of faulty components is produced. However the main brunt of the question is concerned with what happens if the reduction in staff means that there is a higher risk that faulty components will pass quality control procedures and be sent to customers.

Easy marks. The consequences of a business selling faulty products has been a feature of a number of scenarios in recent papers, and so in (c) you should have identified themes of costs of replacing faulty products and loss of sales and reputation. You should always be alert for products, such as braking systems, which may threaten consumer safety.

Examiner's comments. Answers demonstrated lack of planning and repetition, with answers to (a) including comments that were more appropriate to (b). Other failings in (a) included spending time criticising the current system rather than focusing on the attempt to introduce TQM and describing TQM in general terms rather than focusing on the scenario.

(a) (i) <u>Lack of commitment from board</u>

A change to TQM would be significant for GG and it therefore needs to be **led by the board**. The board however has not yet shown a commitment to making any changes. Just holding meetings is insufficient, if, as has happened, no concrete actions result. Holding the meetings in overtime rather than as part of the **normal working week** gives the impression that TQM is a peripheral part of the supervisors' role. The board appears also to be more concerned with other costs than the substantial costs of quality failings that the 20% rejection rate implies.

<u>Rescheduling</u>

The board rejected a practical suggestion from supervisors, to improve the quality of output by **rescheduling work patterns.** One aspect of TQM is to **review production processes** and **make changes to reduce risks of mistakes** being made. The change may also have provided evidence of the extent to which errors are due to lack of attention by staff rather than other factors. The board however seems more concerned with increasing workload, which, if anything, may increase the chances of errors occurring.

<u>Use of quality control staff</u>

The board has also rejected the proposal to **employ quality control staff** on the production line. Again this suggestion clearly relates to TQM. By moving the quality control staff, it emphasises to everyone that maintaining quality is an integral part of the production process rather than a separate activity. It also shifts the focus towards 'getting it right', **preventing rather than detecting errors**. This should **reduce non-conformance costs,** the costs of output being made and then having to be rejected and taken away, and also the costs of employing some quality control staff to monitor output.

<u>Staff motivation</u>

The approach of the board is also likely to result in the **demotivation of production supervisors**. The board has asked them for suggestions but rejected what seem to be sensible recommendations because they do not fit in with the board's agenda for limiting other costs. The supervisors may wonder what the point was of asking them for their suggestions and may therefore not bother about making comments or attempting to improve quality in future.

(ii) <u>Board involvement</u>

The **commitment of the board** should have been made **clear** from the start. Ideally one director should have been appointed as Quality Director. It should be made clear that this is a permanent role and the Quality Director will be responsible for driving a culture of continuous improvement.

<u>Review processes</u>

Every step of the process should be reviewed, in order to see how quality control failures can be prevented. The review should start with previous results of quality checks and focus on investigating stages with a high error rate, or stages where costs of rejection and reworking are particularly high. The review should also examine the system of quality checks, **focusing on the quality checks that take place early on the process**, aiming to identify why early quality checks have failed to pick up defects that later checks have identified

<u>Improvement and redesign of steps</u>

The results and investigations into the reasons for components being defective should then be used as a basis for **improving and redesigning processes to reduce the likelihood of products being defective**. The data may point to some **specific shortcomings**, for example problems in the calibration process, for which allowing more time may reduce errors. They may indicate the possibility of wider changes, perhaps **reduction in the complexity of the product** or simplifying production processes by removing certain steps. The results may also show the need for more **rigorous quality testing earlier in the production process** or indeed involvement of quality staff in production.

<u>Involvement of production supervisors</u>

Involving supervisors in operating circles is a positive step. However the quality circles need to be more fully developed, perhaps meeting more often within normal working hours. The supervisors need to be briefed on what they are expected to contribute. However the briefing should **not be too**

prescriptive and should not limit the scope that the circles have. The presumption should also be that **suggestions supervisors make should be implemented**, unless they are obviously impractical. This is because GG needs to prioritise improving quality over other business issues, supervisors should be best-placed to offer practical suggestions for improvement and adopting their suggestions will ensure supervisors will be committed to leading change in processes.

Involvement of employees

GG also needs to find ways of **promoting commitment to higher quality** by all employees. Possibly the quality circles ought to be widened to include employees as well as supervisors. GG could introduce a **suggestions scheme**, with employees being rewarded for suggestions they make. The results of the quality inspections and investigations should influence the way **employees are trained** if it seems that the same mistakes keep occurring. The board could also **set quality targets** and pay a company-wide bonus if these targets are achieved. Over time the quality targets could be made tougher, in order to promote continuous improvement in processes.

(b) Involvement of quality control in production

If the supervisors' suggestions are adopted, the involvement of quality control staff in production should result in a **reduction of errors during setting up or at other parts of the manufacturing process.** Prevention of errors should mean that the proportion of faulty components that reach the quality testing stages is lower.

Increase in number of errors

However there is also a risk that the reduction in the number of quality control staff will increase the risk of faulty valves that have gone through production being sent to car manufacturers. This may result from the quality control function **reducing the amount of tests it performs** or **carrying out tests more quickly and hence less thoroughly.** The reduction of quality control staff, particularly if combined with pressure on production staff to produce more, may also convey the message that staff need be less concerned about quality. This will also increase the risks of faulty products.

Rejection by manufacturers

Manufacturers are likely to have their own quality testing procedures on GG's valves. These may well **identify at least some of the faulty valves** and compensate for failings in GG's procedures. However manufacturers are likely to require GG to replace the faulty valves. This will increase GG's costs, as well as risking loss of goodwill.

Risks of accidents

If the faulty valves are used in car braking systems, they may cause brakes to fail, resulting in death or serious injury.

Legal costs

If car braking systems fail, GG, as well as the manufacturer, may face **legal action**. GG may have to **incur high legal costs and also face the risks of significant damages** because it knows that its components will be used in brakes, which are vital to car safety. Claimants' chances of success are likely to be improved by the court having the benefits of hindsight that mechanical failure has occurred. Damages may be **more substantial** if the reduction in quality control by GG is held to demonstrate that GG was **negligent.**

Loss of sales

If manufacturers have to reject a high proportion of components from GG, they may eventually **stop buying from GG** and use a more reliable supplier. This risk is enhanced if failure of braking systems is publicly linked with the failure of GG's valves. Manufacturers will be very concerned with threats to their own **reputation and sales.** Toyota, for example, has had significant problems as a result of mechanical failures in its cars. Manufacturers will not wish to use components that have been linked with braking failures.

25   D

(a)   Financial

Sales revenue

In order to monitor performance closely, central management will require **regular information about sales**. Monthly or quarterly sales reports will measure **short-term performance,** when comparisons are made with previous period performance, with performance in the equivalent period in the previous year if sales are seasonal, and with other dealerships. This measure will help central management determine not only the performance of individual dealerships but how successful divisional management has been in monitoring the performance of each dealership.

Return on investment

At the same time the new structure implies autonomy for management over the longer-term. D will need to measure how each division's dealerships are performing over a longer time period, in the light of the resources available. A **return on investment target** can act as a longer term objective, with investment measured in a variety of different ways, for example by floor space or number of staff.

Customer

Repeat business

Customer satisfaction can be measured by the amount of business the dealerships obtain from previous customers. This includes **sales** to customers who have previously purchased cars from the dealerships or subsequent **service business** for dealerships on cars that they have sold. Use of these measures will encourage dealerships to maintain contact with previous customers by sending them information about new products or reminding them about services they offer.

Customer feedback

Customer satisfaction can also be measured by surveying recent customers, **asking them** what they **think of the service provided** or keeping logs of the **number of customer complaints**. This data could provide specific feedback about activities that the business does well, or problems (in terms of services provided or staff) that dealerships need to rectify.

Learning and growth

New makes

Sales of **new makes of cars** should provide a strong indication of how well the dealerships are likely to develop in future. Industry and press coverage, as well as the marketing done by dealerships, should

ensure that new customers are attracted. Dealerships can also measure how many previous customers are persuaded to trade up to the new makes of cars. The success of new makes is likely to be well-publicised in industry journals and dealership performance can be assessed against what has happened in the industry.

New services

The **new services** provided by dealerships, and **measures of how successful** they are, should also indicate future growth. Examples include offers designed to **attract new customers** such as fixed price servicing or services done within a limited timeframe. D should also assess how services that promote longer-term loyalty are doing, for example membership of loyalty clubs or take-up of service plans.

Internal business processes

Rectification work

Rectification work on **cars sold recently** can provide a good indication of the quality of service being provided. The faults being rectified are often likely to be avoidable, since they should have been identified by the dealerships when the cars were checked before being released to customers.

Delays in orders

The number of cars that are not in inventory and have to be ordered specially with **consequent delay in delivery** is an important indication of internal processes. Special orders suggest poor inventory management by the division and a failure to forecast demand accurately. They may also be an indirect indication of lost sales. Some customers may be prepared to wait. Others however may go to a competitor.

(b) (i) ### Lack of transfer pricing

There appears to be **no transfer pricing system** between dealerships, nor any guidelines about the amount of credit customers should receive for a trade-in. Each dealership appears to be credited therefore with the full sales figure, with no distinction being made between the relative proportions within the sales figure of cash received and trade-in credit. As receiving dealerships do not appear to be assessed on the credits they give, it is possible that they are giving excessive credits, to boost their own sales figures.

Rectification work

Company policy means that often the dealership that accepts the traded-in car will not be the dealership that sells it on, although the receiving dealership will be responsible for rectification work. The way the dealerships are organised means that the receiving dealership will normally have a good idea of whether it will be selling on cars it has received. If it is not selling a car itself, maintenance work on it will be a drain on its **profits and labour hours** without the benefit of future sales revenue. The dealership thus has a clear incentive to spend the minimum time on maintenance work, maybe meaning that an inadequate job is done. Defects may not be obvious initially, but may appear some time after sale to the customer, harming D's reputation. In addition the receiving dealership may not always have **staff with the experience** of carrying out work on some cars that are different to the types that it normally sells.

(ii) ### Guidelines on trade-in prices

Guidelines based on **industry standards** could be established for the trade-in prices dealerships are allowed to give customers. Alternatively receiving dealerships could be credited with the cash received from the customer, plus the **difference between a fair market value transfer price and the credit given**, giving the receiving dealerships the incentive to keep trade-in credits to a minimum.

Responsibility for rectification work

One obvious way of remedying this problem will be to make the dealerships that sell the second-hand cars **responsible for the rectification work**. This will ensure that costs and benefits are matched. The selling dealership will have an incentive to ensure the work is done to a high quality to improve the prospect of sale and minimise the risk of subsequent customer complaints. The selling dealership should be able to claim against the receiving dealership for repair work on faults that the receiving dealership should have identified when it accepted the car from the customer.

Charging for rectification work

Alternatively the current system of responsibility for rectification should r̲
dealership that receives the car should be **allowed to charge the dealers**
price for rectification work, based on what external customers would be̲
subsequently be reduced if the rectification work is found to be inadequat̲

26 HH

Text references. Chapters 5 and 7.

Top tips. A clear reminder of P3's place in the performance pillar. Expect more questions that are based on management accounting issues.

Easy marks. Probably the easiest part of the question is (a) (ii), as it gives a fairly wide scope to discuss different measures.

Examiner's comments. Generally this question was done well, although a few students appeared not to know the difference between managing profits and value streams. The one disappointment was students failing to mention overheads, marginal costing and ABC.

Marking scheme

				Marks
(a)	(i)	Up to 2 marks per issues discussed. Issues could include: Encourages focus on whole company performance Differentiation between value and non-value-adding activities Increased customer focus		
			max	5
	(ii)	Up to 2 marks per issue. Issues could include: Activity-based costing Marginal costing Advertising costs budgeting and charging Central overheads Client profitability analysis Target costing Life cycle costing Accounting function reorganisation		
			max	10
(b)		Up to 2 marks per issue. Issues could include: Staff uncertainties/resistance to change Company re-organisation Management performance New targets Management information requirements		
			max	10
				25

(a)

Top tips The scenario emphasises what value streams are, and systems need to focus on what satisfies customers. (a) (ii) allows quite a wide scope to discuss a number of newer management accounting techniques. There are some clear directions in the scenario. For example the fact that overheads are being absorbed into charges should have hinted that you should consider alternative methods such as ABC or marginal costing. As design is an important activity for HH, you should have mentioned life cycle costing. Your answer needs to relate the changes you suggest to the commercial pressures of running the organisation, particularly keeping customers satisfied and limiting central overheads.

(i) Company as a whole

The perception of customers is that HH is selling an integrated service. Staff time and media capacity need therefore to be reported on an integrated basis. Using value streams will mean **reporting the performance of activities across departments** rather than **focusing on the performance of each department**. This would mean that it is no longer necessary to operate a system of internal charging. This would reduce the risk of dysfunctional behaviour, such using supposedly cheaper external suppliers.

Value generating and non-value generating activities

Focusing on value streams should mean a clear distinction being drawn between costs related to **value generation** and other costs. The performance of managers of value streams will be judged solely on the costs generated out of the value stream, and not be influenced by the allocation of additional overheads. Costs such as the costs of central space not directly linked to value generation will be accounted for separately.

Customer focus

Focus on value streams will mean a stronger link between **value for customers** and the costs required to generate that value. It should result in a greater focus on **customer perceptions of value**, the factors that persuade customers to pay the fees charged by H. This should encourage concentration on where the greatest value is added for customers rather than highlighting the internal contribution of individuals.

(ii) Activity-based costs

HH will have to consider how best to account for the costs related to each value stream. An activity-based costing system will focus on **what activities add value** and their **related costs**. This will mean that costs are **directly related to the decisions** made by managers on how to enhance value, rather than managers being held responsible for decisions such as space occupied which do not relate to value generated.

Advertising costs

The **costs of media buying should be budgeted and reviewed** on a centralised basis. The assessment should be on the basis of how cheaply media space can be brought overall. It should be possible to do this as **demand for space from most clients** for campaigns should be **known sometime in advance.** This should mean that the cost of media space no longer influences the measurement of the performance of account executives, and hence will no longer encourage them to bypass the media buying department.

Central overheads

A focus on activity-based costing should also encourage a **close look at central costs** that do not directly generate value. HH needs to revise its policy of appearing to treat these costs as given, to be allocated to departments and recouped on charge-out rates. The most significant central cost is the city-centre site. If it appears to add little value, for example is not used much by clients, then HH's management needs to consider the **relocation of central functions to a cheaper out-of-town site**.

Customer profitability analysis

Focus on value streams should mean information is analysed in terms of the contribution **generated by individual customers or groups of customers**. This requires chargeable hours and revenues for each client to be recorded in detail, and relations with individual clients to be overseen by an account manager. Management should receive details of time billed and work in progress not yet billed.

Target and life cycle costing

Focus on whole value streams should mean focus on the **total value added for clients** and hence the **price that customers are prepared to pay**. This should encourage a target costing approach, establishing this price and then determining total costs and resources to be used on a basis of achieving a **desired profit margin**, rather than calculating price to be charged on the basis of achieving a desired mark-up on costs, including allocated overheads. The control of costs that will be required for target costing to work will be helped by **life-cycle analysis.** This should identify where in a provision of service **most costs are incurred**, for example at the website design stage.

Focusing on the costs and resources used at these stages should help maximise the flow of services in the value streams.

Customer satisfaction analysis

Focusing on value for customers will also encourage a **greater focus of what matters to customers**. This implies more attention being given to non-financial issues, such as the time taken to provide services, the quality of the website and advertising campaigns (benchmarked against competition) and the results of the campaigns.

Reorganisation of accounting function

Focusing on the management of value streams will probably require a **re-organisation of the accounting function.** Fewer, if any, accountants may be attached to departments. Instead accountants may be allocated to a group of client account holders based on services offered to clients within that group.

(b)

> **Top tips.** Change management knowledge could be helpful in answering (b). A significant danger is that although the management accounting system changes, this may not be matched exactly by changes in the organisation structure or management performance measurement. Even if performance measurement does change, managers who can no longer rely on certain methods to manipulate how their own performance is measured will need to be treated carefully.

Staff uncertainties

Staff and department staff may be very uncertain about the purposes of switching to a value chain approach. The uncertainty may be enhanced, and morale threatened, if staff believe that their jobs are in danger. Ahead of changes being made, senior managers must therefore **explain why they are necessary**. Managers should emphasise that changes are required to move HH towards an external, customer orientation, delivering the value that clients require, eliminating waste and no longer being distracted by distortions caused by internal accounting methods.

Company structures

The value streams approach would appear to require a move from a departmental form of organisation to a matrix form of organisation, where individuals are **not just responsible to their department**, but also to the manager responsible for the value stream or client. However staff cannot easily take orders from two or more bosses. A revised authority structure, with the **authority of each manager carefully defined**, needs to be established before changes are made to the accounting system.

Responsibility accounting

The review of the authority of each manager also needs to **define how managers' performance will be assessed**. Managers may well be uncertain about what constitutes successful performance if they are no longer allowed to charge other departments a mark-up for their department's work, or take steps to improve performance such as using **external suppliers or dealing directly with newspapers.** Senior management need to organise management appraisals that **establish objectives** consistent with the value chain approach.

Targets

Moving to a value stream approach implies **extra targets connected with customer satisfaction** as well as financial targets. It may be difficult to decide what these targets should be, how their achievement should be measured and what should happen if they conflict. As a first stage HH should organise a **detailed customer satisfaction survey** to gain a better understanding of which of its activities clients find add most valuable and where it could improve services most. Targets connected with **utilisation of resources** also need to be considered carefully. For example if staff are to provide the knowledgeable service clients require, they need to spend time researching industry and technological developments.

Information required

HH's information systems will need to be adapted to be able to **incorporate relevant information and produce the reports required**. It may be difficult to identify the changes required. The later the changes are made, the more expensive they could be. Managers therefore need to be involved in a consultation

process to define their needs, also bringing in an external consultant to advise on how to reorganise most cost-effectively, based on the experience of similar businesses.

27 Product choice

(a)

Product lifecycle definition

The product lifecycle begins with the initial product specification and ends with the withdrawal of the product from the market. Stages include development, introduction, growth, maturity, decline and senility.

Criteria used to judge products

The criteria being used to judge the investments prior to their **introduction** appear to be based on the financial net present value technique. Products also need to be evaluated against clearly-established criteria that take into account **the company's strategy**. The level of **initial costs** also needs careful consideration. For Product 2 $6,400 million is a large amount of development costs so may cause **significant cash-flow problems.** The issue then arises of how important profits over the whole lifecycle are against the need to recoup the costs quickly. Also significant will be how the knowledge gained from the design and development work may influence the **development of other projects**.

Verification of information

The **realism of the net present value analysis** is very dependent on the quality of the information supplied by the engineering staff and marketing staff. The figures they supply need to be verified, by staff not involved in their production or by internal auditors. They will need to review the **justification behind the assumptions** made, whether the figures appear to be based on **expected, best-case or worst-case** forecasts and how much uncertainty lies behind the figures provided. They also must consider whether some **relevant costs** have been omitted from the analysis, for example costs of establishing new supplier relationships.

The verifiers should also take into account how **accurate previous forecasts** made by the departments have been and whether there are **weaknesses in their information gathering or forecasting processes** that have been identified by previous internal audits but not corrected.

Use of other appraisal methods

Using a higher risk-discounted factor as in the scenario takes into account the risks of the specific investment appraisal. However the **discount factor** is only one of a number of figures in the discount analysis. The company needs to carry out additional **investment appraisals,** using **different assumptions** about marketing and engineering figures, also examining the impact on the figures if the **launch of products is postponed.**

It needs to use other methods of risk analysis to analyse the risks involved. **Sensitivity analysis** will indicate by how much figures have to change before the products make a loss. It also ideally needs some idea of the probabilities of different outcomes, as this will help **calculate expected values** and the **chances of making a loss. Worst-case scenario analysis** will indicate maximum risk levels, which may also influence decisions.

Alternative solutions

You would also have scored marks if you had discussed these issues.

Further analysis

The **decision to commit** to the product over its life cycle is not **irrevocable** as the lifecycle is expected to last some years. **Real options**, including abandonment, may be available during the growth and maturity phase of the lifecycle, and changes in the initial assumptions caused by developments in the fast-moving industry environment may need to be taken into account. The company should therefore have a system in place for **assessing future success** at various stages of the product life cycle. These include when **commitment needs to be made to further costs** beyond the initial costs (for example the Year 2 costs for Product 1) and when **competition** begins to **increase significantly** during the growth stage. The company may also wish to reconsider its policy and maybe **modify the design of the product** to counter competition or to prolong the original expected lifecycle.

Target costing

The quality of the financial analysis may be improved if target or lifecycle costing are used. **Target costing** implies the analysis being **driven by the sales price** that consumers are prepared to pay and the desired profit margin. If costs exceed what is required to achieve the margin, the product will not be manufactured. Assuming the product is manufactured, the company will not be concerned with meeting the initial cost estimates; rather it will be concerned with changing its expectations of what customers are prepared to pay. As customers expect falling prices, so planned costs will have to fall regularly as well. In this example there would be pressure to reduce the manufacturing and distribution costs in later years.

Lifecycle costing

Lifecycle costing would imply going beyond the **development, manufacturing and distribution costs** that are clearly linked in with the product and **tracing elements of all business costs** to the products. Comparison of the total cost figures with expected revenues should give a better understanding of product profitability. Using the complete lifecycle rather than the same base period for each investment will also give a better indication of the investment's long-term importance.

(b)

Top tips. You may have written similar answers to (b) when answering the written parts of investment appraisal questions in F3 *Financial Strategy* where interpretation of calculations is very important. For this paper, you have to bring risk considerations into all parts of your discussion.

Our answer spreads out by starting with the financial risk elements, then moving on to consider other business risks. Some of these could have been generated from your E3 knowledge, illustrating the links between the three Strategic level exams.

Although 3 marks were available specifically for discussion of risk adjusted rates, the majority of the marks were available for other risk factors. Whichever risks you discussed, it's important to use the data selectively to demonstrate why the risks you're discussing are important. Although one mark would have been available for presentation, you could also easily have spent too much time on a lengthy introduction and conclusion.

To: Head of Division
From: Accountant
Date: 20 July 20X7
Subject: Choice between Product 1 and Product 2

You have asked me for a comparison of Product 1 and Product 2 and recommendations about which to choose.

(i) <u>Financial data</u>

<u>Figures at risk-adjusted discount rate</u>

Assuming use of the risk-adjusted discount factor fairly indicates risk would mean accepting Product 1 with a positive NPV and rejecting Product 2 because it has a negative NPV. The **risk-adjusted hurdle rate** represents a method of taking into account the risks associated with the development of a specific project and quantifying their significance based on how seriously the company views them. However the variety of risks involved (discussed further below), and the difficulty of estimating their importance and ranking arguably means that the risk-adjusted rate fails to give a more reliable guide than using the company-wide hurdle rate would.

<u>Sensitivity analysis</u>

Simple sensitivity analysis reveals that Product 2 is much more vulnerable to making a loss if cost or revenue estimates turn out to be **over-optimistic.** Using the hurdle rate Product 1's NPV is $244 million against initial costs of $600 million, whereas Product 2's NPV is $430 million against initial costs of $6,400 million. Therefore the percentage by which Product 1's initial costs would have to increase before it made a loss is much higher than the % that Product 2's costs would have to increase.

<u>Financial risk of Product 2</u>

Having to meet the higher costs of Product 2 may increase the company's financial risk if loan finance is used and **gearing rises.**

<u>Figures at hurdle rate</u>

If however the hurdle rate of 7.5% is used to appraise investments, then Product 2 shows a **higher net present value**. This indicates that the company may be able to make higher net revenues if it chooses Product 2 so long as it accepts the significant risk of making a loss. Whether the company opts for Product 1 or Product 2 will depend on its **risk appetite**; will it prefer higher returns even though it takes greater risks to achieve them.

<u>Product life cycle</u>

Given the industry is changing rapidly, there is a risk that products may become **obsolete before seven years**. The estimated net present value of Product 1 is more vulnerable to a change in its life cycle, since it has the longer life cycle. Revenues from Product 2 begin to flow earlier than from Product 1, although at a fairly low level.

<u>Use of surplus funds</u>

As noted, Product 1 requires a much smaller early investment than Product 2. To improve the comparisons between the two products, we should consider how the spare funds (the funds that would not be needed for Product 1 but would be for Product 2) would be used. We need therefore to consider the **rate of return** and **risk** of other investments for which the surplus funds could be used.

<u>Postponement of Product 1</u>

As Product 1 is a smaller-scale investment, it may be possible to **postpone** it until some years in the future, and fund it out of the eventual receipts from Product 2.

(ii) <u>Business risks</u>

As mentioned, the risk-adjusted discount rate is a means of measuring the levels of strategic and business risks. We need to be sure that sufficient account has been taken of the following risks.

<u>Competitor risk</u>

Certainly we need to consider the **different market profiles** for each product, and the risks that **competitors** will **develop their own products** ahead of us or respond more quickly on one rather than the other, accelerating the product life cycle.

<u>Customer risk</u>

We need to consider not only the likely reactions of customers but the **different profiles of the customer base** for each product.

Supply and manufacturing risk

The **reliability of suppliers and manufacturing arrangements,** and the local infrastructure, needs to be considered carefully. Supply arrangements from China for some companies have been disrupted by problems within China such as electricity rationing. For Product 1 the consequences of problems in China will probably be more severe than problems in Taiwan for Product 2. If manufacturing is taking place in China, disruption there will clearly affect sales, whereas if there are problems with component suppliers in Taiwan, it may be possible to reduce the risk of lost sales by making contingency arrangements to buy components from suppliers in other countries.

Foreign exchange risk

With both products, there may be foreign exchange risks from settling in their suppliers' currencies. However **exchange risk relating to sales** will only apply to Product 2, since Product 1 sales will be in the home market.

(iii) Compatibility with strategy

The investment decision must be **compatible with the company's strategy.** For example we need to assess whether the products are a breakthrough into a new market sector, or whether there is **potential to expand** into other geographical markets. Whether the proposed products are **significantly differentiated** from what the competition is offering may be significant. Product 1 is being sold in the company's retail outlets and the strategic impact on these outlets needs to be considered; will it require them to change their focus or will it utilise any spare capacity that they have.

Recommendations

I would recommend we **choose Product 1** because the risk-adjusted discount rate gives a negative answer for Product 2, and Product 2's profits appear to be much more volatile than Product 1. However I recommend that the final decision is not made until after further consideration is given to whether the risk-adjusted discount rate fairly reflects all the risks involved, and alternative scenarios, based on other assumptions about the figures, are examined.

Alternative solutions

You would also have scored marks in (b) for discussing the risk management process.

Risk management process

Aspects of risk management are also important, particularly risk avoidance and portfolio management.

Risk avoidance

As part of the risk mapping process that we undertake we should have defined what constitute **high likelihood-high consequences risks** that the company should avoid by, for example, not undertaking investment. We need to compare the possible magnitude and the likelihood of making a loss on both products, particularly Product 2, against these criteria to decide whether the risks are too high.

Portfolio management

The company should view investment in both products in the light of its overall portfolio of investments. It should consider how both investments would contribute to ensuring that the company had an optimum mix of **low and high risk investments.** It should also consider the **correlation of both products** with the existing product portfolio – would investing in one ensure that risks were much better spread than investing in the other.

International diversification

The extent of international diversification may be an issue. Product 1 will be sold in the American markets so may be **vulnerable to the American economic cycle**, whereas Product 2 will be sold all over Western Europe and hence diversified over countries with different cycles. Another point is that the risk borne by the retailer will be suffered by our company's outlets for Product 1, but will be shared with third-party retailers for Product 2.

28 VTB

(a)   Plan for personnel requirements

VTB's overall requirements should determine its personnel requirements. If the role of the treasury department is to focus on administration and bookkeeping, staff with qualifications will be needed in this area. If the treasury department's role is to include currency speculation, it will need staff with successful experience in this activity.

A further aspect of planning is the **order** in which **staff are recruited.** If the Treasurer is recruited early in the selection process, he can be involved in planning for staff requirements and the interview process for other members of staff. It will also allow the Treasurer a settling-in period, learning the business while other staff are recruited.

Identify how the requirements can be met

The HR department should **not just consider appointing permanent staff**. Temporary staff may be used to assist in the initial development of the treasury department's systems, or this could be outsourced. If the development is considered a success, there could be scope for making initial temporary appointments permanent.

Assess the actual/required content of jobs

The HR department will need to **decide on the content** of jobs. A **job specification** should be prepared, **setting out the tasks** of the job in detail. Since the team will only be small, it will be important to decide whether all staff members will be required to **multi-task**, or whether individual staff members specialise in different activities with one focusing on accounting, another on dealing with overseas suppliers.

Person specification

The person specification should detail the **experience, skills, qualifications and personal qualities needed** for each of the roles specified. For the appointment of Treasurer, the HR department may require outside advice from a recruitment consultant if it lacks knowledge of the qualifications and experience that the Treasurer should have.

The HR department should also discuss with the Finance Director and Chief Accountant the **remuneration packages and employment terms** that are likely to be offered, based on what they feel will be required to attract candidates fulfilling the person specification and also **linking performance-related elemen**ts to job content.

Advertisement

The Human Resource Department will need to consider which **media and publications** should be used for advertising. They would obviously need to be read by a number of people who fulfil the person specification. How widely the job is advertised is likely to be determined partly by **cost.**

Interview

Only candidates who possess the required skills should be interviewed. If the choice of candidates is insufficient, the **post** should be **readvertised.**

The approach to interviewing candidates should be **consistent** between interviews with candidates facing the same questions. For the Treasurership and other senior roles, interviews should be conducted by a **panel of interviewers.** Because of the importance of the role of the Treasurer, the Finance Director and Chief Accountant should lead the interview process, and the Chief Executive and the Chairman be involved as well.

Selection

Before candidates are selected, the HR department should confirm their **employment histories, references and qualifications** by inspecting exam certificates, confirming with the qualifying body and contacting previous employers and referees (there should be at least two referees). Candidates should also be asked to explain any gaps in employment histories and state whether they have any **convictions for offences involving dishonesty**.

When the decision to recruit is made, the reasons for the choice should be **documented.** The **Finance Director and Chief Accountant** should **approve any changes** to the employment terms and conditions initially decided.

(b)   Responsibilities

The responsibilities of operational managers of the treasury department should include **management of risk.** This should mean that they are **responsible for day-to-day monitoring.** The Finance Director and Chief Accountant should be responsible for **overseeing the treasury department,** rather than delegating this role to internal audit. Internal auditors should provide assurance and review of the treasury department's activities. They should observe the control systems rather than be part of them.

Involvement in commercial decision

By being involved in day-to-day operations, there is a risk that internal auditors will have some responsibility for **approving commercial decisions**. This goes against the principle that internal audit should **not be involved in operational decision-making**.

Expertise

Internal audit may **not have the expertise required** to carry out the day-to-day review of complex treasury transactions.

Independence and familiarity

If internal auditors become involved with the treasury department, there is a risk that they become **too friendly** with members of the department. This could mean that they become too willing to take on trust explanations from treasury staff rather than verifying them.

Self-review

Part of internal audit's brief ought to be reviewing the effectiveness of day-to-day monitoring of the treasury department. However their position will be compromised if they themselves are carrying out the monitoring, since they will be **reviewing their own work.**

Other priorities

Day-to-day monitoring of the treasury department may mean that internal audit has **insufficient time and resources** to carry out other audit work. There may be other risky areas of the business that require substantial internal audit work.

(c)   Strategic objectives

VTB's main strategic objective is to **develop its retail activities**. Its main strategic risks will be linked to that objective. The company's strategy is **not to speculate on the foreign exchange markets**. Instead it should be using the markets to reduce the risks of the commercial transactions it undertakes.

Profits available

The markets for major currencies are generally efficient. It is therefore **difficult to make profits over time by** anticipating the market. VTB may have to invest substantial resources to gain the market intelligence it needs to have a chance of outperforming the market. VTB may have greater opportunities for speculation in the currencies of developing economies, since the markets for these are less mature, and VTB's commercial activities may give it the insights it needs to gain an advantage in these currencies. However this speculation may carry greater risks than dealing in more stable major currencies.

Risk appetite

Speculating on the treasury markets may involve a **higher degree of risk** than VTB's current activities. These risks may be higher than VTB's board or shareholders wish to tolerate. There is no certainty that the currencies in which VTB's treasury function takes positions will appreciate in value.

Motivation of team members

Involving the treasury department in speculative activities may mean that VTB attracts individuals who are **seeking to take high risks in return for high returns**. However VTB's main purpose in setting up the treasury department is not to seek high returns, but to improve the efficiency of its cash management.

29 Derivatives

Text references. Chapter 8.

Top tips. This question requires an in-depth discussion plus knowledge of how to calculate and explain value at risk.

Easy marks. Limited easy marks at the start of the question for explaining the purposes of hedging.

Examiner's comments. Some candidates limited their mark-scoring opportunities in (a) by failing to discuss speculation. Answers to (b) were poor with candidates failing to use the details in the question, not understanding the different uses of the derivatives and clearly not knowing the accounting requirements. The straightforward calculation in (c) was done badly and students need to revise this area.

(a)

Top tips. Note that the answer to (a) doesn't just consider risk from the company's viewpoint but also the investors' viewpoint. The requirement to discuss means that you have to look at both sides of the debate; the basic viewpoints are that Warren Buffett appears to be thinking more of derivatives as means of speculation, whereas corporate treasurers think in terms of derivatives as a method of hedging to **reduce** risks. The 13 marks available mean that you have the chance to discuss in detail the reasoning behind the two viewpoints and reach a conclusion. Hedging may reduce risk, but what problems might involvement in the foreign exchange markets cause? Speculation can lead to excessive losses, but is it possible to reduce risks to a level that's acceptable compared with the returns that may be obtained?

The mention of IAS 39 later in the question should have alerted you to the need to discuss the impact on accounts, but you don't need to go into excessive technical detail; the main points were the problems with measuring fair values and the different treatment of hedging instruments. Bringing in F3 knowledge of the work of treasury departments is also helpful.

Marking scheme

				Marks
(a)		Definition of derivatives and their uses	3	
		Discussion of how hedging manages risks max	4	
		Discussion of speculation. Award marks for discussion of leverage and price movements	4	
		Conclusion	2	
				13
(b)		Up to 2 marks for each risk discussed. Award marks for links to methods to obtain fair values and volatility of fair values		5
(c)	(i)	Definition	2	
		Value of method	2	
				4
	(ii)	Calculation	2	
		Comment	1	
				3
				25

(a)   <u>Definition of derivative</u>

A **derivative** is a financial instrument **settled at a future date**, the value of which changes in response to changes in an **underlying variable**, and which has a **relatively small initial investment** compared with other contracts that respond in similar ways to changes in market forces. Examples of derivatives include foreign exchange, interest rate and commodity derivatives.

<u>Different reasons for using derivatives</u>

The reasons why different views on the use of derivatives exist is that derivatives are used for different purposes. Some organisations use them as a means of **reducing risk** and to **hedge other transactions** they are undertaking. Other organisations use them for **speculative purposes**. Successful speculation can lead to increased return; however with **increased return** comes **increased risk**. However both hedgers and speculators are necessary for markets in futures to function; the involvement of speculators **increases the liquidity of markets** and bridges the gap between hedgers who are selling and hedgers who are buying.

<u>Hedging</u>

Organisations that use futures to hedge are concerned about **future commitments** they are making to deal in the future in foreign exchange, commodities or financial instruments. Because the deal is taking place some time in advance, the eventual receipt or payment may be uncertain. If for example the deal is in a foreign currency, the amount to be received or paid in the home currency will depend on how the **exchange rate** has **moved** in the meantime.

The company will therefore invest in futures so that losses through adverse movements in exchange rates will be matched by gains on the currency future contracts, brought about by changes in price due to the same exchange rate movements. This should **reduce profit and cash flow risks**. **Options** can be used to reduce these risks as well and also allow organisations to **benefit from favourable movements in rates**.

<u>Hedging risks</u>

The risks from hedging derive from the futures investment **not being an exact match** with the original transaction. **Basis risk,** the risk that the futures price movement and the movement of the price of the original transaction will not correspond, may also be significant. If an instrument is held for hedging purposes, its fair value gain or loss is recognised in the income statement, but so also is the gain or loss on the underlying hedged item. This **limits the effect of uncertainties in measurement** on the accounts.

<u>Speculation</u>

Some organisations **buy or sell futures purely to make profits**. They are **not interested in the commodity or instrument** that **underlies the futures transaction**, but instead attempt to make profits from their ability to predict movements in prices of the futures.

Speculation risks

Because the futures market is **highly leveraged**, the speculator can for a small deposit invest in derivatives, whose movements in price are **proportionally much greater** than those of the underlying commodity. As a result the **profit or loss per pound invested is much greater** than speculating on the underlying commodity. Some have also argued that speculation risks are particularly dangerous because they are **poorly understood and complex**. Hence Warren Buffett and others view them as a potential time bomb.

Reduction of speculation risks

Speculation risk can be reduced by employing **treasury specialists** to carry out dealings. However treasury specialists who are employed by an organisation running its treasury department as a **profit centre** may be tempted to **speculate excessively** to improve profits and hence their own reward. In addition even cautious well-informed treasury specialists can be caught by unexpected market changes.

Control of treasury specialists

To reduce this risk the organisation's senior management need to **establish the organisation's risk appetite** in terms of the maximum losses it can sustain and ensure that this is reflected in **effective controls** over the amounts that treasury specialists can risk. However the effectiveness of these controls may be undermined by the difficulties in measuring profits or losses from derivative trading and hence the risks its treasury specialists are taking.

Investors' risks

IAS 39 requires derivatives held for speculation or trading purposes to be carried in accounts at their **fair value**. The risk to investors partly derives from the uncertainties involved in determining fair value. To do so, **significant assumptions** may have to be made, and **judgements** exercised as to what techniques should be used. This means that investors may see a value in the accounts that could have been significantly different under different assumptions, and that accounts **do not disclose fully the risks involved**. This makes judging the situation at the date of the statement of financial position and forecasting the future extremely difficult, and of course the position may have altered significantly since the accounts date.

Conclusion

Thus both viewpoints are potentially true. Derivatives can be a means of risk reduction, but they can also have very serious consequences if not used carefully, or used for speculation, and can also lead to problems for investors trying to assess accounts.

(b)

> **Top tips**. (b) requires an explanation of the impact of fair value accounting on various risks, not just trading risks, again emphasising what we said in the introduction to the kit that you need to think widely about risks. The highlighting of the accounting implications should have led you to cover accounts risks. The question does actually provide the main details of IAS 39 that you need to answer (b).

Accounts risks

The main risk is **loss of reputation or financial penalties** through being found to have produced accounts that give misleading indications of fair value.

Income risks

Income may become **increasingly volatile** depending on the market data and models being used. This volatility is due to a focus on assets and liabilities rather than accounting for income. This may have an **adverse impact on the ability of companies to pay dividends** and on **companies' share price and cost of capital,** as accounts users find it difficult to determine what is causing the volatility.

Systems risks

Adoption of fair value may require investment in new systems, and there may be an **increased risk of systems problems** as systems have to cope with linking of assets with derivatives, accommodating changes in hedge allocations and measuring hedge effectiveness.

(c)

(i)   Value at risk

The **value at risk** model is a statistical method of assessing risk in financial markets. From the viewpoint of the fund manager, value at risk measures the **maximum loss possible due to normal market movements over a given period of time and a given level of probability**, assuming a normal distribution.

In this context the period of time chosen would be one day, reflecting the short length of time financial assets are held before being liquidated. The level of probability chosen will depend on the fund managers' **attitude to risk**; the higher the confidence level, the more **risk averse** the fund manager will be.

Usefulness of value at risk

The value at risk provides an idea of what the potential loss is that is **easily understandable,** and value at risk limits can be used to **control the activities of traders**. A low limit will minimise the risks traders can take. Value at risk does reflect normal market conditions and is less useful in fund markets that could be subject to **sudden shocks**. More sophisticated scenario analysis may also be required.

(ii)   If x = 5% and standard deviation = £60,000

Then Confidence level = 1.65 deviations from the mean

VAR = 0 – (1.65 × £60,000)

VAR = £99,000

The 1.65 is the standard normal value associated with the one-tail 5% probability level. There is a 5% chance that the loss of value each day on the shares will be greater than £99,000. In other words the loss would be expected to be greater than £99,000 one day in every twenty. This appears quite small given the size of the portfolio, but the investor may regard it as excessive. Changing the portfolio may **reduce the standard deviation** and hence the **value at risk** to an **acceptable level**.

30   W Bank

(a)

	4.1%	3.9%		5.6%	
	1-4	1	2-4	1	2-4
	£m	£m	£m	£m	£m
Due to W (W1)	2.6	2.6	2.6	2.6	2.6
Due to P (W2)	(2.45)	(2.45)	(2.35)	(2.45)	(3.2)
Net to W	0.15	0.15	0.25	0.15	(0.6)
Discount factor (W3) 7%	3.387	0.935	2.452	0.935	2.452
NPV to W	0.508	0.140	0.613	0.140	(1.471)
		0.753		(1.331)	

Workings

1 W

£50m × (5% + 0.2%) = £2.6m

2 P

4.1%: £50m × (4.1% + 0.8%) = £2.45m

3.9%: £50m × (3.9% + 0.8%) = £2.35m

5.6%: £50m × (5.6% + 0.8%) = £3.2m

3 Discount factor

Yr 2-4 = Yr 1-4 – Yr 1 = 3.387 – 0.935 = 2.452

(b) (i) Risks for bank

Increases in interest rates

The calculations demonstrate that if interest rates rise, the bank could be making payments to P in years 2-4 that have a **higher NPV** than the payment from P in year 1. This risk appears to be significant, as one of the likely scenarios envisaged by the swaps department results in a net payment to P. The term structure of interest rates will give an unbiased indication of what the market thinks the most likely outcome is.

Counterparty risk

There is the risk that P could **default on its obligations**. However as P is a major quoted company with a good credit rating, this risk appears to be small. The maximum loss is also limited by the requirement for P to pay the net sum rather than the full interest payment to W.

(ii) Increases in interest rates

Diversification

W has **limited its exposure to risk** by having a **varied portfolio of clients wanting fixed and floating positions**. However it will be difficult to maintain the portfolio in balance if interest rates are generally expected to rise or fall, since more companies are likely to seek a swap to a fixed rate if interest rates are expected to rise, or to a floating rate if interest rates are expected to fall.

Counterparty to P

W could hedge **more specifically** and **seek a counterparty to P** that is looking to obtain floating rate finance. However again it may be difficult to find the right counterparty for the size and term of loan if interest rates are expected to rise and clients want fixed rate finance.

Obtaining fixed rate finance

W could attempt to hedge by **obtaining more fixed rate finance itself** to balance up its variable interest rate commitments under the swaps. However as W is a bank, it is already receiving funds from investors who want variable interest rates on their deposits as interest rates are expected to rise.

Credit criteria

W has reduced the risk by only lending to companies that **fulfil its credit ratings**. However the reliability of its credit ratings depends on the strength of the data available. There may be plenty of data about P as a well-known listed company, but there may be less reliable data about smaller clients.

(c) Certainty of interest rate commitment

P is swapping a commitment to **pay an uncertain variable level of interest for a fixed rate**. This will protect P from any rises in the interest rate. However P will not benefit from any falls in the interest rate, although the predictions suggest that the interest rates are unlikely to fall very far.

Certainty of cash flows

P will know the interest rate it will have to pay. This will mean that it can **forecast its finance cost commitments with certainty**. P will also maintain its cost structure if it undertakes the swap, which should help maintain its competitive position if its competitors have fixed rate finance.

Transaction costs

P will have to pay the bank **commission costs**, although these may well be lower than the costs of other methods of hedging, for example the costs of an interest rate guarantee. P may also have to pay a **higher rate of interest** than it would on a loan. However the costs will also be lower than if P repaid its variable rate loan and sought new fixed rate finance. In return P also has the security that the swap is guaranteed by the bank.

31 A

Text references. Chapters 1, 8, 9 and 10.

Top tips. (a) is asking specifically for risks that differ between launching in France and England. For each risk, you would probably get 1 mark for identifying it, 1 mark for discussing how to manage it but it is not that easy to generate ideas from the limited details given.

In (b) A wants floating rate interest so has to pay fixed rate interest and then swap. Since you are given the amount of the loan, you need to calculate the total benefit. However the question does tell you the terms of the swap, so you don't need to work those out.

Easy marks. The benefits and drawbacks of interest rate swaps should be eight of the easiest marks in this exam.

(a) Risks associated with product launch in England

Launch costs

The **actual net present value** will prove significantly **lower** than the expected net present value if launch costs turn out to be the less likely possibility, £145,000.

A should identify the factors that could cause launch costs to be £145,000 and take steps to **avoid these factors materialising**, for example **tight cost control**.

Data risk

We do not know how the data for annual cash flows was compiled, for example the time period over which the probabilities were forecast. Using a **different time period** as the basis for compiling data may have led to a different decision being taken.

A should consider a range of different scenarios, including using **data predicted over different time periods and different market conditions**.

Strategic 'stop' error

By failing to launch in France, A may be committing a 'stop' error – failing to launch in a country with **better long-term potential**. Not launching in France may prevent A from achieving any more than the limited growth available in the domestic market.

A's board should carefully consider the **available strategic options**, taking into account the portfolio of risks that A faces. This should help identify other, more attractive, overseas investment opportunities that A may have.

Risks associated with product launch in France

Exchange risks

A strengthening of the € would mean that the product launch in France would be worthwhile. However if the **€ weakens against the £,** then launching in France would be the wrong decision.

A can reduce this risk by **obtaining finance in France in euros** to fund the launch of the product. This would **match costs of finance against cash flows from the product**, and thus provide a **hedge against currency movements**.

Finance risk

If A decides to raise funds in France, it may find that the finance it can obtain is **more expensive** than it would have available in England because of its better credit history in England.

A may be able to counter this risk by obtaining funding in England and then arranging a **currency swap**.

Market risks

As A is based in England, it may find it more difficult than anticipated to break into the French market if it lacks experience of it. It may not have contacts and also lack an appreciation of **different taste and cultural conditions**. A may also find it **more difficult to withdraw** from the French market once it has made the commitment to enter the market, since it may jeopardise its future chances of success abroad.

A should **reduce this risk** by **undertaking market research** and **employing French staff as agents**, to advise on the French market and to provide means of establishing sales and distribution networks.

(b)   (i)   Benefits of interest rate swaps

Transaction costs

Transaction costs are **low**, being limited to arrangement fees, and potentially much lower than the costs of terminating one loan and taking out another.

Flexibility

Swaps are **flexible**, since they can be arranged in any size.

Credit ratings

Companies **with different credit ratings** can **borrow in the market** that offers each the best deal and then swap this benefit to reduce the mutual borrowing costs. This is an example of the principle of **comparative advantage**.

Capital restructuring

Swaps allow **capital restructuring** by changing the nature of interest commitments. This is helpful if, for example, a company will find it difficult to raise finance at **favourable fixed rates**.

Risk management

Swaps can be used to **manage interest rate risk** by swapping floating for fixed rate debt if rates are expected to rise.

Hazards of interest rate swaps

Risk of default

The swap is subject to **counterparty risk,** the risk that the other party will default leaving the first company to bear its obligations, unless the contract has been guaranteed through an intermediary.

Interest rate risk

If a company takes on a floating rate commitment, it may be vulnerable to **adverse movements in interest rates**. The commitment to the swap arrangements will also mean that a company committed to a fixed rate payment **cannot take advantage of falls in interest rates**.

Costs of hedging

The company will incur the costs of **managing hedging arrangements**.

(ii)   Alternative A

Pay interest at LIBOR + 1.2%

Alternative B

Swap
Pays to bank if swap agreed   (9.4%)
Details of swap
Floating   (LIBOR)
Fixed (W)   8.5%
Net outcome   (LIBOR + 0.9%)

The gain is 0.3% in each of three years, total 0.9%. The 0.5% fee is payable once, therefore net gain = 0.9 % – 0.5% = 0.4%

0.4% × £500,000 = £2,000

32 RGT

Text references. Chapters 8 and 9

Top tips. Note that in this November 2009 question, VYP was facing cash flow difficulties, as was VTB in another question on the same paper. The recent problems that companies have faced as a result of the credit crunch will mean that cash flow issues are likely to be a significant theme of this paper for a while.

(a) is a very typical question on interest rate swaps.

In (b) you need to bring in wider risk issues (appetite, expectations, diversification, prioritisation (short-term liquidity may be the greatest threat that the company faces)).

(c) also discusses some wider issues. Again risk appetite and expectations are factors here. Note that risk appetite is not only concerned with the chances of making a loss, but also what the maximum loss could be. The point emphasised is that reducing or avoiding risk may be more expensive than accepting risk, but that does not mean that taking action to avoid risks was wrong. The favourable circumstances that meant the risk could have been accepted were not certain to occur.

Easy marks. The benefits of interest rate swaps should always be very easy marks.

Examiner's comments. (a) and (b) were done well. (c) was done poorly as many students agreed with the shareholders' viewpoint and failed to discuss the principal issue, that it was based on hindsight.

(a)   (i)

Wants	RGT Fixed	Counterparty Floating	Total
Pays without swap	10%	LIBOR + 1.5%	LIBOR + 11.5%
Pays with swap	LIBOR + 3%	8%	LIBOR + 11%
Bank fee (assume both are charged 0.1%)	0.1%	0.1%	0.2%
Potential gain	0.15%	0.15%	0.3%
Swap			
Pays to bank if swap agreed	(LIBOR + 3%)	(8%)	
Details of swap			
Floating	LIBOR + 3%	(LIBOR + 3%)	
Fixed (W)	(9.75%)	9.75%	
Bank fee	(0.1%)	(0.1%)	
Net outcome	(9.85%)	(LIBOR + 1.35%)	

Working

$10\% - (11.5 - 11/2) = 9.75\%$

Alternative solution

Swap

Pays to bank if swap agreed	(LIBOR + 3%)	(8%)

Details of swap		
Floating (W)	LIBOR + 1.25%	(LIBOR + 1.25%)
Fixed	(8%)	8%
Bank fee	(0.1%)	(0.1%)
Net outcome	(9.85%)	(LIBOR + 1.35%)

Working

$LIBOR + 1.5\% - (11.5 - 11/2) = LIBOR + 1.25\%$

(ii) Benefits of interest rate swaps

Flexibility and cost

Swaps are **flexible**, since they can be arranged in any size, and they can be reversed if necessary. **Transactions costs are low**.

Credit ratings

Companies **with different credit ratings** such as RGT and the counterparty can borrow in the market that offers each the best deal and then swap this benefit to reduce the mutual borrowing costs. This offers them **comparative advantage**.

Capital restructuring

Swaps allow **capital restructuring** by changing the nature of interest commitments. Here the reason for doing so is the expected rise in interest rates, and hence the desire to switch to fixed rate borrowing.

(b) Lower floating rates

One reason may simply be that the floating rates available are **lower than fixed rates**. Managers may take no account of the greater certainty of fixed rates.

Risk appetite

The directors may be prepared to take the risk that floating rates will increase above fixed rates in order to be able to **obtain a potential cost advantage** from floating rates remaining below fixed rates.

Expectations that interest rates fall

Managers may choose floating rate finance because it has the strong expectation that **interest rates will fall**. It may not want to commit to **relatively high fixed interest rates.**

Term of the loan

A company may choose lower floating rates over higher floating rates in a shorter-term arrangement. Even if it is possible that the floating rates will rise, managers may feel it **unlikely** that there will be a **large unpredictable rise**.

Liquidity issues

Even if it is possible that floating rates will increase, a company may prefer to pay floating rates that are lower than fixed rates short-term because it **lacks liquidity**. Managers may believe that the company will be better able to afford higher floating rates in future if they **expect its operating cash flows to improve**.

Diversification

Managers may wish to be funded by a **mix of floating rate and fixed rate debt.** They may believe that the existing proportion of fixed rate debt in the company's financing structure is too high, and leaves the company exposed to a longer-term fall in floating rates.

(c) Criticisms of directors

Commitment to swap

A possible criticism of using a swap is that it **committed RGT to the arrangement** for the period of the swap. It is unlikely that RGT would have been able to trade its commitment when it became clear the swap was unnecessary. RGT may also have been **unable to enter an equal and opposite swap** to cancel out the first swap.

Arguments in favour of swap

Benefit of hindsight

Although the swap now appears to have been the **costliest option**, this may not have been the case when the swap was taken out. Economic indicators at that date may have indicated that **longer-term interest rates were expected to rise,** potentially making floating rate finance expensive.

Predictability of commitment

A certain commitment to a fixed finance cost could make **forecasting and future planning easier.**

Chances of rates rising

The treasury department may have judged when the swap was taken out that the **risk of interest rates rising** was **above acceptable levels**. They therefore chose to **avoid this risk** by entering the swap.

Worst possible outcome

Similarly the directors may believe that the **maximum rate** to which floating interest rates could rise would cause RGT serious problems if it occurred. RGT is facing liquidity problems, and could have **significant problems covering a large floating rate commitment**.

Criteria for judgement

The shareholders appear to fail to understand that judging risk management by whether the policy chosen turns out to be the **lowest cost option** may not be fair. The aim of risk management is sometimes to **avoid a negative risk** rather than choose the best possible outcome. Pressure from shareholders may **distort decision-making by directors** as they weigh possible returns or cost savings against the associated risks.

33 LXN

Text references. Chapters 8 and 9.

Top tips. This question illustrates what we said in the kit front pages about the overlaps between different strategic level exams. The first part of (a) is very much a financial strategy question, and it's perhaps surprising to see it here, but it demonstrates potential overlaps between the different papers.

Hopefully in (b) you weren't put off by the term quality spread differential; all it means is that the two parties share the gains and losses equally. Don't forget to discuss disadvantages as well as advantages in (b)(i). The requirement to draw a diagram in (b) (ii) will have surprised you, and seems fairly superfluous given the requirements in (iii). It's essential to rough a sketch out quickly before you draw the main diagram so that you can make sure you leave enough space for all the detail including two lenders. However, it's easy to spend too long on the diagram so don't got beyond 8 minutes.

In (iii) LXN wants to **obtain floating rate finance** by the synthetic means of the swap, hence initially has to pay **fixed rate**. You should have calculated the total difference as you're asked to evaluate the annual savings. Other methods you could use to calculate the terms of swap are adjusting the fixed rate payment, or saying that the floating rate swap takes place at LIBOR (hence here the fixed rate swap must take place at 4.6%).

You should note that the written parts of this question were worth 15 marks; that's enough to pass it without tackling any of the numbers.

Easy marks. (b) (i) is a straightforward list for five marks.

> **Examiner's comments**. Answers tended to be very good or very bad. Some answers to (a) lacked depth and focus. Poorer answers to (b) showed a lack of understanding of interest rate swaps, whilst some calculations were very badly attempted. 'There are very few numerical topics in the syllabus but it is important that candidates are well-prepared for these.'

(a)   Factors influencing choice of fixed and floating debt

Cost of debt

The respective **current costs** of fixed and floating rate debt, plus any **arrangement or set-up fees**, will influence the decision.

Interest rate expectations

Expectations will be a significant influence, particularly if LXN borrows locally in Euros. Taking out fixed rate debt will eliminate the risk of changes in interest rates causing changes in finance costs. Higher interest rate costs will **not only increase LXN's cost of finance** if the directors choose floating rate debt, but may **decrease demand**, further decreasing profit. On the other hand, expectations of lower interest rates will mean that **floating rate debt** may be a **better option**.

Mix of debt

One way in which LXN can **limit its exposure to interest rate movements** is by having a **mix of fixed and floating rate debt**. If the funding is raised by fixed rate debt, then because the current floating rate debt is redeemable first, after 20X7 LXN could have just fixed rate debt. It would hence be vulnerable to relatively expensive borrowing if rates do decrease, and **termination costs** if it terminates some or all of its loans.

Factors influencing decision to hedge

Attitudes to risk

LXN seems to be very **risk-averse**, and this may increase the likelihood that it chooses to hedge.

Cost of hedging

Purchasing interest rate derivatives will have a **cost**, and LXN will have to decide whether the cost is worth incurring in the light of the **potential magnitude and likelihood** of **losses**. The proposed expenditure and hence loan funding required is €250,000 × 6 × 1.2 = €1.8 million which does not seem very large in the context of €2,000 million assets. If hedging reduces the possibility of financial losses, the company may feel able to **incur more debt**, and the **cost of borrowing** may **fall** because of the decreased risk. If interest rates are expected to remain stable, the **losses from not hedging** are likely to be **small**, not justifying the cost of hedging.

> Alternative solutions
>
> You would also have gained marks if you had discussed the following points.
>
> Tax
>
> If hedging is likely to **reduce variability of earnings**, this may have tax advantages if the company faces a higher rate of tax for higher earnings levels.
>
> External hedging
>
> The directors may be unwilling to undertake external hedging by purchasing derivatives because of the **monitoring** that will be required and the **need to disclose hedging costs** in the accounts in line with IAS 39.
>
> Benefiting from favourable movements
>
> If an interest rate option is purchased, LXN will be **able to gain from favourable movements in interest rates**, and also be **protected from adverse movements**.

(b)   (i)   <u>Advantages of interest rate swaps</u>

(1)   <u>Flexibility and costs</u>
Swaps are **flexible**, since they can be arranged in any size, and they can be **reversed** if necessary. **Transaction costs are low**, being limited to legal fees, and are potentially much lower than the costs of terminating one loan and taking out another.

(2)   <u>Credit ratings</u>
Companies **with different credit ratings** can **borrow in the market** that offers each the best deal and then swap this benefit to reduce the mutual borrowing costs. This is an example of the principle of **comparative advantage**.

(3)   <u>Capital structure</u>
Swaps allow **capital restructuring** by changing the nature of interest commitments without renegotiating with lenders.

<u>Alternative solutions</u>

You would also have gained marks if you had discussed the following points.

(1)   <u>Risk management</u>
Swaps can be used to **manage interest rate risk** by swapping floating for fixed rate debt if rates are expected to rise.

(2)   <u>Convenience</u>
Swaps are relatively **easy to arrange**.

<u>Disadvantages of interest rate swaps</u>

(1)   <u>Additional risk</u>
The swap is subject to **counterparty risk;** the risk that the other party will default leaving the first company to bear its obligations.

(2)   <u>Movements in interest rates</u>
If a company takes on a floating rate commitment, it may be vulnerable to **adverse movements in interest rates**.

(ii)

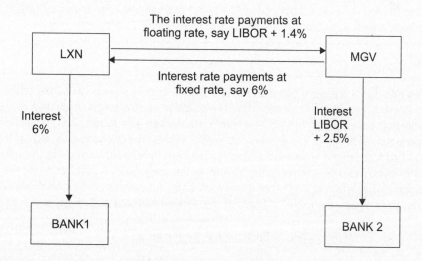

(iii)

	LXN	MGV	
Wants	Floating	Fixed	
Could pay with swap	6%	LIBOR + 2.5%	LIBOR + 8.5%
Would pay without swap	LIBOR + 1.5%	7.2%	LIBOR + 8.7%
Benefit	0.1%	0.1%	0.2%

We are told that gains should be split equally.

	LXN	MGV
Pays to bank if swap agreed	(6%)	(LIBOR + 2.5%)
Details of Swap		
Floating (W)	(LIBOR + 1.4%)	LIBOR + 1.4%
Fixed	6%	(6%)
Net outcome	(LIBOR + 1.4%)	(7.1%)

Working

$$\text{LIBOR} + 1.5\% - \frac{8.7 - 8.5}{2} = \text{LIBOR} + 1.4\%$$

The starting point for this calculation is what LXN pays without the swap.

Without the swap

LXN will pay $(5 + 1.5)\% \times (€250,000 \times 6 \times 1.2) = €117,000$

With the swap

LXN will pay $(5 + 1.4)\% \times (€250,000 \times 6 \times 1.2) = €115,200$

Saving = €1,800

The gain must be considered in the light of the **counterparty risk**, of LXN having to cover payments that MGV has to make. LXN can obviously take steps to assess or limit its exposure, obtaining a credit rating on MGV or seeking an indemnity from MGV's bank.

34 Listed services group

> **Text references**. Chapters 9, 11 and 12.
>
> **Top tips**. If your answer contains most of the points that ours does, you should score well on any questions involving discussion of currency or interest rate risk. Bear in mind however that questions may contain more complex numbers than this one does.
>
> **Easy marks**. (b) as you don't need to carry out any calculations. Any questions on derivatives in this paper will include a discussion element on which you should aim to score well.

(a)

> **Top tips**. (a) is a general question about financial risks so note in (a) (i) the other sources of financial risk as well as interest rate risk and currency risk. The question illustrates that exchange risk is not just about the risk on individual transactions, but also economic risk (longer-term trends) and translation risk (figures shown in the accounts), although this is arguably cosmetic. Whilst (hopefully) you picked up the requirement in (a) (ii) that you had to carry out a calculation, the requirement in both (a) (i) and (iii) to evaluate may have caused you more difficulties. Evaluate implies giving an idea of the magnitude, if possible using the numbers in the scenario to support what you're saying, even if you can't carry out complicated calculations with them. Thus (a) (i) brings in from the scenario the extent of floating rate, foreign currency and short-term borrowings.

(i)   Main sources of financial risk for the group

Based on the information given, which shows only financial liabilities, the main sources of financial risk for the group are **interest rate risk**, **exchange rate risk**, the risk that **short term loans may not be renewed** and the **general financial risk** associated with borrowing (gearing).

Interest rate risk

Most of the group's borrowings are at a **floating rate of interest** (£110 million out of £143 million, or 77%). Because floating rate loans gives the lender the right to increase interest rates in line with general interest rate movements, the company suffers substantial risk that interest rates may increase in the future.

At present the group's **fixed rate loans** (all of which are long term with maturity in more than 5 years) are at a **significantly higher interest rate** than current floating rates. Although part of this excess may be regarded as a premium for the certainty of paying a fixed interest rate, it may also indicate that floating rate interest rates are **likely to rise** in the **medium term** future.

Exchange rate risk

The group reports its results and pays dividends to shareholders in pounds sterling. However, £45 million (31%) of its **borrowings are in foreign currencies** (US dollars and Euros) and there is the risk that the pound will weaken in relation to these currencies, resulting in a higher sterling cost of interest payments and loan repayments.

The group will suffer **similar exchange rate risks** on **its trading transactions** and on its foreign denominated assets.

Risk that short term loans are not renewed

£74m of the group's borrowings (52%) are **due for repayment** within the next year. If the company suffers financial difficulties there may be **difficulty in refinancing its operations**. Further information would be required to evaluate this risk.

Gearing

All companies that borrow suffer from the financial risk that **interest** must be **paid regardless of whether profits are made**. The effect of borrowing is to make the group's profit and cash flow stream more volatile than that of ungeared companies.

(ii) Exchange rate transaction risk

The group's transactions over the next 12 months relating to its foreign currency liabilities are predicted to be:

Liabilities		Loan £m	Rate	Interest/repayment £m
US $ loans: Interest	Fixed	33	7.25%	2.3925
	Floating	8	5%	0.4000
Euro loans: Interest	Floating	4	5%	0.2000
Repayment				1.0000
Total payments				3.9925

If the pound were to depreciate 10% against the US dollar and the Euro, to 90% of its current value, the cost of the payments in pounds would rise to £3.9925/0.9 = £4.4361 million. Additional payments suffered over the next year would therefore be (£4.4361 – £3.9925) million = **£443,600**, which would be charged directly against group profits as an exchange loss. This is referred to as transaction risk.

(iii) How transaction risk relates to translation risk and economic risk in this example

Applied to this example, **translation risk** is the risk that the **statement of financial position values of foreign currency liabilities increase** as a result of a decline in the value of the pound. The current sterling value of foreign denominated liabilities is currently £45 million. If the pound depreciated by 10%, these liabilities would be valued at £45/0.9 = £50 million. The increase in the value of the liabilities would be **£5 million**, which is the translation risk.

Whereas the translation risk depends entirely on what the exchange rates are at the end of the next financial period (one year), there is also the possibility that the **value of a foreign currency liability increases still further** because of longer term movements in exchange rates. This is an example of **economic risk** that, as applied to this example, can be defined as the risk that the **expected present value of foreign currency liabilities increases** as a result of a long term forecast exchange rates.

(b)

> **Top tips**. Key pegs to hang your discussion on in (b) are:
>
> - Purpose (swaps need to be distinguished from other instruments)
> - Cost
> - Matching of exact requirements
> - Whether the organisation can benefit from favourable changes in exchange rates.

Use of derivatives for hedging

A derivative is a security whose **value is derived** from the **price of another asset**, known as the underlying asset. In the context of the current example, the underlying assets are bonds (loan stocks) or currencies and the main types of derivative are forward rate agreements, futures, options and swaps. These can all be used to 'hedge risk', that is reducing the risk associated with using loans and/or foreign currencies.

The derivatives can be **purchased** or **sold 'over the counter'** (OTC), that is by negotiation with a financial institution (a bank), or on **formally regulated exchange markets** which bring together buyers and sellers of standard derivative contracts (futures and options exchanges).

Exchange traded derivatives

The **advantages of exchange traded derivatives** are that they can be **available in smaller contract sizes** and to **organisations with lower credit ratings; transaction costs are low**, and positions can be **closed** at any time by entering into reverse transactions (by selling a futures contract that has previously been purchased). However, because the contract sizes, currencies, time periods and due dates are **standardised** and **limited**, it is usually only possible to obtain approximate hedges.

OTC derivatives

By contrast OTC derivatives can be **tailored by negotiation** to the user's exact hedging requirements. However, positions cannot be so **easily reversed out** if situations change, **regulation is lower, transaction costs** can be **higher** and the **starting size for contracts may be too high** for smaller organisations.

Characteristics of the main types of derivative relevant to the example are given below.

Forward rate agreements

A **forward rate agreement** (FRA) is an OTC contract to lend or borrow a given sum of money in the future at an interest rate that is agreed today. For currencies, the equivalent is the **forward contract:** an agreement to buy or sell a given amount of currency in the future at an exchange rate that is agreed today.

These contracts can be used to **'fix' interest rates or exchange rates** on future transactions, thus **removing the risk of rate movements** in the intervening period. In the example, the company needs to repay a euro loan (of approximately £1 million) next year. The risk of the pound weakening against the euro in the period before the loan is repaid can be hedged by entering into a forward contract to buy £1 million worth of euros at an exchange rate agreed today. The money does not need to be paid until next year, but the exchange rate is fixed today.

Note that removing risk is not always beneficial. If the pound were to strengthen against the euro, the company would have lost the opportunity of making an exchange gain if it fixed its exchange rate using a forward contract.

Futures contracts

Futures contracts are **exchange traded versions** of forward rate agreements and are used in a similar way to hedge risk. The markets are mainly for interest rates rather than currencies.

Options

Options can be obtained for **interest rates and currencies,** for both OTC and exchange traded contracts. In contrast to forward or futures contracts, an option need only be **exercised** (used) if it is **advantageous to the user.** For example, the company has a floating rate sterling loan on which it is currently paying 5% interest. It could purchase an option to pay fixed interest of 7% on this loan. The option would only be exercised if the floating rate rose above 7%. In all other situations the option would be allowed to lapse.

The option therefore offers a guaranteed maximum to the interest paid, while allowing an unlimited reduction in the interest rate. It is known as a **cap.** Because of this flexibility, options are expensive derivatives to purchase.

Swap

A **swap** involves two parties **agreeing to swap payment obligations** on their loans. For example, if the company wished to **reduce interest rate risk**, it may consider swapping its floating rate sterling payments with a party that that was making fixed rate sterling payments on the same principal value of the loan. To **reduce exchange rate risk**, it may agree to swap its interest and repayment on a US dollar loan with a party that has a sterling loan and prefers an obligation in US dollars. This is called a **currency swap.**

35 ZX

Text references. Mainly Chapter 10, though Chapter 11 deals with currency risk and Chapter 9 covers interest rate risk.

Top tips. Make sure you can follow all stages of our answer to (a). (b) brings in control and organisation of the franchisees as well as general issues relating to trading abroad. The verb discuss means that you have to debate whether the risks are significant, bringing in uncertainties and factors that may increase or decrease the risks identified. (c) emphasises that currency and interest rate risks are important topics in this paper. The requirement to evaluate means that you have to show how effective the methods you discuss are likely to be.

Easy marks. (b) is a fairly general discussion on risk. (c) also covers mainstream risks, but with a difference in emphasis to most questions on exchange and interest rate risk which requires thought.

(a)   Expected sterling value of additional profit

Total **number of franchises offered**   = 5 × 5 = 25. Total value = 25 × €100,000 = €2.5m

Value of loans made for franchise costs   = 80% × €2.5 million = €2 million

Value of loans made for property   = €4.8 million

Note: It is assumed that this property loan figure does not need to be multiplied by 80%, as it is the treasurer's estimate.

Total value of loans made   = €2 million + €4.8 million = €6.8 million

Average loan per franchisee   = €6.8 million/25 = €272,000

Annual interest cost of the loans to ZX   = 10% × €6.8 million = €680,000

Annual interest charged to franchisees   = 7% × €6.8 million = €476,000

Therefore, **net annual interest cost to ZX** is (680 – 476) = €204,000

ZX's income from sales made by franchisees is 1% commission + 12% margin on goods sold = 13% × sales value.

Total planned income is 13% × planned sales = 13% × €26 million = €3,380,000

Scen -ario	Sales propor -tion	No. of loan defaults	Sales €	ZX income: 13% × sales, €	Net interest cost €	Cost of loan write-offs* €	Net profit**, €	Prob	Expected value €
1	90%	2	23,400,000	3,042,000	(204,000)	(544,000)	2,294,000	0.1	229,400
2	80%	4	20,800,000	2,704,000	(204,000)	(1,088,000)	1,412,000	0.3	423,600
3	100%	0	26,000,000	3,380,000	(204,000)	0	3,176,000	0.4	1,270,400
4	100%	1	26,000,000	3,380,000	(204,000)	(272,000)	2,904,000	0.2	580,800
								1.0	2,504,200

* Defaults × average loan per franchisee
** Net profit to ZX is ZX income – net interest cost – cost of loan write-offs.

> *Note.* This figure does not include the receipt of €2.5 million for franchise purchases paid by the franchisees. This receipt should be credited to ZX's income statements over the period of the franchise. However, the question does not say for how many years the franchise is valid.

The expected additional profit for ZX is €2.504 million.

The exchange rate at the start of the year is £1 = €1.3939. The Euro is expected to strengthen by 5% over the next year to 1.3939 × 0.95 = £1 = €1.3242.

The average exchange rate for the year is approximately (1.3939 + 1.3242)/2 = €1.3591.

The **expected profit** in £ is therefore 2,504,200/1.3591 = **£1.8425 million**.

The **capital invested** by ZX is loans €6.8 million + working capital £3.65 million.

Using the opening exchange rate of €1.3939, this is £4.878 million + £3.65 million = £8.528 million.

The rate of return earned is 1.8425 / 8.528 = **21.6%**, which is comfortably above the minimum required return for international operations of 15%.

> *Note.* If some portion of the €2.5 million receipt from franchisees were included in profit, the rate of return would be correspondingly higher.

(b)   <u>Risks from expanding into Europe using franchising</u>

Franchising in foreign countries is a form of **foreign direct investment (FDI)** and is subject to the risks associated with this.

<u>Political risk</u>

Because UK is also a member of the European Union (a stable political and economic union), the **political risk** associated with any of the five countries considered is **very small**. The highest risk is probably that increases in corporate or property taxation are introduced in some regions.

<u>Cultural risk</u>

Cultural risk is higher. It is possible that consumers in some locations are **prejudiced** against UK products where there are local alternatives. However, because of this, franchising using national owner-managers may represent a less risky form of investment than the alternative of setting up wholly owned subsidiaries. On the other hand, franchising may prove to be an **unpopular form of business model** in some regions, which is another aspect of cultural risk. In addition it is possible that ZX will **not be able** to attract **sufficient franchisees** as it is not a well-known enough concern. Most franchises are linked to globally known brands.

<u>Currency risk</u>

Any form of investment in Europe will be subject to **currency risk**: the risk that the euro declines in value against the pound, resulting in a **reduced present value of the income stream**. Again, franchising suffers lower risk than investment in wholly owned subsidiaries, although ZX's decision to make **euro loans** to franchisees leaves it exposed (see (c)).

<u>Credit risk</u>

In addition to the normal risks of customers defaulting on debts, ZX bears the risk that its **franchisees will fail** and default on the repayment of the loans it has advanced to them.

<u>Control risk</u>

Franchises are **more difficult to control** than wholly owned investments; in particular they may be unwilling to accept the ZX way of doing things as regards the image projected, store design and product stocking.

<u>Export sales risk</u>

Franchise sales **displace export sales** made by the UK operation or, more indirectly, **divert resources** from the UK.

Lack of goal congruence risk

If franchises are not located carefully, they may end up **competing** with each other.

(c) Management of risks associated with the euro loans

ZX intends to advance fixed interest euro-denominated loans to its franchisees. This will result in three types of financial risk: credit risk, currency risk and, possibly, interest rate risk.

Credit risk

This is the risk that some of the franchisees **default** on the **loans**. In the calculations in (a), this has been accepted as a risk.

Reduction of credit risk

It could be reduced by:

(i)   **Carrying out standard credit control checks** on franchisees.

(ii) **Requiring guarantees** by the directors of the franchisee companies to bank loans.

(iii) **Taking security for the loans** (in the form of charges over the property used for operating the franchise).

However, in taking action to reduce credit risk, ZX must be prepared to negotiate a **reduced margin** from franchisees, or else run the risk of a lower than expected number of franchise takers.

Currency risk

Currency transaction risk is the risk that the **sterling value of loan interest and repayments** is **eroded** if the euro declines in value against the pound. Although this is not predicted to happen in the calculations, there is a substantial risk that it will. Currency risk also applies to the commission remitted by franchisees.

Reduction of currency risk by euro borrowing

The best way to **reduce currency risk** on the **loans to franchisees** is to **finance these loans out of euro (rather than sterling) borrowings**. In that way, if the euro declines, both receipts and payments are reduced. The disadvantage of borrowing in euros is that ZX may **not be able to obtain such a relatively favourable interest rate** as in pounds.

Other methods of reducing currency risk

Alternative ways of hedging currency risk include:

(i)   Forward currency contracts

      These **fix the exchange rates for future receipts and/or payments**. They can be tailored to suit the company's circumstances, but bind the company into a fixed price.

(ii) Futures

      These also **fix the price of a transaction** in the future, but as they are only for standardised amounts, there is likely to be some transaction exposure that isn't hedged.

(iii) Options

      In return for a substantial purchase price, options allow the company to **avoid exchange losses** while **taking advantage of exchange gains**.

(iv) Matching franchise receipts with payments to short-term payables

      That is **EU based suppliers**. This would however reduce the output required from the UK based factory.

Interest rate risk

ZX will suffer from **interest rate risk** if it **grants fixed interest loans** to franchisees while **paying floating rate interest** on the borrowings it makes to finance them. If interest rates rise, ZX would make a loss on this financing arrangement.

Reduction of interest rate risk

This could be avoided by negotiating with its bankers to exchange some of its floating rate borrowings for fixed rate borrowings (probably at a higher rate of interest). Alternatively it could **reconsider its plans** to offer fixed rate finance, and instead **offer franchisees floating rate loans**.

36 Preparation question: Bruce SA

Text references. Chapters 11 and 12.

Top tips. With the forward contract the question indicates you should subtract the amount (the premium). The rate is use is the unfavourable rate for Bruce SA. As it's based **in Europe** and has **received $**, it wants to **buy €** with **the $** it's received. Hence the rate to use is the **higher** rate that means it has to spend more $ (1.2362 – 0.0028 = 1.2334) to obtain each € that it wants. We subtract the 0.0028 as the forward rate is quoted at a premium.

For the money market calculation

- You have to **borrow** in the **foreign currency** to match the foreign currency **receipt**. You will pay off the borrowing with the receipt.
- The amount you borrow is less than you will receive (hence the division) because you will obtain interest by **investing** the amount borrowed in your home market.

As you'll be **receiving $**, you need to **buy € futures** now, and sell them at the later date when you want to buy € with the $ you receive.

For the futures calculation the date of the contract needs to be **after** the date the transaction is due to be settled. (Here the contract is settled mid-September; the September futures date is at the **end** of September.)

The key decisions in the options calculation are to choose the right date – again it needs to be **after** the date the transaction is due to be settled. (The September option, expiring 30 September, is after the mid-September settlement date.) You need to choose the right type of option – here it's a **call** option enabling you to **buy** the **home currency €** that you want using the **foreign currency $** receipt. The option ensures that you can buy at a reasonable price in the worst possible exchange rate scenario. In some calculations, you may have the information available to be able to calculate which option price to choose, but more often, as you do here, you can choose one as an example (if you're told the closing spot rate, then the example option price you choose will be one where you will exercise the option).

Because you're using a traded option, there will be a difference between what receiving from the customer and the amount covered by the option contract, so you have to calculate the **difference** at the **closing spot rate**, having translated the amount of home currency in the option contracts at the **option strike price**. Remember also that the option premium is translated at the **opening** spot rate.

Easy marks. The forward rate calculation should hopefully be straightforward, and you will get easy marks for making the right decisions about which futures and options to choose, and calculating how many contracts.

Hedging using the forward contract

The company should take out a **three month forward contract** to sell $2,350,000 at $1.2362 – $0.0028 = $1.2334

This rate is agreed today for exchange in 3 months, converting to $2,350,000/1.2334 = **€1,905,302**

Top tip. Remember as the exchange rates are quoted as €1 = $X, we have to **divide $** amounts by the exchange rate to obtain amounts in €.

Money market hedging

	Now		*In 3 months*
$	**2** So borrow now $2,342,971	3/12 × 1.2% = 0.3% per 3 months (borrowing rate) × 1/1.003	**1** Will receive $2,350,000

To be able to invest $ borrowed, must sell them now @ 1.2362

| € | **3** So invest now
€1,895,301 | On which interest is received at 3/12 ×
2.2% = 0.55% per 3 months (lending
rate)
× 1.0055 | **4** Due to Bruce
€1,905,725
(effective receipt from hedge) |

Futures market

Set up

(i)   We shall be buying September contracts as they mature after payment date

(ii)   Buy € futures

(iii) Number of contracts

$$\frac{2,350,000/1.2321}{125,000} = 15.3, \text{ say 15 contracts.}$$

Closing prices

Closing futures price is €1 = $1.2439, closing spot rate is €1 = $1.2450.

Outcome

(i)   On futures market

Opening futures price Buy	1.2321
Closing futures price Sell	1.2439
Gain	0.0118
Gain on futures market	0.0118 × 125,000 × 15 = $ 22,125 gain

(ii)   Net outcome

	€
Spot market receipt (2,350,000/1.2450)	1,887,550
Gain on futures market (22,125/1.2450)	17,771
	1,905,321

Option set up

(i)   Contract date

September

(ii)   Type of option

Buy call option as buying €

(iii) Strike price

Say 1.2350

(iv)   Number of contracts

$$\frac{2,350,000 \div 1.2350}{62,500} = 30.4, \text{ say 30}$$

(v)   Premium

$$\text{Premium} = \frac{30 \times 62,500 \times 0.0336}{1.2354}$$

$$= €50,996$$

Closing spot rate

€1 = $1.2450

Outcome

(i) Options market outcome

Spot rate	1.2450
Exercise price	1.2350
Exercise	Yes

(ii) Net outcome

Outcome of options position 62,500 × 30 = €1,875,000

Balance on spot market

	$
Exercise option 62,500 × 30 × 1.2350	2,315,625
Value of transaction	2,350,000
Balance ($ receipt not covered by option contract)	34,375
Translated at spot rate (34,375/1.2450)	€27,610

	€
Options market	1,875,000
Balance on spot market	27,610
Option premium	(50,996)
Net receipt	1,851,614

37 JJ

Text references. Chapters 5, 8 and 11.

Top tips. Most of the scenario relates to part (a) and so each section of your answer needs to relate clearly to the views expressed. JJ has clearly made a mistake in not budgeting for exchange rate risk and the bank cannot be generous because of this mistake. The other point to bring out with the director's views is that waiting and seeing introduces uncertainty and potentially even greater losses. About half the marks here would be available for explaining that the markets price rationally, describing how interest rate parity works and explaining what would happen if market rates are not realistic and investors took advantage.

Easy marks. Most of (c) is standard recruitment good practice for any senior role. The main area of application is the directors' lack of knowledge of the finance sector, which means that it would be wise for them to use a recruitment agency.

Examiner's comments. In (a) poorer answers failed to cover all the comments made by the executive and the bank manager. Answers to (b) were often too general. Some students pointed out that a treasurer would have limited scope in a company like this, but hardly anyone saw the need for more rounded financial skills in the organisation. In (c) a lot of answers focused on the characteristics of a treasurer rather than the steps to be taken when appointing a treasurer.

(a) Chief executive's views

Unexpected cost

The cost of the arrangement to JJ is irrelevant as far as the bank is concerned. The bank has to take the view that JJ should have **allowed for possible movements in foreign exchange rates when budgeting.**

Attitude to exchange risk

The chief executive's attitude to exchange risk is **unclear**. He is concerned about the risk of the USD declining and wishes to mitigate this risk if possible, suggesting he is **risk-averse.** However he is also prepared to **gamble on movements in the spot rate** rather than accepting the rate the bank has set.

Accepting the spot rate at settlement

If the chief executive accepts the spot rate at the date the payment is made, the spot rate may be better than £1 = $1.65, which would lessen any loss. However it is possible, particularly given market expectations, that the rate will be **worse than $1.65**. The effective exchange loss could therefore be **larger** and will also be **uncertain** until the date of settlement. Fixing the rate means that the position is certain and JJ can therefore budget for it.

Bank's view

Prediction of rate

The chief executive may be correct in saying that rates cannot be predicted with complete accuracy. However banks should be able to make a **reliable prediction of the direction** in which interest rates will move. This should be a more accurate prediction than just using today's rate. The forward rate will be based on **interest rate parity**, the idea that differences between spot and forward exchange rates should offset differences in interest rates. Here an expected weakening of the $ suggests that US interest rates are higher than UK rates.

Arbitrage

The bank's argument is strengthened by considering what would happen if market rates were realistic. Investors would realise that they could make a risk-free gain by **investing in one currency and borrowing in another**, and **using a forward contract to obtain a favourable rate** at the end of the period of investment and borrowing. If investors did this, exchange rates would change according to the laws of supply and demand and eventually remove the possibility of risk-free gains.

Bank's own position

The bank will have set the rate, having regard to market expectations and also its own need to make a profit and its own risk exposure. If the rate it sets is less generous than other banks, it will **not attract customers.** Even if the current spot rate is still expected to apply in three months, the bank is still likely to offer a less generous rate, effectively asking JJ to pay a **premium** in return for the bank accepting the risk from exchange rate movements.

(b)   Lack of expertise

At present there appears to be a **lack of financial expertise** on the board, with all of the directors having an electronic engineering background. The arguments put forward by the Chief Executive demonstrate a lack of knowledge of an important area of finance. **Financial issues** facing JJ will become **more complex** if its overseas trade expands. The risk of making costly mistakes such as the failure to budget for exchange risk will increase.

Usefulness of treasurer

However it is questionable whether employing a treasurer at perhaps a high salary represents good value for the company. A treasurer may be able to improve **relations with the company's bank**. There may be scope for the treasurer to make **recommendations to improve working capital management.** However it is unlikely that many areas that the treasury function of a large company would handle would be significant concerns for JJ. There is no evidence that JJ has complex borrowing requirements or faces complex tax issues. Though JJ is beginning to think about using a **forward contract to hedge foreign exchange risk**, at present it does not appear to need to use the complex capital instruments for which specialist treasury advice would be required.

Appointment of finance director or chief accountant

The lack of financial expertise of senior management may be better addressed by appointing a chief accountant or finance director. At present JJ does not seem to employ anyone with **higher accounting skills** in its administration department. A qualified accountant could address problems relating to budgeting and more complex financial accounting issues. A qualified accountant would also have learnt about using financial instruments to hedge exchange risk and could therefore provide the guidance required on the non-complex areas with which JJ is currently concerned.

Costs and benefits

The recruitment decision will be determined by the salary costs versus the tangible and intangible benefits. It is difficult to see how the **significant salary cost of a full-time corporate treasurer** can be

justified by the work the treasurer could do and the savings the treasurer could recommend. JJ may have **more flexibility** when recruiting an accountant as it could weigh up salary costs against the level of experience it is prepared to accept and the responsibilities and authority the accountant is given. At present it seems that recruiting an accountant would provide better value for money, as it would address clear deficiencies in JJ's organisation.

(c) <u>Role and person specification</u>

The directors will need to draw up a **job specification setting out the tasks** of the job in detail. The person specification should detail the **experience, skills, qualifications and personal qualities needed.** JJ's board may require outside advice from a recruitment consultant as it lacks knowledge of the qualifications and experience that the Treasurer should have. The directors also need to consider the **remuneration package and employment terms** that JJ will offer, based on what they feel will be required to attract candidates fulfilling the person specification and also **linking performance-related elemen**ts to job content.

<u>Search process</u>

JJ's board may also consider asking a recruitment agency to undertake the search process. A recruitment agency should have a **good understanding** of which **media and publications** should be used for advertising. An agency may also have suitable applicants on their books, or have knowledge of possible candidates who could then be headhunted.

<u>Interview</u>

Only candidates who possess the required skills should be interviewed. If none of the candidates appears to be what JJ wants, the **post** should be **readvertised.** The approach to interviewing candidates should be **consistent** between interviews, with candidates facing the same questions. Interviews should be conducted by a **panel of interviewers.** Because of the importance of the role of the Treasurer and the need for directors to be happy with the appointment, the Chief Executive should lead the interview process.

<u>Selection</u>

Before the successful applicant's appointment is confirmed , JJ's HR department should confirm the applicant's **employment history, references and qualifications** by inspecting exam certificates, confirming with the qualifying body and contacting previous employers and referees (there should be at least two referees). All applicants interviewed should have been asked to explain any gaps in employment histories and state whether they have any **convictions for offences involving dishonesty**. Anyone admitting to any offences involving dishonesty should not be considered. Applicants might of course lie, but JJ would be able to say that it did ask them and was not told the truth. When the decision to recruit is made, the reasons for the choice should be **documented.**

38 Q

Text references. Chapters 11 and 12.

Top tips. In (a) the most important reason for borrowing in € is to match income and expenditure. Matching of assets and liabilities is less significant if this is a long-term investment, unless the directors are worried about the impact on the statement of financial position.

The fact that you are given data about interest rates in (b) should have highlighted that you needed to use interest rate parity in your calculation and explain the concept. As interest rates in Sri Lanka are higher than the rates for equivalent companies in France (9% v 6%), this means that the Sri Lankan rupee will weaken over time to compensate and prevent arbitrage opportunities.

The cash flows in (c) are the € cash flows which Q then has to transfer into its home currency. Thus the initial cash flow is the receipt in € from the French company, which Q has to repay at the end of the swap arrangement.

(d) asks for an evaluation of the risks. This may mean, as here, concluding that some of the risks are not very large or that they have upsides as well as downsides. There is no indication that Q will assume liabilities for P's payments, which is the main danger.

Easy marks. The points in (a) should have been fairly straightforward.

(a)   <u>Reduction in exchange risk relating to profits or losses</u>

The subsidiary should generate a surplus in €. If the € weakens against the LKR, the value of this surplus in LKR will fall. Borrowing in € and having finance costs in € will mean that the interest costs are **matched** against the surplus. If the € weakens, these payments will become cheaper in LKR and will mitigate the fall in value of the receipt.

<u>Reduction in translation risk</u>

Similarly at the year-end a fall in the value of the € will result in a fall in the value of the subsidiary's assets when they are translated into LKR for the consolidated accounts. If Q also takes out a loan in €, the value of the loan will also fall if the € weakens. If Q is concerned about translation risk because of the reactions of its investors, **matching the subsidiary's assets against the loan** will reduce translation risk.

<u>Abandonment of subsidiary</u>

Obtaining a loan in € could give Q more negotiating power. If pressure from the bank over the loan became too onerous, Q could **abandon the subsidiary and the loan**. However this would damage Q's reputation both in France and probably other countries, including perhaps Sri Lanka. Presumably this possibility has influenced the French banks' reluctance to grant Q funding.

(b)   Exchange rate in 6 years' time

= Current exchange rate × (1 + Sri Lankan interest rate)^6/(1 + Euro interest rate)^6

= 155 × (1 + 0.09)^6/(1 + 0.06)^6

= LKR 183.25

<u>Interest rate parity</u>

The prediction has been made using interest rate parity, which predicts future exchange rate movements on the basis of **differences in nominal interest rates**. Differences in rates will lead to investors holding the currency of the country with the lower interest rates switching to the country with the higher interest rates, ensuring they cannot lose when they switch back by fixing the exchange rates in advance at the forward rate. To stop every investor doing this, the laws of supply and demand will mean that the forward rate would change and would nullify the opportunity for risk-free profit making.

The interest rates used in the calculation are those that will be charged to Q in Sri Lanka and its equivalent company in France. These are comparable because they have been set on the basis of the same level of risk.

(c)

		€m	Exchange rate	Discount factor	LKRm
0	Receipt from French company	20	155.00	1.000	3,100
1	Interest	(2)	159.39	0.917	(292.32)
2	Interest	(2)	163.90	0.842	(276.01)
3	Interest	(2)	168.54	0.772	(260.23)
4	Interest	(2)	173.31	0.708	(245.41)
5	Interest	(2)	178.21	0.650	(231.67)
6	Interest	(2)	183.25	0.596	(218.43)
6	Repayment to French company	(20)	183.25	0.596	(2,184.34)
					(608.41)

(d)   <u>Risk of default by the counterparty</u>

There is a risk that P's investment in Sri Lanka may not be successful and that P may therefore **default on its commitments**. However, unless Q has guaranteed P's interest and principal, it will not be liable for P's debts. Swapping the € principal does not mean Q taking on the liability to the bank for its repayment nor the interest, and Q will merely stop paying the € interest. There may be some administrative difficulties

which Q would need to address as there is no intermediary in the swap arrangement, but these are unlikely to be very costly.

Interest and principal payments

Instead of paying the € interest payments, Q will **make the interest payments on, and repayment of the principal for, the LKR loan.** As Q appears to be a successful business, it should not have difficulty meeting these commitments. If the subsidiary is successful, it will make a contribution that will finance the interest payments.

Repayment of LKR loan and not € loan

At the end of the six years, Q will have to repay the LKR loan rather than the € loan. As the € is expected to strengthen against the LKR over the six years, **having to repay the LKR loan may be cheaper for Q**.

No longer matching

The net contribution from the subsidiary in € will not be matched with the interest payments in €, increasing the **amount unhedged against exchange risk**. However exchange risk has an upside as well as a downside. Again as the € is expected to strengthen against the LKR, Q will benefit from having receipts in €.

Fixed rate

The swap arrangement ties Q to fixed rate borrowing, when possibly a floating rate may offer a **lower interest cost over the period of the loan.**

Difficulty in liquidating the swap

If the subsidiary was not a success and Q wished to close it before the 6 years were up, it would still be **committed to the payments under the swap.**

39   WW

Text references. Chapter 11.

Top tips. It's quite easy to work out what you need to do in (a) (i) from the details in the scenario. Since you're given the exchange rates of other currencies to £, you need to convert all the balances to sterling. The netting off process then takes place in sterling. There are various ways of arranging the settlement, but as the London-based treasurer is arranging matters herself, it seems best to make all the settlements transactions between London and another office. (a) (ii) focuses on costs and complications. The legal and taxation issues are worth mentioning, as it seems that WW may have other centres that are not covered by the multilateral netting exercise.

(b) is a good indication that you need to make sure you understand the significance of all the detail in the scenario. The small balance on the account will only be subject to limited exchange risk. However the large monthly variations may mean that the account does not always remain in surplus.

Easy marks. If you quickly understood how the netting procedure should work, then not only can you score the maximum 11 marks, you can do so in something under the 20 minutes that you would normally allocate to (a) (i), based on the number of marks that it offers.

Examiner's comments. Generally this question was done quite well, although the written parts were done better than the calculations. Some students limited the marks they could score for the calculation by doing a bilateral netting calculation rather than a multilateral netting calculation.

(a)   (i)   Convert the balances to sterling £m

Paying	UK	France	US	Japan	Total receipts (add across)	Total payments (add down)	Net receipt/ (payment)
Receiving							
UK		0.90			0.90	(3.26)	(2.36)
France				0.97	0.97	(2.58)	(1.61)
US	1.93	1.68			3.61	(1.40)	2.21
Japan	1.33		1.40		2.73	(0.97)	1.76

As all transactions are being handled in London, therefore:

France will pay UK £1.61m

UK will pay US £2.21m and Japan £1.76m

(ii)   Advantages

Transaction costs

Netting will reduce the number of transactions that subsidiaries need to make. This will **reduce the transaction costs** that their banks charge, as they will not need to convert cash or pay bank charges.

Administration

There will be time, and potentially cost, savings from the reduced need for administration and invoicing through implementing multilateral netting.

Exchange risk

A **reduction in the amount of currency flows** should reduce exchange risk, by reducing the maximum losses that can arise from currency movements.

Disadvantages

Costs of treasury function

Maintaining a central treasury function to carry out this and other tasks can be **expensive.**

Legal and taxation issues

WW may be liable to regulations that limit or prohibit multilateral netting. It may **also face cross-border taxation complications**. Tax authorities may question the commercial logic of the transactions, particularly if the country is operating exchange controls. WW will need to demonstrate that payments relate to a binding commitment.

Weakness of £

If the £ is weak against the other currencies for a long time, the results of the offices could be **significantly distorted.**

Exchange rate used

Some group companies may **question the exchange rate** being used, if they feel that they are losing out compared with companies in other countries.

Cashflow problems

If one of the offices is having **liquidity problems**, the London treasury department may have to arrange for it to have additional funds to settle its liabilities. This will **increase the number of transactions**, and hence the amount of transaction costs, and maybe also mean that WW incurs more exchange losses.

(b)   Advantages

Consultants and customers

Consultants and customers based in the Eurozone may welcome the fact that their receipts and payments are in their **own currency.** This will mean that they do not face exchange risk, **benefitting from internal**

hedging. However whether this is a significant reason for their choosing to deal with WW is debatable. Consultants could well need the work that WW provides. The main reason for clients choosing to deal with WW appears to be that they wish to use a UK-based consultant with multinational knowledge and expertise. Eurozone customers won't choose a local practice over WW because of small exchange rate advantages.

Exchange rates

Since on average the account will be growing, this may lead to the opportunity to convert large amounts of euros into sterling. Large amounts may have **better exchange rates available.** Alternatively amounts could be left in euros to benefit from forecast gains.

Relative simplicity

There will be a **reduction in foreign currency exposure** without needing to get involved with complicated financial derivatives.

Bank charges

Bank charges should be **reduced,** as movements on the account in the home currency will be less costly.

Disadvantages

Overdraft costs

Although on average the account will show a net surplus, the average figure is quite small compared with the average receipts and payments involved. The monthly variation in receipts and payment could mean that at times the account goes into **overdraft** and this will result in WW incurring further charges, unless it holds a **precautionary balance** on the account.

Exchange risk

The London office may **incur exchange risk** on this account, as **some time** may elapse between agreements with **customers or consultants and payments,** and there may be a difference in the average time between settling receipts and payments. If a payment needs to be made in euros, there are insufficient funds and WW does not want the account to go into overdraft, then WW will need to convert sterling into euros to be able to make the payment. The netting off of receipts and payments will **reduce the net amount** subject to exchange risk, however.

Subsidiary

It may be less costly to use a **subsidiary** in the Eurozone, which would remove the need to use a foreign currency bank account in the UK.

40 KK

Text reference. Chapter 11.

Top tips. The main thing to watch for in (a) (i) is the time period. As well as the costs of the other parties in (a) (ii), it's also important to pick up that there may be problems with the other parties in P. As always also, commitment to a fixed rate means that KK cannot benefit from interest rate movements. (b) was set to get you thinking about the commercial issues connected with this decision, for the manufacturer as well as the purchaser.

In (b) (i) the risk of settling now is losing a large sum of money if the manufacturer defaults. Certain costs will be avoided, but these aren't worth the risks. Note the point in (ii) about the manufacturer accepting the money in advance to ease cash flow.

Easy marks. If you understand money market hedges, there are no significant complications in (a) (i).

Examiner's comments. Pleasingly the calculations in (a) were done well, but students failed to come up with relevant points for (b), indicating that they had not revised financial risk thoroughly enough.

Marking scheme

				Marks
(a)	(i)	2 marks for each calculation on diagram	max	5

(a) (i) 2 marks for each calculation on diagram

max 5

(b) (ii) Up to 2 marks per cost/risk discussed, including:
Costs
Banking costs
Professional costs
Interest rate risk premium
Risks
Interest rate movements
Exchange rate movements
Investment risks in P

max 8

(b) (i) Up to 2 marks per cost/risk discussed, including:
Risks
Exchange rate movements
Non-delivery by manufacturer
Costs
Lost interest
Avoidance of settlement costs

max 7

(ii) Up to 2 marks per issue. Issues could include:
Manufacturer's liquidity
Manufacturer's attitude to exchange risks
Manufacturer's view of exchange rate movements
Liability to bank charges

max $\frac{5}{25}$

(a) (i)

	UK		P
Now	£920,217	@ 2	P$1,840,434
	↓ @ 1.0667**		↑ @ 1.0867*
8 months	£981,595		P$2,000,000

* 8/12 × 13% = 8.67%

** 8/12 × 10% = 6.67%

- Decide how much needs to be invested in the developing country so that total (principal and interest) can be used to repay P$2,000,000 in 8 months' time (13% p.a. = 8.67% for 8 months).

- Convert P$ to £ at spot (£1 = P$2) to give the £ amount required to be borrowed from bank in the UK today.

- Borrow in UK (10% p.a. = 6.67% for 8 months) and work out interest payable.

(ii) <u>Costs</u>

<u>Foreign bank account costs</u>

KK may be charged fees by the bank in P for **opening up, maintaining and closing a deposit account** and **transferring the funds to the vendor**.

Professional costs

KK will have to pay **fees to the lawyer or accountant it uses in P**.

Risk premium from home bank

KK's bank may charge KK a fee for granting the loan. Possibly because of the risks associated with this particular transaction, KK's bank may be including a **premium for risk** within the interest rate it is offering KK.

Forward contract

The cost to KK under the money market hedge may be higher than KK obtaining a **forward contract** from another intermediary.

Risks

Movements in interest rates

KK is committed to paying a **fixed interest rate** on the loan. If bank loan rates fall in the UK over the 8 month period, KK may be able to pay less interest if it obtained a variable rate loan. Similarly in P KK may be able to earn more interest over the eight months if it invested in a variable rate deposit.

Volatility of exchange rates

KK's payment under the money market hedge could be more than it would have been if it took no action and obtained P\$ at the date of payment. If the exchange rate weakened to above 1 GBP = P\$2.0375 (2,000,000/981,594), KK would have to pay less than £981,594.

Risks of investing in P

KK may have difficulties in liquidating the deposit it makes in P. There could be **intermediary risk**, the risk that the accountant or lawyer KK uses embezzles the deposit. **Political or financial instability** may threaten the future of the bank and the security of the investment, and mean that KK is liable for the full amount to the supplier in P as well as having to repay the loan in the UK.

(b)   (i)   Risks

Volatility in exchange rates

By paying now, KK may end up **paying more in £** than it would have done if the P\$ weakens at all. Any rate greater than GBP1 = P\$2 in 8 months' time will mean KK has to pay less than £1 million. The money market hedge provides an unbiased prediction of the likely exchange rate. Since the rate predicted in this way is GBP1 = P\$2.0375, this suggests that it is very likely that KK is better off waiting. The discount KK is offered may not fully compensate for the effects of the movement in exchange rates.

Failure of manufacturer to deliver

By paying in advance, KK is relying on the manufacturer to supply the machinery. If the manufacturer goes out of business in the next 8 months, KK will lose its money. The farming equipment appears to be **new**, and KK does not appear to have evidence of the **reliability of the manufacturer**. If KK pays in advance, it may have trouble obtaining compensation or its money back if the manufacturer goes bankrupt or does not deliver for other reasons. Paying later may give KK the chance to inspect and reject the machinery if it appears to be substandard.

Costs

Lost interest

Bringing the payment forward may result in KK **losing interest** on monies in the bank over the 8 month period, or perhaps having to **increase its overdraft** and therefore face greater interest and charges.

Settlement costs

Settling now would **avoid costs** such as professional fees associated with the money market hedge, and **minimise the bank charges** that need to be paid.

(ii)   <u>Manufacturer's cash flow position</u>

If the manufacturer was **facing liquidity problems** over the next 8 months, obtaining the money now would ease the situation.

<u>Risk</u>

If the manufacturer was financially secure, accepting the payment now would mean that it accepts the exchange risk rather than KK. The manufacturer may normally **invoice in its own currency** to avoid exchange risk.

<u>Likely exchange rates</u>

The manufacturer may **be aware of the predicted exchange rates**, in particular that the most likely situation is that KK will pay less than £1 million. If it is, it could accept the £1 million, and perhaps **arrange its own hedge** which could mean that it received net more than P$2 million.

<u>Bank margins</u>

The manufacturer may also be deterred from accepting the amount by the fact it will have to convert the £ into P$ and thus be **liable for the margins** charged by banks on the transaction rather than KK.

41   G

Text references. Chapters 8 and 10.

Top tips. Economic risk has been tested regularly recently. This question also emphasises that students must know how to do the value at risk calculations.

Easy marks. (c) (iii) is really about the limitations of the value at risk model. As with many other models, you can gain marks by discussing the assumptions, the reliance on historical data and commenting on what the model doesn't show (most likely result, maximum possible loss).

Examiner's comments. Generally answers to this question were poor. Students continued to demonstrate a lack of understanding of economic risk. Few scored full marks on the calculations.

(a)

Top tips. Remember the key point in (a), that economic risk is about long-term competitiveness. Your advice to the directors therefore needs to focus on customer pricing and supply issues, policies also being determined by competitor actions. Note that the question does not ask for measurement of the risks, as this would be a difficult area to evaluate.

<u>Expectations of exchange rate impacts</u>

The view of economic risks will be determined by expectations of how exchange rates are **expected to move in the longer-term.** To some extent this can be modelled using expected changes in long-term interest rates, but other factors will also need to be considered. However changes in exchange rates will only impact on economic risks if they impact on **supply or selling costs.**

<u>Costs of supply</u>

One important determinant of economic risk is how G's American suppliers react to movements in US $ exchange rates. If the **$ rises against other currencies**, G's suppliers will be aware that the costs of their exports will have risen. To avoid damage to their competitive position, they may decrease their prices. If they do so, it will limit the economic impact on G.

<u>Competitive position</u>

An important element of economic risk is whether changes over time result in a **weakening of G's competitive position**. If its direct competitors are using suppliers in the USA as well, impact on competitive position may be limited.

Managing supply costs

The impact of economic risk will also depend on whether the risk can be **avoided**, by **switching to suppliers in other countries or G's home country**. If suppliers in a different foreign country are used, a more favourable foreign currency position for G may be balanced by increases in distribution costs. Other factors to be considered will include quality and reliability, also whether a change of suppliers will impact on consumer demand.

Impact on customers

The impact of economic risk will also depend on the decision G makes about **selling prices**. If it absorbs cost increases due to exchange rate movements, its profits are likely to fall. However if it raises its prices, its profits may or may not fall more, depending on the **impact on consumer demand.** If demand is inelastic, the rise in prices will result in increased revenues. As G is a large retail organisation, its products may well have different degrees of elasticity. It will perhaps have to make perhaps different pricing decisions over its **whole portfolio.**

(b)

> **Top tips**. In (b) the requirement to evaluate means that you have to give some indication of how valid the argument is. The main issue that you need to bring out is that economic risk is less visible but has much more serious long-term consequences than translation risk. However shareholders' views need to be taken into account. You therefore need to explain in your answer what items translation gains and losses affect and how shareholders react to these.

Maximisation of shareholder wealth

The directors have a duty to **maximise shareholder wealth in the longer term.** This hedging policy is seeking to achieve this objective. Arguably therefore directors should not take into account, when establishing policy, the impact of temporary movements in exchange rates that do not have impacts upon cash flows for the period.

Impact of exchange rate changes on income statement

However directors may be concerned about the impact on shareholders, because of the accounting requirements under IAS 21. IAS 21 requires the $ bank balance to be translated at the exchange rate at the date of the statement of financial position, whereas the cost of inventory will be translated at the exchange rate at the date the inventory was purchased. In addition the hedge is against future transactions as well as those reported in the accounting period. Thus the transactions and the hedge **do not fully match**. Also under IAS 21, G has to **disclose the exchange gains or losses** arising from translating monetary assets at the accounting date. The impact of economic exposure need not be disclosed. Though it may result in a fall in profits as directors fear, shareholders will not be able to differentiate the impact of economic risk from other factors affecting the cost of sales.

Impact of exchange rate changes on statement of financial position (SOFP)

The retranslation of the US$ account at the accounting date will also **affect its carrying value in the SOFP**. If the US$ significantly weakens the account will be included at a lower value, **worsening G's asset position and gearing**. This could impact on the financing of G, as finance providers require a higher cost of capital in return for higher perceived risks.

Shareholder reactions

Shareholders may be most interested in the income statement impact. They may be unhappy if a fall in US$ value results in an exchange loss which has been disclosed and which has resulted in **lower earnings per share.** If an exchange gain arises on the $ account, the higher profits may result in shareholders **expecting a higher dividend**, although it would not be based on cash movements.

<u>Disclosure</u>

The company can provide more disclosure than is required by IAS 21 about exchange risks. G may be required, or it may be regarded as good practice locally, to include a **report on risk management within its annual report**. This would include an explanation of its hedging policy. This may help allay shareholder fears, although the fact that G **will not be able to quantify precisely the economic impacts** against which the hedge has been made may mean shareholders have problems judging the directors' actions.

(c)

Top tips. Note from (c) that you won't necessarily be asked to calculate just the daily value at risk. The examiner has commented that value at risk is an important indication of exposure, and so students should be able to calculate it correctly.

(i)   If X = 5% and standard deviation = $450,000

Then Confidence level = 1.65 deviations from the mean

VAR = $450,000 × 1.65 = $742,500

(ii)   30 day SD = daily SD × $\sqrt{30}$ = 450,000 × $\sqrt{30}$ = $2,464,752

30 day VAR = $2,464,752 × 1.65 = $4,066,840

(iii)   <u>Usefulness as indication for directors</u>

<u>Risk appetite</u>

The relevance of the decision to the directors will depend on how they relate to the decision to the risk appetite they have decided is appropriate. 5% is a widely-used measure, but it **may not match G's needs.**

<u>Maximum loss</u>

The VAR figure is a reasonable indication of the **maximum expected loss**, not the maximum possible loss. The directors may wish to consider whether there are extreme factors that could mean the maximum possible loss is significantly different, and try to estimate what it might be.

<u>Historical figures</u>

The value at risk model is **based on historical data,** which may not be a fair reflection of the future economic situation. The unprecedented shocks to the global financial system over the last few years have highlighted this weakness of VAR.

<u>Other assumptions</u>

The VAR model assumes that possible outcomes follow a **normal distribution** and that factors causing **volatility** are **independent** of each other. These assumptions may not apply in practice.

<u>Usefulness as external indicator</u>

The VAR is an **easy to understand and widely used figure** that directors can use to justify their decision to investors, particularly if the loss turns out to be higher than expected.

42 V

Text references. Chapter 11.

Top tips. 9 marks is quite a generous allocation for the three calculations in (a). Certainly the calculations in Question 1 (a) appear to involve rather more work for 6 marks. The only thing that would have complicated the situation in the actual exam was that the paper did not provide the formulae for purchasing power parity and expectations theory (interest rate parity), although the F3 paper does. You therefore need to learn these formulae. The question makes it clear that you need to do the three calculations, but the expectations theory calculation produces (unsurprisingly) the same rate as the forward rate. In (a) (ii) an alternative explanation for the link between interest rates and exchange rates is the international Fisher effect, with high interest rates in a country reflecting an expectation that the country's currency will weaken.

Remember when carrying out any of the calculations in (b) that as the rate is quoted at Y$/C$, and the amount being translated is in C$, you therefore have to **divide** by the exchange rate to arrive at the amount in Y$. Your answer to (b) can be assisted by calculations of what the receipt would be under the forward contract or if the whole amount was left unhedged, as these are other options being considered. The examiner's guidance indicated that the cost of the premium should include the year's interest lost through having to pay the premium in advance. You would not have to make this calculation if you weren't given the interest rates.

You should choose one rate where the option is being exercised, and one rate where it isn't. We have used the current spot rate to demonstrate the impact of the premium on the calculation (though you could have used the prices prediction from (a) as that is the lowest of the three predictions). The spot rate needs to move in the opposite direction to all the predictions for the option to produce a greater net receipt than under the forward contract. Also the rate needs to deteriorate much more than is predicted for the option to be a better choice than leaving the amount unhedged.

Easy marks. The discussion in (c) is about a common decision in currency risk management.

Examiner's comments. Answers to (a) and (c) were generally good. Answers to (b) were not so good, with many students discussing the generic benefits of options rather than the benefits of this particular option.

(a) (i) <u>Inflation rates</u>

Future spot rate A$/B$ = Spot rate A$/B$ × $\frac{1 + \text{country B inflation rate}}{1 + \text{country A inflation rate}}$

Future spot rate Y$/C$ = 2.020 × (1 + 0.08)/(1 + 0.02)

= 2.139

<u>Expectations theory/Interest rate parity</u>

Future spot rate A$/B$ = Spot rate A$/B$ × $\frac{1 + \text{nominal country B interest rate}}{1 + \text{nominal country A interest rate}}$

Future spot rate Y$/C$ = 2.020 × (1 + 0.11/1 + 0.057)

= 2.121

<u>Comparisons of prices</u>

Future spot rate = C$ price/Y$ price

= 420/200

= 2.1

(ii) <u>Expectations theory</u>

The prediction provided by expectations theory is likely to be the most **reliable** and is the prediction on which the forward rate has been based. The theory behind it is that exchange rate will over time move to **counter interest rate differentials.** If they did not, traders could make risk-free gains by borrowing in Y$ and investing in C$. They would ensure they did not lose when

translating C$ back to Y$ to repay their borrowings by fixing the exchange rate in advance at the forward rate. In practice however forces of supply and demand would lead to the forward rate changing to prevent risk-free profit making. Although the forward rate may not be a completely reliable predictor of the future spot rate, banks and other market participants will take particular care to ensure that forecasts are as accurate as possible, since they could make significant losses if they relied on misleading forecasts.

Inflation rates

The prediction based on inflation rates is also based on economic theory, that exchange rates are in equilibrium when the purchasing power of each currency is the same in each country. Spot rates change over time according to inflation rate differentials, with the currencies of countries having high inflation rates weakening against those with lower rates, as inflation brings the value of the currencies down. Expectations theory is likely to provide a better prediction than predicted inflation rates.

Comparisons of prices

Comparisons of prices are likely to provide the least reliable prediction. Prices in different countries will not only be determined by key economic indicators, but by other environmental factors, particularly the **pricing policy** of competitors, also transaction and transportation costs and tax levels.

(b)   Currency option

Option

Spot rate remains at 2.020 Y$/C$

The option will not be exercised, and V will receive net (C$9m/2.020) – (Y$270,000 × 1.057) = Y$4,170,056

Spot rate moves to 2.200 $/£

The option will be exercised, and V will receive net (C$9m/2.150) – (Y$270,000 × 1.057) = Y$3,900,656

Not hedging

If V had not hedged, the receipt would have been (C$9m/2.200) = Y$4,090,909

Forward contract

V will receive (C$9m/2.121) = Y$4,243,281

Alternative calculations
For not exercising the option to produce an equal net receipt to the forward contract, for exchange rate X
(C$9m/X) – Y$(270,000 × 1.057) = Y$4,243,281
X = 1.987
For exercising the option to produce an equal net receipt to leaving the amount unhedged, for exchange rate X
C$9m/X = Y$3,900,656
X = 2.307

Advantages

Removal of uncertainty

The option sets a **floor value**, which V knows it will receive whatever the movements in the exchange rate.

Contract not fulfilled

If the Canadian company does not fulfil the contract, V can **allow the option to lapse**. V would have to fulfil a forward contract if it used that method.

Favourable movements

V **can take advantage of favourable movements** in the exchange rate if the C$ is stronger in a year's time against the Y$ than predicted.

Disadvantages

Premium

The calculations demonstrate that the C$ would have to strengthen against the Y$ for the option to produce higher net receipts than the forward contract because of the large premium that V needs to pay. This is **contrary to all the predicted values**. Although the option is a fallback if the C$ deteriorates, the calculations show that the deterioration would have to be substantial for the option to produce higher receipts than leaving the amount unhedged and not paying the premium.

Cash flow

Having to pay the premium upfront **limits the net receipts on the contract now**. The receipt will only be C$1m/2.02 – Y$270,000 = Y$225,050.

(c)   Factors to consider before changing foreign exchange risk management policy

Advantage

Transfer of risk

As V's foreign customers would have to translate their own currencies into Y$ to pay V, they would have to bear the currency risk. The new policy would mean V **did not face transaction risk.** Because of the time delays between the agreement and payment, the exposure could be significant.

Disadvantages

Speculation gains

The removal of exchange rate risk removes the chance for V to make **speculative gains.** Here V would benefit if over the year the C$ strengthened against the Y$.

Competitive advantage

V has only been able to gain the contract with the Canadian company by agreeing to bill it in C$. Future contracts with this company, along with other contracts with potential Canadian customers, would be jeopardised if V insists on billing in Y$. However the customers may believe that their prices will be influenced by the currency protection measures that V takes if V bills in its home currency. V is also being used by overseas customers for its expertise in its home culture. Therefore it will mainly be competing with firms in its own country, and not local consultancies in the overseas countries.

43   E and N

Text references. Chapters 8, 10-12.

Top tips. An illustration that it is possible to set a currency risk question and not include a single number. (a) is built around the frequency and magnitude of payments, though it is also necessary to establish just what is at risk. This leads on to the recommendation that the unmatched E Pesos receipts are sufficiently large to warrant some hedging. In (b) think of what a local partner would have that N would not have, also why they might fall out. Note agency issues, particularly the cost of monitoring, could be relevant if a joint venture partner is involved. The reaction of finance providers, particularly what the bank in E will do, is the most important element in the discussion about the loan.

Easy marks. The advantages and disadvantages of establishing a joint venture are worth knowing, since they can feature in questions in E3, F3 and ultimately T4, as well as in P3.

Examiner's comments. This question was done less well than the other optional questions. In (a) many students failed to discuss size and frequency and were not able to come up with ways to manage the risks. In (b) students did not see why the two suggestions were different.

Marking scheme

Marks

(a) (i) Up to 4 marks for issues connected with each currency. Issues include:
Currencies need not move in same direction
Number of transactions
Matching
To score high marks, comparison must be clear

max 6

(ii) E Peso Up to 2 marks for per point relating to management techniques. Techniques can include:
Risk acceptance
Matching of payments
Loan finance
Currency swap

max 6

Euro Up to 2 marks for per point relating to management techniques. Techniques can include:
Hedging necessary
Forward contract
Option
Loan
Swap

max <u>6</u>
max 9

(b) (i) Up to 2 marks per advantage and disadvantage discussed, including:
Sharing risk
Cultural help
Spare capacity
Disagreement over terms
Corruption/reputation

max 7

(ii) Up to 2 marks per advantage and disadvantage discussed, including:
Hedging
Ability to resist government pressure
No need for equity investment
Poor terms
Gearing levels

max <u>7</u>
max <u>10</u>
<u>25</u>

(a) (i) <u>Differences in position</u>

There is no guarantee that the E Peso and the Euro will move in **positive correlation** against N's local currency. It's possible that N's local currency may strengthen against one of the two currencies and weaken against the other.

<u>E Peso</u>

The transaction risk connected with the **E Peso** may be limited firstly because the receipts and many of the payments are in E Pesos and N can **match** them. N only needs to be concerned about the transaction risk connected with the surplus of E Peso receipts over payments. In addition the impact of unfavourable currency movements will be limited by the **short timeframe** between the start of the transaction and the settlement. The contract also involves a series of smaller transactions, so the potential exchange loss that relates to each transaction won't be large.

Euro

Transaction risk on the Euro is limited to the **profits** made on the transaction, rather than the **revenues.** However since the notional profits are at a **higher margin** than normal, this will increase the potential exchange loss. In addition the settlement is **annual,** and there will be a **period of up to a year** between the transactions on which the payment is based and the settlement. This allows more time for adverse exchange rate movements, here the Euro weakening against N's home currency.

(ii)   E Peso risk

Natural hedging limits

N can only rely to some extent on natural hedging of receipts and payments. Some hedging is required of the net receipts, since the E Peso currency is weak.

Using E suppliers for other contracts

N could use the E suppliers to supply its manufacturing in its own country as well as supplying its subsidiary in E. Whether this is desirable will depend on its **existing supply arrangements** and also the **terms and reliability offered by the suppliers** in E. When considering terms, N must take into account the costs of, and time taken, delivering parts as the distances are substantial.

Loan

As the E Peso risk will apply for the duration of the contract with the subsidiary, N could hedge the risk by using a loan in E Pesos to establish the subsidiary and **match receipts against loan repayments.**

Currency swap

As an alternative to a new loan, N could use a **currency swap** to restructure the currency base of its liabilities. How desirable this is will depend on the **reliability of counterparties** and **arrangement fees** for any swap arrangements.

Euro

Need for hedging

The level of the payments at risk, and the time period over which exposure applies, means that N needs to take action to hedge the risk. As the payments are for larger amounts, it may be worthwhile to use derivatives. However these are unlikely to be available for the entire four years, and would have to be purchased on an **annual basis.**

Forward contract

If the level of receipts from the foreign government are considered reasonably certain, N could hedge the risk by using a forward contract. This would **remove the uncertainty over exchange rate movements** and be cheaper than some other hedging options. The disadvantages would be that N **could not take advantage of favourable exchange rate movements**, and risks being under-hedged if sales are greater than expected, or over-hedged if less. If over-hedged, it would still have to fulfil the forward contract by dealing in currency at a possibly unfavourable spot rate to make up the shortfall.

Put options

N could use a **put option** to **hedge** the **expected receipt.** The put option would be exercised if the Euro weakened, but N could allow the **option to lapse** if the Euro strengthened, and sell the currency at a favourable spot rate. The main disadvantage with put options may be the **high premium** that has to be paid.

Borrowing

N could take a loan in Euros to hedge the risk with repayment timings matched against the royalty. However the loan would be being taken out **solely to hedge the repayments** rather than to finance the investment in the subsidiary. N's directors may feel that the increased gearing and interest commitments mean that this hedging method is not worthwhile.

Currency swap

Again N can restructure its liabilities by using a **currency swap.** The risks associated with this swap may be lower than the E Peso swap, since the Euro is a more established currency and the choice of reliable counterparties greater therefore.

(b) (i) Entering a joint venture

Advantages

Sharing of risk

Entering a joint venture agreement would mean that the risks of the operation were shared with the joint venture partner, rather than being solely borne by N.

Cultural risk

A joint venture partner will have the **local knowledge** of E that N lacks. A partner will be able to provide the knowledge and contacts that will help in dealing with the government and other regulatory authorities. A partner also may help in dealing with the cultural issues involved in managing local staff and suppliers in E. A locally based partner may be better able to **exercise control over operations** in E.

Manufacturing operations

N may be able to use a joint venture partner in E with **spare manufacturing capability.** This could remove the need to build new facilities.

Disadvantages

Problems over terms

N may find it difficult to **agree terms** with a joint venture partner. Once the contract is in place, the joint venture partner may **renege on its agreement.** N may find it necessary to spend monies and management time **monitoring** the partner to ensure it **fulfils the agreement.** It may also be more **difficult to terminate the arrangement** at the **time** N desires.

Corruption

If the joint venture partner becomes involved in corruption, N may also be legally liable. N could have to pay financial penalties. It could also suffer a **loss of reputation** through an association with corruption, threatening certainly its **chances of winning and retaining contracts with other governments.**

(ii) Loan in E Pesos

Advantages

Hedging

The loan provides a means of **hedging the receipts in E Pesos.** These can be used to meet commitments in E Pesos on the loan.

Governmental pressure

The loan would give N a weapon to **resist pressure from E's government.** E's government may be less inclined to impose on N, if by doing so, it threatens repayments to a local bank. The bank may itself put pressure on the government if it felt its loan was threatened.

Not using equity

A loan would mean that N **would not be committing equity** to finance the investment required. This would minimise its losses if it decided, or was forced, to cease operating in E.

Disadvantages

Terms

The terms of borrowing in E Pesos may not be as favourable as borrowing in other currencies. Because of the economic uncertainties, lenders may demand a **high risk premium**, resulting in **large interest costs** and a **demanding repayment schedule.** The bank in E may also require N's parent company to **guarantee the loan.**

Level of gearing

The extra borrowing may result in gearing levels that are **higher** than N's directors, or its finance providers, deem **desirable**. Other finance providers may react to higher levels and the uncertainties surrounding profits from E by increasing their demands, **again raising N's cost of capital.**

44 N

Text references. Chapters 10 and 11.

Top tips. (a) (i) illustrates an issue that you should always bear in mind in P3 – what are the costs of the method of risk reduction being used. They may be opportunity costs (time taken) as well as financial costs.

In (a) (ii), as the rate is quoted £1 = $X divide the $ amount by the exchange rate. Of the two rates, the rate less favourable to N (1.6050) is chosen and the relevant discount (2.50 cents) is added.

(b) (i) illustrates that economic risks affect home and foreign markets, and sales and purchases. (ii) is a good illustration of how economic risks are risks that can be particularly affected by (1) Lack of information (about competitors' strategic decisions or future shocks) (2) Lack of certainty about the information that is available (long-term movements in interest and exchange rates).

Easy marks. The advantages and disadvantages of forward contracts (or any other hedging instrument) should always be straightforward marks.

Examiner's comments. (a) was generally done well, but answers to (b) were much poorer. In (b) (i) students often failed to discuss the company's competitive position and generally wrote about currency risk. (b) (ii) demonstrated that many students lacked knowledge of economic risk, not understanding its wide-ranging nature.

'Candidates should revise this before the next attempt as this area will be examined in the future.'

Marking scheme

			Marks
(a)	(i)	Advantages – 1 mark per advantage. Consider risk avoidance, cost and flexibility. max	4
		Disadvantages – 1 mark per disadvantage. Consider arrangement costs, problems if original transactions not settled, locked into forward rate.	4
			8
	(ii)	Calculation of costs under forward and spot rates. max	3
		Calculation of difference and conclusion.	1
			4
(b)	(i)	1 mark for each relevant point, including impact on home/foreign sales and supply arrangements.	4
	(ii)	1 mark for each relevant point. Discussion should include uncertainty of assessment, dependence on strategy, dependence on unpredictable economic factors, nature of product and resource markets, switching costs and market imperfections, natural hedging. max	9
			25

(a)   (i)   Advantages of forward contract

Certainty of cash flows

The forward contract **removes the risk** that adverse exchange rate movements will affect the amount in £ that N receives. N can budget for receiving a known amount.

Over-the counter

The forward contract will not be subject to the **requirements and the cost** of a trading exchange.

Tailored to the transaction

The forward contract can be for the **exact amount of the transaction between N and L.**

Settlement date

The contract can be **settled on the same day as the transaction.**

Disadvantages of forward contract

Arrangement costs

It may be **difficult and take time for N to arrange a contract**. The amount is relatively small for a forward contract, and so would not interest some sellers of contracts. Also N's lack of history in the forward market may deter some sellers. The time and costs may outweigh the benefits of the contract.

Default by L

If L fails to settle on the agreed date, N will still be **liable on the forward contract**. N will have to buy dollars at the spot rate, and sell the dollars to the bank at the contracted rate.

Postponement of settlement

Similarly if payment by L is postponed, because of problems meeting L's requirements, the forward contract will still have to be **settled on the agreed date.**

Favourable movements in spot rates

N is committed to settling the forward contract as the contracted rate. If the £ weakens against the US dollar, N **cannot take advantage of the more favourable spot rate.**

(ii)   If **forward contract** used, rate will be 1.6050 + 2.50 = 1.6300

Amount received = 1,755,250/1.6300 = £1,076,840

Under **spot rate**

Amount received = 1,755,250/1.6635 = £1,055,155

Therefore it was beneficial for N to buy the forward contract by £21,685

(b)   (i)   US sales in $

If N invoices further US sales in $ to establish itself in the US market, it will bear the risk of a **long-term decline of the value of the $** against the £.

US sales in £

If N invoices other US customers in £, a strengthening of the £ will mean that its **prices become more expensive** relative to competitors based in the US.

UK sales

N may also be vulnerable even if its future sales are confined to the UK. A strengthening of the £ against the $ will mean that the **prices of systems made by competing US exporters** will become **cheaper**.

Costs of supply

$/£ movements will also affect N if it settles with its suppliers in $. A long-term weakening of the £ against the $ will make the costs of supply more expensive. However if sales are also in $, these will match purchases in $, lessening the impact of exchange rate changes.

(ii)   Nature of economic risks

Economic risks are the risks of exchange rate changes reflecting future cash flows over the longer-term. They **cannot be measured in accounting terms** as they cannot be linked to specific transactions (unlike transaction risks) or figures in the accounts (unlike translation risks).

Dependence on strategic decisions

The level of economic risks will be influenced by the strategic decisions made not only by the **business** itself to maximise its competitive position, but also the decisions made by its **competitors**. These decisions may be difficult to predict.

Interest and inflation rates

Changes in rates will impact upon future exchange rates, but these may be **difficult to forecast over the longer-term**.

Impact of shocks

Unpredictable events, such as the credit crunch, will also impact upon economic risks. The impact of these is made even more uncertain by the impact of financial contagion, how shocks in one economy will affect others.

Impact of movements in other exchange rates

The level of economic risks may not just be affected by **home currency exchange rate movements**. If for example N invoices French customers in €, if the $ weakens against the €, it will become cheaper for French customers to import from the USA if they can pay in $. This will apply even if the £/€ rate remains unchanged.

Results of changes in exchange rates

If N is paying for its supplies in €, a strengthening of the € may ultimately mean it **seeks other suppliers** in a different currency zone, with new levels of currency risk.

Dependence on elasticity of different markets

The impact of exchange rate movements will depend on the **price elasticity** of different markets. This may be difficult to establish, particularly for a company like N that is seeking to establish itself.

Impact of switching costs

Although exchange rate movements may make the prices of the current supplier less attractive, there may be **costs** of finding and making arrangements with a new supplier, and also greater risks associated with a new supplier.

Natural hedges

The impact of economic risk will also depend on the **extent of natural hedging,** how much sales can be matched against purchases, investments against financing.

45 Arbitrage

> **Text reference**. Chapters 8 and 11.
>
> **Top tips.** (a) is simply a question of deciding what to multiply or divide.
>
> The essential point in (b) is that arbitrage relates to exploiting an unexpected difference. The second part of (b) relates to the scenario and hence exchange and interest rates, so you ideally need to use another example in the first half of (b). You may have found it easier to explain how arbitrage works once you had attempted to determine the gain in (c). The main points to bring out in (d) are what each figure represents, and how fairly they measure risk.
>
> **Easy marks.** (d) probably if you concentrate on the usefulness to the organisation. Certainly not (c)!
>
> **Examiner's comments**. In (b) many students confused arbitrage and speculation. Arbitrage involves taking advantage of a short-term opportunity with little speculation being involved.

In (c) only a small number of students produced correct answers. 'It was clear that candidates had not learned this part of the syllabus and did this question out of desperation.'

In (d) most students explained trading limits but not value at risk, probably demonstrating a lack of knowledge of value at risk.

Marking scheme

			Marks
(a)	Calculation of spot rate	2	
	Calculation of forward rate	$\underline{2}$	
			4
(b)	Definition	2	
	Relevance to scenario	$\underline{4}$	
			6
(c)	IRP calculation of true forward rate	1	
	Arbitrage calculation 1 mark per each stage. Award marks for correct principles even if calculations incorrect because of errors in earlier calculations	$\underline{9}$	
			10
(d)	Discussion of trading limits	3	
	Discussion of value of risk	$\underline{3}$	
	To obtain 3 marks uses and limitations must be discussed max		$\underline{5}$
			$\underline{\underline{25}}$

(a)   U$\$$1:Aus$\$$ Y = £1:Aus$\$$Y × US$\$$1:£Y

For current spot rates

US$\$$1   = Aus$\$$2.3180 × $\dfrac{1}{2.0254}$

       = Aus$\$$1.1445

For six month forward rates

US $\$$1   = Aus$\$$2.3602 × $\dfrac{1}{1.9971}$

       = Aus$\$$1.1818

(b)   <u>Arbitrage profit</u>

Arbitrage means **exploiting short-term differences**, maybe between **two markets**, selling in one market and buying in the other. Alternatively it can mean exploiting price differences between **two products**, where the similarities between those products (for example two bonds having a similar maturity and risk) suggests that they should be traded at the same price. Arbitrage differences are **short-term**; as other traders see the opportunities and exploit them, the laws of supply and demand suggest that prices will converge, and the opportunities for exploiting the differences will disappear as equilibrium is reached.

<u>Relevance to scenario</u>

The opportunity for arbitrage profit in this scenario arises because the **difference between the spot and forward exchange rates** does not mirror **differences in interest rates**. Investors can:

- Borrow in one currency
- Deposit what they have borrowed as an investment in the other currency for (say) six months
- Liquidate their investment and convert the proceeds at the forward rate
- Repay the amount borrowed and retain the surplus

(c)

> **Top tips**. Before you get into the calculations for (c), you have to calculate the arbitrage opportunity, using interest rate parity. The opportunity exists because the forward rate suggests that you need more Aus$ to buy each US$ (1.1818) than would be forecast by interest rate parity (1.1405). Curiously interest rate parity not only suggests that the US$ is overvalued; it suggests that the US$ should weaken rather than strengthen forward.
>
> (c) is like a money market hedge, but with complications:
>
> - The US$5,000,000 is the amount you start with now. If we were undertaking a money market hedge, the key amount would be the receipt or payment at the end of the period.
> - To take advantage of the arbitrage opportunity, you need to take out a forward contract to convert the US$ deposit into Aus$ after 6 months. This means that you have to start by **borrowing Aus$ now** and **converting Aus$ into US$ now** to be able to convert them back into Aus$ after 6 months.
> - The need to convert the surplus after the loan has been repaid into a third currency, £, as the business is based in London, so will account in sterling. Here the question supplying the actual exchange rate between £ and Aus$ at the end of 6 months is a clue that you have to do this.
> - It would also be possible to take out a forward contract **now** for the surplus you expect to receive at the forward rate of £1 = Aus$2.3602. The question details make it clear that you would receive a lower amount of £ if you did this (you'd have to pay Aus$2.3602 for each £ rather than Aus$2.32). However that is with the benefit of hindsight; you wouldn't know what the spot rate in six months' time would be when you undertook the original transaction.
> - The transaction costs for the three foreign exchange transactions
>
> (c) is also made more complicated by the fact that the two principal currencies are both $ so you have to make sure you differentiate clearly between Aus$ and US$.
>
> You could also attempt the question by assuming profits are taken today rather than after 6 months.

Ascertain arbitrage opportunity

Using interest rate parity

$$\text{US\$1} \qquad = \text{Aus\$1.1445} \times \frac{1+0.0332}{1+0.0368}$$

$$= \text{Aus\$1.1405}$$

This compares with the rate calculated in (a) of 1.1818 suggesting the US$ is **overvalued forward**.

Therefore we should buy US$ at spot and sell them forward.

This locks in with the rate we shall receive in 6 months' time as forward contracts are binding agreements. To obtain US$5,000,000 now (the maximum permitted for this trader) we need to borrow sufficient Australian $ at the spot rate calculated in (a).

	Now	Interest rate	In 6 months
US $ Dealing currency	4 Take out forward contract to sell, @ 1.1818, US$5,000,000 (1 + 0.0368) = US$5,184,000 This locks in arbitrage opportunity. 3 Invest US$5,000,000	3.68%	5 Liquidate investment + interest received US$5,184,000
	2 Buy US$ @ 1.1445 with Aus$5,722,500 to receive US$5,000,000		6 Sell US$5,184,000 @ 1.1818 to receive = Aus$6,126,451
Aus $	1 Borrow Aus$5,722,500	3.32%	7 Repay Aus$ loan & pay interest Aus $5,722,500(1 + 0.0332) = Aus$5,912,487 Aus$ Surplus = 6,126,451 − 5,912,487 = Aus$213,964
£ Home currency			8 Sell Aus$213,964 @ 2.3200 = £92,226 9 Pay costs of investment (3 × £3,000) = £9,000 Surplus = £83,226

Alternative format for solution

1   **Borrow** Aus$ (5,000,000 × 1.1445) = Aus$5,722,500

2   **Convert to US$** at spot to give US $5,000,000

3   **Invest** US$5,000,000 for 6 months

4   **Take out a forward contract** at 1.1818 to sell the US$ amount expected at the end of 6 months, US$5,000,000 × (1+ 0.0368) = US$5,184,000.

5   After 6 months **liquidate investment**

6   **Convert US$ that have been on deposit plus interest to Aus$,** to give Aus$5,184,000 × 1.1818 = Aus$6,126,451

7   **Repay Aus$ loan and pay interest**. Surplus = 6,126,451 − (5,722,500 × 1.0332) = Aus $213,964

8   **Convert to £,** to give £213,964/2.3200 = £92,226

9   Profit needs to be adjusted by the transaction costs of the three foreign currency transactions (Steps 2, 6 and 8)

Profit = 92,226 − (3,000 × 3) = £83,226

> **Top tips**
>
> - As the US$ spot rate is quoted at US$1 = Aus$1.1445, you **divide** the Aus$ figure by the exchange rate
> - As the six month forward rate is quoted at US$1 = Aus$1.1818, you **multiply** the US$ figure by the exchange rate
> - As the £ spot rate in six months is quoted at £1 = Aus$2.3200, you **divide** the Aus$ figure by the exchange rate

(d) Trading limits

A trading limit, $5,000,000 in the question, limits the size of each transaction undertaken to a monetary amount. Capping all traders in this way, maybe with different limits for each trader, will **limit nominal exposure** from operations.

Nominal value only covers the initial payment transactions, and the total payments may be larger, for example there may be additional **margin** payments on futures transactions. The nominal value also may **not fairly represent the risk** of an individual transaction. For example if another trader working at the organisation is undertaking a transaction in the same market in the opposite direction, the two transactions will be **hedged** and the risks **reduced**, though each will have been limited as if the two transactions were independent.

Value at risk

Value at risk works by determining the potential loss, generally over a whole portfolio, based on the principles that the volatility of market transactions is a **normal distribution**. The value at risk is determined by the **% confidence level** that the organisation wishes to have that the loss will not exceed the value at risk, and the **timeframe** over which the loss may be made – the longer the timeframe the bigger the value at risk. Thus a trader could say that with 95% confidence that the daily loss on the portfolio would not exceed $100,000.

However, particularly with large portfolios, the use of value at risk as a control could be undermined by traders **undertaking individual transactions** for which the chances of losses much greater than $100,000 are much higher, these transactions may be affected by abnormal events and so will not follow the assumed normal distribution. These transactions may not affect the value at risk calculations significantly if the portfolio is large enough.

46 VQR

> **Text references**. Chapter 11.
>
> **Top tips**. This question involves discussion of various issues raised by the chief executive officer, who lacks full understanding of how foreign exchange markets work.
>
> The information you are given indicates that you will need to discuss expectations theory (interest rate parity). Since this is relevant throughout the answer, our answer explains it in detail in the introduction, and refers to it more briefly later on. The marking guide allocated 5 marks for the explanation. The level of detail you are given should have indicated that calculations should be used to support the points you made as relevant.
>
> When dealing with continuously compounded interest rates for part of a year, it is more correct to use x to the power y calculations, but you would also have gained credit if you had adjusted the interest rates by dividing.
>
> You need to assume that there is no concern about the bid/offer spread on the forward exchange rates.
>
> **Easy marks**. Explanation of expectations theory should be fairly straightforward, also why it is risky not to hedge at all. This will often be a possibility that you have to discuss.
>
> The examiner's comments however indicated that many students were unable to define the term adequately.
>
> **Examiner's comments**. Answers were well organised, but calculations were poorly done, indicating inadequate revision of these areas. Written explanations were also often poor.

MEMORANDUM

From: Treasurer
To: Chief Executive Officer
Date: 24 May 20X7
Subject: Financial data

I am writing in response to the questions you raised about the financial data relating to South-East Asia published in the business press. There are two important theories linking exchange rates, interest rates and inflation that need to be considered when determining strategies in this area.

Expectations theory

Expectations theory is based on the hypothesis that the difference between interest rates in the two countries should offset the difference between the spot rates and the forward foreign exchange rates over the same period. The formula is:

$$\text{Future spot rate A/B} = \text{Spot rate A/B} \times \frac{1 + \text{nominal B int erest rate}}{1 + \text{nominal A int erest rate}}$$

(a)   US$ trading forward

The forward rate between the Singapore and US dollars is nearly as predicted by interest rate parity.

$$\text{One month forward rate} = 1.565 \times \frac{1 + 0.0344/12}{1 + 0.0538/12}$$

$$= 1.562$$

> **Top tips**. Because the exchange rates are quoted as US$1 = Sing$X, that means Singapore is Country B in the interest rate parity calculation, the US is Country A.

The reason why the US dollar is quoted forward at a discount or cheaper is that the market has acted to offset the desire that investors in Singapore $ would have to switch to US$, a currency associated with higher interest rates. The Singapore $ has become more expensive in the forward markets to compensate for the lower interest rates in Singapore, a process known as **arbitrage**.

(b)   Forward exchange rates

Again expectations theory can be used to estimate the forward rate.

$$\text{Three month forward rate} = 1.565 \times \frac{1 + 0.0344/4}{1 + 0.0538/4}$$

$$= 1.558$$

We can therefore expect US$3,000,000 × 1.558 = Sing$4,674,000. This compares with a receipt of US$3,000,000 × 1.565 = Sing$4,695,000 on the spot market.

> **Top tips**. As the currencies are quoted at US$1 = Sing$X, you have to **multiply** amounts quoted in US$ to calculate what they are in Sing$.

To guarantee that we receive the minimum of $4,674,000 we should take out a forward contract for the expected receipt at a rate of $1.558, the contract to be performed in three months time.

(c)   Buying Aus$ on spot market

We need to calculate the Sing$: Aus$ crossrates.

Sing$1: Aus$Y = Sing$1: US$Y × US$1: Aus$Y

For current spot rates

$$\text{Sing$1} = \text{Aus$}\frac{1}{1.565} \times 1.311$$

$$= \text{Aus$0.838}$$

For one month forward rates

$$\text{Sing\$1} \quad = \text{Aus\$} \frac{1}{1.562} \times 1.312$$

$$= \text{Aus\$0.840}$$

This indicates that the Australian \$ is expected to depreciate against the Singapore dollar so it may be possible to save money by waiting until Australian dollars are needed and buying them on the spot market some time in the future.

Disadvantages of using the spot market

Risk of adverse movements

Purchasing power parity indicates that the forward rates should in real terms be the same as the spot rates. In practice spot rates will differ from forward rates and VQR could make **gains from favourable spot rate movements**. However VQR may equally make **substantial losses** if rates move **adversely**, and because there is no specialist foreign currency manager, the risks of losses will be too great. By contrast VQR's use of forward contracts allows it to **limit its exposure to losses** by fixing in advance the rates it will use when it comes to pay for imports.

Transaction costs

Transaction costs may also be **higher** if VQR uses the spot market.

(d) Borrowing Sing\$ to pay off Aus\$

It is true that we would be paying lower interest rates on a loan in Sing\$ than a loan in Aus\$. However the difference in the forward rates compensates for this, so it would be **more expensive to buy Aus\$ now** (each one would cost Sing\$1.193) than it would be to set a forward rate to buy them in say a month's time (when each Aus\$ would only cost Sing\$1.190)

In addition if VQR hedges on the money market by buying Aus\$ and placing them on deposit, it would be **matching** the amount deposited with the Aus\$ loan. Although it would suffer higher interest rates than on a Sing\$ loan, it would also benefit from higher interest rates on the deposit. Matching is a further way in which VQR can limit its exposure to losses from exchange rate and interest rate movements.

If you have any further queries, please do not hesitate to get in touch.

47 MNO

Text references. Chapters 9 and 12.

Top tips. This question requires a combination of calculation skills, knowledge in (b) and business decision analysis in (c). (c) gives you the chance to demonstrate your strategic awareness, which we stressed as a key skill in the front pages.

Easy marks. (b) should have been very straightforward if you revised this area well.

Examiner's comments. Few candidates used all the correct rates and attempted to calculate the premium. For (c) students were also uncertain about the most appropriate methods of hedging for small and large companies.

(a)

Top tips. In (a) for futures, as contracts are in £, you have to **divide the receipt** by the **opening futures price** in order to calculate how many contracts.

The question doesn't say anything about the contract size of the option so the simplest assumption is to assume that it's an over-the-counter (OTC) option. (Further confirmation that it's meant to be an OTC option is that it's a put option, implying a right to sell US \$. There are no US\$/£ exchange traded option contracts).

The question also does not tell you any direct information about the premium. You don't actually need the premium information to carry out the calculation, although you should certainly mention that there would be a premium as we have done in our answer. Our alternative solution gives the premium calculation suggested by CIMA, although this method has been questioned.

Futures market

- Buy £ futures
- Number of contracts

$$\frac{1,800,000/1.690}{62,500} = 17.04, \text{ say 17 contracts.}$$

This leaves $(1,800,000/1.690) - (62,500 \times 17) = £2,589$ not covered by contracts.

On futures market

Opening futures price	1.6900	1.6900
Closing futures price	1.6650	1.7200
Movement in ticks	0.0250	0.0300
Loss on futures market	$0.0250 \times 62,500 \times 17 =$	$0.0300 \times 62,500 \times 17 =$
	$26,563 loss	$31,875 profit

Net outcome

	$	$
Spot market receipt	1,800,000	1,800,000
Loss/profit on futures market	(26,563)	31,875
	1,773,437	1,831,875
Translated at closing spot rate	1.665	1.720
	£1,065,127	£1,065,044

Option

We assume that MNO is able to purchase an over-the-counter option that means that the exact amount is covered.

Spot rate moves to £1 = US$1.665

The option will not be exercised, and MNO will receive $1,800,000/1.665 = £1,081,081

Spot rate moves to £1 = US$1.720

The option will be exercised, and MNO will receive $1,800,000/1.675 = £1,074,627.

In practice in either case with the option, MNO will not receive so much because it will have to pay a **premium** for the option. The premium size may well mean that futures are the best method of hedging.

Alternative solution

Premium calculation

Cost = 1.690 – 1.675 = $0.015 per £

Premium = (0.015 × 1,800,000)/1.675 = £16,119

If this figure is used, then the futures market offers the best method of hedging

(b) Tailoring of contracts

The contracts cannot be **tailored to the user's exact requirements**. Futures are dealt with on currency exchanges using **standard contract sizes** and the amount to be hedged may not be an amount that can be hedged using a whole number of contracts. In addition futures are only available for **standard delivery dates** that may not correspond to when the company is receiving or paying currency. This means that the company will have to eliminate its commitments under the futures contracts by **closing out**; undertaking a second futures transaction that reverses the effect of the first one.

Hedge inefficiencies

Having to deal in a whole number of contracts means that there may be an amount that is not hedged by futures, or the futures hedge a larger amount than required. The company can leave the **difference unhedged** and exposed to currency risk, or use a **forward contract** to hedge the difference at a different rate. Hedge inefficiencies are also caused by **basis risk**; the risk that the futures contract price will move by a different amount from the price of the underlying currency. Volatile trading conditions on the futures markets mean that the **potential loss** can be **high**.

Market volatility and liquidity

Futures require a **margin payment corresponding to daily price changes in the futures market.** If the market is volatile the **margin payments** may be for significant amounts.

(c)

> **Top tips**. A good way to approach (c) is to consider key elements of the risk management process; company objectives, the risks that need to be managed, and the availability and effectiveness of risk hedging instruments.
>
> Our answer to (c) brings together in each paragraph the different elements of the requirements – that you have to explain how much hedging is undertaken and what instruments are used to hedge. It seems that some students did not go into enough detail about the different methods used.

Objectives and risk appetites

The strategic objectives and hence the risk appetites of small and large companies are likely to differ significantly. **Small companies** are likely to **concentrate on fewer products and markets**. The key aim is most likely to be using hedging instruments as a means of **minimising exchange transaction risks**. However the risks involved in using some hedging instruments may be considered excessive, for example futures or swaps with significant **counterparty risks**. Small companies may also wish to avoid the **accounting and tax complications** of more complex hedging instruments.

Larger companies by contrast are more likely to achieve their objects by **diversification**, and are likely to tolerate varying levels of risk and return from different activities. This may mean that they are more concerned with being able to take advantage of **possible profits** from derivative usage, for example by using an option so if rates move in a favourable direction the option is not exercised. Ultimately large companies may choose to speculate in **derivatives**, deal in derivatives as a profit-making activity without any link to other underlying transactions.

Incurring exchange risks

Small companies may **incur currency risk** on a limited number of significant transactions in a few currencies. Directors may therefore feel it is worthwhile to **hedge all significant transactions**. To minimise risk, **forward contracts** may well be used as these **guarantee** the exchange rate at which the company will receive or pay monies.

For larger companies, hedging all significant transactions may be **unnecessarily expensive**. Directors will take account of the **currency portfolio** of their transactions. Currency losses through significant payments in a particular currency may be **offset** by significant receipts in the same currency. If the company is undertaking transactions in several major currencies, there is a greater chance that exchange losses on transactions in one currency will be balanced by exchange gains on transactions in another currency.

Incurring interest rate risks

Small companies will be most concerned with the interest rate sensitivities of the debt they need to take out, and their gearing structure is unlikely to be complex. Again they are most likely to be concerned with guaranteeing a borrowing rate on particular sums that they have to borrow and use **forward rate agreements** for that purpose. However they may also want to **use interest rate swaps as** a means of **obtaining finance on better terms**.

Larger companies will be concerned with their overall portfolio, with the **interest rate sensitivities** and **term structure** of their debt and also their investments. This may mean they will use a variety of instruments to hedge different types of finance.

Risk management methods

Smaller companies may not be able to use all the risk management methods available to larger companies. They may not be able to **match receipts and payments** in the same currency for example, or

match investments and borrowings. The commitment required may be excessive; over-the-counter contracts are often of a **minimum size** that may be too large. The **costs** of certain techniques, for example option premiums, may be considered **too high**.

Large companies may be able to employ **specialist treasury personnel** who have a greater level of expertise in using derivatives than would be found in a smaller general finance function. They are also more likely to have directors or senior managers with sufficient expertise to be able to **monitor** treasury activity effectively. They are therefore more likely to use derivatives such as **futures**, **options** and **swaps**.

48 SDT

Text references. Chapter 11 on the financial risks, Chapter 10 on other relevant risks.

Top tips. Note the requirements in (a) require **critical** commentary, which should have indicated to you the need to explain why the director's views were wrong. The main elements in the answer are market efficiency and (insufficient) diversification, both concepts from Financial Strategy, but remember that you may need to use FS knowledge in this paper as well. Don't forget the second part of the question, to discuss potential benefits.

The main problem in (b) appears to have been identifying which figure you had to calculate, indicating you needed to read the question carefully. The **greater** of the two relevant exchange rates is used in every calculation, as in each case SDT is **receiving the foreign currency**, and is having to pay the **higher amount** to obtain each £ that it wants.

(c) is a straightforward look at the higher risks that mean a higher return is required. (d) can bring in debtor management as well as option forward contracts.

Easy marks. Evidently the calculations, as this was the most popular Section B question and many who answered it scored full marks in (b); those that didn't calculated figures the question didn't require rather than made mistakes in calculating the figures the question did require. (c) is a fairly general risk discussion so shouldn't have presented too many problems.

Examiner's comments. This was by some distance the most popular optional question. The question required candidates to comment critically and interpret currency data. About a third of the marks were available for computation.

The main weakness in (a) were failure to discuss the managing directors' views, as required by the question. Many candidates scored full marks in (b), although some failed to score because they did not follow the requirements of the question, and calculated sales value or contribution per unit rather than total contribution.

(a)   The main problems with the Managing Director's views are:

(i)   Conditions for efficiency

The conditions for efficiency are **market liquidity**, **full information** and **freely floating currencies**. In practice liquidity and information available varies between currencies. Many currencies are at most subject to managed floating, floating within limits decided by governments. However conditions for efficiency will apply more to the major currencies in the scenario, and gains and losses from each individual currency may be equally likely.

(ii)   Limited range of currencies

Although the managing director is correct in saying that the risk is diversified, it is not diversified across all currencies. It is possible that the £ may move in an **adverse direction** against each of the three currencies, if for example the UK's inflation rate was higher than other major nations. In fact the currencies quoted are known as the Triad because the countries are similar markets, so in practice there might be **positive correlation between the three** and hence diversification over them will increase the risk of losses.

(iii)   Hedging sales only

Foreign exchange risk is enhanced because it is only in one direction, for **sales**. As purchases are all in £, there is **no matching of sales and purchases** in the same currency which will limit foreign exchange risk.

Currency hedging may be beneficial for the following reasons, although it will incur costs:

(i) <u>Risk limitation</u>

Hedging risk can mean that the **amounts SDT** receives can be **fixed**, and SDT is not subject to **adverse fluctuations**. In an efficient market, prices respond to new information, so shocks may have unexpected effects on exchange rates.

(ii) <u>Size of possible losses</u>

Because SDT exports over 90% of its production, **potential losses** from adverse events could be **very large**.

(iii) <u>Improved forecasting</u>

Fixing the amounts to be received will also help **internal forecasting and budgeting procedures**.

<u>Conclusion</u>

Bearing these considerations in mind, SDT needs to consider hedging risk

(b) (i) (1) <u>A</u>

Contribution = Revenue – Costs

$$= \frac{\text{Export sales}}{\text{Exchange rate}} - \left(\text{Unit variable cos ts} \times \frac{\text{Export sales}}{\text{Unit export sales price}} \right)$$

$= (9{,}487{,}500/200.032) - (2.75 \times 9{,}487{,}500/632.50)$

$= 47{,}430 - 41{,}250$

$= £6{,}180$

<u>B</u>

Contribution $= (82{,}142/1.7775) - (4.80 \times 82{,}142/10.2678)$

$= 46{,}212 - 38{,}400$

$= £7{,}812$

<u>Euro</u>

Contribution $= (66{,}181/1.4784) - (6.25 \times 66{,}181/12.033)$

$= 44{,}765 - 34{,}375$

$= £10{,}390$

(2) <u>A</u>

Contribution $= (9{,}487{,}500/202.63) - 41{,}250$

$= 46{,}822 - 41{,}250$

$= £5{,}572$

<u>B</u>

Contribution $= (82{,}142/1.7750) - 38{,}400$

$= 46{,}277 - 38{,}400$

$= £7{,}877$

<u>Euro</u>

Contribution $= (66{,}181/1.4680) - 34{,}375$

$= 45{,}082 - 34{,}375$

$= £10{,}707$

(ii) <u>Hedging</u>

$$\text{Contribution to sales ratio} = \frac{6{,}180 + 7{,}812 + 10{,}390}{47{,}430 + 46{,}212 + 44{,}765} = 17.62\%$$

Not hedging

$$\text{Contribution/sales ratio} = \frac{5,572 + 7,877 + 10,707}{46,822 + 46,277 + 45,082} = 17.48\%$$

Hedging leads to a higher contribution per sale than not hedging and accordingly SDT should hedge its foreign exchange exposure.

(c) Reasons for generating higher rates of return

Businesses will try to generate higher contributions from export sales as they appear to be riskier than domestic sales.

Foreign exchange risk

Foreign exchange risk will mean that the **receipts are uncertain**, unless the exports are **invoiced in the domestic currency**.

Physical risk

Because of the greater distances, there may be an increased risk of the **goods being lost, damaged or stolen in transit**, or the documents accompanying the goods going astray.

Credit risk

There may be a higher risk in allowing customers credit because **researching their suitability is more difficult** than domestic customers. Payments may be **slower from overseas customers**, and it may be difficult and costly to monitor and pursue customers who fail to pay promptly or at all.

Trade risk

Because of the large distances travelled, there may be a risk that the customers **do not accept the goods** when delivered, or that the order is **cancelled in transit**.

Political risk

Overseas governments may impose a **variety of rules and restrictions**, including **higher quality standards** than are imposed in the company's own domestic market.

Risk mitigation

The effects of all these risks can be mitigated by **hedging techniques** for foreign exchange currency, **insuring against the risks** or reducing the risk of problems by, for example, using **credit reference agencies** to report on customers. However all of these will have **costs**, and increased sales revenues will cover those costs.

(d) Risk

The risk is that SDT will be forced to **buy currency at a poorer spot rate**, in order to be able to sell it to the bank at the forward rate. If the customer subsequently fulfils the contract, SDT may not be able to recoup the loss it has made. Alternatively SDT may take out **another forward contract** up until the time that the customer is expected to pay, but this may be on poorer terms than the original contract. **Transaction costs** will also be incurred.

Risk reduction procedures

(i) Insurance

The risk can be avoided by taking out **insurance** against the possibility of the customers failing to fulfil their obligations, although a premium will be payable.

(ii) Discount

SDT could **reduce the risk of the customers paying late** by offering a **discount for payment on time**; the cost then would be the amount of the discount. Alternatively SDT could specify **penalties** for late payment; this would reduce the cost for SDT if payment was late.

(iii) Hedging

SDT could take out an **option forward contract** that would give it some leeway as to the date the contract will be fulfilled. However there would be **increased transaction costs**, and SDT would have to accept the worst exchange rate over the period the option could be exercised.

49 OJ

Text references. Chapters 11 and 12.

Top tips. The biggest problem you may have found in (a) was setting out the layout clearly. It is useful to plan in advance layouts that might be difficult to fit on a page, for instance layouts with lots of columns as in (a).

(b) requires knowledge of the relationship between forward rates and spot rates and the workings of currency swaps, as well as posing an interesting discussion on whether exchange control risk should affect the discount rate used in investment appraisal.

All three statements in (b) merit at least 6 marks to do justice to the discussion, bringing out the qualifications and problems with the views raised, so you could have been hard-pressed to finish this question in time.

In (b) (i) the distinction that your answer needs to bring out is the difference between an **unbiased** and an **accurate** prediction.

In (b) (ii) the key point is that adjusting the discount rate is an alternative to adjusting cash flows for the effects of exchange controls.

(b) (iii) demonstrates how a swap would work, but to get good marks on this part, it is more important to discuss the problems of swaps and whether other methods (forward contracts) might do the job better.

Easy marks. Difficult to identify as neither the calculations nor discussions are straightforward. Quite a tough question.

(a) (i) <u>OJ Limited: Joint venture NPV</u>

<u>Assumption 1: exchange controls in operation</u>

Year	Project cash SA$'000	OJ's 50% share SA$'000	Cash repatriated SA$'000	Exchange rate £1 = SA$	£'000	Discount factor 16%	PV £'000
0					(450.00)	1.000	(450.0)
1	4,250	2,125	1,062.5	10	106.25	0.862	91.6
2	6,500	3,250	1,625.0	15	108.33	0.743	80.5
3	8,350	4,175	6,862.5	21	326.79	0.641	209.5
		9,550	9,550.0				(68.4)

<u>Assumption 2: removal of exchange controls</u>

Year	Project cash SA$ '000	OJ's 50% share SA$ '000	Cash repatriated SA$ '000	Exchange rate £1 = SA$	£'000	Discount factor 16%	PV £'000
0					(450.00)	1.000	(450.0)
1	4,250	2,125	2,125	10	212.50	0.862	183.2
2	6,500	3,250	3,250	15	216.67	0.743	161.0
3	8,350	4,175	4,175	21	198.81	0.641	127.4
							21.6

(ii) Based solely on these calculations, the joint venture should only proceed if restrictions on repatriation of profits are lifted.

(b) (i) <u>Reliability of forward rates as predictors of spot rates in the future</u>

<u>Forward rate</u>

A forward rate is a rate agreed today at which currency will be exchanged on an agreed future date. Forward rates offered by banks are calculated from **today's spot exchange rate** and **the fixed interest rate in each currency** for the period in question. Because these rates are known with certainty, the forward rate can be fixed with accuracy: any variation from the computed rate would allow speculators to engage in risk-free arbitrage between the money markets and currency markets.

Spot rate

In a **floating exchange rate system**, however, the **spot rate** in the future is **dependent** on many **economic factors** affecting supply and demand for the currency, not just current factors but new events that arise between now and the future date. Factors include balance of payments, capital investment cash flows, interest rates, inflation rates and actions by speculators. The future spot rate is therefore subject to significant uncertainty.

Forward rate as predictor

If consistent patterns emerge, forward rates will be adjusted to take account. The forward exchange rate will be as likely to be above the eventual spot rate as below it. This is, however, completely different from saying that the forward rate is a reliable or accurate predictor of the spot rate. It clearly is **not a reliable predictor** because of the uncertainty in events which might arise between now and the future date. This is particularly likely to be true in a volatile currency such as the South American one in this question.

(ii) Should a higher discount rate be used when there are exchange controls?

The discount rate of 16% is assumed to allow for the time value of money and the normal business risk of the investment but not for the risk of **exchange controls** being **retained**. Since the company is not a public limited company and shareholders are probably undiversified, they are assumed to be concerned with total risk, not just systematic risk. Exchange controls are therefore a relevant risk which must be accounted for.

Allowing for the uncertainty of exchange controls

(1) Risk-adjusted discount rate

The cash flows are **evaluated assuming there are no exchange controls** (Assumption 2) and the **discount rate is increased** to allow for the uncertainty in the timing of the cash flows because of exchange controls.

(2) Two scenarios

Two scenarios are postulated, **one with exchange controls** and one **without**, as in the question. Both are discounted at 16% to allow for business risk, but the discount rate does not need to be increased to allow for exchange control risk, which is already being allowed for by the delayed cash flows in Assumption 1. This method, used in the question, is valid and more detailed than the alternative method.

What is *not* valid is to postulate the scenario with **delayed cash flows** and in addition to **increase its discount rate**. This would be double-counting the exchange control risk.

(iii) Can a currency swap help to minimise the exchange rate risk?

In a currency swap two parties lend each other agreed amounts of different currencies for a given time, the loans being repaid at the end of this period. This has the effect of **fixing the exchange rate in advance** for the repayment date and therefore reduces currency risk.

Terms of swap

Of course there are no 'free gifts' in foreign exchange and the **interest paid** on OJ's loan in SA$ will probably be **significantly higher** than the interest it receives on its sterling loan. In addition, the **swap exchange rate** may well be **higher than 10**. These factors are subject to negotiation between the parties.

Risks of swap

OJ must also consider the **risk** that its **swap partner defaults** on repayment or that **exchange controls prevent the receipt of interest** on its sterling loan. There will also be commission to pay to the intermediary which arranged the swap.

Forward contract

Given that there is a **forward market** for the SA$ then currency risk can be hedged sufficiently without using a swap. As this is OJ's first venture into South America, forward contracts may be easier to manage.

50 YZ

Text references. Chapter 11.

Top tips. A comprehensive question on forward and money market hedging.

Easy marks. As in Question 2, the discussion parts are fairly straightforward and you may want to tackle them first. However, the numerical element is more important in this question, so you will have to attempt the calculations to pass.

Examiner's comments. Many candidates obtained full marks in (a); errors included incorrect treatment of premiums, failing to calculate the interest rates in the money market hedge correctly, and using the wrong spot rate. In (b) some candidates failed to distinguish between forward and money markets, and wasted time by repeating much of their answer under different headings.

(a)

Top tips. You can avoid wasting time in (a) by netting off receipts and payments in the same currency, and only hedging the net amount. € is the **term currency** as it is quoted as £1 = €X and we therefore have to **divide** € amounts by the exchange rate to calculate amounts in £.

Remember that:

- The **bank sells** (and the **company buys**) the **term currency** (€) **low**
- The **bank buys** (and the **company sells**) the **term currency high**

Remember also to **deduct** premiums and **add** discounts from and to the term currency.

When calculating the part year interest rates for the money market hedge, it would be technically better to use the twelfth and fourth roots for 1 and 3 month rates, but the examiner has indicated dividing the annual rates by 12 and 4 is acceptable here.

The company will be concerned with hedging net amounts:

In one month's time 600,000 – 400,000 = €200,000 payment

In three months' time 1,200,000 – 800,000 = €400,000 receipt

(i) Forward currency market

One month

Payment   = 200,000/(1.6186 – 0.0006)
               = £123,609

Three months

Receipt   = 400,000/(1.6202 – 0.0008)
               = £247,005

(ii) <u>Money market</u>

<u>One month</u>

	Now		+ 1 month
€	2 So invest now €199,501	1/12 x 3% = 0.25% per month (lending rate) × 1/1.0025 ←	1 Need to pay €200,000

↓ To be able to invest € must buy them now @ $1.6186

£	3 So need to borrow now £123,255	On which interest is charged at 1/12 × 4.25% = 0.3542% (borrowing rate) × 1.003542 →	4 Due to Bank in 6 months £123,692 (effective cost of hedge)

<u>Three months</u>

	Now		+ 3 months
€	2 So borrow now €396,530	3/12 × 3.5% = 0.875% per 3 months (borrowing rate) × 1/1.00875 ←	1 Will receive €400,000

↓ To be able to invest € borrowed, must sell them now @ 1.6202

£	3 So invest now £244,741	On which interest is received at 3/12 × 3.75% = 0.9375% per 3 months (lending rate) × 1.009375 →	4 Due to YZ £247,036 (effective receipt from hedge)

(iii) <u>Not hedge</u>

<u>One month</u>

Payment = 200,000/1.6192
        = £123,518

<u>Three months</u>

Receipt = 400,000/1.6220
        = £246,609

(b)

> **Top tips**. Don't forget to give a recommendation at the end of your answer to (b). The discussion is primarily about:
>
> - The feasibility of the method
> - The certainty of the results
> - The ability to benefit from favourable exchange rates (only possible on the spot market here)

(i) Advantages of using forward market

If YZ uses the forward market, then the payment is **fixed** and there is no risk of the company suffering losses from adverse movements in the exchange rate. **Cash flow planning** is therefore improved. Evidence suggests that the forward market is an **unbiased predictor** of the spot rate, and anyone using the forward market many times will not lose out compared with not hedging the transactions, and taking a chance on the spot market. Forward contracts can also be **tailor-made** to fit YZ's exact requirements.

Disadvantages of using forward market

A forward exchange contract is binding, and cannot be **terminated** nor its terms **altered** by YZ. For one-off receipts or payments, YZ may lose out on **spot market rates** in one or three months' time not being the same as forward rates. If YZ's customers do not pay on time, YZ will nevertheless have to **honour its own commitment** to the bank. An **option forward exchange contract** (settlement possible on a range of dates) may be available to help overcome this problem.

(ii) Advantages of using money market

Market forces will mean that the premium or discount on a forward contract **reflects the interest differential** between the two. Hence the results of a money market hedge will not be very different from the results of using a forward contract, and a money market hedge is thus **low risk**.

Disadvantages of using money market

YZ is committed to a course of action that it cannot change if **exchange rate movements** mean that it would be better to use the spot market. In addition the operation of money market hedges is **more complicated** than the operation of forward exchange contracts, and possibly further expertise will be required.

(iii) Advantages of using spot market

Not hedging and using the spot market means that YZ can **benefit from unexpectedly favourable exchange rate movements**. As things happened here, YZ would have been better off not hedging the one month payment, but that is said with hindsight.

Disadvantages of using spot market

The spot market carries the **risk of losses** if exchange rates move adversely. Not hedging means that YZ is **uncertain** about what its future cash flow will be.

Recommendation

Hedging would be a prudent course, given the uncertainty about interest rates. There is not much difference in monetary terms between hedging on the forward and money markets, and the decision may depend on the **incidental costs** of both markets.

51 H

Text references. Chapters 13 and 14.

Top tips. If you are asked about a change in risks as here, it is always worth asking whether there are some risks which are being reduced, although generally most of the marks will be for risks that have increased.

Easy marks. You would have gained a few marks in (b) for making points about system design and testing that apply to most companies, but the majority of your answer would need to be focused on H.

Examiner's comments. Answers to (a) were generally better than answers to (b). The main weakness in answers to (a) was identifying too few risks. In (b) some students discussed the whole systems development cycle rather than focusing on the design and testing. The recommendations in many answers failed to relate to the case study.

(a)

> **Top tips**. Note that removal of the element of judgement by legally-trained call centre staff has the upside of removing any bias in judgement, but the substantial downside of removing the opportunity to probe into the kinds of problems that may result in cases being lost. The other major issue is to consider is problems with the system. How easily can they be identified? How easily can the system be corrected (or amended for other reasons, changes in law)? What can H do if the system is a failure?

Upside risks

Better-informed judgements

The expert system may promote better decision-making because the decisions it will make will be based on the judgements of the legal experts employed by H rather than the **less experienced staff currently employed** in the call centre.

Greater consistency

Using a prescribed series of questions and having the decision of whether to proceed **determined by the computer** should mean that decisions are made **objectively** and **consistently** over the whole range of cases. It will remove the possibility of bias adversely affecting the judgements of legal call centre staff.

Lower costs

The **costs and resources** required to take on and train unqualified call centre staff will be lower than the costs of recruiting qualified staff currently. Therefore provided the system does not result in greater costs in other ways (above all through a greater proportion of cases taken on being lost), then profits should increase.

Downside risks

Consequences of incorrect decision-making

If cases are accepted and the client loses, there will be a **waste of staff time** and H will have to pay **costs** to the winning side. If cases where clients would have won are rejected, H's **revenues** will be below what they potentially could have been.

Questions insufficiently wide

The questions staff are told to ask may **fail to cover all the relevant circumstances.** If staff cannot ask discretionary questions, then decisions may be made on the basis of inadequate information, increasing the risk that they are wrong.

No judgements made of information from clients

An 'automatic' questioning approach, rather than an approach that allows staff some discretion in the questions that they ask, may be **less likely to identify problems with what clients are saying**. Currently if staff have doubts about what clients are saying, they can probe further. This may reduce the risks of cases that clients are going to lose going to court.

Incorrect input of information

The information input into the computer for decision may be wrong or misleading. If the clients describe the circumstances of their case poorly, or staff misinterpret what they are saying, clients may be **asked the wrong questions.** New call centre staff's lack of legal training may make this more likely if complex legal issues are involved.

Slowness in discovering problems

If the testing process has not identified major flaws that have increased the risks of incorrect decisions being made, these flaws may not emerge until sometime after the new system starts to operate. Flaws may be reflected in **changes in the proportion of applications accepted or rejected**, or **changes in the proportion of cases accepted and won.** Analysis of patterns could be very time-consuming. It would have to be done on a case-by-case basis and even then the results may not be clearcut. A fall in the proportion of cases accepted (and hence potential fees) may be countered by a rise in the proportion of cases accepted and won. It may be difficult to tell whether cases have been rejected correctly, as these cases will not have gone to court.

Updating system

Updating the system for **changes in legislation or correction of errors** may be very expensive. At present it is relatively simple to update, as it can be done by briefing the legally-qualified call centre staff on a training course. Any changes to the new system will have to go through a **design and testing process** that will be much more expensive and time-consuming. Whilst development is taking place, there may well be an **increased risk of incorrect decision-making** due to the inadequacies of the current system. H may be able to compensate for these by referring more cases to its legal experts, but their time is likely to be expensive.

Commitment to new system

Perhaps the most significant risk that H is taking is that if it implements the new system and it turns out to be completely unsuitable, H cannot go back to the previous system. The legally-qualified call centre staff would have **left by that time.**

(b)

> **Top tips**. One problem in (b) is deciding what areas your answer should cover. The question specifies the design and testing processes, and the examiner commented that some answers were too wide and covered the systems development lifecycle. However training is mentioned in the scenario and receives credit in the mark scheme. The mark scheme also gives credit for mentioning ongoing review after the initial testing.
>
> Key questions for both design and testing are what and who? What should be covered in the design documentation (specific operational aspects as well as the design of the system)? What should the testing cover and what data should be used? Who should be asked for their opinions on the design and who should be involved in the testing process? Here you are trying to identify what the last paragraph of the scenario leaves out. Most importantly it covers the involvement of the experts, but does not mention the involvement of those who will operate the system day-to-day. There are many examples of systems where operational staff were not consulted at all or had their views ignored, and the systems had subsequently to be scrapped because they were impractical to operate.

Design

Documentation

The system documentation drawn up needs to include standard details such as inputs, processing and storage facilities, also program and file design and security. It also needs to **specify the questions that the system will ask.** This should be supported by records of the logic underlying asking the questions. **Training material** will also be part of the documentation. This should be prepared by the systems designer, but H's legally-qualified staff should also have input into it, to ensure it correctly and sufficiently covers relevant law.

Comments by staff

Certainly H's senior lawyers will need to confirm that the **legal logic** underlying the system is sound. However the knowledge engineer **needs to obtain feedback** on whether the questions appear to cover all the areas that interviews by call centre legal staff would currently cover. Ideally therefore current staff should be consulted. However it may be difficult to obtain useful feedback from current staff about the proposed system, as it is likely to result in many of them losing their jobs.

Testing

Testing of systems logic

Before programs are written in detail, the **systems logic developed by the knowledge engineer** should be **reviewed by another IT expert and also by the senior lawyers.** The process should involve following through sequences of questions for different types of case.

Program testing

The programs should be **tested using details of cases that H has previously both taken on and rejected.** The sample of cases that H has taken on should also include both cases that were won and lost. They must **cover all the areas of business** for which series of questions has been developed. Ideally they should **cover as many different permutations of questions as is practicable**.

Analysis of results

The results of the testing should be analysed. Review should focus on computer decisions that were different from those made by the call centre operative. Reviewers should **compare the results of the computer analysis with the records** on the file of the case to see **why differences occurred** and whether they illustrate a flaw in the software's decision-making process.

The review should also examine cases where the computer has **agreed with the operative's decision to take the case on** but the **case was subsequently lost.** The reviewer should consider whether the decision was reasonable on the information given or whether the case details reveal that the questions supporting the computer decision failed to probe a key area.

Lastly cases where the operative made a decision but the computer **identified as needing review** by an expert lawyer should be examined. Individual cases may involve difficult points of law that it is reasonable for a lawyer to check. However too many referrals may indicate problems in the questions supporting the computer-based system.

User testing and training

H's senior lawyers must again be involved in testing the new system, to help ensure its decision-making is legally sound. However they will not be using the system on a day-to-day basis. H must gain assurance that staff who operate the system will do so properly. H must therefore **recruit some new staff for the call centre**, **train them in the new system** and have them **operating the system as part of the testing process**. Queries raised during training or problems that occur when staff operate the system must be fed back to the knowledge engineer and the **system specification amended** if necessary.

Re-testing

If the software has to be amended, it may be **necessary to test all aspects of the software** to ensure that the corrections have not affected other aspects of the software.

Reviewing results when system goes on-line

Identifying problems after the system has gone on-line may result in much more costly and difficult changes than if the problems had been identified in pre-implementation testing. However possibly some problems will **only be identified when the system is in operation**. Therefore H should regard the **period of initial operation** as part of the testing process. Review at this time should include asking call-centre staff to **provide feedback on problems they are experiencing**. Legally-qualified staff should **review the results** of a sample of the first cases put through the computer to see if the decisions appear to be sound. Management should also be alert for **any large differences in the proportion of cases accepted and rejected** that become quickly apparent, or the **referral of a much higher than expected proportion** of cases to H's lawyers.

52 AHB

Text references. Chapters 5 and 14.

Top tips. This is a good example of a question where you do not need much technical knowledge, but which requires clear thought about the issues and good use of all relevant scenario information.

Certainly in (a) (i) the main advantages can be derived from the scenario, the need to test the readiness of both the systems and the people operating them. With any large-scale controls or significant control exercise, cost will potentially be a large disadvantage. That being the case, you also need to ask if some of the objectives can be achieved by cheaper methods, for example here partial testing.

The main point to bring out in (a) (ii) is that the test is not very realistic. The hints in the scenario here include the fact that the test takes place on the quietest day of the year before the call centre is open and that all staff are given warning. Think for example of the fire drills you may have seen. These generally take place without advance warning to test the effectiveness of evacuation procedures if staff are taken by surprise. One point in (a) (ii) is that if you highlight the weaknesses and suggest stronger tests that should have been carried out, these tests could have resulted in more disruption and greater loss of sales. However you don't need to worry too much about this as the focus of the answer is on making the simulation an effective exercise and not debating the costs that were discussed in (a) (i).

In (b) you should bring out the need for both encouragement and enforcement in dealing with the human resource problems.

Easy marks. The examiner's comments that students ignored the childcare and transport issues were surprising, as the scenario clearly highlights them as major staff concerns that AHB needs to address.

(a)   (i)   <u>Advantages</u>

<u>Testing systems</u>

A simulation will test whether **backup systems** will be **available and operate properly** if they are needed and that control systems **operate to minimise the effects of disruption.** The first aspect of this is checking that the **system of back-ups works**, that the files created on the main site have been fully backed-up and can be recreated at the remote site. Secondly the simulation should test whether the website can be **restored within the target timeframe.** Thirdly the test should show whether the hardware and software at the remote site are **robust enough** to be able to handle the online and call centre business for a full day.

<u>Testing staff's understanding</u>

The simulation should also test whether staff understand what they have do if an emergency occurs and how quickly staff can take the action necessary for AHB to resume business as normal. With the systems operators, the main focus will be on how quickly they recreate the data and bring the website back on-line. With call centre staff, the main issue will be whether they can cope with the remote system and the way the remote office is organised. Any weaknesses in staff performance can then be addressed by **briefing or training.**

<u>Disadvantages</u>

<u>Cost</u>

There could be significant costs associated with the simulation. These include the **costs of switching to the remote system**, the **costs of transport to the remote site and any extra labour costs**. Because of the problems with the simulation, systems were not fully operational all day. AHB could have **lost some business** even on a quiet day. If a full simulation was to be more realistic, it would have to take place during a busier working day, **increasing the magnitude of possible losses** from the disruption to business.

<u>Alternative methods</u>

Testing different aspects of operations at different times may be cheaper and less disruptive. The **system of back-ups** could be **tested by itself**. Also the website could go offline outside call centre hours and how long it takes to restore it be tested then.

(ii)   <u>Simulation failing to reflect reality</u>

The major problem with the simulation is that it does not reflect the reality of an actual disaster.

<u>Untypical business day</u>

Even if the staff and systems had been **able to cope on the quietest day of the year,** this may not provide much assurance that they could cope on days when business was much heavier. In addition the test took place when the call centre was **shut** and did not test what would happen if the call centre went down during the working day. A more realistic simulation would have tested what staff would do if they were being pressurised by customers who were having problems booking their holidays.

<u>Staff attendance</u>

The simulation also failed to test what would happen if staff were **not available to be bussed from the primary site**. A big risk for AHB is a disaster occurring overnight and staff still going to the primary site in the morning. To address this risk, the test should have been on a surprise basis, with staff being notified by phone or text that they had to go to the remote site, either under their own steam or by transport provided by AHB. This would test whether **staff details were up-to-date, how quickly staff could get to the remote site and what the impact on operations would be of staff arriving at the remote site at different times.**

<u>Warning in advances</u>

Warning staff in advance may mean that staff whose work is to be tested **take more care** than normal to ensure that there are no problems. For example staff may be more alert than normal of the need to backup work comprehensively.

<u>Back-up arrangements at remote site</u>

There appear to be **no arrangements for backing up the work done** at the remote site. The problems of suddenly having to operate at the remote site may result in an **increased risk of loss of data**. Similarly data could be lost if an actual (rather than a simulated) disaster occurred at the remote site. Arrangements could have been in place to **back up at the primary site** the data processed at the remote site on the day of the simulation. Alternatively and better, AHB should have contingency **back-up arrangements** in place at a further site if it had to operate from the remote site. The simulation could provide an opportunity to test these arrangements.

(b)   <u>Transport arrangements</u>

Staff should be **made aware of the location** of the remote site and briefed on how it can **reached by public transport.** Particularly however if public transport is limited, part of the contingency plan should be provision of transport, either by AHB organising buses itself or supervising a car share scheme. If a car share scheme was operated, AHB would have to ensure that there was sufficient on-site parking and that drivers were properly insured. Essential staff who have to be on site quickly could be allowed to use taxis, at least in the short-term. Part of the preparation for the disaster should be staff making the journey to the remote site, so perhaps AHB could organise training or a staff meeting there.

<u>Staffing measures</u>

The problems over staffing on the day of the simulation indicate that staff are reluctant to work at this site. AHB therefore needs to take measures to deal with this issue.

<u>Contracts</u>

Contracts of employment should specify that staff have to **work at the remote site if necessary**. AHB's HR function should review all contracts to ensure that they do so. Any contracts that do not have this requirement should be amended.

<u>Medical review</u>

H may also **strengthen the requirements for staff to obtain confirmation from their doctor that they had been ill.** It would probably be unrealistic and unpopular for the policy to be applied to illnesses lasting a single day, but it could cut down absences if staff needed to work at the remote site for some time.

Changes in working arrangements

There is however a risk that insisting staff work at the remote site for a significant length of time will result in a **collapse in morale**. Ultimately there could be a large number of staff departures and disruption to the business caused by vacancies and the need to train new staff. AHB therefore needs to show **flexibility** towards staff concerns. It could do this by introducing a **system of flex-time,** so staff hours could fit in with public transport. If this risked leaving the office short of staff at certain times, AHB could **develop the shift pattern** so that there was a greater number of shifts, with staff being required to do a certain number of the less popular shifts.

Incentives

H could also improve staff motivation by compensating staff for the extra travel. This could take the form of **overtime** being paid for travel, particularly to staff who had to travel at times where public transport was poor. AHB could also offer **generous mileage allowances**, perhaps in return for staff sharing their cars with others, or **subsidises** to public transport costs.

Childcare

The problems of staff being absent due to childcare reasons may be very difficult to overcome initially, as staff may not be able to make alternative arrangements very quickly. If staff have to work at the remote site for some time, again AHB could provide **incentives,** for example childcare vouchers. It may also consider allowing staff with children the opportunity to **reduce their hours,** to fit in with school times.

53 T

> **Text references**. Chapters 14 and 15.
>
> **Top tips**. In (a) don't simply say that the Finance Director is wrong. The requirement to evaluate suggests that there may be some points in favour of his view, and these are mentioned in the scenario (seeing the system in practice is perhaps the fairest test and the system is low risk). However from the risk management viewpoint, the system is also of high importance and therefore needs to be tested at various stages of its development.
>
> (b) also requires an evaluation, but for 5 marks it will be a more limited one than in (a). It's grouped around the main attributes of internal audit.
>
> The main areas to consider in (c) are the benchmarking that parallel running provides and the cost implications if the system is unsatisfactory. Given that the Finance Director is basing his arguments on cost, emphasising the costs arising from a poorly performing system is a strong response.
>
> **Easy marks**. (c) should have been fairly straightforward, and the fact that it was done so badly is surprising.
>
> **Examiner's comments**. Most answers were poor. Students failed to relate their answers to the scenario, and seemed to lack understanding of the risks and what a post-implementation review was. Students need to revise information systems more thoroughly and also revise the role of the internal auditor, since these topics will often feature in exams.

(a) Post–implementation review limitations

The Finance Director (FD) appears to be arguing that the post-implementation review cannot fully replicate the system working in practice. Users will only be able to give **informed feedback** when the system comes into use and they are able to see the range of information that the system produces. The system will need to be in operation for some time before the number of queries and errors it produces can perhaps be fairly assessed. Initial problems may turn out to have been due to user unfamiliarity with the system.

Standard software

The basis of the system T has purchased is a standard software package that presumably has a good reputation. T has not had to modify the package very much. Arguably then the **likelihood of the system being unreliable is low.** The implication of the FD's argument is therefore that this low level of risk means that a post-implementation review is unlikely to produce significant feedback that will make undertaking it

worthwhile. However the system is being introduced onto T's hardware, which may lead to problems with compatibility.

Importance of project

Although the likelihood of the system failing may be low, the **impact** if it is not in line with the needs of T is **high.** T is relying on the system not just for accounting reports, but also as the basis of operational decision-making. One of the main aims of a post-implementation review is to **obtain user feedback**. The importance of this system means that it is vital that feedback is sought as early as possible.

Limitations of user feedback

Another significant aim of the review is to ensure that the system **is performing in accordance with specification**. Users may not be able to assess this fairly as they are not used to the system's features. They may not be able to identify if the system is running slowly or is not being operated efficiently. A post-implementation review should be conducted by someone with sufficient expertise to make a reliable assessment.

User needs

A post-implementation review can identify not just problems with the system but issues with **users' perceptions and understanding** of it. T should therefore be able to **identify training needs** and also **obtain further guidance** from the software supplier. It may be more difficult and costly to obtain guidance from the supplier once the three month support period has finished. This should make it less likely that users still have unresolved problems with the system when the help desk facility is no longer available

(b) Independence

Although internal auditors should have provided their opinion on the controls within the system, they should not have been responsible for its **design and implementation.** They thus should be able to take an objective, independent view of how it is operating, since problems will not reflect badly on their judgements.

Knowledge of company

The internal auditors should have the **appropriate knowledge of the company** to be able to conduct the review effectively. They will have detailed knowledge of the accounting requirements of T and so will know what standards the information from the new system needs to meet.

IT skills and experience

The internal auditors may be less able to **judge IT issues** connected with the operation of the package. The new system is a significant advance on the old system, and none of the internal audit team may have had previous experience of such a package. Internal audit may also lack experience of **using computer-assisted audit techniques.**

Priorities

The review appears to be a **valuable use of internal audit time**. The significance of the system to T's future operations means that there is unlikely to be other work on which internal audit time could be better spent.

(c) Failure to provide evidence of errors

Running the old and the new system together enables T's staff to cross-check between the two systems. It provides a means of **verifying the results of the new system and identifying errors quickly,** Errors could have serious consequences, including management decision-making being based on misleading data. They could arise in the new system in a number of ways:

- The modification of the software could have resulted in programming errors
- Data could have been transferred incorrectly between the old and new systems
- Staff could be making errors when inputting data

Staff errors may be a result of inadequate training or poor systems documentation. These errors will be made over a number of accounting periods unless the problems are rectified.

Failure to measure performance standards

The old system also provides a **benchmark of performance** against which the new system can be measured. The new system should be providing reports that are at least as good as the **equivalent reports** provided under the old system. It should also be able to generate one-off reports much more quickly than under the old system.

Costs of resolving processing errors

Although parallel running is a relatively expensive method of systems changeover, the **costs of rectifying problems later on** could also be **very high**. Rectifying processing errors and restoring data will take more time and cost more the more time has elapsed and the greater the number of errors that have been made.

Costs of resolving software problems

The help desk is only available for a short time after the system is installed. Calling the supplier to modify the system subsequently will be **costly and cause further significant disruption to operations and information supply.** It could be even more expensive if problems are serious and the system has to be written off, with the further expense of a new system and maybe temporary reversion to the old, inefficient system.

Change management

The new system represents a significant change in information supply. Staff may be cynical about the benefits it brings. If staff believe that the new system is being imposed on them with a **lack of adequate testing**, they may be **reluctant to use it.** This could also result in inefficiencies and lack of congruence as managers and staff obtain the information they require from other, differing sources.

54 W

> **Text references**. Chapters 13 and 14.
>
> **Top tips**. The risks that the scenario appears to signpost relate to suppliers, manufacturers and quality. The examiner set this question to cover two common real world issues, outsourcing and use of IT to contact suppliers, that are often linked. Reliability is a significant issue with both suppliers and manufacturers, so you have to make sure that your discussion of each is sufficiently differentiated. The question helps you do this by highlighting particular issues with a supplier and manufacturer, which you need to spend time developing.
>
> Although (b) is perhaps more general than (a), it may be difficult to generate 10 marks worth of risks. Both (a) and (b) ask for an evaluation of risks, so you have to indicate how serious the risks might be, the likelihood and consequences of the risks materialising.
>
> **Easy marks**. No particularly easy marks here.
>
> **Examiner's comments**. Answers to both parts were often inadequate. In (a) many students ignored the question requirement to write specifically about manufacturing risks. In (b) answers often included generic risks that were not linked to the scenario. Students clearly need to revise this area.

(a)   Problems with suppliers

Risk

The problems of the suppliers of the memory chips illustrate the potential seriousness of supply problems. W's **supply chain is very complicated** with different suppliers operating in several different countries and some being dependent on others meeting deadlines. The distances involved may increase the risks of delay in supply from some suppliers. There may also be **local problems** affecting individual suppliers, for example natural forces such as flooding or infrastructure difficulties such as power cuts. Delays in supply by even a single supplier can **delay manufacturing** and ultimately, as with the MP3 player, **delay the product launch.** As a result customers will be unhappy and may buy from other manufacturers. Delays may also give competitors the chance to launch their own products before W does.

Risk management

W may deal with the supplier who owns the patent by **buying the patent itself**, or possibly even **buying the supplier,** as the component is a vital part of a key product. The procurement department should review contracts with suppliers generally, and **explore the possibility of tightening the contracts** and being able to **impose greater penalties** if suppliers fail to deliver. **Communications** with suppliers may need to be **more frequent,** certainly if there are indications that suppliers will not deliver on time. The procurement department may consider allowing for longer supplier times as a precaution when planning, even though it makes efforts to ensure suppliers keep delivery times to a minimum. In the longer-term W may wish to simplify its supply chain by **reducing the number of suppliers it uses,** particularly suppliers of standard components, or maybe acquiring other specialist suppliers.

Problems with manufacturers

Risk

One problem with manufacturers is the same as with suppliers, that they will **fail to meet agreed deadlines** in producing the finished goods. A further problem might be that factories can meet the originally agreed dates but **do not have the capacity to increase production** if supply problems occur and manufacturing time has to be shortened in response. Even if factories can deliver more quickly, this may require overtime from staff and the costs may be passed on to W. Once the goods are finished, **delivery to customers may be delayed** through poor organisation or circumstances beyond the factories' control such as poor weather.

Risk management

Again the procurement department should keep contracts with factories under review with a view to **tightening the contracts** and **imposing greater penalties** if the factories do not deliver. W's procurement department should produce a **plan for increasing production,** taking account of **factory reliability, capacity and increased costs.** W should **agree delivery times with the factories, require them to report any delays and investigate complaints** from customers that they have not received their orders. Delays due to circumstances beyond the factories' control should be **insured.** Other possible measures include using suppliers located near to manufacturers where possible, outsourcing logistics to a specialist company or holding safety inventory.

Quality problems

Risk

If there are problems with the **quality of W's products**, W could suffer a loss of reputation, leading to a **significant loss of sales.** This threat is likely to be particularly serious as W has attracted much press interest, and can expect **significant coverage** if there are major problems, particularly with new products. Given the number of suppliers W uses, it may be difficult to ensure that the components it purchases have achieved quality standards. As manufacturing is outsourced, the factories may only feel an incentive to produce to the minimum standards required in their contracts.

The risk of problems occurring may be increased by the **higher rates of production** that the factories are having to achieve because of problems with supply. Possibly **quality checks will not be done or not be done as thoroughly** as a means of saving time.

Risk management

W's research laboratory should carry out **initial quality tests** on demonstration models before the products are released for publicity purposes. W's procurement department must **review factories' plans** to increase production to ensure that they appear realistic. W should insist that **quality checks** are not reduced, and obtain evidence from factories that they have taken place or carry out random checks itself . It can also make clear to suppliers that it will reward quality by **giving reliable suppliers more work.** W must have a **contingency plan** in place if problems arise with new products. It must be able to demonstrate to customers and the media that it takes quality problems seriously by giving **customers refunds** and **keeping the media informed** of steps that it is taking to correct problems.

(b)   Efficiency

If the technology functions properly, EDI should reduce the risk of **delays due to staffing issues.** EDI will simplify the ordering and paying process. The system will place orders and keep records of inventory when received, and carry out recording and invoicing automatically. However the process will be

complicated if W is invoiced for supplies that are **transferred from one supplier to another**. W will not be able to verify whether the delivery has been made and this could cause delays in payment.

Loss of link

The most serious risk is that the **link will be interrupted.** Even with a contingency plan, it could be very **time-consuming** to contact suppliers and manufacturers by other methods and ensure that all transactions are co-ordinated. Because the whole process through to invoicing is dependent on the EDI, **disputes with suppliers** may **increase** if the automatic steps such as delivery recording and invoicing have to be carried out manually.

Quality of information

Although the EDI link may work perfectly, the system will be of little use if the **data exchanged** is **misleading or input late.** Suppliers' systems may accept orders automatically without considering whether they are feasible. As with any information system, the EDI has to be **managed properly** with **deadlines** for data transmission by W and other parties. W's internal audit department should investigate discrepancies between the **commitments** made by suppliers and manufacturers with **actual performance.**

New suppliers

W is dependent upon suppliers having **compatible systems** and being able to cope with the transmission of data via EDI. This will particularly be an issue if W's system is **proprietary** technology. If W wishes to change suppliers, a constraint upon its choice may be the systems of some possible suppliers not being able to operate EDI. Some form of interface may need to be developed. As a result it may not be able to use suppliers who **offer the best prices or the most reliable service**. Technological development of W's products may be delayed because it cannot use suppliers who stock the most advanced components.

Maintenance of systems

Businesses often work to **differing time schedules and time-zones**. W may conduct system maintenance late at night. However, an overseas company in a different time zone may need to access the system at this time.

55 J

Text references. Chapters 6 and 14.

Top tips. In (a) you need to look at how a computer crash could affect the various stages identified – making the original booking, confirmation and signing of the contract and the date for return of the vehicle. The detail given about damage recording should have indicated that this needed to be discussed. There should be paper-based versions of the contracts available that record the damage, but how reliable these are is debatable.

(b) discusses threats to computers in a number of areas. Data protection is clearly important here, and you may be able to think of real-life examples where unsecured computers have been stolen and data illicitly accessed. All the detail that you're given about the extra PC should have hinted to you to discuss compatibility problems, as well as the possibly more obvious issues of viruses and unlicensed use of software.

Easy marks. Like other questions in the September exam, there are no very easy marks, but you can score well by picking up the many hints the scenario gives you about problems.

Examiner's comments. Answers to (a) were poor but answers to (b) were very good. Students who brought in knowledge of the car industry scored well. General answers were not well-rewarded.

Marking scheme

Marks

(a) Up to 2 marks per problems discussed. Problems should relate to:
Bookings of vehicles
Identity of customers
Liability for damage

max   10

(b) Laptop – up to 2 marks per issue discussed. Issues can include:
Poor example
Virus infection
Breach of data protection legislation
Theft of data

max   6

PC – up to 2 marks per issue discussed. Issues can include:
Poor attitude to computer security
Problems of non-standard machine
Central IS support
Recording transactions
Illegal use of software

max   9

15
25

(a) <u>Demand</u>

The system provides a **record of bookings** for all vehicles. If the information was lost, then J would either have to **stop taking bookings** or **risk double-bookings of vehicles.** Either would deter customers from using J in the future.

<u>Due dates</u>

The systems provide the only **easy-to-access record** of when vehicles are due back. The dates could be retrieved manually from contracts but this would be **time-consuming.** J needs to know when vehicles are overdue so that it can take immediate steps to inform the police and minimise the risk of cars 'disappearing' after being stolen.

<u>Damage</u>

The computer contains the up-to-date information about the condition of vehicles. Although the **most recent rental agreement will give an indication of damage** up till when it was taken out, this may be incomplete. All vehicles will thus need to be inspected to provide reliable information for future rental agreements. This will be very time-consuming. However if it is not done, J will **not be able to prove in future disputes that customers caused damage** if there is a possibility that the data on future contracts is incomplete.

<u>Identity confirmation</u>

If the computer data is lost, then J will not be able to ask drivers to **confirm the details of identity** they gave when booking the vehicle. A breakdown of the system will also mean that previous records of the steps taken to confirm identity have been lost as well as the original customer details. This may mean that J cannot prove to insurance companies that valid steps have been taken to confirm identity or competence, and hence the vehicles may be **uninsured** against theft or damage.

<u>Identity details for police</u>

Although J can provide police with customer details shown on the vehicle agreement, the police **may not be able to investigate thefts** without the additional information (confirmation details) stored on the computers.

(b)   <u>Notebook computer</u>

<u>Internal environment</u>

The branch manager is setting a **poor example** to his staff. Not only is he taking unacceptable risks (discussed below) with computer security himself, he is also giving staff the impression that they need not take computer security seriously.

<u>Viruses</u>

Connecting the notebook computer to the branch network could mean that viruses are introduced to the system. The direct connection could mean controls over the system such as firewalls could **fail to prevent the threats** materialising.

<u>Security of data</u>

Under data protection legislation, J will be responsible for the **security and privacy** of customers' data. This means that J needs to exercise strict controls over the locations where the data is held. These controls will be undermined if unauthorised copies are made of the data, and J could be liable as a result.

<u>Theft of computer</u>

The situation will be made worse if the branch manager's computer is **stolen.** This could mean that **unauthorised parties** gain **access** to the data. J will be **liable** to customers whose data has been stolen. If the theft is publicised, future customers may be unwilling to deal with J if they believe that their data will not be held securely.

<u>PC</u>

<u>Internal environment</u>

The findings again indicate **failings in the internal environment**. This time staff are making changes to the system without approval from the head office IS team. Again this suggests a lax attitude toward IS controls and company policy generally.

<u>Lack of standardisation</u>

Problems may arise as a result of the use of a non-standard PC. The PC may not work as efficiently as the other PCs. This could slow down the branch network and have an **adverse impact on the service given to customers.**

<u>IS support</u>

IS support **may not be able to deal with queries** from the branch if the operating system used is not the up-to-date version and IS support does not know about the unauthorised machine.

<u>Recording of transactions</u>

The PC **may not be able to run all the programs** that the other computers run. It may **not therefore record transactions correctly.** The old version of the software may also **corrupt the database** when it makes any changes to the information.

<u>Illicit use of software</u>

The instillation of the software on the extra machine may have been **beyond J's licence.** The CD/DVD drive also gives staff the opportunity to **add unlicensed software** to their machines with the risk of J being **liable for software piracy. Records** of software held maintained by J's IS department could be **incomplete.** The system may also be vulnerable to **viruses** being introduced by unlicensed software if checks are not carried out on it.

56 K

> **Text references.** Chapters 13 and 14.
>
> **Top tips.** In (a) the external auditors will focus on factors having a significant impact on the company's accounts or its future. However the IT considerations that will impact here will also concern the internal auditors. These include awareness of vulnerability, systems maintenance and contingency planning. System security and availability are very important. 15 marks does seem a generous allocation given the requirements of the question.
>
> (b) shows how a risk such as a threat to security can impact hugely on reputation risk, threatening the company's future because of the adverse reactions of customers and credit card companies. Better risk analysis will be important as well as enhanced controls.
>
> **Easy marks.** Some relatively straightforward marks in (a) for thinking about basic IT control categories (continuity/access).
>
> **Examiner's comments.** (b) was generally done better than (a). The fact that the question requirements mentioned external auditors seemed to disconcert some students, although the risk considerations discussed were equally relevant to internal auditors. Some students appeared generally to lack an understanding of how auditors view risks.

Marking scheme

			Marks
(a)	Dependence on IT – fundamental threat to future, need for prevention of threats, back-up and contingency planning.	3	
	Centralisation – lack of segregation of duties, human resource controls, reviews of transactions.	3	
	Illicit access – why might occur, access and virus controls.	3	
	Protection of income – limits need to be enforced.	3	
	Systems development – need for development to reflect customer demands and prevent fraud. Strength of system development process and internal audit involvement.	3	
	Other relevant factors up to 3 marks each	3	
	max		15
(b)	Risks – up to 2 marks per risk discussed, including threats of withdrawal of credit card companies, reputation with customers, unprofitable transactions. max	6	
	Risk management – up to 2 marks per step taken, including risk analysis, isolating problem customers, use of secure third party mechanism. max	6	
	max		10
			25

(a) <u>Dependence on IT</u>

K is totally dependent on its IT systems **functioning reliably**. Without the systems it has no income. Interruption to the systems for any length of time will **threaten the company's future**. Auditors will be concerned whether these risks are being managed effectively by controls **preventing disruption**, for example anti-virus controls. Because of the systems' importance, auditors will want to establish whether the system is completely backed-up, the **extent of contingency plans** and whether contingency arrangements provide the strong controls required.

Centralisation of computer systems

The centralisation of the computer systems may also be a source of significant risk. There may be a **lack of segregation of duties in recording transactions and payments**. It may be possible for the same individual to programme fraudulent charges and make the necessary adjustments to other parts of the system to cover up the fraud. The auditors will therefore consider how much these risks are mitigated by general controls:

- **Human resource controls** over the recruitment of individuals

- **Audit of transactions** by internal audit

- **Analytical or other overall reviews** of transactions or accounts, to identify strange patterns in charges

- **Reviews of computer usage**

Illicit access

A key risk to the system is **access by unauthorised persons**. This could be access to **obtain tracks without paying, obtain customer details, access customer accounts,** or **carry out denial of service attacks** disrupting operations. Auditors will obviously be very concerned with the strength of controls preventing **unauthorised use** such as passwords, and controls, such as up-to-date virus protection software, to prevent viruses affecting the system.

Protection of income

In order to maximise income, K has imposed rules on the number of songs that can be downloaded for free. These limits will only be effective if they are enforced. The auditors will want to ascertain whether the **controls over the number of free downloads** are effective, covering the **complete recording of transactions** and the **prevention of free downloads** when limits are reached.

Development of system

Technology improvements means that K's system will need to develop, to provide a **better service** for customers or to **counter threats to fraud**. Auditors will therefore be concerned with how the **system is developed**. In particular they will want to know how the **need for development is identified**, and how K has **previously handled development** – will lessons learnt from post-completion audits be actioned in future. The **extent of internal audit involvement** will be an important consideration for external auditors, as internal audit work may provide assurance that controls have been adequately tested. However external auditors will also want to obtain assurance that internal audit has sufficient IT expertise to be able to conduct effective testing.

(b) #### Risks

Credit card company risk

K may suffer from the risk that the credit card company will no longer allow customers to pay via K's site, to protect its own reputation. This represents a **threat to revenue**, since some customers will find it more difficult to pay. The problem will be enhanced if other credit card companies also withdraw permission.

Reputation risk

Customers may not wish to use K's website because of fears that they will be **charged fraudulently** and because they fear that fraudsters have **access to their personal data.**

Refunding of payments

K may have to pay refunds to customers, but still be **liable to copyright holders** for the royalties on the downloads.

Alleviation of risks

Risk analysis

K needs to analyse what's happened to see if there is any pattern in the fraudulent charges being made. If the customers who have suffered problems can be easily classified, for example **geographically**, it may be best to stop offering the service to customers with that link until the problem is resolved.

Expert systems

It is possible to purchase expert systems to monitor fraud. Credit card companies use systems that contain **information relating to credit card frauds** over a long period of time. The system can therefore recognise suspicious buying patterns.

Controls over customers allowed to use the service

K can reduce the risks of problems by **recording customer details**. Customers could be asked to **register** and **confirm identity by email**. Alternatively if a fraudulent purchase is identified as coming from a specific computer IT address, then that address should not be allowed to purchase in future.

Secure payment mechanism

The threat to reputation of payment information not being secure can be dealt with by using a **third party payment mechanism** with a reputation for being secure, for example Paypal.

57 FDS

Text references. Chapters 13 and 14.

Top tips. At first glance there does not appear to be much scenario to use, which may be a problem given that both question parts demand consideration of the scenario. However analysis of the limited information does yield various important points:

- We are looking at the situation from the viewpoint of FDS 25, a business unit which is using internal services.

- The scenario emphasises FDS 25 is an investment centre and that meeting budget is a significant issue, so cost control will need to be considered in your answer.

In (a) you need to go through the main stages of systems development. Remember that the shared service centre will be carrying out the detailed development work, but FDS 25 should be able to specify the controls it wants, obtaining advice from the service centre as required. FDS 25 needs to have control mechanisms in place for guiding and monitoring the development. In particular it will want to ensure that the system develops in line with its requirements.

The verb identify in (b) is a lower level verb, limiting what you say about each advantage and disadvantage. Clear headers and short paragraphs will help you score as many marks as possible in this section.

Easy marks. The advantages and disadvantages of outsourcing should represent easy marks as they have been examined before.

Examiner's comments. Students generally scored well on this question, although some lacked knowledge of what a shared service centre was. In (a) some students just discussed project management and failed to mention controls. In (b) students who stated that the risks and benefits of a shared service centre were opposite to those for an outsourcer scored poorly. Layout was also a problem, and in some answers it was difficult to see whether students were referring to outsourcing or a shared service centre.

Marking scheme

			Marks
(a)	1 mark for each relevant control. To score well candidates will need to discuss controls under the main stages of the system development lifecycle		15
(b)	Shared service centre – 1 mark for each relevant advantage or disadvantage discussed. Reward discussions on cost, expertise and flexibility issues	5	
	Outsourcing – 1 mark for each relevant advantage or disadvantage discussed. Reward discussions of cost, expertise and flexibility issues	5	
			10
			25

(a)　Control framework

Steering committee

FDS 25 should set up a steering committee to oversee the **design and implementation** of the **new system**, ensuring that it meets **quality, timing and cost requirements**. The committee should be chaired by a senior manager, and should include a project manager, representatives from the shared service centre and user group representatives from FDS 25.

Role of management team

Given the importance of the investment to support FDS 25's business strategy, FDS 25's management team should be involved in approving the systems before development commences. Management should receive **regular reports** from the **steering committee** about the progress of the project, and **internal audit** about the checks they have carried out. Management should **sign off the project** before it is implemented.

Budgeting

Bringing the project within budget has been highlighted as very important. With the assistance of internal audit, the steering committee should review the **justification on cost grounds** for the **system chosen** and **how realistic** the **detailed budgets** are. The steering committee and senior management should **monitor the progress of costs against budgets** and **discuss overruns** with the service centre if they arise.

Systems design

Analysis

To be effective the design process needs to be based on a detailed analysis of requirements. A **feasibility study** should cover the **benefits and drawbacks** of the **current system, business and user needs**, particularly regarding future developments. The analysis process should examine the extent to which alternative solutions fulfil the **objectives** that the steering committee has defined, and the **costs and time to completion** of each option.

Specification

A key control in the design process is that it should result in a **detailed specification** for approval of the new system covering program and file design, data security and levels of authorisation. **Internal auditors should review the specification** for FDS 25 to ensure the system appears to be providing **complete information**, is **compatible with other systems** within FDS and has **sufficient security controls**. They should also obtain **evidence from users within FDS 25** that they will be happy with the system.

Systems implementation

Testing

The steering committee should specify to the shared service centre the **testing** that it requires to be carried out. As well as **comprehensive testing** by the service centre team, **internal audit** and **FDS 25's users** should test the system and confirm that they are happy with the results of the testing. This is important as FDS 25 is **keen to implement the system quickly to achieve its business objectives**, and so may be tempted to curtail testing.

Organisational controls

Before the new system is implemented, the steering committee needs to obtain evidence that it has been **adequately documented**. FDS 25's staff need to have received **appropriate training** before the system is implemented.

Initial running

The steering committee should ensure that **sufficient time** is planned for the changeover process and that controls over the actual implementation process are adequate, given the method of implementation chosen. Controls will have to ensure that **data is transferred correctly** and that **back-up arrangements** are in place should problems occur when the system goes live.

Post-implementation review

As it seems likely that the system will need to **develop further over time**, the internal auditors should carry out a post-implementation review for FDS 25 to establish whether the new system has **fulfilled users' needs** and whether the **system is performing in accordance with the specification**. The committee should also make a **final comparison of budgeted costs with actual costs**.

(b) (i) Shared service centre

Advantages

Provision of required services

Shared service centres exist to provide **only those services** that their 'customers', here investment centres such as FDS 25, **use**. FDS 25 should not be wasting money paying for unnecessary **risk management and controls** that it doesn't require.

Responsiveness to demands of FDS 25

FDS 25 should be able to **specify** to the service centre the **controls** it wishes to be implemented over **design and implementation**.

Available expertise

The shared service centre may well have developed and implemented similar systems for other divisions, and thus will have **expertise and experience** in developing the system. This should mean that the system is developed efficiently, with little chance of error.

Disadvantage

Availability and cost of service

FDS 25's requirements may be subordinated to those of other parts of the group, and there may be little FDS 25's managers can do. In addition it may not be possible to specify **long-term pricing**. The cost of the services may be determined by group transfer pricing arrangements, and these may mean that the cost increases significantly over time.

(ii) Outsourcing

Advantages

Removal of cost uncertainties

An outsourcing arrangement will mean **costs of purchasing the service should be easy to predict**, and **budgets easy to control**. This is important for FDS 25 as it operates as an **investment centre**.

Service level agreement

A service level agreement should limit uncertainty by setting out the **facilities and level of service** that the service supplier will provide.

Disadvantages

Dependence on supplier

FDS 25 may become very dependent on the outsource supplier as the system is core to its future strategy. If the outsource supplier goes out of business, the loss of IT facilities may mean that FDS 25 may **not be able to achieve its objectives** and its **competitive advantage** may be damaged.

Locked into long-term contract

The service provider may not fulfil the terms of the service level agreement. Also because the system is core to FDS 25's future strategy, it may mean that FDS 25's needs change over time and in the future a **new supplier** may be best able to fulfil FDS 25's requirements. However FDS 25 may not be able to extract itself easily from its contract with the existing supplier.

Confidentiality

Loss of confidential information to a competitor may have severe consequences for FDS 25 given the high-level nature of the system. Using a shared centre avoids the need to transfer data outside FDS.

Monitoring costs

The indirect costs of the arrangement may be higher than expected, including **other transaction costs such as insurance and the internal time resource** involved in monitoring the arrangement.

58 VWS

Text references. Chapters 4, 6 and 14.

Top tips. The scenario does not give very much information about the company and the accounts payable system appears to be a very standard one. You need to try to make the best use of the information to give examples in (a), although there is not that much data you can use. The verb discuss means you have to take the broad purposes and values (mostly derived from the Turnbull guidance) and show that they apply to the accounts payable system.

The scenario provides more material for answering (b). The answer follows a logical sequence, looking firstly at security controls before processing can take place, then controls over processing and lastly controls to minimise threats to the operation of the whole system.

In (c) fraud in a computerised system can come about through false information being input by legitimate means (by staff with the necessary authorisation for example) or altering the programs to generate false payments.

Easy marks. Hopefully you will have revised IT controls well enough to be able to come up with plenty of ideas in (b).

Examiner's comments. Many candidates failed to discuss accounts payable and showed a lack of knowledge of accounts payable systems. Answers were often far too general, with many students just braindumping all they knew about general controls.

Marking scheme

			Marks
(a)	Up to 2 marks for each aspect of purpose/value discussed. To obtain 2 marks, purpose/value must be related to accounts payable		10
(b)	1 mark for control discussed. Award max 6 marks if no reference to payables		10
(c)	1 mark per risk of fraud related to payables	3	
	1 mark per risk mitigation technique that relates to risk identified	3	
	max		5
			25

(a) <u>Purposes of internal control system</u>

The Turnbull report suggests that the main purposes of an internal control system in any area are to **facilitate effective and efficient operations** and **enable the organisation to respond to risks**.

<u>Accounts payable control systems</u>

<u>Safeguarding assets</u>

A key risk for purchases is that payments will be made for **unauthorised or unwarranted purchases**. The control system needs to ensure that payments are:

- **Not made for goods that have not been received**
- Made for orders that have been **properly authorised**
- **Only made to authorised suppliers**.

Another aspect of asset protection is ensuring that supplies are obtained at competitive prices. Given the number of suppliers VWS uses, it should be possible to obtain good terms by threatening to use other suppliers.

<u>Identifying and managing liabilities</u>

Another key risk is that **liabilities** will **not be properly recognised**, leading to disputes with suppliers. Alternatively suppliers may benefit through mistakes, with **cash** being **paid twice** or **being paid to the wrong supplier**.

BPP
LEARNING MEDIA

The system should ensure that **goods and services received are accurately recorded** and that **documentation exists to support all invoices and payments**; accounts payable staff at VWS also need to make sure that invoices and payments are included in the **right suppliers' accounts**. Another part of managing liabilities is to **review regularly suppliers' accounts** to make sure that **available credit** is being **taken**, and **discounts for early payment** are being **accepted**. Staff should also investigate disputed amounts with suppliers to **ensure** that **all credits** to which the business is due **are claimed and received**.

Ensure quality of financial reporting

The accounts payable system is part of the overall accounting system, and it is important for this reason as well that **appropriate liabilities are recognised** and that **payments are recorded**.

Value of internal control system

Reputation and liquidity

Problems with not paying bills mean that suppliers may **decline or tighten credit**, making **trade more difficult** and **impacting on reputation**. Poor cash management can ultimately lead to **liquidity problems**.

Reasonable assurance

Control systems over accounts payable provide reasonable assurance, that the **purposes of the control systems** have been **fulfilled**. They can be undermined by human error, for example entering details into the wrong supplier account. They can also be undermined by **collusion**, for example between accounts payables staff and fake suppliers; **management override of procedures** is also a possible limitation. The control systems may not be able to cope with non-routine transactions, **special one-off orders from suppliers** for example.

Benefits vs costs

The control systems are also only valuable if their **benefits outweigh their costs**. Elaborate authorisation procedures may result in a **lack of flexibility** in dealing with suppliers, and being able to obtain better terms. **Comparison of benefits versus costs** may be **difficult**. Costs of controls, for example salaries, may be apparent, but the benefits, for example in terms of problems prevented, may be difficult to assess since those problems have not materialised.

(b) Supplier authorisation controls

Payables staff should only be able to process invoices and payments for suppliers who have been authorised and who have been given a **payables ledger reference**.

Passwords

The system of passwords used should **differentiate** between the requirements of different types of users. Staff other than payables staff should be able to access some of the information on a **read only basis**. However the system should allow only the accounts payable staff to **change details** on the ledger or to **generate payments**. If access is **attempted unsuccessfully**, the system should **log the attempt** and management review this log.

Matching with order

Invoices should only be entered if they can be matched with specific orders that are already on the system. The system should **match the invoice with the order details** that should already be on the system.

Reasonableness controls

The system should **automatically query and report on all unusual transactions**. For example it should **query any invoice number** that has **already been posted**. It should highlight any payment that results in a **debit balance**; this may indicate that the **payment** has been **made twice**. There may be further **reasonableness checks**, for example **range checks** detecting invoices or orders that are very large for that supplier.

Control totals

Totals should be used to **reconcile different data**, for example the **total of cheques and electronic payments** should **agree with the total of cash paid entries** on the payables ledger control account.

Reports generated

A system of **exception reporting** is vital, highlighting payables or specific invoices that have not been paid for a long time, payables accounts over certain limits or orders that have not been delivered.

Encryption

Because payment data is transmitted electronically, it needs to be **encrypted** into a secret code. This should **prevent hackers gaining access to the data transmitted**.

Virus protection

The systems should be protected from disruption by **anti-virus software** and **on-access virus scanning** that prevents infection by disallowing access to infected items. There should also be policies in place to minimise the risks of viruses being introduced, for example a **ban on unauthorised software**.

Backups

Details on the system should be regularly **backed up** during the day, and backup copies kept away from the main site, along with operating system software. This should enable information to be reconstructed if the system does break down.

Contingency plans

There should be contingency plans, for example backup computer facilities, to enable processing to continue if there is a **major systems breakdown**. Because of the large volume of transactions being processed, it is vital that processing continue with a minimum of delay.

(c) ### False suppliers

Payables staff may be able to enter the **details of non-existent suppliers** onto the system, and then enter false invoice details and make payments to that supplier.

Management should consider **greater segregation of duties**, with staff who enter and update supplier details not being able to process payments on those accounts, and also different staff updating invoice details and generating payments. There should also be reports for **management or internal audit** checking, for example reports showing new supplier accounts that have been opened each period. Controls **matching invoices with orders and goods received** are also important.

Payments for goods not received

Payments may be made to legitimate suppliers for **goods that have not been received**.

Requiring links to be made between **invoices and other data** (orders, goods received) should limit this risk.

Program problems

The writer of the payables ledger computer programs could also commit fraud, by for example **generating electronic payments to himself** rather than suppliers, or **rounding up amounts in control accounts** and paying these through the expenses system.

This risk can be mitigated by **independent testing** of **all programs** and **program changes**.

External hacking

Outsiders could **gain access** to the payables system and arrange for payments to be made to themselves. This particularly applies if outsiders have some access to the computer systems through the Internet.

A **firewall** can **restrict access** to only software and files that are available for public use. The firewall only allows access through a single gateway, and restricts access to the rest of the system by establishing user names and passwords.

59 STU

(a)

(i) Design

Systems design involves the conversion of data into a workable format. It needs to cover:

(1) What the **sources of data** used will be

(2) The **format of input**; the same formats will need to be used across the organisation which has not been the case in the past

(3) The **data warehouse structure**, what structure will be most easy for the users to access

(4) The **format of reports** produced, will these provide the level of detail required for strategic decision-making

Guidance on data security and authorisation levels also ought to be developed at the design stage.

Audit work at design stage

Auditors need to review the evidence that the systems design is **acceptable** to all involved in development, including **users**. They also should review the **adequacy of the systems documentation** and whether the **costs** and **benefits** have been estimated accurately.

(ii) Development

The system needs to be **thoroughly tested by systems development** and **IT staff**. They should assess the **logic of the systems** and **test the programs using test data**. Given that the system may be processing large volumes of data, the **flexibility of the system to cope with peak-time demand and changes to processing routines** should be **investigated**.

Users also need to be involved in the **testing** to assess whether they are able to use the **analytical tools** provided by the system.

Audit work at development stage

Internal auditors will need to be involved in **testing the system** and **review the testing** carried out by other staff. They also need to **review changes to specifications** and **operating instructions** that have resulted from the development process. They will need to ensure that the **new system provides an adequate trail** for managers, themselves and the external auditors.

(iii) <u>Delivery</u>

The **transition** from the current situation will require careful planning. Information on the current systems will have to be transferred, and decisions will be needed on **what information** will be required and **what format** it should be in, as it may not currently be held in a form that can easily used by the new system. In addition all divisions of the company need to start using the SEM at the same time, otherwise the data it uses will not be complete; however this means that the changeover will require a very large IT resource and training commitment.

<u>Audit work at delivery stage</u>

Internal auditors will review whether the **implementation plan is realistic**, particularly given the number of **sites** involved, and that **implementation has been authorised by senior management**. They should again consider the **adequacy** of **documentation** and also the **arrangements** made for maintaining the system once it is operational. The auditors should also be involved in a **post-completion audit,** considering:

- Whether the system has **delivered the expected benefits**
- Whether the **costs have been excessive**
- Any **problems** during the initial operation of the system

(b)

Top tips. (b) demonstrates what we said in the front pages guidance about the need to plan carefully; (b) (i) should focus on the audit implications, and the discussion of other controls should be included in (b) (ii).

In (b) (ii) you could also have discussed organisation controls, since the changes should mean that the board should re-consider how IT support is organised. Changes may include an enhanced central function providing help and setting standards; performance indicators measuring how well the system and the IT function are performing will also be necessary. Discussion of human resource controls over the operators of the system would also have gained marks.

To: Audit committee
From: Accountant
Date: 4 December 20X6
Subject: Auditing computer systems and IT controls

(i) <u>Possible approaches to auditing the system</u>

<u>Importance of accurate data</u>

STU is heavily dependent on the data processed being **accurate and consistent** across the organisation. This means that the internal auditors need to review **the data** itself and also how the data is **processed** by the system.

<u>Reviewing the data</u>

Audit interrogation software allows auditors to extract data from the system for further work. The data extracted can be printed in a form that can be compared with the **data in management reports** produced by the SEM. Audit interrogation software can also perform procedures such as **calculations on large volumes of data,** and thus provide **statistical analysis** of the data within the system. This may **help to indicate the reliability of the data** from the various sites.

Internal audit may use other forms of software to **highlight certain items of data. Resident software** can be used to select automatically certain data for later investigation. **Integrated monitoring software** can highlight certain items (for example certain types of transaction processed at a specific site) if they fall outside limits suggested by the auditors.

<u>Reviewing the system</u>

Test data can be used to check the accuracy of data being produced by the system, by comparing the actual results produced by the system with the expected results. However use of test data may prove problematic in STU's real-time system, as the test data used will have to be reversed.

Embedded audit facilities are audit modules built into the accounting system that allow a continuous review of the data recorded and the manner in which it is treated by the system. An **integrated test facility** creates a **fictitious entity** within the company application; transactions are posted to it alongside regular transactions, and actual results of the fictitious entity compared with what the system should have produced.

Testing controls

In addition internal audit will have to gain assurance on the operation of the key controls that are covered below.

(ii)   Controls over the IT environment

Application controls

Application controls are controls over each **specific application**, and can be grouped into the following categories.

(1)   Input controls

Input controls should ensure the accuracy, completeness and validity of input. Data validation controls include check digits, control totals and checks that the input is within a reasonable numerical range.

(2)   Processing controls

Strong controls over **systems development** should help ensure the **completeness** and **accuracy of processing**. The tests carried out by embedded audit facilities should also provide assurance.

(3)   Output controls

Controls ensuring the completeness and accuracy of output include a list of transactions processed, and investigation and follow-up of error and exception reports.

General controls

General controls relate to the **environment** within which the IT systems **operate.**

(1)   Access controls

Access to the system should be **password protected**; the passwords required should be personal for each user and allow access only to relevant parts of the system. To counter the threat of hacking, passwords should be complex (minimum number of characters, include letters and numbers) and changed regularly.

(2)   Disaster prevention controls

The key central computer facilities should be located in an environment that minimises physical threats by precautions such as **smoke detectors and fire alarms.** Threats from viruses can be reduced by using the **latest anti-virus software, running virus checks** on files received from outside the organisation and **prohibiting the use of unauthorised software.**

(3)   Contingency controls

Daily backups should be taken of the information posted to the system. STU also needs to have **alternative arrangements available** should the system break down. However any alternatives need to be centrally controlled; a return to decentralised systems will wipe out the advantages of the SEM system.

60 CDE

Text references. Chapter 13 on the information systems, Chapter 7 on the management accounting systems.

Top tips. This question is a good illustration of what we said in the front pages about how important it is in this exam to make reasonable recommendations.

Easy marks. (a) (i) just requires a description of different management systems that doesn't really need to be connected to the scenario; this is a straightforward question for a strategic level paper.

Examiner's comments. Descriptions of systems in (a) were generally good, but many candidates failed to score well because they did not make a recommendation. In (b) many answers failed to discuss the cost of the accounting function. Students also failed to appreciate the significance of the question requirement to make recommendations; when these are required, it suggests that there is a need for change, however many answers were in favour of retaining the existing system.

(a)

Top tips. In (a) outline means you have to go through all the different systems **quickly**, with a short paragraph on each. (a) contains some very definite hints about what systems to choose based on CDE's requirements; the lack of integrated data and the need for strategic analysis should have directed you towards choosing an appropriate system and being able to **justify** your choice. You'd obtain 7 of the marks available for outlining the systems, 3 of the marks for making appropriate recommendations. In other words you can go most of the way to passing this question with a good part (a).

(i) <u>Information systems</u>

<u>Transaction processing systems (TPS)</u>

TPS are used for **routine tasks** in which data items or operations can continue. They incorporate the detail but do not provide the summaries that managers need.

<u>Knowledge work systems (KWS)</u>

KWS **facilitate the creation and integration** of new information into a system. They provide communication facilities and access to external facilities, also analytical and graphic facilities to analyse data.

<u>Decision support systems (DSS)</u>

DSS provide a wide range of **alternative information gathering** and **analytical tools** with an emphasis on **flexibility** and **user-friendliness**. They assist in making decisions on issues that are subject to a high level of uncertainty.

<u>Management information systems (MIS)</u>

MIS **transform data** from underlying transaction processing systems into summarised files that are used as the **basis for management reports**. This summarised information is used to assist managers in planning, directing and controlling activities.

<u>Enterprise resource planning systems (ERPS)</u>

ERPS can be used to plan many aspects of operations and support functions. They operate over the whole organisation and across functions, with all departments that are **involved in operations or production** being integrated into one system. Supply chain management software can provide **links with suppliers or customers**. They use **database management systems** so that data is entered once, then transferred across the system, and can be used for **tailored reports**.

<u>Strategic Enterprise Management Systems (SEMS)</u>

SEMS provide data in formats that assist managers in **setting strategic goals, measuring performance** in the light of those goals and **measuring and managing intellectual capital**. They provide more advanced tools such as **balanced scorecard** and **activity-based management** with which to use data, and enable customer, business unit and competitor analysis.

Executive Support Systems (ESS)

ESS summarise and track **strategically critical information** drawn from internal and external sources. They allow managers to move from summarised to more detailed data and also provide facilities such as the ability to **create simulations.** This information is used to help senior managers make **strategic, unstructured decisions.**

(ii)   Recommendation

At present CDE is operating an MIS that however does **not provide sufficient integrated information across the group** and does not help management take **strategic decisions.** CDE requires a system that provides **SEMS or ESS** functions. A SEMS will be geared towards **decision support** and enable management to carry out the **necessary analysis.** An ESS will provide the **flexible tools** that help managers make decisions in a changing environment and for that reason should be the preferred choice, subject to these benefits justifying the **costs** of investment.

(b)

(i)   Relevance of current system

Use of traditional accounting methods

CDE's accounting department currently provides data in traditional formats – budgets, variance analysis and standard costing. Whilst this provides useful information for short-term operational **control purposes**, it is less helpful in providing integrated information for **strategic and business development,** areas where the stock market may feel CDE's performance is lacking judging by its share price performance.

MRP II

MRP has been criticised as providing a mirror to what happens in practice, and hence **allowing inefficiencies to be perpetuated** rather than encouraging improvements. It has been criticised for accounting for long lead times, high inventory, large batch sizes and quality problems and hence building these into the planning process rather than pushing for their elimination.

Budgetary targets

The focus on budgets as a means of analysing performance may be misplaced. It may encourage excessive focus on direct costs that are **uncontrollable** in the short-term. Managers may focus on achieving budgetary targets and not on other relevant measures such as **customer service measures. Budgetary slack** may also be built into the system; we are not told how standard costs are determined by the accounting department, and it may be on the basis of inflated estimates by operational departments.

Rolling budgets

It also appears that **rolling budgets** may not be used, suggesting that the budgeting system may adapt too slowly to the changing environment.

Standard costing

The issue with standards based on material and labour usage is that they may not be revised often enough. Arguably they should be revised as soon as there is any **change in the basis** upon which they are set, which in a changing environment may be quite frequently, to take account of customers' changing demands. In addition standard costing fails to take into account the **balance** between cost control and other aims; it may for example be considered best to pay higher prices for materials to guarantee speedier delivery and hence enhance CDE's ability to operate **just-in-time.**

Cost allocation

The principal problem with using machine hours as a basis for cost allocation is that it suggests that for all CDE's products, machine hours are the **principal determinant** of costs, which is unlikely to be true. There are other factors that will also be significant and will vary between products, such as space, labour or working capital. Using a misleading basis will distort product cost figures.

Role of accounting department

It is felt that the accounting department is too focused on control and analysing past performance. It does not appear to be providing the information about **product market performance** and **customers** that will assist strategic decision-making.

(ii)   ### Improving the system

Implications of just-in-time system

The focus of the just-in-time system that CDE has adopted is on **improvements in productivity and elimination of waste** by obtaining quality components at precisely the time when they are required for use. It follows that the management accounting system needs to focus on key indicators of success or failure in implementing just-in-time. The system of variances used at the moment does not provide all of the necessary information, for example changes in inventory levels.

Lean management accounting

Instead the accounting department needs to take a lean management accounting approach, focusing on performance measurement of **value streams**, activities that **add value** for the **customers**, and which are geared to producing for customers rather than inventory. Product cost is the average cost of the value stream for the quantity produced for the period. Standard costs can still be used to determine **pricing**, but there is less emphasis on them as a means of control.

Backflush costing

The pooling of costs can be done using backflush costing. Backflush costing will significantly reduce the detailed work currently carried out by the accounting department. Use of JIT means that all the costing entries are made at virtually the same moment. Therefore under backflush costing costs will be **calculated and charged when the product is sold**, or when it is **transferred to the finished goods store.** The cost data need not be reported in detail, and inaccuracies in inventory valuation will not be a big issue because inventory is being kept to a minimum.

Activity-based costing

Part of the calculation of costing will be the **allocation of overheads**, and activity-based costing will be a fairer way than the current method. An activity based approach can allocate costs according to value added transactions, for example so-called **change transactions**, activities associated with ensuring customers' requirements are met. The introduction of a system of activity-based costing may increase the costs of accounting, contrary to management's desire to reduce costs, but the benefits of using a much fairer system should more than outweigh the rise in cost.

Role of accounting department

Changes in the methods will be reflected in changes in the role of the accounting department. The focus is likely to be more on adding value, including **providing information** that will **aid strategic decision-making** and **appraising investments** by methods such as **sensitivity** and **what-if analysis**. The accounting department can also provide more useful support by producing a wider range of measures, using the framework of the balanced scorecard. However there are dangers in the accounting department being too focused on helping the operational departments. Excessive identification may lead to a **loss of independence** and **failure to provide any control** in financial management. The best solution may be that the accounting department focuses on the plans and strategies of operational departments, but **rigorously reviews** and **challenges** the assumptions made.

61 AMF

Text references. Chapters 13 and 14.

Top tips. Planning (a) and (b) is important to ensure that you don't repeat yourself; some of the disadvantages of outsourcing are the risks of 'letting go' sensitive information. In (a) you would only have had time to consider a limited number of advantages and disadvantages given that the question asked you to discuss. (ie comment on their likely significance).

Note that some of the advantages and disadvantages discussed do not just relate to the ERPS, but apply to whatever is being outsourced. However the strategic significance of the ERPS also requires discussion.

In (b) again you would only have had time to mention a limited number of points as risks, internal controls and internal audit tasks, although the use of the verb identify suggests your comments on each risk should be limited. (Remember that per the table of question verbs in the front pages 'identify' is a lower level verb). The ultimate risks are loss of reputation and financial consequences, and you need to think what could bring them about. The link between risks and controls is not 1:1, as some controls should cover all the risks, above all the service agreement.

Your comments on internal audit need to bring out the auditors' review of the control environment and the detailed control testing that the auditors should carry out. Internal auditors' work will be inadequate unless they are granted access to the supplier's systems.

The recommended transition process in (c) should mostly be the same as for all major systems development, although the initial implementation needs to be considered carefully.

Note the examiner's comments, indicating common weaknesses in student answers, not just for this question. The discussion in (a) and (b) needed to relate to the supplier **described in the scenario**. Clearly some answers failed to mention the supplier at all. Students also failed to read (c) properly and did not pick up the key point in the requirement that the **supplier had been already chosen;** the question was therefore not about choosing the supplier.

Easy marks. Whatever the contents of your report, you should have made sure you obtained the five marks available for a formal report by including an introduction, conclusion, main heading and structure with subheadings. There should also be a logical flow to the report. The marking scheme specified that the five marks were available for 'structure, style, coherence and presentation.'

Examiner's comments. Many candidates did not obtain the marks for the report format. Discussions about outsourcing were often too general. In (c) a lot of candidates wrote about choosing a supplier rather than the transition to an already chosen supplier.

REPORT

To: Board
From: Management Accountant
Date: 17 October 20X5
Subject: Outsourcing the ERPS system.

Introduction

This report covers:

- The advantages and disadvantages of outsourcing the ERPS system
- Risks of outsourcing and mitigation of risks
- Managing the transition to an outsource supplier

The aims of the ERP system will be to **support the management** of **all business functions** by capturing and then making it available for planning and the production of reports. Outsourcing its development and operations enables us to concentrate on **value-added activities**.

(a)   Advantages of outsourcing

(i)   Consistency with current strategy

Outsourcing will be consistent with the company's overall strategy of limiting internal staffing and resourcing outside wherever possible. It will mean that we do **not to have expend resources recruiting and employing specialist staff**.

(ii)   Expertise

The specialist contractor is likely to have undertaken the **whole range of development activities** for other companies, and thus will have **greater expertise and experience** in developing the system, benefiting from **economies of scale**. This should mean that the system is developed **efficiently**, with less chance of error.

(iii) Costs

An outsourcing arrangement will mean **costs** are **easier to predict** and **budgets easier to control**.

Disadvantages of outsourcing

(i)   Tailoring the system

The system the consultant develops may **not be geared** enough to our needs, either because the consultant recommends an already-developed system that is not appropriate for us, or the consultant has **insufficient knowledge** of our requirements. This may be a crucial factor because of the **strategic importance** of the system, and hence the need for extensive knowledge of our requirements.

(ii)   Flexibility

We may find ourselves tied into a long-term service agreement to use a system that our changing requirements soon **renders inappropriate** for our needs. Although the supplier has a good reputation, there is a risk of **loss of flexibility and inability to respond to changing circumstances**.

Alternative solutions

You would also have scored marks if you had discussed the following disadvantages.

(i)   Loss of staff

Contacts with the consultant over the new system may lead to some of our key staff being **lured away** to work for the consultant.

(ii)   Failure of supplier

If the supplier goes **bankrupt**, AMF's **operations** could be **very seriously disrupted** because of uncertainty over the continued operation of the system.

(iii) Reputation

Our company has the reputation of being at the **forefront of IT development**. This reputation may be jeopardised if the industry learns that we have decided not to develop a key internal IT system ourselves.

(iv)   Costs and resource usage

The arrangement will **not necessarily be cheaper** and, depending on the agreement with the supplier, costs may increase over time. As well as the supplier's charges, we also need to consider **other transaction costs** such as monitoring and insurance, and the internal time resource involved in monitoring the arrangement.

(b)   Risks

Confidentiality

The specialist contractor will be handling the key information about AMF, and there are thus potentially very serious consequences if this information is **leaked to a competitor**.

Business delays

Failure to update information promptly could result in **delays in operations**, for example billing debtors, or decisions being made based on out-of-date information. Ultimately the disruption to production may mean that **customer requirements are not fulfilled**, leading to **financial loss and loss of reputation**.

Dependence

AMF may find itself **locked into the arrangement with the contractor**, and be unable to move to another supplier or to move the system in-house if it's later felt to be desirable.

Controls

Service level agreement

A **tightly drafted service agreement** is the most important control. The agreement should specify **minimum levels of service to be provided**, with **legal guarantees and penalties** for failure to meet those levels of service. Specifications should include **response time** to requests for assistance/information, system uptime percentage and deadlines for performing relevant tasks. The service agreement should also cover **security procedures**, and **make clear the ownership** of the system.

Liaison procedures

A director or senior manager with contract management skills should be responsible for **ongoing liaison arrangements** with the contractor. Staff with **appropriate knowledge** should **liaise on technical aspects** of the system. One possibility would be to **locate a member of staff permanently at the supplier's premises**, to act as liaison between the client and the contractor.

Feedback from operational staff

There should be mechanisms for **feedback from operational staff** so that problems can be quickly rectified. We need to decide whether staff should deal directly with the contractor or use an internal intermediary. An **internal intermediary** has the **advantage** of providing a **single focus for the relationship, better control of costs**, and **better monitoring of usage of service**.

Alternative solutions

You would also have gained marks if you had discussed the following controls.

Monitoring supplier

Press and other information sources about the contractor should be monitored for evidence of any business difficulties or financial problems.

Information technology function

The specialist function retained in-house is potentially a control, as there will be **greater expertise** to liaise with the supplier.

Computer controls

A range of computer controls should be applied to the outsourced systems.

(i)   **Application controls** should be operated over the **input, output and processing** of transaction data by the contractor.

(ii)   **General controls** should be in place over the **recruitment of staff handling sensitive information**, and access controls such as **passwords**. AMF should also **review business continuity controls** operated by the contractor, to ensure that the risk of disruption to AMF's operations is minimised.

Data security controls

Network controls should be operated to **secure data** transferred between AMF and the contractor and prevent hacking.

Internal audit

Control framework

Internal auditors should **consider the adequacy of the control framework**. They should confirm that the **service agreement** is **satisfactory** before it is **signed**, and assess the **adequacy of liaison arrangements**. Internal audit will also review the adequacy of computer controls, and test controls in areas where adverse consequences could be significant, for example **confidentiality breaches**.

Ongoing relationships

Internal audit should inspect records of correspondence between AMF and the service provider, and **confirm** that **concerns raised by AMF** have been addressed **adequately and promptly**.

Information

Internal audit should review the **financial and non-financial information** that the contractor produces to ensure that it is **accurate, complete and fulfils AMF's requirements**. Internal audit will also be concerned with whether the information is **sufficient** to provide a suitable **audit trail**.

Confidentiality

Internal audit should visit the contractor's premises and inspect the arrangements the contractor has for ensuring **security**, including **provisions in staff contracts**. It should have access to the client's systems and staff and carry out tests on the security procedures employed by the contractor.

(c)   Steering committee

This should be **headed** by the **director/manager responsible** for the relationship with the supplier, as well as members of the project planning team, IT support staff, representatives of operational departments and senior staff from the contractor.

Assessment of proposed system

The steering committee should assess whether the proposed system appears to fulfil required criteria, including **level of support** and **security arrangements**, and also consider the **time** and **resources** required for the changeovers, preparing a **budget** for the process.

Project planning team

A **project planning team** should be **responsible** for the transition. Their key tasks will include:

- **Specification** of the **requirements** of AMF that will be embedded in the service agreement of the **internal resources** required to support the project
- **Contacting stakeholders** such as **suppliers and customers** who may be affected
- **Detailed analysis of risk** and specification of a **risk response plan**

Implementation plan

The implementation plan should specify the changeover method. Since the new system will be a fundamental part of AMF's operations, I recommend:

(i)   **Parallel running** be adopted wherever possible, with the complete new and old systems being run in parallel, **processing current data** and **enabling cross checking** to be made. Parallel running should continue until the steering committee is satisfied that the new system is working satisfactorily.

(ii)   For those **parts of the new system** which have **no parallels** with the old system, there should be enhanced checks before the system is operated and monitoring by internal specialist staff and internal audit during the first weeks of operation.

Post-audit

Internal audit should carry out a post-audit on the transition process to **identify learning points** to be applied if other activities are outsourced in the future.

Conclusion

It is fundamental that any agreement between AMF and the supplier is satisfactory to us in terms of the **level of service provided** and the **management of risk**. If the supplier cannot provide the guarantees we require, we should tender elsewhere. Adequate internal controls and internal audit involvement will be necessary, and we should seek information about all the likely costs and resource usage before a decision is reached.

62 KL

Text references. Chapter 14.

Top tips. You need to draw on your P1 and P2 knowledge in (a); this question part is a reminder that Performance Strategy is within the CIMA qualification's Performance (management accounting) pillar.

You should note in (b) the emphasis on *user* needs both as regards the operation of the system and training in it. The answer to (b) also matches the principal accounting and audit problems with their solutions, rather than going into detail about the whole of the systems development process. This demonstrates that the recommendations that (b) requires are relevant for the problems identified.

Easy marks. You can gain credit for using a systematic approach to (b), and linking in problems with corresponding risk reduction measures.

Examiner's comments. A common failing on even good scripts was to write more on part (a) than part (b), which had more than twice as many marks. Other weaknesses in part (a) were writing generally about systems, and proposing that the project start all over again. In (b) many answers failed to discuss how the problems related to the introduction of the new system and standardisation, and the solution of the problems. A number of answers failed to focus on the requirements of the question but were general essays on internal control guidance and computer auditing.

The examiner stated that although the project mentioned in the scenario was the development of a computer system, the question raised a number of points that were applicable generally to project management scenarios.

(a)   Planning the project

If progress and problems are to be communicated effectively, projects must be properly planned. The choice of the new computer system should have been based on a **feasibility study** with alternative solutions assessed. This study should have highlighted **possible problems** with the implementation of the new system, for example the need to have it fully operational before the next year-end.

Once the system had been decided on, the following should have been approved by management:

- **Overall project targets** for costs, timescale or resource usage should have been **established**.
- **Project division**. The **project** should have been **divided** into **activities**, time and cost budgets set and resources allocated for each activity.
- A **framework** should have been set for **monitoring** the project.

The monitoring process

In order for management to monitor the project effectively, the following must be established.

Measurement mechanisms

Time taken can be measured by reference to network analysis or Gantt charts. **Resources** used can be measured by available resources and percentage utilisation. **Costs** can be measured by reference to budgets.

Lines of reporting

It is necessary to establish to **whom progress** should be **reported** and to **whom problems** should be **reported**. As well as reporting to senior management **user departments** should be contacted if **time and budget constraints** mean that **features** they have **requested cannot be implemented**.

Reporting to management

Reporting to management of progress and expenditure should take place every so often as a matter of course and also at the **completion of every major stage** of the project. Additionally **time or budget overruns** or **excess resource usage** should be **reported as soon as they appear likely** to occur.

(b)   The new system may pose the following audit and accounting problems. These are discussed below, together with the actions enabling the risks to be reduced.

Capacity of new system

Assurance is required that the new system will be able to **cope with the volume of processing**.

The **operation** of the whole of the new system should be **tested** prior to implementation using the kind of data volumes from different users that it will have to cope with when operational. In addition the **new system** should be **run in parallel** with the old systems initially, to minimise disruption should the new system be unable to cope with the volume of data.

Local requirements

The new system is replacing a number of systems, and it is possible that **local needs will be ignored**. This may mean the **information available** under the new system is **less** than before, and it may mean the **system cannot cope** with all the **necessary accounting requirements**, for example valuation of stock.

All **users** should be **consulted** about their needs prior to the system being designed. They should also be involved in testing the system to ensure it meets their requirements.

Master files

New master files which contain the appropriate information must be set up but this may be difficult given the **variety of local requirements**.

Design of an appropriate system of master files and coding system should be a **priority** in the development process. Consultation with users is particularly important here.

Transfer of data

There is a risk of **data being lost or corrupted** when being transferred.

Data files from the old system should be **copied** before conversion in the case of failure or corruption. **Master file data** should be **input in stages**, with the data input being copied at each stage. Once the data has been input, it should be printed out and compared with an independent source.

Staff problems

Lack of training of staff and **lack of documentation** of the new system may increase the risk of errors when the system does become operational.

These can be overcome by **proper documentation** and **training**. Documentation of the system should include:

(i)   **Listings** of program instructions, flowcharts, file layouts, input and output documentation, and the **procedures which each program module covers**;

(ii)   **Details of procedures to be followed if a systems crash** occurs;

(iii)   **An operating manual**, containing instructions on setting up and operating the system, and details of error messages and what action to take if they occur.

Training sessions should also help staff. These should include **posting** of **test data**. Attendance records should be kept so that management can ensure that all potential users of the system are trained.

Disaster recovery

Because the group will now be dependent on a single system, the consequences of a **system breakdown** could be **catastrophic**.

There should be **formal plans** for disaster recovery. These should include ongoing controls such as **backup of systems and storage of files** in a remote location. There should also be arrangements for **alternative facilities** to be provided should a catastrophe occur. The plan should cover different types and levels of disruption and should be properly tested.

63 ROS

Text references. Chapter 14.

Top tips. The main advice in (a) is don't jump to conclusions. Remember that although this situation is serious, there are basic techniques and procedures that must be carried out to assess the likelihood of the risk materialising. You have to provide **reasoned** recommendations in the answer rather than resort to inappropriate action with little or no justification.

In (b) it is important to know the main settings of a personnel security policy; however you will gain few marks unless you commented on how effective each section was. Again, be realistic and make practical comments where possible. Remember that programmers are clever people; don't focus the answer on inappropriate actions like simply watching the computer screen to check what they are writing.

(c) emphasises that testing is likely to be ineffective when certain types of viruses are involved. As in previous sections, don't jump to conclusions that the virus will be found – think through the situation carefully and document your answer with clear reasons why testing may not be effective.

Overall this question is quite specific, but it does bring in areas other than computerised systems (fraud, personnel controls), and possibly in the exam a computer fraud may be used as the basis for discussing wider issues.

(b) and (c) are also good examples of questions with complex requirements, and you need to ensure that your answers fulfil the whole requirement. Planning what you'll write, and asking yourself before you start writing whether what you're planning to say answers the question fully, will help you do this.

Easy marks. All parts require careful application to the scenario.

Marking scheme

		Marks
(a)	Up to 2 marks per recommendation made. Actions recommended must relate to scenario	10
(b)	1 mark per feature discussed. Award 0.5 marks max per feature if no comment on effectiveness	6
(c)	Up to 2 marks per aspect of strategy described. Award 1 mark max per aspect if no comment on problems	9
		25

(a) <u>Actions to be taken now regarding the breach of security</u>

The immediate action is to minimise the threat to the company's computer systems.

(i) <u>Dismissal of Mr X</u>

Mr X must be asked to **leave the company immediately** pending further investigation of his claims. He should be escorted from the premises without being allowed to return to his desk or touch any ROS computer. This is to ensure that the virus is not activated.

(ii) <u>Personnel checks</u>

Checks must be made with the personnel department to ensure that **Mr X has signed the standard contract of employment** including the non-disclosure agreements concerning company software. This action will confirm that Mr X was in breach of contract, even if it is later determined that no action can be taken.

(iii) <u>Backup</u>

An **immediate backup** of the software control programme must be taken onto CD-ROM or similar storage media and **stored in a safe**. While backups will be taken each day anyway, this is a precautionary measure to ensure that the most recent copy of the software control program has been duplicated and stored securely.

(iv) <u>Program analysis</u>

The **software control program must be analysed** to try and determine whether Mr X's claims are correct regarding the virus. We should **load the program onto a 'dirty computer'**, that is standalone computer that has no links to any other computer. This will minimise any loss of programs or data caused by the virus. There is no reason to believe that the virus will only destroy the software control program.

(v) <u>Code identification</u>

The **software control program** must be **checked by other programming staff** to see if any of the code appears to relate to a virus. Many viruses have specific signatures which identify them. However, Mr X may well be a skilled programmer and so the virus may be well hidden within the software. If necessary, other programming staff with skill in detecting and removing viruses can be hired to perform this check.

(vi) <u>Program changes</u>

It may be possible to **review recent changes** made to the software control program from the daily system backups. If so, amendments may be traceable to Mr X and then reviewed to determine whether they contain any virus.

(vii) <u>Removal of code</u>

If **suspicious code is detected**, then **attempt to remove it** on the dirty computer. Check that the software still operates after removal.

(viii) <u>Legal advice</u>

If **suspicious code is not detected, take legal advice** on the situation. If necessary, **agree to the terms of Mr X**, asking him to **remove the virus** on the dirty computer. As part of any severance agreement, tell Mr X that he must agree to amend the software at his own cost should any other trace of the virus be found.

(b) The personnel security policy in ROS must include the following features:

(i) <u>Recruitment</u>

Initial recruitment must include the taking of **references from previous employers**. While this will not stop implementing virus software, it will provide an indication of the trustworthiness of the employee. For confidential projects, telephone references may also be obtained to confirm written details.

(ii) <u>Job rotation</u>

Job rotation is important to ensure that **one person does not work too long on one section of code** and possibly implement viruses, and to **ensure that the code is checked** by other individuals. Checking may identify errors in program code as well as viruses.

(iii) <u>Supervision and observation</u>

Supervision may not be effective initially as it is a passive and relatively general activity and may not initially detect any wrongdoing. However, **monitoring of emails** did detect the illegal copying of the program code indicating that this system may be an **effective detection control**.

(iv) <u>Review of computer usage</u>

Reviewing computer usage may be effective where programmers suddenly start to work long or particularly unusual hours, especially with no colleagues around. It is generally easier to amend the code without the concern of someone overlooking the screen while the amendments take place. **Reasons for unusual working hours** must therefore be sought, although many programmers do

work unusual hours. **Actual review of code** may be necessary to try and detect any incorrect programming.

(v)   Enforced vacations

As in any job, **lack of vacations** can be **suspicious** simply because it appears the person does not trust anyone else to continue their work. Lack of vacation may indicate that the code has been amended illegally. However, there is **no guarantee that forcing staff to take vacations** will allow supervisors or other staff **to detect illegal amendments to software**, especially where those amendments are well hidden.

(vi)   Termination procedures

These appear to be adequate in ROS, with Mr X being **denied access to the computer system as soon as the virus situation was discovered**. Allowing any programmer back to a computer after termination of contract may allow them to write new virus code or trigger previously written code.

(c)   Aim of testing strategy

A testing strategy is designed to ensure that **software meets pre-determined objectives** without errors occurring in the input, processing or output of data.

(i)   Strategy approach

The testing strategy is formulated detailing the **approach to be taken to testing**, the **tests conducted**, and the **techniques** to be used. The strategy will ensure that basic objectives are met; however, virus code may not be detected during normal processing so the strategy may fail to test for this.

(ii)   Test plan

The plan **explains what will be tested and when the tests will take place**. If the plan is known in advance then the **virus code** could be **hidden or simply programmed** to remain inactive during testing. Even if the virus can be activated, the test plan may not include appropriate tests, as noted above.

(iii)   Test design

Tests are designed to **check basic input, processing and output** are in accordance with any specification. As a virus will not be on any specification, test design is likely to be ineffective in identifying the virus.

(iv)   Performing tests

Tests are actually carried out. The only possibility of detecting the virus will be if the **results are not exactly as expected**, although given that a timebomb virus will only be active on a given date, actual testing is unlikely to be of any use.

(v)   Documentation

The documentation will simply **show the results of the test**. Although useful in providing a record of testing carried out, if no errors are found then no virus will be recorded.

(vi)   Re-testing

Re-testing, including regression testing, will be performed where **one section of code has been amended**. If the amendment was unauthorised then reviewing the amendment itself will be more effective than actual testing for reasons noted above.

64 Z

(a)   <u>Motive and opportunity</u>

The chief buyer could have been contacted by a supplier and promised a share of illicit gains, which would be a good **motive** to become involved in fraud. As he was responsible for receiving the bid documentation and placing it in secure accommodation, he had the **opportunity** either to substitute envelopes or open envelopes, read the documents inside and put the documents in new envelopes. As the envelopes had so little detail on them, it would be impossible to tell whether the envelopes opened at the meeting were the envelopes in which **bids were sent, or were substitutes.** In addition Z only seems to have the chief buyer's word that Z received four bids. The chief buyer could have **destroyed bid documentation** from other bidders who could have won the contract. The internal auditor, who could have provided **independent scrutiny,** was not involved until late in the process.

<u>K's two bids</u>

K's bid might cause concern because the initial bid was **much lower than the other bids,** but still appeared to be **of sufficient quality** when L's bid was not. Secondly the reason for **increasing the bid by £1m or 50%** is difficult to understand, as there were no other amendments to the bid documentation. There is a possibility that the bid was increased because K somehow discovered that its initial bid was significantly lower than any other. It could **therefore increase its bid** and still win the tender, but with a significantly greater profit margin. The fact that K's second bid was pitched at just the right level to win the tender arouses suspicion. It suggests that K may have known that L's lower bid would be rejected on quality grounds, and that M's bid was higher. The chief buyer would have had an opportunity to inform K that this was the case.

<u>Rejection of L's bid</u>

L's bid was the lowest, but was rejected for other reasons. The reasons given for rejecting the bid appeared to have some substance. However the question remains of **why an inadequate bid was submitted.** Did L make mistakes or was L given misleading information about the bidding process by the

chief buyer? The chief buyer would also have had opportunity to substitute for the document L had submitted a document that he had prepared setting out a bid that would not satisfy the other managers making the decision.

(b) <u>Previous dealings with suppliers</u>

The auditors need to determine whether there is evidence of a link between the chief buyer or any member of the buying team and Supplier K. The auditors should review any previous correspondence that the buying department has had with Supplier K, in order to determine whether such a link exists. If Supplier K has been used in the past, the auditors should ascertain whether there is any evidence of a **close relationship between Supplier K and any of the buying team**. For example, a staff member could have worked for Supplier K in the past or one of his family may have current connections with the supplier.

<u>Bid documentation</u>

The auditors need to find out why differences in the bids submitted by suppliers arose. They should **analyse the details of the bid documents.** In particular they should try to find out why K's first bid differed so significantly from the other bids. K passed the quality threshold that L failed. Therefore K was presumably prepared to accept a much lower profit margin.

The auditors should find out whether there has been any public criticism of K for poor quality, which could indicate that K would not have fulfilled the promises it made. They could ask K to explain why the second bid was £1 million greater than the first bid. If they told K that it could not be accepted as a supplier unless it explained why the two bids differed, that should at least guarantee a response from K, even if K were to give a misleading answer.

If, however, the profit margin on K's original £2 million bid appears reasonable, the auditors then need to consider why the other bids were much higher.

<u>Briefs to suppliers</u>

The auditors need to determine whether differences in the bids from suppliers reflected differences in what the suppliers were told. The auditors should try to **obtain details of the correspondence** with the suppliers who submitted bids. They should see if there are **any differences in the bid specifications sent to each supplier**. They should also compare the bid received from Supplier L with the documentation L was sent, to see if the bid is consistent with what L was told.

<u>Correspondence with other suppliers</u>

The auditors need to discover whether all the suppliers who submitted bids had been included in the bidding process, or whether they had been informed of the contract through some other means. The auditors should thus find out whether any other potential suppliers who did not apparently bid were sent copies of the bidding documents, or whether there is other evidence of suppliers expressing an interest. The auditors should **contact all the suppliers** who did not bid and with whom Z has been in contact about the contract and ask them to confirm that they did not submit a bid. If they say that they did bid, the auditors should request copies as a matter of urgency and try to find out if there is any evidence that the bid documents were received by Z but subsequently 'mislaid'.

<u>Suppliers' bids</u>

As the decision has not been communicated yet to the suppliers, the auditors still have a chance to find out whether there was any **interference with the bids** L and M submitted, which may have led to their rejection. The auditors should therefore contact Suppliers L and M and **request a copy of their bid documents.** They should then compare these copies with the documents that were in the envelopes opened at the meeting. They should ascertain whether the bid M submitted was for £3.2 million and compare the details on the bid documents from L to see whether the two copies are identical.

<u>Opportunities for interference</u>

If it appears that interference did take place with the bids, internal auditors should review who could have accessed them, as anyone with access could have put a bid in a new envelope and forged the required signature. The internal auditor should find out who has **access to the safe** where the bids were kept and whether the safe is normally kept **locked.**

Rejection of L's bid

The auditors should also review the reasons for rejecting L's bid to confirm whether they **appear to be valid,** as on cost grounds L should have been chosen. Although L was offering slightly smaller buses, the auditors should assess whether the difference in size resulted in the buses not being fit for purpose. Likewise the auditors should assess the implications of using the poor quality materials. If the quality of materials meant that the buses had to be repaired more frequently, this would probably be a valid reason for rejecting the bid. If however the differences would just have affected the buses' external appearance, it would be less easy to justify rejecting the bid on these grounds.

(c)   Advantages

Flexibility and cost

It will probably be **quicker to divert internal audit staff** from other work to investigate this potential fraud than it will be to book experienced external audit staff. Using internal audit staff may therefore mean a shorter delay in ordering the buses. Although there may be **opportunity costs** in diverting internal audit staff from other, useful, work, these will probably not be great. External auditors would certainly charge extra fees for the work, as it would not be part of the statutory audit.

Secrecy of investigation

It might be easier for the internal audit department to carry out an investigation without arousing **suspicion**. The internal audit department has ready access to documentation that external auditors lack and **knows K's culture and systems**. Internal auditors should also be able to **exercise appropriate discretion** when carrying out their investigations. External auditors' presence for reasons other than the statutory audit could arouse suspicion.

Disadvantages

Independence

A senior member of the internal audit department was at the meeting at which the **bids were opened and the decision to accept K's bid taken.** It would be very difficult for him to have any involvement in an investigation into a process in which he played some part, as he did not raise any alarm at the meeting despite the suspicious circumstances. More junior internal audit staff may be reluctant to say anything that could be taken as criticism of senior staff for not raising queries earlier.

Lack of experience

None of the internal audit team may have had previous experience of investigating this type of fraud. The external auditors should be able to supply staff with previous experience of fraud investigation and forensic work, who are **more likely to identify irregularities** in the process.

65 Seatown

Text references. Chapters 6 and 15.

Top tips. It's probably best in (a) and (b) to list the information required when you make each point. You need to think about what performance measures are relevant, also whether performance can be compared or benchmarked with other departments or councils. Note in (a) that measures of efficiency need to take into account time taken and distance covered. The examiner's comments confirmed that effectiveness proved to be the most difficult topic to discuss and you were given the most marks for discussing it.

Your answer to (b) needed to recognise that it isn't just a question of measuring quantity of rubbish picked up. Public reaction to litter remaining on the beach has to be taken into account. Thus the quantity of litter not picked up is very important, and also whether any of it is dangerous. Although the tractor sweeping may not pick up much litter, it is justified if it picks up the litter that would concern the public. Likewise the spot checks are looking in particular for the most visible and most hazardous rubbish.

A key point in (c) is the ease of quantification of each criteria.

Easy marks. A rather unexpected question, with limited opportunities to score quick marks.

Examiner's comments. (a) was done well, but (b) and (c) were done poorly, with students appearing to lack understanding of effectiveness.

Marking scheme

		Marks
(a)	Up to 2 marks per issue discussed. Issues could include	
	Economy	
	Labour costs	
	Machinery costs and miles	
	Comparisons with budgets/other services/other councils	
	Efficiency	
	Need to differentiate between sweeping and emptying bins	
	Need to break down figures by areas covered	
	Measure performance against standards	
	max	10
(b)	Up to 2 marks per issue. Issues could include:	
	Quantity of refuse collected	
	Differentiate beaches and bins	
	Links to visitor numbers	
	Success of collection	
	External feedback/indications	
	Frequency bins are emptied	
	Internal audit work	
	max	10
(c)	Up to 2 marks per issue. Issues could include:	
	Accounting/quantitative information	
	Need to consider litter left/not left	
	Problems with target setting	
	Costs of measuring effectiveness	
	Impact of public reaction/reputation issues	
	max	5
		25

(a)   Economy

Costs of labour

Controlling labour costs will be an important element of economy. The council needs to **break labour costs down** for sweeping the sands and emptying the bins. To judge whether the costs are being limited sufficiently, the council will need to **compare actual costs with benchmarks**. These include **comparing actual costs with budget**, with **costs of previous years**, with **comparable costs** for the other areas of the council's activities and **costs incurred by other councils** responsible for beaches. The council's management will need to investigate fluctuations from any of the expected benchmarks.

The council's **management accounting data** should provide most of the information required, assuming that a proper system of budgeting is in place. It should be possible to obtain labour cost information from other councils.

Costs of machinery

Similar comparisons for labour costs should be made for machinery costs such as **vehicle running costs**. The analysis made will need to take into account the cost drivers such as the **number of tractors** and the **number of vehicle miles covered.**

As well as **management accounting cost information and budgets, details of vehicle miles covered** will also need to be maintained.

Efficiency

Efficient use of labour and machines

The council needs to find out how resources are being used. It needs to know **how much time** is being spent **sweeping the sands** and how **frequently bins are being emptied.** The actual frequency of emptying bins should be **compared with the standards** the council set, to review whether bins are being **emptied more frequently** than required or whether the schedule for emptying bins is unrealistic.

It would also be helpful to have **more detail** about how much time is being spent on different areas. Some beaches may be more problematic to clean because of **obstacles** such as rocks. The time and costs spent on these beaches could be reduced by limiting access to them to popular times of the year. To judge efficiency fairly though, the council will also need to take into account the **area of different beaches and the number of litter bins.**

Employees will need to maintain **detailed records of the time spent on each beach** and **when they empty the litter bins.** It will also be important to keep the permanent data, the areas covered by cleaning and the number of litter bins, up-to-date.

(b)   Quantity of refuse collected

The council will need to ascertain how much refuse has been collected. Again it will be helpful if the **refuse collected from sweeping** can be recorded separately from the **refuse collected from bins**, in order to judge both activities fairly. When quantities are reviewed over time, it will be useful to see how much the litter generated is **proportionate to the number of visitors**. The Council should also try to identify whether **other seasonal variations** have a **significant influence** (visitors being less likely to consume food and hence drop food litter during the autumn and winter, and also fewer refreshment kiosks being open during these seasons). The council will need to assess whether more staff resources are needed at the busiest times of the year to keep the litter under control.

Records kept will therefore need to include the quantity of litter disposed of each week. There are various ways in which the number of visitors can be estimated, including **number of users of tourist information centres, car park records** and **estimates based on physical space occupied** by each beach user.

Quantity of refuse not collected

As well as assessing how much litter has been collected, the council needs to have an idea of whether all litter has been **collected from the beach**. Complaints or feedback from beach users will give indications. Management also needs to consider whether litter bins have been **emptied frequently enough** to avoid overflowing. It should be possible to compare records of how frequently litter bins have been emptied compared with the **standards** set by the council. Management should investigate if bins are being emptied less frequently than required by standards.

The council should maintain records of complaints it has received about **litter, ratings made by external parties** and other indications of problems, for example adverse media comment or injuries caused by litter left on the beach. The council should also try to **collect feedback systematically throughout the year from visitors,** for example through issuing questionnaires in tourist information centres.

Spot checks of beaches after sweeping and of bins, particularly during the busiest seasons of the year, by internal audit will also provide evidence of whether litter is being collected thoroughly and promptly. Spot checks of beaches will need to distinguish between different types of litter. Larger items, or items that could cause injury, will be of most concern. This will also help determine whether the standard frequency for emptying bins is appropriate and whether the frequency should vary at different times of the year.

(c)   Measurement of efficiency and economy

Economy is measured **using accounting information** that would be used for the council's financial and management accounts. The time records that are integral to assessing efficiency would also be part of the management accounting system. The information these accounting records provide is largely **numerical and objective.**

Measurement of effectiveness

As discussed above, effectiveness has to take into account both the **quantity of litter picked up** and the **quantity of litter left** on the beach and in the bins. The problem with analysing the amount of litter picked up is that more litter will naturally be picked up at busier times of year. At quieter times there may be less litter generated. However employees may pick up a high proportion and it may be less likely that the bins are overflowing. The data may also give the impression that sweeping is of limited impact compared with emptying bins, but sweeping is more likely to pick up litter that poses a serious risk to users' safety.

The problem with analysing the **amount of litter left** is that it cannot be done on a comprehensive basis **without incurring excessive cost.** Internal audit will not have the resources to carry out checks on any more than a sample basis. The other indicators (complaints, injuries, adverse publicity, even surveys) cannot provide more than a partial picture.

The council may also wish to judge effectiveness in the context of the **adverse impact on the resort's reputation** of beach users finding litter or bins overflowing. This suggests that effectiveness will be of most concern during the peak seasons, where more people are using and staying on the beach, and children are more exposed to litter.

66 LMN

Text references. Chapter 2 covers general risk management issues, Chapter 3 corporate governance and Chapter 16 the role of the audit committee.

Top tips. This question is a very good illustration of our comment in the front pages that questions will cover a variety of organisations. The scenario gives lots of detail about risks and how they are controlled, inevitably for a charity where use of funds for proper purposes and value for money are important.

Note the examiner's comments about the question not being done very well despite being the most popular question in that exam. Some students would have chosen this question because it appeared to be a straightforward corporate governance question. However the fact that this was a charity does complicate the answer, and the question requirements are quite clear that every part needs to be related to the circumstances of a charity. There are no general parts unrelated to the scenario on which easy marks can be scored. Students should have considered these points when choosing questions in this exam, but it seems that many did not.

Easy marks. No very easy parts, but overall a good example of how to illustrate corporate governance in an organisation with relevant information from a scenario.

Examiner's comments. Although this was the most popular optional question, it wasn't done very well, with students being unable to apply corporate governance principles to an organisation that wasn't a listed company and failing to use the information in the scenario. Many answers to (b) focused on the role of the audit committee when the question was about management evaluation of internal controls.

'Candidates should make full use of the reading time to make sure they understand what is being asked.'

(a)

> **Top tips.** In (a) the link between controls and risk management is highlighted in the question details. The discussion in the first part of (a) should be assisted by examples from the scenario, and in the risks-controls you need to include some examples of appropriate controls for LMN. Your answer needs to differentiate clearly, as ours has done by using headers, between purposes and importance so that you can maximise your marks for (a).

Purposes of risk management

Alignment of risk appetite and strategy

LMN's board should consider what **risks** it is prepared to **tolerate** in the light of the organisation's strategy. Risk management comprises the systems and processes for dealing with the risks that the board is prepared to tolerate in order for LMN to fulfil its **strategic objectives**, including its **social goals**.

Develop a consistent framework for dealing with risk

A coherent risk management framework can help LMN **compare risks with obvious financial consequences** (poor cost control, loss of income due to bad debts) with risks whose financial consequences are less obvious (dissatisfied tenants). It also should provide guidelines that can be applied by staff operating across all areas of LMN's activities.

Develop risk response strategies

The risk management process should **identify and evaluate risks** (for example by the high-medium-low method described) and therefore provide the information necessary for management to decide what the best **response to risk** should be – acceptance, control, avoidance or transfer.

Importance of risk management

Improve financial position

The risk management framework can provide a means of judging the **costs of treating the risks** measured against the **benefits**. It can also help LMN's directors judge whether to take advantage of opportunities, for example property investment.

Minimise surprises and losses

By **identifying risks in the risk register**, the risk management process should reduce the occurrence of unexpected shocks. For example identifying **property maintenance** as a risk issue should encourage a programme of regular maintenance designed to deal with the risks associated with the types and ages of property.

Maintain reputation

As LMN is a charity, its reputation as a **good corporate citizen** is very important. Risk management should help it avoid risks to its reputation such as **poor treatment of tenants** or **failing to comply with regulatory requirements**.

Risk management and the internal control system

Internal control is action taken by management to achieve organisational objectives and goals. Internal control thus is bound up with the organisation's strategies, and is therefore also bound up with risk management that is dependent upon the organisation's strategies. Internal control is made up of two elements:

(i) **Control environment**, the framework within which controls operate and within which attitudes towards risk are an important elements. **Communication** between directors and employees is a key element of the control environment.

(ii) **Internal controls**, which should be operated when their **benefits outweigh costs**; controls focused on dealing with the most significant risks will have obvious benefits. Given the risks LMN faces, key controls will include **debtor management**, **maintenance inspections and logs**, **financial appraisal of new investments** and **tenant satisfaction questionnaires**, as well as **accounting**, **compliance** and **cost limitation** controls.

(b)

> **Top tips.** It's necessary to read (b) quite carefully to see what the question wants; an assessment of how much a review by the professional managers contributes to the work of the audit committee, and why therefore the review should be carried out. You should start off by defining what the work of the audit committee is, then consider how much managers' review contributes compared with other sources of information.

Audit committee's role in internal control

Under corporate governance guidelines audit committees are responsible for creating a **climate of discipline and control.** To do this, they have to obtain assurance that internal control is working **effectively** and providing an **adequate response** to the **risks** faced, in particular for LMN, controls over expenditure.

Importance of management review

The management review provides the audit committee with evidence of whether the control systems appear to be **effectively managing the most significant risks**. It also gives the audit committee an indication of the **scope and quality** of management's monitoring of risk and internal control; does it appear to be **adequate** given the risks faced. In the circumstances of LMN, the board of volunteers will wish to gain assurance that the **professional managers** are carrying out their duties effectively and are worth the salaries LMN is paying them. The review should provide **feedback** on weaknesses and should lead to improvements in the control systems.

Other sources of evidence

However management's review of internal control is only one source of evidence that the audit committee should use to gain assurance. LMN's committee should also receive **reports from staff** undertaking important and high-risk activities such as property investment. They should also receive **reports from control functions** such as human resources or internal audit (if any). Feedback from external sources such as **external audit** or **regulatory visits** will also provide information.

(c)

> **Top tips.** In (c) again you can't be too theoretical; any discussion of principles has to be related to how they impact on the audit committee and board's reviews. Selected examples from the scenario information are also needed here to boost the discussion. If you can remember that the board needs to carry out a regular and annual review and the main elements you would have scored well in (c) and gone a long way towards passing this question.

(i)   Review of internal controls

The UK's Turnbull committee emphasises the importance of a regular review and an annual review of internal control as part of an organisation's strategy for **minimising risk, ensuring adherence to strategic objectives, fulfilling responsibilities to stakeholders** and **establishing accountability at its senior levels.**

Regular review

Regular review is an essential part of the strategy for minimizing risks. The audit committee is likely to have responsibility for this review, and as best practice recommends at least **three audit committee meetings a year**; this is thus how often the review should take place. Its findings should be communicated to the board.

The review should cover the following areas:

(1)   Risk evaluation

Whether LMN is **identifying** and **evaluating all key risks**, financial and non-financial. This is a very significant task given the variety of risks faced and also the need to devote limited resources to the most important risks.

(2)   Risk responses

Whether responses and management of risks are appropriate.

(3)   Effectiveness of internal controls

The effectiveness of internal controls in countering the risks. The board should consider how much controls could be expected to reduce the incidence of risks, any evidence that controls have not been operating effectively and how weaknesses are being resolved. The board would consider evidence such as incidence of bad debts, records of property occupation and complaints from tenants.

Annual review

The annual review of internal control should be more wide-ranging, taking into account the **strategic objectives of the charity** and undertaken by the **whole board** rather than just the audit committee. It should examine controls and risk management systems in all major areas:

(1)   Changes in risks

The **changes** since the last assessment **in risks faced**, and the charity's ability to **respond to changes in its environment**. For example the board would consider any changes in LMN's credit ratings, also longer-term trends such as changes in the incidence of low income earners.

(2)   Monitoring

The **scope and quality of management's monitoring of risk and control**, also whether internal audit is required. In particular the review should consider whether the **scope and frequency of the regular review** should be increased.

(3)   Reports

The **extent and frequency of reports** to the board; should reports on high incidence, high likelihood risks be made more regularly.

(4)   Impact on accounts

Significant controls, failings and weaknesses that may materially impact on the financial statements, for example problems over its property portfolio management.

(ii)   Disclosures in the annual report

The report on compliance is a key part of the annual report by which LMN demonstrates its **compliance with regulations** and how it has **fulfilled the differing requirements of its stakeholders**, including tenants, donors, banks and local government.

Responsibility

The board should also **acknowledge its accountability** for LMN's system of control and **reviewing its effectiveness**.

Risk management

The Turnbull report recommends that as a minimum the board should disclose what has been done to **manage risk** and how the board has **reviewed the effectiveness of the risk management process**. The board should explain the limits of the process (it aims at risk management rather than risk elimination) and disclose any **material problems** or **weaknesses** that have been found. It should communicate **risks, objectives, targets** and **measures to counter risks**.

67 SPQ

Text references. Chapter 1 lists the main risks, Chapter 15 covers internal audit's role, Chapter 14 is helpful on the controls and Chapter 4 on ethical issues.

Top tips. Note that (a) stresses the work internal audit does in reviewing the overall control and risk management framework as well as the detailed testing. Consideration of the factors in the COSO framework and CIMA's risk management cycle may help you generate ideas.

(b) is a good illustration of what we said in the front pages about understanding what the question verb requires. The analyse (examine in detail) requirement in (b) means that you have to go beyond the problems with the systems and ask what else the systems development demonstrates about SPQ; make sure your answer clearly identifies the control action.

In (c) we cover the issues, particularly the risks, affecting the running of the specific audit, but also consider the issues affecting this audit's place in the overall plan for internal audit.

In (d) you just about have time to use the principles in considering different solutions to the ethical problem, although don't go overboard on these. You should have made a recommendation about resolving the conflicts at the end of your answer.

Easy marks. (a) is a good start to the question. Similar part questions have been asked on other occasions, so an explanation of internal audit's role may well be worth a few marks in your paper as well.

Examiner's comments. There were many good answers. Poorer answers were too general and failed to relate to the case, particularly in (d). In (a) some candidates failed to relate internal audit to internal control and risk management. Answers to (c) were generally good, although there was a lack of focus on planning and many answers regurgitated textbook learning. A large number of answers to (d) consisted of short bullet points and thus lacked appropriate depth.

(a)   <u>Internal audit's role</u>

Internal audit's evaluation of an organisation's systems and processes is part of the process by which an organisation gains assurance that its **business risks are being effectively managed** and that **internal controls are operating** as planned.

<u>Risk management process</u>

Part of internal audit's remit is to review the **risk management strategies established by management**, the **risk culture** of the organisation and the **reliability of risk assessments** being made. Internal auditors may be able to place reliance on the risk assessments made when planning their own work; however if they are not satisfied, they will have to make their own judgements and report on the inadequacies of the current system to the board and audit committee.

<u>Internal control</u>

Internal audit will also be concerned with how the **systems established by management** to respond to, and manage, risks are working and their work on internal control systems is part of this.

Internal audit will be concerned initially with the **design of internal controls** and the **adequacy of the framework** for reducing risks to acceptable levels. Internal audit will also be concerned with the **operation of controls**, using a combination of **risk assessment and detailed testing**. Not only will internal audit provide a check on operation, it may improve the chances of some controls operating effectively; staff may be more likely to operate controls well if they know that their work might be audited.

<u>Recommendations</u>

The recommendations internal audit make will feed back into the **design and operation** of **risk management and internal control systems**. The recommendations will have regard for the organisation's **strategic objectives** (including the requirement that costs of control are reasonable given benefits) and also the organisation's **risk appetite**.

(b) <u>Risks</u>

<u>Data protection risks</u>

SPQ is possibly vulnerable to the **loss of sensitive data** about customers to competitors or other third parties. It may also have **breached data protection legislation**.

<u>Information systems risks</u>

SPQ may also be vulnerable to interference in the data it holds by the introduction of **viruses**. This would severally impact on its ability to trade on-line.

<u>Accounting information risks</u>

If the problems are widespread there is a risk that management decision-making will be **influenced by incorrect data**. There is also a **compliance risk** that the loss of data will mean SPQ **fails to fulfil legal requirements to maintain proper accounting records**.

<u>Systems development risks</u>

The failure to test systems properly may mean that systems are not fulfilling their objectives and that consequently **resources are being wasted**, either through the systems not providing the **support required** or as here because **resources are having to be used to investigate problems** within the system.

<u>Alternative solutions</u>

You would also have scored marks if you had discussed any of the following risks.

<u>Revenue and counterparty risks</u>

An obvious risk is the risk of **loss of revenue** through failure of customers (or possibly third parties) to pay for goods that have been delivered. There is also a risk of **customers' dissatisfaction** and **loss of sales** if they have ordered goods, but their orders have been intercepted by **third parties**.

<u>Reputation risks</u>

SPQ will be vulnerable to a **fall in its sales**, if its computer problems are made public and as a result **customers lose confidence** in the security of the system. These developments may ultimately **depress the company's share price**.

<u>Controls</u>

<u>Security controls</u>

The whole security system requires urgent review including whether **staff's rights of access to the system** need to change, and whether any current system of **passwords needs to change**. Possibly the passwords currently required are too easily guessed and more **complex passwords or more frequent changes** should be introduced. Other measures include **firewalls**, preventing public access to certain parts of the system.

<u>Accounting information controls</u>

It should **not be possible to delete transactions completely** without a **record being made in the system**, possibly a **dump file**, the contents of which are regularly reviewed and investigated. Also **order and delivery records** should be **matched** to sales and receipts details, and **unmatched orders and delivery notes investigated**.

<u>System testing</u>

The systems development procedures either need to be improved or implemented better, and in particular should **require the approval of the information technology department** and **other users.** The use of a structured methodology would ensure that the system is designed with both business and users' needs in mind. Clearly also a **system of post-audit reviews** should be introduced. If fundamental failure of the systems occur (as perhaps here), there should be a requirement that the system undergo a **complete re-testing.**

<u>Decision-making and review</u>

The governance procedures requiring change may include the requirement for the whole board to approve decisions such as the **introduction of the new systems**, and **improved access** particularly for internal

audit but also for other staff to the audit committee. The UK Corporate Governance Code requires a **regular review** of all internal control systems, including IT systems, by the board.

(c) <u>Strategic issues</u>

The overall audit plan will be influenced by the **organisation's objectives, structure and information flows** and the **risk management system** in place. These will determine which **areas of the organisation** and **which risks** it is most important for internal audit work to cover.

<u>Areas to be covered and extent of coverage</u>

The audit **objectives**, the **order of work**, the **areas** to be covered and **how much and what work** is done will depend on:

(i)   The organisation's **own risk assessment** and **risk assessments undertaken** by **internal audit**

(ii)   The **extent of internal controls** within the area

(iii) Any **specific requests for coverage**, for example by the chief accountant (as here) or the audit committee

(iv)   The **work carried out by external audit**

(v)   The results of **preliminary work** on the audit area including review of previous results and changes in the business environment

(vi)   **Any control breaches identified**

<u>Operational planning</u>

The operational plan will need to cover in detail the **scope and timetabling** of the audit, and also the **staffing and resources** required (including the need for staff with experience or specialist knowledge). If members of the internal audit team have been involved in the design of the system, they should **not** be involved in its audit.

(d) <u>Ethical principles</u>

<u>Integrity</u>

The Head of Internal Audit (HIA) is being asked to tone down the criticisms and **therefore produce a report** that is **potentially misleading** to the audit committee. It may affect the decisions and recommendations the committee makes about the company's risk management procedures and framework if committee members do not have a correct understanding of the **level of risks**.

<u>Objectivity</u>

The HIA is coming under pressure from others to **modify internal audit's recommendations** because of **political pressures** within the company. **Ethical objectivity** requires a consideration of the impact on affected third parties who are unable to influence the decision.

<u>Competence</u>

If internal audit does produce a toned-down report and major problems continue, the **competence of the HIA and the rest of the internal audit department** may be called into question when the problems are discovered, possibly by external audit.

<u>Resolving difficulties</u>

<u>Reporting weaknesses to the chief executive</u>

This course of action would be proper in the sense that the chief executive is the HIA's **immediate superior**. If the chief executive is convinced about the seriousness of the problems, it may be easier to get them corrected. However the chief executive's **previous attitude** suggests that he may forbid the HIA to issue the audit committee with the report in its current form. The chief executive's **previous involvement** also means that the HIA could justifiably bypass him.

<u>Reporting weaknesses to the audit committee</u>

This would resolve the issues of **not supplying the audit committee with information** and aspersions being cast on **internal audit's competence**, and also mean that the HIA had taken a robust attitude to the pressures placed on him. However if there is a **conflict between the audit committee and the chief executive**, it might jeopardise the chances of the necessary improvements being made. **Discussion with audit committee chair** might be a better response than submitting the report directly. As head of the audit

committee, the chair has responsibility for **ensuring the findings of internal audit are properly actioned**, and practically he may be able to advise how best to present the recommendations.

Discussion with finance director

Alternatively the HIA could first discuss the matter with the finance director, as he should be aware of the concerns the chief accountant has. The difficulty might be that the finance director may feel **loyalty to the chief executive** and report the conversation to him.

Recommendation

As a first stage, the best solution would be to **discuss the matter with the audit committee chair** for his advice on the best way to proceed. Although this is not a formal report, notes should be taken of this discussion. Subsequent action can be agreed at this meeting.

68 CFB

Text references. Chapter 15 covers audit risk, Chapter 2 describes the likelihood-consequences matrix. Chapter 16 covers sampling.

Top tips. (a) focuses on audit risk. You therefore need to remember the definition of audit risk when approaching the answer.

Your answer needs at least to state the likelihood / consequences (frequency/severity) matrix before applying this to CFB. The scenario provides four situations that correspond to the four sections of the matrix. For each section of the answer, you should explain audit risk, and then take part of the scenario to show how the internal audit department approaches that risk. You also need to conclude with some comment on how the company should also manage the risk.

Be careful not to be sidetracked into explaining risk from the external audit perspective. Remember, internal audit has a much wider remit than external auditors. Risk analysis is very important in setting priorities and will cover many different areas.

(b) indicates what you are most likely to be asked about sampling; you won't be asked to use one of the sampling methods to select a sample.

Easy marks. You should score well on (b), as this is fairly basic knowledge that does not need to be related to the detail in the scenario.

(a)   **Audit risks** can be ranked according to how likely those risks are to occur and the potential consequences of a risk should they occur as shown in the table below.

		Severity (consequences)	
		High	Low
Frequency (likelihood)	High	Reduce or Avoid	Control systems
	Low	Transfer or reduction	Accept as insignificant

Likelihood High : Consequence High

The risk should be managed by extensive audit testing.

Example

This risk is relevant to the **audit of the computer systems** in CFB. There is a **high likelihood of audit risk** occurring because of the **complicated nature of the computer systems** themselves and the fact that amendments are made on an apparently ad hoc basis. The internal auditor could easily reach the wrong opinion in an internal audit report because the systems may not be understood, recorded incorrectly or not sufficiently well tested before implementation that standard audit tests would fail to detect a material error. The **consequence of the incorrect report** could be that **reliance is placed on the computerised systems** when it should not be.

Risk management

The **risk** will need to be **managed** by **eliminating it as far as possible**. Internal audit staff should have sufficient skill and knowledge on auditing computer systems, and appropriate techniques such as

computer audit software should be used to audit the computer system. The internal auditor will also need to **recommend that appropriate control systems are put in place to prevent risks materialising**. These systems will range from controls over the input of data into the systems, to appropriate backup facilities should the computer system fail.

Likelihood High : Consequence Low

The risk still needs to be **managed by audit testing**, although there can be a **greater emphasis on the company putting appropriate controls in place**. Audit testing will also be at a lower level than for high consequence situations simply because the effect on the company is reduced if the internal audit report is incorrect.

Example

For example, part of the work of the internal audit department is auditing cash sales. There is a **high likelihood of audit risk** occurring in this area simply because **cash is an asset that can be removed from a company easily**. However, CFB receives only **4% of its total income in cash**, so the **consequence of an error in cash is relatively small**. The company would lose some money, but given that fraud would be limited to a small percentage of the total cash income, then overall loss would be minimal.

Risk management

The internal audit department would carry out **specific tests** such as ensuring that the cash received on any one day in the cash sales office agreed to the till roll and then to the bank statements showing deposit of that cash. **Internal controls** would also be **recommended** to try and ensure that cash was not stolen such as cash being counted by two people to prevent one person removing money, and cash being banked by staff not responsible for sales to introduce appropriate segregation of duties.

Likelihood Low : Consequence High

The risk can be **managed** in various ways including **limited testing** or effectively **transferring that risk**.

The fact that audit risk is low implies that that there is a **low risk** that an internal audit report will **provide an incorrect conclusion on a specific area**. The risk could be managed by **transference** – that is accepting the work of other specialists with internal audit simply monitoring those reports.

However, the fact that the consequence of an **incorrect conclusion is high** (here a fall in consumer confidence) means **some work must still be carried out**. If the audit report is wrong, then significant damage could result to the company as incorrect reliance would be placed on that report.

Example

The audit of the operations of CFB provides a good example of this situation. There is a low likelihood of any of CFB's products being sold where the quality is poor because the quality control department regularly samples products, and the internal audit department monitors overall quality from initial input to final output of drinks. However, because quality control testing is limited, it is still possible for internal audit to identify **potentially poor quality of product** from production data but quality control to miss this. It would then be up to internal audit to ask for additional checking.

Risk management

Internal audit work on quality control means that the **quality control process is monitored,** with **reliance being placed on the quality control department**. However, where quality control is limited or the other review indicates a fall in product quality then internal audit must take action.

Likelihood Low : Consequence Low

Appropriate action for internal audit may be simply to **monitor these areas** of the company and provide very **restrictive reporting** on them at all because they are insignificant.

Example

For example, the mixing vats in CFB are **cleaned thoroughly** every three weeks with the discharge being sent into the normal sewer system.

Risk management

Given that the internal audit department has to monitor the effect of CFB's operations on the environment, then this **activity could be checked** to ensure that no harmful chemicals are being released. However, as CFB manufactures fruit drinks, even if a large amount of ingredient was released by accident, it would be

unlikely that any significant environmental damage would result. The consequence of any over release of product is therefore low – no environment is likely to be affected.

(b) <u>Purpose of testing</u>

The purpose of testing is to **test the functioning of the control** on which it has been decided to rely and not the transaction which is the medium of the test. Hence where errors are discovered the monetary value is irrelevant. It is the fact that the error has occurred (and that the control may not be functioning properly) that is important.

(i) <u>Selection of items</u>

Items for testing can be **selected** using **random**, **systematic** or **haphazard selection** of the sample. The first two methods are more acceptable as the question of bias in selection is eliminated.

(ii) <u>Number of items</u>

The number of items that will be tested will be dependent on the following factors.

(1) **Audit risk** – the sample size will be dependent on the degree of reliance to be placed on a test of control and the assessment of control risk. A high degree of reliance will increase the sample size whilst a low assessment of control risk will reduce it.

(2) **Tolerable error rate** – the higher the rate the lower the sample size.

(3) **Expected error rate** – if errors are expected a larger sample will be needed to ensure the tolerable error rate is not exceeded.

(iii) <u>Evaluation of errors</u>

If **errors are found** in testing, they should be **evaluated**. If they all relate to one control, the test may be extended or another control identified upon which reliance can be placed. This would need to be tested in the same way. Alternatively controls may not be relied on if it is felt to be more efficient and effective from an audit point of view to reduce audit risk by extending substantive tests.

69 JJJ

> **Text references**. Chapters 6 and 15.
>
> **Top tips**. This question deals with internal audit planning matters. This question also looks at the issue of outsourcing finance and other functions, albeit from the internal auditor's perspective.
>
> **Easy marks**. There are enough clues in the scenario to enable you to score well in the discussion on cash, inventory and fraud.

(a)

> **Top tips**. (a) covers some mainstream asset management issues but also wider human resource and commercial implications which the internal auditors would cover. The scenario quite clearly highlights areas of concern that of course your answer needs to address, and some areas where problems are quite likely (anything involving cash). Commercial issues are important because of the significant consequences if things go wrong, particularly new developments – here a new product.

<u>Overall approach</u>

Both the **compliance based** and **process based approaches** would be **appropriate** here. The business is well run on the whole and there are specific procedures put in place by management, compliance with which could be assessed. In addition however, due to the nature of the business, it is clear that management and control of cash and inventory are key. These could be the focus of a process based approach. In either case, due to the number of sites involved a risk based approach is likely to be the most effective and efficient.

<u>Specific issues to consider</u>

The key decision to be made is to determine **which sites must be visited** and **which areas are of particular concern**.

Financial matters

On the basis of relative significance to the business as a whole the following sites should receive a routine visit: King's Cross, Marylebone, Hammersmith, Ealing, Gerrards Cross and Thame. Together these six sites contribute 77% of the total turnover of the business.

Particular issues to be addressed include:

(i) Cash management

Whilst there is no information from Head Office to suggest that there is a problem in this area tests should be performed to ensure that **procedures are being followed consistently and correctly**. Checks should be made to ensure that each kiosk manager is maintaining the **physical security** of the cash by, for example, maintaining the twice daily banking of cash.

(ii) Inventory losses

This has been identified as a particular problem at both Kings Cross and Ealing. Work should be performed to try to determine the source of the problems. Possible causes could include:

(1) Poor inventory control

Due to the short product life of the inventory consistent overordering is likely to lead to **inventory losses**. This is perhaps heightened at the King's Cross location where two kiosks share the same store. In this situation it is likely that no one individual is taking overall responsibility for the inventory management. Internal auditors should attempt to find out who has responsibility when they visit the site.

(2) Poor training

Each product should be made to a standard recipe. Where the recipe is not being followed or where errors are being made this will result in **extra inventory** being **utilised and wasted**. The fact that the Ealing branch has had a high level of staff turnover may suggest that staff have lacked training and that the managers have lacked experience in ordering. Internal auditors should check for a sample of the drinks that the **right recipe** is being followed, and **review the personnel records** of staff employed at Ealing.

(iii) Fraud

(1) All sites

The possibility of **theft** needs to be considered. The apparent inventory losses mentioned above could in fact be the result of transactions being made without being recorded with the cash received being misappropriated. The **overall performance** of these kiosks should be **reviewed** to determine whether there are any unexpected falls in revenue in comparison to previous periods.

(2) Princes Risborough

The Princes Risborough site should receive a **surprise inspection** preferably at the start of the morning shift. Whilst Princes Risborough contributes less than 2% of the total revenue of the business matters identified at Head Office have raised some concerns. The failure of the cash takings to reconcile to the cash bankings could be the result of poor control which should be rectified or potentially due to theft. In addition the timings of the transactions have raised suspicions and it is possible that the kiosk is not in operation for the full period of the shift even though the staff members are paid for the full nine hours.

(iv) Commercial matters

The fact that the Gerrards Cross café has failed to sell the newly launched smoothie needs to be **investigated**. At other sites these sales constitute approximately 20% of total revenue and this launch is an important part of the management strategy. Potential reasons could include **poor advertising and promotion** and **inadequate training** on how to make the product. Internal auditors should review **advertising documentation** and **staff training records**.

(v) Operational

A number of issues have been identified in relation to **staff recruitment**, **retention and training**. In particular at the Ealing kiosk an investigation should take place into the reasons behind the recent

loss of managerial staff. Internal audit should carry out a **more general review of the human resources function**, looking particularly at the way that candidates are selected and the training process which they are offered.

(b)

> **Top tips**. Similarly, in (b), many of the issues that the internal auditors would be faced with would be similar to those that an external auditor would face. (b) covers overall systems review and operation of the contracts, as well as more detailed review of value for money and information.

Effect on the activities of internal audit

Review of accounting and internal control systems

Often internal audit is assigned specific responsibility for reviewing the design of the systems, monitoring their operation and recommending improvements. The key difference if the IT function is outsourced is that JJJ will **lose control** over these activities thereby **limiting** the **extent of the work** which the internal auditor can perform directly. Instead it will be the internal auditors' responsibility to **manage the relationship** and **monitor the performance of the service provider**.

Terms of contract

Exactly how the internal auditor will do this would depend on the precise nature of the contract between the two parties. The **terms of the contract** would determine for example the extent to which JJJ has access to **accounting** records prepared by the service organisation and relevant underlying information. It may be useful, therefore, for the internal auditor to be consulted at this stage.

Design of systems

Once the relationship has been established the internal auditor would only have a **limited impact on the design of the system**. Provided that the end product meets JJJ's requirements the way in which these results are achieved and any improvements would be the responsibility of the service organisation. Instead, however it could be the internal auditors' role to monitor the **performance of the service organisation** and determine whether the needs of JJJ are being met on an ongoing basis.

Control environment

In respect of **controls** the internal auditor would still have **responsibility for checking that the overall control environment is strong**. Where services have been outsourced the control environment will be made up of a combination of those operated by JJJ's personnel and those of the service organisation. There are a number of ways in which the internal auditor could monitor the control environment of the service provider including:

- **Information and assurances** regarding the operation of internal controls provided by the service organisation

- **Quality of control**. Assessment of the use of **quality assurance services** (eg the service provider's internal audit function)

- **Actual experience** of adjustments to, or errors in, reports received from the service organisation

- **Reports** from the service providers' external auditors

Examination of financial and operating information

This would normally include **specific enquiry into individual items** including detailed testing of transactions and balances. The result of testing of information provided by the service organisation eg analytical techniques could also be applied to payroll information to establish the validity of processing.

The key issue here is the internal auditors' **access** to the relevant detailed records. In some cases JJJ may not maintain detailed records or documentation initiating transactions for example, purchase invoices. If this is the case the information would be sought from the service company.

Review of economy, efficiency and effectiveness of operations

Financial efficiency or cost saving is probably one of the main reasons why JJJ is considering the outsourcing of its IT function. The internal auditor would have an **ongoing role** in determining whether the

service provider continues to provide **good value for money** by comparing the quality of the service with the negotiated fee.

Special investigations

The internal auditors of JJJ would continue to have **full responsibility for non-IT related special investigations**. Any IT related projects are likely to be the remit of the service organisation as access to their expertise will be one of the main advantages of outsourcing in the first place. The internal auditors may, however, have a role in establishing what those projects should be as they have an in-depth knowledge of the detailed operations and needs of the business.

Compliance with regulations

Under company law JJJ has certain **obligations to maintain proper accounting records**. If JJJ were to use a service organisation the internal audit department might be involved in ensuring that the contractual arrangements are such that company law is complied with. This would include ensuring that the company has **legal ownership of the records and has access to them**.

70 APS

> **Text references**. Chapters 5, 6 and 14 all contain relevant discussion of risks and controls.
>
> **Top tips**. You should be able to see a number of weaknesses in the payroll system. Try and prioritise your answers, as we have, as that part of the question is worth 18 marks and you might run out of time trying to cover them all. Covering six properly should gain you 18 marks (one each for a weakness, consequence and recommendation). SPAMSOAP may help you think up the necessary controls.
>
> Key elements relate to organisational weaknesses, management failing to exercise supervision and threats to the security of assets and data.
>
> (b) is a good illustration of how computerised controls and computer-assisted audit techniques can be covered in questions.
>
> The reference to access controls follows on from the threats to systems identified in (a).
>
> **Easy marks**. It's generally easier to identify weaknesses than to discuss what they mean and how they should be countered. However you will get little or no credit if you just list weaknesses, however long that list is. Presenting what you say in the format we have used demonstrates to the examiner that you are thinking through how the weaknesses should be addressed.

(a)   Weaknesses in the payroll system

Control over time recorded

Weakness

There is apparently **no form of control over what employees record** as their hours. The department supervisors do not appear to authorise the time cards and there is no independent check on whether the hours recorded are the hours worked.

Consequence

The company could be **paying the employee for work which he or she had not done**.

Recommendation

In the first place, the department supervisors should be asked to **authorise the time cards** to ensure that time recorded is reasonable.

However, the supervisor will not always be physically present at the times when employees clock in and out. Therefore in the long term we recommend that the company make use of a **mechanical or computerised clock**, so that employees are required to punch or sign in and out. This will provide an independent check of what hours have been worked.

Segregation of duties

Weakness

There is currently **no segregation of duties** in the wages system. Although the director approves the cheque for the wages, the wages clerk is allowed to create the payroll, which is not authorised until after the cheque has been written, and then put together the wage packets from the cash drawn from the bank.

Consequence

The directors have little control over:

- Whether the **payroll is an accurate reflection** of the clockcards
- Whether the **payslips reflect** what is on the payroll

The wages clerk could **misappropriate cash** from the wages cheque by allocating more cash on the payroll than on the payslips.

Recommendation

In the first instance, some **segregation of duties** should be introduced into the system. Someone other than the person who enters the payroll should make up the wage packets (subject to the point below).

In the longer term, the directors should consider **investing in an integrated payroll system** rather than using a PC. This could automatically record time from the clock machine and create the payroll and the payslips simultaneously.

Cash pay out

Weakness

The wages are **paid in cash** which the wages clerk collects from the bank on wages day.

Consequence

In addition to the possibility of staff misappropriation discussed above, the transfer of a substantial amount of cash between the bank and the premises each week is dangerous and leaves the company highly **susceptible to theft**.

Recommendation

It is common practice for businesses to use **direct bank transfers** to pay wages. We recommend that APS introduces the use of automated banking procedures.

Amendments to wages

Weakness

Wage changes are arranged **informally and orally** with the directors, apparently on an ad hoc basis.

Consequence

This could lead to confusion, particularly given that there are so many staff, and staff **could be paid something other than what has been authorised**. There appears to be **no system for updating the details on the PC** which contains the **payroll details**. It may also lead to some staff receiving wage rises regularly and others being forgotten, which would adversely affect staff morale.

Recommendation

Staff wages should be **reviewed on a systematic basis** (perhaps six monthly) and changes in wages should be authorised in writing. The wages clerk should not process any amendment which is not authorised in writing.

Recruitment

Weakness

Recruitment appears to be undertaken in a **casual, ad hoc manner**.

Consequence

The company could **fall short of the vital resource of staff**, or could employ people of lower skills than required.

Recommendation

The company should set a **recruitment policy**, involve at least two people in each recruitment decision and consider employing a **personnel manager**, see below.

Personnel and policies

Weakness

The company employs 200 people. It has **no written policies towards employees** and no personnel department. Personnel duties are being left to the factory manager.

Consequence

Employment law can be complex, particularly in areas like the EC, and the company could find that it falls **short of regulatory requirements**. It may also be at risk from disgruntled employees taking **legal action** in the event of no company policy to deal with problems arising.

Recommendation

The company should consider forming some **formal policies** towards employees and producing an employee handbook. Given the number of staff it now employs, it should consider employing a personnel manager, possibly on a part time basis, who could also assist with recruitment.

(b)   (i)   Access controls

The most common access control to a computer system is the use of **passwords**. This would be the most appropriate strategy for APS, for whom use of controls such as retinal scans might be a little excessive.

Another important consideration for access is the **physical location of the computer terminals**. They should be contained within lockable rooms. Security will be improved if they are **away from windows**, or they are **not kept on the ground floor**.

Application controls

The application controls which would be used in a payroll system are controls such as:

(1)   **Data entry checks** (for example, values are within a certain range)
(2)   **Total checks** (for example, hash totals, such as the number of employees on the payroll)

(ii)   Test data

Test data is used to ensure that **data is processed correctly by the system**. There are two types that could be used in the payroll system.

Valid data

Valid data could be entered, to ensure that the results are as predicted and expected. This would involve taking the details of an employee or **creating a new employee** and entering details such as pay rates and hours worked which could be valid, and processing them into the system. The required payroll information could be worked out in advance, and agreed to what the system produced.

Invalid data

Invalid data could be entered, to ensure that the system **rejected it and refused to process it** as valid data. This could be varied in several ways.

Examples of invalid data

For example, the test could involve taking a **genuine employee** and changing one detail which was then invalid. Another error could be added to the same test.

71 B Supermarkets

Text references. Chapters 1, 2, 9, 10, 14 and 16.

Top tips. Like some other Section A questions, this has a number of distinct issues covering material across the syllabus. It is important not to get bogged down in any single area.

Easy marks. (b) (i) should have been relatively straightforward if you picked up the comments in the scenario about the loan being expensive and consumer demand being affected by rising interest rates.

Examiner' s comments. Generally this question was done rather badly. In (a) (i) many students exaggerated the impact of the trial hypermarket, saying that it would force the group to seek extra funds or at worst go into liquidation. Students who mentioned that shareholders would be worried about overseas entry barriers and failure to focus by management scored better marks, but only a small number discussed the issues of management ego versus maintenance of shareholder wealth.

In (b) (i) students failed to relate the risks and benefits of the swap arrangement to the case study. For (b) (iii) few students related renewal of short-term borrowing to the interest rate environment.

In (c) (i) many students discussed customer theft and systems issues rather than focusing on staff theft. Answers to (c) (ii) were generally very weak, generic or too vague.

(a)

Top tips. The key to (a) (i) is to realise the significance of the investment for the company and the board. It is not material in financial terms but it has a major impact on the reputation of the directors because it is publicised as the start of a major strategic development. The two issues the answer identifies are that the shareholders may believe that the investment in A is a mistake, and secondly that it undermines their view of the directors (not only could the directors make similar mistakes but they cannot be trusted to tell investors the truth about what they've done).

Making the most of material in both the preseen and unseen is vital for scoring well in (a) (ii). Key points include the fact that B is the first multinational into A, which may make it unpopular anyway. In addition both the preseen and unseen emphasise the need to adapt to local tastes and preferences. A retail consultant is likely to advise doing this, but you need to discuss the chief executive's reluctance to take advice. In particular following strictly the objective of the investment and aggressively promoting B's values is likely to be counter-productive. B is intending to conduct detailed market research, but it may be too late then to adapt its approach and overcome the initial adverse reaction of consumers.

(i) <u>Impact on relationships</u>

The investment may adversely affect relations with investors. Firstly they may have **doubts about the investment** and the way in which it is being made. Secondly they may doubt what the directors are telling them about the investment and there may therefore be a **breakdown in trust.**

<u>Doubts about the investment</u>

<u>Publicity</u>

Although the investment may not be particularly large in financial terms, its symbolic significance is great. It is designed as a **pilot** for the major strategic development of launching expansion into new countries and is being launched with maximum publicity as a sign of the direction that B is going to follow. The investors may feel that the launch is **excessively high-profile**. If the store fails, it will cast doubt on whether **B can deliver expansion** and hence have an **adverse effect on the share price.**

<u>Wrong decision</u>

More fundamentally the investors may believe that the decision to invest in A is mistaken or that the method chosen is wrong (they may believe that B should operate franchises rather than own stores outright). They may believe that the **barriers to entry for a foreign company** are too high, the **customer base is too narrow** and that investment elsewhere would be **more profitable.**

<u>Failure to withdraw</u>

Because the investment is seen as so important, investors may worry that the directors will be **unwilling to admit that it has been a failure and pull out.** Investors may feel that there is a risk that the directors will commit B to a long period of sustaining losses in Country A.

<u>Problems with trust</u>

<u>Directors' priorities</u>

Investors' confidence in directors' decision-making may be generally undermined by the investment in A. They may feel that the strategy of expansion is **excessively risky** and directors are more concerned with overseeing a larger organisation than safeguarding their investment. Investors may also believe that directors are too concerned with **measures of short-term success that are easier to control**, such as increased revenue, rather than building longer-term shareholder wealth. Investors may see the directors as being concerned about **progressing their careers in retailing** and **feeling that managing a larger company will enhance their reputation**.

<u>Misreporting</u>

If investors doubt that the picture of the investment's performance that is being given is accurate, this may generally undermine their trust in the directors. They may believe that directors are putting **excessive spin in their commentary** on the investment's performance. The undermining of trust will be worse if the investors believe that the results of the investment are being **misreported** in the accounts. They may believe that directors have strong motivation to manipulate figures, because this is a high profile investment in a quoted company and their credibility is at stake. If shareholders believe that directors are manipulating the figures relating to the new store, they may be concerned that they have distorted other figures as well.

(ii)   <u>Loyalty to local retailers</u>

B is the first multinational company to attempt to break into A. Local consumers may **react against this** and remain loyal to retail organisations that are based in A. Consumers may feel shopping at local businesses helps **preserve national identity** against external pressures. They may believe that B's values are alien and believe that B will exploit its suppliers and employees. B may also be unpopular if it is believed to be **aiming at affluent consumers** and ignoring the needs of poorer consumers.

<u>Differentiation policies</u>

B is attempting to differentiate itself by **promoting its own values and changing consumer attitudes.** This is a high-risk strategy. It may indicate that B's senior management **has failed to understand customer tastes and preferences** in A. Customers there may find B's style of retailing unappealing and not wish to shop in its stores. B's **approach to marketing** and the language it uses in promotion may not appeal to consumers in A. Taking advice from a retail consultant and modifying B's approach may help to reduce this risk. However if B copies the approaches of existing businesses in A too much, it may not positively differentiate itself sufficiently from them.

<u>Products</u>

B's **standard ranges of products** may not appeal to local consumers, who require products that are clearly aimed at their requirements. Some of B's products may be considered **offensive** by consumers in A. They may not like B selling alcohol or sexually explicit DVDs for example. Not only may individual consumers refuse to shop in the store, B may face **organised boycotts and protests** that will lead to bad publicity and further loss of sales. B could also have problems if it **labels products** in ways that are considered **inappropriate** or local consumers find unfamiliar.

<u>Management style</u>

B's management control style is generally known as **bureaucratic and authoritarian.** B's senior management is likely to take a particular interest in the store in A as it is a flagship store and they cannot afford for it to fail. However they may try to **require store managers to manage in ways that are unfamiliar** in the local culture. Store managers who have been recruited locally may have particular difficulty in fulfilling B's requirements and staff may be **dissatisfied** if they feel they are being treated poorly. Low staff morale may have an adverse effect on operations, for example, standard of service, and may impact upon results.

(b)

Top tips. The swap may appear not to be worthwhile in (b) (ii) given the forecasts, but a crucial point here is that the forecasts are only for one year and rates could rise further over the rest of period. Directors may be prepared to pay the extra interest to remove uncertainty over finance costs over a substantial period. (Remember the value of an interest rate option is higher, the longer the period to expiry.)

In (b) (iii) the most important point is the link between pricing and expectations. B will incur a cost of hedging every time it renews a short-term instrument that is determined by the strength of expectations of interest rate rises. The costs and terms available will change over time, whereas the swap guarantees a single rate which is much more suitable for the long-term commitment that B wishes to make.

(i) <u>Increased finance costs</u>

B's interest costs are 14% of operating profit and it would appear to have scope to bear increased interest costs without there being any threat to **liquidity**. However B's dividend policy is to maintain a dividend pay-out ratio of 50%. An increase in finance costs will mean relatively more going to debt providers and less to shareholders, further **increasing shareholder dissatisfaction.**

<u>Impact of investments</u>

Increased interest costs on floating rate debt will also be mitigated by **increased interest income** (€165 m in the latest accounts) to the extent to which the investments are variable rate investments. If the investments are fixed interest, an increase in interest rate will **reduce their market value**.

<u>Impact on demand</u>

Increased interest rates may also **impact adversely on consumer demand**. Consumers' mortgage payments will increase and consumer spending on high streets is likely to fall. In particular this may hit consumer durable sales in B's hypermarkets as this is discretionary expenditure that consumers don't have to make. This impact may be mitigated by B's discount stores picking up sales, as some consumers seek cheaper deals.

(ii) <u>Interest per annum if B enters the swap</u>

€7,000m × 7.2% = €504m

<u>Interest if B doesn't enter the swap and rates remain unchanged</u>

€7,000m × (1.1 + 3.8)% = €343m

Difference = €171m

<u>Interest if B doesn't enter the swap and EURIBOR rises to 2.0%</u>

€7,000m × (2.0 + 3.8)% = €406m

Difference = €98m

<u>Benefits of committing to fixed interest swap</u>

The payment under the swap arrangement is higher both than it would be if interest rates **remained unchanged** and also if the rates rose in accordance with the Finance Director's estimates. Committing to a fixed interest rate would **remove uncertainty relating to interest rates and profits** over a substantial period, but directors may consider that this benefit involves too heavy a commitment. Their views will firstly be determined what the **probability** appears to be of EURIBOR going above 3.4% and the rate B pays therefore exceeding 7.2%. The directors would also be concerned with the **consequences** for B if rates rose above 7.2%, whether there would be liquidity problems or shareholder anger at a fall in dividends.

<u>Risks of incorrect forecast</u>

The directors would also take into account how reliable the Finance Director's forecast appeared to be. They should consider the **assumptions** underlying the forecast. The fact that most commentators believe that **rates will not increase by as much over the next 12 months** is something directors would take into account, but they would also be aware that is only one year out of six. The Finance Director's forecast appears to have a **significant sensitivity margin**. The

average increase in EURIBOR over the entire period would have to be more than double what the Finance Director predicts for the next year for the swap to be cheaper.

Counterparty risk

Counterparty risk should be minimal as B is making the arrangement with a major commercial bank, which should be financially stable. This may also make it possible for B to **reverse the swap** if it was no longer worthwhile, although there is likely to be a cost in doing so.

(iii)   Short-term nature of instruments

The finance director's assertion about the nature of instruments is correct. Most are designed to hedge for interest rate changes over months rather than years. They are a form of **insurance** for the buyer, where the seller assumes the risk in return for a premium. They are not designed to deal with interest rate changes over a long period, where movements are less certain and the **risks to the provider of the option** would be **greater.**

Renewal of instruments

Costs to B will become **less certain** if a succession of short-term instruments are used. B may find that once the term of the instrument has expired, an instrument offering the same rate is not available or only available at an **increased premium,** because **expectations about rate rises** have **changed.**

Pricing of instruments

The pricing of instruments will take account of **predicted interest rate movements, uncertainties in predictions** and build in a **profit element** as well. Every time B buys a new instrument, it will be paying a premium to the sellers of the instrument that reflects these considerations. The cumulative cost of these premiums over the time period will be greater than the increased interest costs that B will incur if it purchases the fixed interest rate swap.

(c)

> **Top tips.** In (c) (i) the increased ease of carrying out the control procedure may be as important as the procedure being more reliable. If the system is seen as strong, staff may not try to beat it. However did you spot the most significant flaw, that the readers are registering the tags and not the actual inventory.
>
> Note in (c) (ii) that the auditors' work is confined to the pilot scheme in a single store and you should not have discussed work over the whole group. This question is about audit work on a systems development, hence the emphasis on checking the key elements for the system to operate properly, the RFID technology and staff understanding how to use it. Auditors also need to obtain evidence to judge whether the new system is in fact working better than the old one.

(i)   Increase in spot checks

The new technology will mean that it will be simpler to carry out inventory checks. The **portable readers** can be used at any time. They should be **much quicker** and **produce more reliable results** than physical counting. They should also reduce staff time, **removing the need for a number of staff to attend the physical count.** The **frequency** of checks can be increased and it will also be possible to **organise surprise checks** easily, rather than having to arrange a physical count and perhaps giving a fraudster a chance to hide inventory losses.

Manipulation of figures

The new technology should mean that it is **impossible to overstate inventory.** Only inventory that is actually in the warehouse or the stores can be counted. Under the current system staff can check inventory holdings on the computer and **ensure that the physical count records agree with the computer** by recording inventory that has been stolen as still present.

Staff views

The risk of fraud may decrease if staff **believe they will not be able to defeat** the technology. Staff should be told that RFID technology will be used and will be a better system for tracking products.

Limitations on effectiveness

Staff may be able to distort figures in certain ways. They can **take the tags off the goods**, steal the goods and leave the tags in place in the warehouse. The readers would then still **register the tags** and show the goods as still being in inventory. Alternatively the **readers on the doors of the warehouse** could be **switched off** and fail to register movements inwards and outwards of inventory that could then be stolen before the next count.

(ii) Discussions with staff

Internal auditors should **talk to staff who operate the technology** to see if staff's understanding of how it works is correct.

Analytical procedures

Internal auditors should carry out analytical procedures in order to **identify unusual patterns in inventory holdings since the technology was introduced**. Internal auditors should compare differences in levels of particular items within the store over the period of the pilot scheme. Significant differences may indicate a built-in problem with the technology.

Observation of counts

Internal auditors should **observe store staff** when they carry out counts to ensure that they appear to be **using the equipment properly** and **all inventory appears to be counted.**

Testing the technology

Internal auditors should carry out their own **test counts** using the RFID technology and compare the results with the computer records. They should also check the technology is working by **inspecting the readers on the warehouse doors and at stores** to see if they seem to be working and ensuring a **sample of movements of inventory** going into and out of the warehouse and out of the stores **registers** on the readers.

Carrying out physical counts

Internal auditors should also carry out **physical counts and compare the results with the results of their test counts using the RFID technology**. They should also look out for anything unusual in areas where inventory is held, for example inventory that does not have tags on or tags that have become separated from the items carrying them.

Investigation of discrepancies

Internal auditors should review details of test counts conducted by store staff, ascertain whether **discrepancies identified** have been **resolved** and **make further enquiries** if satisfactory explanations have not been received for differences. Internal auditors should also **investigate any differences** their own work has identified.

Review of discrepancies

Internal auditors should also look at the pattern of discrepancies. **Over-counting** should be impossible and may indicate problems with the software. Multiple examples of **undercounting** may indicate staff are not using the technology properly, in particular not standing within range of all the inventory. They should also **compare the number of discrepancies identified** by the RFID technology with the number identified under the old system. If the RFID technology is working properly, the discrepancies should be fewer.

72 M Newspapers 1

Text references. Chapter 1, 2, 6, 11 and 14.

Top tips. The situations relating to (a) and (b) are a contrast. With the postings, there are some controls in place but they need to be reinforced sensibly. In (b) the problem is a total lack of enforcement of controls.

Easy marks. Hopefully in (b) (ii) you picked up on the failings in management – a rulebook that is never opened, permissive local management and central management ignoring the problem previously, which are highlighted in the preseen.

Examiner's comments. Some parts of this question were answered well. (b) (i) was however done poorly, with students failing to fulfil the question requirements. (c) demonstrated again that many students do not have an adequate understanding of financial risk and need to revise this topic better. A number of answers just made the same comments three times.

(a)

Top tips. The obvious risk in (a) (i) is libel but the preseen makes clear that M's brand values are associated with quality news, which makes bad content an even more serious problem.

Note in (a) (ii) that you cannot recommend that all posts be verified as the unseen rules this out. However we believe it would be legitimate for M to keep a particularly close watch on certain stories because of the high risks attached. The unseen scenario suggests that M already has some good controls in place, so enhancing those controls is a sound strategy. You can bring in your own experience here, as you may well have seen websites with notices attached to posts saying report content as offensive. Emphasising the responsibility of users, stating that M will take action and publicly doing so if necessary will help. M must also address the possibility that its controls can be bypassed. Thus you would obtain some marks for discussing sensible password controls.

(i)   Reliability

M's reputation for producing reliable news may be **threatened by allowing subscribers** to post on its site. What subscribers post will **not be subject to the same checks** that a story in M's newspapers would be subject. Subscribers may be more inclined to post doubtful material on M's website than on personal blogs, because of the wider readership it will have. If what is posted is untrue, M will suffer by association, particularly if it is publicly known that M does not carry out checks on the contents of its site. This may affect not just the reputation of the Sunday newspaper, but all publications within M's group.

Values

The **brand values** M promotes of quality reporting and information may be **undermined** by comments on the website that some find offensive, even though the comments are legal. Comments may not be of high quality. The views may be based on dubious sources of evidence or they may be badly written. However there are upsides to allowing controversial comments to be posted. Some newspapers promote their comment facility as **encouraging free speech** with views that do not reflect the position of the papers being allowed.

Libel

M may be subject to the risk of **damages** for libel. M may become liable once the post is made on the site. As posts are not validated in advance, in theory subscribers could post very serious libels. M will remain liable even if it subsequently removes the post, although this may mitigate damages. Those libelled are **more likely to sue M** rather than the person who posted the libel, because they will reckon that M has greater financial resources. They may also be more inclined to sue M in order to deter M from publicising further libels.

Advertising and readership

Some advertisers may not be willing to associate with a site with **doubtful material**. A major reason for the closure of the UK newspaper the News of the World was that advertisers no longer wished to advertise in it. Some readers may **stop accessing it** if they find the content offensive.

Equally, however, if M's site is known to contain strong content, it may **increase the number of readers who access it**.

Competitive advantage

Competitors may **publicise problems that M has**, in order to persuade readers to switch to their papers. For example fans of pop singer J may be angry about the **comments made about her** and may stop buying M's papers as a result. The Sun newspaper, for example, lost a large proportion of its sales in Liverpool after its coverage of the 1989 Hillsborough disaster.

(ii) ## Selective monitoring of stories

Although M considers that editing all posts would be prohibitively expensive, it may be that it has to **monitor posts on particularly controversial stories** where there is a very high risk of seriously offensive or inaccurate posts being made. An example of a high risk story would be the recent paedophilia scandal in the UK associated with the disc jockey Jimmy Savile. M would face massive damages if celebrities were falsely accused on such a story. Possibly M could introduce a time delay, so that posts do not go straight on to the site live, allowing M the scope to block them.

Tightening terms and conditions

M should continue to insist that subscribers **agree to terms and conditions**. As part of this, M should also require subscribers to agree to **take responsibility not only for anything that they post** but **also anything posted from their log-in account**. This will prevent subscribers from claiming that they are not accountable as someone else has used their account.

Monitoring of users

M must have full contact details for all subscribers. M must make it clear that it will **close the account** of anyone who is found to post **offensive or libellous content**. It should block anyone from using the same email address to open a new account. It should also **trace the user back to the credit card details they have supplied** and prevent anyone with that credit card number from opening a new account. M may also **seek compensation** from subscribers whose malicious or reckless posts have resulted in bad publicity or other damage for M.

Reporting of doubtful material

M can attach a facility to all posts, allowing readers of the post to **report the post** if they believe that the post contravenes M's rules. The post can then be **removed automatically** until M's staff have checked it. The problem with this facility is that it may be used excessively, with readers reporting content with which they disagree.

Access controls

M could tighten controls over the security of accounts, to ensure that they cannot be accessed by illegitimate users. M should **not allow the software to remember passwords** so that users do not have to enter them. M should require **passwords to be changed** after a certain length of time. Passwords should consist of a **combination of numbers and upper and lower case letters** to make them less easy to guess. Users should only be allowed to **enter incorrect passwords a certain number of times** before access to the account is halted and the user has to re-register.

Publicity

M can make it clear on its website and when it is challenged that it **requires subscribers to adhere to rules** that prohibit inaccurate or offensive comment and that it will **take appropriate action against subscribers** who contravene its rules. It could also make clear that it will **remove any content that contravenes its rules** as soon as it is identified.

(b)

> **Top tips**. In (b) the main issues are the difficulties of enforcing a stricter policy when much expenditure is discretionary and previous policies have not been enforced. Bringing in the control environment emphasises the importance of firm, but flexible, management. (ii) covers what happens if management is ineffective. (iii) is partly about internal audit but also seeing internal audit work in the wider context of tightening up on expenses and the problems of doing so.

(i) Control environment

The control environment is the **overall attitude, awareness and actions** of directors and management regarding the importance of internal controls. It includes management style and corporate culture and values.

Management style

Management style is particularly important at M because issues such as expense claims are not **closely regulated by rules.** Therefore the onus is on management to be prepared to set fair boundaries and to stand up to staff, to say specific expenditure is not acceptable. If management does not do this, there is a risk of an **anything goes corporate culture.**

Management judgement

At the same time managers cannot be completely inflexible and have to make allowances **for the story and the contacts being established.** If, for example, the paper is seeking the views of a top businessman, it may be necessary to entertain him at an expensive restaurant. However a manager might question other contacts being taken there, on the grounds that it is not necessary to obtain the story.

(ii) Confusion over standards

Journalists may have been unclear as to **what expenses** they could claim. The policies that are in place have never been effectively enforced. Instead if journalists' expense claims have always been allowed, they may have assumed that in practice it will be fine to incur **whatever expenses are necessary to obtain a good story** and management will ignore any questionable expenses. Possibly also they have regarded the generous hotel and travel arrangements as a **perk of their job.**

Weaknesses in local management

Journalists' views on what constitute acceptable expenses have been unchallenged by local management. Local management acknowledge that journalists' attitudes have changed, but managers have **done nothing to curb journalists' increased expectations**. Instead editors' top priority has been **keeping journalists happy**. Editors may be motivated in this by a feeling that they will primarily judged by the quality of stories in their newspapers, and it is worth **paying greater expenses to gain better stories and keep good journalists loyal.**

Weaknesses in central management

The increase in expenses claimed has been apparent to M's central management for some time. However **no action has been taken to enforce the rule book or budgets.** The internal audit work being planned is belated. It also appears that central management has **not given any support to editors** who may have tried to enforce a tighter expenses policy. The delay will make it more difficult to enforce a stricter policy.

(iii) Problems with staff being audited

Staff and managers may be very resentful at being audited, feeling that the expenditure is necessary to do their job. Internal audit may be drawn into a lot of **lengthy and heated discussions** and the audit may not therefore be carried out efficiently. Internal audit may be able to reduce this problem by allowing staff to explain the reasons for their expenditure, but may still face a lack of co-operation from staff.

Stifling of initiative

Auditor visits together with tougher attitudes from management may result in expenditure being reduced. However the system could become **too bureaucratic.** If rules about approving expenditure

in advance are enforced and policed by internal auditors, **opportunities may be lost** if approval cannot be obtained quickly. Staff may become fearful of incurring expenditure which may later be challenged and therefore miss the chance to pursue a good story.

Auditor judgements

Internal auditors may find it difficult to make judgements about what expenditure is **unacceptable or doubtful**, because of **lack of effective guidelines and limitations on the evidence.** The expense claims they review, for example, may show that a claim for meals in an expensive restaurant is supported by valid documentation (that the journalist and contact did go there) but not why that restaurant was chosen (whether it was valid for the journalist to incur that expenditure). Auditors may also have problems judging whether the explanation given for certain expenditure **justifies its level.** For example, buying the latest equipment may make journalists more efficient but does it justify the amount of expenditure made?

Diversion away from other activities

Although the increase in expenses is legitimately a matter of concern, M may be facing more significant risks in other areas. If **internal audit resources** are **limited**, auditors may spend too much time on expenses and not enough on other areas. Possibly a one-off drive to bring journalists' expenses under control may result in a reduction to more acceptable levels and mean that there is less need for regular internal auditor review.

(c)

Top tips. In (c) CIMA's guidance points out that none of the methods are likely to be totally effective. For the UK deal, you have to discuss not only the removal of the exchange risk but also the fact that the deal is a fixed price deal. This means that the risk will be borne by the manufacturer and M will therefore have to compensate the manufacturer by paying a higher fixed price. You can also obtain marks for bringing in from the preseen the issue that the current supplier provides a good service and changing supplier may be a change for the worse. The US$ bank account arrangement is a longer-term arrangement than other money market hedges that you have seen hedging specific transactions. As such, it has to be judged on the interest obtained over time and the longer-term economic risk. If M accepts the risk, it will have control of the amount of extra costs it bears before putting its prices up. What is unpredictable is the effect on demand of a price increase. Again material in the preseen is relevant, that some directors believe that the market for newspapers is declining, and a price increase may hasten the decline.

Switch to UK supplier

Costs

Costs of raw materials

The paper may be more expensive that it would be if M continued to use the **Scandinavian supplier,** which currently supplies M at a **relatively cheap price.** As, however, there are three or four suppliers in competition for M's business, M may be able to negotiate a good deal.

Pricing of deal

The fixed price deal will however have an additional cost element built into it. The supplier will be aware that it will be bearing risks of adverse price movements and not be able to pass these on to M for the period of the deal. The pricing will therefore include a **premium** to compensate the supplier for this risk.

Risks

Exchange risk

Dealing with a UK supplier removes an element of exchange risk for M. It might however increase exchange risk in one way, if **payments in the Scandinavian currency matched receipts in the same currency.** However we are not told that M makes significant sales to the Scandinavian country.

Commodity price risk

The fixed price deal will also **remove uncertainty surrounding commodity price movements** and make cost budgeting by M more straightforward. However M will **not be able to benefit from favourable price movements**.

<u>Reliability of supplier</u>

The supplier M chooses may be **less reliable** than the Scandinavian supplier that M has previously used. The **level of product quality** may be **lower** than its current supplier provides. If the fixed price deal with M is a particularly large one and the supplier's costs significantly increase, this may **threaten the supplier's viability**.

<u>Invest in US$</u>

<u>Costs</u>

<u>Costs of loan</u>

As well as the interest that it has to pay, M will incur other costs if it takes out a loan and makes an investment. It may incur **set-up costs** for both accounts and also **costs for transferring the money to the USA**.

<u>Rate of interest received</u>

The interest received on the US bank account will not completely exceed the increased cost of borrowing. There will therefore be an **opportunity cost** of the return foregone through tying up the money in the bank account rather than making an investment with a better return. Holding a large amount in a hedging account may appear to investors to be a poor use of funds.

<u>Risks</u>

<u>Translation risk</u>

The arrangement will decrease translation risk by **matching the interest on the US bank account with the costs of supply**.

<u>Economic risk</u>

M will be still be subject to economic risk if it continues to use the Scandinavian supplier and its competitors have dealt with exchange risks in other, more effective, ways and hence have lower costs. It can reduce economic risk by **using the monies in the $ investment account to pay for the paper**, but a lower balance in the investment account may mean that M receives a **lower rate of interest**. Longer-term hedging by this method will eventually exhaust the money in the investment account.

<u>Take the risk</u>

<u>Costs</u>

<u>Costs of supply</u>

The costs of the paper may be **lower** over the three year period than if M enters a fixed price deal on less favourable terms.

<u>Costs of changing supplier</u>

M will **not incur the costs of establishing a relationship with a new supplier**.

<u>Risks</u>

<u>Exchange risk</u>

M may **suffer losses through adverse movements in the $.** However it will also **benefit from favourable movements in the $**.

<u>Commodity price increase</u>

M could also be exposed to **increases in the cost of paper**, although again there is an upside risk that paper costs will fall.

<u>Risks of price increase</u>

If M has to increase its cover price as a result of adverse movements in the exchange rate, the impact on demand for its papers will depend on the **price elasticity**. If **competitors** are facing similar supply pressures, the impact on M may be limited if competitors have to put their prices up as well. However price increases may also have the effect of reducing overall the number of customers who pay for newspapers. More customers may obtain news from free papers, free websites or television news programmes.

73 M Newspapers 2

Text references. Chapters 1, 4, 10 and 14.

Top tips. If you had taken this exam and done preparation work on the preseen, this should have helped significantly, as the preseen clearly flagged bribery and plagiarism as possible issues. Knowledge of how the problems at News International in the UK arose and were dealt with is also a significant help in answering this question.

Easy marks. The strategies for dealing with political risk in (c) (i) are more textbook knowledge than some of the other parts of this question (although you still have to choose relevant strategies).

Examiner's comments. (a) (i) was done well but (a) (ii) was done badly: '...many candidates appeared to think that bribery was fine in most circumstances and even came up with helpful suggestions of how it could be carried out in a better way. This was a bit disturbing.'(!!)

(b) (i) was done well, but (b) (ii) poorly. Removing access to the internet would hinder journalists and was unenforceable (journalists need not be at M's premises to use the Internet.) Both parts of (c) were done well, although many answers suggested having a government official on the board, which would change the balance of the board.

(a)

Top tips. (a) (i) follows other recent questions in asking you to discuss ethical issues using CIMA's ethical framework. Do **not** simply explain the 5 categories - this is an approach that students have taken in other questions and have scored zero marks. The correct approach is to apply the relevant categories – integrity (bribery is never fair), objectivity (clear giving into intimidation) and professional conduct (breaking UK law). The other trap in this question is to focus solely on the ethical implications and neglect the commercial implications.

You will score no marks in (a) (ii) if you recommended continuing to pay the bribe. M must also take effective action to improve the ethical environment at N. It may not be necessary for M to reveal that bribery has occurred, but it should be prepared to do so if it seems impossible or undesirable to keep the story secret.

(i) Ethical implications

Integrity

Bribery, even if it is widely practised, shows a lack of integrity. It **breaches the principle of fair dealing.** Newspapers in N's country are only allowed to carry on legitimate commercial activity if they pay bribes. It also breaches the **principle of truthfulness and transparency** that underpin good corporate governance and help M's board to manage M's investment in N effectively**.** M's directors only found out about the bribe when they investigated the regular payment. N's directors did not disclose it first.

Objectivity

N has clearly been **intimidated by threats from the official** to pay the bribe. It is clearly in **N's self-interest** to continue to pay it. Revelation that N has paid the bribe could also damage N. N may therefore also face pressures to take whatever actions are necessary to keep the scandal confidential. This raises questions of whether N would wish to upset the government in any way and whether it would ever criticise, or expose bad behaviour by, the government.

Professional behaviour

Although the law on bribery in N's country may be unclear, M is subject to UK legislation. Bribery of a foreign official is specifically mentioned as an offence in the UK Bribery Act. A company in M's group has clearly breached the law. M would probably also be in breach of the UK newspaper industry's **code of practice.** It would also **breach CIMA's Code of Ethics.**

Commercial implications

Impact on customers and advertisers

N's newspapers could **lose many readers** if the bribery scandal was revealed. There is **public distaste in N's country** for anyone, or any organisation, associated with bribery. The effect on N may also be more serious if readers bought its papers believing **promises of unbiased news.** They may well switch to competitors whom they feel they can trust. Similarly advertisers may **withdraw advertising** from N's papers. A bribery scandal will also **affect the whole group's reputation for reliable reporting.** Readers in other countries may no longer trust what M's papers are telling them.

Cost of bribe

The bribe is for a large amount and further bribes could be for higher amounts. Possibly the money could be saved if the official was **reported to the local authorities.**

Impact on shareholders

Some of M's shareholders may not wish to be associated with a newspaper group that is involved in bribery and may seek to sell their shares. If one of the larger shareholders decides to sell its shares, it could lead to a **significant fall in M's share price.**

(ii) Ceasing to pay bribe

M's management must **instruct N's board to stop paying the bribe immediately.** The bribe appears to be a clear breach of UK law and M will be liable to legal penalties if it continues.

Communication with official

N needs to tell the official that it will no longer pay the bribe. If the official threatens N with closure, N should firstly report the threat to the official's superiors. If the superiors do not take action, because they are also involved in the scandal, N should **threaten to report the scandal publicly**. Revealing the scandal could damage the government at a time when it faces a serious risk of losing office. The threat may therefore mean that the pressure on N is lifted.

Restructuring N's board

M's board has ultimate responsibility for the group. It may legitimately feel that it can no longer trust N's board because it failed to disclose the bribe. M's board may also want to replace N's directors because it feels that they lack credibility in implementing anti-bribery procedures. M's board may thus remove some or all of N's board, replacing them either with **UK executives or local executives recruited from outside who have no links with the bribery scandal.**

Review bribery and corruption policy

The Human Resources Director should review the existing policy to see whether it clearly states what **constitutes bribery and corruption**. All group staff should **sign their acceptance of a revised policy**, to emphasise they understand that M requires its staff to be honest and not corrupt. M's board should also remind all group staff that there will be **zero tolerance** of bribery, and managers and staff found guilty in future will be dismissed.

Whistleblowing channels

M's board should make it clear to staff in all group companies that they should **report any suspicious behaviour** that they see and their careers will not be damaged by doing so. Management should emphasise that staff can contact the board or audit committee.

(b)

Top tips. (b) (i) involves similar considerations to (a), but here you need to discuss in more detail the various ways in which the story could develop. It's important that M takes effective action against the journalist but the need for publicising the issue can be debated. The demand to include the apology on the website may be seen as going too far.

(b) (ii) is perhaps the most difficult part of the question to generate marks. If you couldn't get much beyond using software to search for similar stories, don't worry too much. The exam may include one or two question parts for which most students struggle to generate ideas. The important thing is to put down whatever ideas you can think of and not worry if you think they are only worth, say, 3 out of 9 marks – you should believe that you can make those marks up elsewhere in the paper. Sometimes bringing in your own experience can help too. Many employers insist that staff complete an on-line ethics module, for example. Note also that the question asked about fabrication (making stories up) as well as plagiarism, and you would have limited your mark-scoring opportunities if you failed to discuss this issue as well.

(i) <u>Damage to reputation</u>

If the deception is revealed publicly, either by M or by the South American embassy or newspaper, N and the rest of the M group are likely to suffer **damage to their reputation.** As with revelation of the bribery scandal, there is a risk of losing customers, advertisers or shareholders. The main threat lies from the article being **untrue,** featuring an imaginary charity. How serious a single incident of plagiarism would be taken is debatable. Plagiarism is already **widespread in N's country** and **legal action may not be successful.** Even in the UK, the magazine Private Eye regularly highlights apparent instances of plagiarism in newspapers, but often it does not appear to have much impact on the newspapers concerned.

<u>General impression of M</u>

If the full details of what the journalist had done emerged, it might be difficult to claim the actions were those of a single 'rogue reporter.' The journalist's experiences seem to **demonstrate problems with the overall culture** at N, with journalists being pressurised to provide stories no matter whether they are plagiarised or inaccurate. Some important stakeholders may also believe that N's **internal controls are insufficient,** as they did not identify the problems with the story. Also if the story became public at the same time that the bribes N paid were revealed, both could combine to give the impression of very serious problems with the ethical environment at N and in the M group generally.

<u>Refusing to publish an apology</u>

If M's board believes that it is inevitable or probable that the story will be publicised, it will need to assess which method of publicity will result in the **least damage to the group's reputation.** Refusing to publish an apology may not have any consequences, as the South American newspaper may decide not to publicise what happened. Publication in the South American newspaper by itself may have limited impact as M does not operate on that continent. However there is the risk that international media sources will pick up the story. If they do, M may face serious adverse publicity for not only failing to admit its shortcomings, but also failing to make the donation to the charity.

<u>Publication of apology</u>

If on the other hand N complies fully with the demand of the South American newspaper, the **impact of the damage to its reputation** could be **maximised.** If the statement remains on N's website, it will act as a continuing reminder to readers of poor practice at N. N's competitors are likely to **publicise the deception.** N's advertisers may be less willing to associate with a company that admits poor practice and N could lose substantial advertising income as a result.

<u>Implications of paying a donation</u>

If the journalist is not the only member of staff guilty of deception or plagiarism, N may face similar demands for reparations when other instances are identified. If N pays a donation to the charity, it could set a **precedent.** N could be asked for further sums, and could incur significant costs if it felt obliged to pay them.

Possible strategy

N could attempt to minimise the damage by disciplining the employee or dismissing him but agreeing not to make the reasons public. It could then **negotiate with the South American newspaper** on the basis that it has taken action against the employee and will strengthen its controls to prevent a repeat. N might say that it will make the donation to the charity, but does not therefore need to publicise the case. If the story then leaked out, it could appear that N was guilty of a cover-up, but the damage to its reputation could be minimised if it was known to have taken action and had paid the donation. Alternatively N could offer to pay the donation and publish the apology in the print newspaper but not on the website.

(ii) Evidence gathering

M could insist that all evidence that journalists obtain should be **filed electronically**. Interviews should be recorded digitally and paper documents scanned. Journalists should be made aware that the evidence could be reviewed by management and that stories will not be published without supporting evidence.

Checking staff's work for plagiarism

Managers could carry out **random checks** on stories written by staff. They could enter parts of the article or technical terms into Search engines and see if search results include similar articles. They could also check whole editions using web-based tools that enable comparison against databases containing stories from many different outlets. These tools can be used to **produce an originality report** on stories and any stories with a low originality report should be investigated.

Checking staff's work for fabrication

Stories could also be **checked electronically for fabrications.** Stories could be selected on a risk basis, for example a report of Parliamentary proceedings is less likely to be fabricated than celebrity gossip. Managers could compare stories in N's newspapers with coverage elsewhere of the same subject and investigate discrepancies, for example celebrities appearing to be in two different places at once.

Monitoring coverage of the M group

M's management in the UK should introduce regular central monitoring of all stories in other papers and elsewhere about the group. They should **investigate allegations of plagiarism or fabrication** in other media outlets.

On-line ethics training

M could require all group staff to **undertake on-line ethics training**. It should be easier to ensure that all staff undertake the training if it is done on-line. It will also mean that staff receive consistent messages across the whole group. The ethical training should include situations such as **bribery and plagiarism.** The training should be **validated** by a test at the end, in which staff have to score a certain percentage to pass, or receive additional training.

Monitoring of workloads

The trainee claimed that he plagiarised the article because he was under pressure to **complete several assignments.** Electronic diaries could be used to monitor the workloads of staff, highlighting for possible investigation staff who are **producing a large number of stories** for papers or who are **working very long hours.**

(c)

Top tips. (c) (i) may have been a pleasant surprise for some students who took this paper. It is in line with the examiner's comment that Question 1 will always include financial risk, but it's a reminder that the financial risk section of the syllabus includes political risk. Note that the question doesn't allow you to discuss selling the stake to J but you can discuss other changes in ownership. Negotiations with the opposition party should be possible, although N has to be careful about maintaining objectivity.

(c) (ii) requires a discussion, so here that means points for and against the option of selling to J. Clearly just saying reject the offer because it is too low will not get you six marks – you have to consider the future for N and how different scenarios could affect its value.

(i) Negotiation with local media groups

M's board should ascertain whether any newspaper groups in N's country would be interested in buying N. If N was **owned by a local group,** that would remove the threat of it being nationalised. M may be able to sell N for a fair value to a local buyer and this may be the best way to deal with the investment.

Negotiations with opposition party

M could enter into negotiations with the opposition party before the election takes place. The opposition party may be willing to talk if it believes that N's papers will give it **better coverage** as a result, although M must be very careful not to make any promises that it will clearly support the opposition party if it removes the threat of nationalisation. N could also provide other benefits, for example increased investment and jobs. M could make clear during the negotiations that if the opposition party continues to threaten nationalisation, it might close N immediately if the party wins power. The opposition party may not wish to suffer unpopularity resulting from N's employees losing their jobs and the public no longer being able to buy N's newspapers. It may also be particularly sensitive to claims that it is interfering with the media.

Ownership structure

M may be able to **restructure its investment** in N in a way that will remove the threat of nationalisation. A 50-50 joint venture with a local company might be acceptable to the new government. However M would have to ensure that the changes in practices that the bribery and plagiarism scandals indicate are necessary are enforced. It could still be liable under UK law if N was involved in bribery again, for example. In the longer-term M may **plan to transfer full ownership of N** to a local investor. This should make it more likely that M obtains a satisfactory return from its investment in N.

Production strategies

If negotiations with the opposition party were not possible and M still wished to continue to operate in N's country, it might consider alternative strategies. It could be possible to relocate N so that it was **based in a neighbouring country and transfer the production facilities there**, while still employing journalists based in N's country. This is more likely to be a feasible strategy if the local papers N publishes are weekly rather than daily and there is less deadline pressure.

Financing strategies

The M group will need to repay the loan of £83 million in 2013. It may be advantageous to **undertake a refinancing now**, repaying this loan and taking out a loan from a bank in N's country. The terms may be more favourable and the risk of adverse exchange rate movements may be small. If the government did then nationalise N, M would be able to **default on its loan**. This might make nationalisation less appealing to a new government as a local financial institution would suffer.

(ii) Risks of accepting J's offer

Monetary loss

Accepting J's offer would result in a **clear and certain monetary loss on investment** for M, although it would **guarantee that M realises something from its investment**. This would have an adverse effect on profits and probably dividends for the year. It could well depress M's share price and lead to M's board coming under more pressure from the institutional shareholders. The limited revenues that M will receive from the deal may be **insufficient to fund a significant investment** elsewhere to replace the investment in N.

Other costs of accepting J's offer

M's market price may also be depressed by the **limitation in its opportunities for development**. M would no longer receive profits from newspaper sales in N. It would also **lose valuable revenues** from the advertising on the website. M may also lose other opportunities of developing business in N, for example transferring production of the pan-European newspaper there to take advantage of the lower production costs.

Risks of refusing J's offer

If M continues to operate in N, even if J does his best, he may not be able to protect N from nationalisation. Nationalisation may be on less generous terms than those offered by J and M would therefore make a **bigger loss on the investment.** The value of a continuing investment could also be jeopardised by further revelations about bribery, plagiarism or other misconduct. M may be forced to close its operations in N to limit the damage to the value of reputation of the whole group, just as News International closed the News of the World newspaper in the UK because of the scandals surrounding it.

Change in investment

M could further discuss with J whether the **ownership arrangements** could be **changed** to remove the threat of nationalisation from N. A sale of some of M's stake to J could mitigate losses and remove the threat of nationalisation.

J's credibility

J's attempt to buy the equity means that his future advice to M can no longer be regarded as **objective**, because of his financial interest.

74 F1

> **Text references**. Chapters 1, 2, 6, 8 and 14.
>
> **Top tips**. A major new investment in another continent is a scenario that could come up in any of the 3 strategic level exams.
>
> **Easy marks**. (c) should have been a fairly straightforward systems development question, though it was misinterpreted by many candidates.
>
> **Examiner's comments**. Students often appeared not to have read the question properly, and this particularly undermined answers to (a) and (c). In (a) many students failed to mention CIMA's risk management cycle, although the stages were given in the scenario. Some answers discussed other risks and were not rewarded for this.
>
> (b) and (d) were generally answered well.

Marking scheme

			Marks
(a)	(i)	1 mark per point, up to 4 marks per issues discussed under each heading in the scenario. Points should relate to links between CSR stance and risk to reputation max	8
	(ii)	Up to 2 marks per issue. Issues could include: Publicity about impact on air travel Publicity about contribution to Africa Publicity about advantages for food quality Actions taken to reward/support staff in Africa Actions taken to inform/help UK staff max	8
(b)		1 mark per issue discussed. Max 5 marks under any single heading in question requirement max	10
(c)		1 mark per issue discussed. Max marks under each header: System planning/analysis/design – 5 marks Training and documentation – 2 marks Testing and implementation – 6 marks max	12
(d)		1 mark per issue discussed. Max 8 marks for financial risks, 8 marks for non-financial risks max	12
			50

(a)

> **Top tips.** (a) emphasises the need for you to know the stages of CIMA's risk management cycle. Don't assume you will be given them in the scenario, as you were helpfully in this question.
>
> The emphasis on CSR in the scenario appears to have been designed to get you to focus on reputation issues linked to CSR. Discussion of other potential threats to reputation, for example health issues, was not required. It is difficult not to repeat yourself when answering (a) (i). The way to differentiate your points is for the first stage to emphasise the links with strategic objectives, for the assessment stage to indicate how large the risks are and for the risk response stage to take an overview, mentioning costs, but not going into detail as you do that in (a) (ii).
>
> The main points in (a) (ii) are to emphasise the need for a structured approach to publicising the positive CSR moves that F is taking. The publicity needs to be justified by action, to avoid accusations of hypocrisy.

(i)   <u>Risks</u>

The main risks F faces relate to its revenues, its costs, its environmental performance and its reputation.

<u>Set goals</u>

The board has made the investment in order to **enhance F's social responsibility performance.** A clear upside risk is that the factory will reduce F's use of air travel. F needs to implement new measures, as the steps it has taken so far were insufficient to meet its targets in 2010.

The investment in the factory is also intended to enhance profitability and efficiency. However this has the downside risk of threatening F's reputation because of the possibility of redundancies in the UK.

<u>Identify risk areas</u>

If F's reputation as an eco-friendly company improves as a result of the investment, it could have the **upside risk of increased sales to environmentally-concerned consumers.** There could also be a **decreased risk of criticism** from environmental groups because F is **less reliant on air travel.**

However there is also an **increased risk of criticism** from environmental groups because F will be **selling fruit and vegetables out of season.**

F is also at risk of being criticised for taking **jobs away from its main market** and relocating them to a **lower-wage economy.**

Understand and assess scale of risk

Given current environmental concerns, F is at risk of suffering bad publicity from environmental groups for **operating an unsustainable business model** that is reliant on selling vegetables out of season. They may ignore the reduction in air travel, particularly if F still fails to publish its annual environmental report externally. Whether these criticisms translate into significantly reduced sales to consumers is questionable.

F may also be particularly at risk of being **criticised for exploiting labour in Africa** because of the previous bad publicity about its treatment of its African suppliers. This may be more likely to result in a **consumer boycott and reduced sales,** particularly when combined with the adverse publicity about the UK redundancies.

Develop risk response strategy

F's board appears to be well aware of the need for a **strategy to manage its environmental impact,** as demonstrated by the appointment of the Environmental Effects Manager.

It my now need to consider the need for a **strategy of publicity campaigns** for its CSR policies. Generating this publicity should not cost very much. F may however face a risk of **increased costs,** depending on the actions that are required to justify the publicity.

(ii)   Publicity strategy

F needs to implement a clear publicity strategy that explains clearly its CSR objectives. F should stress publicly that the reasons for establishing the factory in West Africa are to act in a more **socially responsible manner by reducing air travel.** It should also publicise the jobs it is creating and the college courses that are **going to be established,** to demonstrate that it is investing in the African economy. Its CSR stance will be enhanced by greater **transparency,** including publication of its environmental report within its annual report.

Informing UK staff

F needs to keep its UK staff **informed of what is happening** because of the uncertainty over their jobs. In particular it needs to communicate well with the skilled staff who are unhappy about the possibility of working in Africa. It also needs to have a strategy for retaining skilled staff whose expertise F particularly needs. This could include greater financial incentives and limiting the period the staff spend on the 4 weeks-2 weeks regime. F should also make every effort to find alternative employment for UK staff whose jobs will disappear as a result of the switch to Africa, by giving them preference when internal vacancies are advertised.

Employment conditions in Africa

F may be able to **limit the criticism of exploiting labour in Africa** by paying labour of all classes **more than the local market rate.** It should also ensure that other labour conditions, such as hours of work, are generous compared with those offered by other local employers.

Healthy products

To counter the bad publicity from selling out-of-season vegetables, F should **advertise the health benefits of these products.** It should also stress the environmental advantages of freezing the goods where they are harvested.

(b)

Top tips. The examiner hoped that students would draw on their own experiences of studying for CIMA exams when answering this question. It seems that many did and therefore scored highly. The answer needs to discuss the visible indications that the service providers (the colleges) are delivering an adequate service. It also needs to consider the methods by which F can operate some control over the providers.

Governance

F needs to obtain evidence that colleges' management is committed to supporting and promoting the courses. This includes a **strategy of publicising the courses** and a guarantee that courses will not be cancelled because of low numbers and other reasons.

F also needs to establish what arrangements management has in place for **monitoring the quality of courses**. This includes **review of tutor teaching and of the quality of courses notes and support facilities**. The colleges should seek feedback from students, as well as responding appropriately to feedback from F itself.

Staffing

F should obtain evidence from colleges that they will be using tutors with **relevant qualifications and experience** in **the subjects** in the programme. The tutors should be undertaking **continuous professional education.**

F should establish what **contingency arrangements** colleges have if staff go absent or leave suddenly.

F should also confirm with colleges what the staff-student ratio will be on courses and also how much teaching staff are expected to do. F would want to ensure that staff have **sufficient contact and support time with students.**

Support facilities

F should find out what colleges have in terms of **libraries and IT facilities**. F should assess whether these are **adequate to support the planned course programme.**

F should ascertain whether libraries have **purchased up-to-date copies of textbooks,** and whether colleges **plan to upgrade IT facilities**.

Course content

The syllabus needs to be clearly **defined by the college** and publicised to students. The syllabus should include **clear learning objectives** that are related to the requirements that F has. This should be supported by a **detailed learning guide** that enables students to understand what they are expected to know. The course material that students are given should be **clearly linked to the syllabus.**

The exams students sit during the course should **fairly and appropriately test** the knowledge and skills that students have. F's staff should be **involved in the oversight of the exams**. The quality of exams should be **verified by independent external examiners,** who should be academics also with industry experience that is relevant for F's needs.

Placements at the factory or a sandwich structure should be built into the course design for all students, to enable them to experience the practical application of what they are studying. This would also enable F to assess whether students have sufficient knowledge and application skills, and feedback shortcomings to the colleges.

(c)

> **Top tips**. (c) should have been a fairly straightforward question about the development and implementation of an important new IT system. Following the main stages of the systems development lifecycle should have meant you scored heavily.
>
> The examiner's comments indicated however that many students discussed physical inventory management, which was not what the question asked. Though you could relevantly make some mention of the problems with the existing system, the main focus of the answer should have been on the issues associated with the upgrade.

Resource planning

The development of the new system needs to be **timetabled carefully, with deadlines** that match F's requirements as the factory opens. Delays and consequent problems with inventory management could be expensive.

F will also need to ensure that staff with **sufficient IT expertise** are used to design the systems, write the software, and be involved in the testing process.

Analysis

F should ensure that the new system is based on an **analysis of the information F will need in the future**, taking into account the views of management, the accounts team and operational staff. The analysis should include assessment of the training and documentation that will be required for the new system.

The analysis should also take into account the **problems** F has had with its inventory control and information technology. As well as being influenced by the new requirements, will the systems changes attempt to remedy the other current problems with inventory management?

Design and specification

The system design will need to specify the **inputs and outputs required for the system** and incorporate the new basis for inventory management. It will **need to make clear what changes are needed from the old system**.

Management and internal audit should review and sign off the specification, confirming in particular whether it appears to **meet the enhanced information needs** of the business.

Testing

The new system should be **tested by IT staff** and also **operational management and staff** based both in the UK and in Africa. These tests need to obtain evidence that the system will be a sufficient basis for the new approach to inventory management.

Internal audit should also be involved in the testing process. Internal auditors should assess whether the system can generate a sufficient **audit trail** for their needs. They should also review the results of other tests, and whether the development process has taken into account problems found.

Training and documentation

Full user documentation should be prepared for the new system. The documentation should highlight changes from the previous system and should act as a basis for future changes that are required in the system.

A **training programme** for all sales and logistics staff that have to use the system should be timetabled for before the system is implemented. This is likely to involve UK IT staff having to go out to Africa for a period to train local staff.

Implementation

A **direct changeover** to the new system would be risky for F given its previous IT problems, but may be the only practical solution. Parallel running of the old and revised system would be difficult because the two systems do not completely match.

F should conduct a **post-implementation review**, focusing on the number of errors found and whether managers and staff find the information the revised system produces to be for sufficient for their needs. This review may form the basis of a more limited subsequent update of the system.

(d)

> **Top tips**. Note the point about the interest payments matching UK revenues.

UK loan risks

Currency risks

Impact of matching

The interest payments will be in £, **matching the revenues in £** earned from food sales. This will avoid the currency risks arising from the interest payments being in a foreign currency.

Operating risks

F will however be vulnerable to currency risk on the **operating payments** it makes in the local currency, such as staff wages. If the West African currency strengthens, these costs will become more expensive.

Non-currency risks

Borrowing limits

At 31 December 2010 F was close to the limit of its revolving credit facility. Taking out the loan to build the African factory may come close to exhausting the facility and mean that there is a risk that **loan finance will not be available for profitable opportunities** in the UK.

Lack of collateral

F may also face a risk that its UK borrowing opportunities will be restricted by the **reduction in available collateral** resulting from the pledging of UK assets to secure the loan for the factory.

Realisation of security

If the factory is appropriated or destroyed, F will be at risk of **having to realise the UK assets** on which the loan is secured to repay the loan.

Foreign loan

Currency risks

Exchange risks and interest rate

If the currency of the West African country **strengthens against the £,** the interest payments in that currency will become more expensive, as well as the operating expenses (discussed above).

Translation risk

The loan from the government will have to be translated in F's annual accounts at the year-end exchange rate. However the cost of the factory will be translated at the exchange rate on the date of the expenditure on the factory. If the currency of the West African country strengthens against the £, the cost of the factory will no longer be fully offset against the loan. There will be a **translation loss** shown in the accounts, which may concern shareholders.

Non-currency risks

Change in loan terms

A change in government or a change in the policy of the current government may result in **higher interest costs** if the government can charge interest at a floating rate. However the risk of this happening may be limited if the government feels that it would threaten F's servicing of the loan.

Collateral

The pledging of the factory in Africa is **unlikely to concern UK lenders**. Therefore F will face a low risk that its UK borrowing opportunities will be limited by pledging the factory to the government.

Appropriation of factory

The risk of appropriation of the factory by the current or a future government may be **decreased by the loan** that F has with the government. Appropriation would put the repayment of the loan in jeopardy. The government may also be less likely to misappropriate the factory if it threatens local jobs and the local economy.

Interference by government

Again F may only face a **low risk of excessive government intervention** in other ways (through burdensome regulation) if the government fears it will mean F pulling out of the country and the loan being jeopardised.

75   F2

Text references. Chapters 1, 2, 4, 6, 8, 15.

Top tips. The answer to (a) (i) is structured around firstly the press coverage that F has already has, and widens out to consider what will happen if other adverse events occur (regulatory or legal action), and what will happen if sales to other products are affected. The idea that all publicity about the bacteria is bad publicity underlies most of (a) (ii).

(b) is a fairly standard (and predictable given the preseen) question about protection of knowledge assets, but note there is a question about how valuable the asset actually is.

(c) sets out some important issues about the relationship of external auditors to internal auditors and other company staff. The line between what controls are and are not relevant to the financial statements is a blurred one. External auditors would be expected to comment on control weaknesses that have been brought to their attention, even though they may not have a material impact on the accuracy of the accounts. However responsibility for taking steps to remedy problems belongs to management and internal audit.

(d) brings in both transaction and economic risk issues. Supplies could be brought in large enough quantities to require hedging. Mention of competitors should always mean you think about economic and competition risks, even if they are not easy to manage.

Easy marks. The preseen clearly highlighted the recipe as an important asset and students should have been prepared for a question asking about ways to protect it.

Examiner's comments. Answers to some parts were good, but answers to (a) (i), (c) (ii) and (d) were often poor. A common problem was students failing to answer the question set, for example in (a) (i) writing about risks other than reputation risks. Answers to (c) (ii) demonstrated a lack of knowledge of the roles of both internal and external auditors. Also many students wrote about whether internal auditors should cooperate with external auditors, rather than the other way round, which was what the question asked. (d) once again showed that students had not covered financial risk properly, although it will 'always' be a part of the compulsory question. Some students listed hedging techniques, which was not what the question wanted. Others discussed reasons for hedging but did not evaluate the benefits.

(a)   (i)   <u>Adverse press coverage</u>

<u>Likelihood</u>

F has already suffered **adverse press coverage** even if no legal and regulatory action is ultimately taken against it. The fact that a **number of elderly people have been taken seriously ill** makes the story much more newsworthy.

<u>Impact</u>

If papers run frequent food scare stories, older stories may be forgotten quite quickly by most of the public. However the fact that elderly people were taken ill may particularly damage F as it is trying to **increase its sales to welfare organisations** for the elderly. These organisations have a duty to keep track of potential problems and reduce risks where possible, and so sales to this sector may be affected for longer.

<u>Government investigation</u>

<u>Likelihood</u>

The Food Standards Authority will certainly **complete its investigation into the two food products**, because of the possible threat to health. F may also face the threat that the investigation is **extended to other products** if it reveals widespread problems in the Meals Division.

<u>Impact</u>

F will probably suffer a threat to its reputation for **as long as the investigation takes place.** The uncertain situation may damage sales. If F does not stop selling the products, it could also develop a reputation for being **unethical**, putting 'Profits ahead of people.' An adverse verdict may well cause a collapse in the sales for these products. If F is exonerated, this is unlikely to receive the same amount of coverage.

Legal action

Likelihood

F may be liable to legal action by those who have become ill from eating the meals. The **likelihood** of this risk will be related to the **results of the investigation by the Food Standards Authority.** If the authority exonerates F, then legal action is unlikely to succeed. The risk may also be limited if those who suffered ill-health do not have the financial resources to bring a civil action.

Impact

If F settles with claimants before the case comes to court, it could suffer bad publicity for having **acknowledged liability for poor practices**. If legal action does come to court however, the **threat to reputation may be longer-lasting**. Press coverage may keep the story fresh in the minds of the public. Even if F is cleared, evidence in the court case could still damage its reputation.

Loss of sales

Likelihood

As well as affecting sales of the two products, F may suffer a **threat to sales of any of other products,** even if there is no evidence that they could threaten customers' health. The likelihood of this occurring may depend on the attachment the public has to other products and whether they can easily be substituted.

Impact

The impact on sales is **potentially large**, as it may affect any of F's products. The public is unlikely to be concerned about which division of F manufactured the products.

(ii)   All products contain these bacteria

Public fears

The problem with highlighting the fact that all the products contain bacteria is that the public may be scared off by the products by this admission by itself, particularly because of the **link between the bacteria and severe illness.** The public may not appreciate the qualifications about the bacteria being a common organism.

Cooking properly

Emphasising the need to cook the products properly may only act to fix in the public mind the damaging idea that the products need to be **handled with care.** This issue may be made worse by the fact that F has been investigated for **inaccurate labelling,** indicating to the public that they cannot rely on the information on the packaging.

Highlighting concentration in competitors' products

If F emphasises that its competitors' products have higher concentrations, the impact could be a **fall in demand for all products of this type**, F's and its competitors. In addition competitors have an obvious response, that their products are not under investigation, but F's are. F's competitors could use this as a basis of a positive marketing campaign, damaging F's sales, although this might prove to be risky if the competitors' products subsequently suffer the same problems.

Legal defence

If F uses the legal argument that it **complies with all relevant hygiene regulations**, this may not impress the public. Many of the public may believe that F should be concerned with taking effective action to prevent any threat to health and going beyond hygiene regulations if necessary.

Conclusion

This argument is not suitable, as it is unlikely to remove public fears about this type of product.

Negligence by charity

Public fears

A common problem with the other defence is that this argument further reinforces in consumers' minds the **harmful nature of the bacteria.**

Passing the blame

Trying to shift the blame onto any user may be **counter-productive for F**. Some of the public may take the view that F should not be selling products containing these bacteria, particularly as many of the products sold are ultimately for elderly people who are particularly vulnerable to this bacterium.

Appeal of charity

The damage to reputation may be further enhanced by F's attempts to blame the charity. Many of the public are likely to contrast the **good work** the charity is doing with F's aim of **maximising profits**. They may believe the charity must be innocent or believe that F should have liaised more closely with the charity. The public may also dislike F mounting a publicity campaign against charity workers who cannot defend themselves.

Inaccurate instructions

As with the other possible defence, the argument is undermined by the investigation into inaccurate labelling by F and the belief that the information it supplies is **unreliable.**

Conclusion

F may suffer additional damage to its reputation if it uses this argument and therefore it, too, is unsuitable.

(b)   (i)   Impact if recipe is stolen

If someone who knows the recipe joins a rival and leaks it, it may be **difficult for F to detect** that its recipe had been copied. It may not be obvious from the taste of the product or the labelling. However a marketing campaign by the rival promoting the new taste of its pies may be unlikely, since it would draw F's attention to the possibility that copying had occurred. In addition the **advertising costs** may also deter competitors.

Lifecycle factors

How much impact the secrecy of the recipe has on sales now is debatable. The pie has been **established for many years**. Most sales may well be to consumers who have been eating the pies for a long time rather than to new customers. If there is an 'aura' around the pie that helps enhance its sales, this may be due to its 'traditional' taste rather than the secrecy of the recipe. Competitors may have analysed the pie legitimately and produced a recipe for their own pies that is very close to the secret one.

(ii)   Security of tenure

Recording of recipe

The recipe could be held in a **secure location** and brought out only if there was no-one left who knew the recipe. This would mean that F had a fall-back copy to which it could refer. It would also mean that the recipe did not otherwise need to be written down and become more vulnerable to theft as a result.

Non-disclosure agreement

The two individuals who know the recipe could be asked to sign a non-disclosure agreement. Although this would not guarantee **stopping them leaking the recipe**, knowledge that there might be legal consequences might be a deterrent.

Staff issues

One way to stop those who know the recipe leaking it to a rival company is to ensure that they are **content working for F** by rewarding them well. The board therefore needs to monitor the behaviour of those who know the recipe carefully and investigate any indications that they are unhappy. Employment legislation means that F cannot prohibit, for more than a few months, directors or staff joining a rival company.

(c)   (i)   Allocation of internal audit resources

Ultimately the board or the audit committee should decide on how internal audit resources should be allocated. They would take into account the **recommendations of the head of internal audit.** It

is important that internal audit **maintains independence** of the operational departments being audited and does not grant any requests they make automatically. However the operational departments are **stakeholders** of the internal audit function. Therefore internal auditors should carefully consider any reasonable requests that they make.

Role of divisional management

However divisional management is entitled, and should be expected, to raise issues relating to risk management that concern the board. Poor inventory control caused by problems with the IT systems has been a **significant source of loss** for F. It is therefore appropriate for divisional management, and specifically the divisional management accountant, to raise the issue and ask if action can be taken. Investigation by the internal auditors to assess the extent of the problem would be a logical step to take.

Liaison with external auditor

F's staff also have a **statutory duty to co-operate with the external auditors** and supply the information and explanations that they request. Co-operation with the external auditors also assists the efficiency and effectiveness of the external audit process. It appears that the divisional management accountant is informing the external auditor of a matter that would interest the external auditor and is doing so for constructive reasons, to try to resolve the inventory management problem.

(ii)   Co-operation between external and internal audit

Auditing and corporate governance best practice **envisages co-operation between the internal and external audit functions**. The audit committee should exercise oversight over both functions and ensure that there is liaison between them. External auditors may be able to make some use of internal audit work and therefore reduce their own testing. An unnecessarily antagonistic relationship may reduce the efficiency of external audit and push up its costs.

Purpose of external audit

However the statutory purpose of an external audit is to **provide an opinion on the truth and fairness financial statements**. External auditors' work is directed towards providing this opinion and their fees are set on that basis. Co-operating with the internal auditors on review work on IT systems that do not impact on the accuracy of the financial statements goes beyond the terms of engagement for the external auditors. Therefore the fees for the work would have to be negotiated separately.

Monitoring of internal audit

External auditors should also be careful about co-operating with internal auditors, as external auditors have a general duty to maintain independence of management, since they are reporting to shareholders. In particular, as part of their work on the audit of the accounts, the external auditors will **assess the controls** that impact upon the reliability of the financial statements. This includes the internal audit function, with external auditors assessing the **staffing, knowledge and skills of the department, the scope of its work** and **how much reliance** can be placed on what it has done. As a result of this review of controls, external auditors may discuss weaknesses in controls that they have noticed during the audit with management, as a by-product of the audit. They will not however be involved in dealing with the weaknesses, which will be supervised by the board and also involve internal audit.

(d)   Exchange risks

Arguments against hedging

Diversification

F is well-diversified in terms of the countries it uses for supplies and hence the currencies in which it deals. Currency movements against many currencies may be **more likely to even themselves out**. Because many of the supplies that F uses come from a number of countries, F could possibly change its countries of supply as a result of currency movements, although this could mean F is not able to establish long-term relationships with suppliers. It may also impact on the quality of supplies, which is one of F's major strategic concerns. Changing suppliers may also impact on other objectives, for example the CSR objective of reduction of air travel.

Costs

The cost of derivatives to manage specific transaction risks may be **high.** If F used derivatives regularly, it would probably have to employ costly treasury expertise. Use of derivatives would mean that F could not take advantage of favourable currency movements.

Arguments in favour of hedging

Certainty of cash flows

Use of derivatives to manage the risks relating to large transactions with suppliers would mean that the cash flows for F would be **guaranteed.** This would mean **budgeting** would be more predictable and **pricing decisions** would not have to allow for variations in cost.

Competitor reaction

F has assumed that its competitors will react in the same way as it does to managing currency risk. Its competitors may however take **better decisions** when changing their supply policies in the light of currency movements. Competitors may also be **prepared to absorb larger fluctuations in exchange rates** than F before putting prices up. If F increases prices before its competitors do, it may suffer unpredictable falls in demand as a result.

Price taker

F may in any case **not be allowed to pass on currency movements** in the form of price rises. Significant customers, such as large supermarkets, may be able to insist that F keeps its prices down.

Conclusion

Because of the tight margins under which F operates, the **certainty of cash flows** that derivatives on large transactions offer may mean their costs are acceptable. If F continues not to hedge, the board needs to ensure that F has a **flexible supplier management policy** and an **effective strategy for responding to competition**.

76 DEF 1

Text references. Chapters 1, 3, 6, 10 and 11.

Top tips. (a) (i) and (a) (iii) emphasise the need for your revision to include work on the preseen and analysing any obvious weaknesses with the business that the preseen highlights. (b) emphasises something the examiner has made very clear, that financial risk issues may be a significant part of the compulsory question.

Easy marks. If students taking this exam had prepared the preseen thoroughly, they should have come into the exam knowing the strengths and weaknesses associated with the board, discussed in (a) (i).

Examiner's comments. Many students seemed not to have read the scenario carefully enough, and hence failed to identify relevant information for answers. Answers to (a) (iii) lacked depth, as did answers to (b). Once again it appeared that students need to revise financial risk more thoroughly.

(a)

Top tips. Some of the weaknesses in (a) (i) relate to important aspects of governance guidance, for example board mix, the need for non-executive directors and the role of the chairman. However the shareholder arrangement here is unusual and your answer needs to discuss its implications, particularly how all shareholder interests are represented on the board.

The key point in (a) (ii) is transparency. Although there are good reasons for not being transparent with Max, the chairman has to provide the LSGs with the information necessary to make their decision.

In (a) (iii), as with any complex statement you are asked to analyse, an important question will always be whether it is entirely consistent. Here you need to consider consistency with the strategic objectives as well. You also need to assess whether the mission statement is realistic. As it is normally publicly announced, a further important aspect is how the public will react if the company does not fulfil it – particularly if, as here, it includes ethical elements and makes the company vulnerable to allegations of hypocrisy.

(i) Overall structure

The current governance arrangements are very weak as the executives dominate the board. At the moment they can **act in their own interests** instead of the interests of the major shareholders. They can also pursue **excessively risky policies**.

Lack of non-executive directors

Apart from the Chairman, the board **lacks non-executive directors** who can effectively challenge the strategies proposed by the executive directors. Although the Chairman leads the board, he is only one voice. The Chairman alone would find it hard to intervene alone without the backing of the LSGs. Corporate governance reports advise that weight of numbers is an important factor in ensuring non-executive directors have sufficient influence. For example the UK Corporate Governance Code recommends that at least 50% of a board's members should be independent non-executive directors. The lack of non-executive directors also means that key non-executive board committees such as the remuneration and audit committees cannot be used to scrutinise executives.

Chairman

The current chairmanship of the company rotates around the LSGs every two years. While this ensures a measure of stakeholder representation, it does lead to a **lack of continuity** and the danger that the Chairman is less motivated as his term of office comes to an end. Whether all the LSGs always appoint an appropriate person as Chairman may be doubtful as well.

Representation of all LSGs

At present the only person on the board representing the interests of individual LSGs is the Chairman. There is a danger that the Chairman will favour policies that represent the **interests of the LSG he represents**, but not the others. If the board included one non-executive director from each of the four LSGs, it would ensure that their interests were represented equally. It would also give the opportunity for NEDs to have time on the board learning about DEF before becoming Chairman.

Roles of board members

The current executive board members are likely to be focused on **financial and commercial objectives** given their roles. There is a danger that other corporate aims that are important in fulfilling DEF's mission statement will be given less of a priority because they do not have a spokesperson on the board. Having the **Human Resources Director** on the board would ensure that **staff interests are represented** and the need to adopt policies to retain the best staff emphasised. Recruiting a Corporate Affairs Director with responsibility for **fulfilling social and environmental objectives** would mean that these aims are pushed forward.

(ii) Interests of shareholders

There is a danger that DEF's Chairman is acting on his own initiative and not considering the interests of the shareholders. Co-operation with Max may result in the airport being sold at a very favourable price. The LSGs may be happy with this outcome. Adherence to the mission statement, whatever the interests of the LSGs, is not the over-riding duty of directors. However there are valid arguments in favour of not co-operating with Max.

Prudence

Directors certainly have a duty to shareholders to be **cautious in certain circumstances**. The lack of information that Max has supplied about his client may indicate that being cautious in turn about disclosing commercially and personally sensitive information is correct here. It is possible that Max is not being honest. He may be representing a client who would not purchase an interest – a competitor or someone who lacks the resources to purchase a controlling interest.

Non-financial objectives

It is also possible that the Chairman is **correctly interpreting the views** of the LSGs. Obtaining the maximum sales price may not be the top priority for the LSGs. They may instead be most concerned about not being blamed for politically unpopular redundancies if Max's client purchases the site and shuts down the airport. The LSGs may also be worried that closure of an airport and reduction of passenger choice will also be unpopular with voters.

Transparency

In any event it is wrong for the Chairman to suggest keeping details of Max's client's interests confidential from the LSGs. As the LSGs' agents, the Chairman and other directors have a duty of **transparency** towards the LSGs, including disclosure of information relating to issues that fundamentally affect the airport's future. In addition the board needs to meet with representatives from the LSGs to define what their views are about a potential sale and subsequent impacts, since these are not clear at present. It is possible that their views may vary. DEF's board could be left in an extremely awkward position if some, but not all, of the LSGs wish to sell their shares. It is therefore in the board's own interests to clarify the position as soon as possible.

(iii)   Reputation risk

The difficulty with having a mission statement that aims very high, as DEF's does, is that DEF could be accused of **hypocrisy and misleading the public** if it is perceived as failing to fulfil its mission. Passengers may be less likely to use DEF if they feel that promises of quality of service have no credibility. DEF may also be liable to calls for boycotts if it is felt not to be fulfilling the ethical standards set out in its mission statement.

Conflict between commercial and ethical aims

If DEF pursues its mission statement, it may be difficult to develop a clear strategy. There appears to be a **clear potential conflict between achieving commercial success and outperforming other airports**, and being a good corporate citizen. Some critics will take the view that air travel is an activity that has an adverse effect on the local environment and this effect is enhanced near any airport. On this view, DEF running a commercially-successful airport is incompatible with it being a good corporate citizen.

Conflict between cost and quality

If DEF pursues its mission statement's promises of quality, this may be excessively costly. A key strategic objective is that DEF is **financially secure.** Investment in top quality services may not be paid back by increased revenue. Instead profits may be maximised by offering a service that passengers generally find acceptable, even if it is not as good in some aspects as the service offered by other airports.

Other quality issues

DEF's mission statement may have generated expectations from passengers that DEF will be unable to fulfil because of circumstances beyond its control. Local infrastructure or the local environment (vulnerability to adverse weather conditions for example) may mean that travellers to DEF are more likely to be delayed than travellers to other airports.

Staff risks

DEF's stress on its employment of the best people will mean that failure of staff to perform well could **not just undermine the claim** that DEF **employs the best people** but other parts of the mission statement as well. It is likely also that this part of the mission statement is aimed at staff, in order to motivate them. If so, it could be counter-productive if staff do not feel that they are being treated well. Staff will become very demotivated if, for example, they have to **work in very poor conditions**, or they feel that managers are **making it as difficult for them as possible to do their jobs** in other ways.

(b)

> **Top tips.** The requirement to discuss the benefits in (b) (i) includes discussion of whether they are worth anything. Given that there are already policies in place to limit the risk associated with the bureau, the proposal wouldn't actually do much good. The key question in assessing the risks is what will the airlines not included in the proposal do – given that they are trying to limit their own costs, the answer has to be to make the same request.
>
> Unusually (b) (ii) is quite a general requirement, though the examiner's mark scheme indicated that students would get credit for any detail from the scenario that they could include in their answer. The question requirement also states managing foreign currency risk in general. This gives you scope to discuss whether internal or external methods are better for managing specific types of risk, as well as making points about cost and expertise required.

(i)　Benefits

Matching receipts and payments

The principal reason for the proposal is to match US $ receipts from the airline with US$ payments by the bureau. The argument is DEF would only suffer currency risk on the net amount. However DEF **should not need to incur significant currency risk** on the activities of the bureau, since changes in exchange rates will be reflected in the rates offered to passengers. DEF should always make profits on the currency dealings, provided it avoids holding large US$ balances over the longer-term.

Matching Bureau's own receipts and payments

In addition the Bureau's activities will also **hedge themselves** to some extent, as some incoming passengers will wish to exchange their US$ for D$.

Risks

Airlines demanding to pay in US $

The assumption appears to be that all the North American airlines that use DEF will wish to **pay in their own currency to limit their exchange risk**, and that this will result in the 60% hedge. However non-North American airlines may also demand the opportunity to pay in US$ rather than D$, as a more effective way of hedging their own currency risks. If some do so, that will increase the hedge towards 100% and limit the net requirement for US$. Beyond 100%, DEF will be subject to an **exchange risk on a surplus of US$.**

Airlines paying in other currencies

Alternatively other airlines may demand to pay in their own currencies and not US$. It may not be possible to hedge these receipts against payments from the bureau. As a result DEF's **overall exchange exposure may increase** as a result of holding unmatched large surpluses in individual currencies. If DEF does not agree to these requests, it may lose the business of some airlines to competitor airports.

Costs of US$ bank account

If DEF has to **undertake frequent transactions in the US$ bank account,** it may incur significant costs on this account. This contrasts with the current arrangements for the bureau, where the costs of dealing with the bank are factored into the rates charged to customers, with the result that DEF should make a profit.

(ii)　Benefits of internal methods

Cost

Using internal methods will not involve the **costs of arranging external hedging**. It will also not involve the **costs and requirements of specific methods**, for example premiums on options or margin requirements for exchange-traded futures. By contrast any company that has regular receipts and payments in the same currency has automatically established a hedge in that currency without any cost.

Expertise

If a business only uses internal methods, it will **not have to have the expert knowledge** necessary to trade effectively in derivatives. It will have **less need to employ specialist treasury personnel.** The board may find it more difficult to monitor specialist personnel effectively if the directors lack specialist financial knowledge.

Reliance on forecasts

Using internal techniques to **limit the exposure to exchange risk** will mean that the business can be less concerned about forecasts that may be unreliable if exchange rates are volatile, but which must nevertheless be considered when deciding which method to use. If the forecasts are incorrect, the business may not choose the most advantageous hedging method. It may for example choose to buy a more expensive option if exchange rates are expected to be volatile, but then the expected volatility does not occur.

Risk appetite

Using internal hedging methods and limiting the maximum amount of exposure may be **more consistent with the risk appetite** determined by the board. The board may wish to minimise exposure in currency dealings as a long-term policy.

Dealing with economic risk

Using matching wherever possible to **limit net holdings or payments in particular currencies over the longer-term** will **limit exposure to longer-term economic risks**. These relate to negative impacts on **competitiveness** as a result of adverse exchange rate movements over time on currencies where the business has significant long-term surpluses or requirements. External methods can be predominately used to deal with exposure to exchange rate movements for a limited period on specific transactions.

(c)

> **Top tips**. Hopefully in (c) you will have been able to identify the risk of forgeries and employee fraud or error, although you may have found it more difficult to identify how employees could cheat the system. The hints in the scenario about passenger convenience should have led you to consider threats to completing each transaction quickly.

Conversion risk of takings

The risk of adverse exchange rate movements affecting the value of foreign currency takings significantly is minimal. The amounts taken each day in many currencies will be small and the takings are converted to D$ within 24 hours.

Not keeping rates up-to-date

Updating the list of rates used may take time. If it is not done regularly, the margins made by the differences between **shop exchange rates and actual exchange rates** may reduce as actual exchange rates move.

Banking costs

The **costs of maintaining bank accounts** in certain currencies and the **costs of banking small amounts regularly** may be very high relative to the amount of receipts in those currencies.

Lost sales

The time spent converting between currencies, organising the different currencies and calculating the change in D$ may mean that the **average time per transaction is too high**. The outlets affected generate revenues through carrying out large volumes of small transactions. An excessive average transaction time will **reduce the number of transactions and reduce revenues**. Customers may very often not have the patience to wait, or may not have the time, particularly if they are in transit.

Staff errors

There may be a risk that outlets lose money through staff making **calculation errors.** However the amount lost on individual transactions is likely to be small. Any systematic errors should be picked up in the reconciliation process. Also some errors may work out in outlets' favours, with perhaps a neutral effect over time.

Staff fraud

Staff may be able to gain illicitly from foreign currency transactions. They may **ring up the correct amount for a transaction in D$,** subsequently put this money themselves into the till, pocket the foreign currency and exchange it so that they and not the outlet benefit from the rate that customers have been charged. Staff may also be able to take advantage of the rounding required to give change in D$. Daily reconciliation of till takings may not be able to identify problems. The risk of problems not being spotted will be higher if the till software cannot cope with foreign currencies and requires all payments to be entered in D$. Although the amounts staff gain illicitly on each individual transaction may be small, they could accumulate over time if staff are systematic about using the system to their advantage.

Forged currency

If staff are accepting a number of currencies, there is a high risk that purchasers will be **able to use forged currency successfully.** In particular staff may not recognise as forged a note in a currency that they do not see regularly. Whilst retail outlets may have policies for specific notes in a currency, for example checking closely £50 notes in the UK, it is impractical to adopt such policies for too many notes in different currencies. The delays involved, particularly in quick service outlets, may be unacceptable if staff have to check whether they can accept certain notes.

77 DEF 2

Text references. Chapters 1, 2, 3, 10, 11,

Top tips. Quite a varied question. It's important to try to gain some marks for each part, but don't worry too much if you are able to come up with much more material for some parts than for others. Familiarity with the preseen certainly helps at times.

Easy marks. The calculations in (a) do not involve much technical knowledge. It is difficult to say whether any of the discussion parts is significantly easier or difficult than the rest. Possibly it's most difficult to come up with points for (c).

Examiner's comments. (a) (i) was surprisingly done poorly, as it was a straightforward calculation. As well as being incorrect, answers were also often poorly presented. If students answered (a) (i) incorrectly, their answers to (a) (ii) were also likely to be poor. (b) was done well. However (c) on economic risk was, as on previous sittings, done very poorly. The hedging techniques suggested by students were not appropriate. Students must revise economic risk and note that financial risk, particularly, currency risk, will normally feature in Question 1.

(a)

Top tips. The calculations in (a) (i) are not technically difficult but they are quite involved. You have to be very careful to use the correct figures, particularly for security charges which are calculated on the basis of flights arriving and departing.

You could certainly see similar requirements to those of (ii) in E3, F3 and ultimately T4. The decision about S's proposal is difficult. S's flights could utilise most of the spare capacity and loss of the revenue from S is not what DEF needs given its forecast loss. However using the Asian airline as a benchmark demonstrates that if DEF can win more business from other sources, they are likely to be better revenue generators than S will be. As well as the calculations in (a) (i), bringing in some of the financial and quantitative information from the preseen can illuminate your answer.

The preseen information is also important in (iii), particularly details about airport security, facilities available and how easy it will be for DEF to expand. Some knowledge of the air industry, particularly the security restrictions placed on passengers, is also helpful.

(i)   Acceptance of S's proposal

Current revenue

		D$
Landing	4 × 170 × 360	244,800
Passenger load	4 × 1.60 × 117 × 360	269,568
Passenger security	8 × 1.20 × 117 × 360	404,352
Parking	4 × 0.14 × 250 × 360	50,400
		969,120

Proposed revenue

		D$
Landing	13 × 140 × 360	655,200
Passenger load	13 × 0.80 × 117 × 360	438,048
Passenger security	26 × 1.20 × 117 × 360	1,314,144
		2,407,392

Increase in revenue = D$ 1,438,272

Winning the contract with the Asian airline

		D$
Landing	2 × 300 × 360	216,000
Parking	2 × 200 × 360	144,000
Passenger load	2 × 4.00 × 300 × 360	864,000
Passenger security	4 × 1.20 × 300 × 360	518,400
		1,742,400

(ii) Reliability and timescale of S's forecasts

S may have overestimated the demand for flights to DEF. The commitment to increase to 26 flights may not be **sustainable.** Also the increase is going to take place over the next few years and the full increase in revenues will not occur for some time. DEF will suffer an **immediate drop in revenue on existing flights** from S, and will not begin to gain revenue until S starts implementing its plans. This is particularly significant given that DEF is currently making a loss. Although S is undoubtedly right to predict that turnover from outlets and parking will increase, the exact impact on revenues and profits remains unclear.

Dependence on S

If the forecasts are accurate, the revenue from S will rise substantially, but the costs will be kept down. As S's passengers are only allowed cabin baggage, there will be no extra baggage handling costs. S will provide a **guaranteed source of income.** If S relocated to another airport as a result of DEF turning down this deal, DEF would lose about 8% of revenue. If S entered into this arrangement, by contrast, it would become much more difficult for it to relocate to another airport.

However by committing to the contract, DEF will become very dependent on S remaining successful. Around a quarter of the flights at DEF will be by S. If S were to fail, DEF will be left with substantial unused capacity. Dependence on S would also represent dependence on a customer that is making a limited contribution. Assuming current revenue segment percentages continue to apply, S would be taking up around 25% of flight capacity in return for generating around 16% of revenues (2,407 × ((48 + 20 + 15)/48)) /(23,400 + (1,438 × (83/48))).

Utilisation of capacity

S's proposal offers the long-term opportunity to **utilise virtually all the current spare capacity.** Other than S, DEF may only be able to utilise the spare capacity by a **limited expansion of flights** by several different airlines. The limited progress on negotiations with airlines other than S suggest that this could be a very difficult task. If DEF turns down S's offer, it risks an immediate loss of existing business from S, worth about D$1m in aircraft and passenger charges.

Lost opportunities

However if DEF commits to S, that appears to **rule out an increased commitment** to other airlines. Possibly DEF would be able to accommodate the four extra flights from the Asian airline, but the D$1.6m that would generate would be about the maximum extra aircraft and passenger charge revenue it could expect. DEF may not be able to accommodate the North American luxury airline that wishes to operate services from it. The figures suggest that opportunities from other airlines will be **more efficient revenue generators** than S. Winning the contract with the Asian airline will generate D$1.6m in aircraft and passenger charges from 4 extra flights, whereas the contract with S will generate D$1.44m from 18 extra flights. In addition even if S is fully operational, the extra aircraft and passenger charge revenue it will generate in return for using virtually all of DEF's spare capacity will be less than half of DEF's predicted operating loss for 2011. The associated other revenues are unlikely to make up the difference, based on current figures, particularly as S's passengers are likely to be travelling on a low budget and will only spend limited amounts in the retail outlets. Commitment to S would appear to reduce the chances of DEF breaking even again.

Buildings expenditure

DEF would **not appear to need extra finance** at present to fund the expenditure. It has forecast cash balances of around D$3m compared with assumed expenditure of D$800,000. However the facility would not appear to have the potential to generate much extra revenue itself because of its basic nature. It will be some years before it is operating to full capacity. If S's plans do not

materialise, or S withdraws its operations from DEF, **additional expenditure** will be required on the building to bring it up to the standards required by other airlines.

Reaction of other airlines

If the other airlines become aware of the revised terms being offered to S, they may use these in **trying to bargain to reduce their own charges**. The reaction of other airlines may be particularly severe if **operating risks materialise** (see (iii) below) and they believe that their customers are getting a poorer service. DEF's position may be particularly vulnerable on parking charges if S becomes less efficient in turning round its aircraft, and the planes of other airlines are delayed. If S's plans are successful and passenger numbers of other airlines are reduced, then the other airlines may **reduce the number of their flights** to DEF.

(iii)   Aircraft delays

Ceasing to impose parking charges on S may mean that S becomes **slower in turning its aircraft round**, even though it has promised half-hour turnarounds. As S is not monitoring time spent parking, S's staff may become less efficient. This may mean that the **departure of other aircraft is delayed.** Delays may also increase because the runways are being used to capacity and bad weather could cause a backlog of flights. Other airlines and passengers may be less willing to use DEF if the number and magnitude of delays increase.

Security delays

The time taken for passengers to pass through security is already long, and passengers are unhappy as a result. **A rapid and significant increase in passenger numbers may increase delays** and therefore passenger frustration if the security facilities have problems accommodating an increase. Increased passenger numbers may also **jeopardise income** from the fast track service, as more passengers use this service to try to avoid delays, but the increased numbers mean that the fast track service itself slows down. If, to keep waiting times at a reasonable level, more security staff are required to search passengers, then the security team will have **less time to monitor the closed circuit televisions** for possible security problems.

S's passengers

DEF's staff may find it more difficult to deal with security issues relating to S's passengers because S would not be employing staff at check-in facilities. Having passengers check in at an airline's desk provides a **control** that assists monitoring of passenger whereabouts. The check-in desk can also give passengers advice about the **time to allow to go through security and warn them of possible problems.** If problems arise with passengers such as anti-social behaviour, DEF's staff will not be able to deal with representatives from S on-site, and it may take longer to resolve issues,

Hand luggage issues

S's requirement that all baggage is hand baggage could result in **increased security problems and delays** for DEF. S's passengers may pack items that are not allowed by regulations to be carried in hand luggage. However these items may be acceptable if they were packed in baggage that was checked-in and kept in the aircraft hold.

Car parks

Again increased passenger numbers may put pressure on facilities, and local governments may be reluctant to allow DEF to build on more green belt land. Passengers may have to **wait for longer for buses** to take them to the airport. More seriously passengers may find that there is no space in the car parks. If they have to park elsewhere, DEF will **lose car parking income** and passengers are likely to be late for their flights. If car parking problems become widely known, passengers may **prefer to fly from rival airports** where facilities are better.

Reputation risk

DEF's association with a low-cost airline may mean that other airlines and passengers may be less willing to use it, as they may associate it with a **low quality of service**.

(b)

> **Top tips.** If you're wondering how to generate ideas for (b), you need to remember that airport security, like internal audit, is a monitoring role. If you think for a moment what would be the considerations if the Head of Internal Audit reported to the Operations Manager, you will find that key issues are very much the same. The Head of Security, like the Head of Internal Audit, needs to maintain his independence of those he's monitoring. The role of both is so important to organisational risk management that they both need to have direct reporting links to the board.

Advantages

Controllable factors

A key part of **DEF's operations**, and of **passenger experience of the airport,** is its security operations. If the Operations Manager (OM) does not supervise the Head of Security (HS), then the OM cannot be held responsible for this aspect of operations. However efficient security is a source of **competitive advantage,** and is therefore significant from the OM's viewpoint.

Consistent approach

If the OM is in charge of Security, the OM should be able to ensure a **consistent approach** is followed on issues affecting the whole airport, for example **recruitment and treatment of staff.** This can also extend to ensuring that all operations staff, including Security staff, have a **constructive attitude** towards passengers. The OM would be in a position to link demands on security with flight schedules and take actions such as using extra staff at peak times. The OM will be particularly concerned with certain specific issues that are also the responsibility of the HS, for example the handling and security of baggage. The OM will also be **made aware of problems with security** such as staff absence and therefore communicate to passengers what actions they should take.

Disadvantages

Consistency of objectives

The OM will have **targets** relating to the **efficient running of the airport and passenger experience.** Security checks may impede achievement of targets, for example the lengthy delays caused by passengers going through security. The OM may require the HS to use the discretion he has to keep **checks to the minimum required by law**, and perhaps therefore increase the risks of security breaches.

Overstretching

The OM may not have sufficient time to monitor the HS effectively and this may give the HS leeway to pursue his own agenda, which may not be in DEF's best interests. The fact that the current HS's **responsibilities have not been reviewed** since his appointment 20 years ago suggests that not enough attention has been paid to what he has been doing The HS also has been able to maintain his information system in his own way, rather than adopt a more efficient system that is compatible with DEF's other systems.

Independent view

Security's role is to monitor what is happening at the airport and whether operational staff are paying sufficient attention to security. To review operations effectively, the HS needs to be able to take an **independent** view of what is happening and may need to report issues that reflect badly on operations and management. Having the HS report to the OM **undermines this independence**, since the HS may feel constrained in reporting problems, and the OM may play down issues that reflect badly on the OM or the OM's staff.

Board involvement

The consequences of a breach of security are amongst the **most severe risks** that DEF faces. Because these risks are so significant, they must be considered when the board carries out **its regular review of risks.** As it is so important that the Board is kept informed, and determines security policy, therefore the HS ought to **report directly to a board member.**

(c)

> **Top tips.** The main theme of (c) is economic risk. Its appearance in the November 2010 exam here and in Question 4 (c) is not very surprising, as the post exam guide for May 2010 highlighted the topic as a weak area and indicated it would soon be examined again. The details you are given about how the airlines are supplied with fuel and aircraft indicate not just the currency risks they face, but risks that will affect DEF as well.

(i) <u>Transaction and economic risks</u>

DEF will not be liable to currency risk on **specific transactions** since, as the board says, all transactions are priced in D$. However D will be liable to **currency economic risk.** Economic risk refers to the effect of exchange rate movements on the **international competitiveness of the company.** It reflects how future cash flows can be influenced by exchange rate fluctuations.

<u>Impact of D$ on passenger numbers</u>

If the D$ strengthens against other currencies, then holidays in D will become more expensive for foreign holidaymakers. The weakening of other currencies may also affect domestic demand in D, with holidaymakers from D preferring to holiday abroad rather than in D. The effect on DEF of changes in domestic demand is uncertain, as D could gain from holidaymakers in D deciding to go abroad, although fewer holidaymakers take internal flights. As holidaymakers make up the great majority of travellers passing through DEF, there could on balance be a **significant reduction in overall passenger numbers.**

<u>Impact of D$ on retail facilities</u>

Again if the D$ strengthens against other currencies, goods sold in the shops in D$ will effectively become more expensive for foreign travellers. Even if the goods are duty-free, travellers may be **less inclined to buy from the shops.** This may **reduce DEF's income** from the concessions.

<u>Impacts on airlines</u>

Again if the **D$ strengthens against other currencies,** airlines will have to accept reduced margins or increase their prices, **reducing passenger demand.** The same is also true for any of the airline's other costs that are denominated in a foreign currency that strengthens. Thus for example for airlines based in the Euro-zone, a strengthening of the US$ against the euro will increase their fuel costs. Thus DEF may be indirectly affected by currency risks that affect the airlines, even if these risks do not relate to the D$.

<u>Impact on contract with S</u>

If the contract with S fixes the charges, then DEF will **suffer a loss in value in terms of S's currency** if S's home currency strengthens against the D$.

<u>Other economic indicators</u>

Movements in the D$ could influence **movements in interest rates**. If interest rates rise, costs to customers such as mortgage costs could rise, and make passengers less inclined to take expensive holidays abroad.

(ii) <u>Management of economic risks</u>

<u>Dual pricing</u>

DEF could insist that the products and services in its outlets are **priced in more than one currency,** perhaps pricing in euros as well as D$ as it has a lot of custom from Eurozone travellers. This may generate more business as passengers from the Eurozone would not need to incur the costs of changing their money into D$ to purchase from DEF's outlets.

<u>Borrowing in foreign currencies</u>

If DEF does charge airlines in their own currencies, it could hedge the receipts by borrowing in those currencies and using the receipts to pay the interest. However DEF would only be able to borrow up to its **gearing limits.**

Diversification of revenue streams

DEF could develop the activities **generating revenue streams that would not be affected by economic risks**. There may be scope, for example, to become involved in the building development near the airport and develop DEF's property portfolio.

Diversification of routes served

Alternatively DEF could offer discounts to destinations whose currencies influence economic risk levels significantly, for example locations in the USA.

78 Aybe 1

Text references. Chapters 1, 2, 8 and 14.

Top tips. Overall this is a very compartmentalised question, with the three main question parts relating to the three distinct areas discussed in the scenario with no overlap. However Question 1 in the exam may include themes that run throughout the unseen data and affect multiple question parts.

Easy marks. The September exam overall awards few marks for discussion of general factors that are not related to the scenarios. Probably here the risks in (a) are fairly well signposted and identifying four risks and providing one suggestion each on how they should be managed should guarantee 8 marks, even if the examiner is looking for greater depth in discussion of risks (3 marks each) and multiple suggestions for managing each risk

Examiner's comments. Answers to (c) were worse than expected, and this part was often completely missed out. Students appeared to lack knowledge of financial risk. 'It is impossible to avoid financial risk with this syllabus, so it is very important that candidates study it and can do the associated calculations.'

Marking scheme

Marks

(a) (i) Up to 4 marks per risk discussed:
Liability for product problems
Threat to reputation
Supplier risks
Commitment to project

max 12

(ii) Up to 4 marks for responses to each risk discussed max

12

(b) (i) Up to 2 marks per issue. Issues could include:
Selection
Risky projects
Projects with lessons for future
Projects with cost over-runs
Audit of projects before they finish
Audit different managers' work
Investigation
Decision-making processes
Operation of controls
Allocation of costs
Cost overruns/variances

max 8

(ii) Up to 2 marks per issue. Issues could include:
Assessment of managers
Impact on investment decision-making
Fairness of process

max 5

(c) (i) Calculation 3

(ii) Up to 2 marks per issue. Issues could include:
Effectively speculation, not hedging
Ability of director to predict
Use of option

max 6

(iii) Up to 3 marks per issue. Issues could include:
Risk appetite
Commercial issues
Long-term advantage

max 4

50

(a)

> **Top tips.** The risks are fairly clearly signposted in the unseen scenario. Note that the hints given about SPD's dependence on the new contract may equally apply to Q. The threat to reputation is not totally dependent on whether SPD is legally liable – SPD may suffer guilt by association, particularly if it is associated with the speed freak approach to motoring. For P3, you will have studied contract management in the context of outsourced IT suppliers, but they are relevant here as well. The comment about high profitability should alert you to the need to consider other profitable uses of the scarce resource of qualified technicians.

(i) <u>Liability for crashes</u>

If a car **manufactured by Q crashes**, then SPD could be held **liable** for the failure of the circuit board. If a crash happens, it may be difficult to tell whether and why a circuit board has failed and it may be difficult for SPD to prove it was not responsible. This risk is increased by the functioning of the circuit board being dependent on factors beyond SPD's control. It includes a component manufactured by Q, a supplier that SPD has not selected. SPD also has no control over how the circuit board is fitted in the finished car, or how conscientiously the car is maintained.

Reputation risk

Even if SPD is not held liable for problems, it may suffer a serious loss of reputation if cars manufactured by Q have safety problems. Toyota's problems illustrate that potential problems with car safety will be widely publicised. However responsibility for the Gulf of Mexico disaster is allocated, there is no doubt that BP and the other companies involved have all suffered **damage to their reputation.** If there are problems and SPD is blamed by Q or the supplier, this will damage its reputation even if the allegations are unfounded. The risk to reputation is enhanced by how the cars are being marketed. SPD could be criticised for being associated with a car with the appeal that it can supposedly be driven safely at **high speeds**, although the speeds may in fact make it more likely that its components will fail.

Problems with supplier

The component supplier may **not deliver on time** or its components may be unreliable, causing delays in the production process. If the supplier goes out of business, SPD and Q may have **difficulty finding a replacement supplier at short notice.** Particularly if there are only a few suppliers who can manufacture the component, a new supplier may be able to charge a much greater price, **threatening profit margins** on the contract.

Threats to profitability

The contract represents a major commitment of resources for SPD. If Q goes out of business or changes its supplier, SPD will be left with **surplus staff.** Commitment of technicians that are currently employed to the contract may mean that SPD is forced to **turn down more profitable opportunities** because of a lack of resources.

(ii)   Liability for crashes

SPD could build a **failsafe routine** into the circuit board. This would mean that the car could only start if the board was functioning correctly. SPD should also carry out **full and documented quality testing** on the circuit boards. It should either **test the components** it purchases from the supplier itself, or insist that the **supplier provides evidence** that it has tested the components. The agreement with Q should make clear that SPD is not liable for circuit board failure caused by **problems with the manufacturing process at Q** or **inadequate maintenance.** SPD may wish to **insure** against legal costs if the premiums are not excessive, and should hopefully be able to do so if it can satisfy the insurer that it has taken all the steps it can to ensure the circuit boards operate safely.

Reputation risk

SPD should ask Q to ensure drivers are fully warned about the need to drive at safe speeds and the threat to the car's safety of driving too fast. Warnings should be included in sales literature, together with the explanation that the system is designed to **make driving safer** if the car is driven at reasonable speeds. Safety warnings should also be included in the **documents** purchasers are supplied with about the car. The documentation should also include advice to keep the car **well-maintained** and have it **regularly and thoroughly serviced.** New owners could be asked to sign an agreement that the system cannot prevent all crashes.

Problems with suppliers

If SPD is able to have input into the contract with the supplier, it should insist that the contract includes requirements about the **quality and timing of supply,** and that the supplier is **liable for delays caused by its shortcomings.** The contract should also include other requirements imposed on the supplier, for example carrying out quality checks. Its contract with Q should make clear that SPD is **not liable for delays caused by the supplier.** The supplier contract should include a termination clause that SPD or Q can enforce if the supplier **fails to perform satisfactorily.** If problems begin to occur SPD and Q should consult with a view to finding alternative suppliers as soon as possible.

Threats to profitability

SPD's finance department should review Q's accounts and other evidence of its financial status. It should consider how **dependent Q's future profitability** is on the success of this new car, or whether it is very committed to any other makes. SPD should also try to **assess Q's plans for promoting the car**, and whether they are likely to be successful, particularly as it is an expensive

car being marketed at a time of financial stringency. The contract with Q should include provisions for Q to pay **financial penalties** if it terminates the contract prematurely without good reason or fails to order a certain number of boards each year. SPD should also **plan the staffing of the contract** carefully, focusing particularly on the use of technician time, and trying to use lower grade staff for basic tasks wherever possible.

(b)

Top tips. You can bring in knowledge from F3 here as well. The first part of the question is really about what constitutes a good sample. The choice should focus on the projects of greatest concern but all projects should have some chance of being selected. (ii) covers good conduct by the auditors – it is important to obtain feedback from managers even if their explanations are not accepted unchallenged. However the scenario raises wider performance measurement issues which the board needs to address.

(i)   Selection

Important projects

Any projects above a certain size or which involve particularly high risks should be audited, because of the **potential magnitude of the consequences** if they do go wrong.

Projects that had problems

Projects which have **failed to deliver expected benefits**, have **cost too much** or **used too many resources** should be selected for investigation. Here obviously not only the factory building project would be selected, but the other projects where managers had overspent and ignored the budgets should be reviewed. If problems are identified during the course of the project, a post-completion audit could take place before the project ends, and the feedback result in the rest of the project being carried out more efficiently.

Projects providing lessons

Internal audit should focus on projects that are likely to recur in future, to see if they can be **done more efficiently** next time, Internal audit should also examine projects which provide indications of how important aspects of control systems are functioning. With Aybe, where budgets have been ignored, internal audit should consider how **realistic** the budgets were and whether **improvements** need to be made to the **budget-setting process.**

Coverage of managers and departments

Over time internal audit should review the work of **different managers and departments**, to ensure **projects over the whole company** are **reviewed** and managers and departments know that they could be selected for review.

Investigation procedures

Decision-making process

Internal auditors will wish to look at the **key decisions** made during the project. This should be done on the basis of what was **known or what should have been known** at the time. For example it may have been reasonable for managers making decisions about the factory to rely on the work of the quantity surveyor.

Operation of controls

Internal audit should look for evidence that controls that should have operated during the project did so. For example internal audit would normally check that **comparisons** were regularly being made between **phased budgeted expenditure** and **actual expenditure**, and action taken if variances were identified.

Reasonableness of expenditure

Internal audit would also look at the **reasonableness of expenditure** charged to the project. One reason for high costs might be the charging of costs to the project that were not associated with it. Internal audit should compare costs charged against planned expenditure on the project.

Investigation of variances

Whether variances are identified as part of the control process by management or by internal audit, internal audit would investigate **why** they had occurred. They should investigate a number of projects to see if patterns emerge, if the **same managers or departments are responsible for over-runs** or **over-runs occur at the same stage.** They would certainly wish to **investigate the budgeting process** for Aybe to see why it was being ignored.

(ii)   Performance management

The chief executive's comments are surprising, since they appear to suggest that management do not have confidence in the way their **performance is appraised** generally, which is an issue that the chief executive should be addressing. Managers should only be judged on factors that they can control. However the way they **manage risks** should also be **part of the appraisal process.** It is true that managers may be accountable for projects that they agreed should proceed but which turned out to be unprofitable. However the appraisal process should also identify an unduly cautious approach to risk management, resulting in a **failure to invest in projects** that would have been **worthwhile.**

Decisions about investment

A further problem with the chief executive's comments is that they imply that **responsibility for proposing projects** solely rests with lower management. Corporate governance best practice suggests that the **board should consider major investments** itself. Managers would therefore sometimes be required to proceed on significant projects selected by the board that might be subject to an audit.

Fairness of audit process

However the auditors are responsible for reassuring managers that they will be **judged fairly.** They should **obtain feedback** from managers as part of the audit process, although they should assess managers' comments objectively. Auditors' conclusions and recommendations should not be stated in unduly negative terms. Managers should be given a fair chance to respond to the auditors' findings.

(c)

> **Top tips.** In (i) as we aren't told the exchange rate the answer is in US$ rather than C$. In other questions of this type changes in exchange rates may also be an issue. Because the Production Director is talking in (ii) about outguessing the market, this should have alerted you to the issue being that he is recommending a speculative approach – however the futures were bought for hedging, not speculation. Risk appetite plus also experience of speculation may be reasons for ignoring what competitors do, but as copper is such an important element in manufacturing (emphasised in the unseen) its cost will inevitably impact significantly upon pricing policy.

(i)

Difference between selling and buying price	Number of futures	Tonnes in each future	Profit US$
(8,310 – 7,800) ×	150 ×	25	1,912,500

(ii)   Speculation versus hedging

The Production Director is taking a speculative approach to the futures transaction. However the point of undertaking the transaction was to hedge against the price rise of copper and **attempt to fix the net price** that Aybe paid. Selling the future now will leave Aybe unhedged against copper price rises.

Price rises further

The Production Director may be wrong and the **price of futures may rise further.** At present the copper market is volatile and there is no indication why the Production Director believes he knows better than the market. This will mean that Aybe has **not maximised its potential gain** on the future.

<u>Availability and cost of options</u>

If prices go higher and remain high, Aybe may have to opt for an option with a **much higher exercise price** than the current price of the future. If Aybe seeks an option with the lowest available exercise price, the **premium** will be **very high**.

(iii) <u>Risk appetite</u>

The decision of whether to hedge should be linked to the **risk appetite** Aybe's board believes the company should have. The board may believe that not hedging may expose Aybe to risks that are **unacceptably high** for the company and its shareholders. Its competitors may have a different risk appetite and therefore take a different decision. The decision may be complicated by **levels of exchange risk** involved, since futures are priced in US$, whereas copper may be priced in a different currency.

<u>Pricing policy</u>

However the volatility of copper prices may impact upon pricing policies. If competitors hedge, this will give them reasonable certainty in being able to set prices and margins. If Aybe **stops hedging and prices rise,** then either the **increase in costs** will have to be **passed on to customers**, making Aybe's products less competitive, or Aybe will have to **absorb the increase itself** and accept lower margins or even losses. However hedging will have a cost. If competitors pass on this cost to customers, then if Aybe does not hedge and copper prices do not rise, then Aybe may have a cost advantage.

79 Aybe 2

Text references. Chapters 1,4,6,8,10,11 and 13.

Top tips. In (a) you may have analysed the risks discussed in different ways – treated staff risks as a separate item for example. (a) underlines a point to remember for future exams – that the detail you needed to support your answer is almost all in the unseen. If you had taken the May 2010 exam, as part of your preparation you may have considered the possibility that DEC would undertake the investment in the foreign subsidiary, given that it was hinted in the preseen. You may have identified some of the broad risks that you needed to discuss in your answer. However all the risks you discussed needed to be supported by data in the unseen and bring out in particular the points emphasised – lack of profitability, potential problems with government/joint venture, economic risks.

By contrast in (b) you would need to refer back to the details of the capital budget overspend in the preseen – but note the unseen directs you back to this information. It is difficult to find any advantages of the system, but you should have tried to come up with a minimum of two. The discussion highlights some important points about control systems in general. There may be flaws in the **design** of the system (the subsidiary's systems are incomplete) but there appear to be more serious flaws in the **operation** of the systems (unrealistic cost estimates being fed in initially, actual and budgeted data being available but comparisons not being made). You can also get some discussion out of the board's failure to give enough thought to the system and to spend time monitoring it. Remember the Turnbull report stresses that this is an important responsibility of directors.

It seems in (c) (i) that the examiner gave some credit for discussing how the exchange risks between DEC and its subsidiary could be managed, although strictly the question asked about mitigating the exchange risk when trading with other countries. Note that the question asked for a discussion so you needed to indicate how the methods might be used and mention the possible problems.

The examiner's comments about (c) (ii) may have surprised you. They underline that you need to revise the accounting standards relating to financial instruments as their contents are clearly examinable. The problems with using fair value were also examined under the previous (2005) P3 syllabus. (c) (ii) also demonstrates discussion of financial risks may include the impact on the accounts of risks and methods used to manage them.

(d) highlights the emphasis placed by the current syllabus on control mechanisms for the detection and resolution of ethical issues. The discussion though here extends beyond company-wide methods such as an ethical code and into the methods used to prevent fraud. Some of the controls we discuss are purely designed to prevent fraud, but it is also legitimate to discuss ways of detecting fraud, as if they are operating effectively, the certainty of getting caught should deter miscreants.

Easy marks. Some very definite indicators of risk in the preseen material should have helped you come up with some suggestions for (a).

Examiner's comments. The main problems in this question occurred in (b) and (c) (ii). A number of students did not discuss the capital budget overspend in (b). Answers also needed to bring out the lack of links between the inventory system and the sales system. Answers to (c) (ii) demonstrated a lack of knowledge of IAS 39 and fair value. Students need to revise this area and financial risk generally:

'There will almost always be a financial risk element in question 1 as it forms 35% of the syllabus. It is impossible to avoid financial risk with this syllabus so it is very important that candidates study it and can do the appropriate calculations.'

Marking scheme

			Marks
(a)		Up to 4 marks for evaluation of each category of risks discussed. Evaluation should include indication of likelihood/impact. Do not award high marks if there is little or no link to information in the unseen. Risks could include sales, political, ownership, economic, currency, staff, transport, toxic material. max	15
(b)		1 mark per strength/weakness, max of 5 relating specifically to subsidiary, 5 to DEC. Up to 9 marks for weaknesses. max	9
(c)	(i)	Up to 2 marks for discussion of risks, and up to 2 marks for each internal and external hedging method discussed. Award 2 marks for method only if some indication of limitations/difficulties of method.	10
	(ii)	Up to 3 marks for discussion of accounting issues connected with IAS 39/IFRS 9. To obtain 3 marks problems of fair value accounting must be discussed. Up to 3 marks for other accounting issues.	6
(d)		Up to 2 marks per control systems area discussed. Discussion could include control environment, control procedures, ethical code, HR controls, setting remuneration limits, role of accounting function and internal audit. max	10
			50

(a) <u>Product risks</u>

Possibly the most significant threat to the subsidiary's existence is that its operations are **not viable**. It appears to have been established on the basis of sales forecasts that are now appearing to be over-optimistic. Costs have been increased by the **failure to predict demand correctly** and hence the need to **store excess inventory**. If the subsidiary is unviable, it may be difficult to know when to take a decision to cease operating, and there may be **significant termination costs**.

<u>Risks of joint venture partner</u>

Another serious threat to the subsidiary's continued existence is Aybe falling out with its joint venture partner and the **agreement being dissolved**. The subsidiary would have to cease operations. Possible causes of disagreement include **pricing policy**. The partner may wish to offer discounts to establish a presence in local markets, even though the subsidiary's sales staff wish to maintain prices. It may be difficult to assess the likelihood of these disagreements when the contract is signed, as the position on these issues may only become clear once the subsidiary experiences trading difficulties.

Political risks

The subsidiary is also vulnerable to other changes in government policy. The government may introduce **tariffs, tighten exchange control regulations** or **restrict payments for supplies** as well as limiting profit remittances, on the grounds that companies are not charging their subsidiaries a **fair market rate**. It may insist that the subsidiary has to **use local suppliers** or be **managed by local managers**. Although information should be available about the direction of the policy of the existing government, **political risks and uncertainties** could **increase** if there is a **change of government**.

Economic risks

The subsidiary could be affected by the risks associated with inflation, including economic instability and a **weakening of the local exchange rate**. Government action to combat inflation may also impact seriously on the subsidiary. **Rises in interest rates** could reduce expenditure and increases in tax could reduce profits that can be remitted.

Legal and reputation risks

The subsidiary may face **legal action** and a risk to its reputation if staff **do not recycle** components in accordance with stated policy but **throw them away**. This risk may be enhanced if the subsidiary's staff **are not experienced in handling toxic material**. This may result in costly sanctions being taken against the subsidiary and DEC for failing to dispose of components properly and publishing misleading information. It may also cast doubt on the other information DEC publishes.

(b)   Strengths

Inventory and production systems

The systems for inventory and production are operating for the African subsidiary and enabling sales staff to **provide accurate information** about product availability.

Budgeted and actual costs

There appears to be **sufficient information available** for comparisons to be made between **budgeted and actual costs** during the progress of projects such as the factory investment. A phased budget was prepared and actual costs appear to have been recorded while the development was in progress. This comparison was made at the end of the work on the factory, though not before.

Weaknesses

Failure to fulfil needs of business

Systems do not appear to support the strategy of the business and provide information to the board, managers and staff. Information systems are an important part of the risk and control systems of Aybe, which the board should **oversee and monitor**. It seems that the board is failing to pay enough attention to whether the information systems are sufficient to support Aybe's needs.

Lack of confidence of operational managers

Managers with responsibility for capital expenditure clearly have no confidence in the budgeted figures given to them and do not adhere to budgets. This suggests that they have **not had sufficient input** into the budgeting process.

Late development of subsidiary's information systems

The subsidiary's information systems were **not established fully before operations commenced**, but are being developed gradually after trading has started. As a result **establishment costs were not monitored**.

Failure to establish sales control systems

The lack of a sales control systems seems to have led to problems in **establishing sales data**, and **delays in producing export forecasts**. As a result production decisions appear to be being made based on inventory levels rather than customer demand.

Verification of estimates

The systems do not include the requirements to **produce evidence supporting estimates** such as those made by the quantity surveyor. As a result the costs of the factory extension were seriously underestimated.

Tracking of progress

Periodic comparisons have not been made on projects such as the factory extension, although the information appears to have been available.

Board monitoring of progress of investments

The progress of the factory investment was also not reported to the board. Had cost over-runs been reported earlier, the board may have been able to ensure that action was taken to **minimise losses**, rather than being surprised by the size of over-runs when the building was complete.

(c) (i) Risks faced by DEC and its subsidiary

The businesses face **transaction risk** on specific orders from foreign customers. The subsidiary also faces an **economic risk** of its currency declining due to inflation and this resulting in sales prices having to be **maintained at high levels.**

Payment in DEC's currency

Payments for exports could be made in **DEC's currency** rather than that of the African subsidiary or the export customers'. This would avoid the apparently greater risk to receipts of the African subsidiary's exchange rate deteriorating. However export customers may be reluctant to pay in DEC's currency if they believe they may suffer adverse currency risk.

Natural hedging

DEC or its subsidiary could **purchase goods or services from the countries in which its export customers are located or perhaps from the export customers themselves.** The transactions could net off and the currency risk would be reduced, as it would only arise on the difference between receipts and payments in that currency. However this could mean DEC or its subsidiary having to change their **supply arrangements**. The terms available may not be as good as they are currently getting and the **quality of supplies** may be more uncertain.

Forward contract

A forward contract can be purchased to **hedge the amount paid for a delivery of goods in the future**. This could guarantee the exchange rate if the subsidiary is invoicing in the **local currency of the export customer** and then selling the currency it receives in exchange for its currency. However it means that the subsidiary cannot take advantage of favourable exchange rates. It may have to settle the contract by buying the customer's currency itself if the **customer defaults.**

Currency futures

Alternatively DEC or its subsidiary might be able to **take out currency futures** to hedge payments by customers. Because futures contracts are a standard size, they would only be appropriate if payment was for large amounts. A possible problem is that **currency futures** might **not be available** in the currency of the export customer or the African subsidiary. This would make using them a more complex process. DEC and its subsidiary would probably **need to employ specialist treasury expertise** to manage futures properly.

Currency options

Alternatively the subsidiary could use a currency option to fix a limit on the exchange rate for the foreign currency it receives. It could purchase a traded option for amounts fixed by the trading exchange or it could buy an over-the-counter option tailored to the specific amount it should receive. The main advantage of the option contract is that the subsidiary does not have to fulfil it. It will not exercise the option if it can **take advantage of favourable exchange rates** or if its **customer defaults**. The disadvantage is the **cost of the option** is likely to be **larger** than that of **other hedging methods.**

(ii) Transactions

Gains or losses arising on transactions in foreign exchange will be accounted for in the **income statement.**

Payments in DEC's currency

If this method of hedging is used, there will be **no impact on the income statement** as the sales will be in the currency used for the accounts.

Natural hedging

Movements on currency will affect the **income and expenses figures** in the accounts. However these movements will cancel each other out to some extent, depending on how closely receipts match payments.

Derivatives

Currency derivatives will have to be accounted for in accordance with **IAS 39 and IFRS 9.** The main problem, particularly with options, is measuring the contracts at **fair value** at the date of the financial position. **Market price** will be the preferred option, but any market for the derivatives may not be very liquid. Over-the-counter instruments cannot be valued at market price if there is no market, and it may be difficult to obtain information about **recent transaction prices** or the **current fair value of similar instruments**. **Pricing models** requiring debatable assumptions may have to be used.

DEC may be able to use **hedge accounting** if it can offset the derivatives used by the subsidiary to hedge export trading with other instruments.

(d) ### Control environment

The board should consider whether Aybe's control environment encourages ethical behaviour. This has various dimensions, including the board being seen to act ethically. A **code of ethics** and **ethics training** should help. It is also important that unethical behaviour in other areas of the business is not tolerated. Action should be taken for example to prevent components containing **toxic materials being simply thrown away,** as not only is it dangerous but it means that the **CSR report is misleading.**

Personnel policies

Recruitment controls can reduce the likelihood of staff who are likely to act dishonestly being employed. **References** given by applicants should be checked with referees, and applicants asked to explain gaps in employment records as these could indicate a spell in prison. Applicants should also be asked whether they have been **convicted** of any offence involving **dishonesty.** Aybe's employment handbook should make clear that staff who are found guilty of unethical behaviour will be subject to **disciplinary action,** including the threat of dismissal.

Review of remuneration packages

The board needs to review the **performance-related element of remuneration packages** as this appears to be tempting staff to manipulate transactions. It also may be resulting in other behaviour that isn't in Aybe's interests, such as the subsidiary's sales staff being unwilling to reduce prices. To motivate staff, a performance-related element needs to be maintained but this should be linked to an **appraisal of staff behaviour** that includes consideration of whether they have acted ethically. The board should also attempt to establish conditions for obtaining the element that it is possible to fulfil by acting honestly.

Accounting controls

Checks built into the system should highlight **discrepancies** such as the problems with invoice pricing. Staff at the subsidiary should have **compared the order** that was submitted with the **prices** on the inflated invoice. As well as control systems highlighting problems automatically, accounting staff also need to be **vigilant for suspicious transactions**. The manipulation of the invoices was spotted by the alertness of the accounts department.

Internal audit

Internal audit work also should act as a further deterrent to fraud, as it should increase the chances that fraudsters will be **discovered.** Internal audit work should concentrate on areas of **high risk**, such as high value transactions including the **periodic transfer payments**. As the African subsidiary has been recently established, and its staff appear to be under pressure, the risks of problems with its transactions may be high and hence internal audit may need to concentrate on it.

80 PU

(a)   <u>Information strategy</u>

An organisation's information strategy deals with its **information needs**. It ought to support its business strategy. In PU's case, the business strategy revolves around how the coal fired power stations are going to be replaced.

The key information needs to support this strategy will therefore be analysis of the **feasibility, costs and benefits** of the various power generation options, new coal fired stations, gas, nuclear, wind and wave power. The strategy needs to set out how to **obtain and analyse this data**. An information strategy has three elements.

<u>Information systems (IS) strategy</u>

This deals with how the **information needs** will be **satisfied** and what systems will be required. In order to have the information it needs, PU's board needs to consider the following:

- **Employing a management accountant or specialist** in this area to obtain and analyse the data

- **Gathering information from PU's internal accounting systems** on the cost of running the current power stations, as well as any additional costs that will result from the need to comply with new legislation

- **Obtaining data on alternative methods of power generation**, which may involve contacting organisations using these methods, as well as sourcing research papers from the internet or consultants

<u>Information technology (IT) strategy</u>

An IT strategy deals with how the **IS strategy** will be **implemented,** specifically what investment will be made in hardware and software, and what vendor partners will be used.

PU will require the capacity to **store and analyse significant volumes of information**, comparing financial outcomes as well as scenario analysis. Investment in a data warehouse may well be appropriate.

The results of the analysis will ultimately be presented at board level for strategic decision-making, so the systems must be able to generate output in **graphical, summarised format**.

<u>Information management (IM) strategy</u>

The IM strategy deals with **how information will be provided to users** and stored, accessed and controlled.

As noted above, the strategy will need to ensure that the specialists dealing with the information are able to **communicate results** to the board, perhaps delivered as a type of dashboard.

Some of the information will be obtained externally, so **links to information providers** may be needed. However, the stored information will be highly sensitive. **Access** to it thus needs to be **restricted** by use of passwords, physical security etc.

(b)   Currency risks

As PU will be investing and trading in Zee$, a different currency to its domestic one, it will face several types of currency risk.

Economic risks

Economic risk is the threat to **long-term cash flows and competitiveness** as a result of foreign exchange movements. Because the gasification equipment will be manufactured in Zee, the costs of manufacture will be in Zee$. If the Zee$ appreciates against PU's currency, costs will rise without any corresponding increase in revenue, reducing profits.

In addition, the government of Zee is prepared to buy the subsidiary after five years, but the price will be in Zee$. If the Zee$ has depreciated in those five years, the amount PU receives for the subsidiary will be less.

Translation risks

At the end of a financial year, a company must translate all assets and liabilities into its reporting currency. The risk that foreign exchange movements will **reduce the value of an asset or increase the value of a liability** is translation risk. While it does not affect cash flows, it does affect retained earnings and may affect a company's valuation.

PU will be required to consolidate its Zee subsidiary into its financial statements. If the Zee$ falls during the year, the value of the subsidiary will fall. This may **restrict PU's ability to pay dividends,** or **affect investor attitudes,** making it difficult to raise new finance.

Transaction risks

This is the risk that a transaction entered into at one rate is **settled at a different rate,** leading to a loss.

PU's subsidiary will be exporting the gasification equipment back to the home country. PU will therefore run the risk that exchange movements will mean that it ends up **paying more than it planned.** Conversely, the subsidiary will risk **receiving less than it planned**. This is only a risk for the separate entities, at group level any differences will eliminate on consolidation.

As well as currency risk, PU will face several other risks relating to the subsidiary.

Political risks

This is the risk that **government action** will have an adverse effect on an organisation. Political risk is generally higher for companies operating overseas because they are **less familiar with local politics**. Governments are also often inclined to treat overseas companies worse than domestic ones.

Zee is experiencing political unrest. The unequal income distribution may mean that workers are **more inclined to strike**. In extreme cases, instability could lead to **damage to property and equipment.**

There are risks resulting from the fact that 80% of the workforce must be drawn from the population of Zee. There may not be enough workers with **sufficient skills,** which could limit PU's ability to start production. Perhaps PU will need to pay higher wages to attract the workers, which will raise costs.

A change of government may lead to PU's subsidiary **having to trade on less favourable terms,** or even having its **assets seized.** Zee's government may also **change the tax laws,** resulting in the subsidiary paying more tax, or perhaps making it more difficult or expensive to remit funds back to its parent.

Product risks

Product risks result from the **failure of a product to perform as expected**, or be **attractive to customers**. The coal gasification process is a new technology. There is a risk that it will **not work as specified**, or will cause **unexpected environmental or other damage**. This could lead to PU having to write off its investment or pay damages or rectification costs.

Cultural risks

PU is currently focused on its domestic market and has no experience of operating internationally. It is possible that PU's **culture and management practice** will **not translate well** when it runs a business in Zee.

Trading risk

There are a number of risks resulting from the distances involved and time taken in international trade, such as **goods being lost or stolen in transit**, and **increased credit and liquidity risks** resulting from a longer working capital cycle. As PU is trading with its own subsidiary, the key risk is that the gasification equipment is damaged or stolen during transit from Zee to PU's home country.

(c)   (i)   Environmental audit

An environmental audit is an evaluation of how well an organisation is fulfilling its duties as a good corporate citizen in protecting the environment. It includes **reviewing compliance with internal policies and external standards and laws,** as well as ensuring that any **environmental reporting is true, fair and complete**. In PU's case, such an audit will focus on carbon dioxide emissions and PU's reporting requirements.

To carry out this work effectively, PU's internal audit department will need a number of attributes.

Independence

The internal audit function must be independent enough to **produce unbiased reports** and **resist any management pressure** to change or "water down" its findings. This should be safeguarded by **reporting to the audit committee** which, if PU is in line with best practice, will comprise independent non-executive directors.

Skills and knowledge

The staff will need to be **suitably experienced and trained** in how to carry out audits, possibly holding a professional qualification in this area. However, to carry out this assignment, they will also need a **good understanding of environmental issues** and particularly the **requirements of legislation in relation to emissions and reporting.** They will also need a good understanding of the process by which the **information is gathered and reported on** at each power station.

Authority

To carry out an effective audit, the internal auditors will need **sufficient authority to gain access to all relevant staff and records**. They will also need sufficient authority to ensure that any **recommendations** they make, for example improving controls over reporting, are **accepted** rather than ignored.

(ii)   Recommended actions for internal audit

Report to the audit committee

As well as reporting to the Managing Director, the internal audit function will need to submit a report to the audit committee. The head of internal audit may want to meet with members of the audit committee to ensure that they **understand the issue and discuss appropriate follow-up**.

Review controls and recommend improvements

The internal auditors will want to **review the existing controls over emissions reporting,** for example the procedure for checking and sign-off. As these controls have clearly not been effective, they may want to **recommend improvements**, such as requiring an additional check and sign-off before the reports are submitted to head office.

Review prior year returns

The fact that the information submitted is incorrect will raise suspicions that prior year returns from power station N3 may also have been incorrect. Internal audit may therefore wish to carry out **checks on these returns.**

Review returns from other power stations

Assuming that the controls over reporting are similar across the different power stations, the issues at N3 may also be occurring at other power stations. The internal auditors will therefore wish to **prioritise review of other power stations' returns.** They will probably start with those stations showing better than expected figures, as this may be an indication of errors, even if they are not part of the planned rotational audit.

Planned future review

Internal audit will probably schedule a **follow-up visit** to N3 at a future date, perhaps one year ahead, to check that any **control recommendations** have been **implemented** and **returns** are now **correct.**

(d)   False reporting may be a source of risk for a number of reasons.

Reputational damage

If the incorrect reporting becomes public knowledge, PU may gain a reputation for **dishonesty and poor controls**. This may impact on a number of areas of the business including **relationships with suppliers, customers and government**, and ultimately damage profitability.

Financial penalties

The breach of environmental legislation may lead to **fines** being levied, which will lead to further reputational damage as well as a direct financial cost.

Impact on control environment

A high-profile control breach in this area may lead to a general perception within PU that **controls and accurate reporting are unimportant.** The fact that head office seems complicit in this breach will make this risk more serious. This perception could impact on the **general culture and ethos** in PU and therefore undermine control effectiveness throughout the organisation.

Control mechanisms

Internal audit checks

Internal auditors should substantively check reporting, as they do at present. However, rather than audit on a rotational basis, they may use **surprise visits** or focus on those stations with high risk factors, such as a history of error.

Response to errors

Management needs to **respond quickly and decisively to errors**, ensuring that they are corrected and that anyone found to have behaved unethically faces **disciplinary action.** This will send a clear signal about the importance of controls and correct reporting.

Management tone

Management needs to communicate clearly the **importance of following procedures and ethical behaviour**, reinforcing this at every opportunity, and **setting an example** in their own behaviour. The actions of head office in this case are obviously unhelpful.

MOCK EXAMS

348

CIMA – Strategic level
Paper P3
Performance Strategy

Mock Exam 1

You are allowed three hours to answer this question paper.

In the real exam, you are allowed 20 minutes reading time before the examination begins during which you should read the question paper, and if you wish, highlight and/or make notes on the question paper. However, you will **not** be allowed, **under any circumstances**, to open the answer book and start writing or use your calculator during this reading time.

You are strongly advised to carefully read all the question requirements before attempting the question concerned (that is all parts and/or sub-questions).

Answer the compulsory question in Section A.

Answer TWO of the three questions in Section B

DO NOT OPEN THIS PAPER UNTIL YOU ARE READY TO START UNDER EXAMINATION CONDITIONS

SECTION A – 50 marks

Answer this question

Question 1

Preseen case study

Clothing manufacturing in Europe

Since the 1960s there has been a decline in the number of UK and European clothing manufacturers due to competition from cheaper, and sometimes higher quality, imported clothes. The clothing industry generally has become much more fashion conscious and price sensitive. This has led to a reduced number of companies that are still in business in Europe. Some companies have moved all or part of their manufacturing processes to other countries to achieve a cheaper operating base, and up until recently this has allowed them to continue to compete on price.

Many companies have had contracts to supply High Street retailers for over four decades and are highly dependant on retaining these key customers who wield immense buying power over the small manufacturers. A number of family owned manufacturing companies, that had been highly profitable once, have ceased trading, or are operating at very low margins, as a direct result of the High Street retailers being able to dictate terms of business and prices.

An additional factor that has put the main High Street retailers under more price pressure has been the appearance and market growth of new High Street retailers and their new brands, who have procured their goods mainly from overseas sources.

The result is that the few companies that are based in the UK and Europe which are left in the business of clothing manufacturing are having to look very hard at their strategic plans in order for them to manage to maintain their business over the next few years.

History of Kadgee Fashions (Kadgee)

Kadgee was formed in post-World War Two in a European country, and has remained as an unlisted company, although its shares are now held by others outside of the founding family. Kadgee quickly established itself as a high quality manufacturer of both men's and ladies clothes. By the 1960s Kadgee had a turnover equivalent to €25 million, and had nine factories operating in two European countries.

During the late 1960s Kadgee suffered its first major fall in sales, and found that it had large stocks of men's clothes that had been manufactured without specific sales contracts. Kadgee managed to sell off some of the stocks, albeit at below cost price. However, the management decided that it should not manufacture clothes without a firm contract from a retailer in future.

In the early 1970s the range and design of its men's clothing was changed several times, but it continued to make little profit. In 1973, Kadgee sold its men's clothing range and designs and some of its manufacturing equipment to a large listed company. Kadgee decided to concentrate on expanding its ranges of ladies' clothing to meet the growing demands of its main customers (see below).

During the next few years, Kadgee consolidated its position and its profitability increased again. In the early 1980s its then Chief Designer persuaded the Managing Director to expand its clothing range to include a range of girls' clothes. This new limited range was launched in 1982 and was immediately sold out. Kadgee has positioned itself at the upper price range of clothing, and has never tried to mass produce low cost clothing.

During the 1980s Kadgee continued to expand its ranges of ladies and girls' clothes. A further change that occurred was that many of Kadgee's customers were starting to dictate the styles and types of clothing required and Kadgee's designers had to manufacture to customers' specifications.

However, during the 1990s Kadgee suffered a number of setbacks. It also saw many of its competitors suffer losses and cease trading. Kadgee had been able to stay profitable only because of its particular customer base and because it sold high quality clothes that commanded a premium price. However, Kadgee saw its margins on many product lines reduced greatly and also it started to lose many of its smaller customers, who chose to import, at much lower prices, clothing produced in Asia.

Kadgee's shareholders

Kadgee has remained an unlisted company. At the end of 20X5 29% of its shares were held by the company's founder who is no longer on the board, 60% by current directors, 11% by employees. The company has 200,000 shares of €0·10 each in issue and has a total of 400,000 authorised shares. The shares are not traded but the last time the shares were exchanged was eight years ago, when shares were purchased at €8·00 each.

Kadgee's customer base

Kadgee manufactures clothing for a number of European and international clothing retailers, including many well known High Street retailers. It manufactures clothing in the medium to higher price ranges and its customers require top quality designs and finishing to maintain their brand reputation.

The majority of Kadgee's clothing is manufactured for its customers under the customers' own label, for example, clothing manufactured for one of its customers called Portrait is labelled as 'Portrait'.

In 20X5, Kadgee's customer base, analysed by sales value, was as follows:

	20X5 revenue	% of Kadgee's total sales
	€m	%
Portrait	24.0	32.3
Forum	16.8	22.6
Diamond	13.5	18.1
Zeeb	5.1	6.9
JayJay	4.5	6.0
Other retailers of ladies' clothes	7.3	9.8
Haus (children's clothes only)	3.2	4.3
Total	74.4	100.0

Most of Kadgee's contracts are renewed at the start of each fashion season. Kadgee is currently negotiating for clothing sales for the summer season of 20X7.

Human Resources

In the clothing manufacturing business one of the most crucial aspects to achieve customer satisfaction is quality. Kadgee has been very fortunate in having a skilled, very dedicated workforce who have always adapted to new machinery and procedures and have been instrumental in suggesting ways in which quality could be improved. This has sometimes involved a very minor change in the design of a garment and the designers now work much more closely with the operational staff to ensure that the garments can be assembled as quickly and efficiently as possible.

Losses made by Kadgee

Kadgee has suffered from falling operating profit margins due to the pressure exerted by its customers over the last ten years. For the first time in Kadgee's history, it experienced losses for five years through to, and including, 20X2. During this time Kadgee increased its loans and its overdraft to finance operations.

In 20X0, Kadgee refinanced with a ten year loan, which was used to repay existing debt, and also to invest in the IT solutions discussed below, as well as to purchase some new machinery. Kadgee also invested in its design centre (see below), which was completed in 20X1.

During 20X1, the company invested in new IT solutions enabling its customers to be able to track all orders from the garment cutting process right through to completion of garments and through to the delivery to customers' premises.

The IT solutions also enabled Kadgee to monitor its production processes including machine usage, wastage at various stages of production and speed of production through the various stages. This has enabled Kadgee's management to reduce areas that did not add value to the finished garment. The use of TQM throughout the business has also increased Kadgee's efficiency and enabled it to eliminate some other areas which did not add value to the finished garments.

While margins are still low, Kadgee has been operating profitably again since 20X3, albeit at lower margins to those achieved in the past.

Changes in the supply chain

Many of Kadgee's customers have needed to speed up the process of supplying clothing to their shops, so as to meet the demands of the market and to remain competitive. Kadgee has worked closely with its customers in order to achieve shorter lead times from design to delivery of finished products.

In 20X1, Kadgee introduced a new design centre, centralised at its Head Office. The design centre uses Computer Aided Design techniques, which has helped Kadgee's customers to appreciate the finished appearance of new designs. This seems to have helped Kadgee to win new business and to retain its current customers. It has also contributed to Kadgee's ability to speed up the process from design board to finished article. Kadgee has also benefited from working more closely with its customers and this has resulted in additional orders, which Kadgee's customers' would otherwise have procured from overseas sources.

Growing competition from China

During the 1990s and into the 21st century China has had a massive impact on the textile industry. China's manufacturing base is forecast to grow further and this will have a negative impact on many companies operating at a higher cost base elsewhere.

Many European companies have spent millions of Euros establishing manufacturing bases outside their home countries in the last 15 years. Many have opened factories in countries which have much lower operating costs. These include countries such as Turkey, Sri Lanka and Pakistan, as well as Eastern European countries.

The companies which have set up operations in these low cost countries did so in an effort to cut costs by taking advantage of low overheads and lower labour rates, but still managed to maintain quality. However, even the companies that have moved some, or all, of their manufacturing bases and have taken steps to reduce their costs, now have to reconsider their cost base again. This is because of the very low cost of Chinese imports, which they are having difficulty competing against.

Following the relaxation of trade barriers, there has recently been a deluge of Chinese clothing imports into Europe, the UK and the USA.

The quality of Chinese manufactured clothing is improving rapidly and it is now globally recognised that the "Made in China" label represents clothing of a higher quality than many European manufactured garments. Furthermore, the Chinese manufactured garments are being produced at a substantially lower manufacturing cost.

Kadgee has so far been operating in a market that has not been significantly affected by imported goods, as it produces medium to higher priced clothing, rather than cheaper ranges of clothes. However, many of Kadgee's customers are now looking to reduce their costs by either buying more imported clothes or by negotiating substantial price cuts from their existing suppliers. The purchasing power of European retailers being exerted on its suppliers is immense and Kadgee is under much pressure to deliver high quality goods at reduced operating profit margins from all of its customers.

Date: It is now 1 November 20X6.

Appendix 1

Statement of financial position

	At 31 December			
	20X5		20X4	
ASSETS	€'000	€'000	€'000	€'000
Non-current assets (net)		9,830		11,514
Current assets				
Inventory	8,220		6,334	
Trade receivables and rent prepayments	19,404		18,978	
Cash and short term investments	119		131	
		27,743		25,443
Total assets		37,573		36,957

EQUITY AND LIABILITIES

	At 31 December			
	20X5		20X4	
	€'000	€'000	€'000	€'000
Equity				
Paid in share capital	20		20	
Share premium reserve	450		450	
Retained profits	21,787		20,863	
		22,257		21,333
Non-current liabilities				
Loans: Bank loan at 8% interest per year (repayable in 2010)	4,500		4,500	
	21,787		20,863	
		22,257		21,333
Current liabilities				
Bank overdraft	1,520		940	
Trade payables and accruals	8,900		9,667	
Tax	396		517	
		10,816		11,124
Total equity and liabilities		37,573		36,957

Note. Paid in share capital represents 200,000 shares of €0·10 each at 31 December 20X5

<u>Income Statement</u>

	Year ended 31 December	
	20X5	20X4
	€'000	€'000
Revenue	74,420	75,553
Total operating costs	72,580	73,320
Operating profit	1,840	2,233
Finance costs	520	509
Tax expense (effective tax rate is 24%)	396	517
Profit for the period	924	1,207

<u>Statement of changes in equity</u>

	Share capital €'000	Share premium €'000	Retained earnings €'000	Total €'000
Balance at 31 December 20X4	20	450	20,863	21,333
Profit for the period	–	–	924	924
Dividends paid	–	–	–	–
Balance at 31 December 20X5	20	450	21,787	22,257

Appendix 2

Kadgee's Cash Flow Statement

	At 31 December			
	20X5		20X4	
	€'000	€'000	€'000	€'000
Net cash inflow from operations				11,514
Operating profit		1,840		2,233
Add back depreciation	1,965		1,949	
(Increase)/Decrease in inventory	(1,886)		(535)	
(Increase)/Decrease in trade receivables	(426)		(1,526)	
Increase/(Decrease) in trade payables and accruals	(767)		(604)	
		(1,114)		(716)
Net cash flow from operations		726		1,517
Finance costs paid		(520)		(509)
Taxation paid		(517)		(390)
Purchase of tangible fixed assets		(281)		(350)
Dividends paid		–		–
Cash Inflow/(Outflow) before financing		(592)		268
Increase/(Decrease) in bank overdraft		580		(194)
Increase/(Decrease) in cash and short term investments		(12)		74

Unseen case material

The next board meeting of Kadgee is to discuss a number of issues that have arisen from opportunities that Kadgee's Managing Director has recently been investigating, and recommendations that a firm of management consultants recently employed by the Managing Director has made.

Acquisition of Douglas Knitwear

Douglas Knitwear is a family-owned company operating from a single factory in Perth, Scotland, UK. In addition to its exclusive and branded range of knitwear for golfers, which it sells under its own name through up-market department stores around the world, it also supplies some of the same clients as Kadgee with 'own label' knitwear. It additionally has a contract to supply knitwear to one of the UK's large supermarket chains.

The Board of Douglas Knitwear has approached Kadgee's board with a proposal to sell the firm to Kadgee. The board of Douglas Knitwear has made a one-for-one offer, i.e. to sell one Douglas share for one Kadgee share.

Douglas Knitwear has 50,000 shares in issue. All shares are held by members of the Douglas family who, Kadgee's Managing Director has been assured, are all in favour of the merger of the two firms providing the right terms can be negotiated. The present Managing Director of Douglas Knitwear, Michael Douglas, has also made it a condition of the offer that the board retains his present salary and conditions and that he, Michael Douglas, is given a place on the Board of Kadgee.

Kadgee does not have any factories in Scotland. Its nearest factory is 270 miles (435 km) away in the North of England.

Kadgee does not provide knitwear or hosiery to its clients at present and buys in knitted cotton fabrics for blouses and dresses. Clients such as Portrait and Diamond have sourced pullovers, cardigans and socks from other providers. Kadgee's Managing Director feels this is an opportunity to offer a better service that is consistent with the stated policy of several of Kadgee's customers to reduce the number of sources for their products.

Offer to purchase factory

Kadgee's Managing Director has received an offer from a property developer for its factory in Ireland. The proposal is to buy the freehold and to demolish the factory to build office units. The developer is offering €1.9 million for the site which presently houses one of Kadgee's blouse-making operations and employs 90 people. Contracts produced there can be relocated to the remaining factories of Kadgee where sufficient capacity is available.

The developer is prepared to exchange contracts as soon as possible but does not wish to take ownership of the site until September 20X7. A deposit of 10% of the purchase consideration has been offered at exchange.

Kadgee's Operations Director has estimated that most of the machinery at the factory is too old to be worth salvaging although it may be economic to recover some of the warehouse machinery and to use it at one of Kadgee's remaining factories.

Joint Venture in Sri Lanka

Jaffna Enterprises, a Sri Lankan company, has offered to invest in a joint venture to open a factory in Sri Lanka with Kadgee. It will take a year to build and so should be ready to commence production in January 20X8. A preliminary study by Kadgee suggests that the factory could produce apparel at about 30% of the cost of making the same garments in its existing factories and, taking into account the range of garments that might be transferred there, has forecast that overall forecast production costs might fall by 20% per annum. A number of other clothing companies have already transferred production to Sri Lanka.

Jaffna is offering Kadgee 30% of the equity in the joint venture. Jaffna is also negotiating to allocate 30% of the equity to another apparel manufacturer, Rocket, a specialist branded sportswear provider incorporated in another European country. The remaining 40% will be held by Jaffna Enterprises. The CEO will be appointed by Jaffna with one directorship each going to nominees of Kadgee and Rocket. Jaffna already owns and operates several factories in Sri Lanka.

The investment during 20X7 required from Kadgee is €2 million. Kadgee's bankers have indicated that they would be prepared to advance additional loans taking the debt from €4.5 million to €6.5 million but that the additional loan will be charged at 10%.

Design centre

The management consultants have proposed the creation of a separate business unit, incorporated as a separate company, called the Kadgee Design Centre Ltd. Kadgee will hold 60% of the share capital, with other shareholders holding 40%. This will undertake design for Kadgee, its clients and for other apparel firms. It will charge a commercial rate for these services and will rent its present office space from Kadgee at a market rent.

Outsourcing

The management consultants have also proposed outsourcing of logistics (warehousing and transportation of finished clothing) to a major global logistics provider. At present Kadgee employs 42 people in operating its warehouses and in driving the trucks it leases from a finance house.

Risk management function

The management consultants also highlighted various failings in Kadgee's risk assessment processes. As a result the Managing Director is considering whether to establish a risk management function. He does however wish that the function should do more than check for compliance with internal policies. He wishes it to make a clear contribution to Kadgee achieving its objectives.

Governance

As Kadgee is an unlisted company, at present all the directors are executive directors. The Managing Director believes that Kadgee needs to start appointing non-executive directors, as this will make the company more attractive to investors if, as he intends it should, Kadgee seeks a listing in around three years' time. He believes however that the other director/shareholders will be reluctant to see non-executive directors appointed until the company obtains a stock market flotation.

Required

(a)   Discuss the extent to which each of the following proposals impacts upon the risks faced by Kadgee's shareholders:

   (i)   Acquisition of Douglas Knitwear
   (ii)   Sale of the factory in Ireland
   (iii)   The joint venture in Sri Lanka
   (iv)   Creating a separate business unit for design
   (v)   Outsourcing logistics   **(30 marks)**

(b)   Demonstrate to the managing director how the role of the risk management function can extend beyond compliance issues to aiding fulfilment of strategic objectives.   **(10 marks)**

(c)   Discuss the extent to which non-executive directors can contribute to the effectiveness of corporate governance in Kadgee's current situation as an unlisted company that may seek a listing in future.

                                                                                (10 marks)

                                                                       (Total = 50 marks)

SECTION B

Answer TWO of the three questions.

Question 2

(a) Assume you are the Treasurer of AB, a large engineering company. You have forecast that the company will need to borrow £2 million by the end of September 20X3 for at least 6 months. The need for finance will arise because the company has extended its credit terms to selected customers over the summer period. The company's bank currently charges customers such as AB 7·5% per annum interest for unsecured fixed rate borrowing and LIBOR + 0.3% for unsecured floating rate borrowing. You believe interest rates will rise by at least 1·5 percentage points over the next 6 months. You are considering using one of three alternative methods to hedge the risk:

    (i)   Forward rate agreements
    (ii)   Interest rate futures
    (iii)   An interest rate guarantee (a short-term cap)

You can purchase an interest rate cap at 7% per annum for the duration of the loan to be guaranteed. You would have to pay a premium of 0·1% of the amount of the loan. As part of the arrangement, the company will agree to pay a 'floor' rate of 6% per annum.

Required

Discuss the features of each of the three alternative methods of hedging the interest rate risk and advise on how each might be useful to AB, taking all relevant and known information into account. **(12 marks)**

(b) You are contacted by the company's bank and informed that another of the bank's clients, a smaller company in the same industry, is looking for a swap partner for a similar amount of borrowing for the same duration. The borrowing rates applicable to AB and RO are as follows:

	Floating	Fixed
AB	LIBOR + 0.3%	7.5%
RO	LIBOR + 0.5%	8.5%

Required

    (i)   Demonstrate whether a swap would be beneficial to both companies in the situations described below. If a swap is beneficial, recommend how the two companies could co-operate in a swap arrangement to their mutual benefit. The situations are as follows.

        (1)   RO prefers floating rate finance, AB prefers fixed rate finance.
        (2)   RO prefers fixed rate finance, AB prefers floating rate finance.

        Support any recommendations you make with appropriate calculations.

    (ii)   Discuss the advantages and disadvantages of arranging a swap through a bank rather than negotiating directly with a counter-party. **(13 marks)**

<u>Note</u>. A report format is NOT required in answering this question. **(Total = 25 marks)**

Question 3

EWC is a large company in an unregulated sector of the telecommunications industry. It has ambitious plans for sales growth and increased profitability. In support of these goals, senior management has established a flat management structure. Budget targets place employees under considerable pressure but success in achieving and surpassing sales and profitability targets is rewarded by bonuses and share options. Employees who do not achieve their targets do not remain with the company for long.

Performance targets exist for expanding EWC's customer base, sales value and profitability per customer, and geographic and product-based expansion. EWC zealously pursues cost reduction with continual efforts to drive down suppliers' prices. The company aims to eliminate any wasteful practices in management and administration, EWC considers any expenditure that does not lead directly to sales growth to be wasteful and the company minimises its corporate policies and procedures. As a result, EWC has tended to overlook unscrupulous practices in its employees' dealings with customers, competitors and suppliers in the pursuit of its goals. The company is unlisted and reports its profits to shareholders once per year.

Required

(a)   Identify the major types of risk facing EWC that arise from its style of management. Give reasons to support your answer.   **(10 marks)**

(b)   Explain the significance of the control environment in EWC.   **(5 marks)**

(c)   From the perspective of a newly appointed non-executive director, evaluate the financial, non-financial quantitative, and qualitative controls in EWC in the context of EWC's goals and the risks facing EWC.
                                                                                                                                                              (10 marks)

(Total = 25 marks)

Question 4

About 25 years ago, two people visiting a mountain range discovered a large underground cave. The find was considered to be 'exceptional' by the scientific community as the cave was the largest and best preserved example of a 'living cave', that is a cave where specific underground formations such as stalactites were still growing. Years of secret development, involving significant costs that frequently exceeded budget, meant that the cave was opened for public view last year. The development was funded mainly by the national government of the country the cave was located in and a bank loan. The cave is now maintained as a non-profit making Trust, (The CAVE Trust) controlled by a mixture of local people interested in maintaining the cave as well as experienced mountaineers and cave explorers.

Visitors to the cave now pay a fee of about €40 for access to the cave; the fee includes the services of an experienced tour guide. The fee of €40 was derived by the Trust as appearing to be good value for money for guests as well as providing some income to pay for the new tour guides etc. Tickets for cave access are sold near the cave entrance, where a museum and small shop are also located. Visitors pay for tickets using cash, cheques, debit or credit cards. Tickets are issued in numeric sequence, although only a limited number are available for issue each day due to space considerations in the cave. Other income is available from government grants.

Other items of expenditure within the cave include air conditioning and humidity systems to maintain the cave environment, wages of staff, light, heat and power and computer based security systems. Additional expenditure will be required in the next 18 months for extensions to the museum, a restaurant and research areas for school children as well as further development of access to the extensive cave system.

Partly due to lack of experience in the board of management, the actual management accounting system for the Trust is minimal. Information is provided on ticket sales, and expenditure totals at the end of each month.

The national government that provided part of the funding for development of the cave complex has recently indicated that funding will be withdrawn in six months. Unfortunately, the Trust does not have any contingency plan to overcome this loss of income.

Required

(a)   Evaluate the management accounting system at the CAVE Trust and recommend improvements which will help to overcome any weaknesses you identify.   **(11 marks)**

(b)   Explain the audit process for accounting for ticket income in the Trust, recommending the audit tests to be carried out that will help to limit fraud.   **(14 marks)**

(Total = 25 marks)

Answers

DO NOT TURN THIS PAGE UNTIL YOU HAVE
COMPLETED THE MOCK EXAM

362

A plan of attack

We know you've been told to do it at least 100 times and we know if we asked you you'd know that you should do it. So why don't you do it in an exam? 'Do what in an exam?' you're probably thinking. Well, let's tell you for the 101st time. **Take a good look through the paper before diving in to answer questions.**

First things first

What you must do in the first five minutes of reading time in your exam is **look through the paper i**n detail, working out **which questions to do** and the **order** in which to attempt them. So turn back to the paper and let's sort out a plan of attack.

We then recommend you spend the remaining time analysing the requirements of Question 1 and highlighting the key issues in the question. The extra time spent on (a) will be helpful, whenever you intend to do the question, If you decide to do it first, you will be well into the question when the writing time starts. If you intend to do it second or third, probably because you find it daunting, the question will look easier when you come to back to it, because your initial analysis should generate further points whilst you're tackling the other questions.

The next step

You're probably either thinking that you don't know where to begin or that you could have a very decent go at all the questions.

Option 1 (if you don't know where to begin)

If you are a bit **worried** about the paper, it's likely that you believe that case study question 1 looks daunting. We therefore recommend that you do one or both of the optional questions before tackling the case study. Don't however fall into the trap of going over time on the optional questions because they seem easier. You will need to spend half the time available on the case study.

- If you think you can describe interest rate hedging instruments well, but are not sure of the mathematics, do think about attempting **Question 2.** Your answer to (a) can be purely descriptive, and the numbers make up only just over the marks in (b).

- **Question 3** offers some (although not all that much) information to help you generate ideas, and if you think widely across the company's business and those involved in it there is scope for doing well on this question. The detailed requirements will help you structure your answer, and again you need to think broadly, particularly about what constitutes a qualitative control

- **Question 4** is wide-ranging for a section B question, covering management accounting and audit issues. If you don't feel confident with either of these areas, you may avoid the question, although if you read the scenario carefully, you may be able to generate a number of ideas. Both parts will be marked fairly generously and a large number of different points could score marks.

- There is a lot of information in the scenario that you can draw on for part (a) of **Question 1**. Try to think widely about risks and also bring in relevant ideas from E3 and F3.

Option 2 (if you're thinking 'I can do all of these')

It never pays to be over confident but if you're not quaking in your shoes about the exam then **turn straight to compulsory Question 1**. You've got to do it so you might as well get it over and done with. Make sure you answer every requirement and sub-requirement in the question and also make sure you include plenty of examples from the case study. Bear in mind that one thing you are being tested on is an ability to identify and discuss in detail how you would deal with the most important risks.

Once you've done the compulsory question, choose two of the questions in Section B.

- **Question 2** is more of an explanation than a numbers question, so you need to be clear on your terminology. The swap calculations should be fine if you've practised the questions in the body of the kit.

- The shortish scenario in **Question 3** may nevertheless allow you to generate plenty of risks for (a) but remember that it is for only 10 marks and that it is important to explain each risk carefully. (c) requires an evaluation so don't just describe lots and lots of controls; you won't score well unless you say how valuable you think each control is.

- Before you dive into **Question 4,** make sure that you're equally happy with both the management accounting and audit aspects of the question. You need to generate a similar number of points on each part.

<u>No matter how many times we remind you...</u>

Always, always **allocate your time** according to the marks for the question in total and for the parts of the questions. And always, always **follow the requirements exactly**.

<u>You've got free time at the end of the exam.....?</u>

If you have allocated your time properly then you **shouldn't have time on your hands** at the end of the exam. If you find yourself with five or ten minutes spare, however, go back to **any parts of questions that you didn't finish** because you ran out of time.

<u>Forget about it!</u>

And don't worry if you found the paper difficult. More then likely other students would too. If this were the real thing you would need to forget the exam the minute you leave the exam hall and think about the next one. Or, if it's the last one, celebrate!

Question 1

Text references. Chapters 1-3, 5.

Top tips. This question format could be quite common in Section A, with the majority of marks being given for an analysis of the impact on shareholder risks of various business features or developments.

Easy marks. if you knew the main roles of non-executive directors, you should have been to generate sufficient ideas to gain a good mark for (c).

Marking scheme

		Marks
(a)	1 mark per each impact discussed under each heading. Max 7 marks per heading	30
(b)	Up to 2 marks per valid point discussed. Answers can cover any relevant aspect of risk management role. Award high marks for links with strategic objectives.	10
(c)	Up to 2 marks per valid contribution discussed	10
		50

(a)

Top tips. The question asks about changes in risk that impact on shareholders, so your answer must discuss whether and how the opportunities are likely to lead to higher or lower revenues and costs. The other issue of interest to shareholders is voting power, which the acquisition of Douglas will affect.

It's important to plan your answer to (a) in advance so that you don't repeat the same points in detail more than once. Confidentiality for example is a particularly important issue with the design house, but you could alternatively have discussed confidentiality in relation to the Sri Lankan joint venture or the logistics supplier.

(i) Acquisition of Douglas Knitwear

Benefits of diversification

The acquisition would represent a **significant diversification** for Kadgee into knitwear but also into having its own branded product. The Kadgee group will receive revenue from a **larger number of customers** and also across a **wider range of products.** This should reduce the proportionate impact on Kadgee of losing any one of its current contracts, although the loss of monetary revenue may be higher if the acquisition means that Kadgee is supplying the retailer with more products.

Growth opportunities

The merger may offer Kadgee **better chances to expand**. The acquisition provides Kadgee with access to supermarkets, and the availability of this channel may improve Kadgee's chances of successfully developing its own budget clothing range if it decides to expand into this area.

Protection of current deals with retailers

Douglas Knitwear sells to a number of the retailers that Kadgee already supplies. These retailers are looking to reduce the number of suppliers they use, so Kadgee's **ability to provide a greater variety of clothing** should help it **retain current contracts** and maybe gain new ones.

Management synergies

There may be some potential management synergies with the accession of Michael Douglas to the Board of Kadgee. Michael has experience in brand marketing and may lead **more effective promotion** of the Kadgee brand generally. Being able to brand Kadgee products with the Douglas knitwear brand may **enhance Kadgee's appeal.**

Rationalisation of production

The geographical distance and dissimilarity of production processes (knitwear will use different machines and skills from other apparel production) may mean the merger **does not deliver greater production flexibility**.

Change in shareholding patterns

The change in shareholding patterns mean that the current board **no longer commands a majority** of votes (previously they held 60% of shares, with the exchange they will hold 48% (120/250) of shares. There is therefore a theoretical risk that they could be out-voted if all other shareholders combined against them. However they may not be too worried about this risk as an anti-board faction would need the support of the firm's founder to obtain a majority and he may be unwilling to withdraw his support from the board.

(ii)   Sale of the factory in Ireland

Reduced financial risk

Revenue from the sale of the factory in Ireland can be used to **provide finance** for other investments, such as the investment in Sri Lanka. This may be more **acceptable to shareholders** than extra debt finance, which could result in **increased volatility of income** for shareholders.

Cost reduction

Fixed costs associated with the factory such as rent, rates, insurance and maintenance will be **eliminated, improving Kadgee's operational gearing**. There will be some one-off costs associated with the closure such as **relocation of staff**, **dismantling machinery** and **training costs** if required in the factories to which production has been transferred. There is a risk that costs may be higher than anticipated if suppliers decide they cannot supply the other factories and there are therefore cancellation costs.

Capacity

The **reduction in capacity** from **closing factories in Ireland** may mean that Kadgee has less flexibility to meet additional orders that will generate extra profits. The implication is that not all its factories currently have spare capacity.

Staff discontent

Staff at the Irish factory may react to the intended closure by producing fewer goods of a lower quality. This may impact on revenue or result in significant **extra rectification costs**. Some may feel motivated to **sabotage operations.** There may also be an **adverse impact on output and quality** in other factories, with staff feeling less motivated as they are fearful for their jobs.

Developer default

If the developer is forced to **back-out at a late stage,** Kadgee may already have incurred the closure costs while finding itself still **liable for some of the fixed costs** on the factory. Hopefully however the site would appeal to another developer and could soon be sold to someone else, although the **sale price** may be **lower.**

(iii)   Joint venture in Sri Lanka

Reduction in cost base

The fact that other clothing manufacturers already successfully manufacture in Sri Lanka suggests that transfer of production should **reduce production costs,** improving year-end profits. Reducing the cost base may also help Kadgee **protect its revenue streams**, as it will be able to **offer lower prices** to existing customers whilst still maintaining an acceptable profit margin.

Control issues

However the proposed control arrangements will mean that Kadgee does **not have control** over the **strategic development** of the joint venture. If for example it wishes to invest further in Sri Lanka, it may find that its partners are unable or unwilling to do so. Kadgee also lacks control over **operational issues** and may suffer revenue-losing **delays** as a consequence.

Commitment to investment

The initial commitment of $2 million appears comparatively small for a major investment. The consequences of commercial failure or loss of assets would appear to be **acceptably small.** However there is the assumption that Rocket or another investor will join the joint venture. If they do not do so, Kadgee may need to make a further investment of fixed or working capital.

Exchange risks

The currency of Sri Lanka, the Sri Lanka Rupee, will **vary against European currencies**. This means that Kadgee will be contracting costs in the Rupee but receiving its revenues in Euros or other European currency. This creates **exchange rate risk** where a rise in the Rupee would reduce profit margins. This can be avoided by foreign exchange hedging, although this will involve some costs.

Staffing issues

Jaffna Enterprises' experience in managing staff in Sri Lanka should help ensure staff are well-managed and produce goods of the **necessary quality for Kadgee's customers.** However the transfer of manufacturing may threaten the quality of UK production. Staff who are left may be fearful for their own jobs and less willing to co-operate with management.

Resolution of disputes

The ownership arrangements may make the **resolution of disputes** over revenue, cost or risk sharing **problematic.** The multiple jurisdictions potentially involved in legal disputes may mean it becomes very expensive to resolve disputes.

(iv)   Creating a separate business unit for design

Increased revenue earning opportunities

As a stand-alone CAD bureau the design centre will be able to **sell its capacity,** and so recover its costs, from clients beyond Kadgee.

Improved accountability

As a fixed overhead unit there is not presently any account taken of whether the activities of the design centre actually generate **financial benefits** for the shareholders of Kadgee. It has clearly been beneficial to the firm but there is a danger that new designs, samples, prototypes etc are being developed which lead to no additional orders. By charging itself out at an hourly rate the design centre will help management to assess whether its work is **actually delivering profitable contracts.**

Staff retention

Setting up a separate company may reduce the risk of **losing key staff** whose ideas generate the new designs that protect Kadgee's marketplace position. The chances of retaining the management team of the design centre may be improved by giving them the chance to run their own business. The i**ncreased diversity of work and opportunities to build a business** may inspire all the team and also enable Kadgee to attract better staff. The fact that the design centre will be a **separate company** may make it easier to reward employees with **profit-related bonuses** or **share options.**

Priority of Kadgee's interests

If the design centre is to be given complete autonomy, this may mean that on commercial grounds Kadgee's interests do not receive top priority. Kadgee may need to have **priority access** to the design centre for urgent work such as modification of designs whilst in production, as any delay to modification would also result in significant costs of **downtime in the factory** (or of catching up later). However giving this priority to Kadgee may **limit the service** the centre can give to other clients

Impact of transfer pricing

If the design centre charges a market price the effect may be to reduce its usage by Kadgee below the level of usage that would have occurred had the price been lower or nil. If the design centre has more work than it can handle this would represent a sensible allocation of resources. However if it were left with idle capacity because of the lower demand the effect would be **dysfunctional**

because the Kadgee group would not be benefiting from the services of the design centre but still be **paying the costs of maintaining it**. In the same way if the design centre cut back on floor space, or found cheaper premises elsewhere, it could leave Kadgee with the **costs of un-let space** and perhaps also paying a **rental charge** to an external landlord.

Confidentiality of designs

Kadgee could face an increased risk that its **designs** will be **leaked** to, or used for, competitors' products. Similarly non-Kadgee clients of the design centre will naturally wish to be assured that their designs are not revealed to their competitors. Leaking of exclusive designs may result in **legal penalties** for the Kadgee group and also jeopardise relationships with major suppliers. Kadgee may wish to take out **insurance** against these penalties, and include terms in contracts making staff **liable for damages** if they leak designs.

Support by Kadgee

If however the design centre is not a successful business, Kadgee may be faced with the choice of providing **extra financial support** as majority shareholder or accepting the design centre's failure as a business.

(v)   Outsourcing logistics

Reduction in fixed costs

Kadgee should benefit from a **reduction in its fixed cost base**. It has a number of costs that have to be covered if the volume of orders falls (salary costs, operating costs of trucks). Some costs will be incurred even if Kadgee is deriving no benefit from them, for example the costs of empty warehouse space. An outsource provider should be able to offer an arrangement that is better value for Kadgee, particularly if it is **linked to offers processed and items transferred**. Even if there is a fixed cost element in the payment to the outsource provider, the **economies of scale** and the experience effects that the provider enjoys should result in contract prices that are lower than maintaining logistics in-house.

Flexibility

At present Kadgee is considering sourcing some of its production from overseas. This will mean it has to obtain a **global logistics presence.** It should be less costly and less risky for Kadgee to use an established global provider than trying to develop its own capabilities.

Loss of control

Kadgee would lose control over a **strategically important business function**. Problems with logistics could lead to Kadgee losing customers.

Long-term contract

However Kadgee is facing an environment of constant change. An outsourcing contract may have a minimum time period of, say, 5 years. This means that the environment it will operate in may change considerably from the expectations held by the Board at the time the contract was agreed and signed. Volumes of business, locations and service requirements may change. If the contract does not have flexibility or break clauses built into it, Kadgee may have to **pay for service it no longer requires** or be **required to pay compensation** to the partner for early closure of the contract. At the same time **extra payments** may have to be made for **changing the specification** of other parts of the contract.

Risks of delays

Problems in logistics, particularly global supply chains, can lead to losses of revenue for Kadgee and for its clients. Clients may demand penalty fees from suppliers that do not meet delivery dates. A suitable outsource contract can make the **supplier liable for such penalty payments** and allow Kadgee itself to recover money if its operations are disrupted. However the outsource partner may **recognise the uncertainty of the environment** and seek to shift the costs of this on to Kadgee, by for example the use of a standard contract.

Disputes with contractee

Following on from this, Kadgee may have to incur **substantial legal fees** if it wishes to obtain a **tailored contract**. However if it accepts a standard contract, it risks **incurring substantial fees** if a legal dispute does arise.

Costs of monitoring performance

Kadgee will need to incur costs to ensure that the **volumes and timings of collections and deliveries** are **monitored.** If monitoring is inadequate, revenue could be **threatened by late deliveries.** There is also the risk that inventory may be stolen in transit and sold privately at prices that **undercut Kadgee.**

(b)

> **Top tips.** Remember throughout that you are meant to be justifying the role of risk management. Therefore risk management's role in ensuring compatibility of risk responses with strategy needs to be stressed, and you also need to show how the function can improve the efficiency and effectiveness of risk responses. The function should be part of a coherent framework.

Integrated risk management framework

The main role of a risk management function is to ensure that the risk management framework is consistent with the strategic objectives established by the directors and is complete and integrated. This means that the risk management framework should **address the key risks that the company faces** in ways that are **consistent with its overall objectives.** The function for example would assess the benefits of introducing more formal controls in areas where high-calibre staff provide assurance of good quality and weigh these against the costs of more formal procedures in the light of the board's objective to limit costs.

Risk appetite and limits

The risk management function can advise the board on whether Kadgee's current or proposed strategy is in line with the **risk appetite** that derives from the objectives that the board has set. This should involve weighing performance and conformance, the risks that adverse events will happen weighed against the failure to grasp opportunities and generate returns. The proposed Sri Lankan joint venture is a good example of this. It may generate increased risk because of problems of controlling an operation in which Kadgee does not have the sole stake. However it also provides Kadgee with an opportunity to undertake a restructuring of its cost base that will **improve its competitiveness.**

Risk culture

The risk management function can help ensure that a **common risk culture** applies across all operations. This partly involves ensuring existing best practice is spread, for example **quality suggestions by staff** are circulated. Maintaining a common culture is likely to be most important given the likely additions to the group of the Sri Lankan joint venture and Douglas Knitwear. The risk culture may have to be adopted if it is to be applied overseas to a joint venture that Kadgee does not control. Introducing Kadgee's culture into Douglas may also prove challenging if it meets with **resistance from Douglas's management team.**

Roles and responsibilities

The risk management function should also ensure that **risk management responsibilities** are clearly defined and allocated. This includes assessing the performance measurement system to establish whether it measures fairly **achievement of business goals that depend on risk-related decisions**.

Risk indicators and reports

The risk management function should be responsible for establishing a system of risk indicators and reports. It should supply the board with the information it needs to **fulfil governance best practice**, to monitor changing risks and ensure risk management procedures adopt. The risk management function can draw **together information from various sources on key risks**, for example internal reports from sales and design staff who deal directly with customers with external information about the results and future plans of customers. The risk management function should also **monitor indicators** that future risks may materialise, for example **changes in competitor strategy** or problems with the information technology systems.

(c)

> **Top tips.** Strategy, performance scrutiny, risk and performance management are the main headings used in the Higgs report to describe the role of non-executive directors. Again this is a selling exercise; under each heading you need to show clearly the contribution non-executive directors can make.

Business expertise

Non-executive directors can broaden the level of expertise on Kadgee's board, which may at present be fairly limited given the board's owner-manager structure. If Kadgee is to outsource operations and functions, particularly overseas, a non-executive director with experience of a company whose activities have been outsourced, will be able to **advise on the benefits and risks of outsourcing.**

Strategy

A non-executive director should be able to bring an independent viewpoint on strategy to Kadgee's board. At present the board appears to be rather insider-dominated and perhaps unwilling to make waves. A non-executive director may be more inclined to **challenge the strategy** of the board.

Performance scrutiny

A non-executive director can **scrutinise the work done by executive management** and monitor how performance is reported to the board. This will include whether Kadgee is **developing reporting systems** that will be sufficient to provide the reliable information that will be required if it seeks and obtains a listing.

Risk

A non-executive director can also **review the reports on risks and risk management** that derive from the system established by the risk management function. The director will assess whether risks appear to be **adequately managed,** and also that the systems **fulfil the requirements** of **governance best practice** with which Kadgee will have to comply if it obtains a listing.

Directors and management

The non-executive director can assess the performance of directors and managers, and can be responsible for advising on a remuneration structure that **fairly rewards the performance of directors**. He can also advise on what the **concerns of external shareholders** will be if the company seeks a listing and how management will best **demonstrate its accountability** to a new shareholder base.

Question 2

Text references. Chapter 9.

Top tips. Answers to discussion questions like (a) should concentrate on the levels of interest the company will have to pay, the risk of suffering from adverse interest rate movements, the flexibility of the instrument and the cost of using it. You would have been given credit in (a) for using a graph to illustrate your answer.

(b) presented a major problem when it was set. The original wording only covered the situation in (i) (1) where that neither party would benefit, and it was clear that you would need to undertake some sort of swap calculation rather than just saying that neither party would benefit. If you are faced with this situation in an exam, and identify the problem before you get very far into the question, it may be best to do another question. If here however you had already done (a), you would be better off making an attempt at (b), explaining clearly what you had done, the assumptions you made and the problems that you had identified.

(b) mentions that the companies are of different size; in a swaps question this generally indicates that the gains should not be split evenly, but in favour of the larger company. We have split the gains 0.6:0.2, although 0.5:0.3 would have been fine as well. In many questions however you will be told how to split the swap (generally equally).

Easy marks. (a) is quite general; if you tackle it successfully, you can pass the question without scoring very well on the calculations.

Examiner's comments. Generally answers to (a) were good and related well to the question's scenario. Mistakes included failing to recognise that interest rate futures can be traded, commenting that forward rate agreements and futures are options, and not understanding that interest rate guarantees are options.

Marking scheme

					Marks
(a)			Definition of FRA	1	
			Advantages of FRAs	2	
			Disadvantages of FRAs	2	
			Max		4
			Definition of futures	1	
			Advantages of futures	2	
			Disadvantages of futures	2	
			Max		4
			Definition of guarantee	1	
			Advantages of guarantee	2	
			Disadvantages of guarantee	2	
			Max		4
(b)	(i)	(1)	Calculations	2	
			Conclusion – swap not beneficial	1	
					3
		(2)	Swap calculations award marks for potential gain, inclusion of bank fee, swap arrangements, net outcome		6
	(ii)		Advantages and disadvantages – 1 mark per advantage/disadvantage identified		4
					25

(a) (i) <u>FRAs</u>

A forward rate agreement (FRA) would **fix the interest rate on borrowing** at a certain time in the future. If the actual rate is higher than the rate agreed, the bank would pay AB the difference; if lower, AB would pay the bank the difference. FRAs are usually available only for borrowings above $1 million, and AB's borrowing is much larger than that.

Advantages of FRAs

FRAs are **flexible**; they can be arranged for any amounts and any duration. An FRA would protect AB from **adverse interest rate movements** above the rate negotiated. **No premium** is payable on a forward rate agreement.

Disadvantages of FRAs

However the rate the bank will set for the forward rate agreement will reflect expectations of future interest rate movements. As interest rates are expected to rise, the bank may set a higher rate than the 7.5% currently available. AB will **not be able to take advantage if interest rates fall unexpectedly**. It may also be **difficult to arrange a FRA for a period longer than one year**.

(ii)   Interest rate futures

If AB purchases a future, it will be contracting to buy a **specific interest rate commitment** at an agreed price. The terms, amounts and periods of the contract will be **standardised**. The futures price is likely to **vary with changes in interest rates**; as interest rates increase, the price of the future will fall. This acts as a **short hedge** against adverse interest rate movements.

Advantages of futures

AB should be able to hedge the £2 million for a **relatively small outlay**. AB should also be able to obtain futures for the **exact amount** of the borrowing, as the **standard size** of a LIFFE futures contract is £500,000. Futures contracts are easy to liquidate on the open market.

Disadvantages of futures

Interest rate futures are for **fixed periods** with a **fixed settlement date**, so the hedge may need to be adjusted. AB may be liable to **basis risk**, the risk that the price of the futures contract may not move in the expected direction. Futures contracts require a **margin or deposit payment**.

(iii)   Interest rate guarantee

The cap means that the **maximum interest rate** that AB will have to pay during a specific period is 7%. The floor means that the **lowest interest rate** that AB will pay is 6%.

Advantages of guarantee

The cap seems to offer better terms than the forward rate agreement, the rate of which is likely to be above 7.5%. AB will be able to **benefit from falling interest rates**.

Disadvantages of guarantee

The **premium** of 0.1% will be payable whatever the movement in interest rates, and whether or not the option is exercised. The cap also sets a **minimum rate** that AB will have to pay, and AB will not be able to take advantage of interest rates below 6%. However it seems unlikely, given current expectations, that rates will fall that low. The maturity of guarantees is **limited to one year**.

(b)   (i)   (1)   Recommendation

As illustrated below, in this instance the parties will not benefit from a swap and should not therefore undertake one.

	AB	RO	Total
Company wants	Fixed	Floating	
Would pay	(7.5%)	(LIBOR + 0.5%)	(LIBOR + 8%)
Could pay with swap	(LIBOR + 0.3%)	(8.5%)	(LIBOR + 8.8%)
Potential loss			0.8%

(2)   Recommendation

A gain of 0.8% in these circumstances could be made if a swap arrangement was undertaken. As AB is the **larger company**, able to obtain more favourable terms in both markets, the swap has been structured so that it receives 0.6% of the gain and RO receives 0.2%. Under the terms of the swap AB pays 7.5% and RO LIBOR + 0.5%. They then swap amounts, AB paying over LIBOR + 0.5% to RO and receiving 8.3% from RO.

	AB	RO	Total
Company wants	Floating	Fixed	
Pay to bank without swap	(LIBOR + 0.3%)	(8.5%)	(LIBOR + 8.8%)
Pay to bank if swap agreed	(7.5%)	(LIBOR + 0.5%)	(LIBOR + 8%)
Potential gain			0.8%
Split	0.6%	0.2%	
Expected outcome	(LIBOR − 0.3%)	(8.3%)	(LIBOR + 8%)
Swap			
Pay to bank if swap agreed	(7.5%)	(LIBOR + 0.5%)	(LIBOR + 8%)
Swap terms			
Swap floating	(LIBOR + 0.5%)	LIBOR + 0.5%	
Swap fixed(bal fig. working)	8.3%	(8.3%)	
Net paid	(LIBOR − 0.3%)	(8.3%)	(LIBOR + 8%)
Pay to bank without swap	(LIBOR + 0.3%)	(8.5%)	(LIBOR + 8.8%)
Gain	0.6%	0.2%	0.8%

Working

(7.5%) + (LIBOR + 0.5%) + X = (LIBOR − 0.3%)
(LIBOR + 8%) + X = (LIBOR − 0.3%)
X = 8.3%

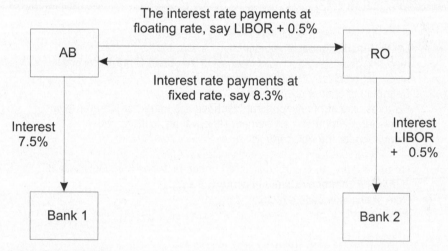

(ii) Advantages of using bank

(1) Finding a counterparty

A bank may be able to find a **counterparty more easily and quickly** than if the company searched for a partner itself. It may also be easy for a bank to reverse a swap if necessary.

(2) Access to counterparty

A bank may have **access to more counterparties** in more markets than if the company tried to find the counterparty itself

(3) Reduced risk exposure

The company is likely to be **less exposed to credit risk** if it deals through a bank. Banks are likely to have better information about the credit risks of counterparties.

Disadvantages of using bank

(1) Cost

Arrangement fees will have to be paid; these will not be necessary if a third party is contacted directly.

(2) Timing

Use of a bank leads potentially to **timing problems** if the company is settling before the counterparty, and the counterparty then defaults.

Question 3

Text references. Chapters 5 – 7.

Top tips. The scenario is a short one for a 25 mark question. However although it is brief, it is quite concentrated and every sentence contains something of significance for your answer. Because the scenario is short, it's easy to use the same material in different parts of your answer and end up repeating yourself. Hence it's particularly important here to read the requirements and then go through the scenario, allocating all the details to the most relevant question part.

Easy marks. Hopefully you were able to use the scenario information to generate a number of risks in (a).

Examiner's comments. Answers to (a) were generally stronger than answers to (b) or (c). Many students showed a worrying lack of knowledge of the control environment in (b), and failed to link unethical working practices to the control environment. Although most students identified the controls in (c), far fewer tried to evaluate them. Students who just wrote 'balanced scorecard' without further explanation did not score any marks.

Marking scheme

			Marks
(a)	Up to 2 marks for each risk identified. Award marks for business, reporting and reputation risks discussed. To obtain 2 marks for risk, risk must be clearly linked to scenario		10
(b)	Definition of control environment	2	
	Features of control environment identified – 1 mark per feature. Award marks for mention of management style, values, culture and foundation for internal controls	3	
			5
(c)	Up to 3 marks per control discussed under each heading. Only award 3 marks if control evaluated in context of EWC	9	
	Role of non-executive director	2	
	max		10
			25

(a)

Top tips. Our answer to (a) starts with the risks connected with staff, then goes on to look at the key risks relating to supplier and customer activity, before focusing on internal and external reporting of this activity and then the external legal risks. Reputation risk is, as often, a good finishing point.

Staffing risks

EWC appears to **tolerate high staff turnover**; targets are important, not the people who achieve them. However this may mean that **human resource costs** are **higher** than they need be, with costs involved in recruiting and training new staff.

Staff risks

EWC's tough attitude to its staff is **unlikely to encourage loyalty and trust**. Staff may seek to **enhance their own performance artificially** in order to achieve short-term targets and hence bonuses, by for example focusing on existing profitable customers and not making the same effort to develop new business requiring greater time investment for more risk. Staff may also be more tempted to **join competitors**, and then aim to take the customers with whom they've been dealing away to the competitors.

Supplier risks

EWC's management practices mean that they are unlikely to develop good relationships with their suppliers and hence **may not be able to rely on the supply chain**. The cost pressure EWC is imposing may also lead to a **reduction in service** from their suppliers, and **disputes** that **disrupt** supply. If EWC changes its suppliers regularly, it will face the **costs of finding new suppliers** and possible problems during the transition if new suppliers have initial difficulties in dealing with EWC's requirements.

Logistics risks

The pressure on costs may increase the risk of **administrative errors** because administration is overworked. This may result in various logistical errors such as not enough inventory being ordered or inventory being sent to the wrong place. These errors may displease customers and result in EWC **losing business.**

Customer risks

The unscrupulous practices towards customers may also **result in lost business**. EWC may have considerable difficulty building up long-term relationships with customers, if they feel that EWC is not treating them fairly, and they can get a better deal from EWC's rivals in a keenly competitive market.

Accounting risks

Failures in the information system may also lead to the accounts **not showing a true and fair view**. If profits and **sales are overstated**, directors and staff may receive **excessive bonuses**.

Legal risks

If staff break the law, then EWC may be at **risk itself from fines and penalties** as well as miscreant staff. This would apply even though EWC is in an unregulated sector, since staff may for example breach **consumer protection legislation** that applies to all businesses.

Reputation risks

If EWC gains a reputation as an unscrupulous operator, then it may find **various business opportunities curtailed**. Potential suppliers and customers may not wish to deal with EWC if they feel the relationship will be unfair. In addition a poor reputation may **jeopardise EWC's chances of obtaining a listing**, which may well be significant to managers and staff holding share options.

(b)

> **Top tips.** In (b) a brief explanation of the control environment may assist your answer but you can't afford to spend half a page on it. The question part is only worth 5 marks, and 4 of those will be for covering specifically EWC's control environment. Note that the answer points out that EWC, in its own way, does have a strong control environment; however it isn't one that encourages ethical behaviour.

Definition

The **control environment** is the overall attitudes, awareness and actions of directors and management regarding internal controls, encompassing management style, corporate culture and values. It provides the background for other controls

EWC control environment

Important aspects of EWC's control environment include the following.

Commercial focus

The important values in EWC's control environment are very **commercial**; they include success at all costs, personal wealth and the need to cut costs and find ways of making more profit.

Efficiency of operations

The philosophy that targets are the only controls that matter may mean that the directors believe that they are operating at **maximum efficiency**. However the board may have judged certain necessary expenditure as unimportant such as **quality control**; this may result in poor quality not being identified and hence customer dissatisfaction.

Organisational structure

The **flat structure** should mean that employees have considerable responsibility, which may **improve their motivation**. It should also mean that they can **respond rapidly to customer needs**. However the flat structure may make it easier for individuals to **override controls**. It could mean that they could easily manipulate profits by **entering false sales invoices before the year-end** and **raising credit notes after the year-end**. It also may be a structure that needs **modification as the company expands**. Decisions about **which new product and geographical markets to develop** need to be taken by senior management taking a wider strategic view, not by sales staff.

Ethical values

There is probably a link between the minimisation of corporate policies and the unscrupulous behaviour. The fact that dubious business practices are not forbidden appears to have led staff to believe that **ethical business behaviour** is **much less important than meeting targets**.

(c)

> **Top tips.** (c) appears to be the most demanding part of the question. The verb evaluate (assess the value of) is a high Level 5 requirement verb, compared with identify and explain in the earlier question parts, which are Level 2 verbs. The examiner requires a realistic assessment of their value and you make the evaluation as a non-executive director interested in higher-level controls and protecting the interests of shareholders and other stakeholders. Key aspects to examine are the impact of controls on strategic decision-making and behaviour.

Financial controls

Quality of information

In order to stay aware of sales, costs and profits, **detailed data** must be being produced and targets be set for each employee. **Value analysis** is also taking place to **identify non-value adding activity**. However the pressure on administration may lead to **poor quality management information** being produced, and lead to managers **taking the wrong business decisions** based on bad information. Although budget targets are tough, they are probably **not considered carefully** and realistic budgets may not be set. There may also be **few or no checks on the quality of the actual information** being compared with budgets.

Sales and profitability targets

Sales and profits targets could complement each other and this would **increase their value**. Setting sales targets means there is an **emphasis on expanding business from existing customers and finding new customers**; profits targets ensure that the **costs of maintaining the customer base are not excessive**. However there is apparently no attempt to address the **undesirable side effects** of these targets. If standards are too demanding, employees may become demotivated and leave. They may also seek to improve their own performance at the expense of other staff, for example **chasing the same customers**.

Non-financial quantitative controls

Expanded geographic and customer base targets

Ambitious targets for expansion appear to be appropriate in a rapidly-developing industry. However targets appear to have been set in every direction without considering whether they can all be achieved together. If cost restrictions mean that not enough time has been spent researching new markets, the targets may turn out to be detrimental because they result in **poor strategic decisions being taken**. EWC may end up **pursuing too many targets** at once or the **wrong targets**, and may as a result lack the resources to service its existing customer base effectively.

Qualitative controls

Failure to measure customer satisfaction

Certain qualitative controls suggested by the balanced scorecard do not appear to be operating, suggesting that qualitative controls will be ineffective, particularly in addressing the risks of losing customers. There seem to be **no attempt to measure business processes** that have the greatest impact on customer satisfaction such as employee performance when dealing with customers. EWC also does not appear to measure what actually matters to customers, for example **customer complaints** and how they are dealt with, or **speed of delivery**.

Reward mechanisms

The reward mechanisms of bonuses and share options reflect the company's objectives, and **do little to encourage ethical, congruent behaviour** as these factors are not taken into account. Arguably they consist of a mix of short-term rewards (bonuses) and longer-term rewards (share options), which make it more likely that successful staff will stay longer. However the **value of share options** is limited at present as EWC is unlisted and there is no ready market for the shares.

Role of non-executive director

Lastly non-executive directors can have an important role in **monitoring strategic development and operations** and **improving the control environment**. The fact that EWC is appointing non-executive directors, when it need not do so as an unlisted company, is a strength. However the corporate governance reports state that non-executive directors need to constitute a **strong and independent body** on the board if they are to be truly effective. A single non-executive director is unlikely to be able to insist on improvements in business ethics. Non-executive directors may **not also be able to obtain assurance about the truth and fairness of the accounts** if the information systems are unreliable.

Question 4

Text references. Chapters 15 and 16 are useful on the audit implications and Chapter 7 on the management accounting aspects.

Top tips. A question illustrating that optional questions may cover more than one syllabus area.

Easy marks. Identifying threats and risks is generally the easiest part of a question like this, and forms the basis of the rest of your answer, so be very alert for risks when you're reading carefully through the scenario, particularly risks to income here and also problems of limited management systems.

Marking scheme

			Marks
(a)	1 mark per weakness identified max	7	
	1 mark per appropriate improvement that relates clearly to weakness max	7	
			11
(b)	Audit planning including risk assessment	4	
	Documentation	1	
	Internal control consideration	1	
	Audit testing 1 mark per well-explained test suggested max	8	
	max		14
			25

(a)

Top tips. (a) is potentially very difficult to 'get into' simply due to the lack of information provided. However, given that scenarios may be relatively short, you will have to draw on your theoretical knowledge to provide outline answers in some situations. The basic sections of a management accounting system in terms of setting sales and expenditure budgets will be known, so these can be mentioned in the answer. Difficulties with the setting of budgets for these areas can then be determined from the scenario to provide useful, if relatively brief, examples to support the comments made.

Weaknesses in and improvements required to the management accounting system

Lack of a management accountant

Possibly the main weakness in the management accounting system is the lack of a management accountant! While some system may have been established in the past to provide basic management information, the lack of appropriate reporting clearly identifies a **lack of expertise** in the Trust. Any revisions to the system will need to be extensive, implying the appointment of a management accountant.

Quality of information

The current system appears to provide some basic monitoring of expenditure only, which will not be sufficient for the future. A **more detailed analysis of costs and income will be needed**. Establishing a new system also implies purchase of additional computer hardware and software, so an appropriate budget will be needed.

Budgets

Given that the Trust will still try to obtain government funding in the future, then **expenditure budgets** will be necessary **to show exactly how the funds would be spent**. Until recently, budgeting would involve cave development and building of the various visitor amenities only. The new management accounting system will have to record the budget initially, and then report expenditure across appropriate budget headings as cave development progresses. The development is likely to involve a high degree of risk, as cost **overruns** were noted in the scenario, so the budget reports would need to show these overruns and provide a basis for further funding applications.

Variance analysis

Monitoring day-to-day running of the Trust should be relatively easy as most of the expenditure is fixed. Budgetary reports will need to **focus on variances** from budgets, although these should be identifiable as increases in staff numbers, additional expenditure on cave humidity control etc.

Determining costs

The current method of setting the ticket price as 'good value' is unlikely to be sufficient, given the reliance on ticket income that the Trust will have in the future. Setting the price will involve determining the following costs:

- **Fixed costs** of running the cave including air conditioning, wages etc.
- **Additional costs** of expanding the cave network
- **Any variable costs**, although these are likely to be limited to light and heat
- **Other discretionary costs** such as marketing may also be included

Total costs are therefore easy to determine and can be used as input into the management accounting system to assist in determining the ticket price in the future.

Setting the ticket price – recommendation

It appears that the total number of tickets that can be sold is already known. Assuming all tickets were sold, then the total costs divided by number of tickets would give the ticket price. However, there is **no information on the demand for the tickets**, meaning that this calculation will not be accurate. Some element of non-sale will have to be determined taking the past 12 months sales since the caves opened, and an estimate of falling demand as the ticket price may well be higher than the current 'good value' price. An initial assumption may be necessary, with subsequent close monitoring of sales following this to determine if the assumption was accurate.

Monitoring guest numbers

The Trust needs to **monitor guest numbers closely** to determine whether **income will be sufficient to meet actual and proposed expenditure**. This information does not appear to be available from the current system. Additional development and therefore costs will be incurred, establishing the link between the guest booking system and the revised management accounting system.

Any new management accounting system will have to **integrate** with the **current guest booking system** to obtain this information. Total income from ticket sales can then be compared to budget in the management accounting system and variance analysis used to determine any deviation from budget.

(b)

> **Top tips.** In (b) you should remember that the main focus on audit work in the syllabus is identifying risk and then testing to ensure that the risks identified do not occur. The main sections of the answer therefore revolve around these two areas. The documentation of systems and internal control are mentioned in the syllabus content, hence require comment in the answer. However, lack of detail is justified partly from the note in the scenario that there are few controls, and partly because documenting and recording controls will be similar for most systems. Audit tests are linked to specific risks, and you should take care to ensure that the question requirement of showing how fraud can be limited is clearly spelt out in the answer.

Audit process for the audit of ticket income in the CAVE Trust

Audit planning

Audit planning is associated with **determining the business risks** for the Trust as a whole and any specific inherent risks and control risks for ticket sales.

Business risk – going concern

The overall business risk relevant to the CAVE Trust is **going concern**. The **withdrawal of funding** from the local government is likely to result in the **closure of the Trust** unless other income sources can be generated. This risk may mean that the Trustees would like to inflate sales income or attempt to minimise costs to try to show the results of the Trust in a favourable light, should negotiations with other providers of finance become necessary.

Inherent risk – cash sales

As some of the ticket sales are made for cash, there is an inherent risk that cash may be either **recorded incorrectly** or **misappropriated** (or both). Cash is a risky asset simply because it can be hidden and moved easily. Audit testing will need to focus on checking that all cash is recorded.

Control risk – lack of management experience

There appears to be **no audit experience** amongst the Trustees of the Trust. This implies that the **control system** will be **weak**, simply because setting up controls is **not a main focus of management**; they are more interested in the cave itself. It is possible that the auditor will not be able to rely on any internal controls, because they will either be missing or inadequate.

Summary of risk analysis

The main area of audit testing must therefore be **checking the completeness of income** – partly because of the potential going concern situation of the Trust and partly due to the nature of cash meaning it is easy to steal. Lack of management controls will affect audit work more from the point of view of limiting control testing and expanding the amount of substantive testing.

Documenting systems

Documenting systems means **recording the accounting system** so that individual transactions can be **followed from their start to end**. The auditor would prepare some form of system notes showing clearly the systems for recording ticket sales from cash and debit/credit cards, along with the controls expected over those systems.

Internal controls

As noted above, the internal control system is likely to be weak. A limited number of reconciliation controls such as agreement of total amount in till to the till roll each day by a person not actually selling tickets may be available. However, the auditor is **unlikely to rely on controls** for testing due to the inherent weaknesses noted above.

Audit testing

Audit testing will focus on ensuring that all transactions are **completely and accurately recorded** in the accounts of the Trust. Additional testing will be required over those areas where cash fraud could take place. Specific tests that will be carried out include:

Risk: Cash income incomplete

(i) For a number of days, **check the cash received in the till to the till roll**. This test will highlight cash fraud because any difference between the cash and the till could indicate cash being removed from the till.

(ii) For the same days, **agree the total amount of sales to the register of tickets actually sold**. This determines tickets sold and provides a check regarding the total income expected to be received.

(iii) **Agree the total cash sales to the bank paying in book**. This test may also identify fraud and money could be removed from the day's cash takings between being taken from the till and recorded on the paying in slip.

(iv) **Agreeing the total of the paying in slip to the bank statement**. This test could, in theory, identify fraud if the whole day's taking were stolen as the money would not appear on the bank statement.

Evaluation of results

If cash fraud is found then the auditor will need to carry out the following additional procedures:

(i) **Ask staff involved** with the sales system **why** the errors could have **occurred** – in other words check that the errors did not simply relate to unintentional mistakes rather than fraud.

(ii) **Attempt to determine the amount of cash fraud** by performing additional tests.

(iii) **Inform the Trustees** verbally of the situation.

(iv) **Make a report** to the relevant authorities for potential fraud.

(v) **Recommend** to the Trustees that **controls noted above are implemented** to try to minimise the likelihood of repeat fraud.

CIMA – Strategic level
Paper P3
Performance Strategy

Mock Exam 2 (September 2012)

You are allowed three hours to answer this question paper.
In the real exam, you are allowed 20 minutes reading time before the examination begins during which you should read the question paper, and if you wish, highlight and/or make notes on the question paper. However, you will **not** be allowed, **under any circumstances**, to open the answer book and start writing or use your calculator during this reading time.
You are strongly advised to carefully read all the question requirements before attempting the question concerned (that is all parts and/or sub-questions).
Answer the compulsory question in Section A.
Answer TWO of the three questions in Section B.

DO NOT OPEN THIS PAPER UNTIL YOU ARE READY TO START UNDER EXAMINATION CONDITIONS

PLEASE NOTE: THE PRESEEN MATERIAL FOR QUESTION 1 OF THIS EXAM IS THE SAME AS THE PRE-SEEN MATERIAL FOR QUESTION 1 OF THE MAY 2012 EXAM [QUESTION 71 IN THIS KIT]

SECTION A – 50 marks

Answer this question

Question 1

Preseen case study

Introduction

B Supermarkets (B) was founded as a grocery retailer in a European country in 1963. Its sales consist mainly of food and household items including clothing. B now owns or franchises over 15,000 stores world-wide in 36 countries. The company has stores in Europe (in both eurozone and non-eurozone countries), Asia and North America. B's head office is located in a eurozone country. B has become one of the world's largest chains of stores.

B's Board thinks that there are opportunities to take advantage of the rapid economic growth of some Asian countries and the associated increases in demand for food and consumer goods.

Structure

The B Group is structured into a holding company, B, and three subsidiary companies which are located in each of the regions of the world in which it operates (Europe, Asia and North America). The subsidiary companies, referred to as "Regions" within B, are respectively B-Europe, B-Asia and B-North America.

Store operations, sales mix and staffing

B operates four types of store: supermarkets, hypermarkets, discount stores and convenience stores. For the purpose of this case study, the definition of each of these types of store is as follows:

A *supermarket* is a self-service store which sells a wide variety of food and household goods such as washing and cleaning materials, cooking utensils and other items which are easily carried by customers out of the store.

A *hypermarket* is a superstore or very large store which sells the same type of products as a supermarket but in addition it sells a wide range of other items such as consumer durable white goods, for example refrigerators, freezers, washing machines and furniture. Hypermarkets are often located on out-of-town sites.

A *discount store* is a retail store that sells a variety of goods such as electrical appliances and electronic equipment. Discount stores in general usually sell branded products and pursue a high-volume, low priced strategy and aim their marketing at customers who seek goods at prices which are usually less than can be found in a hypermarket.

A *convenience store* is a small shop or store in an urban area that sells goods which are purchased regularly by customers. These would typically include groceries, toiletries, alcoholic beverages, soft drinks and confectionery. They are convenient for shoppers as they are located in or near residential areas and are often open for long hours. Customers are willing to pay premium prices for the convenience of having the store close by.

B sells food products and clothing in its supermarkets and hypermarkets at a higher price than many of its competitors because the Board thinks that its customers are prepared to pay higher prices for better quality food products. B also sells good quality consumer durable products in its supermarkets and hypermarkets but it is forced to sell these at competitive prices as there is strong competition for the sale of such goods. B's discount stores sell good quality electrical products usually at lower prices than those charged in its supermarkets and hypermarkets, B only sells electronic equipment in its discount stores. Customers have a greater range from which to choose in the discount stores as compared with supermarkets and hypermarkets because the discount stores specialise in the goods which they sell. B's convenience stores do not have the availability of space to carry a wide range of products and they charge a higher price for the same brand and type of goods which it sells in its supermarkets.

Although B owns most of its stores, it has granted franchises for the operation of some stores which carry its name.

Nearly 0.5 million full-time equivalent staff are employed world-wide in the Group. B tries when possible to recruit local staff to fill job vacancies within its stores.

Value statement and mission

In recognition of the strong competitive and dynamic markets in which it operates, B's Board has established an overall value statement as follows: "We aim to satisfy our customers wherever we trade. We intend to employ different generic competitive strategies depending on the market segment in which our stores trade."

The Board has also produced the following mission statement:

"B practises sustainable investment within a healthy ethical and thoughtful culture and strives to achieve customer satisfaction by giving a courteous and efficient service, selling high quality goods at a reasonable price, sourcing goods from local suppliers where possible and causing the least damage possible to the natural environment. By this, we aim to satisfy the expectations of our shareholders by achieving consistent growth in our share price and also to enhance our reputation for being an environmentally responsible company."

Strategic objectives

The following objectives have been derived from the mission statement:

1   Build shareholder value through consistent growth in the company's share price.

2   Increase customer satisfaction ratings to 95% as measured by customer feedback surveys.

3   Increase commitment to local suppliers by working towards achieving 40% of our supplies from sources which are local to where B stores trade.

4   Reduce carbon emissions calculated by internationally agreed measures by at least 1% per year until B becomes totally carbon neutral.

5   Maximise returns to shareholders by employing different generic competitive strategies depending on the market segment in which B stores trade.

Financial objectives

The Board has set the following financial objectives:

1   Achieve consistent growth in earnings per share of 7% each year.

2   Maintain a dividend pay-out ratio of 50% each year.

3   Gearing levels as measured by long-term debt divided by long-term debt plus equity should not exceed 40% based on book value.

Governance

The main board comprises the Non-executive Chairman, the Chief Executive and nine Executive directors. These cover the functions of finance, human resources, corporate affairs (including legal and public relations), marketing, planning and procurement. There is also one executive director for each of the three regions, being the Regional Managing Directors of B-Europe, B-Asia and B-North America. There are also nine non-executive main board members in addition to the Chairman.

The main Board of Directors has separate committees responsible for audit, remuneration, appointments, corporate governance and risk assessment and control. The Risk Assessment and Control Committee's tasks were formerly included within the Audit Committee's role. It was agreed by the Board in 2009 that these tasks should be separated out in order not to overload the Audit Committee which has responsibilities to review the probity of the company. B's expansion has been very rapid in some countries. The expansion has been so rapid that B has not been able to carry out any internal audit activities in some of these countries to date. The regional boards do not have a committee structure.

Each of the Regional Managing Directors chairs his or her own Regional Board. All of the Regional Boards have their own directors for finance, human resources, corporate affairs, marketing, planning and procurement but their structure is different for the directors who have responsibility for the stores. In B-Asia, one regional director is responsible for the hypermarkets and supermarkets and another is responsible for discount stores and convenience stores. In B-North America, one regional director is responsible for the hypermarkets and supermarkets and another is responsible for discount stores (B does not have any convenience stores in North America). In B-Europe there is one regional director responsible for supermarkets and hypermarkets, one for discount stores and one for convenience stores. In all regions the regional directors have line accountability to their respective regional managing director and professional accountability to the relevant main board director. There are no non-executive directors on the regional boards. Appendix 1 shows the main board and regional board structures.

Treasury

Each of B's three regions has a regional treasury department managed by a regional treasurer who has direct accountability to the respective Regional Director of Finance and professional accountability to the Group Treasurer. The Group Treasurer manages the central corporate treasury department which is located in B's head office. The Group Treasurer, who is not a main board member, reports to the Director of Finance on the main board.

Shareholding, year-end share prices and dividends paid for the last five years

B is listed on a major European stock exchange within the eurozone and it wholly owns its subsidiaries. There are five major shareholders of B, including employees taken as a group, which between them hold 25% of the 1,350 million total shares in issue. The major shareholders comprise two long term investment trusts which each owns 4%, a hedge fund owns 5%, employees own 5% and the founding family trust owns 7% of the shares. The remaining 75% of shares are owned by the general public.

The year-end share prices and the dividends paid for the last five years were as follows:

	200 €	2008 €	2009 €	2010 €	2011 €
Share price at 31 December	47.38	25.45	28.68	29.44	31.37
Net Dividend per share	1.54	1.54	1.54	1.62	1.65

Planning and management control

B has a very structured planning process. Each regional board produces a five year strategic plan for its region relating to specific objectives set for it by the main board and submits this to the main board for approval. The main board then produces a consolidated strategic plan for the whole company. This is reviewed on a three yearly cycle and results in a revised and updated group five year plan being produced every three years.

B's management control system, which operates throughout its regions and at head office, is well known in the industry to be bureaucratic and authoritarian. Strict financial authority levels for development purposes are imposed from the main Board. There is tension between the main Board and the regional boards. The regional board members feel that they are not able to manage effectively despite being located much closer to their own regional markets than the members of the main Board. The main Board members, on the other hand, think that they need to exercise tight control because they are remote from the markets. This often stifles planning initiatives within each region. This tension is also felt lower down the organisation as the regional board members exercise strict financial and management control over operational managers in their regions in order to ensure that the main Board directives are carried out.

Competitive overview

B operates in highly competitive markets for all the products it sells. The characteristics of each of the markets in which it operates are different. For example, there are different planning restrictions applying within each region. In some countries, B is required to operate each of its stores in a partnership arrangement with local enterprises, whereas no such restriction exists within other countries in which it trades. B needs to be aware of different customer tastes and preferences which differ from country to country. The following table provides a break-down of B's stores in each region.

	B Europe	B Asia	B North America
Supermarkets and hypermarkets	3,456	619	512
Discount stores	5,168	380	780
Convenience stores	4,586	35	

B is one of the largest retailing companies in the world and faces different levels of competition in each region. B's overall market share in terms of retail sales for all supermarkets, hypermarkets, discount stores and convenience stores in each of its regions is as follows:

	Market share
Europe	20%
Asia	1%
North America	1.5%

The following table shows the sales revenue and net operating profit earned by B in each of its regions for the year ended 31 December 2011:

	B Europe € million	B Asia € million	B North America € million
Revenue	89,899	10,105	9,708
Net Operating Profit	4,795	743	673

B is constantly seeking other areas of the world into which it can expand, especially within Asia where it perceives many countries have an increasing population and strengthening economies.

Corporate Social Responsibility (CSR)

B is meeting its CSR obligations by establishing environmental targets for carbon emissions (greenhouse gas emissions), careful monitoring of its supply chain, undertaking sustainable investments and investing in its human capital.

Environmental targets for carbon emissions

B's main board is keen to demonstrate the company's concern for the environment by pursuing continuous improvement in the reduction of its carbon emissions and by developing ways of increasing sustainability in its trading practices. A number of environmental indicators have been established to provide transparency in B's overall performance in respect of sustainability. These published measures were verified by B's statutory auditor and are calculated on a like-for-like basis for the stores in operation over the period measured.

In the year ended 31 December 2011, B reduced its consumption of kilowatt hours (kWh) per square metre of sales area as compared with the year ended 31 December 2008 by 9%. The target reduction for that period was 5%. In the same period it reduced the number of free disposable plastic bags provided to customers per square metre of sales area, by 51% against a target of 60%. Its overall greenhouse gas emissions (measured by kilogrammes of carbon dioxide per square metre of sales area) reduced by 1% in 2011 which was exactly on target.

B provides funding for the development of local amenity projects in all of the countries where B stores operate. (An amenity project is one which provides benefit to the local population, such as providing a park, community gardens or a swimming pool.)

Distribution and sourcing

Distribution from suppliers across such a wide geographical area is an issue for B. While supplies are sourced from the country in which a store is located as much as possible, there is nevertheless still a requirement for transportation across long distances either by road or air. Approximately 20% of the physical quantity of goods sold across the group as a whole is sourced locally, that is within the country in which the goods are sold. These tend to be perishable items such as fruit and vegetables. The remaining 80% of goods are sourced from large international manufacturers and distributors. These tend to be large items such as electrical or electronic equipment which are bought under contracts which are set up by the regional procurement departments. B, due to its size and scope of operations, is able to place orders for goods made to its own specification and packaged as under its own brand label. Some contracts are agreed between manufacturers and the Group Procurement Director for the supply of goods to the whole of the B group world-wide.

B's inventory is rarely transported by rail except within Europe. This has resulted in lower average reductions in carbon emissions per square metre of sales area by stores operated by B-Asia and B-North America than for those stores operated by B-Europe. This is because the carbon emission statistics take into account the transportation of goods into B's stores.

Sustainable investments

B aspires to become carbon neutral over the long term. The Board aims to reduce its carbon emissions by investing in state of the art technology in its new store developments and by carrying out modifications to existing stores.

Human Resources

B prides itself on the training it provides to its staff. The training of store staff is carried out in store by specialist teams which operate in each country where B trades. In this way, B believes that training is consistent across all of its stores. In some countries, the training is considered to be at a sufficiently high level to be recognised by national training bodies. The average number of training hours per employee in the year ended 31 December

2011 was 17 compared with 13 hours in the year ended 31 December 2010. In 2011, B employed 45% more staff with declared disabilities compared with 2010.

Information systems and inventory management

In order to operate efficiently, B's Board has recognised that it must have up-to-date information systems including electronic point of sale (EPOS) systems. An EPOS system uses computers or specialised terminals that can be combined with other hardware such as bar-code readers to accurately capture the sale and adjust the inventory levels within the store. EPOS systems installation is on-going. B has installed EPOS systems in its stores in some countries but not in all its stores world-wide.

B's information systems are not perfect as stock-outs do occur from time-to-time, especially in the European stores. This can be damaging to sales revenue when stock-outs occur during peak sales periods such as the days leading up to a public holiday. In Asia and North America in particular, B's information technology systems sometimes provide misleading information. This has led to doubts in the minds of some head office staff about just how robust are B's inventory control systems.

As is normal in chain store groups, there is a certain degree of loss through theft by staff and customers. Another way that loss is suffered is through goods which have gone past their "sell-by" date and mainly relates to perishable food items which are wasted as they cannot be sold to the public. In most countries, such food items which cannot be sold to the public may be sold to local farmers for animal feed.

Regulatory issues

B's subsidiaries in Asia and North America have sometimes experienced governmental regulatory difficulties in some countries which have hindered the installation of improved information systems. To overcome some of these regulatory restrictions, B-Asia and B-North America have, on occasions, resorted to paying inducements to government officials in order for the regulations to be relaxed.

APPENDIX 1

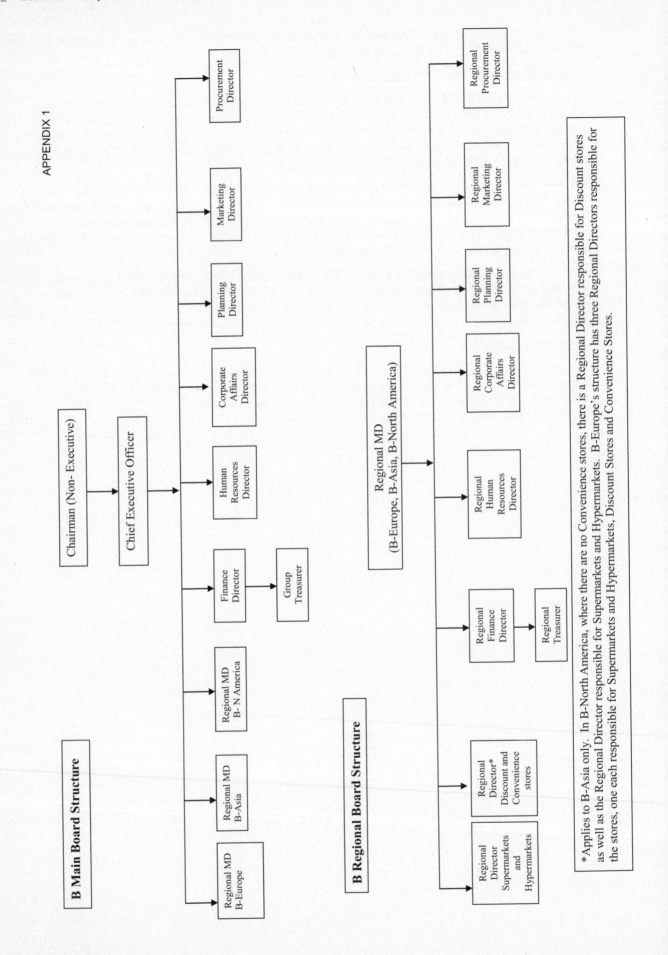

B Main Board Structure

Chairman (Non-Executive)

Chief Executive Officer

Regional MD B-Europe

Regional MD B-Asia

Regional MD B-N America

Finance Director

Group Treasurer

Human Resources Director

Corporate Affairs Director

Planning Director

Marketing Director

Procurement Director

B Regional Board Structure

Regional MD (B-Europe, B-Asia, B-North America)

Regional Director Supermarkets and Hypermarkets

Regional Director* Discount and Convenience stores

Regional Finance Director

Regional Treasurer

Regional Human Resources Director

Regional Corporate Affairs Director

Regional Planning Director

Regional Marketing Director

Regional Procurement Director

*Applies to B-Asia only. In B-North America, where there are no Convenience stores, there is a Regional Director responsible for Discount stores as well as the Regional Director responsible for Supermarkets and Hypermarkets. B-Europe's structure has three Regional Directors responsible for the stores, one each responsible for Supermarkets and Hypermarkets, Discount Stores and Convenience Stores.

B's income statement and statement of financial position.

Income statement for the year ended 31 December 2011

	Notes	€ million
Revenue		109,712
Operating costs		(103,501)
Net operating profit		6,211
Interest income		165
Finance costs		(852)
Corporate income tax		(1,933)
Profit for the year		3,591

Statement of financial position as at 31 December 2011

	€ million
ASSETS	
Non-current assets	57,502
Current assets	
Inventories	7,670
Trade and other receivables	1,521
Cash and cash equivalents	3,847
Total current assets	13,038
Total assets	70,540
EQUITY AND LIABILITIES	
Equity	
Share capital (1)	2,025
Share premium	3,040
Retained earnings	18,954
Total equity	24,019
Non-current liabilities	
Long term borrowings	15,744
Current liabilities	
Trade and other payables	30,777
Total liabilities	46,521
Total equity and liabilities	70,540

Notes:

1   There are 1,350 million €1.50 shares currently in issue. The share price at 31 December 2011 was €31.37.

Unseen case material

Health and safety

In a recent internal report commissioned by the directors of B it was stated that the health and safety laws in the countries in which B operates vary significantly. For example in some countries it is required that all employees whose jobs involve manual lifting are trained so that they can lift objects without risk of injury. The problem is further complicated by the definition of "manual lifting" varying from country to country. Similar issues arise with the need to wear protective clothing and the safe operation of forklift trucks.

B's directors saw the need to provide a safe working environment for B's employees irrespective of the country in which they work. They asked the Human Resources Director to develop a comprehensive safety manual that either matched or exceeded the minimum requirements laid down by law or other regulation in any of the countries in which B operated. Copies of the manual were then distributed to wherever B had employees. All of B's employees are required to adhere to the rules stated in the manual as a condition of their employment. The manual also sets out a number of broad principles, such as making the general manager of each store personally responsible for the safety of everyone employed at that store.

A recent newspaper article published in B's home country accused B of exploiting the weak health and safety rules in some countries. The article provided evidence of unsafe operating practices by describing a recent accident in one of B's stores in Asia. The accident occurred when an employee dropped a heavy box of tinned goods when he was restocking shelves. The crate landed on his foot and this caused a serious injury because he had not been wearing safety shoes. The store's manager then dismissed the employee because his injury meant that he would not be able to work in the foreseeable future. The accident was described on another employee's personal blog and was picked up by the newspaper.

The Regional Human Resources Director in Asia confirmed that the details reported by the newspaper were correct. The employee had not been trained in manual lifting techniques and had lifted the crate carelessly. He did not wear safety shoes because they were not as comfortable as his ordinary shoes. The store's manager had not implemented the health and safety manual that had been issued because he said that compliance with the manual would interfere with the efficiency of the store and that the procedures it contained were unpopular with the employees because they preferred their own methods of work. The Regional Director's report concluded that the store manager's attitude reflected the indifference to health and safety in the workplace that was exhibited by all employees in that region.

Internal audit

The Head of B's Internal Audit department is preparing next year's audit plan. He is aware of the Board's increasing interest in Health and Safety issues and intends to include an audit of the extent to which the procedures and practices stated in B's health and safety manual have been adopted throughout the group.

Feedback from the internal audit staff based at each of the regional offices suggests that managers and staff in some countries are more receptive to supervision and management reviews than others. Some cultures place considerable emphasis on complying with rules and respect for authority while others emphasise individual empowerment.

Currency risk

B's Chairman has been reviewing the risk management arrangements put in place by the corporate treasury department. The Chairman is a little concerned that there do not appear to be any formal systems in place for the management of transaction risks and economic risks arising from movements in the various currencies in which B does business.

The Chairman discussed currency risk with the Group Treasurer and was informed that the B Group as a whole is not heavily exposed to either transaction risks or economic risks. The nature of B's business means that the group is hedged against such risks without the treasury having to take any particular action. The central treasury does, however, maintain a close watch over exposures to currency risks and so it is ready to recommend a change to the currency management procedures very quickly as and when the need arises.

B's Group Treasurer is keen to explore countertrade as a means of managing long-term economic exposures affecting the group. For example, B has recently started to purchase large quantities of clothing from a South American country that has a very volatile currency. The South American country manufactures large quantities of high quality wool and has a tradition of manufacturing woollen goods that are affordably priced. B's Group Treasurer has negotiated contracts with the South American supplier that agree the clothing will be paid for by counter-trade rather than in cash. B is a major buyer of basic commodities such as flour and sugar. It would not be difficult for B to purchase additional amounts of such commodities so that they can then be exchanged for woollen goods. The South American supplier would be able to sell the flour and sugar at a profit in its home country. Each contract would specify clearly the basis upon which woollen goods will be exchanged for commodities.

Required

(a)   (i)   Advise B's directors of TWO risks for the company associated with health and safety in B's stores that could each be categorised as having both high impact and high likelihood. Your answer should include the reasons why you have categorised each of the risks as such.   **(8 marks)**

    (ii)   Discuss the reasons why the procedures stated in the health and safety manual may not have been followed by all employees throughout the B Group.   **(8 marks)**

(b)   (i)   Discuss the factors that the Head of the Internal Audit department should consider when planning an audit of the extent to which all employees of B's stores are complying with the rules and principles as stated in the health and safety manual.   **(10 marks)**

The Head of the Internal Audit department recently sent a memo to all of the internal auditors in the B group that said: "I would like to remind all members of the audit department, irrespective of the country in which they are based, that they should be careful to avoid causing resentment when dealing with other employees"

    (ii)   Discuss the memo sent by the Head of B's Internal Audit department. **(8 marks)**

(c)   (i)   Discuss the Group Treasurer's view that the nature of B's business creates a natural hedge against currency risk. **(8 marks)**

    (ii)   Evaluate the potential risks and benefits to B of the countertrade agreement with the South American supplier. **(8 marks)**

(Total = 50 marks)

SECTION B

Answer TWO of the three questions.

Question 2

The T Group manufactures heavy engineering products. The company has a diverse range of products, each of which requires its own specialised factory. Each factory is established as a separate 100% subsidiary and each is an investment centre. The T Group monitors the performance of each factory using a variety of accounting ratios. One of the key ratios used is return on capital employed (ROCE), calculated using current values where these are available.

T Forge manufactures large metal rollers that are used in industries such as steelmaking and shipbuilding. T Forge occupies a large factory that is situated three miles from the centre of a city of one million inhabitants.

The T Group is presently considering an offer of $52m to buy the land on which T Forge's factory is situated. T Forge will be wound up if this offer is accepted. The buyer will be responsible for dismantling and disposing of the factory and its contents.

When T Forge was first founded it sold most of its output to its home market, but now most of T Forge's customers are located overseas in countries where the quality of engineering training is very poor. These poorly trained engineers have incorrectly rejected T Forge rollers, believing them to be substandard when they are not. The product is of a very high quality, but the current manual production system sometimes leaves cosmetic blemishes on the surface of the rollers that are visible to the human eye. These blemishes have no effect on the operation of the rollers, but there is a growing tendency for customers' engineering staff to reject perfectly good items because the engineers do not have the necessary skills and equipment to distinguish these marks from genuine defects. Roughly 20% of the goods shipped in the year to date have had to be replaced at T Forge's expense because they have failed customers' quality inspections. Rejected rollers are disposed of locally for a tiny fraction of their manufacturing cost because they are too large and heavy to make it cost-effective to return them to T Forge.

T Forge's main competitor is a US company which uses computer numerical control (CNC) machinery to produce rollers that are of the same quality as those produced by T Forge, but they are free of the cosmetic blemishes that are causing T's rollers to be rejected. The T Group's board has asked T Forge's directors to consider investing in CNC lathes similar to those used by the US competitor. These would replace the existing lathes, which are almost 40 years old but which are expected to remain serviceable into the foreseeable future because they are of a very simple construction that is easy to maintain. The replacement lathes would cost $40m and would be depreciated at a rate of 25% on the reducing balance basis. The CNC lathes will not generate any additional sales, but they will prevent the losses associated with customers rejecting goods without good reason because of marks in the metal. The T Group's board believes that the purchase of the CNC lathes would be a positive net present value investment, even after taking account of the opportunity cost of the sale of the factory.

The T Group's board believes that there are three possible strategies to be pursued with respect to T Forge: (1) to carry on as at present, (2) to invest in the new lathes or (3) to sell the land. The board has asked for ROCE to be predicted under each of the first two bases. The T Group's cost of capital is 18% before taxation.

The following budgeted figures are available as the basis for this prediction:

T Forge Budgeted income statement for the year ended 31 August 2013

	$m
Revenue	100
Variable production costs	(30)
Fixed production costs	(25)
Other operating expenses	(11)
Interest	(2)
Profit before tax	32
Tax	(7)
Profit for year	25

T Forge Budgeted statement of financial position as at 31 August 2013

	$m
Property (as at 2011 valuation)	29
Lathes and other manufacturing equipment	nil
	29
Current assets	4
	33
Equity	10
Non-current liabilities	20
Current liabilities	3
	33

Required

(a) Calculate T Forge's budgeted ROCE for the year ended 31 August 2013 if:

(i) The existing lathes are retained; and

(ii) The new lathes were purchased on 1 September 2012.

Note: You should explain any adjustments that you make to the figures shown above in order to calculate ROCE.

(9 marks)

(b) Evaluate the use of ROCE by T Group (i) as a performance measure and (ii) as a tool for decision making.

(6 marks)

(c) Recommend ways other than the investment in CNC lathes in which the management of T Forge could deal with the risk of rollers being rejected because of mistakes in customers' quality control procedures.

(10 marks)

(Total = 25 marks)

Question 3

U is an internet-based company that sells books, DVDs and CDs to consumers. U's customers are required to create an account, to which they register their name, address and credit card details. The customers must also create a password, which they must use whenever they wish to log into their account in order to update their details or place an order. Registered customers can log in and place orders very easily because all of their delivery and payment details are already on file. That feature is one of the main factors behind U's success. The other main factor is that U's software tracks each customer's purchases and uses that information to email recommendations based on past orders. Many customers buy recommended products and the proportion is growing because U's tracking software becomes increasingly accurate as more data is gathered.

U has recently suffered a security breach involving 2,000 of its highest-spending customers. One of U's analysts had been asked to write a report about those customers' buying habits. The report was required urgently and so the analyst copied the customers' files onto a memory stick, which he took home to analyse on his home PC over the weekend. He copied the final report onto the same memory stick, but lost the stick during the train journey into work.

The analyst had one of his flatmates email him a copy of the report, which was still on the hard drive of his home PC, so the report's deadline was met. The analyst did not report the loss of the memory stick because he did not wish to get into trouble for losing the data. He hoped that anybody who found the stick would simply erase the files.

Over the next two weeks, U started to receive complaints from customers that orders were being placed without the account holders' permission. U's policy in these circumstances is to seek clarification from the account holder and suggest that the order could have been placed by a family member who knew the account password. The volume of complaints was higher than usual and the analyst was asked to investigate them to determine whether there was a security problem. The analyst quickly realised that many of the complaints were from the 2,000 customers whose files were on his memory stick and that the person who had found the stick was abusing that information. He admitted the loss of the memory stick and was suspended.

U's customer services department wrote to all of those customers whose accounts had been compromised and offered to cancel any disputed charges on their accounts. The customers were also advised to contact their credit card providers and to study their card statements carefully in case the thief had used that information to defraud them.

Several of these customers complained to a national newspaper and U received many further complaints concerning disputed charges, mainly from customers whose details had not been copied by the analyst.

Required

(a)   Advise U's board on the weaknesses in both the control environment and the internal controls that led to this loss of data. **(12 marks)**

(b)   Recommend, stating reasons, actions that U's board should take to:

(i)   Restore the confidence of its existing and potential customers; **(8 marks)**

(ii) Prevent similar problems occurring in the future. **(5 marks)**

(Total = 25 marks)

Question 4

G is a major clothing retailer, specialising in fashionable clothes for young people. G has shops in every major town and city in its home country. G's customers are extremely conscious of brand names and G must stock the latest products from the biggest and most popular manufacturers in order to remain competitive.

Most of G's most popular brands are imported from the USA. The clothes are expensive to import because the Government in G's country imposes a tariff, which requires G (and all other importers) to pay a tax on all clothing imports. The Government's reason for imposing this tariff is to protect local manufacturers from foreign competition. G is located in a relatively prosperous country and wages are fairly high.

G has been losing sales to a major competitor, which is based in G's home country and has shops in the same towns and cities as G, which sells the same range of clothing but at a lower price. G attempted to compete on price, but stopped doing so when it became apparent that the competitor could undercut any price that G set.

G has investigated the competitor's trading strategy. It appears that the competitor is able to exploit anomalies in the market by buying its inventory in a neighbouring country and bringing it across the border. Two of the countries that adjoin G's home country are not particularly prosperous. Many foreign suppliers, including G's suppliers, supply goods to distributers (and also directly to retailers) in those countries at lower prices than they do in G's home country because they are aware that the final consumers there have low incomes and are not able to pay high prices for brand name clothing. Furthermore, those neighbouring countries do not charge tariffs on clothing imports.

G's home country is part of a trading bloc which includes the neighbouring country from which the competitor is suspected of buying its inventory. There are no physical barriers to regulate the borders between countries within that bloc. Legally, any goods imported from a neighbouring country are subject to tariffs, but G suspects that the competitor has not been declaring these imports to the Government department responsible for collecting tax and so the competitor has benefitted from both cheaper purchase prices and the evasion of the tariff.

Some of G's senior managers have recommended that G should copy its competitor by cancelling all contracts with the major US manufacturers and buying all goods from intermediaries in a neighbouring country. Others recommend reporting their suspicions to the manufacturers and to the Government.

Required

(a)   Discuss the argument that purchasing power parity theory should prevent exporters from charging different prices in different countries. **(5 marks)**

(b)   Discuss the potential risks and benefits to G of buying its inventory from intermediaries in the neighbouring countries. **(10 marks)**

(c)   Recommend actions that the Government in G's home country could take in order to determine whether G's competitor had been evading the tariff on imported clothing. **(10 marks)**

(Total = 25 marks)

Answers

DO NOT TURN THIS PAGE UNTIL YOU HAVE
COMPLETED THE MOCK EXAM

A plan of attack

We've already established that you've been told to do it 101 times, so it is of course superfluous to tell you for the 102nd time to **Take a good look at the paper before diving in to answer questions**.

<u>The next step</u>

You may be thinking that this paper is a lot more straightforward than the first mock exam; however, having sailed through the first mock, you may think this paper is actually rather difficult.

<u>Option 1 (Don't like this paper)</u>

If you are challenged by this paper, it will be best to get the optional questions done before tackling the case study. Don't forget though that you will need half the time to answer the case study.

*   It is very possible to score well in part (c) of **Question 2**, but if you think you'll struggle with the ROCE calculation, we suggest avoiding this question.

*   You may have heard about instance of data loss similar in the scenario in **Question 3**. There are a lot of mark-scoring opportunities here, as there are some fairly obvious points in the scenario and a lot of the controls are straightforward.

*   The last part of **Question 4** is quite unexpected, but if you can think about what a tax investigation might involve, you can score some marks here. The requirement in (a) is fairly straightforward if you've revised PPP.

*   If you've never been very involved in health and safety, don't nevertheless be worried about **Question 1**. Quite a few marks are available for discussing fairly mainstream issues about control systems and audit. Don't miss out the last part of the question, even if you feel you know nothing about countertrade. The arrangement is clearly described in the scenario and you can obtain some marks by making some general points about foreign exchange hedging.

<u>Option 2 (This paper's all right)</u>

Are you **sure** it is? If you are then that's encouraging. You'll feel even happier when you've got the compulsory question out the way, so you should consider doing **Question 1 first**.

*   **Question 1** offers the chance to use mainstream knowledge for this paper to score well. Use any experience you have of being audited in (b) (ii).

*   If you remember your management accounting knowledge from P1 and P2. **Question 2** can offer you a good chance to score well, but you can lose quite a lot of marks if you get the ROCE calculation wrong.

*   A lot of ideas may occur to you when reading the scenario of **Question 3.** If so, you can score very heavily on it as there are plenty of points that you can make.

*   If you can explain PPP, you will get off to a good start on **Question 4**. The last part may seem strange, but if you have an awareness of how a tax investigation might be carried out, you can score well here too.

<u>Once more</u>

You must **allocate your time** according to the marks for the question in total, and for the parts of the questions. And you must also **follow the requirements exactly**.

<u>Finished with fifteen minutes to spare?</u>

Looks like you slipped up on the time allocation. However if you have, make sure you don't waste the last few minutes; go back to **any parts of questions that you didn't finish** because you ran out of time.

<u>Forget about it!</u>

Forget about what? Excellent, you already have.

Question 1

Text references. Chapters 1, 6, 11, 15 and 16.

Top tips. Note how the health and safety breach can be spun out over various areas of the syllabus.

Easy marks. Although the examiner's comments indicated that many students did not cope well with the requirement, (b) (i) is built upon a framework of the fundamentals of audit planning, although the framework does need to be fleshed out by application to the scenario.

Examiner's comments. In (b) students demonstrated an inability to apply their knowledge to the scenario. Most students only made generic points and comments about risk were not specific enough. Short point answers did not score well. In (c) (i) students showed a lack of knowledge of the basics of hedging. Answers to (c) (ii) were often better. although some answers were brief and some students missed out this part entirely. Students must remember that there will always be at least one requirement relating to financial risk in Question 1.

Marking scheme

				Marks
(a)	(i)	1 mark for identification of each risk, up to 4 marks for Justification of each risk	max	8
	(ii)	Up to 2 marks per issue. Issues could include: Inconvenience for staff Staff reluctance Lack of enforcement by management Guidance not followed/understood Inadequate training	max	8
(b)	(i)	Up to 2 marks per issue discussed that clearly relate to this business. Issues could include: Timetabling/coverage of all sites Staffing Prioritisation – identifying high risk stores Differences in extent of work Responses to breaches	max	10
	(ii)	Up to 2 marks per issue. Issues could include: Constructive comments Limit inconvenience Discuss issues with staff Staff not used to audit Staff regard audit as intrusion Some disruption inevitable Staff respond badly to criticisms	max	8
(c)	(i)	Up to 2 marks per issue. Issues could include: Diversification of business Limited timeframe of settlement Local matching Change in supply Matching assets vs liabilities Some risk, but may not justify other hedging methods	max	8

(ii) Up to 2 marks per issue. Issues could include:
Nature of countertrade
Generic commodities
Supplier buy-in
Fixed terms – exchange rates and commodity prices
Changes in supplier
Difficulties with taxation authorities

max   <u>8</u>
<u>50</u>

(a)

Top tips. In (a) (i) it seems best to discuss the risks arising from the health and safety breach. Our answer comments that this breach is itself high likelihood and high impact, and then goes on to analyse the main risks for B that arise from the breach. Note that the legal and reputation risks are distinct so those can be your two risks. It would be possible to gain marks for discussing other risks here, provided you could make a valid case for their being high impact-high likelihood. (The other example quoted in CIMA's guidance is the risk arising from violent confrontation with a shoplifter.)

(a) (ii) focuses on weaknesses in the control environment. Staff indifference is an issue here, but a bigger problem is that the requirements in place are inconvenient for staff. Another key issue arises from B being an international group and hence having problems communicating with staff in some countries, either because the instructions are not clear to them or because local culture works against what B is trying to enforce.

(i) <u>Risks for B</u>

<u>Legal risks</u>

Staff around the world are regularly involved in activities such as lifting heavy objects or driving vehicles that could result in **injury or death** (**high impact**). The fact that staff **frequently undertake** these activities combined with the lax attitude to health and safety in certain parts of the B group means that these risks are also **high likelihood**. If staff are injured or killed, B faces a **high likelihood** of the risk of legal action for compensation, as risks to staff are certainly foreseeable by B. This compensation could be **substantial** if B's failure to enforce proper health and safety procedures is held to be negligent. Similarly in some jurisdictions B will also face a probable risk of criminal prosecution for breaches of health and safety legislation and could be liable again for **substantial penalties or face restrictions on its operations.**

<u>Reputation risks</u>

B also faces a serious risk to its reputation for being a **good employer and a good corporate citizen.** B can expect that there will be a **high likelihood of adverse press coverage**, as allegations of negligence and poor culture at a well-known large company will be seen by the media as a good story. The impact is more difficult to define. Consumers may **boycott B's stores** if the coverage persuades them that it treats its staff poorly. Staff may leave or not be inclined to join B if they feel that their safety is threatened. B has also been very sensitive to fulfilling its CSR obligations, perhaps feeling that it derives a **significant marketing advantage** from being seen as a good citizen. This advantage could be eliminated by bad publicity about health and safety failings and the positive impact of other CSR initiatives nullified.

(ii) <u>Staff reluctance</u>

Staff appear to have been **reluctant to take certain health and safety precautions.** Staff have failed to wear the proper clothing because they do not feel it is comfortable or because it is difficult to wear in hot climates. Staff also appear to prefer to work in their own way rather than follow central diktats. They may also feel that wearing protective clothing is a sign of personal weakness.

<u>Internal environment</u>

The store manager shares staff reluctance to follow health and safety directives. As a result the control environment at the store is poor. The manager is unwilling to insist that staff follow requirements that he knows will be **unpopular with them**. The manager is also more concerned about **store efficiency** than protecting staff's safety. His staff's attitudes are likely to reflect his

own. Some stores have never had an internal audit and this lack of central monitoring may also mean that staff have been given the impression they can ignore directives.

Issuing the manual

Issuing a manual is not adequate by itself to ensure staff compliance, if staff are reluctant to follow central directives. Staff may **not read the manual** or may **ignore what it says.** The fact that a single manual is issued across the group may mean that staff in some countries **struggle to understand the terminology used.**

Lack of training

The fact that staff in some locations have been given potentially dangerous tasks **without being trained in health and safety procedures** may have been taken as an indication that health and safety is not to be taken very seriously. Staff may also fail to understand the requirements of the manual if they have not had previous training in health and safety and the manual is introduced without giving them any extra training. The apparent failure to organise training centrally on the new requirements represents a **lost opportunity to sell the importance of health and safety compliance** to staff.

(b)

Top tips. (b) (i) focuses on certain basic areas of audit planning – staffing, prioritisation and extent of work. Strong evidence could be gained from a surprise visit, although how difficult it will be to make the visit a surprise is debatable.

You may feel at a disadvantage in (b) (ii) if you haven't carried out internal audit work, but most students will be in the same position. The main points are internal auditors can take some steps to build working relationships with staff, but will inevitably cause staff resentment if staff see internal audit as a threat or respond adversely to any criticisms internal audit makes, however justified they are.

(i)   Timing

The Head of Internal Audit (HIA) will need to consider the **timetabling** of the work. Because of the serious risks associated with breaches, it will be necessary to build **visits to every site** into the plan. Internal audit work planned on other, less high-risk matters, may need to be postponed. This may mean carrying out health and safety audit work on some sites **ahead** of when they would be visited for other reasons, in order to complete the work on all sites within the **desired timeframe.**

Briefing of staff

The HIA will need to ensure that internal staff sent on audit are fully **briefed on company and local legal requirements.** They may need to be trained in **particular health and safety practices such as use of equipment.** If the HIA feels there is insufficient specialist knowledge in the internal audit department, it may be necessary to **recruit staff** with the required experience. Audit staff should be instructed to **note all breaches**, including the staff involved and their managers.

Prioritisation

Because internal audit resources will be limited, the HIA will have to decide the order in which sites are visited. This may not be an easy decision. The HIA will be concerned about sites located in **countries with strict health and safety laws** and therefore most serious legal consequences if breaches occur. However such sites may also have a low risk of problems occurring because they enforce strict compliance procedures. The HIA may instead prioritise sites where there have been a **number of accidents or evidence from accident reports of serious breaches, such as at the Asian store**. The HIA will also take into account the comments about indifference to health and safety made in the Regional Director's report.

Types of audit

The way individual sites are audited will also depend on how risky they are. Sites which are considered as low-risk may have audit work carried out on health and safety as part of a more **general internal audit.** Audit work may focus on documented records of compliance and discussions with management about any accidents that have happened.

Sites considered to be higher risk may be audited on a separate visit. If there are concerns, internal audit should try to **visit on a surprise basis**, to see what is happening on site and spot obvious signs of non-compliance, for example a lack of warning notices, or safety equipment and clothing not being available. Internal auditors could also review evidence from **closed circuit television** if available.

Follow up visits

If there is evidence of serious health and safety breaches at some sites, management there must commit to making improvements. Internal audit will need to confirm that promised improvements have been implemented. Therefore the HIA will have to build **follow-up audit visits into the audit plan.** Over time therefore the plan may need to be **flexible**, as internal audit will need to gain assurance as soon as possible that serious risks have been addressed.

(ii) ### Tactful but firm approach

It is important that internal audit does adopt the right approach. The HIA is correct to the extent that taking an overtly antagonistic approach can be counter-productive. Internal audit should try to **establish a positive relationship** with staff, partly by **explaining carefully the purposes of the audit.** However internal auditors should not go to the other extreme and try to be too friendly. If they need to make valid points they should do so clearly and not gloss over weaknesses.

Fitting in with staff

Internal auditors can try to **fit in with local staff** as much as possible. For example they can try to arrange discussions at convenient times for local staff. They should also try to respect local culture in the way they conduct discussions.

Giving staff opportunity to respond

Internal auditors should **discuss any criticisms** that they have with the management and staff involved, to give them the chance to **explain themselves and clarify any misunderstandings**. When internal auditors submit their report, they should **include the comments of local staff** on the points they have raised.

Staff not used to being audited

However there are a number of factors that may lead to staff resentment, whatever steps internal auditors take to mitigate it. Some sites may never have had a health and safety audit before. Some sites have not been visited at all by B's internal auditors. Uncertainty about what is happening may result in staff becoming **defensive**.

Local culture

Staff attitudes towards central management appear to **vary round the world**. Internal auditors may be seen as representatives of distant and out-of-touch head office management, particularly in countries that **emphasise individual empowerment.**

Nature of work

As discussed above, some internal audit visits should be made on a surprise basis, to identify breaches at high-risk sites. This will inevitably mean some **inconvenience and disruption** for local staff because they are not expecting to be visited.

Criticisms made

It seems likely that internal auditors will have to criticise managers and staff at several sites. This may result in **disciplinary action or have other adverse effects** on their careers. Those criticised may therefore feel antagonistic towards internal auditors and argue with them when the results of the internal audit are discussed, even though internal auditors' comments are valid.

(c)

> **Top tips.** The main points in (c) (i) are the opportunities B has for offsetting its cashflows and the short-term over which settlement will take place with the supplier. Bringing in B's strategic objective of increasing commitments to local suppliers mentioned in the preseen is helpful here. You may have wondered in (c) (ii) whether what you knew about countertrade was sufficient to gain 8 marks. However CIMA's post-exam guide states that the question is more about demonstrating understanding of the basics of currency risk and the ability to identify opportunities from unusual situations. You will score some marks for making the basic points about any hedging arrangements, that it removes uncertainty but B will not benefit from favourable movements. The arrangement being direct with the supplier rather than made through a financial intermediary also brings in significant counterparty issues.

(i) <u>Diversification of operations</u>

B operates supermarkets around the world, so to some extent movements on different currencies will **cancel each other out**.

<u>Short timeframes</u>

Settlement with customers in supermarkets will most often be instantaneous and settlement with suppliers will take place quickly. Many of B's purchases will be perishable foods, which will mean that purchases are very regular and balances are settled quickly. B is not likely to be **exposed to significant currency movements**, because of the short-term nature of cash flows.

<u>Local matching</u>

B is aiming to source as much as possible locally and therefore many purchases could be made in the same currency as sales. However local matching will only apply to certain transactions. Some contracts will be with **international manufacturers** and may be denominated in Euros, even though the goods are supplied to the US and Asia.

<u>Ability to change suppliers</u>

Many of the products that B sells are commodities that can be sourced from more than one country. Therefore if a product becomes **more expensive due to currency movements**, it can be sourced from a country where the exchange rate is more favourable.

<u>Assets and liabilities</u>

Part of natural hedging will be the **matching of returns** from assets in a local currency against the **finance costs** of those assets. In the statement of financial position, the impact of exchange rate movements on assets denominated in local currencies will be mitigated by the impact on loans denominated in the same currencies. Thus the extent of natural hedging will partly depend on the sources of B's loan finance.

<u>Conclusion</u>

B's situation means that its exposure will **not be completely hedged.** It may though be sufficiently hedged by natural hedging for other hedging methods to be unnecessary. The treasury operation can monitor the extent to which natural hedging is occurring and take steps if B seems exposed in particular currencies.

(ii) <u>Benefits for B</u>

<u>Fixed terms</u>

Paying with commodities effectively **fixes the exchange rate and removes the uncertainty** associated paying in the volatile currency. It may be difficult to **hedge effectively** against this uncertainty if derivatives are only available at a high price due to the uncertainties involved.

<u>Commodities paid by B</u>

B can easily **obtain the commodities** it needs to pay the South American supplier from sources in many different countries. Because it already buys these commodities, it may be able to **benefit from favourable terms** that it has previously negotiated with its suppliers.

Arrangements with South American supplier

As well as removing uncertainty for B, the countertrade arrangement will also remove transaction risk for the South American supplier. The value of the staple commodity in the South American country should adjust itself as the currency changes and the supplier should therefore be able to make a profit. This may encourage the South American supplier to **maintain a good relationship** with B.

Risks for B

Fixing of exchange rates

Paying in commodities may in the end be **less advantageous** to B than paying in the local currency. Although currency movements may be volatile, over the longer–term they may net in B's favour. B would lose this benefit if it agreed to the countertrade agreement.

Inflexibility of terms

If the terms of countertrade are **fixed for a significant period**, they may become less realistic as time passes. If there are significant swings in worldwide commodity prices that are disadvantageous to B, it may be difficult to renegotiate the contract, although B could purchase futures to hedge against price movements.

Supplier problems

B may have **difficulty terminating the relationship** with the supplier if the supplier does prove to be unsatisfactory or there are other reasons, for example lower prices, for switching suppliers.

Difficulties with taxation authorities

Local tax authorities may raise questions over the value of countertrade arrangements and hence any **sales tax payable**. Disputes with the authorities may be **time-consuming** to resolve and could result in **penalties** being levied.

Question 2

Text references. Chapter 7.

Top tips. The calculation in (a) may appear straightforward for this paper, but it has a number of twists which may result in you scoring low marks if you did not spot them. Traps are:

- Failing to add interest (2) back to arrive at operating profit

- The revalued land – the calculation needed to take account of this revaluation to ensure that fair values of assets are used (52 – 29). The first paragraph of the scenario states that current values should be used when available

- The lathes - they affect both parts of the calculation – profit needs to be adjusted for the depreciation charge, assets need to include the net book value after the depreciation charge

- The rejected production that is no longer produced – we're told this is 20% of valid output. The budgeted cost of sales will include valid and rejected output, so to equal $30m, valid output must cost $25m and rejected output $5m. (ie rejected output is 20/120 of the total figure). As these costs are no longer incurred, presumably to preserve the double entry, current assets must increase as well as operating profit for this amount

One thing the scenario does not explain is how the acquisition of the lathes is to be funded. The assumption appears to be that it is funded out of debt or equity, and any cash surpluses in current assets are untouched.

In (c) the measures you suggest need to address the problems of customers' engineers lacking the skills and equipment to be able to distinguish correctly good output from bad.

Easy marks. Most of the points in (b) should have been revision of what you learnt in P1 and P2.

> **Examiner's comments.** This question was attempted by few students. A surprising proportion of those who did attempt it missed out (a), which inevitably meant they failed the question. Hardly any students adjusted correctly for the value of the land and the lathes. Students must revise ROCE, as answers demonstrated an inability to apply the concept in a complex setting. However marks for (c) were much better.

Marking scheme

			Marks
(a)	1 mark for each element of the calculation and assumptions		
		max	9
(b)	Up to 3 marks for points relating to value of site		
	Up to 4 marks for points relating to value of lathes		
	Up to 2 marks for other issues including comparability, use of accounting profits		
		max	6
(c)	Up to 3 marks per issue. Issues could include:		
	Training customers' staff		
	Provision of equipment		
	Independent assurance		
	Contractual terms		
	Change in sales mix		
		max	10
			25

(a)   1 <u>No investment in lathes</u>

ROCE = <u>Operating profit</u>

        Total assets less current liabilities

= (32 + 2)/((33 + (52 – 29)) – 3)

= 34/53

= 64.2%

<u>2 Investment in lathes</u>

ROCE = <u>Operating profit</u>

        Total assets less current liabilities

= (34 - (40 × 25%) + (30 × 20/120)) /(53 + (40 × 75%) + (30 × 20/120))

= 29/88

= 33.0%

<u>Adjustments</u>

1 Both calculations adjust for the upgrade in the value of the land indicated by the bid (52 – 29)

2 Calculation 2 adjusts profit for the depreciation on the lathes (40 × 25%) and assets for their net book value (40 × 75%).

3 Calculation 2 adjusts profit for the rejected output that will no longer be produced and also adjusts current assets for this amount, as it assumes that the money will no longer be spent   (30 × 20/120).

(b)   Performance measurement

Current value of lathes

At present the measurement of ROCE is being distorted by the lathes being **fully depreciated.** Although they are shown as having no value in the asset part of the calculation, they are nevertheless generating profits and clearly therefore have some economic value.

Change in economic value of land

If land is revalued, T's ROCE will fall despite the fact that it is using the same assets to produce the goods. However including revalued amounts **provides a fairer measure** for evaluating directors' performance, as it takes into account the **opportunity cost** of continuing to use the factory instead of realising its value by selling it.

Other impacts of investment

The ROCE fails to take into account other impacts of the investment being made. These include staff and management resources **no longer being required to deal with rejected output. Relations with customers** may improve. T may also become **more competitive** as its products, like its main competitor's, will be free of blemishes. These factors may all impact on sales in time, but their impact may be difficult to isolate.

Decision-making

Figures used

The calculation does not use the figures that will most concern businesses when making decisions. ROCE uses **historical figures** rather than future figures which will be influenced by the decisions made. ROCE also uses **accounting profits**, which could be distorted by accounting policies, rather than cash flows which are of most concern to the business. It also fails to take into account the **time value of money.**

Distortions by new investment

The value of ROCE is likely to fall if there is a **major investment in non-current assets**, which is desirable from the viewpoint of developing the business. Here ROCE falls because of the decrease in profits caused by the depreciation charge on the lathes, and the increase in assets due to the addition of the net book value of the lathes. These more than outweigh the fall in costs due to output no longer being rejected by customers. However over time the ROCE will start increasing again, due to the fall in net book value of the assets, even though the assets are generating the same depreciation charge and the same cost saving. The most significant measure is the investment generating a positive net value. This should be used as the criteria for decisions by T's directors.

(c)   Education of customers

T needs to address the issue of engineers' **lack of training** meaning they incorrectly identify sound rollers as faulty. T Forge should invite major customers to **send their engineers** to its factory. T Forge staff should explain how the manufacturing process works and demonstrate how marks can appear on rollers, but that these marks are not faults. As part of the demonstration, customers' engineers should be shown a roller that carries these marks but has been tested and been found to be clear of faults.

Supply of equipment

The other main reason for T Forge's products being incorrectly rejected is customers using unsophisticated equipment to test them. T Forge or another company in the T group could **supply more advanced equipment** to customers and could also **train customers' engineers** in using it. This should ensure that proper testing takes place.

Independent assurance

T Forge's position could also be strengthened if it can supply better evidence to customers that rollers with cosmetic blemishes are free from operating faults. It should therefore have at least some of its rollers **quality tested** by an **external expert**. The expert should provide a report that states that rollers with blemishes have been tested, have been found to be free of faults and the blemishes do not impact upon the strength of the rollers.

Contracts with customers

The terms of contracts with customers need to be **tightened.** Terms of sale need to prevent customers from rejecting items because they have cosmetic blemishes. Customers should have to pay for rollers unless they can show there are faults that impede operation.

Change in customer base

Dealing with customers in countries where training and equipment are poor appears to involve significant time and cost for T Forge. Over time it may try to **develop sales in markets** where engineers are trained better and are able to carry out proper quality control inspections.

Question 3

Text references. Chapters 6 and 14.

Top tips. This is a good scenario for a strategic level question. It focuses on a retailer that is similar to major real-life retailers such as Amazon. There have also been a number of high-profile examples of data loss due to lax attitudes towards protecting data security reported in the media.

In (a) the control environment issues are those that resulted in the analyst believing that he could remove the data from the office and failing to take the necessary precautions. To identify the failings in control procedures, you needed to look through what the analyst did and comment on what should have stopped him taking those actions and the mistakes he made.

If you are unsure in (b) how to split your suggestions between (b) (i) and (ii), the answer to (i) should focus on steps that can be publicly announced or are clearly important to the public. U has suffered a very significant loss of reputation, so you will gain credit in (i) for suggesting steps that are likely to restore public confidence. The best way to approach (i) therefore is to imagine you are a customer of U who has learned about the security breach, you want to go on using U because of the convenience but want assurances about security. What can U tell you that will persuade you to continue buying from it? There's also the simpler point that (i) is for 8 marks, (ii) for 5 marks, so the number of points you make for each should reflect this difference.

Note that the theme of improving customer confidence was also tested (in the context of product quality) in another question in the same exam. This underlines its importance in competitive environments, where a loss of confidence is very quickly communicated.

Easy marks. Hopefully you will have been able to pick up the failures by the analyst to keep control over the data that were clearly described in the scenario.

Examiner's comments. Generally this question was done well. Most students failed to mention closing accounts and changing passwords in (b).

Marking scheme

				Marks
(a)		Up to 2 marks per issue discussed. Issues could include: Pressures on staff Poorly trained staff Culture of carelessness Inadequate stress on legal compliance Lack of restrictions on access Removal of data from office Poor security over offsite data Previous issues not investigated		
			max	12
(b)	(i)	Up to 2 marks per issue discussed. Issues could include: Public announcement Closure of accounts affected Reimbursement of customer payments Security review Investigation into fraud		
			max	8
	(ii)	Up to 2 marks per issue discussed. Issues could include: Internal restrictions on data access Restrictions/ controls on offsite data Staff training/disciplinary action		
			max	<u>5</u> <u>25</u>

(a) <u>Control environment</u>

<u>Attitude to staff</u>

The fact that the analyst felt forced to work on the report at home and was afraid to report the loss of data suggests that there is a culture of pressure at U. This may make it more likely that staff **make mistakes** that put security at risk or take **shortcuts that breach security.**

<u>Lack of staff awareness</u>

The analyst made a number of mistakes that suggests that he has **not been properly trained** in **security issues**. Staff appear not to take seriously the threats of identity theft and fraud if data is accessed by an unauthorised person.

<u>Lack of care</u>

The analyst's mistakes may also reflect a **general culture of lack of care** about security matters.

<u>Lack of concern with compliance</u>

U also appears to be paying **insufficient attention to the requirements** of **data protection legislation and best practice.** The data it holds about customers is of varying levels of sensitivity, but U has not attempted to protect data in different ways according to its level of sensitivity.

<u>Internal controls</u>

<u>Access to data</u>

The analyst should **not have had access in the first place** to the data relating to customer credit card details and names and addresses. He did not need it to undertake the analysis of customer buying habits and it does not appear that he would normally need it at work.

Taking home data

The sensitive data should **not have been taken off-site**. However strong on-site controls were, they became ineffective once the data left the office.

Failure to protect data taken home

The analyst took data home on a stick that was **not password-protected**. At least if he had taken it home on an office laptop, the data would have had the password protection on that machine. In addition he did **not control access to the data** on his home computer, as his flatmate was able to access the report on that computer.

Failure to investigate previous complaints

Customers whose details were not copied by the analyst who have complained may be trying to get U to refund the cost of valid purchases. However their complaints may be a sign of **previous concerns about security** that U has not properly addressed before.

(b)   (i)   Underline: Inform customers

U should immediately **inform all customers** whose details were on the memory stick and announce that it has done so. This will be good public relations as far as the affected customers are concerned, and should reassure, and maybe prevent queries from, other customers.

Action in response to complaints

U should also announce that it has **closed the accounts of all customers** whose details were on the memory stick. It should help the customers **create new accounts**. U should also announce a new policy that as soon as it receives any complaints about illicit payments, it should **halt payment on those accounts.** Customers would either be forced to open a new account or, at minimum, to change their passwords. Although it will cause inconvenience to customers, it may improve their confidence in U's procedures if U requires them to **change their password regularly, or change their password** if the account is not used for some time.

Reimbursement of credit card payment

U should **reimburse any fees** that its customers have to pay to open new credit card accounts, to replace those that have been used fraudulently.

Security review

U should announce that it will organise an **investigation** not just into the circumstances surrounding the loss of data, but all aspects of its security. It should state that it will act on recommendations for improvements in its procedures that the investigation identifies. The investigation will have more credibility with customers if it is carried out by an external, independent, consultant or auditor.

Analysis of fraud

U should also announce that it is analysing the illicit payments to see if there are **any patterns,** in particular the **same shipping address** being used to receive goods paid for on different credit cards. If there are, it should state that it will, if necessary, stop shipping goods to suspicious addresses and inform the police. It should also announce that in future it will take action whenever it identifies possible fraud. For example if a complaint is made about an illicit payment and the address to which the goods are shipped is not the customer's normal first choice address, U could place a stop on any more shipments to that address until the complaint is resolved.

(ii)   Limitation of access

Staff should only be allowed to access the data they need for their own work. The system of internal password protection needs to operate at **different levels** for different staff. Only accounts staff should be **allowed to access credit card details.**

Security of offsite data

U's on-site computers should ideally **not have USB sockets** that can be used for memory sticks or staff should be **forbidden from using memory sticks**. Shared files can be transferred over U's network instead. Guidance should prohibit particularly sensitive data such as credit card details from being taken offsite and should state that staff should avoid taking away less sensitive data if

possible. Any data that has to be taken offsite should be taken on **password-protected computers and should be encrypted**.

Staffing issues

The seriousness of the security breach justifies U giving all staff **training that reminds them of the need to maintain data security** at all times. Training will also be needed on any new internal procedures that arise from the security review. U's **disciplinary policy** needs to **threaten sanctions** for **negligence in protecting data**, but also make clear that sanctions will be more severe if a loss of data is not reported immediately.

Question 4

Text references. Chapters 6, 10 and 11.

Top tips. (a) deals with PPP in terms of product pricing (remember the Big Mac example in the text). The main thrust of the answer is that in practice there are a number of other real world issues that will influence pricing.

It helps in (b) to differentiate the risks if the supplies are obtained from the neighbouring country and tariffs are paid (which are risks of supply sourcing) and the risks of acting unethically (prosecutions, threats to reputation). The ethical dilemma of whether to avoid the tariffs is the sort of problem that can also be tested in T4.

(c) is a very unexpected requirement and it is understandable if you struggled with it. The answer tries to go through a process of obtaining evidence, looking at external sources (border records, analytical review on published accounts) before carrying out an audit at the competitor's premises. Making an estimated tax assessment is something that governments often have the power to do and here effectively the government would be calling the competitor's bluff.

Easy marks. The definition of PPP and the problems with it in practice should have provided comparatively easy marks if you had revised it, although the examiner's comments indicated that few students who attempted the question appeared to have done so. The comments made by the examiner in the rest of the report on this exam suggest that it was the second choice optional question for most of the students who attempted it.

Examiner's comments. (a), when attempted, was done more poorly than the other parts, with students showing a surprising lack of understanding of purchasing power parity. Answers to (b) and (c) showed some lack of knowledge and understanding as well. However students who thought carefully about the question and applied their knowledge to the scenario scored well.

Financial risk will be tested in more than one question in every paper and students must therefore show understanding of this area.

Marking scheme

			Marks
(a)	2 marks for explanation of PPP		
	Up to 4 marks for discussing why it may not apply		
		max	5
(b)	Up to 2 marks per issue. Issues could include:		
	Costs of supply		
	Convenience of supply		
	Compensation for poor goods		
	Relationships with previous suppliers		
	Delays in obtaining inventory		
	Government action		
	Reputation risk		
	Internal impact		
		max	10
(c)	Up to 2 marks per issue. Issues could include:		
	Inspection at border		
	Analytical review		
	Surprise audit		
	Inspection of accounting records		
	Estimated assessment		
		max	<u>10</u>
			<u>25</u>

(a)   <u>Purchasing power parity (PPP)</u>

PPP is based on the **law of one price,** that the same goods will be priced at the same regardless of the currency in which they are sold. If a good was priced relatively cheaply in Country A, then traders from other countries would buy up large quantities of the good. Sellers in A would therefore increase prices due to the good's popularity, but eventually demand would fall as prices in A reached the same level as in other countries.

In practice however there are several factors that will mean PPP does not apply in practice.

<u>Competitive strategy</u>

Firms may limit prices to what they think the **market can bear**. This is happening in the neighbouring country where low incomes are keeping down prices. Firms may also keep prices low in order to be able to **enter markets**, particularly if there are significant non-price barriers to entry.

<u>Procurement factors</u>

PPP presupposes free and easy movements of goods between countries. In practice **physical barriers** will deter many firms from purchasing from distant countries. Significant **costs of transporting goods** from other countries will also influence firms' strategy.

<u>Government policies</u>

Governments may also influence pricing by **imposing tariffs**, as the home country government has done. They may also do so indirectly by providing **various kinds of support** to local businesses that enable them to keep their prices low. Governments may also **intervene in foreign exchange markets**, which again will affect relative prices.

(b)   <u>Benefits from buying from intermediaries</u>

<u>Costs of supply</u>

The main benefit to G would be a **fall in prices paid** to purchase the goods. G would also benefit from lower costs if it follows its competitor's strategy, fails to declare the goods to the authorities and avoids tariffs. As G has previously attempted to compete on price, this is likely to be a significant advantage.

Ease of supply

If G wished to obtain supplies of an existing line speedily, it would be **quicker to buy and transport from the neighbouring country** and costs of transport will also be lower

Risks to G

The risks to G partly depend on whether it declares the goods and pays the tariffs. Even if G pays the tariffs, there are some risks.

Comeback to intermediaries

If there were problems with goods, G may find it **more difficult to obtain compensation** from intermediaries. If goods were unsatisfactory, G would have to rely on consumer protection legislation in the neighbouring country, whereas contractual terms with the supplier may provide stronger protection against substandard goods.

Relations with suppliers

G would **lose the benefit of any goodwill** that it has **built up with its American suppliers**.   The suppliers may have granted G **preferential supply arrangements**, enabling G to obtain some brands for exclusive sale in G's home country. Manufacturers may **take G to court** to stop G undermining their supply arrangements with other companies. They may also refuse to deal with G in future.

Delays in obtaining inventory

When suppliers introduce new ranges, G would not able to obtain them until intermediaries in the neighbouring countries have obtained them and then G would need to buy and transport them. Other competitors in G's home country, who deal with the overseas suppliers directly, may therefore have the **new ranges available sooner.** As G is selling fashionable goods, any lag in having the goods available may make a big difference to sales. Intermediaries may **not also stock all the brands** that G requires, or be able to **supply the volume of goods** that G requires.

If G fails to pay the tariffs, it faces additional risks.

Action by government

If G is found guilty of tax evasion, its country's government may **levy fines and penalties** that exceed any previous cost savings that G may have had. G's directors may also face criminal charges and actions from professional institutes to which they belong.

Damage to reputation

G's business reputation may be seriously damaged if it is **publicly exposed as avoiding tariffs**. Customers may boycott G if they do not feel they can trust what G is telling them. Suppliers may be unwilling to deal with G.

Damage to internal environment

G may suffer a number of internal problems if it fails to pay tariffs. Some directors or staff may not approve of what they see as dishonest conduct, and this may result in **disputes or employees leaving the company**. Some staff may see this as a general indication that dishonest conduct will be ignored if it benefits the business and may **act illegally or unethically in other ways.**

(c)   Border patrols

The government could **stop the competitor's lorries** at the border between the two countries and note the volume of clothing that was being imported. It could check that the competitor had paid tariffs on this clothing, although the competitor might be careful to do so as it knows its lorries have been stopped. The spot check however would also give the authorities an idea of the volume of clothing that the competitor was importing from the neighbouring country.

Analytical review

The government could carry out analytical procedures on the competitor's accounts. They could attempt to calculate what the **gross profit percentage should have been**, based on sales, the assumptions that all the clothing was purchased in the neighbouring country and the assumptions that the competitor legitimately paid tariffs. If cost of sales appears to be much less than this, the authorities could investigate further.

Audit of competitor's records

The government could carry out a **tax audit** of the competitor's books. The government probably would be able to insist on doing this at any time and should certainly have the power if there were suspicions that the competitor was evading tax. If there was a strong suspicion of fraud, the government might be able to organise a **surprise visit**, which would limit the opportunity the competitor had to conceal information.

The inspectors could **compare tariffs paid with evidence of goods had been received** including goods in inventory, goods received records and details of purchases recorded in the accounting records. Discrepancies between the purchases on which tariffs have been paid and what appear to be actual purchases, or discrepancies between different records of goods would suggest the competitor had been evading tariffs. Inspectors would also investigate further if there was inadequate supporting documentation for the purchases shown in the accounts.

Estimated tariff

The government could make an **estimated assessment** for the competitor based on the tariffs it should have paid on what its purchases appear to be. If the competitor cannot provide evidence that the assessment is wrong, this probably indicates that it has previously not been paying the correct amounts.

CIMA – Strategic level
Paper P3
Performance Strategy

Mock Exam 3 (November 2012)

You are allowed three hours to answer this question paper.
In the real exam, you are allowed 20 minutes reading time before the examination begins during which you should read the question paper, and if you wish, highlight and/or make notes on the question paper. However, you will **not** be allowed, **under any circumstances**, to open the answer book and start writing or use your calculator during this reading time.
You are strongly advised to carefully read all the question requirements before attempting the question concerned (that is all parts and/or sub-questions).
Answer the compulsory question in Section A.
Answer TWO of the three questions in Section B.

DO NOT OPEN THIS PAPER UNTIL YOU ARE READY TO START UNDER EXAMINATION CONDITIONS

Pre-seen case study

V, a private limited company in a European country (SK), which is outside the Eurozone, was founded in 1972. The currency in SK is SK$. V is a travel business that offers three holiday (vacation) products. It has a network of 50 branches in a number of major cities throughout SK.

History of the company

V achieved steady growth until six years ago, when it found that its market share was eroding due to customers increasingly making online bookings with its competitors. Direct bookings for holidays through the internet have increased dramatically in recent years. Many holidaymakers find the speed and convenience of booking flights, accommodation or complete holidays online outweighs the benefits of discussing holiday alternatives with staff in a branch.

V's board had always taken the view that the friendly direct personal service that V offers through its branch network is a major differentiating factor between itself and other travel businesses and that this is highly valued by its customers. However, V found that in order to continue to compete it needed to establish its own online travel booking service, which it did five years ago. Until this point, V's board had never engaged in long-term planning. It had largely financed growth by reinvestment of funds generated by the business. The large investment in IT and IS five years ago required significant external funding and detailed investment appraisal.

Much of V's business is now transacted online through its website to the extent that 60% of its revenue in the year ended 30 June 2012 was earned through online bookings.

Current structure of V's business

V offers three types of holiday product. These are known within V as Package, Adventure and Prestige Travel. V only sells its own products and does not act as an agent for any other travel companies. It uses the services of other companies engaged in the travel industry such as chartered airlines and hotels which it pays for directly on behalf of its customers.

Package

"Package" provides holidays mainly for families with children aged up to their late teens. These typically are for accommodation in hotels (where meals are part of the package) or self-catering apartments (where no meals are provided within the package).

Adventure

"Adventure" caters for people aged mainly between 20 and 30, who want relatively cheap adventure based holidays such as trekking, sailing and cycling or who wish to go on inexpensive back-packing holidays mainly in Europe and Asia.

Prestige Travel

"Prestige Travel" provides expensive and bespoke holidays mainly sold to couples whose children have grown up and left home. The Prestige Travel product only provides accommodation in upmarket international hotel chains in countries across the world.

All three of these products provide holidays which include flights to and from the holiday destinations and hotel or self-catering accommodation. V has its own customer representatives available at the holiday destinations to provide support to its customers. All-inclusive holidays (in which all food and drinks are provided within the holiday price) are offered within each of the three product offerings.

Support products

V supports its main products by offering travel insurance and foreign currency exchange. The travel insurance, which is provided by a major insurance company and for which V acts as an agent, is usually sold along with the holidays both by branch staff and by staff dealing with online bookings.

Currency exchange is available to anyone through V's branches irrespective of whether or not the customer has bought a holiday product from V. A new currency exchange product is provided by V through which a customer purchases an amount of currency, either in SK's home currency (SK$) or else in a foreign currency and this is credited on to a plastic card. The card is then capable of being read by automated teller machines (ATM's) in many countries across the world allowing the customer to withdraw cash in the local currency up to the amount that has been credited on to the card.

Marketing of products

V relies for the vast majority of its business on the literature, available in hard copy and online, which it provides on the holiday products it sells. Exceptionally, V is able to offer some of its existing holiday products at discount prices. These may be offered under any of the three main products offered but they are mostly cut-price holiday deals which are available under the Package holiday product label.

Sales structure

Staff in each of the 50 branches accept bookings from customers and all branches have direct IT access to head office. Online enquiries and bookings are received and processed centrally at head office, which is located in SK's capital city.

Branch managers have some discretion to offer discounts on holidays to customers. V offers a discount to customers who buy holidays through its online bookings. The branch managers have authority to reduce the price of a holiday booked at the branch up to the amount of the online discount if they feel it is necessary to do so in order to make the sale.

Financial information

V's revenue, split across the holiday and support products offered, for the financial year ended 30 June 2012 is summarised as follows:

	Revenue SK$ million
Package	90
Adventure	60
Prestige Travel	95
Support products	5

The overall net operating profit generated in the financial year to 30 June 2012 was SK$35 million and the profit for the year was SK$24 million, giving a profit to sales ratio of just under 10%. V's cash receipts fluctuate because of seasonal variations and also because V's customers pay for their holidays shortly before they depart.

Further details, including extracts from V's income statement for the year ended 30 June 2012 and statement of financial position as at 30 June 2012 are shown in Appendix 1.

Financial objectives

V's key financial objectives are as follows:

1. To grow earnings by, on average, 5% a year.
2. To pay out 80% of profits as dividends.

Foreign exchange risk

V has high exposure to foreign exchange risk as its revenues received and payments made are frequently in different currencies. It normally settles hotel bills and support costs, such as transfers between hotels and airports in the local currencies of the countries where the hotels are located. It normally pays charter airlines in the airline's home currency. Scheduled airline charges are settled in the currency required by the particular airline.

V is exposed to fluctuations in the cost of aircraft fuel incurred by airlines which are passed on to travel businesses. It has often been necessary for V to require its customers to make a supplementary payment to cover the cost of increases in aircraft fuel, sometimes after the customer had thought that the final payment for the holiday had been made.

Board composition and operational responsibilities

The Board of Directors comprises five people: an Executive Chairman (who also fulfils the role of Chief Executive), a Finance Director, an Operations Director, an IT Director and a Human Resources Director. The Executive Chairman founded the business in 1972. He has three grown-up children, two of whom successfully pursue different business interests and are not engaged in V's business at all. The third child, a son, is currently taking a "year out" from study and is going to university next year to study medicine.

The branch managers all report directly to the Operations Director. In addition, the Operations Director is responsible for liaising with airlines and hotels which provide the services offered by V's promotional literature. The IT Director is responsible for V's website and online enquiries and bookings. The Finance Director is responsible for V's financial and management accounting systems and has a small team of accountancy staff,

including a part-qualified management accountant, reporting to her. The Human Resources Director has a small team of staff reporting to him.

Shareholding

There are 90 million SK$0.10 (10 cent) shares in issue and the shareholdings are as follows:

	% holding
Executive Chairman	52
Finance Director	12
Operations Director	12
IT Director	12
Human Resources Director	12

Employees

V employs 550 full-time equivalent staff. Turnover of staff is relatively low. High performance rewards in terms of bonuses are paid to staff in each branch if it meets or exceeds its quarterly sales targets. Similarly, staff who deal with online bookings receive a bonus if the online bookings meet or exceed quarterly sales targets. V's staff, both in the branches and those employed in dealing with online bookings, also receive an additional bonus if they are able to sell travel insurance along with a holiday product to customers.

Employee development for staff who are in direct contact with the public is provided through updates on products which V offers. Each member of branch and online booking staff undertakes a two day induction programme at the commencement of their employment with V. The emphasis of the induction programme is on customer service not on details relating to the products as it is expected that new staff will become familiar with such product details as they gain experience within V.

Safety

V publicly states that it takes great care to ensure that its customers are as safe as possible while on holiday. To date, V has found that accidents while on holiday are mainly suffered by very young children, Adventure customers and elderly customers. There has been an increase in instances over the last year where customers in resort hotels have suffered severe stomach complaints. This has particularly been the case in hotels located in resorts in warm climates.

Executive Chairman's statement to the press

V's Executive Chairman was quoted in the national press in SK in January 2012 as saying, "We are maintaining a comparatively high level of revenues and operating profit. This is in a period when our competitors are experiencing very difficult trading conditions. We feel we are achieving this due to our particular attention to customer service. He cited V's 40 years of experience in the travel industry and a previous 99% satisfaction rating from its customers as the reasons for its success. He went on to state that V intends to expand and diversify its holiday product range to provide more choice to customers.

Board meeting

At the next board meeting which took place after the Executive Chairman's statement to the press, the Operations Director expressed some concern. He cast doubt on whether V was able to provide sufficient funding, marketing and IT/IS resources to enable the product expansion to which the Executive Chairman referred. The Operations Director was of the opinion that V places insufficient emphasis on customer relationship marketing. The Finance Director added at the same meeting that while V presently remained profitable overall, some products may be more profitable than others.

The Executive Chairman responded by saying that V's high level of customer service provides a sufficiently strong level of sales without the need to incur any other marketing costs. He added that since V achieved a high profit to sales ratio, which it has managed to maintain for a number of years, it really didn't matter about the profits generated by each customer group.

Retirement of the Executive Chairman

The Executive Chairman formally announced to the Board in July 2012 that he intends to retire on 30 June 2013 and wishes to sell part of his shareholding in the company. The Board members believe the time is now right for V, given its expansion plans, to enter a new stage in its financing arrangements, in the form of either debt or equity from new providers.

Extracts from V's income statement and statement of financial position

INCOME STATEMENT FOR THE YEAR ENDED 30 JUNE 2012

	Notes	SK$ million
Revenue		250
Operating costs		(215)
Net operating profit		35
Interest income		3
Finance costs		(4)
Corporate income tax	1	(10)
Profit for the year		24

STATEMENT OF FINANCIAL POSITION AS AT 30 JUNE 2012

	Notes	SK$ million
ASSETS		
Non-current assets		123
Current assets		
Inventories		3
Trade and other receivables		70
Cash and cash equivalents		37
Total current assets		110
Total assets		233
EQUITY AND LIABILITIES		
Equity		
Share capital	2	9
Share premium		6
Retained earnings		60
Total equity		75
Non-current liabilities		
Long-term borrowings	3	50
Revenue received in advance		3
Current liabilities		
Trade and other payables		35
Revenue received in advance		70
Total liabilities		158
Total equity and liabilities		233

Notes

1. The corporate income tax rate can be assumed to be 30%.

2. There are 90 million SK$0.10 (10 cent) shares currently in issue.

3. 30% of the long-term borrowings are due for repayment on 30 June 2014. The remainder is due for re-payment on 30 June 2020. There are debt covenants in operation currently which restrict V from having a gearing ratio measured by long-term debt divided by long-term debt

SECTION A – 50 marks

Answer this question

Question 1

Unseen case material

<u>Customer safety</u>

V has received a large claim for compensation on behalf of customers who had travelled to a country that had been a popular holiday destination for many years but which suffered from civil unrest in July 2012 which is the peak holiday season. The unrest included protests, fighting with the police, and the destruction of government offices throughout the country. Initially the unrest was in the capital city but it later spread to other towns throughout the country, including the holiday resort towns. None of V's customers were injured during the unrest.

When the unrest started a large number of customers who had booked to travel to that country contacted V to seek advice. V reassured them, on the basis that there had been no violence in any of the country's holiday resorts, and advised that they should go on holiday as planned. V's home government had not advised its citizens against travelling to the holiday resorts in the country in question. The terms of the travel insurance that V had sold to most of its customers state that the cost of a holiday booking will only be refunded on safety grounds if the government has advised against travel.

During the holiday season there was an unexpected series of violent protests in the country's major holiday resorts. V advised its customers to remain within their hotels during the protests and that flights would be provided to bring them home as soon as order had been restored. Most customers were brought home before their original scheduled return date, but some were delayed and did not return home until several days after their due date.

V compensated customers by refunding the cost of the hotel accommodation for any days that were lost because of the early return. Many customers were dissatisfied with this and got together and responded to a newspaper advertisement published by a large law firm that offers its clients a "no win – no fee" arrangement. The law firm has written to V to request a meeting to discuss an out of court settlement. The letter states that the settlement should include full refunds of the cost of all holidays and compensation for the stress suffered. Additionally it seeks compensation for loss of earnings for the customers who returned home late.

No win – no fee services are offered by some law firms in order to attract clients who cannot afford to pay for legal advice. The law firm pursues the client's case. If it is successful then the law firm claims all legal fees from the defendant, along with the client's compensation. If the case is lost then the law firm does not make any charge.

<u>Information technology</u>

V's online booking system is not particularly sophisticated. It was developed five years ago when V's board reluctantly took the view that it needed to offer customers the option of booking online. The site itself has not been modified at all during that time.

Customers can interact with V's booking system 24 hours a day, seven days a week ("24/7"). However, V's system cannot make a final booking with a charter airline or with a holiday hotel outside of normal office hours. Any 'out of hours bookings' are not processed until the next working day. The information is held on V's server but reservations are not made with the airlines or hotels until it is processed.

V has recently run into problems with this system. There have been several cases where customers have booked a holiday using V's online system but then received an email 48 hours later to tell them that either the airline or the hotel has rejected the booking because there were no places available for the dates requested. This problem arises on popular destinations because other travel companies use the same airlines and hotels and these competitors' websites can communicate directly with the airline and hotel systems on a 24/7 basis.

V's Finance Director has contacted the major airlines and hotels in order to discuss a permanent connection to their systems, so that customer bookings could be made immediately regardless of the time of day. Unfortunately, the airlines and hotels are not willing to permit such an arrangement because V has not updated its software since its online booking system was first installed. That has led to an increasing number of errors

that have had to be resolved by the airline or hotel contacting V's head office staff by telephone or email and having the booking confirmed. The airlines and hotels would be unwilling to permit V to offer a 24/7 online booking facility unless it upgraded its systems to the latest industry-standard software.

V's board is concerned that an upgrade could prove disruptive and expensive and is considering abandoning online bookings altogether.

Currency risk

All of V's sales are priced in SK$. The company's costs are ultimately fixed in terms of either USD or the local currency of the country in which the holiday is based.

The terms and conditions imposed by the hotels and charter airlines permit them to charge V (and all other travel companies) a supplementary amount to cover any increased cost associated with rising aircraft fuel prices (which are set in USD) or increased hotel and other local costs (which are set in local currencies). These supplementary charges can be made at any time up to the customer's date of travel.

V has copied the industry practice of warning customers at the time of booking that it may be necessary to pass on the cost of any increase in the cost of fuel or other holiday charges. V has frequently charged customers as much as an additional 10% of the cost of their booking because of such additional costs. All such supplements have to be settled by the customer prior to departure.

V's Sales Manager has asked whether it would be possible to offer customers guaranteed fixed prices, with no fuel or currency supplements. This would mean that any increases would be borne by V and would consequently reduce profits, or to cover this V could set higher selling prices at the time of booking to allow for potential increases. The Sales Manager argues that it is impossible to know how this will affect customer demand.

Required

(a) (i)   Explain why it is difficult for V to advise its customers properly with respect to the threats arising from civil unrest. **(8 marks)**

     (ii) Recommend, stating reasons, a set of procedures that V should have in place to deal with the possible outbreak of civil unrest in any of the countries to which it sends its customers. **(9 marks)**

     (iii) Evaluate the risks for V arising from the existence of law firms which advertise "no win – no fee" services in the national press. **(8 marks)**

(b) (i)   Evaluate the risks to V arising from the company's existing online booking arrangements. **(6 marks)**

     (ii) Advise V's IT Director on the steps that should be undertaken in order to upgrade V's online booking system to offer a 24/7 connection to airline and hotel systems. **(9 marks)**

(c) Advise V's directors on the difficulties associated with evaluating the impact of currency movements on demand for holidays. **(10 marks)**

(Total = 50 marks)

SECTION B

Answer TWO of the three questions.

Question 2

H is a company that manufactures basic electronic components such as capacitors and printed circuit boards for the IT industry. The company has recently appointed K as a non-executive director. K was the founder and chief executive of a quoted executive recruitment consultancy and employment agency. She has stood down from that role and has accepted the position on H's board in order to seek fresh challenges.

H's board meets twice every year for a formal discussion of company strategy. These meetings tend to look back at H's performance for the previous half-year. This discussion mainly focusses on a report based on the monthly management accounts for the previous half year and then briefly considers the future impact of these. Monthly management accounts are presented to the board at their monthly board meetings.

K has attended two of the meetings relating to strategy. At the conclusion of the second meeting she expressed two concerns about the half-yearly board meetings. Firstly the meetings focus on feedback rather than feed forward. K argued that the board should be constantly forward looking and aiming to identify new opportunities. K believes that historical summaries of past performance distract from the need to plan for the future. Secondly, K believes that the half-yearly meetings focus on details associated with the existing business model rather than strategic direction. She believes that it would be a more productive use of the board's time at these meetings to work towards identifying strategic opportunities that might be pursued over the next three to five years. When she was chief executive of her employment agency the board met at least once per year and frequently more often to think about new strategies that might be pursued.

H's Production Director has complained that K has really misunderstood the board's responsibility for the management of H. The Production Director believes that her first argument is invalid because the distinction between feedback and feed forward control is more about day to day tactical management rather than strategic management. The Production Director believes that feed forward is more about fine tuning rather than strategic management. The Production Director also believes that K's comments about strategic direction demonstrate a very limited understanding of manufacturing electronics. H must respond and react to the requirements of the IT industry. H cannot really innovate. The life cycle of the company's products is such that changes to H's strategic direction happen infrequently. The Production Director has suggested that K should restrict her comments to the information prepared for consideration by the full board, especially as she has come from the service sector and has no real understanding of manufacturing.

Required

(a)   Evaluate the respective arguments put forward by K and by the Production Director concerning the need for H's full board to be forward looking rather than focussing on past performance.   **(8 marks)**

(b)   Evaluate K's argument that H's board should review the company's strategic direction at its half-yearly meetings.   **(8 marks)**

(c)   Evaluate the Production Director's argument that K should not comment on the manner in which H is run because of her background and lack of experience in a manufacturing company.   **(9 marks)**

(Total = 25 marks)

Question 3

U is an administrative assistant in the treasury department of a multinational company. U was checking some current market valuations when she noticed an anomaly in the rates associated with the USD/GBP exchange rates.

The spot rate for converting GBP to USD was 1.556 USD to the GBP. The three month forward rate for converting USD back to GBP was 1.499 USD to the GBP.

U's bank was prepared to lend GBP at a fixed rate of 5.08% per annum. The bank was also prepared to offer a fixed rate for USD deposits of 5.12%.

U printed these figures out and spoke to the company treasurer because she believed that there was an arbitrage opportunity. The treasurer agreed that U's figures indicated that an opportunity existed, but said that the opportunity would have disappeared in the time that it had taken her to walk across the office.

U asked why the multinational company did not pay greater attention to the possibility of arbitrage opportunities. The treasurer replied that "Arbitrage is a full-time occupation and it is a rather risky commercial venture. I am happy to leave the potential profits to the arbitrageurs who have made it their business to trade in that way". The treasurer also stated that the company's treasury department is a cost centre and that he had no desire to make it into a profit centre.

Required

(a)   Calculate the potential gain that could have been made by the company if it had borrowed GBP 10m in order to exploit the anomaly that she had identified.   **(6 marks)**

(b)   (i)   Evaluate U's argument that the company could profit from this opportunity.   **(4 marks)**

        (ii)   Evaluate the treasurer's argument that arbitrage is a risky commercial venture.   **(8 marks)**

(c)   Evaluate the treasurer's view that it is better for the company's treasury department to operate as a cost centre rather than as a profit centre.   **(7 marks)**

(Total = 25 marks)

Question 4

F is a member of the internal audit department of D, a courier company. F has recently completed a compliance audit of the extent to which the company's delivery vans are being maintained in accordance with the company's policy.

Each of D's depots has a full-time mechanic. The company's policy is that the depot mechanic is required to check each van's fluid levels and give a road test on a monthly basis. The Depot Manager is responsible for ensuring that every van has been checked in this manner.

One of D's delivery drivers was recently involved in a road traffic accident. The police report relating to this accident indicates that the van's brakes had failed because of a leak in the brake pipe. The delivery driver has been charged by the police with an offence because it is illegal to drive a vehicle with defective brakes.

D's Transport Manager has reviewed the van's maintenance log. The log shows that the depot mechanic had not inspected the van during the six weeks before the accident. The Head of Internal Audit has reviewed F's report and has noticed that although F had visited the depot shortly before the accident occurred he had reported that policies were being adhered to.

The Head of Internal Audit has asked F to explain why he gave a positive report when records prove that policies had not been adhered to. F explained that the Depot Manager had admitted that the vans had not been inspected as frequently as company policy required because the depot mechanic had been absent for two weeks because of ill health. There were no other qualified mechanics available to carry out these inspections and the depot's repair budget was insufficient to pay for the vans to be inspected by a third party. The Depot Manager had asked F not to note this omission in the audit report because it would lead to disciplinary action, which would harm the Depot Manager's career. F agreed not to report the missed inspections provided that the Depot

Manager promised that all of the vans would be inspected as soon as possible when the depot mechanic returned to work.

The Head of Internal Audit was dissatisfied with F's behaviour alleging F had not acted in an independent manner. F denies that accusation because he has no connection to the Depot Manager or any of the depot's other staff. Additionally, F has pointed out that the Depot Manager could easily have falsified the maintenance records to conceal the fact that the vans had not all been inspected on schedule and a negative internal audit report would simply encourage Depot Managers to falsify their records in future.

Required

(a)   Evaluate the Head of Internal Audit's assertion that F had not behaved in an independent manner.

(7 marks)

(b)   Discuss the implications of F's behaviour for the governance of D.   **(8 marks)**

(c)   The Head of Internal Audit wishes to conduct a thorough investigation into the level and frequency of the inspection of the company's delivery vans.

Recommend the tests that the internal audit department could conduct to ensure that the depot mechanics are inspecting vehicles in accordance with company policy. You should explain the purpose of the tests that you have recommended.   **(10 marks)**

(Total = 25 marks)

Answers

DO NOT TURN THIS PAGE UNTIL YOU HAVE
COMPLETED THE MOCK EXAM

426

A plan of attack

We've already established that you've been told to do it 101 times, so it is of course superfluous to tell you for the 102nd time to **Take a good look at the paper before diving in to answer questions**.

<u>The next step</u>

You may be thinking that this paper is a lot more straightforward than the first mock exam; however, having sailed through the first mock, you may think this paper is actually rather difficult.

<u>Option 1 (Don't like this paper)</u>

If you are challenged by this paper, it will be best to get the optional questions done before tackling the case study. Don't forget though that you will need half the time to answer the case study.

- Don't let the control systems terminology used in **Question 2** worry you too much. There's enough detail given in the scenario to make clear what the different viewpoints are. You can help yourself in (a) and (b) by asking what the limits are on the views discussed. (c) is not a bad question at all on the contribution made by non-executive directors.

- If you tackled Question 45 Arbitrage in the main body of the kit, that will be a significant help in tackling **Question 3.** However if you haven't, the calculation is a money market hedge calculation without complexities. You can also get marks for giving a definition of arbitrage. It's Ok to use knowledge from F3 as well as P3 in this paper, and if you can do that, (c) offers good mark-scoring opportunities.

- If you can approach part (a) of **Question 4** thinking about what independence really is (which may not be what everyone in the scenario thinks it is) that will help you see what might undermine it. (b) is an exercise in scenario analysis. There are 10 marks for (c), so if you're really struggling to think up tests, it might be worth avoiding this question. Remember however that you have to explain the purpose of each test, so if you can do that for all your suggestions, that will help you score marks.

- It helps in part (a) (i) of **Question 1** to think about recent news coverage you may have seen of civil disturbances. (a) (ii) is about contingency planning, so if you can remember the key elements from other contexts, that will help here. The term no-win, no-fee services is explained for (a) (iii) and it helps here to think about how lawyers operating on this basis generate business. Systems development knowledge is helpful in answering (b). Note carefully the requirements in (c) – the question is about the uncertain link between currency movements and the demand for holidays and you have to consider what contributes to these uncertainties.

<u>Option 2 (This paper's all right)</u>

Are you **sure** it is? If you are then that's encouraging. You'll feel even happier when you've got the compulsory question out of the way, so you should consider doing **Question 1 first**.

- If you are confident of your knowledge of corporate governance, **Question 2** is a good applied question on what the board does and what non-executive directors can contribute.

- **Question 3** has some similarities to Question 45 Arbitrage in the kit, so if you did that question well and have read recent articles on this area published by CIMA , you would most likely choose this question.

- **Question 4** will test your understanding of independence, but you may feel that there is plenty of material in the scenario you can use. It pays to be slightly wary of (c), as you'll have to generate a number of ideas and also explain them – single line suggestions for tests won't be enough.

Once more

You must **allocate your time** according to the marks for the question in total, and for the parts of the questions. And you must also **follow the requirements exactly**.

Finished with fifteen minutes to spare?

Looks like you slipped up on the time allocation. However if you have, make sure you don't waste the last few minutes; go back to **any parts of questions that you didn't finish** because you ran out of time.

Forget about it!

Forget about what? Excellent, you already have.

Question 1

Text references. Chapters 1, 2, 8, 10.

Top tips. It isn't the kind of background knowledge we would normally suggest you need to have, but knowledge of what happened during the UK and Arab Spring riots in recent years is quite helpful in answering (a) (i).

You should be able to score well in (a) (ii) by discussing key elements of disaster planning. These include having a clear strategy in place, obtaining information if problems arise, communicating with staff and customers (particularly staff who will be dealing with customers) and arranging transport away from affected areas.

The impact of legal claims is a very regular exam topic. As always, you need to consider reputation issues as well as the costs and damages resulting from legal action. Our answer focuses on why dissatisfied customers may be more likely to make claims if they can use no-win no-fee firms as opposed to firms where they will have to pay costs if they lose.

(b) (i) also brings in reputation issues, emphasising that any failure in customer service can be widely publicised. In (b) (ii) you need to focus on the steps that need to be taken rather than discussing the issues arising in relation to the upgrade of the system.

Your answer to (c) needs to bring out why there is no automatic link between changes in exchange rates and demand for holidays. You should remember that competitor reaction is an important influence on the level of economic risk. If you have studied economics before, and recalled the factors that influence price elasticity of demand (for example whether the good is a luxury, time horizon, availability of substitutes and pricing policies of competitors), that is helpful here.

Easy marks. Perhaps (a) (ii) and (b) (ii), where you can adapt frameworks (contingency planning, systems development) that you have used in other questions.

(a)   (i)   <u>Time delays between booking and holidays</u>

The conditions that result in civil unrest during a holiday **may not exist** when the customers book that holiday. They may result from a subsequent change of government or government imposing unpopular policies. They may be a consequence of a specific event. Riots in London in 2011 began after a protest at the police shooting a suspect dead.

<u>Incomplete intelligence</u>

V's knowledge of what is going in the country may be limited. Its representatives there may only have **knowledge of what is going on in their own localities** and that may be incomplete. V is forced to rely on the advice given by the government of its own country, on the grounds that it has **better intelligence.** This reliance is reinforced by the terms of V's insurance policy, that bookings will only be refunded if the government has advised against travel. In the scenario given, the government saw no reason to advise tourists to stay away from the country. In any event organisers of protests mostly do not publicise their plans in advance.

<u>Uncertainty of developments</u>

If trouble starts in one location within a country, there may be considerable uncertainty about **how far it could spread and how quickly**. The riots in the holiday towns appear to have been unexpected. People who take part in riots do not act in a predictable way. During the 2011 UK riots there appears to have been a **'copy-cat' effect**, with rioters imitating what had happened elsewhere. Mobile technology enabled these riots to be organised very quickly. How far disturbances spread may also depend on the **speed and strength of the reaction of the authorities**. During the 2011 UK riots some locations, such as major shopping centres, that appeared to be at risk were patrolled by a strong police presence and remained peaceful.

<u>Terms of advice</u>

It is also difficult for V to decide on the **nature and strength of the advice** it should give. Its advice that holidays could go ahead was based on the situation at the time. If it had given stronger advice not to travel, it could then have been liable for refunds that might not have been necessary if the resorts were not affected by the violence. If V had advised customers not to travel and it then turned out that there was no trouble where customers had planned to go, customers might be

annoyed at V for being over-cautious. Some customers are also prepared to book holidays in countries where political instability is a possibility and are happy to take the chance that it will not affect where they are going.

(ii) Contingency plan

V should have a contingency plan in place in its home country, so that if serious unrest occurs, it can immediately have **sufficient staff** available to provide information and assistance for customers who are affected. The staff involved should be clearly briefed on what their **responsibilities** are. V must also keep other staff, who are in direct communication with customers, **informed** and should also post information on its **website** as a further channel of communication. They should be given enough details to be able to discuss the situation broadly, but should also know where in V to direct specific queries.

Obtaining information and advice

As part of the plan, V should also be aware of **where to obtain information** about what is happening in the country so that it can give the right advice. This includes **liaison with embassies**, which may be in the best position to advise V. V should also ensure that staff are aware **of local news sources.** This should be supplemented, if trouble does start, with other sources that are available. For example, during the 2011 UK riots, interactive maps were available on the Google Maps website that showed satellite views of what was happening in the streets during the rioting. V should also, of course, know whom to **contact at airlines and other transport providers** and maintain constant contact with them if trouble happens and it appears customers may need to be evacuated as soon as possible.

Communication with representatives

Communication must be maintained with V's representatives in troubled areas. Local representatives may have **information that is not available from 'official sources'**, but may not have information about the **wider situation** in the country that V's home country staff can obtain. There must be **two-way communication** even before trouble starts. V must brief local representatives if it has news of possible problems in an area. The local representatives should contact V with any intelligence they have of impending disorder, or if they are getting queries from worried customers. If trouble does start, constant **communication** is vital. V must offer clear guidance from its home country but also take account of what the representatives report. V must also ensure that local representatives have a number of **different communication methods available**, including email, mobile phones and access to landlines, so that if one method becomes unavailable, representatives can communicate in another way.

Advice to customers

V should be **proactive** in giving advice to its customers who are in locations affected, as it has legal and ethical responsibility for their safety. Where customers are based in the same location as customer representatives, this should be straightforward, as the customer representatives will be the point of advice and should be able to contact customers **easily.** For countries where there are no customer representatives, V needs to establish how many of its customers are in areas affected by conflict and who they are. V should have **contact details**, such as mobile phone numbers for customers who are in unstable locations, for example those on backpacking holidays. Customers in this situation should also be advised about **contacting V and who to contact locally** in the event of unrest. The advice given should prioritise customer safety over everything else. Advising customers to stay in their hotels is an example of sensible advice.

Travel planning

In conjunction with its local representatives, V should work out plans to get customers to **airports, or out of the country by alternative routes by road or sea, as quickly as possible**, to avoid customers being at risk and facing uncertainty for a long period. Ideally V should be able to identify alternative transport arrangements if one option is blocked by disturbances. However any plans made will need to be flexible. Transporting customers while disturbances are going on may pose an unacceptable threat to their safety and it may be wise to wait until order is restored.

(iii) <u>Costs and management time</u>

Key risks to V are incurring the **costs of legal fees and damages or out-of-court settlements**. Management time will be taken dealing with claims and speaking with lawyers whether or not V eventually wins a case.

The existence of no win-no fee firms is likely to mean that V suffers a **greater volume of claims** for the following reasons.

<u>Publicity</u>

No-win no-fee firms publicise their services vigorously, with adverts aimed at the national press or other media that potential litigants view. This advertising can **draw unhappy customers' attention** to the fact that compensation may be available and encourage them to sue V.

<u>Risk for customers</u>

Dissatisfied customers may be more inclined to pursue action using no-win no fee firms than other solicitors because for them **only upside risk** is involved. They will not incur any costs if they lose and will receive some compensation if they win.

<u>Customers' financial resources</u>

No-win no-fee firms will also facilitate claims from customers whose **financial resources are limited**. Customers may be unwilling to incur the costs of using other legal firms. However they may pursue legal action if they believe they will not incur any costs if they do so.

<u>Nature of claims</u>

As the rewards no-win no fee firms obtain will depend on the **size of the settlement,** it may encourage them to **pursue a number of different claims for each client**. Here V is not only facing claims for the direct costs of all holidays, but also indirect costs of lost earnings and the difficult-to- quantify costs of stress suffered.

<u>Reputation risks</u>

V may also suffer a loss of reputation that may result in **loss of sales**. As part of their advertising, no-win, no-fee firms are likely to **highlight their previous successes** and **draw attention to alleged flaws** in the way V treats its customers that they were able to exploit, such as insurance terms that are too restrictive. This bad publicity may deter customers from booking with V in future, although this will depend on how V deals with claims compared with other travel agents. If V's compensation policies are in line with other travel agents, the reputation risk will not be as great as if V's policies are stricter.

(b) (i) <u>Loss of current bookings</u>

V's sales may be adversely affected by failings in its systems. Possibly the **time delay** between the customers making bookings and V contacting hotels or airlines has meant that rooms or flights that had been available when the bookings were made were no longer vacant.

<u>Impact on customer retention</u>

There is also no guarantee that customers will book other holidays with V. They may try to **book alternative holidays** with other companies. More generally they may be **dissatisfied** with having a booking they thought they had made successfully rejected later. They may, in future, look to book holidays with V's competitors, who can offer them more reliable online bookings.

<u>Bad publicity</u>

As well as losing business from individual, dissatisfied, customers, V may suffer wider damage if customers **complain publicly**. Sites such as Trustpilot provide online forums for customers to comment on travel companies. If a lot of customers complain about problems with bookings, customers reading the forums may be wary about using V.

<u>Airlines and hotels refusing to deal with V</u>

Airlines and hotels currently have to take time and maybe incur costs through having to resolve problems caused by V's faulty software. There is a risk that these may eventually cause the companies to **refuse to deal with V** or give **V's competitors preferential treatment.** Possibly also

the airlines or hotels may make it a condition of continuing to deal with V that V **pays compensation** for any errors it makes.

(ii) <u>Liaison with airlines and hotels</u>

V needs to ascertain from airlines and hotels what features the software it buys needs to have in order for them to allow V to have a **permanent connection**. There is a danger that it may spend money on a system that **does not meet the requirements of the airlines or hotels**, or it may incur **excessive costs on unnecessary features**.

<u>Choice of software supplier</u>

Choice of the right supplier is a key step in the upgrade process. If V is being forced to upgrade to industry-standard software, its choice of supplier may be very restricted. The comments of hotels and airlines suggest that V needs to choose a supplier that has already supplied other travel firms with the most advanced software. It seems V will need a standard system but also one where it can **choose the modules** it needs. V will also need to take into account the **level of investment** it will need in **new hardware** to make its systems **compatible** with the new software. Other factors to consider include the **help with development** offered by the supplier, the **on-going support available,** the **training** the supplier provides and the **terms** on which updates will be available.

<u>Testing</u>

The system needs to be tested both by **staff involved in on-line operations** and other staff who would need to **act as customers.** V would have to work with the supplier to ensure that the testing environment **modelled the systems that airlines and hotels** would use. Use of an experienced supplier should mean that an appropriate testing environment was readily available. V would also need to determine with the supplier the **evidence of satisfactory testing** it would need to supply to airlines and hotels to convince them to allow V 24/7 access.

<u>Documentation and training</u>

V needs to ensure that the supplier provides **full and clear documentation** for V's staff. V should also organise a **systematic training programme** in the new system in conjunction with the supplier, ensuring particularly that staff who deal with online bookings are trained in the system before it goes live.

<u>Implementation</u>

A **pilot operation**, with a hotel or airline with which V enjoys good relations, will enable V to **identify any remaining problems** and provide additional evidence for other airlines and hotels to convince them to allow 24/7 online bookings. V needs to try to ensure that issues are resolved before the new system is used generally. If problems remain once the system goes live and the airlines and hotels still have to deal with errors caused by V's systems, then they may withdraw facilities for 24/7 connection and it may be difficult to convince them to restore the connections.

(c) <u>Sensitivity to costs</u>

V will find it difficult to gauge the **overall impact of exchange rate movements** because impacts will vary significantly by type of holiday. For example customers who have to pay for their own food and drinks abroad will face the risks of the currency they have to use becoming more expensive, whereas customers who **purchase all-inclusive holidays** will not face this risk. The **price elasticity of the demand for different types of holiday** is also likely to **vary.** The demand for Package holidays is likely to be more price-sensitive than the demand for Prestige Travel holidays, where the content of the holiday is more likely to be a significant differentiator.

<u>Demand for different types of holiday</u>

There may be an uncertain **substitute effect for holidays,** with demand for V's holidays in countries whose currencies have appreciated falling but being compensated to some extent by demand rising for V's holidays in countries with cheaper currencies. In addition, if customers are worried about the impact of exchange risk, they may consider holidaying in their own home country. It again will be difficult to gauge the effect of this on V. Customers may choose holidays offered by V or its competitors. They may choose cheaper holidays at home than they would had they gone abroad, or they may choose higher quality holidays at home and so spend the same amount that they would have spent on an overseas holiday.

Timing

Major shocks that have a significant impact on exchange rates and will clearly impact on customers' plans are rare. Much more commonly **exchange rates vary continuously over time but individual variations are small**. It may therefore be difficult to gauge the point at which the cumulative impact of exchange rate movements starts to impact upon customer demand. Many customers will also be **booking holidays months in advance** and exchange rates could change between when customers book holidays and when they take them.

Forecasts

Similarly it will be difficult to gauge how much **forecasts of future exchange movements** impact upon consumer decisions. V will find it difficult to judge how much notice customers take of forecasts, and the point at which forecast movements begin to change customers' holiday decisions. The situation may be complicated by how **reliable forecasts are**. Customers may make plans on the basis of forecasts that turn out to be inaccurate.

Competitor reaction

The impact of exchange rate movements upon demand for V's holidays will also depend on **competitor reaction**. Competitors will be facing the same decisions about how to **factor into pricing** exchange rate movements and their decisions may be different from those of V. The demand for V's holidays may also be affected by other competitor action such as **marketing**. If, for example, competitors heavily market all-inclusive deals in locations with strengthening exchange rates where V does not offer all-inclusive deals, the negative impact on demand for V's holidays in those places may be particularly severe.

Setting higher prices vs charging a supplement

The position V faces is complicated by having to assess the **relative impact of the different methods** it can use to adjust for adverse exchange rates. Charging higher, but guaranteed, fixed prices may result in fewer customers booking holidays. However customers who do book fixed price holidays will not face the risk of being charged supplements. If customers are charged supplements because of higher exchange rates, this may result in their **being dissatisfied** with the service V has provided and also feeling that they **cannot be certain** when they book holidays with V how much they will cost. Both of these factors could result in a fall in demand in the future for V's holidays, but it will be difficult to gauge by how much.

Indirect impacts of exchange rate movements

Exchange rate movements may also affect other factors that influence demand for holidays. In particular countries may respond to movements in their exchange rates by **increasing interest rates.** This may reduce consumer demand, perhaps on holidays generally, or particularly on holidays abroad.

Question 2

Text references. Chapters 3 and 5.

Top tips. A possible prompt in (a) is that K comes from outside H. Her comments about planning for the future link into the external opportunities and threats that will impact upon H.

Whilst in (a) you need to question the Production Director's views, it's important to discuss K's views critically in (b). Possibly the Production Director has a better understanding of the likely timescale of strategic change for H.

Easy marks. (c) should be the easiest part of the question if you revised non-executive directors. To score high marks though, you would need to relate your answer to what K can bring to H.

(a) Views of K and Production Director (PD)

The views of K and the PD are not necessarily incompatible. Both feedback and feedforward controls are important aspects of the board's role.

PD's views

Need for feedback

The feedback stage is an important part of the control process. CIMA's risk management cycle includes the stage of **continuous review and refinement of systems**. Systems need to incorporate both **positive feedback**, which promotes continuous improvement, and negative feedback, which is designed to correct problems and return performance to what was planned.

Avoiding future mistakes

Review of major projects or developments after they have been completed can ensure that **problems are resolved** and **mistakes do not recur** on future projects. For example, a post-completion audit of a major project would review whether expenditure and resources used have been excessive and whether the project has delivered the expected benefits.

Performance measurement

The board needs to review H's financial performance, as it will be held accountable for it. Details in the management accounts and comparisons with budgets will also help the board **assess the performance of subordinate managers.** However only reviewing financial indicators may lead to important non-financial measures of success being ignored. The PD has highlighted that H's strategy is to respond and react. If H had attempted to measure its innovation and learning for example, this might have highlighted the need for greater focus on new products.

K's views

Feedforward control

Feedforward control is the forecasting of differences between actual and planned outcomes and the implementation of prior action to **avoid adverse outcomes.** These outcomes may take place over the longer-term, so to see feedforward in terms of day-to-day tactical management is too limiting a definition. In addition, future outcomes may be affected by changing environmental conditions that have not applied in the past but which will have a bearing on future plans.

Changes in IT industry

H's board needs to be aware of **developments in the IT industry** if it is to manufacture products that meet industry requirements in future. Fundamental changes to IT may mean that some of H's products become **obsolete**, others require **modification** that will take time to develop. If H does not react quickly enough and change its product base, demand may fall significantly. Identifying this fall after it has happened, when the board reviews the management accounts, may mean that it is too late to take effective action. Modifying the product base, perhaps making fundamental alterations to production processes to be able to produce new or changed products, is a longer-term strategic decision, not a day-to-day one.

Customer issues

A backward looking assessment also does not take into account changes in **customer demands and profile**. Existing customers may wish to **renegotiate supply arrangements** and place tighter requirements on H. It may be less easy to attract new customers because of H does not offer what they want and its competitors do. Also judgement on performance is measured purely in financial terms. The board does not appear to consider **customer satisfaction or quality measures.**

Supply issues

H also needs to be aware of possible future issues with supply. This might include changes to the materials used or **possible shortages.**

Competitor action

The board also needs to anticipate what its **competitors are likely to do**. Competitors, for example, may be **able to gain a cost advantage** by moving their production facilities to another country. Given that H manufactures only basic components, it is likely to be competing on price. If competitors are then able to charge lower prices because of their cost advantage, this could seriously affect demand for H's products. Again only taking action after reduced sales have become apparent in the management accounts may be too late.

(b)   Strategy setting

Corporate governance guidance highlights the central role of strategy setting in the work of boards. IFAC/CIMA guidance stresses the need for boards to be concerned with **performance** as well as conformance and compliance. A focus on performance means considering strategic decisions, use of resources and value-adding activities. Risk management models such as the Enterprise Risk Management (ERM) stress the need to link strategic and risk management objectives. The ERM also highlights the need for boards to consider the **general strategic direction of the business** as well as strategies relating to particular markets and specific business units.

Need to consider other issues

H's board must spend time considering strategic issues. However there may be dangers in **focusing excessively on medium to longer-term strategic opportunities.** The board may not spend enough time on considering issues that are affecting strategy currently. Focusing on the external environment may lead to the board becoming detached from the issues H will have in implementing its strategy.

Limits to strategic development

K is trying to **apply the board model** she adopted at the recruitment agency she ran. Rapid developments in the recruitment sector and the need to anticipate competitors may well have justified the focus on new strategies that K's agency's board had. There may be **less need** for H to make **rapid changes in strategy.** The PD may be correct in saying that changes in H's strategic direction will happen less frequently and K has not fully understood the electronics industry. H's board may need to focus more on keeping existing strategies under review than making the frequent changes of strategy that K's agency made. Possibly also H's board may spend more time on considering **strategies for specific elements of its operations** and less time on reviewing the overall strategic direction of the whole company than maybe K's agency did.

Strategic committee

Twice yearly board meetings may not give H's full board sufficient time to review strategic issues. H could consider **establishing a strategic committee** as a regular board committee. This committee could undertake regular reviews of strategy and provide data that would **expedite and better inform the main board's decision-making.** The meeting schedule of the strategic committee can be more flexible than the meeting of the full board.

(c)   Responsibility

As a member of a single board, K has the same legal responsibility for its decisions as the executive directors. Attempts to restrict K's contribution may result in K feeling that she is **unable to discharge her responsibilities** in the way she ought to do and may lead to K feeling that she cannot continue to act as a director. If it is felt that K's background and experience is not relevant and means that her contribution can only be limited, then she should not have been appointed to the board in the first place.

Strategic contribution

A key role of non-executive directors is to **challenge and contribute to the direction of strategy.** Although K comes from outside the company and industry, this may mean that she is able to review the way the board works **objectively** and with a **fresh perspective**, because she is distant from the day-to-day affairs

of H and has no existing interests to protect. K has had experience of developing strategy within a listed company, which should give weight to her views. The impression is that the board's method of considering strategy has become inflexible and the existing directors have become set in their ways. Even if some of K's suggestions are unrealistic, the questions she asks may result in the directors reviewing whether they need to spend more time looking at future challenges.

Information considered by the board

As well as challenging executives on strategy, non-executive directors also have a responsibility to question whether the board is **operating effectively**. The PD's comment that K should be content with reviewing the information prepared for the board is too restrictive. K has a duty to consider whether the **information being provided for the board is sufficient** and to ask for the board to have more information if she feels it is required.

Similarities of approach

The PD is mistaken in seeing K's background in a service industry as irrelevant to a manufacturing company. K has acted as a Chief Executive and brings general experience of running a business. This is not just relevant to the service sector. For example, the ways boards in both sectors should approach analysing their companies' activities are similar. Both should involve the **identification of value-generating activities and cost-drivers**.

Human resources experience

An important aspect of running H is **effective management of its human resources**. K's contribution in this area may be particularly strong, because of her background in running the recruitment agency. H's existing board may not have extensive experience of this area.

Gaining knowledge and experience

Possibly the PD has grounds for seeing K's comments at present as **naive**. However K has an obligation to become **better informed about H**, the environment and markets in which it operates and the issues it faces. This process will enable K to make a **more effective, credible contribution** when taken together with her other skills and experience.

Question 3

Text references. Chapters 8, 9 and 11.

Top tips. In (a) to take advantage of the arbitrage opportunity, you need to take out a forward contract to convert the US$ deposit into £ after 3 months. This means that you have to start by **borrowing £ now** and **converting £ into $** to be able to convert them back into £ after 3 months. One trap in the question is that the interest rates quoted are annual interest rates, but the period covered in 3 months, hence 5.12%/4 = 1.28% and 5.08%/4 = 1.27%.

In (b) (i) how long the short-term differences last will depend on the efficiency of the market – in a truly efficient market differences will disappear instantaneously as the treasurer suggests. In theory pure arbitrage ought to be risk-free, but imperfections in knowledge or arrangements for settling transactions may result in the risks discussed in (b) (ii).

Easy marks. If you remembered what you studied in F3 as well as P3, (c) should offer very easy marks. Remember the focus on control including HR controls to recruit the right people and limits on, and scrutiny of, their activities when they are trading. This question also illustrates the importance of reading articles that are published by CIMA. If students had read the two articles on arbitrage that were published in 2012, that would have helped them answer this question.

(a)

	Now	Interest rate	In 3 months
$	4 Take out forward contract to sell, @ 1.499, $15.56m (1 + 0.0128) = $15.759m	5.12%pa	5 Liquidate investment + interest received $15.759m
Dealing currency	This locks in arbitrage opportunity. 3 Invest US$15.56m		
	2 Buy $ @ 1.556 with £10m to receive $15.56m		6 Sell $15.759m @ 1.499 to receive = £10.513 m
£	1 Borrow £10m	5.08%pa	7 Repay £ loan & pay interest 10m (1 + 0.0127) = £10.127m £ Gain = 10.513 – 10.127 = £0.386m

---

Alternative format for solution

1 **Borrow** £10m

2 **Convert to $** at spot of 1.556 to give $15.56m

3 **Invest** $15.56m for 6 months

4 **Take out a forward contract** at 1.499 to sell the $ amount expected at the end of 3 months, $15.56m × (1+ 0.0128) = $15.759m.

5 After 3 months **liquidate investment**

6 **Convert $ that have been on deposit plus interest to £,** to give $15.759m/1.499 = £10.513m

7 **Repay £ loan and pay interest**. Gain = £10.513m – (£10m × 1.0127) = £0.386m

---

Top tips.

- As the £ spot rate is quoted at $1.556 = £1, you **multiply** the £ figure by the exchange rate

- As the three month forward rate is quoted at $1.499 = £1, you **divide** the US$ figure by the exchange rate

---

(b) (i) Arbitrage profit

Arbitrage means **exploiting short-term differences**, maybe between **two markets**, selling in one market and buying in the other. Alternatively it can mean exploiting an opportunity in a single market when an **asset's known price differs from the price at which it should be trading.** In this example the difference arises because the difference between the spot rate now and the forward rate being offered does not reflect the difference in UK-US interest rates.

Elimination of arbitrage opportunity

For as long as the differences remain, the company can exploit them and make a profit. However arbitrage differences are **short-term**. In foreign exchange markets, for example, they exist only when **purchasing power parity or the law of one price** is not operating. As other traders see the opportunities and exploit them, the laws of supply and demand suggest that prices will converge. The opportunities for exploiting the differences will disappear as equilibrium is reached. This may not happen instantaneously as the Treasurer suggests, but it is likely to happen quickly, due to global financial markets and the Internet allowing instant access to information.

(ii) Nature of opportunities

Some types of arbitrage should not involve any risk of incurring financial loss. If for example one currency is available **more cheaply on one financial market** than another, dealers can make a risk-free profit by buying in the cheaper market and selling in the dearer market. However there may be

other risks involved. Arbitrage may involve short-selling, agreeing to sell products that the dealer does not yet own. Questions have been raised about the ethics of this, and some market regulators have the power to ban short-selling. A dealer may be able to exploit an arbitrage opportunity to deal in a company's shares because he has **inside information** that it is illegal for him to use to his advantage.

Possession of knowledge

However in order to exploit arbitrage, speculators have to understand what they are doing. If they identify what they think is an arbitrage opportunity but does not exist, they could end up making a loss. They may not, for example, take into account the possibility that the forward rate used in an arbitrage arrangement has conditions attached that mean it is to the bank, and not the dealer's, advantage. It is possible that the **gains expected from arbitrage** may be reduced by a failure to estimate correctly the **costs of dealing**, for example brokers' fees. The treasurer correctly draws attention to the need for **knowledge and experience** in order to guarantee exploiting arbitrage opportunities effectively. There will also be costs of **obtaining information** and **maintaining IT systems** to monitor markets.

Execution risk

In order for arbitrage to be risk-free, settlement of the two transactions has to take place **simultaneously**. If this does not happen, the speculator will be **exposed to market risk,** the risk that movements in market prices will result in losses. **Price movements** may generally be **small**, but a large shock, for example a currency devaluation, could lead to significant losses.

Product risk

Arbitrage can take place between two products, where similarities between those products suggest they should be traded at the **same price.** However there may be differences between those products due to transaction and other costs and taxes, which may limit opportunities for arbitrage gains.

Counterparty risk

If a speculator is undertaking transactions with different counterparties, there is the risk that one of the counterparties will **fail to meet its commitments.** This will leave the speculator making one transaction and not being able to carry out the other transaction immediately. The speculator may be forced into a second transaction on **less favourable terms**. The speculator may also face **liquidity problems** resulting, for example, from a large payment commitment which the speculator cannot immediately meet with the corresponding receipt.

Leverage risk

Risk levels will also depend on leverage – the **level of initial investment required** to make a commitment to buy or sell. If leverage is high and the level of initial investment is small, then even small adverse changes in price could result in large losses.

(c)   Operating as a cost centre

Advantages

Staffing

Operating the department as a profit centre may impose unrealistic targets upon staff who do not have the necessary treasury skills and experience. Operating as a cost centre and **limiting expectations** may be more compatible with existing staff's capabilities.

Disadvantages

Limitation of responsibilities

In a cost centre managers only have an incentive to **keep the costs of the department** within **budgeted spending targets**. There may be little incentive to **demonstrate commercial awareness**, for example in more **effective management of working capital**.

<u>Operating as a profit centre</u>

<u>Advantages</u>

<u>Profits</u>

The first advantage is that the expertise in the treasury department can be used to **make money** for the business. Having this opportunity may also motivate and help retain staff.

<u>Market prices</u>

If the department is to be a true profit centre, then it should **charge market prices** for its services to other departments. This may provide management with a better indication of the **value of its activities.** However it may be difficult to put realistic prices on some services, for example arrangement of finance or general financial advice.

<u>Disadvantages</u>

<u>Possibility of losses</u>

Running a treasury department as a profit centre speculating on markets can expose a company to a **risk of very significant losses**. Even financial institutions with considerable expertise in their treasury departments have proved vulnerable to the activities of a single rogue trader.

<u>Risk appetite</u>

Even if a treasury department is profitable, its staff may be taking **risks** that directors would regard as excessive. However directors may not fully understand the risks treasury is taking. Expertise in treasury issues will therefore be required at **board or senior management level**.

<u>Resourcing the treasury department</u>

If a treasury department is to make profits consistently, it will need to be adequately resourced and this will be costly. It will involve recruitment of staff with the **knowledge and experience** to exploit opportunities and their salary costs may well be high. Staff will also need to be provided with access to **information of sufficient quality** to enable them to do their jobs effectively.

<u>Supervision</u>

Because of the risks potentially involved from a treasury department operating as a profit centre, directors need to ensure that its activities are properly supervised. Controls will need to be more elaborate than if the department was a cost centre just undertaking hedging activities. The managers of the treasury department need to impose and enforce **limits** on staff, both in terms of the **activities** that staff can and cannot carry out and **financial limits** on their trading. In a number of cases where organisations have incurred large losses, traders broke trading limits but their managers ignored this because for a time the traders were making profits.

Question 4

Text references. Chapters 4, 15 and 16.

Top tips. In (a) the main points to bring out are that independence is predominantly a state of mind, not a legalistic approach to establishing connections.

In (b) it may help to go back to the basic definition of governance – the system by which companies are directed and controlled. F's behaviour highlights various flaws in controls, with budgeting working against effective operation of controls and managers and staff being more concerned with protecting themselves and their colleagues.

In (c) internal auditors need to maintain scepticism and realise the limitations of tests that they are carrying out. As well as reviewing the logs, auditors need to ascertain how reliable they are. Hence they seek independent evidence (inspecting the vans themselves and talking to drivers) and also try to see whether there are any indications that the logs may have been falsified. Auditors also should not carry out tests that will only provide weak evidence. For example, observing mechanics carrying out tests will not give any real assurance to auditors, since the mechanics will know they are being observed and make sure they conduct the tests thoroughly.

Easy marks. You could get certainly 2 marks in (c) just for mentioning the inspection of vehicle logs that F carried out.

(a)   <u>Nature of independence</u>

F may have **no friendship or previous working connection** with anyone in the depot. However his interpretation of independence is mistaken. Independence is a **state of mind**, the avoidance of being swayed by inappropriate influences. It appears here that independence has been impaired due to a **familiarity threat.** F's judgement has been compromised because of his knowledge of D and his sympathy with D's employees.

<u>View of company</u>

The first influence that seems to have compromised F is that he appears to have allowed his judgement to be **influenced by his views of how D controls its activities and treats its staff.** It looks like F was influenced by the fact that D's failure to provide the Depot Manager with a large enough budget meant that no replacement mechanic could be used to carry out the tests. F thus believed that it would be **unjust** for the Depot Manager to be disciplined, and so chose a course of action that would avoid this happening.

<u>Sympathy for Depot Manager</u>

F also appears to have been unduly influenced by his **sympathy for the Depot Manager**. F seems to have taken into account the stress the Depot Manager seemed to be under. He thus seems to have accepted the explanation given by the Depot Manager **without verifying whether it was true**, thus **failing to show any professional scepticism**. F also allowed the Depot Manager to provide a guarantee that turned out to be **worthless.**

<u>Actions taken</u>

The other indication of F's lack of independence was that he **deliberately filed a false report**. This could not be justified as an objective course of action, as he failed to report properly on what he had found. It also demonstrated a **lack of integrity.** It may have been possible for F to take other actions that were legitimate. He could for example have reported his concerns about lack of financial resources to the audit committee.

(b)   <u>Corporate governance in D</u>

F's behaviour calls into question a number of the mechanisms that senior management use to maintain control over D.

<u>Budgeting</u>

F's sympathy with the Depot Manager seems partly to derive from a belief that budget limitations prevented the Depot Manager **arranging the tests to be done by hiring a third party**. This seems to indicate that tight budgeting may be **preventing other important controls from being operated** and may result in **dysfunctional behaviour** by depot management. The maintenance check is clearly a key safety check and the consequences of an accident resulting from inadequate maintenance could be severe. There should be sufficient flexibility in the budget to ensure that proper checks can take place and vans are properly maintained.

<u>Human resource controls</u>

The Depot Manager feared disciplinary action despite there perhaps being some reason for checks not taking place. This suggests a **culture of coercion and inflexibility** within the company, which however may not ensure compliance if staff regard it as **too strict**. Here F seemed to sympathise with the Depot Manager and thus devised a way to circumvent the system, giving a clean report in return for obtaining assurance that testing would take place. There may well be other instances of **collusion** between staff that are undermining other controls.

<u>Position of Depot Managers</u>

F's behaviour and comments raises the issue of how much Depot Managers can be relied on to **ensure compliance with company policy.** The depot manager that F dealt with showed poor judgement and maybe a willingness to find a convenient excuse for not complying with an important policy. Worse, F's suggestion that Depot Managers might **falsify maintenance records** not only means that important maintenance work is not done, it implies a **culture of dishonesty** that casts doubt on other actions by depot managers and also the information they provide.

Position of internal auditors

F' s actions also raise questions over the role of internal audit. Internal audit review is a key control, supporting successful **senior management monitoring of activities**. However if other internal auditors have been as lenient as F, internal audit work may be valueless. It may give management false assurance that compliance has taken place when controls have not been operated and perhaps dangerous conditions exist. Also if external auditors assess the work done by internal audit and find that it is inadequate, their audit will have to be **more extensive** than if they could place reliance on the results of internal audit work.

Whistleblowing arrangements

F's behaviour may also indicate that D does not have sufficient channels for employees to raise concerns about behaviour or company policies.

(c)   Review of the maintenance logs

Reviewing the maintenance logs of at least a sample of vans, as F did, could identify failures to inspect other vans often enough. The records should clearly show whether vans have been **inspected monthly.** Inspection of the records should also demonstrate whether the Depot Manager had reviewed the tests carried out on the van, since the records should show evidence of a review having been done. It may also be possible to **verify what is in maintenance logs** by inspecting other records. For example, if maintenance checks indicate that new parts need to be ordered, internal auditors could trace these to a purchase invoice.

Accident reports

The internal auditors should **review any records at the depots of other accidents**. To confirm whether these records are accurate, they should obtain corroborative evidence, such as obtaining from finance staff details of legal or insurance claims for damages. They should assess whether the accidents could have been due to mechanical failures resulting from a lack of maintenance. They should inspect the maintenance logs of these vans for the period immediately before the accident to see if maintenance inspections were carried out, what they found and whether repair work was done if the inspections indicated it was required.

Maintenance of delivery vans

The auditors could **inspect the fleet of vans** and note any that appeared to have been **poorly maintained**. They could check the **brake fluid levels** in vans. They could then **investigate the maintenance logs** to see whether they have been **inspected monthly**, what recent inspections have found and whether any work had been done on the vans subsequently. This should give an indication of whether the inspections have been done thoroughly and what was done as a result.

Discussions with delivery drivers

The internal auditors could talk to van drivers to see if they had had any **problems with their vans,** whether they had reported them and if they knew what action had been taken as a result. The van drivers would clearly not want to drive defective vehicles. The auditors could then compare what the van drivers had told them with the maintenance records on the vans to see if the maintenance reports had found any problems.

Availability of mechanics

The internal auditors should also ascertain when mechanics were absent from **work due to holiday or illness.** If mechanics were away for a long period of time, the auditors should **investigate the alternative arrangements** that were made to carry out the inspections or whether nothing was done, as happened at the depot F visited. The auditors should **review van maintenance logs** in the light of this information, as if inspections are shown as being done when no-one was apparently available to do them, this could be a sign that maintenance logs are being forged.

Review pattern of testing

When they inspect the maintenance logs of individual vehicles, the auditors should note the dates the vans were inspected. They should then collate this information for all the logs they have seen and assess whether there are any **unusual patterns**. For example, if a depot has a significant number of vans, and they are all shown as being inspected on the same day, this could mean that the inspections are not very thorough or not being done at all.

MATHEMATICAL TABLES
AND EXAM FORMULAE

444

PRESENT VALUE TABLE

Present value of £1 ie $(1+r)^{-n}$ where r = interest rate, n = number of periods until payment or receipt.

Periods (n)	Interest rates (r)									
	1%	2%	3%	4%	5%	6%	7%	8%	9%	10%
1	0.990	0.980	0.971	0.962	0.952	0.943	0.935	0.926	0.917	0.909
2	0.980	0.961	0.943	0.925	0.907	0.890	0.873	0.857	0.842	0.826
3	0.971	0.942	0.915	0.889	0.864	0.840	0.816	0.794	0.772	0.751
4	0.961	0.924	0.888	0.855	0.823	0.792	0.763	0.735	0.708	0.683
5	0.951	0.906	0.863	0.822	0.784	0.747	0.713	0.681	0.650	0.621
6	0.942	0.888	0.837	0.790	0.746	0.705	0.666	0.630	0.596	0.564
7	0.933	0.871	0.813	0.760	0.711	0.665	0.623	0.583	0.547	0.513
8	0.923	0.853	0.789	0.731	0.677	0.627	0.582	0.540	0.502	0.467
9	0.914	0.837	0.766	0.703	0.645	0.592	0.544	0.500	0.460	0.424
10	0.905	0.820	0.744	0.676	0.614	0.558	0.508	0.463	0.422	0.386
11	0.896	0.804	0.722	0.650	0.585	0.527	0.475	0.429	0.388	0.350
12	0.887	0.788	0.701	0.625	0.557	0.497	0.444	0.397	0.356	0.319
13	0.879	0.773	0.681	0.601	0.530	0.469	0.415	0.368	0.326	0.290
14	0.870	0.758	0.661	0.577	0.505	0.442	0.388	0.340	0.299	0.263
15	0.861	0.743	0.642	0.555	0.481	0.417	0.362	0.315	0.275	0.239
16	0.853	0.728	0.623	0.534	0.458	0.394	0.339	0.292	0.252	0.218
17	0.844	0.714	0.605	0.513	0.436	0.371	0.317	0.270	0.231	0.198
18	0.836	0.700	0.587	0.494	0.416	0.350	0.296	0.250	0.212	0.180
19	0.828	0.686	0.570	0.475	0.396	0.331	0.277	0.232	0.194	0.164
20	0.820	0.673	0.554	0.456	0.377	0.312	0.258	0.215	0.178	0.149

Periods (n)	Interest rates (r)									
	11%	12%	13%	14%	15%	16%	17%	18%	19%	20%
1	0.901	0.893	0.885	0.877	0.870	0.862	0.855	0.847	0.840	0.833
2	0.812	0.797	0.783	0.769	0.756	0.743	0.731	0.718	0.706	0.694
3	0.731	0.712	0.693	0.675	0.658	0.641	0.624	0.609	0.593	0.579
4	0.659	0.636	0.613	0.592	0.572	0.552	0.534	0.516	0.499	0.482
5	0.593	0.567	0.543	0.519	0.497	0.476	0.456	0.437	0.419	0.402
6	0.535	0.507	0.480	0.456	0.432	0.410	0.390	0.370	0.352	0.335
7	0.482	0.452	0.425	0.400	0.376	0.354	0.333	0.314	0.296	0.279
8	0.434	0.404	0.376	0.351	0.327	0.305	0.285	0.266	0.249	0.233
9	0.391	0.361	0.333	0.308	0.284	0.263	0.243	0.225	0.209	0.194
10	0.352	0.322	0.295	0.270	0.247	0.227	0.208	0.191	0.176	0.162
11	0.317	0.287	0.261	0.237	0.215	0.195	0.178	0.162	0.148	0.135
12	0.286	0.257	0.231	0.208	0.187	0.168	0.152	0.137	0.124	0.112
13	0.258	0.229	0.204	0.182	0.163	0.145	0.130	0.116	0.104	0.093
14	0.232	0.205	0.181	0.160	0.141	0.125	0.111	0.099	0.088	0.078
15	0.209	0.183	0.160	0.140	0.123	0.108	0.095	0.084	0.074	0.065
16	0.188	0.163	0.141	0.123	0.107	0.093	0.081	0.071	0.062	0.054
17	0.170	0.146	0.125	0.108	0.093	0.080	0.069	0.060	0.052	0.045
18	0.153	0.130	0.111	0.095	0.081	0.069	0.059	0.051	0.044	0.038
19	0.138	0.116	0.098	0.083	0.070	0.060	0.051	0.043	0.037	0.031
20	0.124	0.104	0.087	0.073	0.061	0.051	0.043	0.037	0.031	0.026

CUMULATIVE PRESENT VALUE TABLE

This table shows the present value of £1 per annum, receivable or payable at the end of each year for n years

$$\frac{1-(1+r)^{-n}}{r}.$$

Period s (n)	1%	2%	3%	4%	5%	6%	7%	8%	9%	10%
					Interest rates (r)					
1	0.990	0.980	0.971	0.962	0.952	0.943	0.935	0.926	0.917	0.909
2	1.970	1.942	1.913	1.886	1.859	1.833	1.808	1.783	1.759	1.736
3	2.941	2.884	2.829	2.775	2.723	2.673	2.624	2.577	2.531	2.487
4	3.902	3.808	3.717	3.630	3.546	3.465	3.387	3.312	3.240	3.170
5	4.853	4.713	4.580	4.452	4.329	4.212	4.100	3.993	3.890	3.791
6	5.795	5.601	5.417	5.242	5.076	4.917	4.767	4.623	4.486	4.355
7	6.728	6.472	6.230	6.002	5.786	5.582	5.389	5.206	5.033	4.868
8	7.652	7.325	7.020	6.733	6.463	6.210	5.971	5.747	5.535	5.335
9	8.566	8.162	7.786	7.435	7.108	6.802	6.515	6.247	5.995	5.759
10	9.471	8.983	8.530	8.111	7.722	7.360	7.024	6.710	6.418	6.145
11	10.368	9.787	9.253	8.760	8.306	7.887	7.499	7.139	6.805	6.495
12	11.255	10.575	9.954	9.385	8.863	8.384	7.943	7.536	7.161	6.814
13	12.134	11.348	10.635	9.986	9.394	8.853	8.358	7.904	7.487	7.103
14	13.004	12.106	11.296	10.563	9.899	9.295	8.745	8.244	7.786	7.367
15	13.865	12.849	11.938	11.118	10.380	9.712	9.108	8.559	8.061	7.606
16	14.718	13.578	12.561	11.652	10.838	10.106	9.447	8.851	8.313	7.824
17	15.562	14.292	13.166	12.166	11.274	10.477	9.763	9.122	8.544	8.022
18	16.398	14.992	13.754	12.659	11.690	10.828	10.059	9.372	8.756	8.201
19	17.226	15.679	14.324	13.134	12.085	11.158	10.336	9.604	8.950	8.365
20	18.046	16.351	14.878	13.590	12.462	11.470	10.594	9.818	9.129	8.514

Periods (n)	11%	12%	13%	14%	15%	16%	17%	18%	19%	20%
					Interest rates (r)					
1	0.901	0.893	0.885	0.877	0.870	0.862	0.855	0.847	0.840	0.833
2	1.713	1.690	1.668	1.647	1.626	1.605	1.585	1.566	1.547	1.528
3	2.444	2.402	2.361	2.322	2.283	2.246	2.210	2.174	2.140	2.106
4	3.102	3.037	2.974	2.914	2.855	2.798	2.743	2.690	2.639	2.589
5	3.696	3.605	3.517	3.433	3.352	3.274	3.199	3.127	3.058	2.991
6	4.231	4.111	3.998	3.889	3.784	3.685	3.589	3.498	3.410	3.326
7	4.712	4.564	4.423	4.288	4.160	4.039	3.922	3.812	3.706	3.605
8	5.146	4.968	4.799	4.639	4.487	4.344	4.207	4.078	3.954	3.837
9	5.537	5.328	5.132	4.946	4.772	4.607	4.451	4.303	4.163	4.031
10	5.889	5.650	5.426	5.216	5.019	4.833	4.659	4.494	4.339	4.192
11	6.207	5.938	5.687	5.453	5.234	5.029	4.836	4.656	4.486	4.327
12	6.492	6.194	5.918	5.660	5.421	5.197	4.988	4.793	4.611	4.439
13	6.750	6.424	6.122	5.842	5.583	5.342	5.118	4.910	4.715	4.533
14	6.982	6.628	6.302	6.002	5.724	5.468	5.229	5.008	4.802	4.611
15	7.191	6.811	6.462	6.142	5.847	5.575	5.324	5.092	4.876	4.675
16	7.379	6.974	6.604	6.265	5.954	5.668	5.405	5.162	4.938	4.730
17	7.549	7.120	6.729	6.373	6.047	5.749	5.475	5.222	4.990	4.775
18	7.702	7.250	6.840	6.467	6.128	5.818	5.534	5.273	5.033	4.812
19	7.839	7.366	6.938	6.550	6.198	5.877	5.584	5.316	5.070	4.843
20	7.963	7.469	7.025	6.623	6.259	5.929	5.628	5.353	5.101	4.870

AREA UNDER THE NORMAL CURVE

This table gives the area under the normal curve between the mean and the point Z standard deviations above the mean. The corresponding area for deviations below the mean can be found by symmetry.

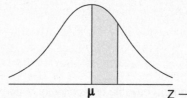

$Z = \frac{(x - \mu)}{\sigma}$	0.00	0.01	0.02	0.03	0.04	0.05	0.06	0.07	0.08	0.09
0.0	.0000	.0040	.0080	.0120	.0160	.0199	.0239	.0279	.0319	.0359
0.1	.0398	.0438	.0478	.0517	.0557	.0596	.0636	.0675	.0714	.0753
0.2	.0793	.0832	.0871	.0910	.0948	.0987	.1026	.1064	.1103	.1141
0.3	.1179	.1217	.1255	.1293	.1331	.1368	.1406	.1443	.1480	.1517
0.4	.1554	.1591	.1628	.1664	.1700	.1736	.1772	.1808	.1844	.1879
0.5	.1915	.1950	.1985	.2019	.2054	.2088	.2123	.2157	.2190	.2224
0.6	.2257	.2291	.2324	.2357	.2389	.2422	.2454	.2486	.2517	.2549
0.7	.2580	.2611	.2642	.2673	.2704	.2734	.2764	.2794	.2823	.2852
0.8	.2881	.2910	.2939	.2967	.2995	.3023	.3051	.3078	.3106	.3133
0.9	.3159	.3186	.3212	.3238	.3264	.3289	.3315	.3340	.3365	.3389
1.0	.3413	.3438	.3461	.3485	.3508	.3531	.3554	.3577	.3599	.3621
1.1	.3643	.3665	.3686	.3708	.3729	.3749	.3770	.3790	.3810	.3830
1.2	.3849	.3869	.3888	.3907	.3925	.3944	.3962	.3980	.3997	.4015
1.3	.4032	.4049	.4066	.4082	.4099	.4115	.4131	.4147	.4162	.4177
1.4	.4192	.4207	.4222	.4236	.4251	.4265	.4279	.4292	.4306	.4319
1.5	.4332	.4345	.4357	.4370	.4382	.4394	.4406	.4418	.4429	.4441
1.6	.4452	.4463	.4474	.4484	.4495	.4505	.4515	.4525	.4535	.4545
1.7	.4554	.4564	.4573	.4582	.4591	.4599	.4608	.4616	.4625	.4633
1.8	.4641	.4649	.4656	.4664	.4671	.4678	.4686	.4693	.4699	.4706
1.9	.4713	.4719	.4726	.4732	.4738	.4744	.4750	.4756	.4761	.4767
2.0	.4772	.4778	.4783	.4788	.4793	.4798	.4803	.4808	.4812	.4817
2.1	.4821	.4826	.4830	.4834	.4838	.4842	.4846	.4850	.4854	.4857
2.2	.4861	.4864	.4868	.4871	.4875	.4878	.4881	.4884	.4887	.4890
2.3	.4893	.4896	.4898	.4901	.4904	.4906	.4909	.4911	.4913	.4916
2.4	.4918	.4920	.4922	.4925	.4927	.4929	.4931	.4932	.4934	.4936
2.5	.4938	.4940	.4941	.4943	.4945	.4946	.4948	.4949	.4951	.4952
2.6	.4953	.4955	.4956	.4957	.4959	.4960	.4961	.4962	.4963	.4964
2.7	.4965	.4966	.4967	.4968	.4969	.4970	.4971	.4972	.4973	.4974
2.8	.4974	.4975	.4976	.4977	.4977	.4978	.4979	.4979	.4980	.4981
2.9	.4981	.4982	.4982	.4983	.4984	.4984	.4985	.4985	.4986	.4986
3.0	.49865	.4987	.4987	.4988	.4988	.4989	.4989	.4989	.4990	.4990
3.1	.49903	.4991	.4991	.4991	.4992	.4992	.4992	.4992	.4993	.4993
3.2	.49931	.4993	.4994	.4994	.4994	.4994	.4994	.4995	.4995	.4995
3.3	.49952	.4995	.4995	.4996	.4996	.4996	.4996	.4996	.4996	.4997
3.4	.49966	.4997	.4997	.4997	.4997	.4997	.4997	.4997	.4997	.4998
3.5	.49977									

This table can be used to calculate $N(d_1)$, the cumulative normal distribution functions needed for the Black-Scholes model of option pricing. If $d_1 > 0$, add 0.5 to the relevant number above. If $d_1 < 0$, subtract the relevant number above from 0.5.

EXAM FORMULAE

Valuation models

(i)   Present value of an annuity of £1 per annum, receivable or payable for n years, commencing in one year, discounted at r% per annum:

$$PV = \frac{1}{r}\left[1 - \frac{1}{[1 + r]^n}\right]$$

(ii)   Present value of £1 per annum, payable or receivable in perpetuity, commencing in one year, discounted at r% per annum:

$$PV = \frac{1}{r}$$

(iii)   Present value of £1 per annum, receivable or payable, commencing in one year, growing in perpetuity at a constant rate of g% per annum, discounted at r% per annum:

$$PV = \frac{1}{r - g}$$

Notes

Review Form – Paper P3 Performance Strategy (01/13)

Name: _____   Address: _____

_____

_____

How have you used this Kit?
(Tick one box only)

☐ Home study (book only)

☐ On a course: college _____

☐ With 'correspondence' package

☐ Other _____

Why did you decide to purchase this Kit?
(Tick one box only)

☐ Have used the complementary Study text

☐ Have used other BPP products in the past

☐ Recommendation by friend/colleague

☐ Recommendation by a lecturer at college

☐ Saw advertising

☐ Other _____

During the past six months do you recall seeing/receiving any of the following?
(Tick as many boxes as are relevant)

☐ Our advertisement in *Financial Management*

☐ Our advertisement in *PQ*

☐ Our brochure with a letter through the post

☐ Our website www.bpp.com

Which (if any) aspects of our advertising do you find useful?
(Tick as many boxes as are relevant)

☐ Prices and publication dates of new editions

☐ Information on product content

☐ Facility to order books off-the-page

☐ None of the above

Which BPP products have you used?

Text	☐	Success CD	☐	Interactive Passcards	☐
Kit	☑	i-Pass	☐	Home Study Package	☐
Passcard	☐				

Your ratings, comments and suggestions would be appreciated on the following areas.

	Very useful	Useful	Not useful
Passing P3	☐	☐	☐
Planning your question practice	☐	☐	☐
Questions	☐	☐	☐
Top Tips etc in answers	☐	☐	☐
Content and structure of answers	☐	☐	☐
'Plan of attack' in mock exams	☐	☐	☐
Mock exam answers	☐	☐	☐

Overall opinion of this Kit   Excellent ☐   Good ☐   Adequate ☐   Poor ☐

Do you intend to continue using BPP products?   Yes ☐   No ☐

The BPP author of this edition can be e-mailed at: nickweller@bpp.com

Please return this form to: Stephen Osborne, CIMA Publishing Manager, BPP Learning Media, FREEPOST, London, W12 8BR

Review Form (continued)

TELL US WHAT YOU THINK

Please note any further comments and suggestions/errors below.